HANDBOOK ON
Using Administrative Data for Research and Evidence-based Policy

HANDBOOK ON

Using Administrative Data for Research and Evidence-based Policy

Shawn Cole
Iqbal Dhaliwal
Anja Sautmann
Lars Vilhuber

Copyright ©2020 by Shawn Cole, Iqbal Dhaliwal, Anja Sautmann, and Lars Vilhuber.

Published by the Abdul Latif Jameel Poverty Action Lab, 400 Main Street E19-201, Cambridge, MA 02142, USA

The individual chapters are copyright by their authors or as noted. Chapters are licensed under the terms of the Creative Commons Attribution - Non-Commercial 4.0 International License (https://creativecommons.org/licenses/by-nc/4.0/), which permits use, sharing, adaptation, and redistribution in any medium or format, as long as you give appropriate credit to the original author(s) and the source, provide a link to the license, and indicate if changes were made. You may do so in any reasonable manner, but not in any way that suggests the licensor endorses you or your use. You may not use the material for commercial purposes. Use by governmental entities is not considered commercial use.

ISBN 978-1-7360216-0-6 (print)
ISBN 978-1-7360216-1-3 (ebook)
DOI: 10.31485/admindatahandbook.1.0

Cite this Handbook as:
Cole, Shawn, Iqbal Dhaliwal, Anja Sautmann, and Lars Vilhuber (eds.), *Handbook on Using Administrative Data for Research and Evidence-based Policy*. Cambridge, MA: Abdul Latif Jameel Poverty Action Lab. 2020.

To read this book online and download printable PDFs, visit admindatahandbook.mit.edu.

This book is typeset in Charter and Helvetica.
Cover design by Elizabeth Bond. Interior layout and design by Elizabeth Bond, Anja Sautmann, and Evan Williams.

Contents

About the Editors vii

About J-PAL ix

Acknowledgements x

Foreword xi
Daniel L. Goroff

1 **Using Administrative Data for Research and Evidence-Based Policy: An Introduction** 1
Shawn Cole, Iqbal Dhaliwal, Anja Sautmann, Lars Vilhuber

Special Topics

2 **Physically Protecting Sensitive Data** 37
Jim Shen, Lars Vilhuber

3 **Model Data Use Agreements: A Practical Guide** 85
Amy O'Hara

4 **Collaborating with the Institutional Review Board (IRB)** 113
Kathleen Murphy

5 **Balancing Privacy and Data Usability: An Overview of Disclosure Avoidance Methods** 145
Ian M. Schmutte, Lars Vilhuber

6 Designing Access with Differential Privacy   173
   Alexandra Wood, Micah Altman, Kobbi Nissim, Salil Vadhan

Case Studies

7 Institute for Employment Research, Germany: International Access to Labor Market Data   243
   Dana Müller, Philipp vom Berge

8 Ohio and the Longitudinal Data Archive: Mutually Beneficial Partnerships Between State Government and Researchers   283
   Joshua D. Hawley

9 New Brunswick Institute for Research, Data and Training: A Ten-Year Partnership Between Government and Academia   311
   Donna Curtis Maillet, James Ted McDonald

10 The Private Capital Research Institute: Making Private Data Accessible in an Opaque Industry   347
   Josh Lerner, Leslie Jeng, Therese Juneau

11 Aurora Health Care: Using Electronic Medical Records for a Randomized Evaluation of Clinical Decision Support   385
   Laura Feeney, Amy Finkelstein

12 The Stanford-SFUSD Partnership: Development of Data-Sharing Structures and Processes   417
   Moonhawk Kim, Jim Shen, Laura Wentworth, Norma Ming, Michelle Reininger, Eric Bettinger

13 **City of Cape Town, South Africa: Aligning Internal Data Capabilities with External Research Partnerships** 467
 Hugh Cole, Kelsey Jack, Derek Strong, Brendan Maughan-Brown

14 **Administrative Data in Research at the World Bank: The Case of Development Impact Evaluation (DIME)** 503
 Arianna Legovini, Maria Ruth Jones

15 **The Use of Administrative Data at the International Monetary Fund** 541
 Era Dabla-Norris, Federico J. Díez, Romain Duval

16 **Using Administrative Data to Improve Social Protection in Indonesia** 563
 Vivi Alatas, Farah Amalia, Abhijit Banerjee, Benjamin A. Olken, Rema Hanna, Sudarno Sumarto, Putu Poppy Widyasari

Index 588

About the Editors

Shawn Cole is the John G McLean Professor of Business Administration at Harvard Business School. Shawn is a Co-Chair of J-PAL's Innovations in Data and Experiments for Action Initiative (IDEA). His research examines agriculture, corporate finance, banking, and consumer finance in developing countries. He has conducted randomized evaluations in education, financial literacy, agricultural risk management, and ICT for agriculture. He received a Ph.D. in economics from the Massachusetts Institute of Technology in 2005, where he was an NSF and Javits Fellow, and an A.B. in Economics and German Literature from Cornell University.

Iqbal Dhaliwal is the Global Executive Director of J-PAL and co-chair of IDEA. Based at MIT, he works with the Board of Directors to develop J-PAL's strategic vision, with leadership of the seven regional offices to coordinate J-PAL's worldwide research, policy outreach, capacity building, and operations, and with funding partners to secure resources for J-PAL worldwide. He has setup many partnerships for J-PAL with data providers and implementing partners. He is a co-PI on a very large randomized evaluation in India that used both survey data and large admin datasets to help a state government reduce health care absenteeism. Iqbal has a deep appreciation of the concerns and constraints of data providers in governments as he began his career as a member of the Indian Administrative Service (IAS) formulating policy and implementing programs across many assignments. Later as a Director in an economic consulting firm in Chicago, he analyzed numerous very large data sets to provide critical insights to private sector clients in manufacturing, health, banking and automotive sectors. He has a BA in economics from the University of Delhi, an MA in economics from the Delhi School of Economics, and an MPA in international development from Princeton University.

Anja Sautmann is a Research Economist in the World Bank's Development Research Group (Human Development Team). She is interested in how households and individuals make decisions, from healthcare for children to daily consumption to marriage, and how incentives and individual behavior shape optimal policy design. Before joining the World Bank, Anja was an Assistant Professor at Brown University (2010-2017) and the Director of Research, Education, and Training at the Abdul Latif Jameel Poverty Action Lab at MIT (2017-2020) and Director of IDEA. She received her Ph.D. in Economics from New York University and her undergraduate degree in Economics from Ludwig Maximilians Universität in Munich, Germany. She is an affiliate of the CESifo research network.

Lars Vilhuber is the Executive Director of the Labor Dynamics Institute at Cornell University, and a faculty member in Cornell University's Economics Department. He is also the American Economic Association's Data Editor. Lars is a Co-Chair of IDEA. His research interests relate to the dynamics of the labor market. He also has extensive experience in the application of privacy-preserving publication and access to restricted data. He is chair of the scientific committee of the French restricted-access system CASD, member of the governing board of the Canadian Research Data Centre Network (CRDCN), and incoming chair of the American Statistical Association's Committee on Privacy and Confidentiality. Lars has an undergraduate degree in Economics from Universität Bonn and a Ph.D. in Economics from Université de Montréal.

About J-PAL

The **Abdul Latif Jameel Poverty Action Lab (J-PAL)** is a global research center working to reduce poverty by ensuring that policy is informed by scientific evidence. Anchored by a network of more than 225 affiliated professors at universities around the world, J-PAL draws on results from randomized impact evaluations to answer critical questions in the fight against poverty. Many of the randomized evaluations conducted by J-PAL affiliated professors have used administrative data. J-PAL builds partnerships with governments, NGOs, donors, and others to share this knowledge, scale up effective programs, and advance evidence-informed decision-making. Many of these partnerships have also helped make administrative data available for research. J-PAL was launched at the Massachusetts Institute of Technology in 2003 and has regional centers in Africa, Europe, Latin America & the Caribbean, the Middle East & North Africa, North America, South Asia, and Southeast Asia. In 2019, J-PAL launched the Innovations in Data and Experiments for Action Initiative (IDEA) to improve access to and use of administrative data for evidence-based policymaking.

Acknowledgements

The editors of the Handbook would like to thank the Alfred P. Sloan Foundation for providing financial support that made this work possible. We would also like to express our thanks to all the authors who contributed to the Handbook and provided invaluable feedback and workshopping, as well as Steven Glazerman, Jennifer Sturdy, and Torsten Walter for insightful comments and review.

We thank Jim Shen for his work managing the Innovations in Data and Experiments for Action Initiative (IDEA) and the creation of the Handbook, while also coauthoring two chapters in this book, Evan Williams for creating or co-creating many of the accompanying materials for the Handbook, such as the webinar series, and providing invaluable assistance from organizing the chapter review process to proof-reading, Sam Friedlander for staffing IDEA early on, and the many J-PAL staff members who provided additional feedback on the various components of this Handbook.

Elizabeth Bond designed the Handbook cover and other associated materials and Theresa Lewis provided copy editing for the Handbook. We appreciate their attention to detail and hard work that helped turn 16 distinct chapters into a cohesive whole. Additional thanks go to Aparna Krishnan (Project Director, J-PAL South Asia) and Claudia Macías (Associate Director of Policy, Training and Research, J-PAL Latin America & the Caribbean) for their continuing support of IDEA.

Foreword

by Daniel L. Goroff
Vice President and Program Director
Alfred P. Sloan Foundation

This is an important Handbook, compiled by an important institution, on an important topic. The Alfred P. Sloan Foundation is therefore a particularly proud sponsor of the Innovations in Data and Experiments for Action Initiative (IDEA) of the Abdul Latif Jameel Poverty Action Lab (J-PAL), which has taken on this endeavor, and of work on administrative data generally.

Many think of J-PAL as an advocate for randomized controlled trials (RCTs). This is true, of course, and the world is better for it. Others realize that J-PAL stands for more than econometric improvements. J-PAL is also about collective responsibility, for example. By bringing the laboratory model to the social sciences, J-PAL promotes new ways of designing, staffing, documenting, crediting, and replicating experiments that produce reliable results. Indeed, researchers leading this movement seem to have priorities that go beyond producing yet another paper for their own CVs. The shared goal they pursue instead—relentlessly and with great integrity—is to discover meaningful answers to important questions.

How is J-PAL bringing about this reorientation of empirical social science as a profession? Taking a page from the behavioral economists, nudges tend to succeed by making change seem easy, attractive, social, and timely. As a replacement for how lone professors have traditionally worked with their graduate and postdoctoral students, the laboratory model goes a long way on each of these four dimensions, thus providing a new technology for producing reliable research results. Among those interested in empirical evidence, there is ample demand for such results, too, as the world struggles with everything from poverty to pandemics and from prejudice to polarization. Large-scale surveys, a traditional source of insights about matters like these, are no longer seen as fully adequate to the task due to rising costs, slow turnaround, sampling frame challenges, and declining response rates.

So, when it comes to generating empirical evidence, we have a novel production technology together with weakening competition and robust demand for the outputs. What about the inputs? Besides the laboratory labor, there is also a need for data. Wait—don't we usually think of research data as a product of this process? Suitably refined and polished, after all, we store those data sets away in repositories in case someone else ever wants to admire them. This Handbook is not about that, but rather about the new and promising role that administrative data is beginning to play as an enabler of exciting research.

What counts as administrative data? There are many definitions. I, for one, take it to mean any information not originally collected for research purposes. That includes transaction descriptions and other records compiled while conducting public or private sector business of all sorts. Unlike when dealing with well-designed and well-curated research data sets, no metadata, comparison groups, representative samples, or quality checks can be assumed.

Some therefore refer to administrative data as *digital exhaust*. That characterization certainly evokes origins as an unintended byproduct but fails to convey the potential value. Others speak of *found data*. That brings to mind an oasis stumbled upon in the desert. Unlike exhaust but more like an oasis, many like to classify administrative data as a public good.

I argue that this Handbook suggests a better metaphor—at least implicitly. The contributors' more explicit goal is, of course, to help facilitate and promote the use of administrative data in the production of high-quality empirical evidence. In terms of nudging researchers in that direction, this is already an attractive and timely proposition. In fact, commercial applications of administrative data are all the rage throughout the rest of society. Without more active roles for independent researchers and academic standards in this data revolution, there is a danger that only a few large and rather secretive institutions will either know—or think they know—what is going on in the world.

The challenge is that, as a goal to nudge toward, repurposing administrative data for use by researchers has been neither easy nor social. The Handbook chapters that follow present many examples of how the process can be made less burdensome for individuals and more beneficial for society. One way of appreciating the value of such advice is to consider the potential costs incurred without it:

Fixed Costs

Some holders of administrative data charge researchers for access. Even data that are supposed to be public by law, like the federal tax returns of charitable organizations, may only be available in bulk for a fee. Voter rolls and company registers must be purchased in certain states but are free to download in others.

Even after paying any such initial fees, administrative data sets usually need extensive preparation and attention prior to computing any statistics. The cleaning, documenting, linking, and hosting of files can be quite demanding. If the information is private or proprietary, then setting up an enclave or other protections also incurs expenses.

The case studies in this Handbook detail how much time and effort it can take to manage administrative data even before any research can begin. Currently, every investigator tends to start anew by negotiating their own access, doing their own cleaning, and making their own linkages with little incentive to share anything other than the final findings. We can do better. The lessons this Handbook proffers, and the coordination it suggests, show how.

Marginal Costs

Beyond routine maintenance, the budget implications of calculating one more statistic from a well-prepared, well-proportioned, and well-hosted data set should be pennies at most. But there are other costs as well. When dealing with confidential information, for example, it follows from theorems described in this Handbook that every new query answered about a given data set leaks some privacy and depletes the *privacy loss budget* that should be fixed in advance. Even if the data set has nothing to do with people, every new query leaks some validity, too, and depletes the *statistical significance loss budget* that should also be set in advance. The chapters on disclosure avoidance methods and differential privacy explain how query mechanisms that satisfy ϵ-differential privacy control the rate at which simply trying to answer the questions that researchers submit about a given data set eventually and inevitably uses up the privacy loss and statistical significance budgets. Once spent, responsible curators are supposed to stop accepting queries altogether.

Remember this next time you hear that open data sets are a "public good" just like lighthouses or unpatented discoveries. Open data may serve the public good to be sure. Technically speaking, however, a research data set is not only excludable but also rival in the sense that with use it gradually loses its ability to generate safe and reliable evidence. This has consequences regarding the provision of administrative data for research purposes that the Handbook explores and that I will revisit below.

For now, note that we can only slow the rate at which privacy and validity evaporate with data use. No technological advances or other cleverness can prevent such leakage altogether, according to the theorems. What to do? Moving to new data sets, say either resampled ones or "set-asides" reserved from the original, can not only refresh budgets but also provide new perspectives. Another strategy is rationing direct access to data that would otherwise be overused. Exploratory research can be performed on high-quality synthetic data without impacting privacy or validity budgets at all. Tentative statistical or modeling conclusions obtained that way can then be sent to validation, or verification, servers for confirmation. These servers do access the original data but are designed to use only small portions of the privacy or validity budgets. The only researchers able to query the original data would be those whose explicit, important, and pre-registered hypotheses cannot be tested otherwise due to linkage or other requirements. Such a regime has been shown not only to generate publishable results but also more reliable results than research based on p-hacking, data dredging, selective reporting, and other common practices.

Transaction Costs

Negotiating a Data Use Agreement (DUA) often requires considerable time, tact, and trust. As described in the chapter on data use agreements, legal technicalities and bills can be formidable but surmountable. All may seem to go well until some new player or policy sends everything back to square one. Case studies in this Handbook highlight just how to engineer mutually beneficial relationships between data holders and data users by avoiding or overcoming such frictions.

Economists who study transaction costs suggest that, when frictions are onerous, the solutions are often institutional. There is a role here for intermediaries who can deal with entire sectors of similar data holders on the one hand and with entire classes of data users on the other. This has to be more efficient than everyone negotiating pairwise agreements one at a time.

Examples range from the Institute for Research on Innovation and Science (IRIS) at the University of Michigan, which processes, protects, and provides administrative data gathered from universities about grant expenditures, to the Private Capital Research Institute (PCRI), which does the same with data from private equity firms as described in the PCRI's chapter in this Handbook. Some refer to such intermediaries as *Administrative Data Research Facilities*. The staff of each includes experts on data governance who also know the data-holding sector and the data-using sector well enough to deliver valuable benefits to both.

Opportunity Costs

Professors lament that, absent such intermediaries, the time and effort they spend trying to secure administrative data keeps them from pursuing more valuable tasks few others can address. This has particularly been the case, for example, in their quest for social media data held by tech platforms. Arguably, researchers have paid insufficient attention to challenges such as protecting privacy, identifying specific hypotheses suitable for testing with the data if obtained, compensating for the fact that such data do not constitute a representative sample of a well-defined population other than the users of a particular platform, devising ways to combine administrative data with survey or experimental data, etc.

Indeed, obsession with "getting the data" may blind researchers to other approaches or considerations. Most administrative data, after all, are only observational. Unless it describes suitable treatment and comparison groups, such data can rarely, if ever, yield robust causal conclusions. Running a well-designed RCT can, of course. RCTs usually require not just access to administrative data, but also the active cooperation of administrators in carrying out an experiment. Chapters in this Handbook provide examples from around the world where concentrating on how to answer an important question, instead of just how to obtain an attractive data set, has paid off handsomely.

***

Faced with all these costs, researchers naturally look for funding to cover expenses. That includes making proposals to grant-making organizations like the Alfred P. Sloan Foundation. When describing my work there, I often say that I am in the public goods business. That framing, when invoked in discussions of open data as a pure public good, suggests that the provision of data depends on solving a collective action problem, that is, a game where the natural Nash equilibrium fails to be Pareto efficient.

Under such circumstances, social science lore recommends nudging players to take their social obligations seriously and to internalize more of the benefits that might accrue to others. J-PAL and similar groups have made progress this way, as described above, motivated by compelling goals like the alleviation of poverty and supported by substantial grants from private and public sponsors. But while philanthropy can proudly provide start-up funds, the sustainable provision of public goods ultimately depends on fundamental shifts in cultural, institutional, or legal support.

In other words, calling a commodity a "public good" may sound like praising it as worthy for funding. But to a grant-maker, the technical term "public good" just signals that, short of tax dollars or philanthropic support, financing will be difficult and sustainability will be very difficult. Cases where grants do help a community solve a collective action problem and provide a public good can be very productive, compelling, and gratifying, of course. The Handbook describes excellent examples, including the tools, systems, knowledge, and access mechanisms that facilitate research on administrative data.

Not everything of social value has to be a public good like this in the technical sense. As chapters in the Handbook indicate, conducting research on a data set—administrative or not—uses up its evidentiary value, especially if the data describes sensitive information about individuals. Talk of budgets, in this case for privacy and validity, evokes the way economists usually analyze the provision of commodities other than public goods.

From this point of view, we have a familiar scarce resource problem—but with high initial costs, low marginal costs, and the potential to enable a wide range of valuable activity over time. Solutions to such problems are often called infrastructure projects, particularly ones that result in reduced transaction costs, too. Monopolies or duopolies tend to play a role, justified by the positive externalities associated with sound infrastructure. Financing is not necessarily that much easier than for a public good but can also generate significant social benefit if designed well. Like railway or communications nodes, institutional intermediaries in this case could be connected to form an efficient network that traffics in administrative data by following trusted standards and practices.

Building these nodes, whether they are called Administrative Data Research Facilities or not, thus represents capital investment in research infrastructure. The Alfred P. Sloan Foundation's enthusiasm about providing data for economics research is, like the chapters that follow, based on realism both about the economics of research data and about the promise of administrative data in particular. Others wishing to join this adventure may similarly find inspiration in this Handbook's account of how capital and labor can be organized to help answer important questions by transforming administrative data into high-quality evidence.

CHAPTER 1

Using Administrative Data for Research and Evidence-Based Policy: An Introduction

Shawn Cole (Harvard Business School)

Iqbal Dhaliwal (J-PAL, Massachusetts Institute of Technology)

Anja Sautmann (World Bank)

Lars Vilhuber (Cornell University)

1.1 The Potential of Administrative Data for Research and Policymaking

Over the course of our careers, we, the editors of this Handbook, have been witness to extraordinary changes in economics, economic research and evidence informed policymaking. One of them has been the rise of research in applied microeconomics and development economics that focuses on working closely with policymaking and implementing organizations and creating an evidence base for better social programming. Two key factors have contributed to this trend: increased availability of new data sources, and the rapid growth in the

Copyright © Shawn Cole, Iqbal Dhaliwal, Anja Sautmann, and Lars Vilhuber.
Cite as: Cole, Shawn, Iqbal Dhaliwal, Anja Sautmann, and Lars Vilhuber. "Using Administrative Data for Research and Evidence-Based Policy: An Introduction." In: Cole, Shawn, Iqbal Dhaliwal, Anja Sautmann, and Lars Vilhuber (eds.), *Handbook on Using Administrative Data for Research and Evidence-based Policy*. Cambridge, MA: Abdul Latif Jameel Poverty Action Lab. 2020.

use of experiments (randomized control trials or randomized evaluations) in the social sciences. These developments have enabled many new avenues of research.

Recent studies using administrative data show, for instance, how behavioral factors can lead to decision biases, and how these biases can be addressed with better policy design. Improved ways of presenting information have been shown to significantly raise eligible earned-income tax credit (EITC) benefits claims (Bhargava and Manoli, 2015), and reduce uptake of costly payday loans (Bertrand and Morse, 2011). New experimental research has also contributed to the credible assessment of the long-run effects of landmark social programs, such as the effects of Medicaid health insurance in the US on hospital visits, conditional cash transfers through PROGRESA in Mexico on health, or the PACES school voucher program in Columbia on educational outcomes (Taubman et al., 2014; Gertler and Boyce, 2003; Angrist, Bettinger and Kremer, 2006). Through a better understanding of the pathways of impact, such studies can help improve the design and performance of these programs.

Randomized trials and research evaluating policy impacts more generally have dramatically improved the quality and breadth of evidence used to inform better policymaking. Just within the J-PAL network, affiliated researchers have conducted over 2,000 randomized evaluations and scale-ups of evaluated programs have reached over 500 million people. Moreover, a good number of studies, including the ones cited in the preceding paragraph, make use of existing data sources, typically from administrative databases. Yet it is also our experience that this type of research frequently involves complex and costly original data collection. For example, the large-scale surveys that accompany many randomized evaluations typically consume a large share of the financial and staff resources devoted to the research project overall. A lack of relevant, reliable, and comprehensive data that researchers can access has been a limiting factor for new studies and consequently the spread of evidence-informed policy.

At the same time, there are a wide variety of data sets already in existence, from patient-level health care data in the US to geotagging for police vans and garbage trucks in India (Doshi et al., 2016; The Times of India, 2020), which could dramatically reduce the cost and complexity of policy-relevant research – including randomized control trials – and speed up the formation of an evidence base for policy-making. Administrative data are sometimes referred to as *organic data* (Groves, 2011) because they are generated as part of normal business processes. Decision-makers at firms and in government are often already using such data to better understand problems and issues of the populations they serve. Based on such analytics, new policies are implemented or new questions defined. As a natural next step, carefully designed, systematic research with administrative data, often carried out in partnerships that include academic researchers, firms, and governments, may carry out in-depth analyses, conduct experiments, and develop and field supplemental surveys to test specific mechanisms or hypotheses. This type of innovative research can dramatically expand the insights gained from the data and their feedback to policy.

An increasing fraction of academic studies conducted in high-income countries and published in the most prestigious journals in Economics now use administrative data (see Figure 1.1; Chetty, 2012; and Einav and Levin, 2014). In general, however, researcher access to administrative data sets remains difficult and idiosyncratic (Card et al., 2011), and the potential of administrative data especially in low- and middle-income countries is far from exhausted. This Handbook is motivated by our view that easier access to and an increased use of administrative data sets by researchers could dramatically improve the quantity and quality of available evidence on social programs and policies.

The potential benefits of greater access to administrative data are growing exponentially as the scope of data held at governments, non-governmental organizations (NGOs), and private firms is multiplying. For example, both the government and private firms in the US gather salary and employment data, for labor market reports and payroll processing, respectively (Abowd et al., 2009; Grigsby, Hurst and Yildirmaz, 2021). The data volume processed for these purposes every few months is equivalent in volume to the decennial census of the entire US population. Digital collection of data at the point of

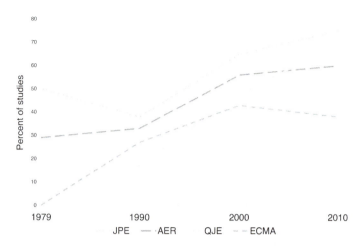

Figure 1.1: Share of studies conducted in high-income countries that use administrative data, among studies published in the four top US journals in Economics (Journal of Political Economy, American Economic Review, Quarterly Journal of Economics, Econometrica). Source: Chetty (2012). Reproduced with permission.

origin (as opposed to *ex post* digitization of administrative forms and reports) has already become the norm in high-income countries and is on that path elsewhere in the world.

Administrative data often have very useful properties. They can measure certain features objectively, such as distance traveled, price paid, locations visited, or contacts with a system or provider. This can avoid social desirability or recall biases of survey data. Checks and balances like biometric capture or automatic geotagging can additionally make administrative data more reliable and accurate than self-reported information. These properties themselves may have the potential to make the use of administrative data useful for policy; for example, biometric records used to monitor public health workers in India improved attendance by 15 percent, even when consequences for absentee staff were in practice limited (Dhaliwal and Hanna, 2017).

Broad coverage and routine collection as part of day-to-day operations also often make administrative data more representative and may solve an Achilles' heel of many potential surveys and experiments: attrition.

The size of administrative data sets can make it possible to run experiments with more treatment arms, and to detect even effects that are small or heterogeneous between groups, without loss of statistical power.

Finally, completely new types of data open exciting new areas of research to improve policies and programs. For example, utility billing, cash register scanning, or phone usage data have provided insights into day-to-day behavior at previously unheard-of levels of detail. The large volume of such data also makes them much more amenable to cutting-edge analysis methods like machine learning, allowing for new classes of insight and inference such as artificial intelligence.

Although firms and NGOs are increasingly making data under their control accessible, governments have long been at the forefront of making data available for research. Examples include labor statistics and social insurance data, but also census data and national, state, and district-level household and firm surveys. When researchers and governments work closely together to conduct research based on administrative data, uniquely fruitful research-policy partnerships can arise that generate innovative, policy-relevant studies. As an early and particularly impressive example, chapter 16 by Vivi Alatas, Farah Amalia, Abhijit Banerjee, Benjamin A. Olken, Rema Hanna, Sudarno Sumarto, and Putu Poppy Widyasari of this Handbook describes a series of ambitious, nationally representative experiments on the targeting and delivery of social protection programs in Indonesia. This body of work arose out of a decades-long collaboration between academic and World Bank researchers, the national statistical agency of Indonesia, and the Government of Indonesia and had significant influence on Indonesia's policies. These types of partnerships are a promising and important development in social policy research.

Governments, but also NGOs, have begun to see it as part of their mandate to make the information they use for internal programming publicly available. Chapter 13 by Hugh Cole, Kelsey Jack, Derek Strong, and Brendan Maughan-Brown describes how the City of Cape Town (CCT) articulates this mandate in its *Data Strategy* by describing administrative data as a "collection of public assets," which should be used to "maximise public benefit". Individual data sets may not be able to provide value infinitely: as pointed out in the foreword by Daniel L. Goroff and in chapter 6 by Alexandra Wood, Micah Altman, Kobbi Nissim, and Salil Vadhan, the value of any data set for generating new statistically valid analyses as well as the ability to protect individuals from identification depletes with use. However, administrative data most often constitute a *flow* of data that is generated at regular intervals or continually over time. Therefore, the value of the agreements, systems, tools, and materials that create or facilitate access to such a recurring or continuous flow of data persist for much longer. A given access mechanism can continue to be used as data covering new time periods become available, and is moreover often flexible enough to be adapted or repurposed as new data types become available for research access.

Public access to data, especially generated by governments and donor-funded organizations, is often considered a value in itself, because it provides transparency on the information being collected and the programs that use this information. Many recent legal reforms reflect this view, such as the Foundations for Evidence-Based Policymaking Act of 2018 in the US or the Digital Economy Act 2017 (Part 5, Digital Government) in the UK, and their equivalents in many other countries. Beyond that, it also enables the broadest possible use of the data in studies on social policies, including by researchers who may not have the resources to collect their own data. In this manner, removing access barriers to data can play an important role in enabling early-career researchers, those working in low-income countries, or those at less well-resourced institutions, to engage in ambitious, high-quality scientific work. At the same time, with a well-designed access mechanism, the organizations providing the data can benefit as well, by having their stored data accessed, cleaned, and analyzed by a broad set of users to provide new insights on key challenges and problems faced by the programs and beneficiaries in their local context.

↳ Benefits!

1.2 Why is the Analysis of Administrative Data Still Relatively Rare?

In light of the tremendous benefits, it is our view that the use of such data for policymaking and research still remains far below its true potential.

Even though most organizations are now collecting administrative data in digital form, many do not yet have the in-house capacity to aggregate and analyze these data before they are overwritten or destroyed after having served their operational purposes. There is often no systematic approach to incorporating data analysis into strategic or operational decision-making. When organizations are analyzing data, it is often for short-term program monitoring, for example through highly aggregated dashboards, rather than carefully designed research. Many data providers, particularly at the sub-national level, are also unfamiliar with the idea of making data available externally, and sometimes lack a clear legal mandate. As a result, these data providers do not have standardized procedures, and are often reluctant to share data at all. At the same time, many researchers have little experience interacting with data providers, having been trained in the traditional model of collecting original data or using secondary (public-use) data in research. In addition to the challenge of negotiating complex data access agreements, researchers face unfamiliar technical hurdles, such as working with data warehouses.

In individual cases, researchers have negotiated one-off or ongoing access to a wide variety of data, in some cases producing influential policy lessons. But they frequently navigate this process without any systematic guidance. Access is often fragile and may depend on the championship of a single individual in the organization. We have also observed organizations with no data use policies and little awareness of the risks of sharing personally identifiable information (PII); in such instances, personal data may unwittingly be exposed to unnecessary risks.

From our own work and that of others, we identify three key challenges for the expanded use of administrative data in research and policy analysis: making the data usable, addressing confidentiality and privacy, and balancing value and costs.

1.2.1 Making Data Usable for Analysis

Many data providers collect data in outmoded files and disconnected databases, and the data are often not in formats amenable to systematic data analysis (Groves and Schoeffel, 2018; Hand, 2018). Data providers interested in research with administrative data would have to commit resources to overhauling their systems and collecting or digitizing key outcomes of interest, and they may not even readily know what type of staff or consultants to hire, what guidelines to set, and how to manage such staff. Data cleaning and data preparation can be especially complex if the goal is to link administrative data with other sources of information (such as survey data) to better understand the extent of the problem, for effective monitoring, or to conduct experiments.

When data linkage, cleaning, curation, and documentation are not performed by the data provider, they must be done by researchers. This work is typically time-intensive but offers limited professional or personal reward; data curation is not an intrinsic part of funded research and is not usually recognized academically. Upon completion of the research, there is little incentive to share prior data curation work with the data provider or other researchers. This leads to duplication of effort and an increased risk of mistakes. Making data usable can be a significant hurdle even for experts. For example, in chapter 7 Dana Müller and Philipp vom Berge estimate that the preparation of a given data set for analysis—de-identification, documentation, and test data preparation—takes between fifteen and sixty person-days.

1.2.2 Protecting Privacy While Promoting the Accessibility and Utility of Data

The unique value of administrative data for policy-relevant analysis and research is often in the level of detail and the personal relevance of the information the data hold. Sources range from medical records to location tracking to employment history. However, these contents also render the data sensitive and make it particularly important to prevent unauthorized access. The privacy of respondents (individuals, such as patients or job seekers, but also firms, hospitals, doctors, etc.) is therefore a key priority when providing research access to administrative data. Respondents whose data appear in administrative data sets have rarely explicitly consented to participate in academic research, and data collection by government agencies, but also by private companies, frequently does not provide individuals with the option to remove or withhold information.

Protecting such personal information is increasingly required by law, but it is also an ethical obligation. Both when a legal framework exists and in cases in which legislation governing the collection and use of the data is imprecise or even absent,[1] data providers therefore typically endeavor to keep the identity and attributes of the individuals, firms, and institutions in the data confidential. When there is no clearly defined process or mandate for providing data for research purposes to individuals outside the immediate set of staff responsible for the data, data providers will justifiably be conservative about whom they entrust with access.

A range of tools are available to protect personal information in administrative data, and these tools are a focus of both the thematic chapters as well as the case studies in this Handbook. However, those mechanisms require expertise to implement, and they also affect how the data can be used. An important instance of this is the editing of data to reduce the chance that a person or computer could identify, or attempt to identify, specific people or attributes of those people. Aggregating, coarsening, or removing personal details in the data are standard tools of statistical disclosure limitation (SDL), but the increase in protection almost always comes at the cost of reducing the data's utility for analysis (see chapter 5 by Ian M. Schmutte and Lars Vilhuber);

---

[1] Notable examples in which privacy is only minimally protected includes information about the employees of the United States federal government or property tax records in many US counties.

in fact, some types of research are only possible when individuals are personally identified. This includes experiments in which different interventions are provided to different groups to assess their effects: it is typically necessary to at least temporarily work with identified data in order to know who received which program or program variant.

Most other security requirements also have the potential to reduce the set of data users either in principle or in practice: data may be protected by requiring access with a specific device, at specific times, or at a unique location such as a secure room (see chapter 2 by Jim Shen and Lars Vilhuber); or the data provider may restrict access to certain groups, such as researchers affiliated with an academic institution. The data provider therefore needs to weigh these restrictions against the likelihood of data breaches occurring and the damage that would result, and this can be a challenging exercise. A focus of the many case studies in this Handbook, and a large number of implementations documented elsewhere, is to find feasible solutions that are useful for researchers, sustainable to data providers, and respectful of respondents' privacy.

1.2.3 Value vs. Cost

The processes involved in both making data usable and protecting individuals' privacy can be relatively simple, but may also require significant resources, and it may not always be clear at the outset which it is. Some data providers may perceive risks of making data accessible for research (such as the reputational risk of publications being negatively received by the public or their superiors, or the legal and ethical risk associated with possible data breaches) while not being sure as to what the benefits of research will be and how it will feed back into decision-making. This is compounded by the fact that data providers may not have a full view of how data analysis can improve strategic and operational decision-making or what research is possible; or they attribute low value to the insights that could be generated, perhaps because they do not internalize the generalizable lessons from such research.

Researchers may also not always know how to add value for data providers. Developing dashboards drawing on the data, creating summary statistics or research briefs that give the provider or the general public a sense of the provider's activities, suggesting implementable measures to streamline operations, and generally helping the data provider to assess and showcase the value-added, are activities that are not part of the regular skill set of academic researchers.

On the researcher side, significant time and effort may be needed to negotiate and obtain data access when robust and well-documented request and access procedures for administrative data are not yet established. Prominent universities or researchers may be at an advantage (real or perceived) in terms of the resources they can devote to this work. The investment may discourage some potential users, including those from low-income countries. Successful data access mechanisms must be able to address all these points: provide value to both data providers and researchers, commit resources to policy-relevant analysis and to translating research insights into actionable recommendations, and deliver fast and streamlined data access and use.

Another salient feature of administrative data access is that the costs are frontloaded. Once a data set has been cleaned and curated, the data are readily available for use in any number of research projects. Similarly, establishing data access procedures can be a costly and time-intensive process, including finding solutions for privacy issues, creating buy-in from all stakeholders, and defining and formulating responsibilities, conventions, and rules. However, this initial investment could enable much faster access requests in the future. The cost hurdle is in many cases too high to overcome for a single researcher or a single research project even if the continued use of the data would justify this cost. Two possible solutions are either to distribute the costs among several research teams who will get access to the data, or to dedicate resources at the data provider to covering the initial fixed costs of creating access and overcoming capacity bottlenecks.

1.3 This Handbook

While the questions outlined above are challenging, many institutions have developed effective and replicable solutions to share administrative data with researchers. These institutions have made data usable and put data security measures and privacy policies in place in a manner that created long-term value for both data providers and researchers. The Handbook draws inspiration from these successes.

To date, much of the existing literature has focused on high-level considerations and the restricted-access data landscape (see the list of additional resources at the end of this chapter) but has very little practical information. In particular, there is a lack of tangible, concrete advice for sub-national organizations that wish to make confidential administrative microdata accessible in a responsible fashion, even though researchers, governments, NGOs, and private firms have consistently expressed interest in learning from experiences around the world. There are gaps on a range of topics: drafting data use agreements, cleaning and linking data sets, implementing secure computer systems and managing the data infrastructure, designing an application workflow for granting access to multiple researchers, analyzing data for decision-making, and facilitating collaborations between researchers and data providers.

With this Handbook, we aim to close these gaps and to provide researchers and data providers with guidance on best practices in legal and technical areas; and perhaps just as importantly, we hope to furnish a set of compelling examples of success that can serve as inspiration for others. We believe that the practical and actionable lessons from these cases can provide valuable information to other institutions, data providers, and researchers on how to securely and easily share, access, and analyze administrative data. Additionally, as mentioned at the beginning of this introduction, we see an incredible opportunity in combining the use of administrative data with field experiments and supplemental survey data, something which to date is relatively rare and for which almost no guidance exists. Several chapters in this Handbook therefore make explicit reference to this goal. We hope that this will inspire innovative experiments based on administrative data that will generate insights on the impact of policies and programs worldwide.

The first part of the Handbook consists of in-depth and practical thematic chapters on technical and legal issues surrounding administrative data access. The second part provides structured case studies of different data access mechanisms and research projects that illustrate how to succeed in a wide variety of legal and technical environments. We here briefly describe each of them.

1.3.1 Different Levers for Protecting Sensitive Data: The Thematic Chapters

The thematic chapters of the Handbook provide guidance on four topics: how to align administrative data use and institutional review board–compliant research, how to craft data use agreements (DUA) between data providers and researchers, how to protect the data physically, and how to use computational and statistical techniques to conceal the identity of individuals in the data. In this manner, these chapters cover a set of interlinked ways of protecting personal data: physical, legal, and analytical.

Chapter 2 discusses the hardware and software necessary to provide secure access to data, covering topics such as data encryption, user authorization through security tokens, biometric identification, and secure-room setups. Along with standard safety measures such as password protection, physical security shields the data primarily from unauthorized access, be it malicious hacking or inadvertent looks taken at someone else's screen. Data providers can stipulate or provide the necessary hardware and software in order to keep data secure.

Analytical techniques to protect data deter or prevent unauthorized use. A range of such statistical disclosure limitation methods are described in chapter 5. The chapter covers techniques to avoid inadvertent identification of individuals, either from the data directly or from summaries, analyses, or visualizations. SDL provides methods to "blur" the data so that individual observations may be obfuscated, but aggregates or analyses (such as averages, counts, or model-based parameters) remain within certain bounds and can be used for meaningful analysis and comparison. Traditional SDL methods are already widely in use, and the chapter describes methods that allow data custodians to assess how much to modify the data to achieve sufficient protection and how much subsequent analyses might be affected.

A relatively new approach to this question is differential privacy, described in chapter 6. Differentially private methods provide strong promises to prevent outside parties from learning whether any individual is in the data, regardless of the background information available to others. In this it differs from traditional methods, which typically protect against specific, rather than general, methods of breaching privacy. Differentially private methods are being used more and more for releases of tabular data, for instance by the US Census Bureau (Machanavajjhala et al., 2008), Google (Erlingsson, Pihur and Korolova, 2014), Apple (Differential Privacy Team, 2017), SafeGraph (SafeGraph, 2020), but can also be challenging to implement. Chapter 6 provides an overview and details on the advantages and challenges of implementing differential privacy.

The chapters on data use agreements and institutional review boards (chapter 3 by Amy O'Hara and chapter 4 by Kathleen Murphy, respectively) broadly fall under legal protections. Legal protections primarily serve to regulate the use of the data by authorized users.

An important element of legal data protection is the data use agreement (DUA) between the researcher and the data provider, which governs how the data are used and accessed, and can require researchers to implement, or be subject to, physical and analytical protections. A DUA can also stipulate reviews or audits, as well as sanctions in cases of violations. Conversely, the DUA can specify what data uses are permitted, when the data needs to be provided, and how results can be published. In this manner, DUAs ensure that the interests of the data provider, the researcher, and the individuals in the data are preserved. Chapter 3 describes the process of drafting a DUA and provides a flexible template.

Lastly, chapter 4 describes the process of US federal regulatory review of individual research projects for the protection of subjects and specifically the principles and guidelines that institutional review boards (IRBs) apply in such review. In the US and elsewhere, ethics review is required for most research with human subjects. From the perspective of the data provider, a requirement of IRB approval, potentially built into the DUA, can serve as an opportunity for an external and unbiased review of the balance between the burdens and benefits of the research and any risks to which individuals in the data might be exposed. The IRB can thus help the data provider and the researcher assess the risk that a data breach or misuse of the data might bring and oblige the researcher to think through data security and analysis strategies that help minimize these risks. Conversely, the chapter also clarifies whose interests or what uses of data an IRB does not protect and which therefore need to be regulated in other ways if any party of the administrative data collaboration wishes for such regulation.

1.3.2 Data Protection in Practice: The Five Safes in the Case Studies

In practice, any solution for creating administrative data access needs to take into account the unique circumstances of the data and data provider in question. Factors to consider include

- the intended uses of the data and analysis;
- the different interests of all partners;
- idiosyncratic issues, needs, or requirements of the data provider and the researchers involved;
- specifics of the location and the legislative and institutional frameworks; and
- the content and structure of the data.

The general guidance provided in the thematic chapters addresses these needs only partially; successful solutions employ the available set of tools in creative ways and combine different protection methods into a coherent whole. As illustrated in chapter 7, some data providers may decide to provide a menu of various combinations of SDL, physical security, and legal constraints to cover various degrees of analytical fidelity and feasibility of research projects.

To showcase such solutions, we have selected an array of case studies that have implemented robust, innovative, and sustainable data access mechanisms and processes. Table 1.1 gives an overview of all the case study chapters. We asked the authors to describe their data protection solutions using the Five Safes framework (Desai, Ritchie and Welpton, 2016) as an organizing principle.[2] Each of the *safes* describes one aspect in which an access model reduces the risk of unauthorized release of personal information.

Safe projects describe how the data provider goes about assessing projects for appropriateness. In order to ensure data protections that are commensurate with the risk involved, and more generally to ensure ethical conduct of the research, safe projects may include, for example, a requirement of ethics (IRB) review but also a policy-focused review by data provider staff.

Safe people discusses what criteria are used for identifying researchers who are granted data access. For example, affiliation or training requirements may be a tool to ensure that the user has the necessary qualifications to draw accurate conclusions from the data or that the researcher is not subject to a financial conflict of interest. Safe projects and safe people often interact; for example, when data can be used by only a select group of people whose intentions and qualifications are assured, it may not be necessary to review each individual project before granting access. As an edge case, consider the World Bank (chapter 14 by Arianna Legovini and Maria Ruth Jones), where the research staff with data access are directly employed by the organization; the World Bank applies its internal standards of ethical conduct to all staff but does not require external ethics review.

Safe settings describe the environment in which data access is permitted and shows how physical security is implemented in practice. The

---

[2]The Five Safes framework is broadly and internationally used as a guiding principle by national statistical agencies (Australian Bureau of Statistics, 2017; Statistics Canada, 2018) and provinces and individual agencies (see e.g., Province of British Columbia, BC Ministry of Citizens Services, n.d.). Altman et al. (2015) suggest an alternative framing.

Table 1.1: Case studies at a glance

Chapter 7: Institute for Employment Research (RDC-IAB)
Data provider: national government agency
Data access: varies by dataset, includes access to web-based remote submission, secure rooms at IAB and partnering universities, secure computers at universities.
A clear legal mandate allows RDC-IAB to distribute German labor market data through a sophisticated network of remote access points housed at national and international research institutions.

Chapter 8: Ohio Longitudinal Data Archive (OLDA)
Data provider: state agencies
Data access: research center at a public university provides data for download to approved users
A long-running and successful administrative data partnership that first emerged in 2007. In the last five years, 28 published studies have used data accessed through OLDA.

Chapter 9: New Brunswick Institute for Research, Data, and Training (NB-IRDT)
Data provider: provincial government social protection agencies
Data access: research center at a public university provides access to approved users
A relatively new partnership that has seen rapid growth and expansion in the data that it makes available to researchers, with specific legal mandates for data access and sharing.

Chapter 10: Private Capital Research Institute (PCRI)
Data provider: private firms and publicly available data
Data access: remote access to data stored at a university-affiliated data archive
Meticulous data cleaning work and relationship building in an industry that tends to be secretive, as well as sophisticated data protection policies, led to the creation of a comprehensive database on private capital.

Chapter 11: Aurora Health Care
Data provider: private company
Data access: data is directly transferred to the researchers
A proactive researcher team helped a private firm think through data protection and cleaning issues to enable a randomized control trial that measures sensitive health outcomes.

Chapter 12: Stanford-San Francisco Unified School District (SFUSD) Partnership
Data provider: school district
Data access: research center at a private university provides data for download to affiliated faculty
A well-established and mature partnership with streamlined application and review processes that hosts comprehensive data on students, teachers, and schools, and supports data access for multiple projects each year.

Chapter 13: City of Cape Town (CCT)
Data provider: city government
Data access: approved researchers access a server owned by the city government
A new data policy led to a productive cooperation between the City and academic researchers to create systematic data access.

Chapter 14: Development Impact Evaluation (DIME), World Bank Group
Data provider: variety of public and private partners
Data access: data is transferred directly to DIME
DIME's group of development economists and analysts apply best practices of research developed over time in partnerships with many different data providers.

Chapter 15: International Monetary Fund (IMF)
Data provider: variety of international government partners
Data access: data is held by national governments or transferred directly to IMF
As part of its mandate, the IMF helps governments overhaul their tax records and systems and conduct research on the tax data.

Chapter 16: Government of Indonesia
Data provider: national government agencies
Data access: data is held by the government or transferred directly to researchers
A long-term research partnership with the government enabled multiple nationally representative experiments to improve the targeting of social programs.

concrete implementation choices showcased in the case studies complement the overview of the different methods provided in chapter 2 and illustrate the diversity of possible approaches.

For example, in the Ohio Longitudinal Data Archive (OLDA) partnership (chapter 8 by Joshua D. Hawley), data access may occur from the researcher's own computer, but the file transfer protocol only admits identified devices that were previously registered. The Research Data Center at the Institute for Employment Research (RDC-IAB)—chapter 7—requires that all users access the data through hardware that fulfills a specific set of client specifications, and until 2018, required a dedicated thin client, a stripped-down device that has no functionalities other than logging onto the central data server.

How stringent the physical protection measures are may again partly depend on what groups of people are given access (safe people), but also on how sensitive the data are (safe data), either for privacy or intellectual property reasons; for example, only secure rooms or similar physical access-restricted setups can reliably protect from unauthorized parties snapping images of a user screen.

Safe data covers how analytical protection methods, such as those described in chapter 5 and chapter 6, are implemented to minimize disclosure risk when the data are stored or viewed. These methods protect from inadvertent disclosure by data provider staff, by researchers accessing the data, or during data transfer. They may also protect from unauthorized attempts to identify individuals in the data by users who were given data access. IRB review is often more straightforward when personal information is protected in this manner, which provides an incentive for researchers to prefer analytical protection methods.

While disclosure protection procedures such as the masking of identifiers are in principle straightforward, the case study examples often reveal complexities in the details. As an example, chapter 11 by Laura Feeney and Amy Finkelstein describes their work with Aurora Health Care. Aurora implemented a de-identification system in which personally identifiable information is replaced by an anonymous ID number before any data were shared. However, as new patients appear in the data, the de-identification procedure needs to create new, unique anonymous numbers for the patients and, moreover, the system must be able to link different data sets via this unique ID in order to combine a variety of data sources. At the same time, the procedure must not inadvertently allow a reconstruction of the underlying information; for example, the ID number cannot be calculated in a deterministic way from the person's date of birth or similar information. In successful partnerships, privacy expertise contributes not only to solving issues such as this one but also to identifying challenges before they occur.

Safe outputs are about minimizing the disclosure risk that stems from the *publication* of analytical results and other outputs, again by applying the tools of SDL outlined earlier. The information of individuals must remain hidden as researchers describe the data or cases in the data, create tables, or display graphs. Safe outputs can even mean withholding the name of the data provider in order to protect the research partners or the individuals whose data are used in the research.

Again, safe outputs interact with the other four safes. For example, where the selected researchers have significant data expertise and their proposals undergo IRB review, the data provider may rely on the DUA to stipulate only *ex post* review of outputs for disclosure risk as described in chapters 5 and 6. By contrast, in cases where the user base is broader, the data provider may choose to permit data analysis only in-house (i.e., through remote access) and only release publishable results to the user after performing SDL review, possibly requiring alterations of outputs such as summary tables or regression coefficients.

Implicit in each case study is a global assessment of the risks involved. These risks are typically not explicitly articulated (except in some instances through the legal framework) but risks guide the data protection choices made by each data provider. Thus, each case study represents a particular set of choices guided by the tradeoff between ease of access on the one hand and the unmitigated risks on the other.

In addition to discussing their particular implementation of the Five Safes framework, each case study also describes how the data were made usable, the institutional setup, the specific legal framework for data access and data use, sustainability (outreach activities undertaken, revenue generated or accounted for, and metrics for success), and aspects of robustness and reproducibility. These round out the data access mechanism examples and point the reader to a diverse range of solutions.

The chosen structure allows readers to either engage with individual chapters, or to focus on specific aspects of administrative data access across multiple case studies. For instance, the reader may want peruse specifically the section that describes how *safe people* are selected in each chapter.

1.3.3 Institutional Models of Access

As discussed above, in many situations where administrative data could be analyzed for research and policy purposes, there is an initial hurdle to overcome in which researchers and data providers face a range of one-off costs and activities. The structure and requirements of this process are described in the section on institutional setup in each chapter. On the data provider side, once an application process has been created, permissions have been obtained, and a data set cleaned, additional users could access the data at low additional expense. On the researcher side, investments may have to be made upfront as well, from building skills to learning about the data structure to forming a relationship with a data provider. Afterwards, multiple research projects may become possible with the same data provider, and skills are transferable to projects with different data providers.

Relatedly, one data provider might be able to supply many different data sets or periodically update the same data sets over many time periods, creating panel data for the same individuals or repeated cross-sections of representative samples. It is often beneficial for creating new research and policy insights to link different types of data and combine, for example, labor market data with education data. The OLDA provides an example of this (chapter 8).

In all these cases, there are significant economies of scale or scope when creating administrative data access. Accordingly, many success-

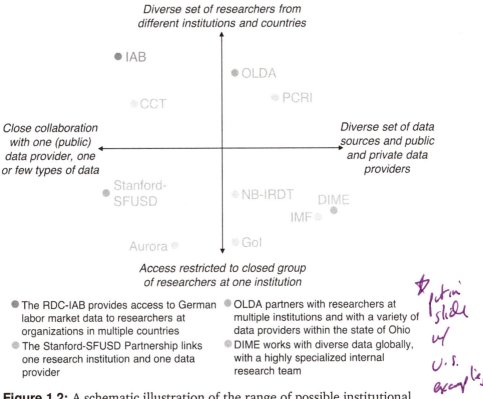

Figure 1.2: A schematic illustration of the range of possible institutional arrangements for a data provider, realizing economies of scale and scope at different levels.

ful data access mechanisms bundle access, for example by managing multiple users, tapping multiple data sources within an organization, combining data sets from multiple data providers, or conducting multiple projects within the same or similar government-researcher partnerships.

Our case studies span data from the public and the private sector and many different data-hosting organizations from governments and international institutions to academic research centers. However, not by coincidence, most of our case studies describe data access mechanisms that in one way or another harness benefits from specialization, bundling, or scale economies.

Figure 1.2 provides something of a taxonomy in regard to specialization and scope by placing the different access models of the case studies on two axes: the diversity of data or data providers and the diversity of users. There is the greatest potential for realizing specialization benefits or economies of scale when all researchers are affiliated with the same organization or when all data is similar and comes from the same data provider. The former means for example that user access protocols or security requirements can be tailored to one specific set of users, whereas the latter means that they can be customized and automated for the needs of one data provider, but also that staff will be able to develop deep expertise regarding the data and its idiosyncrasies. Economies of scope are more likely to be realized when many different users access the same data or when the same team of experts works with many different types of data sets or data providers, for example by building transferable expertise or utilizing systems and infrastructure to capacity.

In one type of model for administrative data access, these benefits are realized by **a center or unit in long-term partnership with an institutional partner** that provides different data sets or the same type of data over many periods of time. Excellent examples in our case studies are chapter 12 by Moonhawk Kim, Jim Shen, Laura Wentworth, Norma Ming, Michelle Reininger, and Eric Bettinger describing the Stanford-San Francisco Unified School District Partnership or chapter 7 describing the RDC-IAB. In these settings, relationship-building between the data intermediary and the data provider and careful design of the legal and institutional framework ensure that policy interests and research conducted with the data are closely aligned.

A dedicated data access center can provide additional value by creating access for data provider staff for policy analysis (or conducting such analysis) and by maintaining policy engagement after the research ends. Appropriate data use agreements can encourage researchers to contribute data cleaning, data documentation, or policy analysis to the center. Since the partnership is close and the data and its possible uses are well circumscribed, data extraction processes can typically be streamlined and partially automated, and DUAs can follow a template, facilitating and speeding up access for the benefit of all parties. Vibrant administrative research centers can also create a local ecosystem of like-minded experts and provide technical training and attractive prospects for high-caliber researchers and staff.

Many **mature systems for research data access are hosted by universities that collaborate with specific governments**. Aside from the Stanford-SFUSD Partnership and the RDC-IAB, another example of this in the Handbook is the OLDA. The advantages of hosting the data at academic institutions are many: they often have an ethics review board (IRB) or can provide support for ethics review, they manage grants, they can supply space and an existing computing infrastructure, and can provide channels to other researchers as well as audiences (conferences, seminars, plenary discussions, events, etc.). Postdoctoral researchers and graduate and undergraduate students can contribute their skills to the data work; access to the data for their own research may provide additional incentives. Universities are often seen as more independent and less political or partisan than other policy research organizations such as think tanks. Chapter 8 describes how OLDA's institutionalization as a center at Ohio State University facilitated long-term research projects across legislative cycles and associated changes in policy priorities.

An alternative model involves locating a **data-sharing center within the data provider** as done in by the RDC-IAB (chapter 7) and the City of Cape Town (chapter 13). This has the advantage of ensuring that the data provider maintains a high level of oversight and control. It also can allow a wider user base since academic partnerships often restrict access to affiliated researchers. On the other hand, this type of access mechanism cannot take full advantage of the resources and capabilities of academic partnerships. Government entities, for example, may have limited resources and are often prohibited from accepting grant financing.

In some cases, hybrid models are employed where a **university research center embeds staff with the data provider**, thus supplying the staff resources and university access while the data remains under the control of the data provider. This is an approach that the Abdul Latif Jameel Poverty Action Lab (J-PAL) has used in the past in a partnership with the Government of Tamil Nadu through the IDEA Lab in South Asia. Another path, taken by the Private Capital Research Institute (PCRI, chapter 10 by Josh Lerner, Leslie Jeng, and Therese Juneau), is to create an **entirely separate non-profit organization** with its own governance structures, while only housing the final data at a university-affiliated data archive. Such an approach may achieve some of the benefits of university location, such as trust in academic independence and clear governance, without incurring some of the bureaucratic and overhead expenses associated with universities.

Yet another type of successful data access model does not rely on a data intermediary but instead makes use of the benefits of specialization by assembling a **team of experts and researchers who interact with a wide range of potential data providers**. Chapter 14 describes how the Development Impact Monitoring and Evaluation unit (DIME) at the World Bank conducts research projects with a range of government and private sector data providers. Chapter 15 by Era Dabla-Norris, Federico J. Diez, and Romain Duval illustrates how the International Monetary Fund (IMF) works with many different national governments streamlining, standardizing, and analyzing tax data.

The DIME and IMF chapters highlight what a specialized researcher team can do in terms of ensuring high-quality data collection, integration with experiments, and cutting-edge best practices for data analysis, such as building systems to ensure that individual researchers make their results reproducible. This model may be particularly interesting for large policy organizations, such as international multilaterals and NGOs or similar institutions, but the model can also be attractive for a small team of academic collaborators or for private companies with capacity for a research group. Large organizations can take full advantage of a coordinated team of highly trained researchers who can build expertise for specific types of administrative data and apply that expertise in a range of partnerships with different data providers. One potential downside can be that researchers external to the organization have no or only restricted access to the data. DIME was able to successfully avoid this issue through collaborations between internal and external researchers, which can serve as an encouraging example to other organizations who take similar approaches. In this way, external researchers can contribute to the exchange of ideas and increase the amount of research that can be done beyond the limits imposed by internal research capacity.

1.3.4 Balancing Interests and Creating Value for All Partners

An important aspect of setting up administrative data access for research and policy analysis that is successful in the long term is to ensure that the interests of all stakeholders are served. Stakeholders include the individuals whose information are contained in the data, but also the data provider and data intermediaries, the researchers who are conducting the data analysis, the academic and policy communities, and the general public.

Protections for personally identifiable information were discussed in detail earlier. However, data providers often have other reasons besides privacy to protect the content or provenance of administrative data and steer the research taking place. Data on the operation of large-scale policy programs, taxation or spending, and other information are often sensitive for political, legal, criminal justice, or national security reasons. Private companies have an interest in protecting their brand name, maintaining the trust of their customers and clients, and keeping legal rights over valuable data they own or create. Differences in priorities and interests can even occur within the same data-providing organization. For example, as the authors of chapter 13 point out, those charged with storage and governance of the data are often more conservative in the uses they consider permissible than the branches of the organization that provide services and whose operations would benefit from better data analysis.

The case studies describe a variety of ways in which data access mechanisms can resolve these tensions. For example, the PCRI (chapter 10) has data use agreements with private companies that keep the firm's name anonymous and ensure that any analysis done with the data is for non-profit, academic research, and the data can never be directly accessed by users. These reassurances have enabled the PCRI to assemble an impressive amount of data from a famously reserved industry. Chapter 15 explains that the immunity of the IMF greatly facilitates cooperation with governments and tax authorities, because the IMF protects data from any access outside the Fund itself, including by members of the same country or government that supplied the data. In the national context, most statistical agencies are required to protect their data and are exempt from responding to requests by law enforcement, for example. The United Nations' Fundamental Principles of Official Statistics, first adopted in 1994, requires in Principle 6 that "individual data ... be strictly confidential and used exclusively for statistical purposes" (United Nations, 2014). An external data intermediary and the right legal framework could emulate such guarantees in other contexts.

Several data intermediaries in the case studies have also established formal review by the data provider to ensure alignment of any research projects with policy goals: the OLDA has a multi-stage review process starting with a one-page proposal and in the Stanford-SFUSD Partnership, the school district conducts what they call ABC review (alignments, benefits, and costs). Chapter 8 also mentions that being able to fall back on a formal review process is helpful when dealing with unusual data requests, possibly from powerful actors, as it protects all parties from misuse—of the data as well as of the resources invested to curate and provide the data.

When instituting a review process, it is important to ensure that the interests of researchers and the public are both protected, meaning that the independence of the research is guaranteed, in order to maintain full credibility of research findings. For example, data use agreements might specify that identifying details of the data provider may be withheld, but the data provider cannot revoke permission to use the data *ex post*. Without this protection, academic freedom is curbed, and researchers may spend time and resources on a project that they later cannot publish; in the long run, such approaches would likely stifle research use of data and introduce systematic biases in research results.

Public data providers, such as government agencies, are bound to uphold the interest of citizens and the public good. In the eyes of a public servant, this goal may conflict with costly investments in data analysis with uncertain benefits. The strongest incentive for undertaking more formal access to administrative data is therefore often an explicit legal mandate. Chapter 8 gives a compelling description of the role of federal funding as a signal of endorsement by the national government, which spurred action at the state level to make Ohio's labor data accessible. Similarly, chapter 7 on the RDC-IAB and chapter 9 by Donna Curtis Maillet and James Ted McDonald on the NB-IRDT describe the legal mandate of those institutions to create access to vital administrative data under these institutions' care. The City of Cape Town (chapter 13) underwent a concerted shift in institutional priorities with a formal new data policy that put the focus on open access to data.

Lastly, systematized access to administrative data can be designed in such a way that the data intermediary or the researchers who benefit from access to the data for their own research agenda give back and provide value to the data provider in the form of technical expertise, policy advice, or data analysis. The OLDA, for example, has a sophisticated outreach program with *data days* and a Workforce Success Measures dashboard for the public. Researchers could also provide training and capacity building for the data provider. The City of Cape Town requires researchers to share tools and analysis files with CCT staff.

A last important trade-off concerns the streamlining of access and the opportunities to combine administrative data with identified data, for example to conduct experiments. Automated disclosure avoidance measures make it simpler to protect data, but restrict access to personally identifiable information. The power of administrative data for experiments lies in the potential to not just analyze the data but actively combine the identified data with other sources to conduct experimental interventions. The earliest established administrative data centers have focused almost exclusively on making data available for observational research. This has the advantage that identifiers can be removed from the data early and, consequently, research use has typically been low risk for the privacy of those in the data. In many cases, observational studies allow the data provider to take a relatively light-touch role in the request and access process. However, observational research foregoes the significant potential and advantages of conducting randomized control trials in which administrative data are used to assess the effects of certain policies.

This Handbook contains compelling examples of creating systematized, ongoing capacity to conduct randomized field experiments using administrative data. As far as research undertakings go, these are perhaps the most complex. In particular, close cooperation between the researcher and the data provider is typically necessary. On the one hand, the research and program delivery teams need to know the identity of individuals in the study sample in order to link administrative data with treatment group assignment. This may require more involved procedures to satisfy legal or ethical mandates for the protection of individual data. On the other hand, the data provider will often also act as the program provider. For an experiment, this requires implementing the randomization procedure and adhering to the assignment of study participants into different treatment groups.

There are currently few experiments that involve large samples and the systematic use of administrative data. However, chapter 12 on the Aurora Health Care cooperation shows that a close research partnership and the right data curation procedures can allow compelling experiments while making only de-identified data accessible to researchers. Chapter 16 showcases the collaboration of the Government of Indonesia with a team of academic and non-academic development economists, which has linked large-scale randomized trials to an ongoing policymaking agenda. The chapter points out that administrative data can play a role at multiple stages of an experiment—be it to provide the sampling frame or to monitor the reach of interventions and provide important program outcome data. The multi-year collaboration between J-PAL Southeast Asia and the Government of Indonesia involved both using administrative records to evaluate interventions and implementing data collection for experiments as part of a national statistical survey. These chapters give a glimpse of the possibilities that open when researchers and policy organizations truly work as partners in using administrative data for policy analysis.

1.4 Further Reading

For information beyond the scope of this Handbook, we refer readers to a number of excellent starting points on a range of topics: the various challenges of making data available securely (see Reuter and Museux, 2010; Harron et al., 2017; ADRF Network, 2018; Future of Privacy Forum, 2017); resources on data held by national statistical offices (NSO) and the initial creation of integrated data systems, including (in the US) work by Actionable Intelligence for Social Policy (AISP); and guides for the European context, which include case studies of national statistical agencies (OECD, 2014; Bujnowska, 2019).

The existing literature also provides high-level guidance on numerous topics, including the following: methods to transparently select and authorize access applications at scale and to evaluate whether researchers are trustworthy (for a new approach, see Levenstein, Tyler and Davidson Bleckman, 2018); data use agreements that fit within the broader legal framework (some limited guidance provided by Kanous and Brock, 2015; Kuchinke et al., 2016; Alter and Gonzalez, 2018); access modalities such as providing a secure computing infrastructure with local or remote access (Weinberg et al., 2007; Vilhuber, 2013, 2017); tools to apply statistical disclosure limitation to the output of analysis conducted using the organization's data (Liu, 2020; Dupriez and Boyko, 2010; Duncan, Elliot and Salazar-González, 2011); complementary data publication mechanisms such as public-use or scientific-use data (Bujnowska, 2019); and how to publish information on and access modalities for confidential data (Abowd, Vilhuber and Block, 2012).

References in Chapter 1

Abowd, John M., Bryce E. Stephens, Lars Vilhuber, Fredrik Andersson, Kevin L. McKinney, Marc Roemer, and Simon Woodcock. 2009. "The LEHD Infrastructure Files and the Creation of the Quarterly Workforce Indicators." In *Producer Dynamics: New Evidence from Micro Data.* , ed. Timothy Dunne, J. Bradford Jensen and Mark J. Roberts. University of Chicago Press. https://www.nber.org/chapters/c0485.

Abowd, John M., Lars Vilhuber, and William Block. 2012. "A Proposed Solution to the Archiving and Curation of Confidential Scientific Inputs." *Lecture Notes in Computer Science*, 216–225. Berlin, Heidelberg:Springer. https://doi.org/10.1007/978-3-642-33627-0_17.

ADRF Network. 2018. "ADRF Network Working Group Reports." https://www.adrf.upenn.edu/our-work (accessed 2020-10-05).

Alter, George, and Richard Gonzalez. 2018. "Responsible Practices for Data Sharing." *The American psychologist*, 73(2): 146–156. https://doi.org/10.1037/amp0000258.

Altman, Micah, Alexandra Wood, David O'Brien, Salil Vadhan, and Urs Gasser. 2015. "Towards a Modern Approach to Privacy-Aware Government Data Releases." *Berkeley Technology and Law Journal*, 1967. https://doi.org/10.2139/ssrn.2779266.

Angrist, Joshua, Eric Bettinger, and Michael Kremer. 2006. "Long-Term Educational Consequences of Secondary School Vouchers: Evidence from Administrative Records in Colombia." *American Economic Review*, 96(3): 847–862. https://doi.org/10.1257/aer.96.3.847.

Australian Bureau of Statistics. 2017. "Managing the risk of disclosure: the Five Safes Framework." Report 1160.0. https://www.abs.gov.au/ausstats/abs@.nsf/Latestproducts/1160.0Main%20Features4Aug%202017 (accessed 2020-09-01).

BC Ministry of Citizens Services. n.d.. "Privacy, Security and the Five Safes Model." https://www2.gov.bc.ca/gov/content/data/about-data-management/data-innovation-program/privacy-security (accessed 2020-09-01).

Bertrand, Marianne, and Adair Morse. 2011. "Information Disclosure, Cognitive Biases, and Payday Borrowing." *The Journal of Finance*, 66(6): 1865–1893. https://doi.org/10.1111/j.1540-6261.2011.01698.x.

Bhargava, Saurabh, and Dayanand Manoli. 2015. "Psychological Frictions and the Incomplete Take-Up of Social Benefits: Evidence from an IRS Field Experiment." *American Economic Review*, 105(11): 3489–3529. https://doi.org/10.1257/aer.20121493.

Bujnowska, Aleksandra. 2019. "Access to European Statistical System Microdata." In *Data-Driven Policy Impact Evaluation: How Access to Microdata is Transforming Policy Design.* , ed. Nuno Crato and Paolo Paruolo, 87–99. Cham:Springer International Publishing. https://doi.org/10.1007/978-3-319-78461-8_6.

Card, David E., Raj Chetty, Martin S. Feldstein, and Emmanuel Saez. 2011. "Expanding Access to Administrative Data for Research in the United States." American Economic Association Report January. https://www.aeaweb.org/content/file?id=13

19.
Chetty, Raj. 2012. "Time Trends in the Use of Administrative Data for Empirical Research." http://www.rajchetty.com/chettyfiles/admin_data_trends.pdf (accessed 2018-07-19).

Desai, Tanvi, Felix Ritchie, and Richard Welpton. 2016. "Five Safes: Designing data access for research." https://uwe-repository.worktribe.com/output/914745 (accessed 2020-01-30).

Dhaliwal, Iqbal, and Rema Hanna. 2017. "The devil is in the details: The successes and limitations of bureaucratic reform in India." *Journal of Development Economics*, 124: 1–21. https://doi.org/10.1016/j.jdeveco.2016.08.008.

Differential Privacy Team. 2017. "Learning with Privacy at Scale." *Apple Machine Learning Journal*, 1(8). https://machinelearning.apple.com/2017/12/06/learning-with-privacy-at-scale.html.

Doshi, Jalpa A., Franklin B. Hendrick, Jennifer S. Graff, and Bruce C. Stuart. 2016. "Data, Data Everywhere, But Access Remains a Big Issue for Researchers: A Review of Access Policies for Publicly-Funded Patient-level Health Care Data in the United States." *eGEMs (Generating Evidence & Methods to improve patient outcomes)*, 4(2): 8. https://doi.org/10.13063/2327-9214.1204.

Duncan, George T., Mark Elliot, and Juan-José Salazar-González. 2011. *Statistical confidentiality: principles and practice. Statistics for Social and Behavioral Sciences*, New York:Springer-Verlag. https://doi.org/10.1111/j.1751-5823.2012.00196_11.x.

Dupriez, Olivier, and Ernie Boyko. 2010. "Dissemination of Microdata Files - Principles, Procedures and Practices." The World Bank Working Paper 005. http://ihsn.org/dissemination-of-microdata-files (accessed 2019-11-15).

Einav, Liran, and Jonathan Levin. 2014. "Economics in the age of big data." *Science*, 346(6210). https://doi.org/10.1126/science.1243089.

Erlingsson, Úlfar, Vasyl Pihur, and Aleksandra Korolova. 2014. "RAPPOR: Randomized Aggregatable Privacy-Preserving Ordinal Response." *Proceedings of the 2014 ACM SIGSAC Conference on Computer and Communications Security - CCS '14*, 1054–1067. https://doi.org/10.1145/2660267.2660348.

Future of Privacy Forum. 2017. "Understanding Corporate Data Sharing Decisions: Practices, Challenges, and Opportunities for Sharing Corporate Data with Researchers." Future of Privacy Forum. https://fpf.org/wp-content/uploads/2017/11/FPF_Data_Sharing_Report_FINAL.pdf (accessed 2020-10-05).

Gertler, Paul J., and Simone Boyce. 2003. "An Experiment in Incentive-Based Welfare: The Impact of PROGRESA on Health in Mexico." Royal Economic Society 85. https://ideas.repec.org/p/ecj/ac2003/85.html (accessed 2020-11-10).

Grigsby, John, Erik Hurst, and Ahu Yildirmaz. 2021. "Aggregate Nominal Wage Adjustments: New Evidence from Administrative Payroll Data." *American Economic Review*, Forthcoming. https://www.aeaweb.org/articles?id=10.1257/aer.20190318&&from=f (accessed 2020-11-10).

Groves, Robert. 2011. ""Designed Data" and "Organic Data"." https://www.census.gov/newsroom/blogs/director/2011/05/designed-data-and-organic-data.html (accessed 2020-09-01).

Groves, Robert M., and George J. Schoeffel. 2018. "Use of Administrative Records in Evidence-Based Policymaking:." *The ANNALS of the American Academy of Political and Social Science*. https://doi.org/10.1177/0002716218766508.

Hand, David J. 2018. "Statistical challenges of administrative and transaction data." *Journal of the Royal Statistical Society: Series A (Statistics in Society)*, 181(3): 555–605. https://doi.org/https://doi.org/10.1111/rssa.12315.

Harron, Katie, Chris Dibben, James Boyd, Anders Hjern, Mahmoud Azimaee, Mauricio L Barreto, and Harvey Goldstein. 2017. "Challenges in administrative data linkage for research." *Big Data & Society*, 4(2): 2053951717745678. https://doi.org/10.1177/2053951717745678.

Kanous, Alex, and Elaine Brock. 2015. "Contractual Limitations on Data Sharing Report prepared for ICPSR." Inter-University Consortium For Political And Social Research, https://doi.org/10.3886/contractuallimitationsdatasharing.

Kuchinke, Wolfgang, Christian Krauth, René Bergmann, Töresin Karakoyun, Astrid Woollard, Irene Schluender, Benjamin Braasch, Martin Eckert, and Christian Ohmann. 2016. "Legal assessment tool (LAT): an interactive tool to address privacy and data protection issues for data sharing." *BMC medical informatics and decision making*, 16(1): 81. https://doi.org/10.1186/s12911-016-0325-0.

Levenstein, Margaret C., Allison R. B. Tyler, and Johanna Davidson Bleckman. 2018. "The Researcher Passport: Improving Data Access and Confidentiality Protection." https://hdl.handle.net/2027.42/143808.

Liu, Fang. 2020. "A Statistical Overview on Data Privacy." *arXiv:2007.00765 [cs, stat]*. http://arxiv.org/abs/2007.00765 (accessed 2020-08-31).

Machanavajjhala, Ashwin, Daniel Kifer, John M. Abowd, Johannes Gehrke, and Lars Vilhuber. 2008. "Privacy: theory meets practice on the map." 277–286. https://doi.org/10.1109/ICDE.2008.4497436.

OECD. 2014. "Expert Group for International Collaboration on Microdata Access: Final Report." http://www.oecd.org/sdd/microdata-access-final-report-OECD-2014.pdf (accessed 2018-10-09).

Reuter, Wolf Heinrich, and Jean-Marc Museux. 2010. "Establishing an Infrastructure for Remote Access to Microdata at Eurostat." 249–257. Springer Berlin Heidelberg. https://doi.org/10.1007/978-3-642-15838-4_22.

SafeGraph. 2020. "Stopping COVID-19 with New Social Distancing Dataset." https://www.safegraph.com/blog/stopping-covid-19-with-new-social-distancing-dataset (accessed 2020-11-03).

Statistics Canada. 2018. "Information on Statistics Canada Privacy Framework." https://sencanada.ca/content/sen/committee/421/BANC/Briefs/BANC_SS-1_REF_StatisticsCanada_e.pdf (accessed 2020-10-05).

Taubman, Sarah L., Heidi L. Allen, Bill J. Wright, Katherine Baicker, and Amy N. Finkelstein. 2014. "Medicaid Increases Emergency-Department Use: Evidence from Oregon's Health Insurance Experiment." *Science*, 343(6168): 263. https://doi.org/10.1126/science.1246183.

The Times of India. 2020. "Chennai's waste management to go hi-tech." https://timesofindia.indiatimes.com/city/chennai/chennais-waste-management-to-go-hi-tech/

articleshow/78376635.cms (accessed 2020-11-10).

United Nations. 2014. "Fundamental Principles of Official Statistics." A/RES/68/261. https://unstats.un.org/unsd/dnss/gp/fundprinciples.aspx (accessed 2020-09-01).

Vilhuber, Lars. 2013. "Methods for Protecting the Confidentiality of Firm-Level Data: Issues and Solutions." *Labor Dynamics Institute*. https://digitalcommons.ilr.cornell.edu/ldi/19.

Vilhuber, Lars. 2017. "Confidentiality Protection and Physical Safeguards." https://hdl.handle.net/1813/46207 (accessed 2018-11-04).

Weinberg, Daniel, John M. Abowd, Sandra Rowland, Philip Steel, and Laura Zayatz. 2007. "Access Methods for United States Microdata." U.S. Census Bureau, Center for Economic Studies Working Paper 07-25. https://www2.census.gov/ces/wp/2007/CES-WP-07-25.pdf (accessed 2020-09-21).

Special Topics

CHAPTER 2

Physically Protecting Sensitive Data

Jim Shen (J-PAL, Massachusetts Institute of Technology)

Lars Vilhuber (Cornell University)

2.1 Introduction

Within the Five Safes framework, safe settings rely heavily on the physical environments in which data are stored, processed, transmitted, and accessed, and from which researchers can access computers that store and process the data. However, it is also the setting that is most dependent on rapidly evolving technology. In the 1980s, it was common and considered secure enough to send around floppy disks, which researchers then inserted into stand-alone desktop computers in a locked room. Forty years later, network technologies allow for superior security combined with greater ease of access.

Possibly because technological advances happen faster than legal frameworks change, data custodians and policymakers may not be aware of the most current technological possibilities when crafting the legal and contractual framework for data access. This chapter will attempt to capture a snapshot of the technologies available and in use

---

Copyright © Jim Shen and Lars Vilhuber.
Cite as: Shen, Jim, and Lars Vilhuber. "Physically Protecting Sensitive Data." In: Cole, Shawn, Iqbal Dhaliwal, Anja Sautmann, and Lars Vilhuber (eds.), *Handbook on Using Administrative Data for Research and Evidence-based Policy*. Cambridge, MA: Abdul Latif Jameel Poverty Action Lab. 2020.

as of 2020, as well as characterize the technologies along a multi-dimensional scale, allowing for some comparability across methods. This is followed by several examples, both from the case studies in this handbook as well as others that are of particular relevance.

As a caution, by the time that this chapter is being read, the range of possibilities may yet again have expanded (rarely does it contract). The difficulty of implementing any given data access mechanism is contingent on the local conditions, skills, and available resources. Due to the many possible factors that go into a technological choice, it is not feasible to make a comprehensive set of recommendations for data providers and researchers. However, this chapter can provide recommendations for a minimum baseline of security features that data access mechanisms should include and a framework for evaluating the tradeoffs between addressing likely threats while maintaining useful access and minimizing costs.

Readers must note that physical security is only one component of protecting individuals in data and safely using data for research and cannot be considered on its own. The various technical measures described in this chapter are always implemented within the context of an overall access mechanism and cannot be evaluated or ranked independently. Each case study in this handbook is an example of a global approach to implementing data access mechanisms, of which the technology used is one component.

For illustrative purposes, this chapter utilizes a simplified structure in which data providers, researchers, and possibly third parties are the actors involved in the process of storing and hosting data and computers. The introductory chapter and chapter 3 on data use agreements (DUA) provide a more refined view of the various roles.

2.2 Types of Security Threats

There are a variety of security threats, each with different levels of likelihood, severity, and considerations, that are unique to the specific context of every data sharing agreement and access mechanism.[1] Depending on the context, actions taken to address any given threat may be required, for practical or legal reasons, regardless of the burden on researchers or the cost of implementing the solutions. Data providers and researchers looking to establish new data access mechanisms should carefully judge the likely threats, including their severity and the cost-effective ways of addressing them.

The archetypical threat to any computer system is the active, unauthorized access by adversarial actors (commonly referred to as hackers). There are two main mechanisms in which this occurs. Adversarial actors can exploit technical vulnerabilities in the data access mechanism, such as improperly secured computer systems and networks. Threat actors can also utilize social engineering,[2] which is the use of deception to manipulate individuals to reveal credentials to unauthorized users.[3] There are many possible incentives for adversarial actors to compromise data: exploiting specific data (targeted attacks), inflicting financial or reputational harm (targeting organizations), seeking financial or reputational gain (attacks of opportunity), or attacking for its own sake (functionally random targeting). One cannot assume that any particular set of data is not of interest for adversarial actors merely due to the contents of the data or the organization that holds the data; many types of stolen electronic data have direct monetary value, and the attack itself can be the objective when adversaries are motivated by ideological reasons (Ablon, 2018).

---

[1] Cichonski et al. (2012) provides definitions, which are adopted here.
[2] https://csrc.nist.gov/glossary/term/social_engineering (accessed 2020-10-10).
[3] It is called phishing (https://csrc.nist.gov/glossary/term/phishing) when an e-mail or website is used to deceive an individual.

> One example of a data breach due to adversarial actors exploiting technical vulnerabilities is the Equifax data breach of 2017.[a] Equifax neglected to apply security patches on their servers, leading to adversarial actors compromising Equifax computer systems and the private information of over 147 million people.[b]
>
> ---
> [a] https://epic.org/privacy/data-breach/equifax/, accessed 2020-10-10.
> [b] FTC, https://www.ftc.gov/enforcement/cases-proceedings/refunds/equifax-data-breach-settlement, accessed 2020-10-10.

A related security threat is an unintentional breach where data are left unsecured by authorized users. In this scenario, the data are breached not by any deliberate attempt by adversarial actors to gain access but by behavior of authorized users that leaves data exposed, such as the loss of a device that contains or can access data. These breaches can still lead to adversarial actors acquiring confidential data. Collectively, deliberate attacks by adversarial actors and unintentional breaches can both be categorized as unauthorized access.

> There are numerous examples of data breaches through the loss of laptops containing unencrypted data. Whether from employees of a government agency, such as the Department of Veterans' Affairs (Bosworth, 2006) or the National Institutes of Health (Greenemeier, 2008), or staff at universities (Stanford Report, 2008), most of these are probably inadvertent: the laptop stolen was the target for its resale value, not for the (probably unknown) value of the data it contained. Not all incidents are due to loss of electronic media; physical confidential records can also be lost by theft or accidents (CBC News, 2019).

The third main category of security threats is internal: authorized users become bad actors and use the data in unauthorized ways. Unlike the other two threats, this is a situation where the threat comes from within the framework of the data access mechanism. This is an inherent risk of granting data access to outside users. Users may wish to conduct analyses that are unauthorized by the data provider, exploit the data for personal gain unrelated to the analytical use of the data, or suffer lapses in judgement regarding the protection of the data. This kind of threat is in part addressed through non-technical means, in particular the choice of safe people and contractual and legal sanctions. However, restrictive data access mechanisms serve to address this threat as well.

> The Facebook–Cambridge Analytica scandal[a] is an example of the misuse of data by otherwise authorized users. While the initial collection and analysis of Facebook user data by developers was within the bounds of Facebook's terms of service, a researcher subsequently provided the data to Cambridge Analytica in violation of those terms.
>
> [a]See Confessore (2018) for an overview.

2.3 Technical Features of Data Access Mechanisms

There are a variety of technical tools that can be used to protect against these security threats and are important for the implementation of secure data access mechanisms. This section provides a non-exhaustive introduction to a list of important tools, systems, and concepts. These tools broadly correspond to protecting three components of data access mechanisms: the transfer and storage of data, the researcher's access to the data, and the secure locations for data access. The chapter then proceeds to describe commonly used data access setups, the protections they provide, and their advantages and disadvantages.

2.3.1 The Basics

All computer systems should follow the basic computer security mechanisms. While this may be standard practice for any centrally managed computers, many researchers at universities, corporations, and government agencies may be self-managing their laptops. At a minimum, all computers should use a firewall and antivirus software, be encrypted with secure passwords, and apply basic computer hygiene, such as not using USB drives or other devices unless they are owned by the user (for example, see guidance by Microsoft[4] and Apple[5]). When using storage servers, operating systems need to be kept up-to-date with security patches. Data providers and researchers looking to implement new data access mechanisms, or to review existing ones, should consult with their institutions' IT and security staff.

2.3.2 Storage of Data

Physical Media

Physical media is any device used to store data: hard drives, solid-state drives, and removable media. Removable media include devices such as USB drives, DVDs, and external hard drives. Removable media are typically used in the transfer of data between parties, such as from a data provider to a researcher. They are often disallowed on secure access or analysis systems. On-site storage may be in the form of directly attached physical media or network drives.

Cloud Service

The use of cloud storage services[6] can provide storage solutions that also serve as transfer mechanisms. Mechanisms similar to cloud storage can be implemented by data providers or intermediaries by using open-source software such as Nextcloud[7] and is becoming more common, in particular in combination with cloud computing. Utilizing cloud storage services may place the data under the control of a third party, which may be prohibited depending on the data sharing agreement or relevant legal constraints. Files may be encrypted on cloud storage services.

---

[4] https://support.microsoft.com/en-us/help/4092060/windows-keep-your-computer-secure-at-home (accessed 2020-10-10).

[5] https://support.apple.com/en-ca/guide/mac-help/flvlt003/mac (accessed 2020-10-10).

[6] As of 2020, Amazon Web Services, Box, Dropbox, Google Drive, and Microsoft OneDrive are all vendors of cloud storage services.

[7] https://nextcloud.com (accessed 2020-10-10).

Reliability as a Criterion

Reliability of storage refers both to preventing data loss as well as maintaining system uptime. The risk of data loss can be mitigated by using one or more of the following techniques. Multiple disks can be organized in a redundant array (RAID) such that the failure of any one (or sometimes multiple) disk(s) does not result in the loss of data. Robust automated backup strategies tailored to the risk tolerance as well as any legal or DUA requirements can be used. Backup strategies involving manual action (plugging in a USB drive in combination with scheduled backup software) are fallible but may be considered as a last resort.

When using servers to store data, maximizing system uptime is important to allow for the uninterrupted use of data for research. Specialized storage servers allow for maintenance, including hot-swapping the hard drives, while the server remains available for use. Similarly, having a USB drive with a current backup available mitigates the downtime should data be lost.

Online storage services implement all of these techniques as a normal part of their businesses and may be one way for researchers utilize reliable data storage if compliant with DUAs. Furthermore, the ability to retrieve a backup copy or a previously versioned copy need not be implemented at every point. For instance, it may be sufficient for the data provider to implement backups for key data files. In case of data loss, the researcher can simply request a new copy of the file. However, researchers will still need to be able to back up their own code and derivative files.

2.3.3 Encryption

Encryption is a cornerstone of information security. Fundamentally, encryption is a process of encoding information using a process that prevents other parties from reading it unless they have the encryption key. Data can be encrypted at rest (when not being used or while stored on hard drives or USB drives) and in transit (while being transferred over a network or on physical media such as DVDs or USB drives).

CHAPTER 2

Even though using encryption may decrease convenience (a password or a hardware key needs to be used each time decryption occurs), utilizing encryption for data and devices should be mandated as a minimum-security feature as part of any data access mechanism. In almost all cases, there is no added monetary expense for encrypting existing data and devices; in return there is a substantial increase in protection against unauthorized access. IT staff, where available, should be well versed in these techniques. Individual researchers, if receiving data, should consult with IT staff on how to implement an appropriate strategy. While utilizing encryption is a basic computer security best practice, it is of particular relevance for data access mechanisms due to the many methods of using encryption for storing and transferring data.

Security in the context of data storage is the prevention of unauthorized data access should an adversary gain access to the storage device. On top of data access controls for users, the storage mechanism itself needs to be properly configured. Keeping the data fully encrypted when not in use, known as encryption at rest, provides protection in the event that an adversary gets access to the storage device. When an entire hard drive is encrypted and needs to be unlocked before being used it is called full-disk encryption (FDE), and it can be implemented with both hardware or software methods.[8]

FDE occurs once when systems (servers, laptops) are booted up and can be combined with biometric authentication. Data encryption may require that a hardware token be present any time data are processed, but such a hardware token may be embedded in the computer or attached as a USB device.[9] File-level encryption can also be employed when using online storage systems. Operating system–level FDE

---

[8] In the case of hardware-based encryption, the disk needs to be decrypted before the operating system can boot, whereas operating system–based encryption relies on features of the operating system once it is booted. In practice, the differences from a user perspective are minimal.

[9] For instance, Windows BitLocker supports the use of both a trusted platform module built into modern computer motherboards as well as a startup key stored on removable media (https://docs.microsoft.com/en-us/windows/security/information-protection/bitlocker/prepare-your-organization-for-bitlocker-planning-and-policies #bitlocker-key-protectors accessed 2020-10-10).

is built into all major operating systems: FileVault[10] on MacOS, BitLocker[11] on modern Microsoft Windows operating systems, and various systems on Linux OS.[12] If not using FDE, users can encrypt individual data files (file-level encryption) or virtual disks, both of which would only be decrypted when in use. Popular software for file-level encryption, such as GnuPG,[13] are free and easy to use and available for all major operating systems. For virtual encrypted disks, VeraCrypt[14] can be used.

In settings where cloud services are allowed, it is worthwhile to investigate the encryption practices of the cloud vendor. Many cloud vendors offer enterprise services that can meet higher standards of security suitable for meeting regulatory or legal requirements or can prevent the service provider from decrypting the data. However, while the cloud service may encrypt any data stored on its servers, the cloud storage service may be able (or even legally obligated) to decrypt the data. A work-around is to use additional file-level encryption before making the data available on the cloud service, and this may be mandated by the data sharing agreements.

2.3.4 Transfer of Data

Unless researchers access data at the data providers' computers and premises, data needs to be transferred.

Transfer by Physical Media

Physical media intended for data transfers such as USB drives and DVDs should always be encrypted. USB keys can be purchased with hardware-based encryption. When using physical media, the decryption keys (passwords) should always be transmitted separately; this

---

[10] https://support.apple.com/en-us/HT204837 (accessed 2020-10-10).
[11] https://docs.microsoft.com/en-us/windows/security/information-protection/bitlocker/bitlocker-overview (accessed 2020-10-10).
[12] https://help.ubuntu.com/community/Full_Disk_encryption_Howto_2019, accessed 2020-10-10.
[13] https://gnupg.org/index.html (accessed 2020-10-10).
[14] https://www.veracrypt.fr/en/Home.html (accessed 2020-10-10).

prevents an unauthorized user who manages to obtain either the decryption key or the physical media from accessing the protected data.

Secure Network Protocols

For data access mechanisms that rely on electronic transfers between the data custodian and researcher, using an encrypted transfer protocol is a minimum-security practice that should be followed at all times. Some obsolete but commonly used transfer protocols do not use encryption and are therefore vulnerable to data being read in transfer. Any transfer protocols should be encrypted in transit. There are many network protocols used for transferring data or establishing secure connections between computers. Data may be transferred peer-to-peer or may require the use of an intermediary party that sometimes is not a signatory to the DUA. Secure peer-to-peer transfer can use the SSH File Transfer Protocol (SFTP) or authenticated transfer via HTTPS (the same protocol used by banks and most modern websites, which encrypts the data sent between the client and the server). Transfer over virtual private networks is also encrypted, regardless of transfer protocols, including for shared directory mounts (Windows shares, NFS). In settings where cloud services are allowed, data transfers are always encrypted. Encrypted cloud services can fulfill the requirement for a minimally secure electronic transfer protocol.

Note that while the transfer may be encrypted, both intermediate as well as final endpoints should use encrypted storage. As with cloud services, it may be useful to use file-level encryption to ensure that any intermediate storage locations do not compromise the security of the transfer mechanism.

2.3.5 Data Access Controls

Data access controls are of particular relevance for systems where multiple researchers utilize the same computing resources for access to or analysis of data. Access control regulates what users can view or use in a computing environment, preventing unauthorized users from accessing confidential data. Access controls can be implemented by setting user permissions on directories at the operating system level on a computer. Another method is to use a virtual machine, which is a completely isolated computing environment running on a host computer. A host computer can run multiple virtual machines, with each researcher or research project having a specific virtual machine. Each virtual machine is configured to provide access only to a specific (limited) set of data files as defined by the access permissions of the research team. In addition, software availability or network access can be customized on a per-project basis. Containers, popularly known as Docker,[15] or Linux techniques such as chroot[16], achieve similar goals with varying degrees of isolation and performance penalties.

2.3.6 Virtual Private Networks

When using virtual private networks (VPNs), an encrypted channel is established between two computers over public networks. Once set up, the connection is as secure as though the computers were connected on the same local, private network. The VPN ensures that a minimum-security level is achieved by all other network connections, such as shared network drives or remote desktop access, as these all occur within the same encrypted channel. This is useful for data access mechanisms that allow researchers to access data from many possible locations as well as for data transfers. As typically implemented, users must authenticate themselves with usernames, passwords, and often a secure token (2FA) to access the VPN. Many universities have VPN services that allow researchers to access university networks from a remote location. There are VPN configuration settings built into the Windows Server operating system as well as open source options. These can be useful in instances where a data sharing partnership has to implement a VPN from scratch, such as establishing a VPN service at a data provider location that is sharing data for the first time.

---

[15] https://www.docker.com/ (accessed 2020-10-10).
[16] https://help.ubuntu.com/community/BasicChroot (accessed 2020-10-10).

2.3.7 IP Address Restrictions

When any network is involved, network access controls may be implemented. One way to ensure that only an authorized system has access to a remote system is to restrict the IP address of the devices that are allowed to connect to the server. This can be useful for performing data transfers as well as for remote access to data. There are two types of restrictions: blacklisting and whitelisting. Blacklisting blocks known or potential bad actors but otherwise does not restrict connections to the server; whitelisting only allows authorized users access to the server and is the primary use of IP restrictions in an access control mechanism. This is frequently an option built into the software for managing the server. For example, software used for managing SFTP can restrict the IP addresses that it will accept connections from. For data providers and researchers, this can be restricted to specific devices that the researcher registers with the data provider as the access computer. Other more sophisticated network access controls may also be implemented as dictated by any one of the involved parties' IT security staff. Restricting the IP address to specific devices can help protect against both unauthorized users, who would need to gain access to an authorized device, as well as allow for the monitoring of the whitelisted devices to guard against misuse of the data.

2.3.8 Remote Desktop

Remote desktop software (also referred to as virtual desktop infrastructure, VDI) enables users to connect to another computer's desktop over a network. This can be used in data access mechanisms when the researcher does not have direct access to the data and performs the analysis remotely on a separate computer. Data custodians must configure the analysis computer to allow for incoming remote desktop connections, and the access provider must supply the appropriate software and network infrastructure to support the remote desktop connections from the access computer. Password and other authentication requirements help protect against access by unauthorized users. Analysis computers (typically servers) configured for remote desktop access typically run Microsoft or Linux operating systems; access to the remote desktop exist on a variety of platforms, including cell phones and Apple computers. Vendors of such systems include Microsoft,[17] Citrix,[18] VMware,[19] and NoMachine.[20] Remote desktop connections are often channeled through a VPN for additional security.

The use of remote desktop software allows a researcher to use an analysis computer remotely with the desktop environment of the analysis computer displayed on the client device (the access computer). The data custodian retains full physical control over the analysis computer. This can help prevent the misuse of data by authorized users. The use of remote desktop software can be valuable in instances where the data custodian has decided to not allow researchers to hold the data, in research data centers accessing data stored elsewhere, or when an access provider is supporting researchers across a wide geographical area, such as supporting international research on data that cannot leave the country of origin. The access computers do not need to be capable of running statistical software or intensive analysis; the analysis will occur on the server that hosts the data and software packages. At the same time, the analysis computer (hosted by the data provider) must be capable of supporting multiple, simultaneous researchers running analysis software. Remote desktops are reliant on active internet connections. While remote desktops are robust to network disconnects (users can simply reconnect to the running session and continue where they left off), the user experience degrades when network connections are unstable or slow.

2.3.9 Thin Clients

Thin clients are a special case of an access computer running remote desktop client software. The primary benefit of thin clients is the extension of hardware control to the researcher's desktop by the data

---

[17]https://www.microsoft.com/en-us/p/microsoft-remote-desktop/9wzdncrfj3ps (accessed 2020-10-10).
[18]https://www.citrix.com (accessed 2020-10-10).
[19]https://www.vmware.com (accessed 2020-10-10).
[20]https://www.nomachine.com (accessed 2020-10-10).

provider. Very secure implementations of thin clients can prohibit any usage beyond displaying information from the server and accepting mouse and keyboard input from the user. Thin clients typically operate without local storage, preventing users from saving data to the client. Thin clients can be secured against unauthorized access with various login and authentication requirements that may be more stringent than the controls on researcher's own system. Thin clients may be housed within a specific access location or provided directly to the researcher.

Generally, researchers would not procure their own thin clients, as they have no utility outside of facilitating remote access. Rather, they are typically provisioned by data custodians or access providers. The management and infrastructure needed to support thin clients may require expenses over and above the cost of providing remote desktop services.

However, one of the main advantages of dedicated hardware thin clients is that they are cheaper and simpler than regular computers. As of the time of writing, thin clients can cost as little as US$100 for the hardware itself, in contrast with the cheapest entry level computers, which are several hundred dollars. Thin clients can be sourced from many manufacturers of enterprise hardware both as standalone devices for the user to configure as well as full-fledged hardware and software package solutions configured by the vendor (the latter costs more than solely procuring the hardware). Thin clients can be purchased from most business PC vendors, including Dell[21] and HP,[22] as well as some custom-produced solutions, such as the SD-Box[23] developed by, and produced for, the Centre d'accès sécurisé aux données (CASD).[24]

---

[21] https://www.dell.com/en-us/work/shop/wyse-endpoints-and-software/sc/cloud-client/thin-clients, accessed 2020-12-10

[22] https://www8.hp.com/us/en/cloud-computing/thin-clients.html (accessed 2020-10-10).

[23] https://www.casd.eu/en/technologie/sd-box (accessed 2020-10-10).

[24] https://www.casd.eu/en (accessed 2020-10-10).

2.3.10 Biometric Authentication

Biometrics[25] are physical, biological, and sometimes behavioral features unique to individuals. Biometric authentication is the use of biometric features to verify the identity of individual users based on stored information about authorized users. One of the most common biometric technologies in current use is fingerprint scanners for consumer electronics such as laptops and smartphones. Other commonly used technologies include facial recognition, retinal or iris recognition, and voice identification. Biometrics can be used to control access to secured locations as well as to secure individual devices, helping to prevent unauthorized access. The main components of such an access system include the biometric sensor itself, which is connected to a database that contains the set of validated users, and either the physical or electronic lockouts for a given system (e.g., entering a room or logging into a computer), which are controlled by the biometric sensor.

Biometric authentication techniques can serve both as a primary form of identification as well as a layered two or multiple factor authentication techniques, such as in conjunction with passwords or other devices. While some devices come with built-in biometric authentication, such as the aforementioned fingerprint scanners, implementing additional biometric authentication requires significant resources. In particular, the initial enrollment of users' biometrics typically requires the physical presence of the individuals.

2.3.11 Physical Access Cards

Physical access cards are electronic cards that identify the card bearer for a physical access control system. An access mechanism for devices or rooms secured by a card reader validates the user's card against a database that has a set of valid cards and subsequently opens the locks on the system or room. The cards can be outfitted with magnetic stripes, barcodes, chips, or other systems for interfacing with the

---

[25] https://csrc.nist.gov/glossary/term/biometric (accessed 2020-10-10).

card reader. Physical access cards are commonly used by organizations, including universities and government agencies, and can have the advantage of using existing infrastructure to support the creation of secure access rooms for researchers receiving administrative data. Unlike with biometric authentication, access cards can be easily lost or given to others and have a greater potential for misuse. Older systems may also be vulnerable to cloning attacks in which the magnetic stripe is copied to an unauthorized card. Protecting the access cards themselves is primarily a policy and training issue.

2.3.12 Secure Rooms

Rooms that house computing systems (both for storage and for access) can be secured against unauthorized access. Rooms can be constructed in ways that prevent unauthorized access and can be outfitted to monitor usage and users. Secure rooms may be required to have fully enclosed walls that extend from floor to ceiling, have a small number of possible entryways, and have doors, windows, air vents, and other possible entryways secured by bars, mesh, or other methods. Doors and walls may need to satisfy minimum specifications in terms of materials, construction techniques, and thickness to increase protection against physical attacks. For instance, reinforced doors and walls offer increased protection compared to regular home and office construction materials. Door hinges, access panels, partitions, windows, and other possible ways of entering the room can be installed from the inside of the secure room to prevent their removal from the outside. Additional requirements may extend to physically securing devices within the room. Computers may be required to have no outside network connections (air-gapped network) or no network connection at all. These restrictions are typically only utilized when mandated by data providers or required by law for the sharing of data. Building secure rooms is a costly endeavor, as few offices will meet these specifications without additional construction and hardening. Not all university campuses will have secure rooms, and when they do, there will often only be one secure room. Thus, access to secure rooms typically entails both long-distance and local travel, reducing overall accessibility.

2.4 Typical Access Mechanisms

The above technological methods can be combined in various ways, yielding an access mechanism. The case studies in this handbook each implement one or more of these access mechanisms. This section provides four archetypal examples of data access mechanisms. These are broad categorizations of how data access mechanisms can be set up and are not exhaustive of all possibilities.

2.4.1 Remote Execution

Under a remote execution model, a researcher submits a request to have the analysis executed on the confidential data by the data custodian.[26] The researcher does not directly access the data and can only view output shared by the entity executing the analysis code. Data custodians maintain full control over the data and have the opportunity to check the researchers' code prior to execution as well as the output produced by the code prior to transferring to the researcher.

Remote execution requires that the data custodian maintains a mechanism for executing researchers' code, either through an automated service or technical staff manually executing the analysis. The remote execution systems may also conduct disclosure avoidance checks on the output before sending it back to the researchers. These checks may also be conducted in automated fashions or manually. In some cases, data providers prepare test files: data files that have the same variables and table structures as the real data but contain fictitious values.

The data custodian creates and maintains the systems to facilitate the transfer of the necessary files through customized web portals or code upload facilities. While the input code and the output results by definition are non-sensitive files, electronic data transfer mechanisms or secure network protocols may still be useful tools. In some instances, cost is recovered by charging researchers.

---

[26]Remote execution systems are non-interactive. See Virtual Data Enclave for remote systems in which access is interactive.

Remote execution gives strong protection against adversarial actors via the data access mechanism (breaches of a data provider occurring outside of the data access mechanism can still occur), though query attacks, in which attackers create overlapping queries or tabulations that reveal sensitive data, may still be possible (Asghar and Kaafar, 2019). Researchers have no opportunity to accidentally disclose research data. Data providers have strong protection against misuse of the data, as they have the opportunity to vet every analysis code prior to executing it or transferring the results back to the researcher. The tradeoff for the data provider is the cost of providing the necessary resources (systems and staff time) to conduct the analysis.

Remote execution systems may integrate throttles and delays to prevent resource abuse or query attacks. For instance, the number and runtime of analysis jobs for users may be severely limited or carry an hourly cost. Researchers need to specify the analysis carefully, and iterative or exploratory analysis may be inhibited or reduced. For some researchers, this may be perceived as an impediment; however, for researchers working under a preregistration paradigm, the same restriction may be neutral or even perceived as an advantage.

2.4.2 Physical Data Enclave

In a physical data enclave model, researchers must enter an access-controlled location (the data enclave) to analyze the data. The data provider can act as its own data custodian or appoint a trusted third party to run the enclave on the data provider's behalf; enclaves under the control of the researcher are described under Researcher-Provided Infrastructure. The data custodian can choose to use on-site storage and computing at the data enclave or on a remote server that can only be accessed by thin clients located within the data enclave; in this case the connection to the remote server typically uses secure network protocols, virtual private networks, or an encrypted direct connection. The data custodian typically has staff or automated systems to ensure that only authorized researchers enter the location, which may be secured with biometric authentication or physical access cards. Sometimes, the access rooms themselves satisfy specific security requirements (secure rooms). Output vetting may ensure that only safe outputs are removed from enclaves.

The data custodian has most of the security benefits of remote execution by maintaining full control over the data in the entire research process. Because the data remains under the control of the data custodian and secure rooms restrict physical access to approved users, the data custodian is secured against unauthorized access. Physical data enclaves remove the potential bottleneck and additional expense of requiring dedicated staff on the part of the data provider to actually run the analysis on behalf of the researcher.

However, physical data enclaves still impose restrictions on the flexibility of researchers. Instead of waiting for someone to run the remote execution for them, researchers must schedule visits and travel to a physical location. Capacity limits may restrict the number of users that can access the data at the same time. In more basic implementations, a physical data enclave can be as simple as a locked room that only authorized users can enter. Meeting more stringent security requirements can impose a substantial initial start-up cost on new sites. This cost is often borne by the researchers' institution, and is too large for individual researchers to incur.

2.4.3 Virtual Data Enclave

A virtual data enclave is conceptually similar to a physical data enclave. Data custodians still maintain servers that house the data. However, the requirement to access the data from a secure room is relaxed. Researchers have many choices for access, sometimes unrestricted, and may be able to utilize their normal office or home to access the data via remote access. There are two basic approaches to the remote access mechanism: either using remote desktop software that the researcher can install on their own computer or dedicated thin clients rented from, or provided by, the data custodian. As with physical enclaves, the data custodian typically also requires the use of secure network protocols or virtual private networks to access the data.

Virtual data enclaves retain most of the security benefits of physical data enclaves, except for physical control of the environment from which researchers access the data. In particular, as with physical data enclaves, data or output cannot be removed from the secure environment. While virtual enclaves remain robust against unauthorized release of the data by keeping data stored in a secured environment and requiring authenticated access, it is possible for unauthorized individuals to view and potentially interact with the restricted access environment. For instance, unauthorized users could illicitly view the screen of an authorized user using the access system (known as shoulder surfing), or authorized users could share credentials with unauthorized users. Note that legal and contractual requirements may make such behavior explicitly illegal.

The virtual data enclave model does not require researchers to travel to specific facilities to perform their research, though some restrictions may still apply (IP addresses, university offices). While there may still be incentives to share costs for thin clients, most virtual data enclaves are affordable for individual researchers.

2.4.4 Researcher-Provided Infrastructure

In some data sharing arrangements, the researcher provides the on-site storage and analysis infrastructure. The data provider will transmit the data to the researcher through a secure transfer mechanism (physical media, over secure network protocols, or a cloud service). Providers typically require that data be encrypted at various stages of processing.

When the analysis environment is under the physical control of the researcher, the data provider has a significantly reduced ability to monitor usage of the data. More so here than in other models, the data provider depends on the contractual agreement with the researcher for preventing the misuse of the data, typically through a DUA specifying safe settings and the nature of safe outputs.

This process allows researchers more flexibility and rapid turnarounds on research findings. The overall cost is typically much lower, as the data provider only has to provide the data and the staff necessary to transfer data to the researchers. Separate staff or systems are not needed to control exit or entry of people and to monitor analysis outputs, since this is delegated to the researcher. Data providers may choose to conduct on-site inspections to verify adherence to contractual agreements of the safe setting, verify at-rest encryption protocols, or require attestation of post-project destruction of data. Some providers require that researchers submit their output for approval, which requires staff time.

2.5 Five Aspects of Data Access Mechanisms

Actual implementations of data access mechanisms have many degrees of freedom in combining the technical components outlined at the start of this chapter. The four typical access mechanisms combine these technical components in specific ways. Each of the case studies in this handbook is a variation of the four typical access mechanisms. In order to summarize the salient features of data access mechanisms, each of the data access mechanisms are categorized in five aspects:

- The level of **researcher agency over analysis computers** refers to any technical restrictions on usage of the analysis computers.
- The **location of analysis computers and data** refers to the physical location of researcher-accessible computers used to analyze the data; for simplicity, this context assumes that the analysis computers are at the same location as the data.
- The **location of access computers** refers to the physical location of the computers (endpoints) that researchers use to access the data, which may be the same or separate from the analysis computers.
- The level of **access security** refers to the overall physical security arrangements for the environment and access computers from which researchers can access the data.
- The **range of analysis methods available** to researchers refers to any restrictions on the types of statistical analysis that researchers can perform on the data.

For each aspect, a data access mechanism is classified into three categories. These are weakly aligned with how restrictive it may be on the researcher, or conversely, how much control the data provider exerts; these range from high to low, but the mapping is not always exact. However, in all cases, there are distinct variants, which are described in the sections below. For convenience, a simple visualization has been defined that maps the level of restrictions to colors (with the most restrictive category of each aspect being the lightest while the least restrictive is the darkest), allowing a visual comparison of multiple access mechanisms.

Note that "control" is deliberately not framed as guaranteeing greater security. The level of security of any data access mechanism is dependent on a large number of factors of which the technological features are merely one component. Proper implementation and maintenance of the technical infrastructure, compliance with restrictions outlined in the DUA, the training of users and staff, and other factors all contribute to the actual security of a data access mechanism.

When proposing and negotiating a potential DUA, evaluating the physical security arrangements along the five aspects outlined can help researchers and their data providers craft robust mechanisms to protect data when transferring and using data for research.

Each of the five aspects of data access mechanisms have specific interactions with physical security. Such interactions are highlighted further in the descriptions of the five aspects and examples provided. In all cases, relaxing restrictions increases risk with respect to physical security (safe settings) but can be mitigated by measures in the other safes of the Five Safes framework discussed in this chapter, allowing data providers to maintain an acceptable risk-cost-usability trade-off. The five aspects are not fully independent but neither are they tightly aligned. Thus, it is possible to combine low restrictions on the location of analysis computers with any level of agency over their configuration or have highly restricted access environments combined with a wide range of restrictions on analysis methods.

2.5.1 Researcher Agency Over Analysis Computers

One of the key controls leveraged by data providers is the level of agency that researchers have over the analysis computer. This is typically implemented through restrictions on operating system configuration and software installation; the effect on researchers is the potential restrictions on the software that they can utilize.

Data providers may choose to grant researchers only low or medium agency over analysis computers in order to increase computer and network security and as a mechanism for disclosure control. By restricting what users can do, such controls can help harden the analysis computers against direct threats from adversarial actors or researchers unwittingly installing malware on the analysis computers.

In a **low agency setting**, researchers will be limited to the software that the data provider chooses to allow and will not have administrative privileges over the analysis computer.[27]

A **medium agency** setting may allow researchers some choice of software or limited system configuration. For instance, researchers may be able to install or request the installation of supplemental packages for pre-approved software (R, Stata) but may not be able to change system parameters such as which network to use. Typically, data providers (or data intermediaries) have direct administrative control of such computers.

In the **high researcher agency** settings, researchers have few restrictions on how the analysis computer can be configured. They may have administrative privileges to the analysis computer and few, if any, restrictions on the software that can be installed. The researcher may own and physically control the analysis computer or may be granted administrative privileges to a computer that is owned by the data provider or third party. Data providers may still mandate technical solutions such as the use of monitoring, operating system patch management software, or anti-virus software.

---

[27]These restrictions can affect not only the base software itself but also third-party additions for those software such as third-party packages for Python, R, and Stata.

Table 2.1: Examples of researcher agency over analysis computers

Researcher Agency	Example
Low Agency	In the Statistics Canada Real Time Remote Access (RTRA) system, researchers can only use SAS and cannot directly view the data with no exceptions allowed.
Medium Agency	The Federal Statistical Research Data Centers (FSRDC) network has a specific set of software on their secure computing network that is made available to researchers. Additional software can be requested, which must be approved by program managers and security analysts.
High Agency	In the National Center for Education Statistics (NCES) restricted-use data license, the researcher must set up a secure data room in accordance with NCES requirements. Researchers provide the analysis computer, retaining full administrative control and the freedom to use any software.

The advantage of low researcher agency is the reduced likelihood of inadvertent or intentional unauthorized use of data. The cost of low or medium agency is varied. Restrictions on software may increase training expenditures for researchers. Restrictions on physical attributes of the analysis computers may increase the expense of providing more storage or limit computationally intensive analyses, slowing down research. A low researcher agency agreement shifts most of the burden of maintaining the analysis computer onto the data provider. Thus the increased security of low agency is gained through slower research and higher costs for the data provider.

2.5.2 Location of Analysis Computers and Data

The location of the researcher-accessible data and the analysis computer defines who is considered the data custodian within a data access mechanism. Note that this is distinct from agency over the analysis computer: the analysis computer may be physically located with researchers, but the researcher may have low agency over that computer. The selected examples also abstract from situations where data storage and computing capabilities are in separate locations, as these situations are rare.[28] The party that houses the analysis computers and data has physical control. As such, they will need to provide the physical infrastructure and technical staff to store the data and facilitate access.

The default situation is for the **data provider** to have custody of the analysis computer and data, acting as the data custodian. This may occur when there are specific legal or policy requirements for the data's location and security or if the data provider is best positioned to act as such in terms of technical capabilities. Data providers who have existing infrastructure that they can repurpose or have access mechanisms established as part of their existing work may find this option to be particularly attractive. Furthermore, by acting as their own data custodian, transferring data is not a task that the data provider needs to consider.

Data providers can choose a **third-party** data custodian. In general, third-party data custodians (also called data intermediaries) interact with multiple researchers and may interact with multiple data providers. Third parties may have better or specific technical expertise, lower cost structures for the same level of security, and may leverage economies of scale in security and access mechanisms. Third parties can be government statistical agencies, acting on behalf of provincial or administrative government agencies, data centers at universities, or commercial entities. They may also have expertise in combining data from multiple sources while protecting the privacy of each source. For instance, government departments responsible for immigration and taxes may not be legally allowed to share data with each other, but they may each be able to transfer the data to a trusted third party. University-based third parties tend to be more familiar with the requirements and use cases of researchers, enabling these third parties to be more responsive to the needs of researchers: an area of expertise that can be of interest to data providers. For instance, university-based third parties may have expertise in survey management and data

---

[28] All computing platforms, as of the writing of this chapter, require that data be transferred to the analysis computer's memory, thus necessarily co-locating data and analysis.

archiving or in high-performance computing. Entities without their own research agendas may be particularly appealing as third parties, as that removes one of the incentives for the misuse of the data by an external data custodian.

In some cases, the distinction between these two categories becomes blurred. A data provider with substantial expertise in making their own data accessible may offer this expertise to others, thus acting as third-party data custodian.[29]

Finally, individual **researchers** can act as the data custodian. This is still quite frequently used, in particular when no previous data access existed. For the researcher, acting as the data custodian enables more flexibility for accessing the data without traveling or remote access systems. Most of the cost of maintaining IT infrastructure and security fall onto the researcher, subject to other conditions in the overall data access plan; in addition, researchers assume the risk and liability associated with housing data. Security provisions include keeping analysis computers offline with no external network connections or other provisions. The enforcement of the DUA becomes a key mechanism for preventing the misuse of the data. Researcher agency over the analysis computer may also be limited, despite the researcher having physical control of the analysis computer. For instance, some data providers (often commercial companies) provide researchers with fully encrypted and remotely managed laptops. While the laptop and data are located with the researcher, the researcher has only low agency over the analysis computer.

In all cases where the data provider relinquishes the data custodial role, data are transferred. While secure data transfer mechanisms exist, this is an additional risk within the overall framework; as described earlier, the cost is typically low to null.

---

[29]The United States Federal Statistical Research Data Center (FSRDC) network makes data from five US government agencies available to approved researchers. These include the Census Bureau, which created the FSRDC system in the 1980s as a network to provide access to Census Bureau data only. The FSRDC's data and analysis computers continue to be located within the secure computing center of the Census Bureau itself (U.S. Census Bureau, n.d.*b*).

Table 2.2: Examples of analysis computer and data locations

Data Location	Example
Data Provider	The Institute for Employment Research (RDC-IAB) (on-site access) house all highly confidential RDC-IAB data on their own servers, which are accessed remotely by researchers from various locations.
Third Party	The Private Capital Research Institute (PCRI) serves as a trusted third party for its data providers (private capital firms) and in turn contracts with a third party (National Opinion Research Center, NORC) to maintain the analysis computers and data access mechanism.
Researcher	The Aurora Health Care and MIT data exchange has the data and analysis computer located with the researcher. Researchers must store the data in accordance with security requirements outlined in their DUA.

For data providers, transferring control of the data and analysis computers to a third party or directly to researchers might be desirable when support for many researchers is a burden for the regular business of the data provider. By transferring the data to another party, a data provider may no longer be responsible for the cost of providing computational infrastructure for data storage and analysis. However, the data provider may see some additional costs for enforcing access restrictions, such as needing to conduct site visits once physical custody of the data has been transferred. Data providers will rely on the enforcement of DUAs when giving others custody of data.

Location of Access Computers

In many cases, the analysis computer may not be physically accessible to the researcher. This section therefore distinguishes access computers and restrictions that might be imposed on them as to their location and type. As a special case, the access computer can be coincidental with the analysis computer. Access computers can be located with the non-researcher data custodian, a third-party access provider, or the researcher. The location of the access computer is not necessarily aligned with the ownership of the access computer. For instance, a researcher may be assigned a computer that serves as an access computer but which is owned by the data provider. The security of the access computers is discussed in the next aspect, which is distinct from the locational aspect.

If the access computer is located with the **non-researcher data custodian**, which can be the data provider or a third-party custodian, the researcher must travel to that location.

Data providers can choose a **third-party** access provider. Note that the third-party access provider need not be a data custodian. Researchers may still have to travel to a separate location. The key role played by third-party access providers is control over physical access to the access computers. In some cases, third-party access providers may also have the technical capability to maintain sophisticated network connections that are beyond the scope of individual researchers, such as VPN setups with dedicated encrypted endpoints. In other cases, it may simply be a way for multiple researchers to share the cost of using a mandated technical solution.[30]

Finally, access computers can be located with the **researcher**. Trivially, locating the analysis computer with the researcher makes the access computer co-incidental. However, there are numerous cases where the access computer is with the researcher while the analysis computer is not. Examples include any web-based access, most remote execution systems, and many remote desktop systems: researchers use their own computers to access the portal while all computation occurs elsewhere. In almost all cases, locating access computers with researchers allows them to work from a location of their choice, though in some cases this may be restricted to a designated university office.

In general, the closer access computers are located to the data provider, the higher the security arrangements that apply. However, the two aspects are not perfectly correlated. In particular, access computers located with researchers can have very different security arrangements.

---

[30]The French CASD charges rent for its thin clients, and researchers sometimes locate such a thin client in a lab for shared access.

Table 2.3: Examples of access computer locations

Access Location	Example
Data Custodian	The New Brunswick Institute for Research, Data and Training (NB-IRDT) is an example of locating access computers with the data custodian. Researchers wishing to use data held by NB-IRDT must travel to one of the NB-IRDT campuses to utilize the access computers. The access computers, in turn, connect over secure networks to the central analysis computers.
Third Party	The SafePod Network (SPN) in the United Kingdom is an example of locating access computers with a third-party access provider. Each individual SafePod, located at academic institutions, houses an access computer that provides remote access to the UK Administrative Data Research Network (University of Bristol, n.d.).
Researcher	The RDC-IAB Job Submission Application (JoSuA) system is a web interface that researchers can use from their own computers to submit analysis files to the IAB-RDC for execution on IAB systems.

Security of Access Computers

In addition to the location of access computers, the security of access to those computers can vary substantially. This aspect encompasses both the location where the access computer resides and the type of access computer. Security of access is categorized in three levels: high, medium, and low security. Data providers and researchers looking to establish new data access mechanisms should weigh the additional resource costs and barriers to research incurred by increasing access location security with the additional protections that higher security access locations provide.

In instances where a party other than the data provider maintains the access location, data providers typically have the right to approve the security arrangements, conduct audits, or otherwise directly verify that the operator is in compliance with the mandated security requirements.

A **high security access location** has strong specifications for physical security, requiring the use of a secure room, typically requiring additional hardening of the room beyond just access controls, physical monitoring by video or access location staff, in addition to any electronic monitoring on the access computer itself. The additional protections and monitoring guard against unauthorized access as well as the removal of unauthorized outputs from the access location.

If not already existent at the access location, data custodians or access providers will require expertise from IT and security specialists to assist with defining the specifications and implementation of the features of high security access rooms.

A **medium security access location** has a defined location with access restricted to approved researchers. These can be rooms secured with keycards, biometrics, or a simple lock and key restricted to approved staff. Such restrictions may be designed to prevent a limited set of unauthorized access attempts or to inhibit shoulder surfing. Medium security access rooms may incur additional costs for the location administrator, requiring dedicated space and staff to maintain the access location itself, but may also be as simple as a designated locked room at a university research institute.

A **low security access location** has few or no access controls. Simple restrictions might include broad geo-restrictions (campus-only) or procedures to follow. Data providers may mandate storing the access computer in a locked room or the use of IP address restrictions. When no access restrictions are imposed, researchers are free to use access computers from any location.

In addition to the locational security described above, the **type of access computer** can also range from high security to low security. Highly secure access computers (which do not contain data) may still include fully encrypted operating systems, the use of VPNs, remote desktop software, secure network protocols, and encryption or requiring biometric authentication of the access computer. This can take the form of dedicated thin clients. Low security access computers are typically allowed for remote submission or web portal-type access, where any computer, in any location, is allowed.

Table 2.4: Examples of access computer security

Access Security	Example
High Security	The FSRDC network maintains a network of 29 locations (U.S. Census Bureau n.d.b). While these secure rooms are located at partner organizations (universities, research centers, Federal Reserve Banks), the rooms themselves are under the control of the US Census Bureau and none contain any data. Each secure room contains multiple thin clients. Researchers travel (across campus or to a partner organization) to use the thin clients to access analysis computers located within the secure computing center of the Census Bureau (U.S. Census Bureau, n.d.*b*).
Medium Security	Data distributed under the NCES restricted-use data license must be kept in a locked room with access restricted only to licensed researchers, and the security arrangements are subject to random audits by NCES.
Low Security	In the Stanford-SFUSD Partnership, data are stored on secured servers at Stanford. However, researchers can access the data from anywhere as long as they take reasonable and appropriate efforts to keep the data secure from unauthorized access as specified in their DUA.

This section combines the type of access and location into one aspect, since the ultimate convenience to researchers arises from a combination of the two security measures. For instance, a data provider might provide researchers with a dedicated secure laptop, which can only be used to remotely access the analysis computers and nothing else. While there may be no location restrictions imposed on the researcher, the secured computer does not hold any data and this may be considered to be a de-facto **medium** security solution.

The terms of the remote access will be defined in the DUA between the researcher and the data provider. The risks of locating the access computers but not the analysis computers away from the data provider are smaller. Because access computers contain no data, even if encrypted, the risk of inadvertent disclosure (for instance, if stolen) is reduced. Remaining risks include shoulder surfing and credential sharing, which can be mitigated by using third parties to control access. There is substantial convenience for researchers from having the access computer closer to their usual place of work, increasing the speed of research. The growth of networks of research data centers, where access is shared amongst many users while data are mostly remote, is testament to the demand among researchers and the acceptability of the risk for many data providers.

2.5.3 Range of Analysis Methods Available

The final aspect of data access mechanisms is the set of analysis methods available to researchers. Analysis methods can be unrestricted, subject to limited restrictions, or under extensive restrictions. Methods range from simple tabulations to complex machine learning algorithms via standard econometric techniques.

These restrictions can be implemented for technical or security reasons but mainly serve to ensure that researchers cannot misuse the data or generate unsafe output. This aspect of data access mechanisms is distinct from the agency that researchers have over the analysis computer and is closely related to the statistical protection of the data (see chapters 5 and 6), affecting safe data and outputs.

Restricting the analysis methods available to the researcher is primarily intended to protect the outputs of any analysis, preventing reidentification and other misuses of the data. Generally, the goal of restrictions on methods is to relax or automate output checks. Setting up such systems requires a high degree of technical sophistication and resources available to data custodians. Few off-the-shelf implementations of restricting analysis methods are available. While this may be intended as a physical restriction on safe projects, researchers and data providers looking to establish new data access mechanisms should be clear on what restrictions may be placed on analysis methods and plan the research project accordingly.

When analysis methods are **unrestricted**, researchers can use the full set of methods available in the software that are provided on the analysis computer, including any tabulation or regression analysis. Note that the ability to report on the results obtained via these methods might still be restricted, depending on what is considered safe output.

Table 2.5: Examples of range of analysis methods available

Analysis Methods	Example
Highly Restricted	The Statistics Canada Real Time Remote Access system only allows users to employ a set of approved SAS commands. There are further limits on the number of variables and observations that can be included in analysis.
Limited Restrictions	The RDC-IAB on-site and JoSuA systems broadly allow for most econometric techniques, but certain Stata commands are censored and unavailable to researchers.
Unrestricted	OLDA places no limitations on the methods that researchers can use. OLDA relies on disclosure review, as mandated in their DUA, to ensure safe outputs.

Furthermore, the ability to access any method, for instance through add-on packages distributed through repositories such as the Statistical Software Components (SSC) archive at Boston College for Stata or the Comprehensive R Archive Network (CRAN) for R, may depend on the agency the researcher has over the analysis computer.

When **limited restrictions** are imposed, some methods might be prevented, even if the software is available, by censoring elements of those software programs. In particular, the ability to inspect individual records may be limited.

Analysis methods may be **highly restricted**. Restrictions can include limiting the methods available to researchers to a whitelisted set of commands or, in more extreme examples, limit researchers to the use of tabulator software that can only provide conditional tables. Most researchers will perceive this to impose strong limitations on their ability to conduct research as usual, but such methods are sometimes used to reach a wide range of users while allowing for more relaxed conditions on the rest of the Five Safes framework.

CHAPTER 2

2.6 Specific Data Access Mechanisms Along the Five Aspects

This section evaluates several data access mechanisms along the five aspects. Some of these have already been referenced for individual aspects, but the following content provides a comprehensive picture of all aspects. These include case studies in this handbook as well as outside examples. They are chosen to provide a spectrum of access mechanisms, focusing on variability in the five aspects, not representativeness. Each example provides a "badge" summarizing the five aspects visually.

2.6.1 New Brunswick Institute for Research, Data and Training (NB-IRDT)

The NB-IRDT serves as a third-party data custodian for the Province of New Brunswick, Canada to make de-identified personnel and health data available to researchers. The data and analysis computers are located at the central NB-IRDT facility, and

> Researcher Agency: Medium
> Data Location: Third-Party
> Access Location: Data Custodian
> Access Security: High Security
> Analysis Methods: Unrestricted

researchers may travel there or to satellite NB-IRDT data centers to access the data via thin clients in secure rooms from which mobile devices and outside materials are banned. Thus NB-IRDT serves as a non-researcher data custodian as well as a third-party access provider to provincial data with high security. Researchers have medium agency over the analysis computers: access to common statistical programs is provided and researchers can request other software packages. The NB-IRDT allows researchers unrestricted analysis methods, relying on manual disclosure control to ensure safe outputs.

The NB-IRDT requires over two dozen staff[31] located with the data custodian, including multiple data analysts, system administrators, and

---
[31] https://www.unb.ca/nbirdt/about/team.html, accessed 2020-10-10.

other technical staff to set up and maintain the data access mechanism. For more information, see chapter 9.

2.6.2 Research Data Center at the Institute for Employment Research (RDC-IAB)

The RDC-IAB is an entity within the German Federal Employment Agency, separate from the administrative databases. It thus acts as an internal third party for the Employment Agency. The RDC-IAB uses three different access models, each with unique implementation. Notably, more sensitive data are subject to greater protections while maintaining usability for researchers.

The most restrictive access method is RDC-IAB on-site access, which makes de-identified individual data available to researchers. The RDC-IAB maintains the data and analysis computers. Researchers have low agency over the analysis

Researcher Agency: Medium

Data Location: Third-Party

Access Location: Third-Party

Access Security: High Security

Analysis Methods: Limited Restrictions

computers, being restricted to approved statistical software; other user-provided software is not allowed, and third-party packages for authorized software must be approved and installed by RDC-IAB staff. Access computers (thin clients and secure workstations) are located at the RDC-IAB headquarters and guest RDCs at various trusted institutions around the world, which then act as third-party access providers. The access locations are subject to high security with physical monitoring of researchers and room access controls.

The JoSuA remote execution system allows researchers to utilize the same microdata, though they cannot view the data directly. Researchers are limited to viewing the de-identified output from their analysis, and there are some

Researcher Agency: Medium

Data Location: Third-Party

Access Location: Researcher

Access Security: Low Security

Analysis Methods: Limited Restrictions

CHAPTER 2

restrictions on Stata commands.

In return, controls around access computers and locations are relaxed: Researchers utilize their own computers to use the JoSuA interface, and there are no restrictions on access locations. The data and analysis computer remains located with the RDC-IAB, and researchers are subject to the same limitations on their agency over analysis computers and available analysis methods.

The RDC-IAB also makes data products (scientific use files) available for direct download by researchers using a secure download platform, which are further anonymized variants of the microdata available in the other two access methods. The researcher's institution acts as the data custodian by hosting the data and the analysis computer, with the researcher's institution having high agency over the analysis computer. The access computers and access location are also at the researcher's institution. The RDC-IAB DUA for downloading the scientific use files requires a medium security access location. The building and room are required to have some level of access control or monitoring against unauthorized access; options range from receptionists and security guards to admission with simple key locks. Also note that scientific use data can only be accessed by European research institutions.

> Researcher Agency: High
> Data Location: Researcher
> Access Location: Researcher
> Access Security: Medium Security
> Analysis Methods: Unrestricted

The RDC-IAB has a staff of over two dozen people,[32] not counting staff at guest RDCs. Each data center requires at least one staff member, as well as additional staff to maintain the data products and approve projects. For more information, see chapter 7.

---

[32]https://www.iab.de/839/section.aspx/Bereichsnummer/17, accessed 2020-10-10.

2.6.3 Ohio Longitudinal Data Archive (OLDA)

OLDA is a third-party data custodian that provides de-identified, individual-level data to researchers on behalf of the state of Ohio. The data are initially located at OLDA before ultimately being transferred to researchers' analysis computers

Researcher Agency: High
Data Location: Researcher
Access Location: Researcher
Access Security: Low Security
Analysis Methods: Unrestricted

via an SFTP server. The researchers have full agency over the analysis computer, which also serves as the access computer. The computer must be physically located in the researcher's university office, and the IP address must be registered with OLDA. There are no specific requirements imposed on the researcher's office (low security). Researchers have unrestricted analysis methods available to them.

Approximately a dozen full-time staff maintain the data access mechanism. OLDA relies on the statistical protections of the data (safe data), the security of researchers' institutions, and disclosure avoidance methods applied to outputs to keep data protected. For more information, see chapter 8.

Private Capital Research Institute (PCRI)

The PCRI data access mechanism provides researchers access to highly sensitive business information about private capital firms. Organizationally, PCRI serves as a third-party data custodian, but in turn uses the National Opinion Research Center

Researcher Agency: Medium
Data Location: Third-Party
Access Location: Researcher
Access Security: Low Security
Analysis Methods: Limited Restrictions

(NORC) and in some cases the FSRDC system as a third-party location for the data and analysis computers. Researchers have low agency over the analysis computers: users are restricted to the Stata on the

NORC servers (see FSRDC for restrictions there). Researchers can only use thin clients that are provided to them by NORC. There are no formal restrictions on the location of the access computers, although researchers are required to use their best efforts to prevent unauthorized access. PCRI and NORC implement limited restrictions on the analysis methods available within Stata, prohibiting certain commands and sample sizes.

PCRI itself has three full-time and six part-time staff to make the data usable for researchers, but relies on the preexisting resources at NORC for the data access mechanism. For more information, see chapter 10.

2.6.4 Federal Statistical Research Data Centers (FSRDC)

The United States Federal Statistical Research Data Centers (FSRDC) network hosts data from multiple federal statistical agencies partners, serving as third-party data curator and access provider. The data and analysis computers are hosted at the Census Bureau's computer center, which is separate from operational systems. Researchers have medium agency over these computers; users are restricted to authorized software but have the ability to request approval for additional programs. Analysis methods are unrestricted. Access computers are thin clients located in secure rooms built by, and located on, the campuses of partner institutions; however, the secure rooms remain under the control of, and are considered part of, the Census Bureau. Thus, while the system seems to have third-party access providers, it is in fact a model where the Census Bureau acts as its own access provider (U.S. Census Bureau, n.d.*b*). Nevertheless, FSRDC serves as an interesting hybrid model.

Researcher Agency: Medium

Data Location: Data Provider

Access Location: Data Custodian

Access Security: High Security

Analysis Methods: Unrestricted

As of January 2021, there are 30 FSRDC locations. Each has at least one full-time staff member, and the entire IT infrastructure is maintained by Census Bureau IT staff. Initial startup costs reach hundreds of thousands of dollars. Partner institutions cover part of the cost of maintaining each RDC location (U.S. Census Bureau, n.d.*a*). For more information, see U.S. Census Bureau (n.d.*a*, n.d.*b*).

2.6.5 Statistics Canada Real Time Remote Access (RTRA)

The RTRA system provides access to several Statistics Canada data sets. The data and analysis computers remain with Statistics Canada. Researchers have low agency over the analysis computers and are restricted to using SAS. Access computers are not restricted: researchers can use any computer to submit jobs. Analysis methods are heavily restricted: users are limited to specific commands within SAS, restricted numbers of procedure calls per day, class variables, and other controls on the SAS environment (Statistics Canada, 2018).

Researcher Agency: Low
Data Location: Data Provider
Access Location: Researcher
Access Security: Low Security
Analysis Methods: Highly Restricted

The RTRA system is maintained by Statistics Canada, a major national statistical agency. Additional controls include automated controlled rounding of the outputs (safe outputs) and identification of safe users: registration and a contract are required for access, and researchers must be affiliated with a government department, non-profit organization, or an academic institution. Note that Statistics Canada also partners with the Canadian Research Data Centre Network to provide access similar to the FSRDC system but with different data and unrestricted analysis methods. For more information, see Statistics Canada (2018).

2.6.6 SafePod Network (SPN)

The SafePod Network in the United Kingdom makes de-identified administrative data from several UK administrative data providers available for researchers. A SafePod is a prefabricated room with a single thin client with remote access.

> Researcher Agency: Low
> Data Location: Third-Party
> Access Location: Third-Party
> Access Security: Medium Security
> Analysis Methods: Unrestricted

Analysis computers and data are located with the data provider, accessible through secure VPN connections (University of Bristol, n.d.). Each data provider decides about the agency level that researchers have over analysis computers and restrictions on analysis methods. For instance, at the Office for National Statistics, researchers have medium agency over the analysis computers and no restrictions on analysis methods (Office for National Statistics, 2020). The unique aspect of the SafePod is the security of the access locations. SafePods are a minimalistic yet robust implementation of a medium security location (an access-controlled space with CCTV monitoring) that can exist within low security environments such as university libraries.

SafePods are relatively cheap, requiring only a suitable location to place a prefabricated room and can use existing staff members to manage access to the SafePod. While the SafePod is still a physical location that requires installation and ongoing staff and maintenance, it is an example of innovation for more access locations to provide protection against the various security threats at a lower cost than a traditional full-scale research data center. For more information, see Office for National Statistics (2020); University of Bristol (n.d.).

2.6.7 National Center for Education Statistics (NCES) Restricted-Use Data License

The NCES, a part of the United States Department of Education, allows researchers to apply for a restricted-use data license for de-identified, individual-level data on education. Under the terms of the license, the researchers serve as data custodians and receive

> Researcher Agency: High
> Data Location: Researcher
> Access Location: Researcher
> Access Security: Medium Security
> Analysis Methods: Unrestricted

the data on an encrypted CD from NCES. Analysis and access computers are co-incidental, located with the researcher, and subject to certain security configuration requirements for computer and storage of data Researchers have high agency over the analysis computer and are not restricted in the choice of analysis methods. NCES mandates a medium level of security for the access location, requiring that the location must be a locked room with access restricted to authorized users but without additional specifications for security. The security arrangements must be approved by NCES prior to the receipt of restricted-use data and are subject to unannounced inspections (National Center for Education Statistics, 2019).

The NCES restricted licenses require minimal resources for the data access mechanism; using physical media minimizes the technical resources needed to establish and harden a transfer mechanism. Researchers can utilize their existing university resources to set up the access location. NCES relies on its disclosure review process (safe outputs) to protect against misuse. For more information, see National Center for Education Statistics (2019).

2.6.8 Summary of Examples

Table 2.6 provides a summary of the five asppects of the data access mechanisms covered in this chapter. Additionally, it includes data access mechanisms from case studies in the rest of the Handbook that

Table 2.6: Summary of Access Mechanisms Along the Five Aspects

Data Access Mechanism	Researcher Agency Over Analysis Computer	Location of Data and Analysis Computer	Location of Access Computer	Access Security	Range of Analysis Methods Available
IAB RDC (chapter 7)	Medium	Third-Party	Third-Party	High Security	Limited
IAB JoSuA (chapter 7)	Medium	Third-Party	Researcher	Low Security	Limited
IAB SUF (chapter 7)	High	Researcher	Researcher	Medium Security	Unrestricted
OLDA (chapter 8)	High	Researcher	Researcher	Low Security	Unrestricted
NB-IRDT (chapter 9)	Medium	Third-Party	Data Custodian	High Security	Unrestricted
PCRI (chapter 10)	Medium	Third-Party	Researcher	Low Security	Limited
Aurora (chapter 11)	High	Researcher	Researcher	Low Security	Unrestricted
Stanford-SFUSD (chapter 12)	High	Researcher	Researcher	Low Security	Unrestricted
CCT (chapter 13)	High	Researcher	Researcher	Low Security	Unrestricted
DIME (chapter 14)	High	Researcher	Researcher	Low Security	Unrestricted
FSRDC	Medium	Data Provider	Data Custodian	High Security	Unrestricted
NCES	High	Researcher	Researcher	Medium Security	Unrestricted
RTRA	Low	Data Provider	Researcher	Low Security	Highly Restricted
SPN	Low	Third-Party	Third-Party	Medium Security	Unrestricted

were not covered in this chapter due to having very similar implementations as those described above. Note some case studies, such as the International Monetary Fund, utilize a wide range of access mechanisms (varying across different data providers) and are not categorized in this table.

2.7 Guidance for Data Providers and Researchers

For data providers with the capacity and resources to implement sophisticated technological solutions, several acceptable solutions that balance high security with relatively broad accessibility and convenience exist. The RDC-IAB on-site access model with international access, the NB-IRDT as a provincial system, and the national FSRDC network represent traditional, highly secured, and technically sophisticated methods of provisioning access today. The UK SafePod Network is an endeavor to reduce the technological cost of such a system. If some restrictions on analysis methods are acceptable, the Statistics Canada RTRA and the RDC-IAB JoSuA remote-access system can be accessed from a wider range of locations and with fewer resources required. While these mechanisms may be costly, they can also have great benefits as shown in several of this handbook's case studies. Similarly, economists have been able to make tremendous progress on very challenging questions by using micro-data in Scandinavian countries, which often includes detailed information on individuals' educational records, test scores, employment, and assets and liabilities (Maret-Ouda et al., 2017; Cesarini et al., 2017).

Data providers with limited experience in security may consider establishing safe access protocols a daunting task. There are many examples of relatively simple but effective data access mechanisms with typically lower costs. Mechanisms such as the NCES restricted-use data license at the national level, OLDA at the state level, and the Stanford-SFUSD partnership at the city level leverage greater scrutiny on non-technological aspects with lower technological requirements and allows the researcher to carry much of the burden of maintaining the access infrastructure. Protection of data at rest and in transit with the use of encryption and secure transfer mechanisms are relatively cheap to accomplish; the threat of adversarial actors can be mitigated with a small investment in the proper physical resources. Another possibility is to partner with academic researchers. Universities, by and large, have highly refined data security policies. Many are designed to enable research to use, for example, HIPAA-protected data, which is tightly regulated by US federal law. Hence, data providers may choose to delegate data protection to academic institutions.

While there is the temptation to always maintain the strongest possible protections across all aspects, under the right circumstances a data provider can allow researchers more flexibility in various aspects while maintaining the overall security of the system. Perhaps the most direct example of this is the differences between the RDC-IAB on-site access versus remote access models. The same projects, people, and outputs are allowed in both models, while additional statistical anonymization for the data are made available via the remote access system. As a result of this change, the IAB can switch from a high security access system to no requirements for access security in the remote-access system. This has the benefit of allowing much broader access to the data for researchers, with the associated increased utility of the data and additional potential for researchers generating findings relevant for policymakers.

The necessary aspects of a data access mechanism and the restrictions that are placed on the researchers' access to the data should be considered in the context of the other parts of the Five Safes framework. The proper protections of the data with the researcher and the fulfillment of the other aspects of the Five Safes framework to the data provider's satisfaction allows the use of data access mechanisms that provide the researchers with a high level of flexibility. DIME at the World Bank, OLDA, the Stanford-SFUSD Partnership, Aurora Health Care and MIT, and the City of Cape Town and J-PAL partnership are all examples where the data providers (across a spectrum of high-, medium-, and low-income countries) directly transfer sensitive, individual-level data and confidential government data to researchers.

A final related point is that the enforcement of the terms of the DUA is an important factor in determining the flexibility in the data access system. More sophisticated DUAs and greater strength of enforcement enables increased flexibility in the data access mechanism while maintaining strong protections. This corresponds to a trade-off between the investment in physical infrastructure and human resources necessary for tight control over a data access mechanism versus the investment in the institutional and legal framework of data access. In the partnerships above, the necessary protections in the data access mechanism are established in large part by the DUA.

CHAPTER 2

About the Authors

Jim Shen is the Senior Manager for the Innovations in Data and Experiments for Action Initiative (IDEA) at the Abdul Latif Jameel Poverty Action Lab based at MIT. He was the Data Manager for the Center for Education Policy Analysis (CEPA) from January 2015 to August 2019 where he managed the CEPA data warehouse. He was responsible for the day-to-day operations of the CEPA data warehouse, serving as the point of contact for Stanford researchers utilizing San Francisco Unified School District (SFUSD) data and SFUSD staff for data exchanges. Jim holds a BA in history and international relations and an MA in political science from the University of California, San Diego.

Lars Vilhuber is the Executive Director of the Labor Dynamics Institute at Cornell University, and a faculty member in Cornell University's Economics Department. He is also the American Economic Association's Data Editor. Lars is a Co-Chair of IDEA. His research interests relate to the dynamics of the labor market. He also has extensive experience in the application of privacy-preserving publication and access to restricted data. He is chair of the scientific committee of the French restricted-access system CASD, member of the governing board of the Canadian Research Data Centre Network (CRDCN), and incoming chair of the American Statistical Association's Committee on Privacy and Confidentiality. Lars has an undergraduate degree in Economics from Universität Bonn and a Ph.D. in Economics from Université de Montréal.

References in Chapter 2

Ablon, Lillian. 2018. "Data Thieves: The Motivations of Cyber Threat Actors and Their Use and Monetization of Stolen Data." https://www.rand.org/pubs/testimonies/CT490.html (accessed 2020-08-24).

Asghar, Hassan Jameel, and Dali Kaafar. 2019. "Averaging Attacks on Bounded Noise-based Disclosure Control Algorithms." arXiv 1902.06414 [cs]. http://arxiv.org/abs/1902.06414 (accessed 2020-07-19).

Bosworth, Martin H. 2006. "VA Loses Data on 26 Million Veterans." https://www.consumeraffairs.com/news04/2006/05/va_laptop.html (accessed 2020-07-13).

CBC News. 2019. "CRA loses box of 'sensitive' taxpayer information in truck accident | CBC News." https://www.cbc.ca/news/politics/cra-boxes-accident-1.5395078 (accessed 2020-07-13).

Cesarini, David, Erik Lindqvist, Matthew J. Notowidigdo, and Robert Östling. 2017. "The Effect of Wealth on Individual and Household Labor Supply: Evidence from Swedish Lotteries." *American Economic Review*, 107(12): 3917–3946. https://doi.org/10.1257/aer.20151589.

Cichonski, Paul, Tom Millar, Tim Grance, and Karen Scarfone. 2012. "Computer Security Incident Handling Guide: Recommendations of the National Institute of Standards and Technology." National Institute of Standards and Technology Special Publication 800-61r2, https://doi.org/10.6028/NIST.SP.800-61r2.

Confessore, Nicholas. 2018. "Cambridge Analytica and Facebook: The Scandal and the Fallout So Far." *The New York Times*. https://www.nytimes.com/2018/04/04/us/politics/cambridge-analytica-scandal-fallout.html (accessed 2020-07-13).

Greenemeier, Larry. 2008. "Security Breach: Feds Lose Laptop Containing Sensitive Data – Again." https://www.scientificamerican.com/article/security-breach-lost-laptop/ (accessed 2020-07-13).

Maret-Ouda, John, Wenjing Tao, Karl Wahlin, and Jesper Lagergren. 2017. "Nordic registry-based cohort studies: Possibilities and pitfalls when combining Nordic registry data." *Scandinavian Journal of Public Health*, 45(17_suppl): 14–19. https://doi.org/10.1177/1403494817702336.

National Center for Education Statistics. 2019. "Restricted-Use Data Procedures Manual." https://nces.ed.gov/statprog/rudman/.

Office for National Statistics. 2020. "Accessing secure research data as an accredited researcher." https://www.ons.gov.uk/aboutus/whatwedo/statistics/requestingstatistics/approvedresearcherscheme (accessed 2020-10-05).

Stanford Report. 2008. "Stanford alerts employees that stolen laptop had personal data." http://news.stanford.edu/news/2008/june11/laprelease-061108.html (accessed 2020-07-13).

Statistics Canada. 2018. "Real Time Remote Access - System limitations." https://www.statcan.gc.ca/eng/rtra/limitation (accessed 2020-06-17).

University of Bristol. n.d.. "SafePod." http://www.bris.ac.uk/staff/researchers/data/safepod/ (accessed 2020-06-18).

U.S. Census Bureau. n.d.*a*. "Federal Statistical Research Data Centers." https://www.census.gov/fsrdc (accessed 2020-06-21).

U.S. Census Bureau. n.d.*b*. "Hosting an RDC at your Institution." https://www.census.gov/about/adrm/fsrdc/about/hostrdc.html (accessed 2020-06-21).

CHAPTER 3

Model Data Use Agreements: A Practical Guide

Amy O'Hara (Georgetown University)

3.1 Overview

What are data use agreements? Data use agreements (DUA)—also referred to as data sharing agreements or data use licenses—are documents that describe what data are being shared, for what purpose, for how long, and any access restrictions or security protocols that must be followed by the recipient of the data. Other contracts, such as non-disclosure agreements, may be used to guarantee confidentiality over sensitive discussions, information, and data.

This chapter explains how to develop a DUA to access administrative data for a research project. The chapter documents specific questions to consider when developing an agreement and points to useful templates and guides.

There are at least two parties to such agreements: the data provider and the data requestor. The data provider is responsible for permitting data access on behalf of the collecting agency or data subjects.

Copyright © Amy O'Hara.
Cite as: O'Hara, Amy. "Model Data Use Agreements: A Practical Guide." In: Cole, Shawn, Iqbal Dhaliwal, Anja Sautmann, and Lars Vilhuber (eds.), *Handbook on Using Administrative Data for Research and Evidence-based Policy*. Cambridge, MA: Abdul Latif Jameel Poverty Action Lab. 2020.

> What if the data provider does not require any formal documentation? The researcher should write a letter describing the data requested, the planned uses, and a summary of the data management plan. The letter should clearly state the proposed use of the data, redistribution of the data, and methods for data retention or destruction at the project's end. Researcher and data provider should then sign and date the letter. Alternatively, the researcher can simply send the letter and obtain a return receipt.

The data provider is bound by law, regulation, or policies that may be very specific regarding access to direct identifiers (name, date of birth, social security number) and sensitive information (health conditions, grades, or test scores). The data requestor is a researcher pursuing data access for a specific purpose. Researchers at universities must typically go through a review of the DUA by an Office of Research or Sponsored Programs or the Office of the General Counsel and possibly by university information security specialists.

In some circumstances, the data provider may utilize a separate data custodian or data intermediary to offer data on their behalf, adhering to all required laws, regulations, and policies. Custodians and intermediaries support data access, reducing the burden for data providers by handling requests, reviews, and provisioning to researchers. Projects involving multiple information sources will require multiple DUAs, potentially involving a variety of terms and conditions. DUAs may also become more complex for multi-site research projects when different teams of researchers will need to access data and collaborate. Intermediaries can be particularly useful in these circumstances for facilitating data access, by coordinating between different data providers and researchers.

Depending on the data provider, other forms of documentation can be used. Examples include memoranda of understanding (MOU), data use agreements, and data exchange letters. These have different structures and levels of detail, but all of these instruments will state the legal framework for data access, what the requestor may do with the data (e.g., scope of the study, restrictions on redistribution), security controls, and constraints on publishing. The data requestor should always prepare some form of documentation for data access, even if the data provider does not require it.

3.1.1 Relating the DUA to the Five Safes Framework

The Five Safes framework used throughout this handbook is an approach for structuring aspects of data access. The five safes are safe projects, safe people, safe settings, safe data, and safe outputs.[1]

Safe projects have governance measures over project scope and sensitivity with review and approval processes that involve institutional review boards (IRB) or ethics boards. Data providers must determine who are *safe people* through policies, screening, and training, and may require affiliation to an educational or non-profit institution, proof of research competence (e.g., grants received, curriculum vitae), and citizenship or tenure in the relevant country. Safe settings and data involve the researcher's interface and work environment, potentially restricting what an analyst can see, what an analyst can do, the analyst's computing environment, and the analyst's physical location (see also chapter 2). Safe data and outputs protect the privacy of data subjects by reducing re-identification risks both during access and after publication. Such protection occurs through statistical disclosure limitation methods such as rounding, aggregating, and suppression (obscuring unique observations in tables, figures, or maps) or formal, mathematical privacy protections (see chapters 5 and 6).

At a high level, a DUA should address all five safes. It should include intended data uses to define the safe project; terms for data access and handling for a safe setting; and terms for output publication and release for safe outputs. DUAs are essential to define acceptable data uses, linkages, and topics of analysis. Agreements may also detail roles and responsibilities for the data provider and researchers (defining safe people) and cover safe data by including a list of data elements and any reporting or disposition requirements. There are many permutations

---

[1] See Desai, Ritchie and Welpton (2016) for more information on the Five Safes framework including examples for each dimension.

on such restrictions;[2] any requirements as well as penalties for failing to comply with them should be included in the DUA.

Such an agreement strives to protect all parties by specifying the terms and conditions for data access and use. DUAs are risk mitigation tools, clarifying expectations between the parties. Data providers are often reluctant to enter data sharing arrangements, as they may be fearful of the liabilities resulting from use of the data that could result in harm to their program, agency, or the data subjects. Through DUAs, data providers can specify controls on data handling and notification measures in case of data mismanagement. DUAs also solidify the roles and responsibilities of researchers and their institutions, clarifying liability issues in advance.

The following sections describe how to (1) prepare for a data sharing arrangement, (2) negotiate a sound agreement, and (3) comply with the signed agreement, based on review of guides and best practices across multiple domains.[3] Some of these refer to a researcher negotiating a DUA with a data provider for the first time, but the considerations for this case contain pointers for establishing good processes and developing templates and examples for subsequent DUAs.

3.1.2 Preparation

Creating DUAs can be time-intensive. In some cases, negotiations fall apart after months or years of discussions. Advance planning can help both researchers and data providers achieve sound DUAs. DUAs can be initiated by the researcher or data provider.[4] Data providers may have different or expedited procedures when sharing data with a researcher, an evaluator, or contractor working on their behalf.

If a data provider has an established data request process, a researcher must review their terms and requirements, offering additions or edits

---

[2]See Goroff, Polonetsky and Tene (2018) for a comprehensive discussion of possible methods.
[3]See Appendix B for a set of these guides.
[4]See Yates et al. (2018) for a checklist from the data provider's perspective.

as appropriate. Data providers should be aware of the laws, regulations, and policies permitting use of their data, and, upon receiving a first request, determine whether data request procedures already exist in their organization. Data providers (such as government agencies or private companies) may have Offices of General Counsel that have preferred templates or formats. Some data providers will be reluctant or unable to modify their request processes. Data request and access procedures may not always be publicly available, though some agencies and organizations have data request procedures on their websites, and this can significantly speed up and simplify the request process.

3.1.3 Understanding the Available Data

Researchers need to be able to identify the correct data source: the agency or organization who holds the data content needed for their planned analysis. This may be difficult in settings where data descriptions are not readily available. Can data users determine whether the data are fit for use? Can they ascertain what data is captured by data providers, how the data are coded, and whether such capture and coding are documented consistently across time?

Well-prepared data users will typically do this by reviewing a data description, a codebook, or a data dictionary. Data providers should consider preparing such materials or working with pilot data users to do so. A data sample may provide a better understanding of the data content. If documentation or a sample is unavailable, program rules, regulations, and forms can be used to provide background.

However, a field on an application or benefits form does not automatically mean the information is cleaned or stored by the agency. Prior analyses of the same data by other studies or at other sites can provide helpful information on availability and usability of the underlying data. Researchers should seek out such studies and providers may want to keep a record of research conducted with their data to facilitate future use.

3.1.4 Understanding the Costs of Obtaining Data

Both parties should consider what is possible, and what is likely, in terms of the timeframe the agreement will cover. This includes when data delivery can occur, how data will be extracted from administrative systems, and what expenses might arise during the term of the data sharing arrangement. Agreements can take up to a year to negotiate from drafting to execution, especially if there is no history of the two parties exchanging data before. Even organizations with past data sharing relationships or with established processes may have a queue of requests, which may create delays. After achieving a signed agreement, researchers should anticipate for the time between approval and delivery: the processes for fulfilling the request may be intensive. For example, data providers will need time to document and format the requested data and additional time may be needed to pull data from multiple databases or from inactive storage. That process may be especially lengthy if the request is novel. Data providers may also require notification or approvals before any output releases or publications.

Many administrative agencies are resource constrained, needing to prioritize program needs over research requests. In this situation, they may decide to charge fees for data preparation and extraction. Being transparent about timeframe and cost and making the data use agreement as clear as possible helps set expectations between the parties.

3.1.5 Consideration for the Data Subjects

Researchers should consider potential benefits, costs, and risks for the data subjects in the planned project and think of how to communicate the project to the data subjects, including an explanation of why their data are needed. The researchers should be prepared to explain what data will be used, whether the data will be linked with other information, and who will have access to the data. They should also be able to explain the project in direct language (free from jargon) for the subjects or their parents or guardians and provide a finite project timeline. This is useful for purposes of establishing an informed consent

> Researchers may consider preparing (and data providers may consider requesting) an engagement matrix that maps project steps with different forms of external input to build trust with the data subjects (Future of Privacy Forum and Actionable Intelligence for Social Policy, 2018). Engagement could involve simply informing subjects about the project, seeking their input, or active collaboration during the project. Communicating with the subjects could include interviews, advisory committees, working groups, town halls, social media discussions, or press releases. Researcher and data provider may also consider a transparency checklist[a] as part of each project,[b] to add legitimacy to the project and its results when completed. A transparency checklist can accompany publications resulting from the analysis to clarify how the data, code, and other study materials were handled upon project completion.
>
> [a] http://www.stat.columbia.edu/~gelman/research/published/checklist.pdf (accessed 2020-12-15).
> [b] See Aczel et al. (2020) guide and checklist.

procedure as well as the conduct of ethical research when consent is not required and for communication with the public (e.g., in contexts where the research informs public policy). The ethical and transparent conduct of research supports future use of the data and establishes trust with the public and data subjects.

3.1.6 Investigating the Data Sharing History for Data Providers and Researchers

Researchers might inquire whether the data needed for the project have been successfully shared by the data provider before. In relevant cases it can be helpful to build on a copy of the previous data use agreement, provided by the agency or by researchers who have accessed data in the past.[5] For a researcher, requesting data access with a past protocol in hand is a strong position. When approaching

---
[5] Some jurisdictions may require a formal written request or even a Freedom of Information Act request to share the DUAs.

an agency with a set process for data sharing, the researcher should review the process and forms and know which office in the organization approves requests. If requesting an unusual extract or approaching an agency that has never permitted research access before, researchers should identify some data sharing examples within their department or in other localities to review terms and conditions in their agreements. Data providers on the other hand can ask researchers about past performance information on quantitative research projects. This could include their history of using administrative data or examples of their data management plans and approaches when handling sensitive data. This information can help the data provider determine whether the researcher has the capacity to protect the data, deliver the results they have proposed, and whether they have been good partners in the past (or whether they have been involved with data breaches).

3.1.7 Understanding the Legal Context

It is important to have an understanding of the legal framework that governs the use of the data. This may involve laws at the national, subnational (state, province), and local level. In the case of private data providers, it may involve notions of copyright and legal responsibility. If the data provider and the research institution are not located in the same country, this includes the legal framework in both countries. If the server hosting the data is based in a third country, additional requirements may affect the data provider (e.g., the General Data Protection Regulation (GDPR) in the European Union). The degree of regulation varies across countries, and data protection laws (and interpretations of them) change frequently. The parties should work with legal and privacy professionals to identify the legal authority for data access. This is especially important when requesting individually identified data, as defining what constitutes personal data varies across jurisdictions.

Investigating the legal framework helps researchers form realistic expectations regarding scope and conditions for the DUA. Moreover, it is important that researchers (or their institutions) are aware of the legal setting, so they can ensure compliance with all applicable laws, especially if the data provider has limited legal experience approving data sharing and data use by researchers.

3.1.8 Thinking through the Analysis and Publication Process

Considering the project goals and timeline, the researcher should assess how much time it will take to clean, harmonize, and link data—all necessary steps before conducting analyses or publishing results. Time required for each of these steps can depend on the past experiences of the researcher (or their institution) with a particular type of data. Researchers should allow ample time to prepare data for use after receipt, possibly in collaboration with the data provider. The researcher should also allocate time to prepare findings for release and identify disclosure avoidance techniques to protect against re-identification of the data subjects in project outputs. Data providers should be prepared to review outputs and be familiar with common disclosure avoidance protocols (see chapter 5).

3.1.9 Taking a Broad Interpretation of Data

Data includes information directly from administrative databases on program participants or clients, regardless of the extent to which it is processed, linked, or contains identifiers. But data also refers to metadata about the system, files, and content as well as statistical information that will be published through the project, such as descriptive statistics, coefficients, or visualizations. A sound data use agreement covers all of these. See the concepts of safe data and safe outputs in section 3.1.1 on relating the DUA to the five safes framework.

3.2 Negotiating the Data Use Request

With preparations complete, the data provider and researchers can pursue a DUA for an individual project. The data provider ultimately decides whether and how access will be granted: a researcher with clear plans and expectations and a data provider with established and transparent processes are equipped to engage effectively. This section includes some pointers and considerations for the pursuit of a DUA by a researcher, especially in a first-time engagement. From the provider perspective, many of the points below are about information the researcher needs, and data providers can facilitate the DUA process by making this information available either publicly or to the individual researcher. Data providers may also face similar issues if they are requesting data from other agencies or organizations.

3.2.1 Getting the Right People Involved

The researcher needs to communicate with the right decision-makers within the data providing organization about the project and upcoming request. Note that administrators may support the idea of the project but may be unaware that their data systems lack necessary data elements to complete the analysis. An administrator might not have a full view of the complexities of their data systems and structures, which may make it difficult or impossible to identify or derive the data needed for the analysis without technical assistance. Similarly, substantial resources from the data provider may be required to extract data from multiple systems and, if a longitudinal study is planned, from active and inactive storage. It is therefore important to consult the data provider's technical staff on each request. Researchers will need to engage their Office of Sponsored Research, IRB, and sometimes Office of General Counsel. When working in a foreign country, many parties may need translations (even if the researcher does not).

3.2.2 Asking Questions About the Process

The researcher should discuss with the data provider how the negotiation will proceed before submitting the request. Does the data provider have an iterative process? Will they counter or iterate on the request? If one part of the request is denied, will the rest proceed or will the whole request be returned? Does the data provider require an IRB or ethics board review and approval from their end, or do they require that a researcher obtain IRB approval from their institution before requesting or accessing data? What is the signature process for all parties to the agreement? Who are authorized individuals permitted to sign on behalf of the researcher's or data provider's organization? Will the data provider require background checks on researchers?

3.2.3 Understanding the Reasons Behind a Negative Response

Data providers say no for many reasons. It is important to understand what the "no" means in order to determine how best to respond. The researcher should determine whether the response is stemming from a legal, policy, or cultural barrier.

Organizations without existing systems for data sharing may turn down a request because they lack clear internal roles and responsibilities or resources to administer the agreement development, data exchange, and relationship monitoring. Obtaining funding or external resources can help to support the process.

A request denial may also come from a key decision-maker who may feel that the risks of data sharing overwhelm potential benefits. They may have concerns about unauthorized uses, breaches, negative publicity, or privacy concerns raised by their legislatures or clients. Decision-makers may be afraid that problems will be discovered in the data or have trepidation about what the results of the study will show. Such concerns are described in "Why Data Providers Say No...and Why they Should Say Yes" (National Neighborhood Indicators Partnership, 2018). The engagement matrix and transparency check list, described in the breakout box on communication tools for engaging subjects and the public, can help in this area.

If data are inaccessible due to a legal barrier, the researcher should find the section of the statute or code that prohibits access and determine whether access would be permitted in the case that the researcher were under contract with the agency or producing an output for that agency. In instances where access would have been permitted, the parties may consider discussing a mutually beneficial contractor relationship between the researcher and data provider. Otherwise, the researcher may determine whether a separate legal interpretation of the statute or regulation would be appropriate or whether the law effectively prohibits access. Even when there are not legal barriers, there may be policy barriers. This happens when a written policy prevents access. The parties should investigate whether a waiver or a policy change are feasible.

When there is no law or written policy blocking access, there still may be cultural barriers. Data providers (or individuals at the data provider) may reject a request because such sharing has never taken place before or was done only in special circumstances. They may also lack the resources to entertain the request: they may have already shared the data with another research team or their own in-house experts are looking into the same or related research topic. The researcher can try to identify why the agency is reluctant and explore the risks that data sharing poses to them. They can discuss with the data provider how controls over the mode of access, users, uses, and outputs may mitigate these risks and how the project can produce benefits for the provider. Negotiating parties can refer to the various sections in this handbook for examples on successful data use agreements, as well as the technical possibilities (see chapters 2 and 5), which might allay fears and uncertainties.

3.2.4 Trying to Find Mutual Interests

It is helpful to think through the interests of the organization as well as the interests of individual decision-makers, such as the program manager, agency leader, chief information security officer, and so on.[6] Consider what the agency needs to do: improve program administration, increase efficiency, reduce costs, and help program participants. What can the research team produce for the data provider? This could be clean data, documentation, code, a report, or a dashboard. Researchers should ask what the data provider's unanswered questions and needs are.

3.2.5 Drafting the Request

Does the agency have a posted process, pre-specified forms, or a template? If none exists, the researcher should try to get an example of a successful request and be attentive to detail in formulating a new request. Be sure to include processes and requirements of the data provider, such as review requirements.

Guides that provide templates are available from various domains. Appendix A to this chapter provides one template. Other examples are listed below:

- "Data Sharing: Creating Agreements" (Jarquín, 2012) from the Colorado Clinical and Translational Sciences Institute includes specific questions to help determine which sections should be included in a DUA from a clinical health perspective.
- *Legal Issues for IDS Use: Finding a Way Forward* (Petrila et al., 2017) is an expert panel report informing state and local governments that want to integrate data. This report explains why politics and relationships matter and walks through the legal considerations for preparing a MOU or Data Use License. The document includes links to a sample agreement made with two states and one county as well as a data license template from a federal agency for health and human services data.
- "Guidelines for Developing Data Sharing Agreements to Use State Administrative Data for Early Care and Education Research" (Shaw, Lin and Maxwell, 2018) includes examples with early childhood

---

[6]See Coburn, Penuel and Geil (2013) for a discussion of maintaining mutualism in a research partnership.

research from two states, along with links to checklists and toolkits. This research brief also includes "advice from researchers" sections throughout.

3.2.6 Signing the Agreement

Complications can arise during the signature process for agreements. Late edit insertions may require further rounds of review. When the document is signed by all parties (i.e., fully executed), both sides must monitor staffing changes in their organizations to keep the signatories current. Most agreements describe how changes to the executed agreement may be requested (e.g., in writing to the signatory, within fifteen days of a new appointment). If the researcher changes institutions, they must discuss the DUA update process with the original institution, new institution, and data provider so expectations are clear. Both the original signatory and the researcher should determine whether the original DUA will be terminated once a new DUA with the gaining institution is signed. The researcher must follow data management and security protocols if data transfer to their gaining institution is required, checking with institutional information security specialists if terms of transfer were not explicit in the original DUA.

3.3 Compliance

Once the agreement is signed, the work is not done. The researcher should develop a plan to ensure compliance with the terms in the agreement and implement measures to demonstrate compliance per DUA requirements. Monitoring data processing controls, lists of approved users, updates to storage locations, upcoming releases, and review of publications requires coordination across the research team. Even if the data provider is not tracking these things, the researcher should.

The researcher should review the agreement terms regularly to be sure the necessary data are accessible and the project is on track for completion within the stated scope and timeline. If the researcher discovers a need for additional data elements, an extension, or broader scope, they need to pursue a modification to the agreement. Since such modifications are common, the data provider may consider developing a template.

When using the data, the researcher should remember that this is a contractual arrangement and an opportunity to build trust between the parties. Working collaboratively with the data provider to understand the data will help build this relationship. Administrative data were not originally collected for research use, so researchers should ask questions if the data do not look as expected. Seeking clarification or correction can avoid misuse of the data and keep the data provider involved.

3.4 Summary

No matter the size of the project or the volume of data needed, all parties should invest the time in preparing a sound data use agreement. Agreements enable safe projects. The topics covered in this chapter have been put in to practice through all the case studies in this volume. The process is well described in chapter 12 on the Stanford-San Francisco Unified School District Partnership. Appendix A provides a sample text for consideration when writing DUAs, and Appendix B lists additional toolkits and guides on the DUA process.

About the Author

Amy O'Hara is a Research Professor in the Massive Data Institute at the McCourt School of Public Policy at Georgetown University, and the Director of Georgetown's Federal Statistical Research Data Center. She also leads the Administrative Data Research Initiative at Georgetown, improving secure, responsible data access for research and evaluation. She was previously a senior executive at the US Census Bureau where she negotiated DUAs for federal, state, and local administrative data. Her current research focuses on population measurement, data governance, and record linkage. She received her PhD in Economics from the University of Notre Dame.

References in Chapter 3

Aczel, Balazs, Barnabas Szaszi, Alexandra Sarafoglou, Zoltan Kekecs, Šimon Kucharský, Daniel Benjamin, Christopher D. Chambers, Agneta Fisher, Andrew Gelman, Morton A. Gernsbacher, John P. Ioannidis, Eric Johnson, Kai Jonas, Stavroula Kousta, Scott O. Lilienfeld, D. Stephen Lindsay, Candice C. Morey, Marcus Munafò, Benjamin R. Newell, Harold Pashler, David R. Shanks, Daniel J. Simons, Jelte M. Wicherts, Dolores Albarracin, Nicole D. Anderson, John Antonakis, Hal R. Arkes, Mitja D. Back, George C. Banks, Christopher Beevers, Andrew A. Bennett, Wiebke Bleidorn, Ty W. Boyer, Cristina Cacciari, Alice S. Carter, Joseph Cesario, Charles Clifton, Ronán M. Conroy, Mike Cortese, Fiammetta Cosci, Nelson Cowan, Jarret Crawford, Eveline A. Crone, John Curtin, Randall Engle, Simon Farrell, Pasco Fearon, Mark Fichman, Willem Frankenhuis, Alexandra M. Freund, M. Gareth Gaskell, Roger Giner-Sorolla, Don P. Green, Robert L. Greene, Lisa L. Harlow, Fernando Hoces de la Guardia, Derek Isaacowitz, Janet Kolodner, Debra Lieberman, Gordon D. Logan, Wendy B. Mendes, Lea Moersdorf, Brendan Nyhan, Jeffrey Pollack, Christopher Sullivan, Simine Vazire, and Eric-Jan Wagenmakers. 2020. "A consensus-based transparency checklist." *Nature Human Behaviour*, 4(1): 4–6. https://doi.org/10.1038/s41562-019-0772-6.

Coburn, Cynthia E., William R. Penuel, and Kimberly E. Geil. 2013. "Research-Practice Partnerships: A Strategy for Leveraging Research for Educational Improvement in School Districts." William T. Grant Foundation. https://wtgrantfoundation.org/library/uploads/2015/10/Research-Practice-Partnerships-at-the-District-Level.pdf (accessed 2020-10-05).

Desai, Tanvi, Felix Ritchie, and Richard Welpton. 2016. "Five Safes: Designing data access for research." https://uwe-repository.worktribe.com/output/914745 (accessed 2020-01-30).

Future of Privacy Forum, and Actionable Intelligence for Social Policy. 2018. "Nothing to Hide: Tools for Talking (and Listening) About Data Privacy for Integrated Data Systems." https://fpf.org/wp-content/uploads/2018/09/FPF-AISP_Nothing-to-Hide.pdf.

Goroff, Daniel, Jules Polonetsky, and Omer Tene. 2018. "Privacy Protective Research: Facilitating Ethically Responsible Access to Administrative Data." *The ANNALS of the American Academy of Political and Social Science*, 675(1): 46–66. https://doi.org/10.1177/0002716217742605.

Jarquín, Paige Backlund. 2012. "Data Sharing: Creating Agreements." Colorado Clinical and Translational Sciences Institute & Rocky Mountain Prevention Research Center. http://trailhead.institute/wp-content/uploads/2017/04/tips_for_creating_data_sharing_agreements_for_partnerships.pdf.

National Neighborhood Indicators Partnership. 2018. "Why Data Providers Say No...And Why They Should Say Yes." https://www.neighborhoodindicators.org/library/guides/why-data-providers-say-noand-why-they-should-say-yes (accessed 2020-07-15).

Petrila, John, Barbara Cohn, Wendell Pritchett, Paul Stiles, Victoria Stodden, Jeffrey Vagle, Mark Humowiecki, and Natassia Rozario. 2017. "Legal Issues for IDS Use: Finding a Way Forward." University of Pennsylvania, Actionable Intelligence for Social Policy. https://www.aisp.upenn.edu/resource-article/legal-issues-for-ids-use-finding-a-way-forward/ (accessed 2020-10-05).

Shaw, Sara, Van-Kim Lin, and Kelly Maxwell. 2018. "Guidelines for Developing Data Sharing Agreements to Use State Administrative Data for Early Care and Education Research." Administration for Children & Families OPRE Research Brief 2018-67. https://eric.ed.gov/?id=ED602071 (accessed 2020-10-05).

Yates, Deborah, Tim Beale, Stewart Marshall, and Martin Parr. 2018. "Designing data sharing agreements: a checklist." Open Data Institute. https://gatesopenresearch.org/documents/2-44 (accessed 2020-10-05).

Appendix

Appendix A

Sample Text for Agreement Components

Often, simply establishing that a proposed agreement covers all the important components can be a major impediment. To assist with this, below is a list of agreement sections with example language sourced from a range of successful data use agreements; this is offered as a starting point, not legal advice.

Title
Data Use Agreement for [Data/System] Access between Party 1 and Party 2

Parties and Purpose
This Agreement is between Party 1 [Office, Agency, Department, Institution] and Party 2 [Office, Agency, Department, Institution]. Party 1 and Party 2 are entering into an Agreement that will allow the exchange of data and clarification of data access and use. Party 1 will provide data collected to Party 2 for the purposes of [specify].

Authority
Party 1 is a(n) [specify] organization whose mission is [specify]. The authority for Party 1 to enter into this Agreement is [xxx]. This authority permits the release of [data] to [specify]. The [law/code] permits disclosure of [data] for [specify] functions. Party 2 is an [specify] organization whose mission is [specify].

Terms and Conditions
Description of planned data use by Party 2, consistent with Purpose above.

- Treatment of data anomalies, including technical assistance from Party 1 and redelivery as needed
- Terms for data storage, treatment of original data, handling of Personally Identifiable Information, and data linkage protocols

- Conditions for storing modified data (including integrated, recoded, de-identified, and derived data) during and after the project
- Terms for storage of researcher generated files (including retention/archiving, e.g., To the extent permitted by law, the original data received from Party 1 will be retained by Party 2 for [specify period].)

Data Elements

The following data will be provided under this Agreement: [Specify list of data elements from named programs/systems, noting which time periods, populations, and/or geographies are sought.]

Approved Research Uses

[Describe project objectives, intended data use, expected linkages.]

Roles & Responsibilities

Party 1 agrees

To transfer to Party 2 via [specify, e.g., secure File Transfer Protocol or appropriately encrypted disk], data from [specify] for the years [specify], as described in [Data Elements]. The delivery of [specify] data will occur before [specify]. To disclose data only for the authorized uses in [Terms and Conditions]. To comply with all applicable federal and state laws and regulations relating to the use and disclosure, the safeguarding, confidentiality, and maintenance of the data. To provide adequate documentation and support of transferred files for Party 2 to be able to interpret the data for the uses permitted in this Agreement, including definitions of variables/data dictionary, a record layout, record count, and record length. To allow Party 2 to link with [specify] data to complete their analysis. To allow Party 2 to use the data at the Processing Sites listed in this Agreement for the projects listed in [Approved Research Uses] in this Agreement.

Party 2 agrees

To access, hold, use, and disclose data only for the authorized uses in [Terms and Conditions]. To comply with all applicable federal and state laws and regulations relating to the use and disclosure, the safeguarding, confidentiality, and maintenance of the data. To ensure that all data users comply with the requirements of this Agreement. To immediately report within [specify] any use or disclosure of Protected Data other than as expressly allowed by this Agreement. Notice shall be given to the contact [specify]. Any changes in planned use of the data must be submitted to Party 1 in writing and receive written approval.

Duration, Amendments, and Modifications

This Agreement is effective on the date it is signed by both parties. The Agreement shall terminate [specify number of months/years] following the date on which it becomes effective. If, at the end of [same number of months/years above], the parties wish to continue the relationship, they must execute a new Agreement.

The parties shall review this Agreement at least once every [specify] or whenever a [State/Federal/Local] statute is enacted that materially affects the substance of the Agreement, in order to determine whether it should be revised, renewed or canceled.

Notwithstanding all other provisions of this Agreement, the Parties agree that

a. This Agreement may be amended at any time by written mutual consent of both parties and
b. Either party may terminate this Agreement upon thirty (30) days written notice to the other party.

Termination

Either party may terminate this Agreement for any reason on [specify number of days] business days' notice to the other party. Each party may terminate this Agreement with immediate effect by delivering notice of the termination to the other party, if the other party fails to perform, has made or makes any inaccuracy in, or otherwise materially breaches, any of its obligations, covenants, or representations, and the failure, inaccuracy, or breach continues for a period of [specify number of days] business days' after the injured party delivers notice to the breaching party reasonably detailing the breach.

Ownership of Developed Intellectual Property

If either party develops any new Intellectual Property in connection with this Agreement, the parties shall enter into a separate definitive Agreement regarding the ownership of that new Intellectual Property.

Resolution of Disagreements

Should disagreement arise on the interpretation of the provisions of this Agreement, or its amendments and/or revisions, that cannot be resolved at the operating level, the area(s) of disagreement shall be stated in writing by each party and presented to the other party for consideration. If agreement on interpretation is not reached within thirty (30) days, the parties shall forward the written presentation of the disagreement to respective higher officials for appropriate resolution.

Confidentiality and Non-Disclosure

Party 2 shall use appropriate safeguards to protect the data from misuse and unauthorized access or disclosure, including maintaining adequate physical controls and password protections for any server or system on which the data is stored, ensuring that data is not stored on any mobile device (for example, a laptop or smartphone) or transmitted electronically unless encrypted, and taking any other measures reasonably necessary to prevent any use or disclosure of the data other than as allowed under this Agreement. Party 2 shall ensure that any agents, including subcontractors, to whom it provides the data agree to the same restrictions and conditions listed in this Agreement. Party 2 will not attempt to identify any person whose information is contained in any data or attempt to contact those persons.

IT Security

[Specify Statutes or Acts] protect the confidentiality of the data. Party 2 will comply with all laws applicable to the privacy or security of data received pursuant to this Agreement.

Publication/Disclosure Rules

Party 2 will ensure that any study, report, publication, or other disclosure of data provided under this Agreement is limited to the reporting of aggregate data and will not contain any information identifiable to a private person or entity. Aggregate data for purposes of this Agreement will mean datasets consisting of no fewer than [specify cell restrictions or alternative disclosure limitation methods]. [Include citation and/or disclaimer language if desired.]

The dissemination and use of publicly released reports, articles, and other products derived in whole or in part from the data will not be discontinued due to the expiration or termination of this Agreement. Furthermore, the use of data linked to other data as part of the projects described in Attachment B will not be discontinued due to expiration or termination of this Agreement.

Party 2 agrees to provide Party 1 with an advance copy of any publication resulting from the data use not less than [specify number of days] prior to the submission or disclosure of the publication, to permit Party 1 to reasonably comment, update, or otherwise propose modifications or edits to the draft publication and to ensure there is no disclosure of confidential data. If Party 1 does not respond to Party 2's submission of materials for its review for [specify period], Party 2 may proceed to publish or present these materials.

Limitations on Liability
In no event shall either party be liable to the other party under this Agreement or to any third party for special, consequential, incidental, punitive, or indirect damages, irrespective of whether such claims for damages are founded in contract, tort, warranty, operation of law, or otherwise or whether claims for such liability arise out of the performance or non-performance by such party hereunder.

Monitoring and Breach Notification
In the event of an actual or suspected security breach involving its information system(s), Party 2 will immediately notify Party 1 of the breach or suspected breach and will comply with all applicable breach notification laws. The parties agree to cooperate in any breach investigation and remedy of any such breach, including, without limitation, complying with any law concerning unauthorized access or disclosure.

Remedies in Event of Breach
The parties recognize that irreparable harm may result in the event of a breach of this Agreement. In the event of such a breach, the non-breaching party may be entitled to enjoin and restrain the other from

any continued violation. This section shall survive termination of the Agreement. In the event that a breach is identified and it is determined by the non-breaching party that (a) individual or public notification is required and (b) that the requirement for notification is substantially caused by the other party, the party responsible for the breach shall be liable for the reasonable costs incurred by the other party to meet all federal and state legal and regulatory disclosure and notification requirements, including, but not limited to, costs for investigation, attorneys' fees, risk analysis, and any required individual or public notification, fines, and mitigation activities.

Signatures
Party 1 Name, Title, Date
Party 2 Name, Title, Date

Additional sections, as appropriate

Contacts
Party 1's designated contact concerning this Agreement is Name, Title, Address, Phone, Email. Party 2's designated contact concerning this Agreement is Name, Title, Address, Phone, Email.

User Training
Party 2 will annually sign an acknowledgment that all individuals authorized to have access to disclosed data have been instructed, as specified by Party 1 in [specify], with regard to the confidential nature of the data, and that each authorized individual has taken Party 1's [specify training]. Party 2 will take all necessary steps to ensure that the individuals who have access to data comply with the limitations on data use, access, disclosure, privacy, and security set forth in this Agreement. Such steps will include, but not be limited to, requiring each individual with access to data to acknowledge in writing that he/she understands and will comply with such limitations [specify Non-Disclosure Agreement terms, as applicable].

Public Information
To promote organizational transparency, and in support of data discovery for current and future researchers, Party 2 may publish non-

sensitive data documentation to public-facing websites. This documentation may include a project abstract, description, or summary of results.

Use of Name

Neither party will use the other party's name, logos, trademarks, or other marks without that party's written consent.

Community Stakeholders

The parties agree to engage community stakeholders in the course of this research project. No confidential data will be released or discussed with third parties, but the parties may agree to disclose de-identified aggregate reports to support their initiatives and engage community stakeholders.

Costs

This project shall not result in the transfer of funds from one party to another. Party 1 agrees to provide technical assistance to Party 2 to develop and deliver the initial data extract. If the parties determine that additional staff or supports are necessary at any stage of this research project, Party 2 agrees to seek funding to support those needs.

CHAPTER 3

Appendix B

Toolkits and Guides

Links to these online resources can be found in the Online Appendix at admindatahandbook.mit.edu/book/v1.0/dua. html#dua-appendix.

California Accountable Communities for Health Data-Sharing Toolkit

This toolkit is produced by the University of California Berkeley Center for Healthcare Organizational and Innovation Research and sponsored by the California Health and Human Services Agency and University of California Berkeley, School of Public Health. This report summarizes seven parameters for data sharing, Purpose/Aim, Relationship/Buy-in, Funding, Governance and Privacy, Data and Data-sharing, Technical Infrastructure, and Analytic Infrastructure while observing that parties will have varying levels of maturity and expertise across these categories.

CMS Administrative Simplification: Covered Entity Guidance

This clickable guide helps identify whether an organization or individual is a covered entity under the Administrative Simplification provisions of HIPAA. It is a good example of a straightforward tool that aids decision-makers to understand what laws apply to whom.

Department of Education Data Sharing Tool for Communities

This toolkit is designed to simplify the complex concepts of FERPA. It covers three primary focus areas: understanding the importance of data collection and sharing, understanding how to best protect student privacy when collectively using personally identifiable information from students' education records that are protected by FERPA, and understanding how to manage shared data using integrated data systems. It includes a sample MOU and sample consent form.

Health Care Systems Research Network DUA Toolkit

This toolkit includes a useful flowchart called "When do I need a DUA?" and a good glossary of terms, especially for health or healthcare projects.

National Association of County & City Health Officials (NACCHO) Data Sharing Framework
This report titled "Connecting the Dots: A Data Sharing Framework for the Local Public Health System" focuses on DUA content areas needed by local public health officials. It includes a case study involving data access in a Colorado community.

National Governors Association, Improving Human Services Programs and Outcomes Through Shared Data
More for policymakers than practitioners, this brief includes short examples of how data sharing helped states and their residents in Indiana, Kentucky, Maryland, Massachusetts, North Carolina, Pennsylvania, Rhode Island, South Carolina, Virginia, and Washington.

National League of Cities Sharing Data for Better Results Guide
Prepared with Stewards of Change, this guide was written for officials, agency leadership and managers. It highlights their incentives to share data, what information can be shared, and who can receive the information with specific examples across domains including education, health, mental health, substance abuse, human services, and criminal justice. They include sample MOUs from two counties, a city, and a state and have an appendix listing major federal laws and regulations.

Sharing Data for Social Impact: Guidebook to Establishing Responsible Governance Practices
Produced by Natalie Evans Harris, a program fellow with the Beeck Center for Social Impact and Innovation, this guide is for those who take action on the data and drive impact. The guide focuses on three phases: building the collective, defining the operations, and driving impact.

Agreement Collections

NNIP's Collection of Example Data-Sharing Agreements
This collection of agreements comes from multiple domains including

labor and human services, department of motor vehicles, criminal justice, education, housing, and health and healthcare. It also includes some generic agreements and other materials, such as an information security incident protocol, breach plan, and sample confidentiality pledge.

Data2Health Data Use Agreement Library

An analysis of DUA practices across 48 Clinical and Translational Science Award (CTSA) institutions, this collection includes DUA templates, forms to request DUAs, and policies and guidance documents.

Drexel Data Sharing Agreement Repository (DataSAR)

This repository is a collection of DUAs, samples, contracts, use policies, and forms. It can be filtered by domain and discipline. This collection is aligned with Drexel's Licensing Model and Ecosystem for Data Sharing Initiative.

Contracts for Data Collaboration

This collection contains DUAs for domestic and international government administrative data and private sector information. The site also includes a guide describing forms of collaboration and explains how they categorized DUAs based on Who, What, When, Where, Why, and How the data sharing was occurring.

Administrative Data Research Initiative Data Sharing Index

This index, a collection of standards, guides, and templates, is searchable by geographic categories including city, county, state, or federal and domain categories such as education, health, housing, human services, justice, or workforce.

CHAPTER 4

Collaborating with the Institutional Review Board (IRB)

Kathleen Murphy (Northwestern University, ret.)

4.1 Introduction

This chapter is focused on the institutional review board (IRB),[1] an administrative body created at a university or other organization to review research to ensure ethical protection of participants involved. This chapter describes what the IRB does and does not do and what researchers, data providers, and related stakeholders can expect from IRB review of research that involves humans. While all research uses information in various formats that is "data," for the purpose of this chapter, the focus will be on research that accesses and uses administrative data in different forms, formats, and contexts. This may include research activity where administrative data are the central feature or

---

Copyright © Kathleen Murphy.
Cite as: Murphy, Kathleen. "Collaborating with the Institutional Review Board (IRB)." In: Cole, Shawn, Iqbal Dhaliwal, Anja Sautmann, and Lars Vilhuber (eds.), *Handbook on Using Administrative Data for Research and Evidence-based Policy*. Cambridge, MA: Abdul Latif Jameel Poverty Action Lab. 2020.

[1] There are various names for similar boards such as Research Review Board (RRB) (Chicago Public Schools, 2020), Research Ethics Committee (REC) (NHS Health Research Authority, 2020) or some similar naming convention for boards established to conduct ethical and regulatory review of human research.

where the data are part of a larger project. There may be different contexts such as international research or collaborative research (or both) where there are different regulatory requirements, as well as different review processes. Some data-driven projects will include only existing administrative data, while others include retrospective or prospective data alone or in conjunction with other research methods, such as experimental interventions, surveys, interviews, or observation. Some projects only involve the analysis of data, while others can include multiple iterations of experimental and comparison interventions as well as innovative analysis of multiple data sets, which are linked by a subset of identifiers. In the United States, the IRB review of such projects takes all of these design factors into consideration in the context of a well-established ethical and regulatory process as described in section 4.5.

The goal of this chapter is to provide researchers, data providers, data stewards, and other stakeholders with the tools they need to understand the IRB process. The chapter provides a practical understanding of what an IRB considers and how an IRB processes human research including data driven proposals. This includes how an IRB considers data acquisition, data management, data storage, and data retention in the conduct of research. The chapter references the ethical principles as well as the application of the federal, state, local, and institutional guidelines for research in as much as the IRB has oversight of these principles and guidelines in the United States. The text includes discussion of related international considerations, which may inform ethical and regulatory deliberation. Finally, the chapter provides practical strategies for collaborating with the IRB, which has oversight of the research.

There are a number of resources in the literature that identify the advantages of big data and administrative data for conducting research. That is not reiterated here except to endorse that the ease of use, reduced burden on participants and researchers and the long-term availability of administrative data makes this approach a logical way to contribute to the knowledge base. For additional information see Feeney et al. (2015); Connelly et al. (2016); Collmann and Matei (2016). For more detailed descriptions of the use of administrative data for public policy and the public good see for example Card et al. (2011); Collmann and Matei (2016); Figlio, Karbownik and Salvanes (2016).

4.2 What is the IRB?

The ethical guidance and regulatory requirements for IRB review of all human research includes the ethical principles of the Belmont Report (United States 1978) and the US Department of Health and Human Services (HHS) Office for Human Research Protections (OHRP) regulations found in the part of the Code of Federal Regulations (CFR) referred to as "Title 45: Public Welfare, Part 46—Protection of human subjects, Subpart A—Basic HHS Policy for Protection of Human Research Subjects" or 45 CFR 46 (Code of Federal Regulations, 2017a; Office for Human Research Protections, 2016b). Throughout this chapter, regulatory citations are in reference to this section of the CFR.

The IRB is an administrative body that reviews human research (defined by 45 CFR 46.102 (e)(1)) to ensure the ethical protection of participants from the reasonably foreseeable risks of harm caused by research. The harms the IRB considers include physical, psychological, social, legal, and economic risks as well as community or group harms. For example, an inadvertent disclosure of sensitive or identifiable information is a common risk in social and behavioral research because the disclosure can result in social, psychological, or legal harm. All IRBs include the risks that need to be considered in the conduct of research in the protocol and consent templates, as well as in reviewer guides and on their websites. See for example, University of California, Irvine[2] and the Northwestern University[3] protocol templates.

An IRB or ethics review process may be part of an academic institution; a medical facility; a federal, state, or local agency; or any other organization or commercial entity that chooses to conduct human research. Entities that receive federal funds for any reason and conduct human

---

[2]https://research.uci.edu/compliance/human-research-protections/irb-members/assessing-risks-and-benefits.html (accessed 2020-12-15).

[3]https://www.irb.northwestern.edu/templates-forms-sops (2020-12-15).

research are required by federal mandate in the United States to have an IRB.

IRB membership and the organization and function of an IRB is defined in the regulations 45 CFR 46: 107, 108. An IRB will consist of a minimum of five members of diverse backgrounds and expertise, including scientists and non-scientists, in order to provide complete and adequate review of human research. In IRBs with a large volume of projects, minimal risk research activity is generally reviewed by full-time employed IRB office staff who are also board members and qualified to review. Greater than minimal risk studies must always be reviewed at a convened meeting referred to as Full Board review.

Table 4.1: Categories of review conducted by an IRB

Review Type	Regulatory Authority	Risk	Description
Exempt	Ethical principles of Belmont (respect for persons, beneficence, and justice)	Minimal risk (often anonymous or deidentified data)	Briefer application and typically reviewed in the IRB office
Expedited	Belmont and 45 CFR 46.111	Minimal risk (identifiable, personal or sensitive information)	Reviewed in the office by one or more IRB members. If expedited reviewer does not approve, the study may go to the full board
Full Board	Belmont and 45 CFR 46.111	Greater than minimal risk (could include minimal risk research that does not fit in exempt or expedited review categories)	All studies involving prisoners and certain research with vulnerable populations regardless of risk such as children, fetuses, and neonates. Projects can only be disapproved at a convened meeting

In addition to the internal organization or agency-based IRB, organizations and independent researchers that do not have their own IRB can contract with independent IRBs which can be both commercial or non-profit. Independent IRBs also can serve in the role as a central IRB where multiple (academic or clinical) institutions are conducting the same research and either want to contract with an independent IRB or are required by regulation to rely on one IRB for oversight of the whole project. The reliance agreement process, where one IRB agrees to rely on another IRB for oversight, can be with a commercial IRB or with an IRB that is, for example, located in an academic institution where that IRB has agreed to serve as the IRB of record for a multisite project. For the regulatory guidance on the reliance process see 45 CFR 46.114.

Independent IRBs also may be an option for a data provider who would like to submit research projects for ethical oversight when there is no federal requirement to do so. This chapter is not focused on independent or central IRBs but for more information about central IRBs and institutional IRBs see Wandile (2018).

At the center of the ethics review process is the Belmont Report (National Commission for the Protection of Human Subjects of Biomedical and Behavioral Research, 1979), which summarizes the ethical principles and guidelines IRBs use when reviewing research involving human subjects. Three core principles are identified:

1. *Respect for persons* allows individuals to be self-directed and make informed, voluntary decisions about whether they wish to participate in research and is the fundamental ethical rationale for the consent process and the elements of the consent document.
2. *Beneficence* assesses the risks and benefits of participating in research, recognizing the obligation of the researcher to minimize risks while maximizing the benefits of participation.
3. *Justice* directs investigators to recruit and enroll those who would benefit from the outcome of the research and to not impose undue risks on those who would not otherwise be helped by the research.

The principles of the Belmont Report are codified in federal regulations 45 CFR 46 to protect the rights and welfare of humans recruited to participate in federally funded research activities. Although the federal regulations specifically apply to non-exempt research projects in

CHAPTER 4

organizations that receive federal funds, academic institutions have routinely applied these same regulatory guidelines to federally and non-federally funded or even unfunded projects, simply because the regulatory standards are ethically reasonable.

It is in the context of these ethical principles and regulatory requirements that IRBs are charged with the responsibility of reviewing research involving human participants. The definition of human research is discussed in section 4.3 in more detail, but it is in this context that the IRB has the authority to approve, monitor, modify, and disapprove all research activities that fall within its jurisdiction. These regulations apply to research conducted in the United States or by US-based researchers conducting research in another country.

4.3 IRBs and International Research

Human research can take place anywhere in the world and there are over 1,000 laws, regulations, and guidelines on human research protections in 133 countries (Office for Human Research Protections, 2020). OHRP annually compiles the most relevant regulations and agencies[4] that regulate research in each country. Some, though not all countries, have regulations and guidance regarding social and behavioral research activities. Countries that do have such guidance tend to have more restrictive data protection rules and regulations than those in the United States. For example, in the European Union, the General Data Protection Regulation (GDPR)[5] (European Parliament and Council of the European Union, 2016) covers the protection of all personal data of which research data are but a subset. GDPR special category data include race and ethnic origin; religious or philosophical beliefs; political opinions; trade union memberships; biometric data used to identify an individual; genetic data; health

---

[4]https://www.hhs.gov/ohrp/sites/default/files/2020-international-compilation-of-human-research-standards.pdf (accessed 2020-12-15).

[5]GDPR is legislation in the European Economic Area that protects persons with regard to the processing of personal data and on the free movement or sharing of those data. GDPR is comprehensive, encompassing all personal data not just research data.

data; and data related to sexual preferences, sex life, and/or sexual orientation. Similarly, the consent documents in the countries of the European Economic Area (EEA) have more prescriptive and restrictive requirements than in the US (Office for Human Research Protections, 2018). Whatever the country, researchers need to be cognizant of the local country regulations that may apply. For example, *respect for persons* as articulated in the Belmont Report applies in other countries, it just may be defined differently.

In addition, when research is taking place in a country where the regulations are different, researchers in the United States will be held to the standard of what is referred to as equivalent protections (45 CFR 46.101(h)); additional guidance can be found in Office for Human Research Protections (2016a). This means the researcher based in the US (who is subject to review by an IRB) and conducting research internationally is responsible for utilizing strategies to mitigate risk and protect participants at the level that would be required if the research was conducted in the United States. One example is the age of majority and consent to participate in research. In most US states the age of majority and consent is 18, while in some countries, such as Germany, Italy, Paraguay, and Ecuador, the age of consent is 14. A US researcher conducting research in Paraguay will be expected to use 18 as the age of consent to participate by the IRB. Another example, the Family Educational Rights and Privacy Act (FERPA) is a US law (20 U.S. Code § 1232g; 34 CFR part 99) and not applicable in other countries; however, if using education data from another country where education data does not have privacy and confidentiality protections, the IRB will expect that the research will apply equivalent protections as would exist under FERPA. In this example, data providers, data stewards, and researchers would need to address the use and collection of data in relation to minors when requesting IRB review.

4.4 What an IRB Does Not Do

Just as important as what the IRB does do, is what it does not do. As stated earlier, the mission of an IRB is the protection of participants in research from risks associated with the research. To do this, an IRB must contribute to the development of training, policies, and practices that facilitate this purpose. However, there are a number of related oversight and regulatory activities required for some research activities that are **not** the purview of the IRB, though they contribute to the IRB process.

The IRB does not manage the grants or mechanisms for funding the research and is not involved in developing conflict of interest management plans. Additionally, while the IRB in some institutions may serve as the privacy board, as is the case for biomedical research, this is not a regular IRB function The IRB typically does **not** have the responsibility to create or finalize data sharing agreements such as data use agreements (DUAs) and data transfer agreements or other contracts such as non-disclosure agreements (NDAs). Finally, data safety plans for sensitive restricted data are most often developed outside of the IRB. However, non-disclosure agreements and data safety plans have implications for the IRB review of the data management plan in the protocol (the specific and detailed design for how a research study will be conducted, which is submitted to the IRB for review).

The IRB will conduct an administrative review of these agreements and plans and, when applicable, hold the researcher accountable. For example, if there is a reported conflict of interest as part of the COI management plan where the principal investigator (PI) is prohibited from conducting data analysis because of a vested interest in the outcome, the IRB will make sure that is written into the protocol and reflected in any consents that are in use. Similarly, when applicable, the IRB will require that the DUA be uploaded into the IRB record and that the data protections outlined in the data sharing agreement are written into the IRB protocol. However, the IRB is not a signatory or even an intermediary in these agreements. The designated official on the institution side is the responsible party for signing the DUA or NDA, and for processing the funding, evaluating conflict of interest, or establishing the appropriate data security mechanism. While data providers can rely on the IRB monitoring and enforcing any of these activities as they relate to data protection and protection of participants, the IRB is not the responsible party for initiating them.

In addition, researchers need to know their own institutional policies and practices as to where each of these related activities fit with IRB review. For example, in some institutions, the IRB review may not proceed until the DUA is in place. In other institutions, the finalizing of the DUA is contingent on the IRB approval. While both the IRB and the data sharing agreement processes can typically be started at the same time, the researcher and data provider need to know what the sequence is for final approval. A key point is in all research requiring approval, the data security evaluation and compliance with FERPA or the Health Insurance Portability and Accountability Act (HIPAA) regulations must be in place before IRB approval can be processed.

4.5 What the IRB Will Do to Ensure the Protection of Participants

The first order of ethical challenge in all research is the risk of harm. When it comes to the use of administrative data in research, the risk of harm stems from the potential for violations of privacy, confidentiality, or informed consent (even if the research project as a whole may expose participants to additional risks). All of the stakeholders in data-driven, human research that are subject to IRB need to start with the federal regulations that govern the IRB review of research. The criteria for IRB review are articulated in 45 CFR 46.111 (Code of Federal Regulations, 2017b). This part of the regulation outlines seven specific elements that **must** be in every non-exempt research project protocol, which all IRBs use to determine whether research can be approved. The following have been abbreviated from the regulations for the purpose of this handbook; **all of the following** must be met:

(1) "Risks to subjects are minimized by using procedures that are consistent with sound research design and that do not unnecessarily expose subjects to risk." (45 CFR 46.111(a)(1)(i))

To evaluate sound research design in a data driven project, the IRB will consider whether the variables of the data set, the sample size,

CHAPTER 4

and the proposed analysis are consistent with the intended purpose of the study. There must be scientific merit to the study and there must be consistency between the purpose and the data being used.

(2) "Risks to subjects are reasonable in relation to anticipated benefits, if any, to subjects, and the importance of the knowledge that may reasonably be expected to result." (45 CFR 46.111(a)(2))

A primary risk to the subjects directly related to the use of administrative data or linkage of such data with survey data is the re-identification of participants, either by an external party or by one of the stakeholders in the project. This is in addition to any other risks associated with the project unrelated to the use of administrative data, such as the risks to participants due to the intervention itself. The IRB will work with researchers to anticipate risks to individual participants and to ensure there are adequate mechanisms in place to protect participants from harm, such as loss of income, retaliation, or punishment. Risk mitigation with administrative data is often focused on levels of access and security with regard to the collection, transfer, storage, and access management of data. In addition to protecting subjects from the risks of disclosure to outside parties, projects may also need to mitigate the risks of reidentification by the data provider; the researcher and data provider may consider an arms-length agreement, which prevents the data provider from accessing the identified data and provides another measure of protecting subjects. There are multiple ways to protect individuals and their related information through technology and by de-identifying that data. The researcher will work with the IRB, in addition to their institution's general counsel and IT where appropriate, to manage the risks and security procedures for working with administrative data.

For example, in a study where a researcher collaborates with a bank to evaluate a microfinance program, it is possible for researchers to uncover fraud or deception by individual participants in the course of the project. Logically the bank will want to know that information, but that places the participant at risk of harm by having participated in the research. In this example, it would not be unusual for an IRB to require a research team to state in the protocol that the DUA must prevent access to, or sharing of, identifiable information with the bank or must otherwise restrict the bank's use of linked administrative data to protect participants from retaliation or punishment.

(3) "Selection of subjects is equitable." (45 CFR 46.111(a)(3))

This means that for all research, the data being used or collected are a logical reflection of the purpose of the study and representative of the population most likely to benefit from the study. For data-driven projects that analyze a set of existing data, this would not generally be an issue. The primary concern in this case is that the data used must be logically connected to the purpose of the research project. However, some projects may use an existing administrative data set to select a study sample as in the case of randomized controlled trials that use administrative data as a census to select participants. This selection process should be free of biases; any biases could lead to the benefits and burdens of the research being unequally distributed. This can be an issue if there are biases within the administrative data. The IRB will consider the usage of administrative data for sample selection as it relates to the Belmont Report principle of justice: the people selected to be recruited to participate in the research are those most likely to be affected by the problem being studied and to benefit from the research.

(4) "Informed consent will be sought from each prospective subject or the subject's legally authorized representative, in accordance with, and to the extent required by, 45 CFR 46.116" (45 CFR 46.111(a)(4))

The typical standard for research with human subjects is that there is signed written consent. With projects where the data were originally collected for purposes other than research, consent for the data to be used for future research is rarely part of the original agreement between those subjects and the data collector. If consent is present, oftentimes the agreement that the data can be used for research is buried in the details at the end of the Terms of Service as to belie the concept of "informed" consent. Similarly, governments rarely use "consent" in the IRB sense of the term when collecting administrative data, as they

CHAPTER 4

do not obtain data for research purposes. Instead, in the US, the government may use terms like Privacy Impact Assessments (PIAs), System of Records Notices (SORNs), and Computer Matching Agreements (CMAs) to alert the public to additional uses of data. These protocols do establish a legal floor for the use of the data, but they do not reflect the ethical intent of informed consent as articulated in the federal regulations. For projects that only use retrospective administrative data, an IRB will typically look for an explanation in the research protocol for why it is not possible or reasonable to obtain written consent. In research projects that combine administrative data with survey data or other direct subject contact, the informed consent procedure for the new data collection can also include consent to the use of the administrative data. To that end, the researcher needs to decide whether individuals who meet the criteria for the ongoing research activities are free to decline the use of the administrative data and still participate in the rest of the study. If use of the data is a mandatory requirement for participation, that needs to be stated in the consent. If it is optional, then it needs to be added to the consent form as an "optional element" to make it clear that it is not a requirement of participation.

(5) "Informed consent will be appropriately documented or appropriately waived in accordance with 45 CFR 46.117." (45 CFR 46.111(a)(5))

This is referred to by IRBs as documentation of consent and the rationale is consistent with element 4 that the standard practice is signed written consent. However, there are many circumstances in which a waiver of documentation of consent is appropriate either because it is not practical, such as with a phone interview or an online survey, or for safety reasons in which written consent would endanger the person to have their name attached to a study. This is most likely to occur with participants who are vulnerable. For example, interviews with sex workers in countries where it is illegal or with individuals in domestic violence shelters could be at heightened risk if their names were on a document.

(6) "When appropriate, the research plan makes adequate provision for monitoring the data collected to ensure the safety of subjects." (45 CFR 46.111(a)(6))

Monitoring data collection is not an issue for projects using existing data in isolation or data that will be collected anonymously, especially if the data are used retrospectively. However, this may apply to a study that uses administrative data to observe participants over time during their participation in a project. For example, consider a randomized controlled trial that uses administrative data to study the implementation of a new social policy. As part of the assessment, the study uses unemployment records, medical records, or other sources to assess measures related to socio-economic status, employability, and markers of depression. In such a scenario, the IRB will typically require real time monitoring of those data so that researchers can intervene in outstanding circumstances. Some examples where intervention is warranted include the instance of a participant reporting suicidal ideation, lack of ready access to food, clean water, or health care, or any increased risk of harm caused by a change in the policy being studied. In situations where it is unclear that the benefits to society outweigh the harm to participants, the research may need to be stopped to protect the participants. The only way to recognize the harm is to monitor the data as they are generated. The IRB expects researchers to recognize the probability and the magnitude of the harm and to address it in the protocol. While monitoring data may not be an issue, the protocol needs to address why that is the case.

(7) "When appropriate, there are adequate provisions to protect the privacy of subjects and to maintain the confidentiality of data." (45 CFR 46.111(a)(7))

Confidentiality is a key factor for IRB deliberation of all research including projects using administrative data. Unintended disclosure of sensitive, private information is one of the primary risks of participation in research, and appropriate measures to manage the risk must be in place to protect participants and their related data. The more sensitive the data being used or collected, the more robust the data protection plan must be. Several of the chapters in this handbook discuss in detail the different strategies available to protect subject privacy and confidential data; those details will not be reiterated, but this chapter emphasizes that appropriate strategies must be elements provided in the protocol for IRB review.

The above seven elements are required for IRB approval of a research project. There is far more detail about the specifics of what is required with informed consent including when it can be altered or waived (Code of Federal Regulations, 2017d) and how it must be documented in the actual regulations. It is important to note that while all IRBs are using the same federal regulations, there may be different interpretations of the application of the regulations, especially around the requirement of consent and when it can be altered or be waived. Data providers can rely on the IRB review process to address each of the seven elements required for IRB approval and to approve only those projects that have adequate protections in place. Researchers, on the other hand, need to understand the basic regulatory requirements and to work with their own IRB to understand how the principles and regulations are being applied to their specific study. Similarly, researchers can go a long way in helping themselves navigate the IRB process by addressing each of the specific regulatory requirements in their protocol and related documents submitted to the IRB. The rest of this chapter is focused on the practical concerns for IRBs regarding specific research projects, the IRB related questions that must be asked and answered, and the manner in which IRBs think about the answers.

4.6 Considerations of the IRB

Being able to understand how and what the IRB considers when reading over a new project will inform the researcher what to include when submitting a new project proposal to the IRB. If the project proposal is framed how an IRB considers projects, the review process will likely be more collaborative and quicker, with far fewer changes requested.

4.6.1 Is the Study Human Research or Not Human Research (nHR)?

The first consideration is whether IRB review is needed and involves two questions to come to a conclusion. To decide whether a project is human research the following questions are considered in sequence by an IRB. If the answer to **any** of these questions is no, the study is not human research (nHR) and it does not require IRB review. For additional guidance, the OHRP provides decision charts[6] (Office for Human Research Protections, 2020) to help map the process of how to think about the question, "Is an Activity Human Subjects Research Covered by 45 CFR Part 46?"

1. **Is it research?** In this context research is defined as a systematic investigation designed to contribute to generalizable knowledge (45 CFR 46.102(l)). There are two concepts to consider: systematic collection of information and generalizable knowledge. If a project does not meet both requirements then it does not require IRB review as it is not a research activity and is therefore not human research. It should be noted that generalizability can be a nuanced concept that is more multifaceted than just statistical generalizability, although data driven projects tend to be most closely linked to statistical generalizability (Lee and Baskerville, 2003). Nonetheless, when there is a systematic investigation (secondary analysis) of existing data and the investigation is intended to contribute to generalizable knowledge, the activity is research.

2. **Does the research involve human subjects?** It is possible to have a systematic collection of data that are routinely collected about people such as birth, death, taxes, participation in programs, insurance cost, medical care, etc. This collection of data is not for research purposes so while it is systematic, it is not research at the outset, because it is not intended to contribute to generalizable knowledge. Managing the data does not change that assessment. In the course of working with one (or many) administrative data

---

[6]https://www.hhs.gov/ohrp/regulations-and-policy/decision-charts/index.html (accessed 2020-12-15).

sets over time, the data provider or researcher may also use these data for activities that do not constitute research. For example, if a researcher assists a government data provider in managing their administrative data both for a research project and to improve the government's internal processes, the latter usage is not a research activity. Managing and organizing data to make data more accessible is still not intended to contribute to generalizable knowledge, so this would not meet the definition of research.

For research to be considered human subjects research, the investigator must be conducting research about a living individual. The federal definition of "human subject" includes that the researcher "(i) obtains information . . . through intervention or interaction with the individual, and uses, studies, or analyzes the information . . . ; or (ii) obtains, uses, studies, analyzes, or generates identifiable private information" (45 CFR 46.102(e)(i–ii)).

There is a regulatory "or" so if either factor is true (intervention/ interaction *or* identifiable private information) then the study is considered to involve human subjects. However, the timing of when the interaction or identifiable information occurs matters. If data were collected for non-research purposes and the data source removed the identifiers from the data before providing it to the researcher, it is research but without human identifiers, so there are no people for the IRB to protect. On the other hand, if the researcher receives identifiable data and is the one to remove the identifiers, then the human subjects have come into contact with the research and the study would require IRB review. The details of the lifecycle of the data matter for IRB review. For additional guidance, the OHRP has produced decision charts[7] to help IRBs, institutions, and researchers.

While an activity might not meet the federal definition of human research, some institutions may still require researchers to undergo the IRB process; researchers must be aware of their local IRB policies and practices. In addition, many journals, conferences, and workshops require documentation of IRB review; in response, most IRBs have de-

---

[7] https://www.hhs.gov/ohrp/regulations-and-policy/decision-charts/index.html (accessed 2020-12-15).

veloped an abbreviated process for submitting a description of nHR and the IRB will verify whether additional IRB review is necessary, and provide documentation of this process for the researcher

If a study is determined to be human research, there are additional questions to be considered regarding IRB review.

4.6.2 Is the Study Federally Funded?

In addition to the Department of Health and Human Services, there are 19 other federal agencies that are signatories to 45 CFR 46 and include the OHRP regulations for the protection of humans in research in their own regulations. The issue of federal versus non-federal funding (including no funding) is important for two reasons. The first is that most non-exempt federally funded projects are under the purview of 45 CFR 46 and therefore require IRB review. In addition, even if a project is not federally funded, institutional policy may require IRB review. In particular, this is the case if the institution where the research is occurring has a Federalwide Assurance under which there is an agreement that all research will be subject to 45 CFR 46 (Office for Human Research Protections, 2017). Data providers may also require an IRB review, even absent federal funding, as a condition for supplying data for research projects. While most academic institutions have an IRB, private organizations and private individuals are not compelled to use IRB review if their research is not federally funded. For example, private corporations like Amazon, Facebook, and Google can conduct research without IRB review, as they are not constrained in the same way by the federal regulations.

4.6.3 Is the Researcher an Agent Such That the Institution is Engaged in HR?

The follow up to the funding question is the question of engagement in the research. It is possible to be a collaborator on a research project and not be engaged in the IRB sense of the term. If an institution is not engaged, then IRB review is also not needed. Engagement centers around the question of agency and whether the researcher is an agent of the institution or organization for which the local IRB has oversight. The definition of "agent" will be defined by the institution or organization, not by the individual. The guidance from OHRP about engagement states, "In general, an institution is considered *engaged* in a particular non-exempt human subjects research project when its employees or agents for the purposes of the research project obtain: (1) data about the subjects of the research through intervention or interaction with them; (2) identifiable private information about the subjects of the research; or (3) the informed consent of human subjects for the research." (Code of Federal Regulations, 2017c) There are nuances to *engaged* and OHRP has detailed guidance regarding what it means to be engaged and examples of *not engaged* in research. The examples in the guidance are helpful to researchers, data providers, and IRBs to consider.

In addition, where there are multiple researchers collaborating on the same research study, some of the researchers and their institutions may not be engaged in HR if their role does not involve access to actual people or identifying information. In multi-site projects, determining who is an agent and what institutions are engaged can get complicated. Engagement is ultimately a decision that is up to the IRB of each institution. Neither can an outside IRB or other external party decide whether another IRB should be involved. Data providers, data stewards, and researchers need to be clear that it is never the place of one institution's IRB to decide for another that they are not engaged. Data providers, data administrators, and any relevant stakeholders, including researchers, need to know that individual researchers will always be held accountable by their own IRB for verification of engagement. Note that this is distinct from determining the IRB of record for a multi-site research project.

4.6.4 Is the Project Exempt From the Regulations or Non-Exempt (Expedited or Full Board Review)?

The final question is directly related to the level of review. There are three primary distinctions between projects that are eligible for exempt review and those eligible for non-exempt review: risk of harm as it relates to identifiability of the data, vulnerability of the participants, and matters of research consent and waiver of consent.

Identifiability of the Data and Retention of the Identifiers

The most common difference between exempt and non-exempt research is related to the level of risk of harm to participants. *Minimal risk* and *greater than minimal risk* are the two levels of risk that IRBs consider. Minimal risk is defined in the regulations[8] as "... the *probability and magnitude of harm or discomfort anticipated in the research are not greater in and of themselves than those ordinarily encountered in daily life or during the performance of routine physical or psychological examinations or tests.*" Anything else is considered as greater than minimal risk.

The probability and magnitude harm are the important concepts related to an assessment of the difference between minimal risk and greater than minimal risk. The magnitude of harm relates to the nature of the harm and the vulnerability of the participants in the research and is somewhat more concrete than assessing the probability of harm. For the IRB, magnitude of harm starts with what could possibly go wrong and then what would be the actual harm to the participant. For projects using administrative data, a common risk of harm is the possibility of linking research information directly to an individual. This can be further exacerbated when combining administrative data with primary data collection. If there is a loss of privacy and confidentiality, the IRB always considers the types of harm that may be related to psychological, legal, social, economic, group, or community harms

---

[8] https://www.law.cornell.edu/cfr/text/45/46.10245 CFR 46.102 (j) (accessed 2020-12-15).

with regard to the actual content of the information. Even if reidentification occurs, the level of harm that may result can vary depending on the information in the data. In addition, even if the data collected in a study have been de-identified, there needs to be an assessment of the probability of the re-identification. De-identification is a first line of defense against many harms, but it is not infallible. As technology, software, and algorithms improve, it is increasingly possible to reidentify people based on just a few concrete data points (see chapter 5 for more details).

With personally identifiable or sensitive information, the researcher will be required to provide the IRB with a rigorous data protection and data management plan minimizing the risk of identification or re-identification of participants. The relevant margin that the IRB needs to consider is the additional risk of harm that occurs due to the use of the data for the proposed research project. While collecting and storing the original data may entail risks, these would be incurred with or without the research. From this perspective, the use of an isolated data set under an appropriate data management plan typically does not appreciably change the risk of individuals in the data. Probability and magnitude of harm become more challenging for IRBs, data providers, and researchers when the research is combining multiple data sets. This applies both to combining different sources of administrative data as well as when combining administrative data with primary data collection. The researcher needs to specifically communicate to the IRB not only the risk of each data set in use but also the probability and magnitude of harm of any combined data set. It is important that data providers, data stewards, researchers, and IRBs are informed, informative, and realistic about the probability and magnitude of harm in a study that is engaging in secondary analysis of one or more data sets. That discussion must include the reality of the protection afforded by de-identification as well as the robustness of the overall data protection plan if identifiers are retained. In that regard, it is always a good strategy to include a statement in the research protocol: even if re-identification could be possible, the principal investigator commits to ensuring that the study team will not re-identify participants.

> It should be noted that anonymous and de-identified data are not subject to the GDPR of the European Union provided that the research team had no role in the collection of the data with identifiers and has no access to the identifiers going forward. If identifiers are collected by the research team, the definition of "special categories" of data require a more robust data protection plan.

De-Identified Data, Risk, and IRB Review De-identified data once contained identifiers, but by the time of the new use they no longer contain sufficient identifiers to link information to specific individuals with any degree of certainty. The level of IRB review for de-identified data is contingent on who originally collected the data and whether the data are coded or whether a key exists. IRBs need to know when, where, and how the data were de-identified in the life cycle of the research. The IRB will take note of whether the producer of the data (Institution A) is removing the identifiers or whether the recipient of the data (Institution B) is removing identifiers. If Institution B is receiving de-identified data from Institution A, with no access to a code or key and no one on the study team had anything to do with the original collection of the data, it is probable that such a study would not meet the definition of human research. If the study personnel from Institution B were involved with the original collection, will have access to the key of identifiers, or will be removing the identifiers, the study could be exempt. Such a study could be reviewed by expedited procedure if, for example, the PI from Institution B is listed on the original grant proposal as a Co-PI.

Identifiable Private Information and Restricted Data The regulatory code defines identifiable private information as follows: *"Private information* includes information about behavior that occurs in a context in which an individual can reasonably expect that no observation or recording is taking place, and information that has been provided for specific purposes by an individual and that the individual can reasonably expect will not be made public (e.g., a medical record)" And

CHAPTER 4

"Identifiable private information is private information for which the identity of the subject is or may readily be ascertained by the investigator or associated with the information" (45 CFR 46.102 (e)(4)(5)).

Restricted data is a distinction that is at the discretion of the holder of the data. Restricted data are typically described as both private and identifiable by source of the data or data steward. This means there is a process that the researcher must go through in order to obtain access to and use the data. The definition of "restricted" is made by the data source, not by the IRB; the IRB will respect the designation and the level of review required by the source.

The study protocol submitted to the IRB must specify the type of data, the source of the data, and whether the identifiers (if any) will be removed or retained. If there are identifiers or if there is a plan to retain identifiers long term, there must be a data protection plan that specifies where the data will be stored, for how long, and who will have access. The greater the risk to participants of inadvertent disclosure of identifiable private information, the more robust the data protection plan must be.

Vulnerability of the Participants

The second consideration for IRBs in determining whether a project is exempt or non-exempt is regarding the perceived vulnerability of the study population. Vulnerable populations[9] are defined in the regulations (45 CFR 46 Subpart B, C, and D), including children, prisoners, and other groups of people who are considered to need additional protections due to social or economic conditions. Most human research with vulnerable populations is likely to be non-exempt and subject to regulatory review, although it can depend on the purpose of the study and whether any of the information is already publicly available.

---

[9]For vulnerable populations under Federal protection see 45 CFR 46 Subpart B regarding pregnant women, human fetuses, and neonates, Subpart C regarding prisoners, and Subpart D regarding minors. Other vulnerable populations identified by IRBs might include situations in which there might be a power differential such as student and instructor, employee and employer; a cognitive or physical disability; or difference that requires additional protections such as literacy, SES, language, or other social status.

Consent and Waiver of Consent

The third consideration that distinguishes exempt from non-exempt studies is the issue of informed consent. Exempt projects have a consent process but are not required to meet the documentation or other requirements for consent as detailed in 45 CFR 46.116 and 45 CFR 46.117 criteria. A waiver of consent or waiver of documentation of consent is not necessary; instead, participant consent may be achieved through distribution of information sheets.

If a study contains personally identifiable information, there is an increased risk of harm, so the study will likely be considered non-exempt. Non-exempt review includes a regulatory requirement for the IRB to review consent. For example, with a non-exempt study that proposes to use administrative data that was obtained without consent, the IRB has to determine whether consent is needed at the point of the research or whether it can be waived. The standard regulatory requirement for all HR is for there to be an informed consent process and a signed written document. For the IRB to waive consent, there are specific regulatory criteria—all of which must be met. Researchers must address in their study protocol the following criteria as part of a rationale for the request for the IRB to waive consent 45 CFR 46.116(f)(3):

i. "The research involves no more than minimal risk." Researchers should use the regulatory definition of minimal risk (see section 4.6) in a study specific way in the rationale for the request for a waiver. There is no option for waiver of consent for studies determined to be greater than minimal risk.
ii. "The research could not practicably be carried out without the requested waiver or alteration." This refers to the research design. Often there is not a reasonable or feasible way to ask hundreds of people for the consent to use their administrative or other pre-existing data that have been or will be collected over time, because the current research team does not have access to the individuals from which the data were originally collected. The more distant the researcher is from the initial collection of the data, the more likely an IRB will grant a waiver of consent based on this criterion,

provided there is a robust data protection plan.

iii. "If the research involves using identifiable private information..., the research could not practicably be carried out without using such information... in an identifiable format." While similar to practicability, this criterion relates more directly to the retention and use of identifiers. From an IRB perspective, this is usually the key part of the ethical deliberation to waive consent for identifiable private information. While the IRB will typically respond more favorably if the researcher plans not to retain identifiers, sometimes the identifiers are needed to connect different data files and data collected over time. For instance, randomized controlled trials often remove but store the identifying information separately from the rest of the data so that subjects can be reidentified in the future as needed, such as in the case of adverse events that need to be remedied. If the identifiers need to be retained, the IRB simply requires the researcher to provide the rationale for why the identifiers are needed and the plan for how the identifiers, or the key to the identifiers, will be kept separate from the actual data. It is also useful to provide a plan for the end-of-study removal of identifiers.

iv. "The waiver or alteration will not adversely affect the rights and welfare of the subjects." People have a fundamental right to consent to participate in research. In order to provide a rationale for why a waiver of consent does not affect rights and welfare, the protocol needs to address the issue of protection of privacy of the individual and confidentiality of the data. For example, depending on the original source of the contact information, it could be ethically feasible to justify a waiver consent for using retrospective data to identify potential participants for recruitment to research. Similarly, if all the other elements are addressed and the raw data are to be de-identified (if the benefit of the study is greater than the risk to participants of using their information without consent) this could be a circumstance when rights and welfare would not be placed at risk. Alternatively, when a wavier could adversely affect rights and welfare, it is unlikely to be granted. For example, in a situation where the research poses greater than a minimal risk to the subjects and the researchers are performing a direct intervention or otherwise interacting with the subjects, the subjects are available and there are no logistical hurdles to obtaining the waiver of consent. Similarly, it would be unusual for an IRB to waive a parent's right to consent (give permission) for their minor child to participate in research because parents, as guardians for their children, have a fundamental right to determine consent for the child to participate in research. Although waiving parent permission is not a welfare issue per se, waiving parent permission could be considered to negatively affect the parent's rights.

v. "Whenever appropriate, the subjects or legally authorized representatives will be provided with additional pertinent information after participation." Access to participants after the study depends entirely on the research project. In a study that performs primary data collection, notifying participants through some sort of report or posting on a website may be feasible. However, it can also be true that providing a summary to participants is not possible due to passage of time, or is not appropriate due to the relevance of the findings to the individual. This can happen with a project where the researchers do not have direct access to the subjects in the data, as can be the case for studies only using administrative data. Feasibility and appropriateness are considered by the IRB when determining whether researchers need to provide additional information to the subjects of a study.

All of these criteria for granting a waiver of consent use the regulatory "and," meaning that all criteria must be addressed. Researchers who are requesting a waiver of consent need to be proactive about addressing all five of the criteria.

4.7 Strategies for Communicating with the IRB

Working with the IRB should be a collaborative process. While the IRB's authority to approve or reject proposed research projects may frustrate researchers, it is important to emphasize that the purpose

CHAPTER 4

of the IRB is to protect participants and ensure that human research meets the requisite ethical and regulatory criteria.

At any given time, IRB staff are reviewing potentially hundreds of projects from different disciplines, with differing funding sources, and with different regulatory requirements. A project protocol that clearly and directly addresses the criteria from the perspective of the IRB will undergo a more efficient and effective review process.

Communicating effectively and constructively with the IRB is key to getting studies reviewed in a productive and timely manner. The following are some strategies for communicating with an IRB:

1. The protocol templates required by IRBs are constructed to address the ethical and regulatory considerations that must be present for IRB approval. Although protocol templates may vary between IRBs in terms of format and the order of the elements, they are all designed to collect the information required to consider any project in light of the 45 CFR 46.111 criteria.
2. Because IRBs must consider whether a project is exempt or nonexempt, it is important to focus particular attention on the specific interactions with participants and/or their identifying information. The IRB is less concerned about the theory underlying the purpose of the project and more focused on the risks to participants. This includes needing specific detail of the how, when, why, and where of interactions with participants or their identifying information.
3. The protocol should indicate whether current study staff are related or unrelated to the original collection of the data. The protocol should be specific about who is doing what on the study.
4. The IRB needs to know the details of the data collection, access, storage, and management of any retrospective or prospective data used by the research project. There should be data collection instruments or a data dictionary, or both, included with the other study documents. If the information collected is identifiable and sensitive, there needs to be commensurate plan for mitigating risk of harm to the participants.
5. The protocol should address what identifiers will be collected, received, or accessed by the study team. In addition, the retention of

identifiers over the life of the project must be addressed. The IRB will focus on the risk associated with retaining identifiers as well as the risk associated with re-identification of de-identified data. The IRB will also want to know about the risk to participants associated with combining multiple data sets.

6. If the study is collaborative or multi-site, there needs to be a description of what each collaborator and site is doing on the project and a specific articulation of what each collaborator is doing in terms of IRB review. Questions that should be addressed include: what part of the research is happening at what institution, organization, or country, and by whom? If all institutions or organizations are doing the same thing, who is conceptually in charge of the research? For studies subject to the Revised Common Rule's Cooperative Research Provision (45 CFR 46.114), which institution will be the IRB of record?

7. Identify the type of data sharing agreement and the process for establishing it. The process will vary by institution or organization, so researchers should know what policies and procedures apply. The data sharing agreement is not an IRB function, but it can affect the IRB process.

8. Every protocol submitted to the IRB for review stands on its own merit and every IRB has their own way of applying the regulations. Just because one IRB found a project to be exempt, does not mean that another IRB will find the same. Similarly, even within the same IRB, just because one reviewer determined that a project did not need IRB review, that does not mean that another reviewer would come to the same conclusion. Consistency within and between IRBs is a challenge, especially with complicated research: the collaborative process is therefore an important feature. The more information the IRB has to work with, the more consistent the results of the review.

The part of a protocol that relates to the use of administrative data is often easy to write and fast to review if it contains all the relevant information. Researchers facing pushback from an IRB should be able to have a dialogue with the reviewers where the IRB can explain its

CHAPTER 4

decisions and why it is making certain recommendations or requesting specific protections.

The goal of this chapter has been to provide a practical guide to researchers and other stakeholders on managing IRB procedures. It is important to emphasize that while this chapter addresses a wide variety of potential problems and concerns, in practice almost every university where research takes place has a well-functioning IRB, which performs the critical, but typically routine, work of providing oversight of research. Nearly all research proposals are able to satisfy IRB concerns, though they may sometimes require some adjustment to satisfy the principals laid out above.

About the Author

Kathleen Murphy, PhD, MSW, MLIS, is a Certified IRB Professional, retired from Northwestern University IRB in 2019 after serving as a Board member, Vice Chair, and Manager of the Social and Behavioral IRB. She came to Northwestern as the first Social Science Data Librarian in 2006. Prior to Northwestern, Kathleen was a clinical social worker in private practice specializing in work with children. She has taught clinical practice and quantitative and qualitative methods for many years. Kathleen has served on different IRBs over the years and the opinions and perspectives included here are based on her experience and are not presented as the perspective of any given IRB.

References in Chapter 4

Card, David E., Raj Chetty, Martin S. Feldstein, and Emmanuel Saez. 2011. "Expanding Access to Administrative Data for Research in the United States." American Economic Association Report January. https://www.aeaweb.org/content/file?id=1319.

Chicago Public Schools. 2020. "The Research Review Board." https://www.cps.edu/research/Pages/Research.aspx (accessed 2020-07-03).

Code of Federal Regulations. 2017*a*. "45 CFR 46 Subpart A—Basic HHS Policy for Protection of Human Research Subjects." https://www.ecfr.gov/cgi-bin/retrieveECFR?gp=&SID=83cd09e1c0f5c6937cd9d7513160fc3f&pitd=20180719&n=pt45.1.46&r=PART&ty=HTML#sp45.1.46.a (accessed 2020-09-22).

Code of Federal Regulations. 2017*b*. "45 CFR §46.111 Criteria for IRB approval of research." https://www.ecfr.gov/cgi-bin/retrieveECFR?gp=&SID=83cd09e1c0f5c6937cd9d7513160fc3f&pitd=20180719&n=pt45.1.46&r=PART&ty=HTML.#se45.1.46_1111 (accessed 2020-09-15).

Code of Federal Regulations. 2017*c*. "45 CFR §46.116 General requirements for informed consent." https://www.ecfr.gov/cgi-bin/retrieveECFR?gp=&SID=83cd09e1c0f5c6937cd9d7513160fc3f&pitd=20180719&n=pt45.1.46&r=PART&ty=HTML#se45.1.46_1116 (accessed 2020-09-15).

Code of Federal Regulations. 2017*d*. "45 CFR §46.117 Documentation of informed consent." https://www.ecfr.gov/cgi-bin/retrieveECFR?gp=&SID=83cd09e1c0f5c6937cd9d7513160fc3f&pitd=20180719&n=pt45.1.46&r=PART&ty=HTML.#se45.1.46_1117 (accessed 2020-09-15).

Collmann, Jeff, and Sorin Adam Matei. 2016. *Ethical Reasoning in Big Data: An Exploratory Analysis. Computational Social Sciences*, Switzerland:Springer.

Connelly, Roxanne, Christopher J Playford, Vernon Gayle, and Chris Dibben. 2016. "The role of administrative data in the big data revolution in social science research." *Social Science Research*, 59: 1–12. https://doi.org/10.1016/j.ssresearch.2016.04.015.

European Parliament and Council of the European Union. 2016. "Regulation (EU) 2016/679." https://eur-lex.europa.eu/legal-content/EN/TXT/HTML/?uri=CELEX:32016R0679&from=EN (accessed 2020-09-15).

Feeney, Laura, Jason Bauman, Julia Chabrier, Geeti Mehra, and Michelle Woodford. 2015. "Administrative Data for Randomized Evaluations." J-PAL North America. https://www.povertyactionlab.org/resource/using-administrative-data-randomized-evaluations (accessed 2020-01-30).

Figlio, David N., K. Karbownik, and K.G. Salvanes. 2016. "Education Research and Administrative Data." In *Handbook of the Economics of Education*. Vol. 5 of *Chapter 2*, 75–138. Elsevier. https://doi.org/10.1016/B978-0-444-63459-7.00002-6.

Lee, Allen S., and Richard L. Baskerville. 2003. "Generalizing Generalizability in Information Systems Research." *Information Systems Research*, 14(3): 221–243. https://doi.org/10.1287/isre.14.3.221.16560.

National Commission for the Protection of Human Subjects of Biomedical and Behavioral Research. 1979. "The Belmont report: ethical principles and guidelines for the protection of human subjects of research." Department of Health, Education, and Welfare. https://www.hhs.gov/ohrp/regulations-and-policy/belmont-report/read-the-belmont-report/index.html.

NHS Health Research Authority. 2020. "Research Ethics Committees in the UK." https://www.hra.nhs.uk/about-us/committees-and-services/res-and-recs/research-ethics-committees-overview/ (accessed 2020-07-03).

Office for Human Research Protections. 2016*a*. "Equivalent Protections." https://www.hhs.gov/ohrp/international/equivalent-protections/index.html (accessed 2020-09-15).

Office for Human Research Protections. 2016*b*. "Federal Policy for the Protection of Human Subjects ('Common Rule')." https://www.hhs.gov/ohrp/regulations-and-policy/regulations/common-rule/index.html (accessed 2020-09-15).

Office for Human Research Protections. 2017. "Federalwide Assurance (FWA) for the Protection of Human Subjects." https://www.hhs.gov/ohrp/register-irbs-and-obtain-fwas/fwas/fwa-protection-of-human-subjecct/index.html (accessed 2020-08-21).

Office for Human Research Protections. 2018. "Compilation of European GDPR Guidances." https://www.hhs.gov/ohrp/international/GDPR/index.html (accessed 2020-09-15).

Office for Human Research Protections. 2020. "Human Subject Regulations Decision Charts." https://www.hhs.gov/ohrp/regulations-and-policy/decision-charts/index.html (accessed 2020-09-15).

Wandile, Pranali M. 2018. "Central IRB vs. Institutional IRB—Advantages and Disadvantages for Multicenter Trials." *Clinical Researcher*, 32(4): 28–38. https://doi.org/10.14524/CR-17-0009.

CHAPTER 4

Appendix

A data-only protocol template can be found in the Online Appendix at admindatahandbook.mit.edu/book/v1.0/irb.html #irb-appendix.

CHAPTER 5

Balancing Privacy and Data Usability: An Overview of Disclosure Avoidance Methods

Ian M. Schmutte (University of Georgia)
Lars Vilhuber (Cornell University)

5.1 Introduction

The purpose of this Handbook is to provide guidance on how to enable broader but ethical and legal access to data. Within the Five Safes framework (Desai, Ritchie and Welpton, 2016), data providers need to create *safe data* that can be provided to trusted *safe people* for use within *safe settings* (chapter 2), subject to legal and contractual safeguards (chapter 3). Related, but distinct, is the question of how to create *safe outputs* from researchers' findings before those findings finally make their way into the public through, for example, policy briefs or the academic literature. The processes used to create safe data and safe outputs (manipulations that render data less sensitive and therefore more appropriate for public release) are generally referred to as

---

Copyright © Ian M. Schmutte and Lars Vilhuber.
Cite as: Schmutte, Ian M., and Lars Vilhuber. "Balancing Privacy and Data Usability: An Overview of Disclosure Avoidance Methods." In: Cole, Shawn, Iqbal Dhaliwal, Anja Sautmann, and Lars Vilhuber (eds.), *Handbook on Using Administrative Data for Research and Evidence-based Policy*. Cambridge, MA: Abdul Latif Jameel Poverty Action Lab. 2020.

statistical disclosure limitation (SDL).[1] This chapter will describe techniques traditionally used within the field of SDL, pointing at methods as well as metrics to assess the resultant statistical quality and sensitivity of the data. Newer approaches, generally referred to as *formal privacy methods*, are described in chapter 6.

At their core, SDL methods prevent outsiders from learning too much about any one record in the data (Dalenius, 1977) by deliberately and judiciously adding distortions. Ideally, these distortions maintain the validity of the data for statistical analysis but strongly reduce the ability to isolate records and infer precise information about individual people, firms, or cases. In general, it is necessary to sacrifice validity in order to prevent disclosure (Goroff, 2015; Abowd and Schmutte, 2015). It is therefore important for data custodians to bear this trade-off in mind when deciding whether and how to use SDL.

One key challenge for implementing privacy systems lies in choosing the amount or type of privacy to provide. Answering this question requires some way to understand the individual and social value of privacy. Abowd and Schmutte (2019) discuss the question of optimal privacy protection (see also Hsu et al., 2014 in the specific context of differential privacy). For an illustration, see Spencer and Seeskin (2015), who use a calibration exercise to study the costs (measured in misallocated congressional seats) of reduced accuracy in population census data.

Part of the social value of privacy arises from its relationship to scientific integrity. While the law of information recovery suggests that improved privacy must come at the cost of increased error in published statistics, these effects might be mitigated through two distinct channels. First, people may be more truthful in surveys if they believe their data are not at risk (Couper et al., 2008). Second, work in computer science and statistics (Dwork et al., 2015; Dwork and Ullman, 2018; Cummings et al., 2016) suggests a somewhat surprising benefit of differential privacy: protection against overfitting.

---

[1]Other terms sometimes used are "anonymization" or "de-identification," but as this chapter will show, de-identification is a particular method of SDL, and anonymization is a goal, never fully achieved, rather than a method.

There are three factors that a data custodian should bear in mind when deciding whether and how to implement an SDL system in support of making data accessible. First, it is necessary to clarify the specific privacy requirements based on the nature of the underlying data, institutional and policy criteria, and ethical considerations. In addition, the custodian, perhaps in consultation with users, should clarify what sorts of analyses the data will support. Finally, SDL is often part of a broader system to protect sensitive data that can also involve access restrictions and other technical barriers. The broader system may allow for less stringent SDL techniques when providing data to researchers in secure environments than would be possible if data were to be released as unrestricted public use data.[2] This implies that the chapter will not provide a recommendation for a "best" method, since no such globally optimal method exists in isolation.

Rather, this chapter provides an overview of the concepts and more widely used methods of SDL. Relative to other primers that cover similar material, this text focuses more closely on the advantages and disadvantages of various methods from the perspective of data users. This chapter can serve as a reference that data providers and data users can employ to discuss which forms of SDL are appropriate and will satisfy the needs of both parties. In particular, there is a focus on how common SDL tools affect different types of statistical analysis as well as the kind of confidentiality protections these tools support, drawing heavily on Abowd and Schmutte (2015). SDL is a broad topic with a vast literature, starting with Fellegi (1972). Naturally, this brief summary is not a replacement for the textbook treatment of SDL in Duncan, Elliot and Salazar-González (2011). Finally, SDL methods must be implemented and deployed, and the chapter provides pointers to existing off-the-rack tools in a variety of platforms (Python, R, and Stata). Readers might also consult other summaries and guides, such as Dupriez and Boyko (2010), World Bank (n.d.), Kopper, Sautmann and Turitto (2020), and Liu (2020).

---

[2]Chapter 7 on the RDC-IAB provides a good illustration of how various SDL methods are combined with different access methods to provide multiple combinations of analytic validity and risk of disclosure.

CHAPTER 5

5.2 Purpose of Statistical Disclosure Limitation Methods: Definitions and Context

A clear and precise sense of what constitutes an unauthorized disclosure is a prerequisite to implementing SDL. Are all data items equally sensitive? How much more should one be able to learn about certain classes of people, firms, villages, etc.? Note that even when trusted researchers (*safe people*) can be sworn to secrecy, the ultimate goal is to publish using information gleaned from the data, and the final audience can never be considered trusted.[3]

The key concepts are privacy and confidentiality. Privacy can be viewed, in this context, as the right to restrict others' access to personal information, whether through query or through observation (Hirshleifer, 1980). Confidentiality pertains to data that have already been collected and describes the principle that the data should not be used in ways that could harm the persons that provided their information.

> For example, Ann, who is asked to participate in a study about health behaviors, has a *privacy* right to refuse to answer a question about smoking. If she does answer the question, it would breach *confidentiality* if her response was then used by an insurance company to adjust her premiums (Duncan, Jabine and de Wolf, 1993).

Harris-Kojetin et al. (2005) define disclosure as the "inappropriate attribution of information to a data subject, whether an individual or an organization" (Harris-Kojetin et al., 2005, p. 4). They proceed to describe three different types of disclosure. An *identity disclosure* is one where it is possible to learn that a particular record or data item belongs to a particular participant (individual or organization). An *attribute disclosure* happens if publication of the data reveals an attribute

---

[3]In the United States, 62% of individuals are aware (and possibly resigned) that government and private companies collect data on them, and seem to believe that there is little benefit to them of such collection: 81% think so when companies do the data collection, and 66% when the government does so (Auxier et al., 2019).

of a participant. Note that an *identity disclosure* necessarily entails *attribute disclosure*, but the reverse is not the case.

> In the hypothetical health study, if Ann responds that she is a smoker, an *identity disclosure* would mean someone can determine which record is hers and therefore can also learn that she is a smoker—an *attribute disclosure*. However, an attribute disclosure could also occur if someone knows that Ann was in the study, they know that Ann lives in a particular zip code, and the data reveal that all participants from that zip code are also smokers. Her full record was not revealed, but confidentiality was breached all the same.

With these concepts in mind, it is necessary to ask whether it is sufficient to prevent blatant all-or-nothing identity or attribute disclosures: usually not, as it may be possible to learn a sensitive attribute with high, but not total, certainty. This is called an *inferential disclosure* (Dalenius, 1977; Duncan and Lambert, 1986).

> Suppose Ann's health insurer knows that Ann is in the data and that she lives in a particular zip code. If the data have 100 records from that zip code and 99 are smokers, then the insurer has learned Ann's smoking status with imperfect but high precision.

In addition to deciding what kinds of disclosure can be tolerated and to what extent, in many cases it may also be meaningful to decide which characteristics are and are not sensitive. Smoking behavior may nowadays be regarded as sensitive, but depending on the context, gender might not be. In the case of business data, total sales volume or total payroll are highly sensitive trade secrets.

Generally, the county in which the business is located or the industry in which the business operates might not be sensitive, but consider a survey of self-employed business people: the location of the business might be the home address, which might be considered highly sensitive. These decisions on what is sensitive affect the implementation of a privacy protection system.[4]

However, additional care must be taken because variables that are not inherently sensitive can still be used to isolate and identify records. Such variables are sometimes referred to as *quasi-identifiers* and they can be exploited for *re-identification* attacks. In business data, if the data show that there is only one firm operating in a particular county and sector, then their presence inherently leads to identity disclosure. Many of the traditional approaches to SDL operate in large part by attempting to prevent re-identification.[5] Garfinkel (2015) discusses techniques for de-identifying data and the many ways in which modern computing tools and a data-rich environment may render effective de-identification impossible, reinforcing the growing need for formal privacy models like differential privacy.

SDL methods may be required for legal and ethical reasons. Institutional review boards (IRBs) require that individual's well-being be protected (see chapter 4 on IRBs). Legal mandates may intersectwith ethical concerns, or prescribe certain (minimal) criteria. Thus, the US Health Insurance Portability and Accountability Act of 1996 (HIPAA) (U.S. Department of Health & Human Services, n.d.) has precise definitions of variables that need to be removed in order to comply with the law's mandate of de-identification (Department of Health and Human Services, 2012). The European Union General Data Protection Regulation (GDPR) came into effect in 2018 and has defined both the way researchers can access data and the requirements for disclosure limitation (Cohen and Nissim, 2020; Greene et al., 2019; Molnár-Gábor, 2018). Similar laws are emerging around the world and will define both minimal requirements and limits of SDL and other access controls. The California Consumer Privacy Act (CCPA) (Marini, Kateifides and Bates, 2018) and the Brazilian Lei Geral de Proteção de Dados (LGPD) (Black, Ramos and Biscardi, 2020) came into effect in 2020,

---

[4]There is a large and robust literature in economics on the value of privacy. For an overview of ideas in this literature, we recommend Varian (2002) and Acquisti, Taylor and Wagman (2016).

[5]Thus the occasional reference to methods as *de-identification* or *anonymization*, though these terms can sometimes be misleading in regard to what they can actually achieve.

and India is currently considering such a law (Panakal, 2019).

Finally, note that there is a parallel concept of non-statistical disclosure limitation that is a complementary part of secure data dissemination. This applies to the metadata—like codebooks, data descriptions, and other summary information—that can leak potentially sensitive information. For example, data documentation might reveal that only certain geographic areas were included in a particular collection, information that could be used as an element in a re-identification attack. While typically not considered quantitative disclosure avoidance, some of the same concepts described here can apply to such metadata as well. For instance, removing mention of the collection area from the documentation is akin to suppression, while only revealing broad regions of data collection is akin to coarsening.

5.3 Methods

There are many different SDL methods, and the decision of which to use depends on what needs to be protected, how their use will affect approved analyses, and their technical properties. At a high level, think of an SDL system as a mechanism that takes the raw confidential data, D, as inputs and produces a modified data set, $\tilde{D}$. The researcher then conducts their analysis with the modified $\tilde{D}$. Ideally, the researcher can do their analysis as planned, but the risk of disclosure in $\tilde{D}$ is reduced.

Researchers generally need to consider all of the design features that went into producing the data used for an analysis. Most already do so in the context of surveys where design measures are incorporated into the analysis—often directly in software packages. Some of these adjustments may already take into account various SDL techniques. Traditional survey design adjustments can consider sampling. Some forms of coarsening may already be amenable to adjustment using various clustering techniques (Moulton, 1986; Cameron and Miller, 2015).

More generally, the inclusion of edits to the data done in service of disclosure limitation is less well supported by, and less well integrated in, standard research methods. Abowd and Schmutte (2015) argue that the analyses of SDL-laden data are inherently compromised because the details of the SDL protections cannot be disclosed. If the details cannot be disclosed, the consequences for inference are unknowable and, as they show, may be substantial. Regression models, regression discontinuity designs, and instrumental variables models are generally affected when SDL is present. The exact nature of any bias or inconsistency will depend on whether SDL was applied to explanatory variables, dependent variables, instruments, or all of the above. Furthermore, it is not always the case that SDL induces an attenuating bias.

With these goals in mind, following Abowd and Schmutte (2015), this chapter distinguishes between *ignorable* and *non-ignorable* SDL systems. Briefly, SDL is *ignorable* for a particular analysis if the analysis can be performed on the modified data, $\tilde{D}$, as though it were the true data. In a non-ignorable analysis, the result differs in some material way when $\tilde{D}$ is substituted for D. When the SDL method is *known*, then it may be possible for the researcher to perform an *SDL-aware* analysis that corrects for non-ignorability. However, SDL methods are generally not ignorable except in certain specific applications.

The chapter briefly outlines several of the methods most commonly used within national statistical offices. For interested readers, Harris-Kojetin et al. (2005)[6] describe how SDL systems are implemented in the US statistical system, while Dupriez and Boyko (2010) offers a more multinational perspective.

5.3.1 De-Identification

In general, it is good practice to remove any variables from the data that are not needed for data processing or analysis and that could be considered direct identifiers. This is often referred to as de-identification. What constitutes "direct identifiers" may differ on the context, but generally comprises any variable that might directly link to confidential information: names, account or identifier numbers, and

---

[6]As of the writing of this chapter in August 2020, WP22 is being revised and updated, but has not yet been published.

sometimes exact birth dates or exact geo-identifiers.[7] HIPPA defines sixteen identifiers that must be removed in order to comply with the law. It may be necessary to preserve identifiers through parts of the data processing or analysis if they are key variables needed for record linking. In field experiments, the identities of treatment and control units may need to be merged with an administrative data set. It is also sometimes necessary to use direct identifiers to link records between surveys and administrative data, or precise geographic coordinates may be needed to compute distances as part of the analysis. If possible, the data provider should facilitate record linking while the data are secure and before they are shared with the research team.

5.3.2 Suppression

Suppression is perhaps the most common form of SDL and one of the oldest (Fellegi, 1972). In their most basic form, suppression rules work as follows:

1. Model the sensitivity of a particular data item, table cell, or observation (disclosure risk).
2. Do not allow the release of data items that have excessive disclosure risk (primary suppression).
3. Do not allow the release of other data from which the sensitive item can be calculated (complementary suppression).

Suppression rules can be applied to microdata: the sensitive observations are removed from the microdata, or to tabular data, where the relevant cells are suppressed.

In the case of business microdata, a firm that is unique in its county and industry might be flagged as having high disclosure risk and eliminated from the data. Another less damaging possibility is that just the sensitive attributes are suppressed, so a researcher would still know that there was a firm operating in that industry and location but not the other attributes. For tabular data, the principle is the same. Continuing with the business application, suppose there is one large firm

---
[7]See guidance in World Bank (n.d.) and Kopper, Sautmann and Turitto (2020).

CHAPTER 5

and several smaller competitors in a given industry and location. If the cell is published, it might be possible for its local competitors to learn the receipts of the dominant firm to a high degree of precision.

Cell suppression rules based on this sort of reasoning are called *p-percent rules*, where *p* describes the precision with which the largest firm's information can be learned. A conservative estimate of this occurs when the largest firm's value is *(1-p)%* of the cell's value.

A variant of this rule takes into account prior precision *q* (the "pq percent rule"). Another rule is known as the *n,k* rule: a cell is suppressed if *n* or fewer entities contribute *k* percent or more of the cell's value. These rules are frequently applied to statistics produced by national statistical agencies (Harris-Kojetin et al., 2005). Simpler rules based entirely on cell counts are also encountered, for instance, in the Health and Retirement Study (Health and Retirement Study, n.d.). Tables produced using HRS confidential geo-coded data are only allowed to display values when the cell contains three or more records (five for marginal cells).

If a cell in a contingency table is suppressed based on any one of these rules, it's original value could be backed out by using the information in the table margins and the understanding that table cells need to sum up to their margins. Some data providers therefore require that additional cells are suppressed to ensure this sort of reverse engineering is not possible. Figuring out how to choose these *complementary suppressions* in an efficient manner is a non-trivial challenge.

In general, cell suppression is not an ignorable form of SDL. It remains popular because it is easy to explain and does not affect the un-suppressed cells.

Data suppression is clearly non-ignorable, and it is quite difficult to correct for suppression in an SDL-aware analysis.[8] The features of the data that lead to suppression are often related to the underlying phenomenon of interest. Chetty and Friedman (2019) provide a clear

---

[8] One approach is to replace suppressed cells with imputed values, and then treat the data as multiply-imputed.

illustration. They publish neighborhood-level summaries of intergenerational mobility based on tax records linked to Census data. The underlying microdata are highly sensitive, and to protect privacy the researchers used a variant of a differentially privacy model. Chetty and Friedman show that if they had instead used a cell suppression rule, the published data would be misleading with respect to the relationship between neighborhood poverty and teen pregnancy, because both variables are associated with neighborhood population. Hence, the missingness induced by cell suppression is not ignorable.

Suppression can also be applied to model-based statistics. For instance, after having run a regression, coefficients that correspond to cells with fewer than n cases may be suppressed. This most often occurs when using dichotomous variables (dummy variables), which represent conditional means for particular subgroups.

> In a regression, a researcher includes a set of dummies for interacting occupation and location. When cross-tabulating occupation and location, many cells have less than five observations contributing to the coefficient. The data provider requires that these be suppressed.

5.3.3 Coarsening

Coarsening takes detailed attributes that can serve as quasi-identifiers and collapses them into a smaller number of categories. Computer scientists call this *generalizing*, and it is also sometimes referred to as *masking*. Coarsening can be applied to quasi-identifiers to prevent re-identification or to attributes to prevent accurate attribute inference. When applied to quasi-identifiers, the concern is that an outsider could use detailed quasi-identifiers to single-out a particular record and learn to whom it belonged. By coarsening quasi-identifiers, the set of matching records is increased, raising uncertainty about any re-identified individual's true identity. In principle, all variables can serve as quasi-identifiers, and the concept of *k-anonymity* introduced by Sweeney (2002) is a useful framework for thinking about how to implement coarsening and other microdata SDL. *K-anonymity* is discussed in section 5.4.1.

Coarsening is common in microdata releases. Generally, it may make sense to consider coarsening variables with heavy tails (earnings, payroll), residuals (truncate range, suppress labels of range). In public-use microdata from the American Community Survey, geographic areas are coarsened until all such areas represent at least 100,000 individuals (U.S. Census Bureau, 2011). In many data sources, characteristics like age and income, are reported in bins even when the raw data are more detailed. Topcoding is a common type of coarsening in which variables, such as incomes above a certain threshold, are replaced with some topcoded value (e.g., US$200,000 in the Current Population Survey). When releasing model-based estimates, rounding (another form of coarsening) can satisfy statistical best practice (not releasing numbers beyond their statistical precision) as well as disclosure avoidance principles by preventing inferences that could be too precise about specific records in the data.

Whether coarsening is ignorable or not depends on the analysis to be performed. Consider the case in which incomes are topcoded above the 95th percentile. This form of SDL is ignorable with respect to estimating the 90th percentile of the income distribution (and all other quantiles below the 95th). However, coarsening age is not ignorable if the goal is to conduct an analysis of behavior of individuals around some age or date-of-birth cutoff. Coarsening rules should therefore bear in mind the intended analysis for the data and may be usefully paired with restricted-access protocols that allow trusted researchers access to the more detailed data. See Burkhauser et al. (2011) for an example of the impact of topcoding on estimates of earnings inequality.

5.3.4 Swapping

The premise behind the technique of *swapping* is similar to suppression. Again, each record is assigned a level of disclosure risk. Then any high-risk record is matched to a less risky record on a set of key variables, and all of the other non-key attributes are swapped. The result is a data set that preserves the distribution among all the key variables used for matching. If the original purpose of the data was to publish cross-tabulations of the matching variables, swapping can produce microdata that are consistent with those tabulations. This approach is more commonly used in censuses and surveys of people or households and rarely used with establishment data.

Swapping is ignorable for analyses that only depend on the matching variables, since the relationships among them will be preserved. However, swapping distorts relationships among the other variables and between the matching variables and the other variables. In the example above, the swapping would be non-ignorable in the context of a study of how smoking behavior varies across zip codes. In general, statistical agencies are not willing to publish detailed information about how swapping is implemented since that information could be used to reverse-engineer some of the swaps, undoing the protection. Hence, SDL-aware analysis may not be possible and inference validity negatively affected.

> For example, consider the hypothetical health study again, and now suppose the known factors are Ann's zip code, gender, race, ethnicity, age, smoking behavior, and the size of her household. Ann's record might be classified as high risk if, for example, she has a very large household relative to the rest of the other respondents who are also from her zip code. If the data are used to publish summaries of smoking behavior by age, race, and gender, then Ann's record would be matched to another record with the same age, race, gender, and smoking behavior, and the values of the household size and zip code attributes would be swapped.

5.3.5 Sampling

Sampling is the original SDL technique. Rather than the full confidential microdata, publishing a sample inherently limits the certainty with which attackers can re-identify records. While sampling can provide a formal privacy guarantee, in modern, detailed surveys, sampling will not in general prevent re-identification. In combination with other tools, like coarsening, sampling may be particularly appealing because, while it is non-ignorable, researchers can adjust their analysis for the sampling using familiar methods. Sampling is often used in conjunction with other methods, including with formally private methods, to amplify the protection provided.

5.3.6 Noise Infusion

Noise infusion can refer to an array of related methods, all of which involve distorting data with randomly distributed noise. There is a key distinction between methods where the microdata are infused with noise (input noise infusion), versus methods where noise is added to functions or aggregates of the data before publication (output noise infusion).

Noise infusion was developed as a substitute for cell suppression as an approach to protecting tabular summaries of business data. Originally proposed by Evans, Zayatz and Slanta (1998), the basic approach assigns each microdata unit (a business establishment) a multiplicative noise factor drawn from a symmetric distribution (e.g., centered on one) and multiplies sensitive (or all) characteristics by that factor. Tabular summaries can then be made from the distorted characteristics. As cell sizes increase, the distortions applied to each unit average out. Thus, while small cells may be quite distorted and thus protected, large cells usually have little distortion. Most cells no longer need to be suppressed. These approaches are used in the US Census Bureau's Quarterly Workforce Indicators (Abowd et al., 2009, 2012) and County Business Patterns with a truncated distribution. When the noise distribution is unbounded, for instance Gaussian, noise infusion may be differentially private (see chapter 6 on differential privacy).

Noise infusion has the advantage that it mostly eliminates the need to suppress sensitive records or cells, allowing more information to be revealed from the confidential data while maintaining certain confidentiality protections. Noise infusion also generally preserves the means and covariances among variables. However, it will always inflate estimated variances and can lead to bias in estimates of statistical models and in particular regression coefficients. Hence, noise infusion is generally not ignorable. If the details of the noise distribution can be made available to researchers, then it is possible to correct analysis for noise infusion. However, information about the noise distribution can also help an attacker reverse engineer the protections.

5.3.7 Synthetic Data and Multiple Imputation

Synthetic data generation and multiple imputation are closely related. In fact, one particular variant of synthetic data as SDL (partially synthetic data) is also known as "suppress and impute" (Little, 1993). Sensitive values for some or all records are replaced by (multiple) imputations. More generally, fully synthetic data (Rubin, 1993) replaces all values with draws from a posterior predictive distribution, estimated given the confidential data. For an overview, see Raghunathan, Reiter and Rubin (2003), Little, Liu and Raghunathan (2004), and Drechsler (2011).

Synthetic data have been used in the Federal Reserve Board's Survey of Consumer Finances to protect sensitive income values (Kennickell, 1998), and in the US Census Bureau's American Community Survey microdata to protect data from group quarters such as prisons and university residences (Hawala and Rodriguez, 2009). The US Census Bureau's LODES data, included in the OnTheMap application, uses synthetic household data (Machanavajjhala et al., 2008). Synthetic data can be used in conjunction with validation servers: researchers use the synthetic data to create complex model-based estimation and then submit their analysis to a remote server with access to the confidential data for validation of the results. Such a mechanism has been used by the US Census Bureau in collaboration with Cornell University for confidential business microdata (Kinney et al., 2011) and for survey data combined with administrative data (Abowd, Stinson and Benedetto, 2006). The term is sometimes used as well for test data for remote submission systems, which typically makes no claims as to the validity; it is simply constructed to replicate the data schema of the confidential data to test statistical code.

5.3.8 Examples of SDL Methods

Table 5.1 shows how the various methods can be combined, drawing on examples both from this Handbook as well as from other frequently used data sources.

5.4 Metrics

The design of an SDL system depends on determinations about what constitutes an acceptable level of disclosure risk, balanced with the proposed uses of the data. There are many different ways to describe and measure disclosure risk. A commonality these systems share is the ability to determine the uniqueness of a record, or combination of attributes in the data, that then intuitively predicts the ease with which a record could be distinguished to re-identify the respondent (perhaps aided by a linked data set). Likewise, there are many different ways to assess whether the released data are suitable, or fit, for their intended use. These quality measures are often based on how closely the released data match the true data on certain statistical summaries, and it will be important for researchers and data custodians to agree on what are the most relevant summaries.

5.4.1 Disclosure Risk

Early definitions of disclosure risk were based on rules and guidelines derived from institutional knowledge, assessment of summary measures, and re-identification experiments (Harris-Kojetin et al., 2005). Statisticians have subsequently developed more formal models to measure risk of re-identification for specific types of publication and with particular threat models. For instance, Shlomo and Skinner (2010)

Table 5.1: Summary of SDL methods

	In this Handbook	Removal of Direct Identifiers	Removal of Quasi-Identifiers	Suppression	Coarsening	Swapping	Sampling	Noise Infusion	Synthetic Data
IAB On-Site Access	✔	✔	✘	✔	✔	✘	✔	✘	✘
IAB Scientific Use Files	✔	✔	✔	✔	✔	✘	✔	✘	✘
OLDA	✔	✔	◻	✔	✔	✘	✘	✘	✘
NB-IRDT	✔	✔	—	✔	✔	✘	✘	✘	✘
PCRI	✔	✔	—	✘	—	✘	✘	✘	✘
Aurora Public-Use File	✔	✔	◻	✔	✔	✘	✘	✘	✘
Stanford-SFUSD	✔	◻	✔	✔	✘	✘	✘	✘	✘
City of Cape Town	✔	◻	—	—	✔	—	✘	✘	—
DIME (World Bank)	✔	◻	✔	—	—	—	—	✘	—
Survey of Consumer Finances	✘	✔	—	✔	✔	✘	✔	✘	✔
American Community Survey	✘	✔	—	✘	✔	✔	✔	✘	◻
Quarterly Workforce Indicators	✘	✔	✘	✔	✔	✘	✘	✔	✘

Notes: ✔ = Yes, ◻ = Partially, ✘ = No, — = No Info

model re-identification risk in survey microdata when an attacker is matching on certain categorical variables.

Recently, computer scientists and statisticians have introduced more general concepts of disclosure risk and data privacy. Latanya Sweeney proposed the concept of k-anonymity (Sweeney, 2002) which defines disclosure risk in terms of the number of records that share the same combination of attributes. If a single record is uniquely identified by some combination of attributes, disclosure risk is high. Sweeney says that a data set can be called k-anonymous if for all feasible combinations of attributes, at least k records have that combination. Intuitively, increases in k reduce the risk that observations can be singled out by linking other data sets that contain the same attributes. The concept of k-anonymity can provide some guidance when thinking about how to implement the SDL systems described above. For example, if records are uniquely identified by age, race, and gender, then one might collapse age into brackets until there are at least $k > 1$ records for each such combination.

However, k-anonymity does not protect against attribute disclosure. If all k observations with the same combination of attributes also share the same sensitive attribute, for example, smoking behavior, then the published data do not fully prevent disclosure of smoking behavior. Recognizing this, Machanavajjhala et al. (2007) introduce the concept of ℓ-diversity. The idea is that whenever a group of records are identical on some set of variables, there must be a certain amount of heterogeneity in important sensitive traits. If a certain group of records matches on a set of quasi-identifiers and also all share the same smoking status, then to achieve ℓ-diversity, one might alter the reported smoking behavior of some fraction (ℓ) of the records—a form of noise infusion.

5.4.2 Data Quality

When the released data or output are tabular (histograms, cross-tabulations) or are a limited set of population or model parameters (means, coefficients), a set of distance-based metrics (so-called "ℓ_p distance" metrics) can be used to compare the quality of the perturbed data. Note that this is a specific metric, as it is limited to those statistics taken into account—the data quality may be very poor in non-measured attributes! For $p = 1$, the ℓ_1 distance is the sum of absolute differences between the confidential and perturbed data. For $p = 2$, the ℓ_2 distance is the sum of squared differences between the two data sets (normalized by n the number of observations, it is the Mean Squared Error, MSE).

In settings where it is important to measure data quality over an entire distribution, the Kullback-Leibler (KL) divergence measure can also be used. The KL-divergence is related to the concept of entropy from information theory and, loosely, measures the amount of surprise associated with seeing an observation drawn from one distribution when one expected them to come from another distribution. Other metrics are based on propensity scores (Woo et al., 2009; Snoke et al., 2018). More specific measures will often compare specific analysis output, a task that is quite difficult to conduct in general. Reiter, Oganian and Karr (2009) propose to summarize the difference between regression coefficients when analyses can be run on both confidential and protected data in the context of verification servers.

5.5 Tools

For data providers faced with the need to start providing safe data for use by external researchers, a growing number of software packages are available that implement the methods described in this chapter. The Inter-university Consortium for Political and Social Research (ICPSR) has a checklist that may be of use in early development of an SDL system (ICPSR, 2020). The listing of tools below is incomplete but will provide practitioners with a place to start. A fully developed SDL system will have unique requirements and may require custom programming. Nevertheless, many tools are useful across a wide range of applications.

Statistics Netherlands maintains the ARGUS software for SDL (Hundepool and Willenborg, 1998), including τ-ARGUS to protect tabular data (De Wolf, 2018), and μ-ARGUS for protecting microdata (Hundepool and Ramaswamy, 2018). The software appears to be widely used in statistical agencies in Europe. An open-source R package, sdcMicro, implements a full suite of tools needed to apply SDL, from computation of risk measures, including k-anonymity and ℓ-diversity, to implementation of SDL methods and the computation of data quality measures (Templ, Kowarik and Meindl, 2015; Templ, Meindl and Kowarik, 2020).

Simpler tools, focusing on removing direct identifiers, can be found at J-PAL for Stata (stata_PII_scan) and R (PII-scan), and at Innovations for Poverty Action (IPA) for Python or Windows (PII_detection) (J-PAL, 2020b,a; Innovations for Poverty Action, 2020).

A number of R packages facilitate generation of synthetic data. Raab, Nowok and Dibben (2016) and Nowok, Raab and Dibben (2016) provide synthpop, a flexible and up-to-date package with methods for generating synthetic microdata. The R package simPop (Templ et al., 2019) can also generate synthetic populations from aggregate data, which can be useful for testing SDL systems on non-sensitive data. In some cases, one might also consider using general-purpose software for multiple imputation for data synthesis.[9]

Many of the methods described in this chapter are technical and require statistical and programming expertise. If that expertise is not already available among staff, some institutions provide guidance to researchers who wish to apply SDL techniques.

5.6 Conclusion

There is now a greater demand for all kinds of data. More than ever before, scholars and analysts have the tools to use data to better understand the economy and society and to inform policy. Alongside these advances, data custodians find themselves under pressure to make databases available to outsiders. However, the pressure to make data

---

[9]See "Multiple imputation in Stata" or the mice package in R (Buuren and Groothuis-Oudshoorn, 2011).

available is not always accompanied by the resources, tools, or expertise needed to do so safely.

The same advances driving these new demands have a darker side. Computing power together with the availability of detailed outside data make it easier than ever for attackers to exploit improperly protected data. Therefore, when making data available for research, agency stewards must take great care to also protect the subjects in the data. This chapter provides an overview of techniques traditionally used to modify the data to achieve that goal. There is a legitimate concern that some of the methods discussed here cannot protect against all possible attacks made possible with modern computing power. Those concerns animate the discussion of formal methods that yield provable privacy guarantees elsewhere in this Handbook.

About the Authors

Ian M. Schmutte is Associate Professor in the Department of Economics at the University of Georgia. Ian is currently working with the US Census Bureau on new methods for protecting confidential data. His research has appeared in the *American Economic Review*, *Journal of Labor Economics*, *Journal of Human Resources*, *Journal of Business & Economic Statistics*, and the *Brookings Papers on Economic Activity*.

Lars Vilhuber is the Executive Director of the Labor Dynamics Institute at Cornell University, and a faculty member in Cornell University's Economics Department. He is also the American Economic Association's Data Editor. Lars is a Co-Chair of IDEA. His research interests relate to the dynamics of the labor market. He also has extensive experience in the application of privacy-preserving publication and access to restricted data. He is chair of the scientific committee of the French restricted-access system CASD, member of the governing board of the Canadian Research Data Centre Network (CRDCN), and incoming chair of the American Statistical Association's Committee on Privacy and Confidentiality. Lars has an undergraduate degree in Economics from Universität Bonn and a Ph.D. in Economics from Université de Montréal.

Disclaimer

The views expressed in this paper are those of the authors and not those of the US Census Bureau or other sponsors.

Acknowledgements

This chapter draws on Abowd et al. (2019) and the INFO7470 class at Cornell University (Abowd and Vilhuber, 2016). We gratefully acknowledge the support of Alfred P. Sloan Foundation Grant G-2015-13903 and National Science Foundation (NSF) Grant SES-1131848 for the earlier work.

References in Chapter 5

Abowd, John M., and Ian M. Schmutte. 2015. "Economic analysis and statistical disclosure limitation." *Brookings Papers on Economic Activity*, 221–267. https://doi.org/10.1353/eca.2016.0004.

Abowd, John M., and Ian M. Schmutte. 2019. "An Economic Analysis of Privacy Protection and Statistical Accuracy as Social Choices." *American Economic Review*, 109(1): 171–202. https://doi.org/10.1257/aer.20170627.

Abowd, John M., and Lars Vilhuber. 2016. "Session 12: Statistical Tools: Methods of Confidentiality Protection." Labor Dynamics Institute, Cornell University Presentation 45060. https://hdl.handle.net/1813/45060.

Abowd, John M., Bryce E. Stephens, Lars Vilhuber, Fredrik Andersson, Kevin L. McKinney, Marc Roemer, and Simon Woodcock. 2009. "The LEHD Infrastructure Files and the Creation of the Quarterly Workforce Indicators." In *Producer Dynamics: New Evidence from Micro Data.* , ed. Timothy Dunne, J. Bradford Jensen and Mark J. Roberts. University of Chicago Press. https://www.nber.org/chapters/c0485.

Abowd, John M., Ian M. Schmutte, William Sexton, and Lars Vilhuber. 2019. "Introductory Readings in Formal Privacy for Economists." Labor Dynamics Institute, Cornell University Document 2662639, https://doi.org/10.5281/zenodo.2662639.

Abowd, John M., Martha Stinson, and Gary Benedetto. 2006. "Final Report to the Social Security Administration on the SIPP/SSA/IRS Public Use File Project." U.S. Census Bureau 1813/43929. http://hdl.handle.net/1813/43929.

Abowd, John M., R. Kaj Gittings, Kevin L. McKinney, Bryce Stephens, Lars Vilhuber, and Simon D. Woodcock. 2012. "Dynamically Consistent Noise Infusion and Partially Synthetic Data as Confidentiality Protection Measures for Related Time Series." U.S. Census Bureau, Center for Economic Studies 12-13, https://doi.org/10.2139/ssrn.2159800.

Acquisti, Alessandro, Curtis Taylor, and Liad Wagman. 2016. "The Economics of Privacy." *Journal of Economic Literature*, 54(2): 442–492. https://doi.org/10.1257/jel.54.2.442.

Auxier, Brooke, Lee Rainie, Monica Anderson, Andrew Perrin, Madhu Kumar, and Erica Turner. 2019. "Americans and Privacy: Concerned, Confused and Feeling Lack of Control Over Their Personal Information." Pew Research Center. https://www.pewresearch.org/internet/2019/11/15/americans-and-privacy-concerned-confused-and-feeling-lack-of-control-over-their-personal-information/ (accessed 2020-07-17).

Black, Kate, Gretchen A. Ramos, and Giovanni Biscardi. 2020. "6 Months Until Brazil's LGPD Takes Effect – Are You Ready?" *The National Law Review*. https://www.natlawreview.com/article/6-months-until-brazil-s-lgpd-takes-effect-are-you-ready (accessed 2020-08-08).

Burkhauser, Richard V., Shuaizhang Feng, Stephen P. Jenkins, and Jeff Larrimore. 2011. "Estimating trends in US income inequality using the Current Population Survey: the importance of controlling for censoring." *The Journal of Economic Inequality*, 9(3): 393–415. https://doi.org/10.1007/s10888-010-9131-6.

Buuren, Stef van, and Karin Groothuis-Oudshoorn. 2011. "mice: Multivariate Imputation by Chained Equations in R." *Journal of Statistical Software*, 45(3): 1–67. https://doi.org/10.18637/jss.v045.i03.

Cameron, A. Colin, and Douglas L. Miller. 2015. "A Practitioner's Guide to Cluster-Robust Inference." *Journal of Human Resources*, 50(2): 317–372. https://doi.org/10.3368/jhr.50.2.317.

Chetty, Raj, and John N. Friedman. 2019. "A Practical Method to Reduce Privacy Loss When Disclosing Statistics Based on Small Samples." *Journal of Privacy and Confidentiality*, 9(2). https://doi.org/10.29012/jpc.716.

Cohen, Aloni, and Kobbi Nissim. 2020. "Towards formalizing the GDPR's notion of singling out." *Proceedings of the National Academy of Sciences of the United States of America*, 117(15): 8344–8352. https://doi.org/10.1073/pnas.1914598117.

Couper, Mick P., Eleanor Singer, Frederick G. Conrad, and Robert M. Groves. 2008. "Risk of disclosure, perceptions of risk, and concerns about privacy and confidentiality as factors in survey participation." *Journal of official statistics*, 24(2): 255. http://www.scb.se/contentassets/ca21efb41fee47d293bbee5bf7be7fb3/risk-of-disclosure-perceptions-of-risk-and-concerns-about-privacy-and-confidentiality-as-factors-in-survey-participation.pdf.

Cummings, Rachel, Katrina Ligett, Kobbi Nissim, Aaron Roth, and Zhiwei Steven Wu. 2016. "Adaptive Learning with Robust Generalization Guarantees." *CoRR*, abs/1602.07726. http://arxiv.org/abs/1602.07726.

Dalenius, Tore. 1977. "Towards a methodology for statistical disclosure control." *Statistik Tidskrift*, 15: 429–444.

Department of Health and Human Services. 2012. "Methods for De-identification of PHI." *HHS.gov*. https://www.hhs.gov/hipaa/for-professionals/privacy/special-topics/de-identification/index.html (accessed 2020-08-26).

Desai, Tanvi, Felix Ritchie, and Richard Welpton. 2016. "Five Safes: Designing data access for research." https://uwe-repository.worktribe.com/output/914745 (accessed 2020-01-30).

De Wolf, Peter-Paul. 2018. "τ-ARGUS." [software]. http://research.cbs.nl/casc/tau.htm (accessed 2020-08-17).

Drechsler, Jörg. 2011. *Synthetic Datasets for Statistical Disclosure Control: Theory and Implementation. Lecture Notes in Statistics*, New York:Springer-Verlag. https://doi.org/10.1007/978-1-4614-0326-5.

Duncan, George, and Diane Lambert. 1986. "Disclosure-limited data dissemination." *Journal of the American Statistical Association*, 81(393): 10–18. https://doi.org/10.1080/01621459.1986.10478229.

Duncan, George T., Mark Elliot, and Juan-José Salazar-González. 2011. *Statistical confidentiality: principles and practice. Statistics for Social and Behavioral Sciences*, New York:Springer-Verlag. https://doi.org/10.1111/j.1751-5823.2012.00196_11.x.

Duncan, George T., Thomas B. Jabine, and Virginia A. de Wolf, ed. 1993. *Private Lives and Public Policies: Confidentiality and Accessibility of Government Statistics*. National Academies Press. https://doi.org/10.17226/2122.

Dupriez, Olivier, and Ernie Boyko. 2010. "Dissemination of Microdata Files - Principles, Procedures and Practices." The World Bank Working Paper 005. http://ihsn.org/dissemination-of-microdata-files (accessed 2019-11-15).

Dwork, Cynthia, and Jonathan Ullman. 2018. "The Fienberg Problem: How to Allow Human Interactive Data Analysis in the Age of Differential Privacy." *Journal of Privacy and Confidentiality*, 8(1). https://doi.org/10.29012/jpc.687.

Dwork, Cynthia, Vitaly Feldman, Moritz Hardt, Toni Pitassi, Omer Reingold, and Aaron Roth. 2015. "Generalization in Adaptive Data Analysis and Holdout Reuse." In *Advances in Neural Information Processing Systems 28.*, ed. C. Cortes, N. D. Lawrence, D. D. Lee, M. Sugiyama and R. Garnett, 2341–2349. http://papers.nips.cc/paper/5993-generalization-in-adaptive-data-analysis-and-holdout-reuse.pdf.

Evans, Timothy, Laura Zayatz, and John Slanta. 1998. "Using Noise for Disclosure Limitation of Establishment Tabular Data." *Journal of Official Statistics*, 14(4): 537–551.

Fellegi, I. P. 1972. "On the Question of Statistical Confidentiality." *Journal of the American Statistical Association*, 67(337): 7–18. https://doi.org/10.2307/2284695.

Garfinkel, Simson. 2015. "De-Identification of Personal Information." National Institute of Standards and Technology Internal Report 8053, https://doi.org/10.6028/nist.ir.8053.

Goroff, Daniel L. 2015. "Balancing privacy versus accuracy in research protocols." *Science*, 347(6221): 479–480. https://doi.org/10.1126/science.aaa3483.

Greene, Travis, Galit Shmueli, Soumya Ray, and Jan Fell. 2019. "Adjusting to the GDPR: The Impact on Data Scientists and Behavioral Researchers." *Big Data*, 7(3): 140–162. https://doi.org/10.1089/big.2018.0176.

Harris-Kojetin, Brian A., Wendy L. Alvey, Lynda Carlson, Steven B. Cohen, Steve H. Cohen, Lawrence H. Cox, Robert E. Fay, Ronald Fecso, Dennis Fixler, Gerald Gates, Barry Graubard, William Iwig, Arthur Kennickell, Nancy J. Kirkendall, Susan Schechter, Rolf R. Schmitt, Marilyn Seastrom, Monroe G. Sirken, Nancy L. Spruill, Clyde Tucker, Alan R. Tupek, G. David Williamson, and Robert Groves. 2005. "Statistical Policy Working Paper 22: Report on Statistical Disclosure Limitation Methodology." U.S. Federal Committee on Statistical Methodology Research Report. https://nces.ed.gov/FCSM/pdf/spwp22.pdf (accessed 2020-12-15).

Hawala, Sam, and Rolando Rodriguez. 2009. "Disclosure avoidance for group quarters in the American Community Survey: Details of the synthetic data method." http://hdl.handle.net/1813/47676 (accessed 2020-08-17).

Health and Retirement Study. n.d.. "Disclosure Limitation Review." University of Michigan. https://hrs.isr.umich.edu/data-products/restricted-data/disclosure-limitation-review (accessed 2020-08-09).

Hirshleifer, Jack. 1980. "Privacy: its origin, function, and future." *The Journal of Legal Studies*, 9(4): 649–664. https://doi.org/10.1086/467659.

Hsu, Justin, Marco Gaboardi, Andreas Haeberlen, Sanjeev Khanna, Arjun Narayan, Benjamin C. Pierce, and Aaron Roth. 2014. "Differential Privacy: An Economic Method for Choosing Epsilon." *2014 IEEE 27th Computer Security Foundations Symposium*, 398–410. https://doi.org/10.1109/CSF.2014.35.

Hundepool, Anco, and Leon Willenborg. 1998. "ARGUS, Software Packages for Statistical Disclosure Control." 341–345. Heidelberg:Physica-Verlag HD. https://doi.org/10.1007/978-3-662-01131-7_45.

Hundepool, Anco, and Ramya Ramaswamy. 2018. "μ-ARGUS." [software]. http://research.cbs.nl/casc/mu.htm (accessed 2020-08-17).

ICPSR. 2020. "Disclosure Risk Worksheet." University of Michigan Document 156095. http://hdl.handle.net/2027.42/156095 (accessed 2020-08-21).

Innovations for Poverty Action. 2020. "PovertyAction/PII_detection." https://github.com/PovertyAction/PII_detection (accessed 2020-08-30).

J-PAL. 2020a. "J-PAL/PII-Scan." https://github.com/J-PAL/PII-Scan (accessed 2020-08-30).

J-PAL. 2020b. "J-PAL/stata_PII_scan." https://github.com/J-PAL/stata_PII_scan (accessed 2020-08-30).

Kennickell, Arthur B. 1998. "Multiple imputation in the Survey of Consumer Finances." https://www.federalreserve.gov/econresdata/scf/files/impute98.pdf (accessed 2020-10-05).

Kinney, Satkartar K., Jerome P. Reiter, Arnold P. Reznek, Javier Miranda, Ron S. Jarmin, and John M. Abowd. 2011. "Towards Unrestricted Public Use Business Microdata: The Synthetic Longitudinal Business Database." *International Statistical Review*, 79(3): 362–384. https://doi.org/10.1111/j.1751-5823.2011.00153.x.

Kopper, Sarah, Anja Sautmann, and James Turitto. 2020. "J-PAL Guide to de-identifying data." J-PAL Global. https://www.povertyactionlab.org/sites/default/files/research-resources/J-PAL-guide-to-deidentifying-data.pdf (accessed 2020-08-08).

Little, Roderick JA. 1993. "Statistical analysis of masked data." *Journal of Official Statistics*, 9(2): 407–426. http://www.scb.se/contentassets/ca21efb41fee47d293bbee5bf7be7fb3/statistical-analysis-of-masked-data.pdf.

Little, Roderick J. A., Fang Liu, and Trivellore E. Raghunathan. 2004. "Statistical disclosure techniques based on multiple imputation." In *Applied Bayesian modeling and causal inference from incomplete-data perspectives.*, ed. Andrew Gelman and Xiao Li Meng, 141–152. Wiley. https://doi.org/10.1002/0470090456.ch13.

Liu, Fang. 2020. "A Statistical Overview on Data Privacy." *arXiv:2007.00765 [cs, stat]*. http://arxiv.org/abs/2007.00765 (accessed 2020-08-31).

Machanavajjhala, Ashwin, Daniel Kifer, Johannes Gehrke, and Muthuramakrishnan Venkitasubramaniam. 2007. "L-diversity: privacy beyond k-anonymity." *ACM Transactions on Knowledge Discovery from Data*, 1(1). https://doi.org/10.1145/1217299.1217302.

Machanavajjhala, Ashwin, Daniel Kifer, John M. Abowd, Johannes Gehrke, and Lars Vilhuber. 2008. "Privacy: theory meets practice on the map." 277–286. https://doi.org/10.1109/ICDE.2008.4497436.

Marini, Alice, Alexis Kateifides, and Joel Bates. 2018. "Comparing privacy laws: GDPR v. CCPA." Future of Privacy Forum. https://fpf.org/wp-content/uploads/2018/11/GDPR_CCPA_Comparison-Guide.pdf (accessed 2020-06-20).

Molnár-Gábor, Fruzsina. 2018. "Germany: a fair balance between scientific freedom and data subjects' rights?" *Human Genetics*, 137(8): 619–626. https://doi.org/10.1

007/s00439-018-1912-1.

Moulton, Brent R. 1986. "Random group effects and the precision of regression estimates." *Journal of Econometrics*, 32(3): 385–397. https://doi.org/10.1016/0304-4076(86)90021-7.

Nowok, Beata, Gillian M. Raab, and Chris Dibben. 2016. "synthpop: Bespoke Creation of Synthetic Data in R." *Journal of Statistical Software*, 74(1): 1–26. https://doi.org/10.18637/jss.v074.i11.

Panakal, Dominic Dhil. 2019. "India's Proposed Privacy Law Allows Government Access and Some Data Localization." *The National Law Review*. https://www.natlawreview.com/article/india-s-proposed-privacy-law-allows-government-access-and-some-data-localization (accessed 2020-06-20).

Raab, Gillian M., Beata Nowok, and Chris Dibben. 2016. "Practical Data Synthesis for Large Samples." *Journal of Privacy and Confidentiality*, 7(3): 67–97. https://doi.org/10.29012/jpc.v7i3.407.

Raghunathan, Trivellore E., Jerry P. Reiter, and Donald B Rubin. 2003. "Multiple Imputation for Statistical Disclosure Limitation." *Journal of Official Statistics*, 19(1). http://www.scb.se/contentassets/ca21efb41fee47d293bbee5bf7be7fb3/multiple-imputation-for-statistical-disclosure-limitation.pdf.

Reiter, Jerome P., Anna Oganian, and Alan F. Karr. 2009. "Verification servers: Enabling analysts to assess the quality of inferences from public use data." *Computational statistics & data analysis*, 53(4): 1475–1482. https://doi.org/10.1016/j.csda.2008.10.006.

Rubin, Donald B. 1993. "Discussion: Statistical disclosure limitation." *Journal of Official Statistics*, 9(2): 461–468. http://www.scb.se/contentassets/ca21efb41fee47d293bbee5bf7be7fb3/discussion-statistical-disclosure-limitation2.pdf.

Shlomo, Natalie, and Chris Skinner. 2010. "Assessing the protection provided by misclassification-based disclosure limitation methods for survey microdata." *Annals of Applied Statistics*, 4(3): 1291–1310. https://doi.org/10.1214/09-AOAS317.

Snoke, Joshua, Gillian M. Raab, Beata Nowok, Chris Dibben, and Aleksandra Slavkovic. 2018. "General and specific utility measures for synthetic data." *Journal of the Royal Statistical Society: Series A (Statistics in Society)*, 181(3): 663–688. https://doi.org/10.1111/rssa.12358.

Spencer, Bruce David, and Zachary H. Seeskin. 2015. "Effects of Census Accuracy on Apportionment of Congress and Allocations of Federal Funds." *JSM Proceedings, Government Statistics Section*, 3061–3075. https://www.ipr.northwestern.edu/our-work/working-papers/2015/ipr-wp-15-05.html.

Sweeney, Latanya. 2002. "Achieving k-anonymity privacy protection using generalization and suppression." *International Journal on Uncertainty, Fuzziness and Knowledge-based Systems*, 10(5): 571–588. https://doi.org/10.1142/s021848850200165x.

Templ, Matthias, Alexander Kowarik, and Bernhard Meindl. 2015. "Statistical Disclosure Control for Micro-Data Using the R Package sdcMicro." *Journal of Statistical Software*, 67(4). https://doi.org/10.18637/jss.v067.i04.

Templ, Matthias, Alexander Kowarik, Bernhard Meindl, Andreas Alfons, Mathieu Ribatet, and Johannes Gussenbauer. 2019. "simPop: Simulation of Synthetic Populations for Survey Data Considering Auxiliary Information." https://CRAN.R-project.org/package=simPop (accessed 2020-08-17).

Templ, Matthias, Bernhard Meindl, and Alexander Kowarik. 2020. "sdcMicro: Statistical Disclosure Control Methods for Anonymization of Data and Risk Estimation." https://CRAN.R-project.org/package=sdcMicro (accessed 2020-08-17).

U.S. Census Bureau. 2011. "Final Public Use Microdata Area (PUMA) Criteria and Guidelines for the 2010 Census and the American Community Survey." https://www2.census.gov/geo/pdfs/reference/puma/2010_puma_guidelines.pdf.

U.S. Department of Health & Human Services. n.d.. "Health Information Privacy." https://www.hhs.gov/hipaa/index.html (accessed 2020-06-23).

Varian, Hal R. 2002. "Economic Aspects of Personal Privacy." In *Cyber Policy and Economics in an Internet Age.* , ed. William H. Lehr and Lorenzo M. Pupillo, 127–137. Boston, MA:Springer US. https://doi.org/10.1007/978-1-4757-3575-8_9.

Woo, Mi-Ja, Jerome P. Reiter, Anna Oganian, and Alan F. Karr. 2009. "Global Measures of Data Utility for Microdata Masked for Disclosure Limitation." *Privacy and Confidentiality*, 1(1): 111–124. https://doi.org/10.29012/jpc.v1i1.568.

World Bank. n.d.. "DIME Wiki: De-identification." https://dimewiki.worldbank.org/wiki/De-identification (accessed 2020-08-08).

CHAPTER 6

Designing Access with Differential Privacy

Alexandra Wood (Harvard University)

Micah Altman (Massachusetts Institute of Technology)

Kobbi Nissim (Georgetown University)

Salil Vadhan (Harvard University)

6.1 Introduction and Overview

This chapter explains how administrative data containing personal information can be collected, analyzed, and published in a way that ensures the individuals in the data will be afforded the strong protections of *differential privacy*.

It is intended as a practical resource for government agencies and research organizations interested in exploring the possibility of implementing tools for differentially private data sharing and analysis. Using intuitive examples rather than the mathematical formalism used in other guides, this chapter introduces the differential privacy definition and the risks it was developed to address. The text employs modern privacy frameworks to explain how to determine whether the use of

---

Copyright © Alexandra Wood, Micah Altman, Kobbi Nissim, and Salil Vadhan.
Cite as: Wood, Alexandra, Micah Altman, Kobbi Nissim, and Salil Vadhan. "Designing Access with Differential Privacy." In: Cole, Shawn, Iqbal Dhaliwal, Anja Sautmann, and Lars Vilhuber (eds.), *Handbook on Using Administrative Data for Research and Evidence-based Policy*. Cambridge, MA: Abdul Latif Jameel Poverty Action Lab. 2020.

differential privacy is an appropriate solution in a given setting. It also discusses the design considerations one should take into account when implementing differential privacy. This discussion incorporates a review of real-world implementations, including tools designed for tiered access systems combining differential privacy with other disclosure controls presented in this Handbook, such as consent mechanisms, data use agreements, and secure environments.

Differential privacy technology has passed a preliminary transition from being the subject of academic work to initial implementations by large organizations and high-tech companies that have the expertise to develop and implement customized differentially private methods. With a growing collection of software packages for generating differentially private releases from summary statistics to machine learning models, differential privacy is now transitioning to being usable more widely and by smaller organizations.

6.1.1 Organization of this Chapter

We place differential privacy in a general framework—introduced by Altman et al. (2015) and an alternative to the Five Safes framework (Desai, Ritchie and Welpton, 2016) used throughout this Handbook—that involves selecting combinations of statistical, technical, and administrative controls to mitigate risks of harm to individuals resulting from access to data. The framework discusses differential privacy as an approach to employ together with other tools, including consent mechanisms, data use agreements, and secure environments. Some of the content in this chapter (Sections 6.1–6.3) is excerpted from, adapted from, or otherwise based, in part, on Wood et al. (2018) and Altman et al. (2015).

The chapter is organized as follows: Section 6.2 explains the differential privacy guarantee in more detail using stories to illustrate what differential privacy does and does not protect. Section 6.3 places differential privacy in a general framework of complementary privacy controls and characterizes principles for selecting differential privacy in conjunction with other controls. These principles include calibrating privacy and security controls to the intended uses and privacy risks associated with the data, and anticipating, regulating, monitoring, and reviewing interactions with data across all stages of the lifecycle (including the post-access stages), as risks and methods will evolve over time. Section 6.4 presents succinct summaries of several deployment cases. These provide selected concrete examples of data dissemination that illustrate some key design choices and their implications.

More technical discussions of several topics are included in an extensive online appendix. A discussion of different technical approaches to disseminating data with differential privacy can be found in Appendix A, which also characterizes the key design choices and trade-offs across them. Appendix B elaborates on the implications of differential privacy for data collection, use, and dissemination with a special emphasis on how differential privacy affects data collection and data repository practice and policy. Appendix C provides a list of selected tools and resources for implementing differential privacy protections.

Section 6.2 is recommended for policymakers as well as for analysts and communications professionals seeking to explain differential privacy to policymakers, data users, and data subjects. Sections 6.3 and 6.4, in combination with Appendix B, are recommended for organizational directors and principal investigators responsible for identifying where differential privacy is appropriate as part of a project or organization-level data-protection strategy. Appendices A, B, and C are recommended for those with a technical background aiming to design and deploy differential privacy addressing specific data dissemination requirements.

6.1.2 Motivation: Formal Guarantees are Needed to Protect Data against Growing Privacy Risks

Government agencies and research organizations are utilizing increasingly greater quantities of personal information about individuals over progressively longer periods of time. Powerful analytical capabilities, including emerging machine learning techniques, are enabling the mining of large-scale data sets to infer new insights about human characteristics and behaviors and driving demand for large-scale data sets for scientific inquiry, public policy, and innovation. These factors are also creating heightened risks to individual privacy.

A number of measures have been developed for sharing sensitive data while protecting the privacy of individuals. These interventions encompass a wide range of legal, procedural, and technical controls, from providing access to only trusted researchers, using data enclaves, and imposing restrictions as part of data use agreements, among others. One category of controls is a collection of *statistical disclosure limitation (SDL)* techniques, which are widely adopted by statistical agencies, research organizations, and data analysts to analyze and share data containing privacy-sensitive information with the aim of preventing users of the data from learning personal information pertaining to an individual. Statistical disclosure limitation encompasses a wide range of methods for suppressing, aggregating, perturbing, swapping, and generalizing attributes of individuals in the data.[1] SDL techniques are often applied with the explicit goal of *de-identification* (i.e., redacting or coarsening data with the goal of increasing the difficulty of linking an identified person to a record in a data release).[2]

Differential privacy is motivated by an ever-growing number of real-world examples of data releases that were thought to be sufficiently protective of privacy but were later shown to carry significant privacy risks. Over time, changes in the way information is collected and analyzed, including advances in analytical capabilities, increases in computational power, and the expanding availability of personal data from a wide range of sources, are eroding the effectiveness of traditional SDL techniques.

For over a century,[3] statistical agencies have recognized the need to protect against uses of data that would threaten privacy, and, for most of this time, the primary focus of formal protections has been to prevent re-identification (for an overview, see Willenborg and

---

[1] For an overview of traditional SDL techniques, see Harris-Kojetin et al. (2005) and chapter 5 in this handbook.

[2] For an introduction to de-identification techniques, see Garfinkel (2016).

[3] See, e.g., Chapter 2 Section 25 of the Thirteenth Census Act (The Statutes at Large of the United States of America, 1909).

De Waal, 1996). Re-identification attacks gained renewed attention in the privacy research literature in the late 1990s (Sweeney, 1997) and have become increasingly sophisticated over time, along with other emerging types of attacks that seek to infer characteristics of individuals based on information about them in the data (Narayanan and Shmatikov, 2008; de Montjoye et al., 2013; Calandrino et al., 2011). In particular, successful attacks on de-identified data have shown that traditional technical measures for privacy protection may be vulnerable to attacks devised after a technique's deployment and use. Some de-identification techniques, for example, categorize attributes in the data as (quasi-)identifying (e.g., names, dates of birth, or addresses) or non-identifying (e.g., movie ratings or hospital admission dates). Data providers may later discover that attributes initially believed to be non-identifying can in fact be used to re-identify individuals. De-identification hence requires a careful analysis—not only of present data sources that could be linked with the de-identified data toward enabling re-identification but also of future data sources and other hard-to-anticipate future sources of auxiliary information that can be used for re-identification.

Moreover, there are privacy attacks beyond record linkage attacks on de-identified records. A recent example illustrating the evolving nature of privacy attacks is the reconstruction and re-identification of the 2010 Decennial Census database. This example demonstrates that even publications of statistical tables transformed using traditional statistical disclosure limitation techniques may be vulnerable to privacy attacks.[4]

> In a paper published in 2018, researchers revealed that the underlying confidential data from the 2010 US Decennial Census could be reconstructed using only the statistical tables published by the US Census Bureau (Garfinkel, Abowd and Martindale, 2019). Researchers demonstrated a type of attack, called a *database reconstruction attack*, that leveraged the large volumes of data from the published statistical tables in order

---

[4]This example is reproduced from Fluitt et al. (2019).

to narrow down the possible values of individual-level records. The researchers were able to reconstruct with perfect accuracy the sex, age, race, ethnicity, and fine-grained geographic location (to the block-level) reported by Census respondents for 46 percent of the US population (Abowd, 2019). Researchers also showed that, if they slightly relaxed their conditions and allowed age to vary by up to only one year, these five pieces of information could be reconstructed for 71 percent of the population (Abowd, 2019).

Further, the researchers showed that the reconstructed records could be completely *re-identified*. They were able to assign personally identifiable information to individual records using commercial databases that were available in 2010 (Abowd, 2019). They concluded that, with this attack, they could putatively re-identify 138 million people, and they confirmed that these re-identifications were accurate for 52 million people, or 17 percent of the US population (Abowd, 2019).

These findings are startling. In 2012, the last time the Census Bureau performed a simulated re-identification attack on census data sets, the re-identification rate was only 0.0038 percent (Ramachandran et al., 2012). The test attack using the data published for the 2010 Decennial Census demonstrates that previous risk assessments underestimated the re-identification risk by a factor of at least 4,500 (Ramachandran et al., 2012).

The demonstration of a database reconstruction attack on the statistical tables published by the Census Bureau is just the latest in a long line of attacks illustrating the privacy risks associated with releasing and analyzing large volumes of data about individuals. In particular, it is a real-world manifestation of the growing risks from combining and analyzing multiple statistical releases—broadly referred to as risks from *composition* (Ganta, Kasiviswanathan and Smith, 2008; Fluitt et al., 2019). The modern mathematical understanding recognizes that any research output increases disclosure risk.⁵ Although some increases in disclosure risk may be small, they accumulate, potentially to the point of a severe privacy breach. Taken together, the outputs may enable an accurate reconstruction of large portions of the data set, as seen in the reconstruction and re-identification of the 2010 Decennial Census database.

Producing accurate statistics while protecting privacy and addressing risks from composition is a challenging problem (Dwork et al., 2016). It is a fundamental law of information that privacy risk grows with the repeated use of data, and this applies to any disclosure limitation technique. Traditional SDL techniques—such as suppression, aggregation, and generalization—often reduce accuracy and are vulnerable to privacy loss due to composition.⁶ A rigorous analysis of the effect of composition is important for establishing a robust and realistic understanding of how multiple statistical computations affect privacy.

Privacy attacks such as these have underscored the need for privacy technologies that are immune not only to linkage attacks but to any potential attack, *including attacks that are currently unknown or unforeseen*. It is now understood that risks remain even if many pieces of information are removed from a data set prior to release. Extensive external information may be available to potential attackers, such as employers, insurance companies, relatives, and friends of an individual in the data. In addition, ex post remedies, such as simply "taking the data back" when a vulnerability is discovered, are ineffective because many copies of a set of data typically exist; copies may even

---

⁵Note that the fact that small risks can combine dramatically is a key insight essential to differential privacy. Differential privacy provides a quantification of privacy risk, and provable guarantees with respect to the cumulative risk from successive data releases. Some risk assessment frameworks, such as the Five Safes framework as originally proposed, make an assumption that "many research outputs pose no disclosure risk because of their functional form" (Desai, Ritchie and Welpton, 2016, pg. 13). Traditional disclosure avoidance methods do not provide ways to quantify the accumulation of privacy risk from multiple uses and releases of data.

⁶See Ganta, Kasiviswanathan and Smith (2008). The impression that these techniques do not suffer accumulated degradation in privacy is merely due to the fact that these techniques have not been analyzed with the high degree of rigor that has been applied to differential privacy. For a discussion of privacy and utility with respect to traditional statistical disclosure limitation techniques, see Chen et al. (2009).

persist online indefinitely.[7]

6.1.3 Features of the Differential Privacy Guarantee

Differential privacy is a strong definition (or, in other words, a standard) of privacy in the context of statistical analysis and machine learning, protecting against the threats described above, including those of unknown attacks and cumulative loss. Tools that achieve the differential privacy standard can be used to provide broad, public access to data or data summaries in a privacy-preserving way. Used appropriately, these tools can, in some cases, also enable access to data that could not otherwise be shared due to privacy concerns and do so with a guarantee of privacy protection that substantially increases the ability of the institution to protect the individuals in the data.

With differential privacy, statements about risk are proved mathematically—rather than supported heuristically or empirically. The definition of differential privacy also has a compelling intuitive interpretation: inferring information specific to an individual from the outcome of an analysis preserving differential privacy is impossible, including whether the individual's information was used at all.

Differential Privacy Is a Standard, Not a Single Tool

Differential privacy is a standard which many tools for analyzing sensitive personal information have been devised to satisfy. Any analysis meeting the standard provably protects its data against a wide range of *privacy attacks*, i.e., attempts to learn private information specific to individuals from a data release.[8]

---

[7] As an example, in 2006 AOL published anonymized search histories of 650,000 users over a period of three months. Shortly after the release, the New York Times identified a person in the release and AOL removed the data from their site. However, in spite of the withdrawal by AOL, copies of the data are still accessible on the Internet today.

[8] The authors distinguish protection against *privacy attacks*, which involves the attacker making use of the intended "advertised" functionality of a data access mechanism, from protection against *security attacks*, which involves an attacker attempt-

Differential Privacy Is Designed for Analysis of Populations, Not Individuals

Differentially private analyses can be deployed in settings in which an analyst seeks to learn about a population. For example, when statistical estimates (such as counts, averages, histograms, contingency tables, regression coefficients, and synthetic data) are computed based on personal information, the privacy of the individuals in the data needs to be protected.

The Differential Privacy Guarantee

It is mathematically guaranteed that the recipient of a data release generated by a differentially private analysis will make essentially the same inferences about any single individual's private information, whether or not that individual's private information is included in the input to the analysis.

The differential privacy guarantee can be understood in reference to other privacy concepts, such as opt-out and protection of personally identifiable information (PII):

- Differential privacy protects an individual's information essentially as if their data were not used in the analysis at all (i.e., as though the individual opted out and the information was not used).
- Differential privacy ensures that using an individual's data will not reveal essentially any PII that is specific to them. Here, *specific* refers to information that cannot be inferred about an individual unless their information is used in the analysis. Information specific to an individual would be considered PII under a variety of interpretations.[9]

---

ing to exploit unintended implementation vulnerabilities (e.g., by circumventing access control mechanisms). Differential privacy does not generally provide protection against security attacks, which should be addressed using complementary controls like encryption and access control.

[9] For an example of an analysis of this relationship with respect to the Family Educational Rights and Privacy Act's (FERPA) definition of PII, see Nissim et al. (2018).

CHAPTER 6

Differentially Private Analysis Requires the Introduction of Statistical Noise

To achieve differential privacy, carefully crafted random statistical noise must be injected into statistical and machine-learning analyses.[10]

Protecting Privacy Increases the Uncertainty of Results

The introduction of statistical noise to protect privacy necessarily reduces the accuracy of statistical analyses. As the number n of observations in a data set grows sufficiently large, the loss in accuracy due to differential privacy can become much smaller than other sources of error such as statistical sampling error. However, maintaining high accuracy for studies on small or modest-sized data sets (or modest-sized subsets of large data sets) is a challenge. As a consequence, all results computed using tools for differentially private analysis will be approximate. Conversely, any system that produces exact results without any random modifications cannot meet the differential privacy standard.

Preventing Cumulative Privacy Failure Requires a Budget for Privacy Loss, Which in Turn Limits Utility

Every computation leaks some information about the individual records used as input regardless of the protection method used. To prevent cumulative privacy failure, the privacy loss that accumulates over multiple computations must be calculated, tracked, and limited. Differential privacy provides explicit, formal methods for defining and managing this cumulative loss, referred to as the *privacy-loss budget*.

The inevitability of privacy loss implies that there is an inherent tradeoff between privacy and utility as the former degrades with an increase of the latter. Formal frameworks for statistical disclosure limitation

---

[10]The choice of noise addition technique—whether statistical noise is used to blur individual data points, the output of a computation, or intermediate computations—is a delicate algorithmic question; a variety of noise addition techniques have been developed for differentially private analysis with the purpose of guaranteeing differential privacy while minimizing the overall inaccuracy introduced.

(such as differential privacy) are distinct from traditional, less formal approaches in that formal frameworks quantify this trade-off explicitly: what can be learned about an individual as a result of their private information being included in a differentially private analysis is strictly limited and quantified by a privacy loss parameter, usually denoted *epsilon* (ε). Further, many tools for differentially private analysis are designed to make efficient trade-offs between privacy and utility.

6.1.4 An Illustrative Scenario: Publishing Education Statistics

The scenarios in this section illustrate the types of information disclosures that are addressed when using differential privacy.

> Alice and Bob are professors at Private University. They both have access to a database that contains personal information about students at the university, including information related to the financial aid each student receives. To gain access, Alice and Bob were required to undergo confidentiality training and to sign data use agreements restricting the disclosure of personal information obtained from the database.
>
> In March, Alice publishes an article based on the information in this database and writes that "the current freshman class at Private University is made up of 3,005 students, 202 of whom are from families earning over US$350,000 per year." Alice reasons that no individual's personal information will be exposed because she published an aggregate statistic taken over 3,005 people. The following month, Bob publishes a separate article containing these statistics: "201 families in Private University's freshman class of 3,004 have household incomes exceeding US$350,000 per year." Neither Alice nor Bob is aware that they have both published similar information.

CHAPTER 6

> A clever student Eve reads both of these articles and makes an observation. From the published information, Eve concludes that between March and April one freshman withdrew from Private University and that the student's parents earn over US$350,000 per year. Eve asks around and is able to determine that a student named John dropped out around the end of March. Eve then informs her classmates that John's parents probably earn over US$350,000 per year.
>
> John hears about this and is upset that his former classmates learned about his parents' financial status. He complains to the university and Alice and Bob are asked to explain. In their defense, both Alice and Bob argue that they published only information that had been aggregated over a large population and does not identify any individuals.

This story illustrates how the results of multiple analyses using information about the same people, when studied in combination, may enable one to draw conclusions about individuals in the data. Alice and Bob may each publish information that seems innocuous in isolation. However, when combined, the information they publish can compromise the privacy of one or more individuals. This type of privacy breach is generally difficult to prevent by Alice and Bob individually, as it is likely that neither knows what information has already been revealed or will be revealed by others in future. This problem is referred to as the problem of *composition*.

Suppose, instead, that the institutional review board at Private University only allows researchers to access student records by submitting queries to a special data portal, which responds to every query with an answer produced by running a differentially private computation on the student records.

> In March, Alice queries the data portal for the number of freshmen who come from families with a household income exceeding US$350,000. The portal returns the noisy count of 204, leading Alice to write in her article that "the current freshman class at Private University is made up of 3,005 students, approximately 205 of whom are from families earning over US$350,000 per year." In April, Bob asks the same question and gets the noisy count of 199 students. Bob publishes in his article that "approximately 200 families in Private University's freshman class of 3,004 have household incomes exceeding US$350,000 per year." The publication of these noisy figures prevents Eve from concluding that one student with a household income greater than US$350,000 withdrew from the university in March. The risk that John's personal information could be uncovered based on these publications is thereby reduced.

This example hints at one of the most important properties of differential privacy: it is robust under composition. If multiple differentially private analyses are performed on data describing the same set of individuals, then the guarantee is that all of the information released will still be differentially private. Notice how this scenario is markedly different from the previous hypothetical in which Alice and Bob do not use differentially private analyses and inadvertently release two statistics that in combination lead to the full disclosure of John's personal information. The use of differential privacy rules out the possibility of such a complete breach of privacy. This is because differential privacy enables one to measure and bound the cumulative privacy risk from multiple analyses of information about the same individuals.

However, *every* analysis, regardless of whether it is differentially private, results in *some* leakage of information about the individuals whose data are being analyzed, and this leakage accumulates with each analysis. This is true for every release of data, including releases of aggregate statistics. In particular, the example above should not be understood to imply that privacy does not degrade after multiple differentially private computations. In fact, as indicated in Section

6.2.4, privacy risks accumulate with each release or analysis involving an individual's data. For this reason, there is a limit to how many analyses can be performed on a specific data set while providing an acceptable guarantee of privacy. Therefore, measuring privacy loss and understanding quantitatively how risk accumulates across successive analyses are critical. In the context of the example above, measures need to be established, such as restricting the overall number of queries to which researchers may apply to Private University's database.

6.1.5 What Types of Analyses are Performed Using Differential Privacy

Differentially private algorithms are known to exist for a wide range of statistical analyses, such as count queries, histograms, cumulative distribution functions, and linear regression; techniques used in statistics and machine learning, such as clustering and classification; and statistical disclosure limitation techniques, like synthetic data generation, among many others.

Count Queries Differentially private answers to count queries (i.e., estimates of the number of individual records in the data satisfying a specific condition) can be obtained through the addition of random noise (Dwork et al., 2016).

Histograms Differentially private computations can provide noisy counts for data points classified into the disjoint categories represented in histograms or contingency tables (i.e., cross-tabulations) (Dwork et al., 2016).

Cumulative Distribution Function (CDF) There are differentially private algorithms for estimating the entire CDF of a dataset (or the distribution from which it is drawn) (Bun et al., 2015). These algorithms introduce noise that needs to be taken into account when statistics such as median or interquartile range are computed from the estimated CDF.[11]

Linear Regression Differentially private algorithms for linear regression introduce noise in a variety of different ways, and the choice of which algorithm is best will depend on properties of the underlying data distribution (e.g., the amount of variance in the explanatory variables), the sample size, the privacy parameters, and the intended application (Wang, 2018; Alabi et al., 2020).

Clustering Researchers are developing a variety of differentially private clustering algorithms (i.e., algorithms for grouping data points into clusters so that points in the same cluster are more similar to each other than to points in other clusters) (Stemmer and Kaplan, 2018), and such tools are likely to be included in future privacy-preserving tool kits for exploratory analysis by social scientists.

Classification and Machine Learning Theoretical work has shown it is possible to construct differentially private algorithms for a large collection of classification tasks, such as identifying or predicting to which set of categories a data point belongs based on a training set of examples for which category membership is known (Blum et al., 2005; Kasiviswanathan et al., 2011), and subsequent work has developed more practical methods for differentially private machine learning, including deep learning (Abadi et al., 2016).

Synthetic Data Generation Research has shown that in principle it is possible to generate differentially private synthetic data that preserves a vast collection of statistical properties of the original data set.[12] A significant benefit is that once a differentially private synthetic data set is

---

[11]For data over an ordered domain, a cumulative distribution function depicts for every value x an estimate of the number of data points with a value up to x. For a more in-depth discussion of differential privacy and CDFs, see Muise and Nissim (2016).

[12]See, for example, Blum, Ligett and Roth (2013). Synthetic data are data sets generated from a statistical model estimated using the original data. The records in a synthetic data set have no one-to-one correspondence with the individuals in the original data set, yet the synthetic data can retain many of the statistical properties of

generated, it can be analyzed any number of times, without any further implications for privacy. As a result, synthetic data can be shared freely or even made public in many cases. For example, statistical agencies can release synthetic microdata as public-use data files in place of raw microdata. However, significant challenges remain with respect to both the level of random noise introduced and computational efficiency for general-purpose differentially private synthetic generation in practice, particularly for high-dimensional data.[13]

6.2 How Differential Privacy Protects Privacy

6.2.1 What Does Differential Privacy Protect?

Intuitively, a computation protects the privacy of individuals in the data if the computational output does not reveal any information that is specific to any individual subject. Differential privacy formalizes this intuition as a *mathematical definition*. Similar to showing that an integer is even by proving that it is the result of multiplying some integer by two, a computation is shown to be differentially private by proving it meets the constraints of the definition. In turn, if a computation can be proven to be differentially private, one can rest assured that using the computation will not unduly reveal information specific to a data subject.

To see how differential privacy formalizes this privacy requirement as a definition, consider the following scenario.

---

the original data. Synthetic data resemble the original sensitive data in format and, for a large class of analyses, results are similar whether performed on the synthetic or original data.

[13]Intuitively, preserving more statistical information (e.g., all entries of a high-dimensional variance-covariance matrix) requires spreading the privacy-loss budget more thinly and thus introducing greater noise. There are much more complex methods that can detect and exploit relationships between the statistics to introduce less noise, but those methods can be computationally infeasible on high-dimensional data.

> Researchers have selected a sample of individuals across the US to participate in a survey exploring the relationship between socioeconomic status and health outcomes. The participants were asked to complete a questionnaire covering topics such as where they live, their finances, and their medical history.
>
> One of the participants, John, is aware that individuals have been re-identified in previous releases of de-identified data and is concerned that personal information he provides about himself, such as his medical history or annual income, could one day be revealed in de-identified data released from this study. If leaked, this information could lead to an increase in his life insurance premium or an adverse decision for a future mortgage application.

Differential privacy can be used to address John's concerns. If the researchers only share data resulting from a differentially private computation, John is guaranteed that the release will not disclose anything that is *specific to him* even though he participated in the study.

To understand what this means, consider a thought experiment, which is illustrated in Figure 6.1 and is referred to as *John's opt-out scenario*.[14] In John's opt-out scenario, an analysis is performed using data about the individuals in the study, except that information about John is omitted. His privacy is protected in the sense that the outcome of the analysis *does not depend on his specific information,* because it was not used in the analysis at all.

John's opt-out scenario differs from the scenario depicted in Figure 6.2, referred to as the *real-world* scenario, in which the analysis is based on John's personal information along with the personal information of the other study participants. The real-world scenario involves some potential risk to John's privacy as some of his personal information could be revealed by the outcome of the analysis, because it was used as input to the computation.

---

[14]Figure 6.1 is reproduced from Wood et al. (2018).

CHAPTER 6

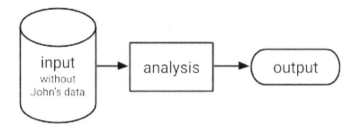

Figure 6.1: John's opt-out scenario

Differential privacy aims to protect John's privacy in the real-world scenario in a way that mimics the privacy protection he is afforded in his opt-out scenario.[15] Accordingly, what can be learned about John from a differentially private computation is (essentially) limited to what could be learned about him from everyone else's data *without his own data being included in the computation*. Crucially, this same guarantee is made not only with respect to John but also with respect to every other individual contributing their information to the analysis.

For a precise description of differential privacy and the mathematics underlying the construction of differentially private analysis, the reader is referred to the literature listed in Appendix C. In lieu of the mathematical definition, this chapter offers a few illustrative examples to discuss various aspects of differential privacy in a way that is intuitive and generally accessible.

6.2.2 Privacy Protection Is a Property of an Analysis—Not a Data Release

Throughout this chapter, we refer to the general concept of an *analysis* that performs a computation on input data and outputs the result (illustrated in Figure 6.2).[16] The analysis may be as simple as deter-

---

[15]The use of differentially private analysis is *not* equivalent to the traditional use of opting out. On the privacy side, differential privacy does not require an explicit opt-out. In comparison, traditional use of opt-out requires an explicit choice that may cause privacy harms by calling attention to individuals that choose to opt out. On the utility side, there is no general expectation that using differential privacy would yield the same outcomes as adopting the policy of opt-out.

[16]Figure 6.2 is reproduced from Wood et al. (2018).

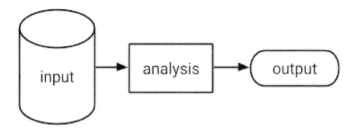

Figure 6.2: An analysis (or computation) transforms input data into some output.

mining the average age of the individuals in the data, or it may be more complex and utilize sophisticated modeling and inference techniques.

We focus specifically on analyses that transform sensitive personal data into an output that can be released publicly. For example, an analysis may involve the application of techniques for aggregating or de-identifying a set of personal data in order to produce a sanitized version of the data that is safe to release. How can the data provider ensure that publishing the output of this computation will not unintentionally leak information from the privacy-sensitive input data?

A key insight from the theoretical computer science literature is that *privacy is a property of the informational relationship between the input and output,* not a property of the output alone.[17] In other words, one can be certain that the output of a computation is privacy-preserving if the computation itself is privacy-preserving. The following examples show why this is the case.

Consider the following statistic: a representative ninth-grade GPA at City High School is 3.5. One might naturally think that this statistic is unlikely to reveal private information about an individual student. However, one needs to know *how* the statistic was computed to make that determination. For instance, if the representative ninth-grade GPA was calculated by taking the GPA of the alphabetically first

---

[17] This insight follows from a series of papers demonstrating privacy breaches enabled by leakages of information resulting from decisions made by the computation. See, for example, Kenthapadi, Mishra and Nissim (2013). For a general discussion of the advantages of formal privacy models over ad hoc privacy techniques, see Narayanan, Huey and Felten (2016).

student in the school, then the statistic completely reveals the GPA of that student.[18] Alternatively, a representative statistic could be based on average features of the ninth graders in the school—using the most common first name, the most common last name, the average age, and the average GPA to produce "John Smith, a fourteen-year-old in the ninth grade, has a 3.1 GPA." Suppose that coincidentally a student named John Smith subsequently joins the ninth-grade class. Although his name appears in the published statistic, one knows with certainty that the statistic does not reveal private information about him, because it was not based on his student records in any way.

These examples are clearly contrived, and no reasonable analyst would publish either statistic. On a fundamental level, however, the examples demonstrate that when trying to decide whether a data release can be made public, one needs to consider the computation used to produce that release and not the release by itself. Thus, when thinking about privacy in the context of statistical releases, one should think about it as a computational property, especially if the goal is to make rigorous, formal claims about the data. This is one of the properties of differential privacy. If a computation can be proven to be differentially private, the researcher can rest assured that using the computation will not unduly reveal information specific to a data subject. Adopting this formal approach to privacy yields several practical benefits for users, including robustness to auxiliary information, composition, and post-processing, as well as transparency—each discussed in turn below in Section 6.2.3.

6.2.3 Methodology Example: Limiting Privacy Loss from Participation in Research

In the earlier example featuring Professors Alice and Bob at Private University, differentially private analyses add random noise to the

---

[18]One might object that the student's GPA is not traceable back to that student unless an observer knows how the statistic was produced. However, a basic principle of modern cryptography (known as Kerckhoffs' principle) is that a system is not secure if its security depends on its inner workings being a secret. In this context, it is assumed that the algorithm behind a statistical analysis is public (or could potentially become public).

statistics they produce.[19] This noise masks the differences between the real-world computation and the opt-out scenario of each individual in the data set. This means that the outcome of a differentially private analysis is not exact but an *approximation*. In addition, a differentially private analysis may return different results, even if performed twice on the same data set. Because researchers intentionally add random noise, analyses performed with differential privacy differ from standard statistical analyses, such as the calculation of averages, medians, and linear regression equations.

> Consider a differentially private analysis that computes the number of students in a sample with a GPA of at least 3.0. Say that there are 10,000 students in the sample, and exactly 5,603 of them have a GPA of at least 3.0. An analysis that added no random noise would hence report that 5,603 students had a GPA of at least 3.0.
>
> However, a differentially private analysis adds random noise to protect the privacy of the data subjects. For instance, a differentially private analysis might report an answer of 5,521 students when run on the data; when run a second time on the same information, it might report an answer of 5,586 students.
> In a differentially private analysis, the added noise makes every potential answer almost as likely whether John's data are used in the analysis or not. This is done by controlling the likelihood ratio of any answer with John's data included or excluded.

A differentially private analysis might produce many different answers given the same data set. Because the details of a method providing differential privacy can be made public, an analyst may be able to calculate accuracy bounds that show how much an output of the analysis is expected to differ from the noiseless answer.

---

[19] In other differentially private computations noise may be added to intermediate results of a computation or at the data collection process. The latter is referred to as the *local model* of differential privacy.

An essential component of a differentially private computation is the privacy loss parameter, usually denoted by the Greek letter ε (epsilon). This parameter determines how much noise is added to the computation. Choosing a value for the privacy loss parameter can be thought of as a tuning knob for balancing privacy and accuracy. A lower value for ε corresponds to stronger privacy protection and also a larger decrease in accuracy, whereas a higher value for ε corresponds to weaker privacy protection and also a smaller decrease in accuracy. The following discussion establishes an intuition for this parameter. It can be thought of as limiting how much a differentially private computation is allowed to deviate from the opt-out scenario of an individual in the data.

Consider the opt-out scenario for a certain computation, such as estimating the number of HIV-positive individuals in a surveyed population. Ideally, this estimate should remain exactly the same whether or not a single individual, such as John, is included in the survey. However, ensuring this property *exactly* would require the total exclusion of John's information from the analysis. It would also require the exclusion of Gertrude's and Peter's information in order to provide privacy protection for them. Continuing with this line of argument, one comes to the conclusion that the personal information of *every* surveyed individual must be excluded in order to satisfy that individual's opt-out scenario. Thus, the analysis cannot rely on any person's information and is completely useless.

To avoid this dilemma, differential privacy requires only that the output of the analysis remain *approximately* the same whether John participates in the survey or not. Differential privacy allows for a deviation between the output of the real-world analysis and that of each individual's opt-out scenario. The privacy loss parameter ε quantifies and limits the extent of the deviation between the opt-out and real-world scenarios, as shown in Figure 6.3 below.[20] The parameter ε measures the effect of each individual's information on the output of the analysis. It can also be viewed as a measure of the additional privacy risk an individual could incur beyond the risk incurred in the opt-out scenario.[21]

---

[20] Figure 6.3 is reproduced from Wood et al. (2018).
[21] ε is a unitless nonnegative quantity measuring probability log-ratio.

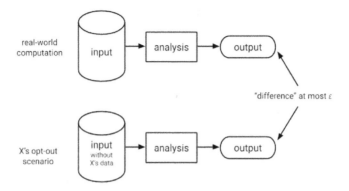

Figure 6.3: Differential privacy. The maximum deviation between the opt-out scenario and real-world computation should hold simultaneously for each individual X whose information is included in the input.

Note that in Figure 6.3 John has been replaced with an arbitrary individual X to emphasize that the differential privacy guarantee is made simultaneously to *all* individuals in the sample, not just John.

Choosing a value for ε can be thought of as tuning the level of privacy protection required. This choice also affects the utility or accuracy that can be obtained from the analysis. A smaller value of ε results in a smaller deviation between the real-world analysis and each opt-out scenario and is therefore associated with stronger privacy protection but less accuracy. For example, when ε is set to zero, the real-world differentially private analysis mimics the opt-out scenario of each individual perfectly. However, as argued at the beginning of this section, an analysis that perfectly mimics the opt-out scenario of each individual would require ignoring all information from the input and accordingly could not provide any meaningful output. Yet when ε is set to a small number, such as 0.1, the deviation between the real-world computation and each individual's opt-out scenario will be small, providing strong privacy protection while also enabling an analyst to derive useful statistics based on the data.

Simple conventions for choosing ε have not yet been developed; the current best practice for choosing ε is to explore the trade-off between the choice of ε and the utility provided by an analysis for every application, as well as to consider the potential risks to individuals and the level of risk the data owner might be permitting given their legal, contractual, and ethical obligations. It is expected that as the use of differentially private analyses in real-life applications increases, the accumulated experience will shed light on how to reach a reasonable compromise between privacy and accuracy. As a rule of thumb, however, ε should be thought of as a small number, between approximately $1/100$ and 1.[22]

This chapter has discussed how the privacy loss parameter limits the deviation between the real-world computation and each data subject's opt-out scenario. However, it might not be clear how this abstract guarantee relates to privacy concerns in the real world. Therefore, in this section, a practical interpretation of the privacy loss parameter is discussed as a bound on the financial risk incurred by participating in a study.

Any useful analysis carries the risk that it will reveal information about individuals (which in turn might result in a financial cost). The following example shows that while differential privacy necessarily cannot eliminate this risk, it can guarantee that the risk will be limited by quantitative bounds that depend on ε.

> Gertrude, a 65-year-old woman, is considering whether to participate in a medical research study. While she can envision many potential personal and societal benefits resulting from her participation in the study, she is concerned that the personal information she discloses over the course of the study could lead to an increase in her life insurance premium.
>
> For example, Gertrude is apprehensive that the tests she would undergo as part of the research study would reveal that she is

---

[22] In general, setting ϵ involves making a compromise between privacy protection and accuracy. The consideration of both utility and privacy is challenging in practice and, in some of the early implementations of differential privacy, has led to choosing a higher value for ϵ. As the accuracy of differentially private analyses improves over time, it is likely that lower values of ϵ will be chosen.

> predisposed to suffer a stroke and is significantly more likely to die in the coming year than the average person of her age and gender. If such information related to Gertrude's increased risk of morbidity and mortality is discovered by her life insurance company, it will likely increase her premium substantially.
>
> Before she decides to participate in the study, Gertrude wishes to be assured that privacy measures are in place to ensure that her involvement will have a limited effect (if any) on her life insurance premium.

Gertrude's life insurance company may raise her premium based on something it learns from the medical research study, even if Gertrude does not herself participate in the study. The following example is provided to illustrate such a scenario.[23]

> Gertrude holds a US$100,000 life insurance policy. Her life insurance company has set her annual premium at US$1,000 (i.e., 1 percent of US$100,000) based on actuarial tables that show that someone of Gertrude's age and gender has a 1 percent chance of dying in the next year.
>
> Suppose Gertrude opts out of participating in the medical research study. Regardless, the study reveals that coffee drinkers are more likely to suffer a stroke than non-coffee drinkers. Gertrude's life insurance company may update its assessment and conclude that as a 65-year-old woman who drinks coffee, Gertrude has a 2 percent chance of dying in the next year. The insurance company decides to increase Gertrude's annual premium from US$1,000 to US$2,000 based on the findings of the study.

In this hypothetical example, the results of the study led to an increase

---

[23] Figures in this example are based on data from US Social Security Administration (2011).

CHAPTER 6

in Gertrude's life insurance premium, even though she did not contribute any personal information to the study. A potential increase of this nature is likely unavoidable to Gertrude because she cannot prevent other people from participating in the study. This type of effect is taken into account by Gertrude's insurance premium in her *opt-out scenario* and will not be protected against by differential privacy.

Next, consider the increase in risk that is due to Gertrude's participation in the study.

> Suppose Gertrude decides to participate in the research study. Based on the results of medical tests performed on Gertrude over the course of the study, the researchers conclude that Gertrude has a 50 percent chance of dying from a stroke in the next year. If the data from the study were to be made available to Gertrude's insurance company, it might decide to increase her insurance premium from US$2,000 to more than US$50,000 in light of this discovery.
>
> Fortunately for Gertrude, this does not happen. Rather than releasing the full data set from the study, the researchers release only a differentially private summary of the data they collected. Differential privacy guarantees that if the researchers use a value of $\varepsilon = 0.01$, then the insurance company's estimate of the probability that Gertrude will die in the next year can increase from 2 percent to at most 2.04 percent, as per the equation:
>
> $$2\% \cdot (1 + 2 \cdot \varepsilon) = 2\% \cdot (1 + 2 \cdot 0.01) = 2.04\%^a$$
>
> Thus, Gertrude's insurance premium can increase from US$2,000 to US$2,040, at most. Gertrude's first-year cost of participating in the research study in terms of a potential increase in her insurance premium is at most US$40.
>
> Note that this analysis *does not* imply that the insurance company's estimate of the probability that Gertrude will die in the next year must increase as a result of her participation in the

> study, nor that if the estimate increases it must increase to 2.04 percent. What the analysis shows is that if the estimate were to increase, it would not exceed 2.04 percent.
>
> Consequently, this analysis *does not* imply that Gertrude would incur an increase in her insurance premium or that if she were to see such an increase it would cost her US$40. What is guaranteed is that if Gertrude should see an increase in her premium, this increase would not exceed US$40.
>
> ---
> ^{a}The approximate calculation provided in this example only holds for small ε, using $e^{2 \cdot \varepsilon} \approx 1 + 2 \cdot \varepsilon$. See Table 6.1 for an exact formula.

Gertrude may decide that the potential cost of participating in the research study, US$40, is too high and she cannot afford to participate with this value of ε and this level of risk. Alternatively, she may decide that it is worthwhile. Perhaps she is paid more than US$40 to participate in the study or the information she learns from the study is worth more than US$40 to her. The key point is that differential privacy allows Gertrude to make a more informed decision based on the worst-case cost of her participation in the study.

It is worth noting that should Gertrude decide to participate in the study, her risk might increase even if her insurance company is not aware of her participation. For instance, the study might determine that Gertrude has a very high chance of dying next year, and that could affect the study results. In turn, her insurance company might decide to raise her premium, because she fits the profile of the studied population (even if the company does not believe her data were included in the study). On the other hand, differential privacy guarantees that even if the insurance company knows that Gertrude *did* participate in the study, it can essentially only make inferences about her that it could have made if she had not participated in the study.

One can generalize from Gertrude's scenario and view differential privacy as a framework for reasoning about the increased risk that is incurred when an individual's information is included in a data analysis. Differential privacy guarantees that an individual will be exposed to

CHAPTER 6

essentially the same privacy risk regardless of whether their data are included in a differentially private analysis. In this context, think of the privacy risk associated with a data release as the potential harm that an individual might experience due to a belief that an observer forms based on that data release.

In particular, when ε is set to a small value, the probability that an observer will make some inference that is harmful to a data subject based on a differentially private data release is no greater than $1+\varepsilon$ times the probability that the observer would have made that inference without the data subject's inclusion in the data set.[24] For example, if ε is set to 0.01, then the probability of any adverse event to an individual (such as Gertrude being denied insurance) can grow by a multiplicative factor of 1.01 (at most) as a result from participation in a differentially private computation (compared with not participating in the computation).

As shown in the Gertrude scenario, there is also the risk to Gertrude that the insurance company will see the study results, update its beliefs about the mortality of Gertrude, and charge her a higher premium. If the insurance company infers from the study results that Gertrude has probability p of dying in the next year, and her insurance policy is valued at US$ 100,000, this translates into a risk (in financial terms) of a higher premium of $p\times$ US$ 100,000. This risk exists even if Gertrude does not participate in the study. Recall how in the first hypothetical, the insurance company's belief that Gertrude will die in the next year doubles from 1 percent to 2 percent, increasing her premium from US$1,000 to US$2,000, based on general information learned from the individuals who did participate. Also, if Gertrude does decide to participate in the study (as in the second hypothetical), differential privacy limits the change in this risk relative to her opt-out scenario. In financial terms, her risk increases by US$40 at most, since it can be shown that the insurance company's beliefs about her probability of death change from 2 percent to no greater than $2\% \cdot (1+2\cdot\varepsilon) = 2.04\%$,

---

[24]In general, the guarantee made by differential privacy is that the probabilities differ at most by a factor of $e^{\pm\varepsilon}$, which is approximately $1 \pm \varepsilon$ when ε is small.

when $\varepsilon = 0.01$.[25]

Note that the above calculation requires certain information that may be difficult to determine in the real world. In particular, the 2 percent baseline in Gertrude's opt-out scenario (i.e., Gertrude's insurer's belief about her chance of dying in the next year) is dependent on the results from the medical research study, which Gertrude does not know at the time she makes her decision whether to participate. Fortunately, differential privacy provides guarantees relative to every baseline risk.

> Without her participation, the study results would lead the insurance company to believe that Gertrude has a 3 percent chance of dying in the next year (instead of the 2 percent chance hypothesized earlier). This means that Gertrude's insurance premium would increase to US$3,000. Differential privacy guarantees that if Gertrude had instead decided to participate in the study, the insurer's estimate for Gertrude's mortality would have been at most $3\% \cdot (1 + 2 \cdot \varepsilon) = 3.06\%$ (assuming an ε of 0.01), which means that her premium would not increase beyond $3,060.

Calculations like those used in the analysis of Gertrude's privacy risk can be performed by referring to Table 6.1.[26] For example, the value of ε used in the research study in which Gertrude considered participating was 0.01, and the baseline privacy risk in her opt-out scenario was 2 percent. As shown in Table 6.1, these values correspond to a worst-case privacy risk of 2.04 percent in her real-world scenario. Notice also how the calculation of risk would change with different values. For example, if the privacy risk in Gertrude's opt-out scenario were 5 percent rather than 2 percent and the value of epsilon remained the same, then the worst-case privacy risk in her real-world scenario would be 5 percent.

---

[25] The reason that the multiplicative factor is $1 + 2 \cdot \varepsilon \approx e^{2 \cdot \varepsilon}$ rather than $1 + \varepsilon \approx e^{\varepsilon}$ is that posterior beliefs can be expressed as a ratio of two probabilities, each of which can change by a factor of at most e^{ε}. The factor of 2 was incorrectly omitted in the original paper (Wood et al., 2018) describing this example.

[26] Table 6.1 corrects a calculation error appearing in the original paper (Wood et al., 2018).

Table 6.1: Maximal change between posterior beliefs in Gertrude's opt-out and real-world scenarios. The notation $A(x')$ refers to the application of the analysis A on the dataset x', which does not include Gertrude's information. As this table shows, the use of differential privacy provides a quantitative bound on how much one can learn about an individual from a computation. The entries in the table are calculated using the formula $q = \min(e^{2\varepsilon}q', 100 - e^{-2\varepsilon}(100 - q'))$, where q' is the posterior belief given $A(x')$ and q is the upper bound on the posterior belief given $A(x)$, both expressed as percentages.

posterior belief given $A(x')$ in %	value of ε					
	0.01	0.05	0.1	0.2	0.5	1
0	0	0	0	0	0	0
1	1.02	1.11	1.22	1.49	2.72	7.39
2	2.04	2.21	2.44	2.98	5.44	14.78
3	3.06	3.32	3.66	4.48	8.15	22.17
5	5.10	5.53	6.11	7.46	13.59	36.95
10	10.20	11.05	12.21	14.92	27.18	73.89
25	25.51	27.63	30.54	37.30	67.96	89.85
50	50.99	54.76	59.06	66.48	81.61	93.23
75	75.50	77.38	79.53	83.24	90.80	96.62
90	90.20	90.95	91.81	93.30	96.32	98.65
95	95.10	95.48	95.91	96.65	98.16	99.32
98	98.04	98.19	98.36	98.66	99.26	99.73
99	99.02	99.10	99.18	99.33	99.63	99.86
100	100	100	100	100	100	100
	maximum posterior belief given $A(x)$ in %					

The fact that the differential privacy guarantee applies to *every* privacy risk means that Gertrude can know for certain how participating in the study might increase her risks relative to opting out, even if she does not know *a priori* all the privacy risks posed by the data release. This enables Gertrude to make a more informed decision about whether to take part in the study. For instance, she can calculate how much additional risk she might incur by participating in the study over a range of possible baseline risk values and decide whether she is comfortable with taking on the risks entailed by these different scenarios.

6.2.4 Strengths of Differential Privacy Over Traditional SDL Approaches

This discussion outlines some of the key features of differential privacy that enable it to overcome the weaknesses of traditional approaches and provide strong protection against a wide range of privacy attacks.

Differential Privacy is Robust to Auxiliary Information

As illustrated by the re-identification attack on the 2010 Decennial Census database described in Section 6.1.2, effective privacy protection requires taking auxiliary information into account. A data provider designing a differentially private data release need not anticipate particular types of privacy attacks, such as the likelihood that one could link particular fields with other data sources that may be available. When using differential privacy, even an attacker utilizing arbitrary auxiliary information cannot learn much more about an individual in a database than they could if that individual's information were not in the database at all.

Currently, differential privacy is the only framework that provides meaningful privacy guarantees in scenarios in which adversaries have access to arbitrary external information. Releases constructed in a differentially private manner provide provable privacy protection against any feasible adversarial attack, whereas de-identification concepts only counter a limited set of specific attacks.

Differential Privacy is Robust to Composition

When evaluating privacy risk, it is important to recognize that privacy risk accumulates with each release or analysis involving an individual's data. Under what has come to be called the fundamental law of information recovery, releasing "overly accurate answers to too many questions will destroy privacy in a spectacular way" (Dinur and Nissim, 2003; Dwork et al., 2017; Dwork and Roth, 2014). This is true whether or not any privacy-preserving technique is applied and regardless of the specific privacy-preserving technique in use.[27] A reconstruction attack, such as the reconstruction of the 2010 Decennial Census database presented in Section 6.1.2, is an example of a privacy attack that leveraged composition.

One of the most powerful features of differential privacy is its robustness under composition; in other words, the combination of multiple differentially private analyses preserves differential privacy (Dwork et al., 2016; Ganta, Kasiviswanathan and Smith, 2008). Differential privacy provides provable bounds with respect to the cumulative risk from multiple data releases, and is the only existing approach to do so. Recall that the definition of differential privacy is equipped with a numeric parameter $\varepsilon > 0$ that bounds privacy risk.[28] Furthermore, one can reason about—and bound—the overall privacy risk that accumulates when multiple differentially private computations are performed on an individual's data. As a simple example, imagine that two differentially private computations are performed on data sets containing information about the same individuals. If ε_1 bounds the privacy risk of the first computation and ε_2 bounds the privacy risk of the second computation, then the cumulative privacy risk resulting from these computations is no greater than the risk associated with an aggregate parameter of $\varepsilon_1 + \varepsilon_2$. In other words, the composition of the two differentially private analyses is also a differentially private analysis with privacy risk at most $\varepsilon_1 + \varepsilon_2$. Importantly, no coordination is needed between the two mechanisms for this bound to hold.

The example above is a simple instance illustrating how analysts can bound the total disclosure risk due to multiple differentially private disclosures. Often, better bounds can be achieved via applying a set of tools known as *composition theorems*. The fact that the total dis-

---

[27] For further discussion see Wood et al. (2018); Altman et al. (2015).
[28] See Section 6.2.3 for further discussion of how ϵ quantifies privacy risk.

closure risk can be bounded—without having mechanisms coordinate their actions—allows for a rigorous management of privacy risks across multiple disclosures and access points. As an example, a registry such as the Epsilon Registry suggested by Dwork, Kohli and Mulligan (2019) can hold information about the value of the privacy parameter ε used in implementations of differentially private data releases and hence serve as a basis for bounding the total disclosure risk.[29]

Differential Privacy is Robust to Post-Processing

It is also important to evaluate whether an approach to privacy that is being considered can be made ineffective through post-processing, i.e., via further analyzing a data release that purports to preserve privacy. For example, Machanavajjhala and Kifer (2015) describe post-processing vulnerabilities for some algorithms that satisfy k-anonymity. The demonstration of a reconstruction attack on the 2010 Decennial Census database presented in Section 6.1.2 is an example of a privacy attack that employed post-processing: while the released data tables purportedly preserved privacy, analyzing the releases enabled the reconstruction of individual respondents' records.

Differential privacy is an example of an approach that is robust to post-processing. To understand what this means, consider a scenario in which an analyst applies a post-processing transformation B on the output of the ε-differentially private analysis A. For instance, after a data publisher adds noise to a collection of statistics using a differentially private tool, they might wish to round the statistics or replace negative statistics with zero before publishing them. In such cases, the resulting analysis $(B \circ A)$ is also ε-differentially the risk to privacy. A data publisher can even share details about the analysis A, the transformation B, and the value of ε without increasing privacy risk. Importantly, the guarantee that $(B \circ A)$ is ε-differentially private holds for any transformation B—even one that is designed with an intention to breach privacy.

---

[29]The proposal for an Epsilon Registry is intended to be a publicly available bulletin board where firms would disclose information about their deployment of differential privacy. *See* Dwork, Kohli and Mulligan (2019).

Differential Privacy Does Not Rely on Security by Obscurity

Differentially private tools also have the benefit of transparency, as maintaining secrecy around a differentially private computation or its parameters is not necessary. This feature distinguishes differentially private tools from traditional de-identification techniques, which often require concealment of the extent to which the data have been transformed and thereby leave data users with uncertainty regarding the accuracy of analyses on the data. This approach can enable public scrutiny of the privacy-preserving techniques used. Further, the amount of noise added by differential privacy can be taken into account in the measure of accuracy, unlike traditional techniques that keep the information needed to estimate the privacy error secret.

6.2.5 What Does Differential Privacy *Not* Protect?

The following example illustrates the types of information disclosures that differential privacy does not aim to address.

> Ellen is John's friend and knows that he regularly consumes several glasses of red wine with dinner. Ellen learns that a research study had found a positive correlation between drinking red wine and the likelihood of developing a certain type of cancer. Based on the study and her knowledge of John's drinking habits, she might conclude that he has a heightened risk of developing cancer.

It may seem that the publication of the research results enabled a privacy breach by Ellen, as the study's findings helped her infer new information about John's elevated cancer risk of which he himself may be unaware. However, Ellen would be able to infer this information about John regardless of his participation in the medical study (i.e., it is a risk that exists in both John's opt-out scenario and the real-world scenario). Risks of this nature apply to everyone, regardless of whether they shared personal data through the study or not. Differential privacy is a concept specifically designed to allow for studies such as in this example. Therefore, differential privacy does not guarantee that *no* information about John can be revealed. The use of differential privacy only protects the information that is *specific* to him, i.e., information about John that cannot be inferred unless an analysis received his personal information as part of the input.

This and similar examples demonstrate that any useful analysis carries a risk of revealing some information about individuals. However, such risks are largely unavoidable. In a world in which data about individuals are collected, analyzed, and published, John cannot expect better privacy protection than is offered by his opt-out scenario, because he has no ability to prevent others from participating in a research study or to prohibit a release of public records. Moreover, the types of information disclosures enabled in John's opt-out scenario often result in individual and societal benefits. For example, the discovery of a causal relationship between red wine consumption and elevated cancer risk can inform John about possible changes he could make in his habits that would likely have positive effects on his health.

6.3 Aligning Risks, Controls, and Uses: Where Is the Use of Differential Privacy Appropriate?

This section discusses factors to take into account when evaluating whether differential privacy is an appropriate tool to be applied within a specific context, as well as factors in determining whether differential privacy should be deployed alone, in combination with other controls, or as part of a tiered access system. As an overview, Table 6.2 provides some of the key factors that weigh in favor of, or against, an appropriate use of differential privacy. For example, use cases involving statistical analysis of a population or large groups and the possibility of significant and lasting informational harms to individuals weigh heavily in favor of the adoption of differential privacy.

Table 6.2: Considerations when deciding whether to use differential privacy for a particular use case

Use cases where DP is more likely to be appropriate	Use cases where DP is not appropriate	Use cases where DP is challenging
• Informational harm derives from making inferences about individuals or small groups • Intended use is statistical analysis of population or large groups • Sensitivity of information is high • Information and analyses are highly structured • Datasets are large • Types of analyses to be conducted are known in advance • Composition effects are important • Release of (low-dimensional) synthetic data is acceptable or preferred	• Informational harm derives from making inferences about large groups • Intended use is individual inference or individual intervention • Intended control is purpose limitation • Intended control is computation limitation[1] • Datasets are very small (e.g., less than a few dozen observations)	• Supporting data linking • Supporting data cleaning • Estimating complex statistical models efficiently • Datasets are small (e.g., dozens to thousands of observations)[2] • Differentially private analysis not yet available • Intended output is high-dimensional synthetic data

[1] A control on computation is designed to "limit the direct operations that can be meaningfully performed on data. Commonly used examples are file-level encryption and interactive analysis systems or model servers. Emerging approaches include secure multiparty computation, functional encryption, homomorphic encryption, and secure public ledgers, eg blockchain technologies." (Altman et al., 2018).
[2] For a real-world example, see the Opportunity Atlas case study presented in Section 6.4.2.

To help guide a systematic analysis of the relevant factors within a specific use case, this discussion follows a framework for selecting privacy controls based on a systematic analysis of harm, informational risk, and intended analytic uses as presented by Altman et al. (2015).

6.3.1 Selecting Privacy Controls Based on Harm and Informational Risk: A Framework

Altman et al. (2015) propose a framework for selecting reasonable and appropriate privacy and security measures that are calibrated to the intended uses, threats, harms, and vulnerabilities associated with a specific research activity.[30] For applying this framework in practice, Altman et al. (2015) recommend a life-cycle approach to decomposing the factors at each information stage, including the collection, transformation, retention, access and release, and post-access stages. A diagram from Altman et al. (2015) illustrating a partial conceptualization of this framework is reproduced in Figure 6.4. The x-axis represents the sensitivity of the information, or the maximum level of expected harm to an individual in the data resulting from uncontrolled use of the data. The y-axis represents the post-transformation identifiability, or the potential for others to learn about individuals based on the inclusion of their information in the data. Examples range from data sets containing direct or indirect identifiers to data shared using expertly applied rigorous disclosure limitation techniques backed by a formal mathematical proof of privacy (e.g., user-level differential privacy with a low value of ε).

These factors—the level of expected harm from uncontrolled use of the data and the post-transformation identifiability of the data—suggest minimum privacy and security controls that are appropriate in a given case, as shown by the shaded regions in Figure 6.4. The subsets of controls within each region illustrate some possible combinations of controls from the more comprehensive set of procedural, economic, educational, legal, and technical controls (some of which are covered in other chapters of this Handbook). For data associated with only negligible or minor and fleeting harms, the use of differential privacy without any additional controls may be appropriate, but for more significant and lasting or even life altering harms, notice and consent mechanisms as well as terms of service may also be required. Obtain-

---

[30]In this framework, evaluating the intended uses of the data involves an assessment of the types of uses or analytic purposes intended by each of the relevant groups of data users and how privacy controls implemented at each stage enable or restrict such uses. An evaluation of the threats involves assessing potential adverse circumstances or events that could cause harm to a data subject as a result of the inclusion of that subject's data in a specific data collection, storage, use, or release. Privacy harms are injuries sustained by data subjects as a result of the realization of a privacy threat, and privacy vulnerabilities are defined as characteristics that increase the likelihood that threats will be realized. See Altman et al. (2015).

CHAPTER 6

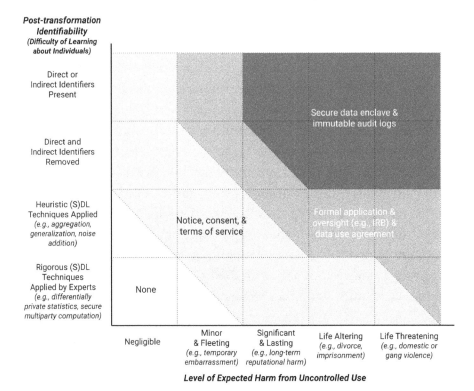

Figure 6.4: Calibrating privacy and security controls

ing consent is particularly important when using data for secondary uses not initially disclosed to the data subjects or when the selected value of ε is large. For data associated with potentially life-threatening harms, a formal application and oversight process, such as an institutional review board or restricted data access committee, together with a data use agreement may be necessary. As Figure 6.4 illustrates, in many cases, the use of differential privacy allows data analysis projects to be carried out safely with fewer additional privacy and security controls than would be required with other approaches.

Altman et al. (2015) note that the design of a real-world data management plan should consider a wide range of available interventions and incorporate controls at each stage of the lifecycle, including the post-access stage, and not be limited to the choices of controls illustrated in Figure 6.4. "[A]lthough the data transformation and release stages typically attract the most attention, threats and vulnerabilities arising from other lifecycle stages should not be ignored. For example, privacy risks may be present at the collection stage if the data collection process could be observed by an adversary; data retained in long-term storage are vulnerable to unintended breaches; and, increasingly in a big data world, external, independent publication of auxiliary information may create new or unanticipated privacy risks long into the post-access stage" (Altman et al., 2015). Further, one should note that some of the regions in Figure 6.4 are divided by a diagonal line; these areas correspond to situations in which an actor could decide between different choices based on factors related to the intended uses of the data or existing institutional or contractual requirements. It is also important to observe that the recommendations reflected in this diagram may differ from current practice. For example, Altman et al. (2015) argue that data that have been de-identified using simple redaction or other heuristic techniques should in many cases be protected using additional controls.

6.3.2 Considerations When Deciding Whether to Use Differential Privacy

As summarized in Section 6.3.1, differential privacy fits into a broader framework of privacy and security controls that should be applied across the information life cycle to appropriately mitigate risks of informational harm. Within a coherent set of information controls, differential privacy's primary role is as a formal criterion for disclosure control that ensures limitations on types of *inferences* that can be made about individuals and small groups based on the outputs of computations. In other words, implementations of differential privacy (especially in the curator model as discussed and contrasted with other models for differential privacy in Appendix A) modify summary information before it is published in order to prevent others from learning any information that is unique and specific to any individual who was part of the group being summarized.

In the context of designing a secure and private information system, differential privacy is used as part of a collection of controls aimed at mitigating informational harm while enabling some types of information uses. Differential privacy is usually neither sufficient protection on its own nor uniquely necessary—and in some cases differential privacy may simply not be appropriate for the intended use.

Three considerations are critical in deciding whether to use differential privacy: (1) how are recipients of protected information intending to use it, and how well do differentially private analyses support these intended uses; (2) what is the nature and degree of informational risk to be mitigated, and are there serious harms that could arise from learning about individuals; and (3) what complementary and alternative controls are available for protecting the data? Each of these questions is discussed in turn below.

How Well Does Differential Privacy Fit the Intended Uses of the Data?

Evaluating the intended uses of the data involves answering a series of sub-questions, including (a) what level of inference is intended; (b) what types of questions, queries, or models must be supported; and (c) how much accuracy is needed?

What Level of Inference is Intended? Differential privacy is a standard that was designed to support statistical analysis of populations or large groups yet prevent inferences about (and thus interventions targeted to) individuals and very small groups. Consider, for example, the collection, analysis, and sharing of public health information related to the COVID-19 pandemic. Differentially private analyses can be applied in tasks such as estimating the extent to which large communities adhere to social distancing, measuring the efficacy of infection rate reduction measures like social distancing and masks, identifying large disease clusters, and selecting and fitting statistical models of disease transmission.[31] If performed with differential privacy these analyses would yield valuable and meaningful statistics while providing strong

---

[31] See, e.g., Google's COVID-19 Community Mobility Reports (Aktay et al., 2020), https://www.google.com/covid19/mobility (accessed 2020-12-17).

protection for the privacy of individual medical results, locations, social encounters, etc. If analysis at the individual level is desired (e.g., to identify specific individuals for testing or quarantine) disclosure control methods other than differential privacy should be used. Researchers who intend to prevent certain types of learning about large groups, such as information that could be used to discriminate on the basis of protected group status, should be aware of limitations; while differential privacy protects information that is specific to groups consisting of a small number of individuals, the use of differential privacy alone does not provide protection against group-level inference for larger groups.

What Types of Questions, Queries, or Models Must be Supported?
In theory, with the exception of learning about individuals or small groups, differential privacy could be used to compute any form of answer for any purpose, as it is a constraint on inference, not on purpose or computation (Altman et al., 2018). And in practice, as outlined in Section 6.1.5, a large number of analyses can be performed with differential privacy guarantees.

However, there are some limitations on the current understanding of how to perform certain classes of tasks privately (e.g., the use of differential privacy in analyzing records of textual data is currently limited); how to measure the accuracy or utility of protected results; and how to optimize the privacy versus utility trade-off. Even where algorithms to perform specific calculations are known, robust software that implements these methods may not yet be available. Generally, differentially private tools limit both the *number* and *form* of analyses that are possible. Most differentially private tools that provide interactive access to data by design support a limited range of model specifications or statistical operators. For example, a particular tool may allow one to pose queries that can be expressed in terms of counts on definable subsets of the data set (which allows for contingency tables and hence fitting logistic regression models) but not to run any arbitrary statistical model. Similarly, an analyst can apply any model to a non-interactive, synthetically generated data set, but only a limited range of models will return accurate or useful results. Further, it is generally more difficult to apply differential privacy if the methods used by analysts are qualitative, unstructured, or do not lend themselves to rigorous mathematical definitions. Certain queries, such as estimating the number of individuals with specific attributes, are quite straightforward. However, in-depth data cleaning is difficult to define in a sufficiently formal way to apply differential privacy protections to the process.

Appendix C lists currently available software tools for differentially private computation. In general, these tools support a wide range of summary tabulations and summary statistics, the generation of synthetic data sets for some forms of multivariate analysis, and selected applications such as geospatial or location-based analysis. If the intended analyses fall outside of the capabilities of existing tools, one should anticipate that considerably more effort will be required to deploy an effective system in order to support such analyses. This is the case even if the core algorithms for those calculations are already known. Those following this approach should engage experts in differential privacy as part of the design and deployment process.

What is the Required Level of Accuracy? Differential privacy provides a quantifiable trade-off between privacy and utility (or accuracy). The amount of noise that differential privacy needs to introduce for a *single count query* is on the order of $1/\varepsilon$ in which ε is the privacy-loss parameter. At minimum, the data set being analyzed must have at least $1/\varepsilon$ observations to obtain meaningful results. For most analyses, however, the size of the data set must be much larger than $1/\varepsilon$ to obtain useful results, and how much larger will depend on a number of factors including how many statistics are being calculated, the complexity of the statistical model, the dimensionality of the data, and the particular differentially private algorithm being used. Thus, it is difficult to provide a rule of thumb. In practice, one can run experiments on non-sensitive synthetic or public data as a way to evaluate the accuracy of a tool or algorithm for a given application ahead of time. (Using experiments on the *sensitive* data to select an algorithm or set its parameters may leak information that violates differential privacy.)

When operating within the framework of existing tools, one should plan to test that outputs remain useful for the intended purposes. There are many different measures of utility and, even if an algorithm does a good job at trading off between utility and privacy, the utility loss for a particular use case may be quite different than the average loss.

What Is the Nature and Degree of Informational Risk to be Mitigated?

Another factor to consider when deciding whether to adopt differential privacy is the nature and degree of informational risk to be mitigated. Figure 6.4 illustrates an approach to conceptualizing whether differential privacy is a suitable control to use given different levels of harm associated with uncontrolled use of a particular data set. Some of the relevant questions to consider involve the sensitivity of the information and the potential for risks to accumulate with multiple releases of information about the same individuals or groups of individuals.

How Sensitive are the Data? When evaluating informational risk, consider the sensitivity of the information or its potential to cause harm to individuals, groups of individuals, or society at large. Generally, information should be treated as sensitive when it reveals information specific to an individual (even partially or probabilistically and possibly in combination with other information) and such inference is likely to cause significant harm to an individual, group, or society.[32] Informational harms "may occur directly as the result of a reaction of a data subject or third parties to the information, or indirectly as a result of inferences made from information" (Altman et al., 2015). Appli-

---

[32]For an extended discussion and framework for assessing information sensitivity, see Altman et al. (2015).

cable laws[33] and institutional policies[34] may provide some guidance regarding sensitivity, but data may be sensitive and have the potential to cause harm, even if the data do not include categories of information traditionally considered sensitive (Altman et al., 2015). Other key factors increasing informational risk include the number of independent attributes associated with each subject in the data, the scope of intended analytic uses, the number of individuals included in the data, and the size and diversity of the population observed (Altman et al., 2018). Risks can also grow due to characteristics related to time, such as an increase in the amount of time between collection and analysis, in the period of time over which data are collected, and in the frequency of collection (Altman et al., 2018).

Does Composition of Multiple Releases Pose a Significant Threat?
Privacy risk inevitably grows as more computations are released. Differentially private protection mechanisms have the advantage that risk composes predictably and slowly across multiple releases. In contrast, when information is released through other mechanisms, multiple releases could result in sudden and catastrophic loss of privacy.

Absent formal protection mechanisms, it is not possible to definitively assess composition risks ex ante. As general guidance, composition effects are of greatest ex ante concern under the following conditions: (a) data are collected from the same individuals by uncoordinated data controllers, (b) releases are updated frequently, (c) many releases are performed over time, (d) releases are high-dimensional, or (e) prior

---

[33] See, e.g., Regulation (EU) 2016/679 of the European Parliament and of the Council on the protection of natural persons with regard to the processing of personal data and on the free movement of such data, and repealing Directive 95/46/EC (General Data Protection Regulation) (2016) OJ L119/1, Article 9 (providing that the "[p]rocessing of personal data revealing racial or ethnic origin, political opinions, religious or philosophical beliefs, or trade union membership, and the processing of genetic data, biometric data for the purpose of uniquely identifying a natural person, data concerning health or data concerning a natural person's sex life or sexual orientation shall be prohibited," unless one of the delineated exceptions in Paragraph 2 of the Article applies).

[34] See, e.g., Harvard University Information Security, Handout—Research Data Security Levels with Examples, https://security.harvard.edu/handout-research-data-security-levels-examples (accessed 2020-12-17).

releases cannot be reliably recalled.[35]

Alternatively, if the data controller is aware of all potential auxiliary information, it could attempt to assess the cumulative privacy risk post-computation but prior to release. Or, if harm to individuals is readily detected, the data controller could purchase insurance to compensate such harm ex post. These caveats notwithstanding, in the modern information environment, composition risks are generally substantial and ex post formal protections are typically infeasible.

What Complementary and Alternative Controls are Available for Protecting the Data?

As illustrated in Figure 6.4, various controls can be complementary to differential privacy. Some examples include contractual approaches for enforcing purpose restrictions, vetting and oversight of analysts for the purpose of privacy budget allocation, and encryption and other information security restrictions on private databases, especially if now exposed to a different set of users through a publicly available differentially private interactive query mechanism. Other tools may be used as an alternative for purposes that differential privacy does not support, such as the role that access via a secure data enclave can play as part of a tiered access system.

Further, a single mode of access will generally not be appropriate for the needs of all users. Different communities of users seek answers to different questions and may have different quality and accuracy requirements even when addressing the same question. It is therefore essential to understand end user usages of inferences and their implied utility and quality criteria (as discussed in Appendix A). An analyst should take these factors into account in particular when allocating the privacy budget across analyses and when selecting the specific interactive and static publication mechanisms to be included.

Tiered access will generally be necessary to accommodate a wide range of desired uses of the data. For a given set of data, access may be made

---

[35]For discussions of how data privacy risks accumulate, see Altman et al. (2018); Fluitt et al. (2019).

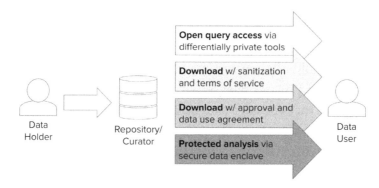

Figure 6.5: An example of a tiered access model

available to different categories of users through different modes of release. Figure 6.4 demonstrates how controls can be selected at each tier. For example, data associated with potential harms that are only minor and fleeting could be released to the public after traditional statistical disclosure limitation techniques, such as aggregation and generalization, have transformed the data. Users who seek to obtain the full data set, including direct and indirect identifiers, would be required to submit an application to an institutional review board or other oversight body, and their use would be subject to the terms of a data use agreement. This approach makes it possible to calibrate data releases to the risk profile of a data set as well as specific uses intended by different data users. Figure 6.5 provides an example of such a tiered access model (see also Sweeney, Crosas and Bar-Sinai, 2015; Crosas, 2019).

6.3.3 Regulatory and Policy Compliance

Statistical agencies, companies, researchers, and others who collect, process, analyze, store, or share data about individuals must take steps to protect the privacy of the data subjects in accordance with various laws, institutional policies, contracts, ethical codes, and best practices. In some settings, tools that satisfy differential privacy can be used to analyze and share data while both complying with legal obligations and providing strong mathematical guarantees of privacy protection for the individuals in the data (Nissim et al., 2018). Indeed, differentially private tools provide privacy protection that is more robust than that provided by techniques commonly used to satisfy regulatory requirements for privacy protection.

That said, privacy regulations and related guidance do not directly answer the question of whether the use of differentially private tools is sufficient to satisfy existing regulatory requirements for protecting privacy when sharing statistics based on personal data. This issue is complex because privacy laws are often context dependent, and there are significant gaps between differential privacy and the concepts underlying regulatory approaches to privacy protection. Different regulatory requirements are applicable depending on the jurisdiction, sector, actors, and types of information involved. As a result, data sets held by an organization may be subject to different requirements. In some cases, similar or even identical data sets may be subject to different requirements when held by different organizations. In addition, many legal standards for privacy protection are to a large extent open to interpretation and therefore require a case-specific legal analysis by an attorney.

Other challenges arise as a result of differences between the concepts appearing in privacy regulations and those underlying differential privacy. For instance, many laws focus on the presence of personally identifiable information (PII) or the ability to identify an individual's personal information in a release of records. Such concepts do not have precise definitions, and their meaning in the context of differential privacy applications are especially unclear. In addition, many privacy regulations emphasize particular requirements for protecting privacy when disclosing individual-level data, such as removing PII, which are arguably difficult to interpret and apply when releasing aggregate statistics. While in some cases it may be clear whether a regulatory standard has been met by the use of differential privacy, in other cases—particularly along the boundaries of a standard—there may be considerable uncertainty.

Regulatory requirements relevant to issues of privacy in computation rely on an understanding of a range of different concepts, such as PII, de-identification, linkage, inference, risk, consent, opt-out, and purpose and access restrictions. The definition of differential privacy can arguably be interpreted to address these concepts while accommodating differences in how they are defined across various legal and institutional contexts (Wood et al., 2018). For instance, when differential privacy is used, it can be understood as ensuring that using an individual's data will not reveal essentially any PII specific to them.[36] Differential privacy arguably addresses record linkage in the following sense. Differentially private statistics provably hide the influence of every individual (even small groups of individuals). Although linkage has not been precisely defined, linkage attacks seem to inherently result in revealing that specific individuals participated in an analysis. Because differential privacy protects against learning whether an individual participated in an analysis, it can therefore be understood to protect against linkage. Furthermore, differential privacy provides a robust guarantee of privacy protection that is independent of the auxiliary information available to an attacker. Indeed, under differential privacy, even an attacker utilizing arbitrary auxiliary information cannot learn much more about an individual in a database than they could if that individual's information were not in the database at all.

The foregoing interpretations of the differential privacy guarantee can be used to demonstrate that in many cases a differentially private mechanism would prevent the types of disclosures of personal information that privacy regulations have been designed to address. Moreover, differentially private tools often provide privacy protection that is more robust than that provided by techniques commonly used to satisfy regulatory requirements for privacy protection. However, further research is needed to develop methods for proving that differential privacy satisfies legal requirements, and setting the privacy loss parameter ε based

---

[36]Note that the reference to "using an individual's data" in this statement means the inclusion of an individual's data in an analysis, and the use of the term "specific" refers to information that is unique to the individual and cannot be inferred unless the individual's information is used in the analysis. Furthermore, the use of the word "essential" in the statement "will not reveal essentially any PII specific to them" means that, compared with an opt-out scenario where no information specific to an individual is leaked, some small leakage of such information (inevitably) occurs. The parameter ϵ bounds this leakage.

on such requirements is needed.[37] In practice, data providers should consult with legal counsel when considering whether differential privacy tools—potentially in combination with other tools for protecting privacy and security—are appropriate within their specific institutional settings.

6.4 Case Studies

Differential privacy is a relatively new concept, first presented in the theoretical computer science literature in 2006 and now seeing early stages of application in real-world settings. This section provides short case studies on three implementations of differential privacy: the 2020 Decennial Census, the Opportunity Atlas, and the Dataverse Project. This discussion focuses on describing aspects of the context in which these differentially private solutions were developed, as well as the design choices that were made with respect to the relevant contextual factors.

This selection of case studies, though limited by the small number of practical implementations of differential privacy to date, aims to reflect a range of different scenarios. The first case study involves a national statistical agency publishing statistical data products from a census, the second involves a team of researchers developing a web-based visualization tool for exploring sensitive administrative data analyzed as part of a research study, and the third describes the functionalities of a general-purpose differential privacy tool being developed for use by data providers and analysts who do not have expertise in differential privacy. Although none of these examples directly describe sharing data from sub-national agencies, they carry real-world lessons relevant to employing differential privacy in such contexts.

Each of the case studies reflects one point in the space of design factors discussed in Section 6.3 and Appendix A. These factors are summa-

---

[37]For an extended discussion of the gaps between legal and computer science definitions of privacy and a demonstration that differential privacy can be used to satisfy an institution's obligations under FERPA, see Nissim et al. (2018).

rized in Table 6.3. The remainder of this section expands upon critical features of each case and their implications.

6.4.1 The 2020 Decennial Census

In September 2017, the US Census Bureau announced its decision to deploy differential privacy in the disclosure avoidance mechanism for the 2020 Decennial Census (Garfinkel, 2017). This decision was motivated in part by the composition effects revealed by a reconstruction attack on the 2010 Census data release (see Section 6.1.2) and the confidentiality and data publication mandates that bind the US Census Bureau.[38]

In many ways, the data from the US Decennial Census is an excellent fit for differential privacy. Compared to most survey data, it is low-dimensional (i.e., only asks a few questions of each respondent) and the sample size is very large (minimizing the relative impact of the noise added for differential privacy). These features normally would allow for a straightforward application of standard differentially private algorithms (e.g., those which add independent noise to each cell of different cross-tabulations). However, there are a number of other features of the Decennial Census data products that have created challenges and debate among stakeholders over the transition to differential privacy (Garfinkel, Abowd and Powazek, 2018; Hawes, 2020; boyd, 2020).

First, these data products have a long history of being used for a vast and diverse range of applications, such as apportioning seats in the US House of Representatives, redistricting, funding allocations, provision of local emergency resources, and social science research. To minimize the impact on data users and the software they use, the Census Bureau has decided to produce differentially private data products that have the same form as the traditional products and consist of tables that are

---

[38] Specifically, the US Constitution mandates the Decennial Census (U.S. Const. art. 1, 2.), and it is carried out by the US Census Bureau, bound by Title 13 of the US Code, which prohibits Census Bureau employees from "mak[ing] any publication whereby the data furnished by any particular establishment or individual under this title can be identified" (13 U.S.C. § 9(a)(2)).

Table 6.3: Design choices in case study implementations of differential privacy

	2020 Decennial Census	The Opportunity Atlas	Dataverse repositories
Risks & Sensitivity	**Sensitivity:** Data subject to stringent statutory protections. Trust in confidentiality critical to collecting sensitive information from respondents. **Risks:** Concerns about composition effects and reconstruction attacks motivated adoption of DP.	**Sensitivity:** Data subject to stringent statutory protections. **Risks:** Prior methods of de-identification and redaction judged not to sufficiently mitigate risk.	**Sensitivity:** General-purpose system designed to support analyses of data of varying degrees of sensitivity. **Risks:** Vary by data source. DP provides stronger mechanism to mitigate risk than pre-deposit redaction and deidenfication.
Tiered Access Controls	Part of a tiered access system that has historically included custom tabulations service for institutional clients; and Research Data Centers for access by vetted individuals to private data.	Original data sources remain available to vetted users through federal Restricted Data Center mechanism.	Part of a tiered access model that also supports access to private data with vetting and restricted license.
Trust & Publication Models	Curator model, based on prior data collection design, with cleaning before DP applied. Focus on non-interactive publication of tables.	Curator model applied to previously collected data, with cleaning and linkage (between Census and IRS data) before DP-like methods applied.	Curator model, based on previously collected and deposited data. Supports both non-interactive releases of summary statistics and interactive queries.
Budget Allocation	Must allocate budget and optimize accuracy for broad range of current and future analyses.	Budget analysis focused on balancing privacy vs. societal utility, leading to choice of a rather large epsilon.	Provides recommended choices of epsilon based on sensitivity of data. Choice to allow per-analyst budgets requires semi-trusted and accountable analysts.
Estimating Uncertainty	Adopting DP has made noise addition explicit, whereas data users had previously treated Census tables as if they have no error.	Designed to produce uncertainty estimates (taking privacy noise into account) together with quantities of interest, and estimates also calculated in a DP-like manner.	Important to expose uncertainty estimates from noise due to privacy, both before and after release.
Granularity	Focused both on individuals and households, as appropriate to data measurement design	Focused on individuals.	Determined by data depositor.

exactly consistent with an underlying synthetic data set (rather than a collection of noisy statistics that would be produced by a standard differentially private algorithm), along with other information that needs to be published exactly (e.g., the state population totals). This required the design of custom differentially private algorithms by experts at the Bureau (Garfinkel, Abowd and Powazek, 2018; Abowd et al., 2019).

Second, the sources of error in the Decennial Census data products (in particular, disclosure avoidance) have historically not been made explicit and have been largely ignored by data users. Differential privacy is transparent about its noise addition and thus creates concern among stakeholders for the potential impact on their applications. Reconstruction attacks (Dinur and Nissim, 2003) tell us that the data products cannot be simultaneously accurate for all possible uses and maintain privacy, leaving the Bureau with the challenging problems of deciding which users and uses to prioritize for accuracy and then optimizing the algorithm and its privacy-loss budget allocation accordingly. To this end, the Bureau published a Federal Register Notice (Bureau of the Census, 2018) to understand what aspects of their data products were most important for data users and also released a series of demonstration products showing the impact of potential versions of their differentially private algorithms on past Decennial Censuses.[39]

Referring to some of the other design choices discussed in Appendix A, the plans for the 2020 Decennial Census are utilizing a curator model (with the US Census Bureau as the trusted curator) with a noninteractive publication model corresponding with the pre-existing data collection and dissemination design. However, historically, access to data from the Decennial Census has not been limited to the public-use products discussed above but have also been made available through other means, including a custom tabulation service for institutional clients and Federal Statistical Research Data Centers for access by vetted individuals. Thus, the planned use of differential privacy fits within an existing tiered access system. It remains to be seen whether and how

---

[39] See United States Census Bureau, https://www.census.gov/programs-surveys/decennial-census/2020-census/planning-management/2020-census-data-products/2020-das-updates.html (accessed 2020-12-17).

interactive differential privacy will play a role in subsequent accesses to data from the 2020 Census. Similar to past Census disclosure avoidance systems, the planned algorithm is to be applied after data cleaning edits are performed (Garfinkel, 2017). It will enforce privacy at the granularity of individuals as well as at the granularity of households for publications that are based on household characteristics.

Consider the application of differential privacy to the Decennial Census in contrast with another data product from the US Census Bureau— namely, the Post-Secondary Employment Outcomes (PSEO) data (Foote, Machanavajjhala and McKinney, 2019). This data product includes estimates of the cumulative distribution function of earnings for different subsets of the national student population, based on linking college transcripts with Longitudinal Employer-Household Dynamics (LEHD) data. In contrast with the Decennial Census products, this was a new product first released in 2018, so there was no history of entrenched data use that constrained the form of the data release. As a result, it was possible to employ standard differentially private algorithms (namely, binning the earnings within each subset and adding noise to the counts in each bin). Note that the linking of transcript data with LEHD data is done prior to the application of the differentially private algorithm. The PSEO release used a privacy-loss parameter of $\varepsilon = 1.5$ (US Census Bureau Center for Economic Studies, n.d.).

6.4.2 The Opportunity Atlas

[Margin note: Look of δ include]

The Opportunity Atlas is a web-based visualization tool for exploring social mobility data. It was published as the result of a collaboration between the US Census Bureau, Harvard University, and Brown University (Chetty et al., 2018). The database contains data relevant to understanding children's economic outcomes in adulthood for every Census tract in the United States. Researchers and policymakers can use the Opportunity Atlas to understand how individuals' prosperity or poverty is rooted in the neighborhoods in which they grew up and how interventions can be targeted in certain neighborhoods to help more children rise out of poverty.

The Opportunity Atlas is based on data about over 20 million children and their parents, compiled from multiple statistical and administrative data sources. Census data sources include the 2000 and 2010 Decennial Censuses and the American Community Survey. Administrative data sources included de-identified data from IRS income tax returns and data on students receiving Federal Pell Grants, obtained from the US Department of Education's National Student Loan Data System.

Raj Chetty and John Friedman, Director and Co-Director of the Opportunity Insights research team, respectively, developed the privacy protection mechanism for the Opportunity Atlas in consultation with the US Census Bureau and the Harvard University Privacy Tools Project (Chetty and Friedman, 2019). Consistent with the US Census Bureau's broader efforts to modernize its approach to disclosure limitation (as discussed in Section 6.4.1) and the legal protections for both Census and IRS data,[40] the Opportunity Atlas was produced using a method inspired by differential privacy.

Linkage, analysis, and disclosure avoidance were performed in Census facilities. There was a single set of analyses to perform to generate the Opportunity Atlas, and a privacy budget was not reserved for future analyses. They ran simple linear regressions on the data from the Census Bureau and IRS in order to predict child income rank from parent income rank in each Census tract, broken down by race, gender, and other variables. This created challenges for a differentially private solution, as the sample sizes were small (on the order of tens, hundreds, and thousands), and there was sometimes a very small variance in the explanatory variable. However, despite these challenges, the Opportunity Atlas achieved good results using a differential privacy–inspired method. In terms of accuracy, this approach performed better than

---

[40]The raw data from the Census Bureau is protected by Title 13 of the United States Code, which prohibits "mak[ing] any publication whereby the data furnished by any particular establishment or individual under this title can be identified" (13 U.S.C. § 9(a)(2)). Pursuant to Title 26, the IRS shares federal tax returns and return information with the Census Bureau for statistical purposes, and the Census Bureau is prohibited from disclosing such tax return information except in "a form which cannot be associated with, or otherwise identify, directly or indirectly, a particular taxpayer" (26 U.S.C. 6103(j)(4)).

some traditional statistical disclosure limitation techniques. Indeed, the researchers found that traditional count suppression would have caused them to miss strong relationships that relied on small counts (e.g., between teenage birth rates for black women and the proportion of single parents in Census tracts) (Chetty and Friedman, 2019). The Opportunity Atlas also includes uncertainty estimates (standard errors), which are also calculated in a differential privacy–inspired manner.

Chetty and Friedman suggest selecting the privacy-loss parameter (ε) using the framework of Abowd and Schmutte (Abowd and Schmutte, 2019), equating the marginal societal benefit of increased accuracy with the marginal cost due to reduced privacy. Given the small sample sizes of the Opportunity Atlas and the importance of accurate data for policymaking, the Opportunity Atlas used (with approval of the Census Bureau Disclosure Review Board) a value of ε that is significantly larger than is typically considered in the differential privacy literature. Specifically, they used $\varepsilon = 8$ for each of several statistics published for each demographic group within a tract.

The Chetty-Friedman method is a general technique, in that it applies to many different statistical estimators (not just simple linear regression). However, it is not formally differentially private, and its privacy properties rely on the same analysis being carried out on many different cells (e.g., many Census tracts as in the Opportunity Atlas). For the specific case of simple linear regression, subsequent work has developed formally differentially private methods that are competitive with the Chetty-Friedman method, and thus may be applied even to releases that do not have the cell structure of the Opportunity Atlas (Alabi et al., 2020).

6.4.3 Dataverse Repositories

The Harvard University Privacy Tools Project[41] and the OpenDP initiative[42] have been developing a vision for how differential privacy can be incorporated into research data repositories like Dataverse, ICPSR, and Dryad to help human-subjects researchers safely share and analyze sensitive data (Gaboardi et al., 2016; The OpenDP Team, 2020). Although these solutions have not yet been deployed at the time of this Handbook, software to support the projects are under active construction and may be available for use in the near future. Thus, this section outlines how differential privacy might fit into some of the ways that research data repositories are used, employing a lightly edited extract from the OpenDP whitepaper (The OpenDP Team, 2020). For concreteness, the text is written as specific to using OpenDP software in Dataverse repositories but can be generalized to other repositories and underlying differential privacy software.

Dataverse (King, 2007; Crosas, 2011, 2013; King, 2014), developed at Harvard's Institute for Quantitative Social Science (IQSS) in 2006, enables researchers to share their data sets with the research community through an easy-to-use, customizable web interface, keeping control of, and gaining credit for, their data while the underlying infrastructure provides robust support for good data archival and management practices. Dataverse has been installed and serves as a research data repository in more than fifty institutions worldwide.

Dataverse repositories (like most general-purpose data repositories) currently have little support for hosting privacy-sensitive data. Data sets with sensitive information about human subjects were supposed to be "de-identified" before deposit. Unfortunately, as discussed in Section 6.1.2, research in data privacy starting with (Sweeney, 1997) has demonstrated convincingly that traditional de-identification does not provide effective privacy protection. The current alternative to open data sharing in repositories is that researchers depositing a data set (*data depositors*) declare their data set restricted: the data set would

---

[41]Harvard University Privacy Tools Project, http://privacytools.seas.harvard.edu (accessed 2020-12-17).

[42]OpenDP, http://opendp.io/ (accessed 2020-12-17).

not be made available for download, and the only way for other researchers to obtain access would be through contacting the data depositor and negotiating terms on an ad hoc basis. This approach is also unsatisfactory, as it can require the continued involvement of the data depositor, the negotiations can often take months, and thus it impedes the ability of the research community to verify, replicate, and extend work done by others.

OpenDP can enable Dataverse to offer additional ways to access sensitive data as illustrated by the following use cases.

1. Enabling variable search and exploration of sensitive data sets deposited in the repository

Dataverse already automatically calculates variable summary statistics (counts, min/max, means, etc.) when a tabular file is deposited. These summary statistics for each variable can be viewed using the Data Explorer tool, even without downloading or accessing the data file. As OpenDP is integrated with Dataverse, a data depositor should be able to generate a differentially private (DP) summary statistics metadata file using an OpenDP user interface. To do this, the data depositor would select "Generate DP Summary Statistics" after the tabular data file is ingested in Dataverse, launching the OpenDP interface. Then they would select the privacy-loss parameter for their data file, and OpenDP would create the differentially private summary statistics file and Dataverse would store the newly created metadata file associated with the sensitive tabular data file. Once the data set is published, an end user would be able to view the summary statistics of the sensitive data file using the Data Explorer tool without ever accessing or downloading the actual data file.

2. Facilitating reproducibility of research with sensitive data sets

At least a third of the data sets deposited in Dataverse are replication data and code associated with a published scholarly paper. With OpenDP, data depositors or owners could create a differentially private release on a sensitive data set, which could be used to computationally reproduce the results of the published paper while protecting the privacy of the original data set. In this case, like in Use Case 1 above, a data depositor would select a privacy-loss parameter through the OpenDP user interface and use OpenDP's statistical query interface to select and run the statistics of choice to create the appropriate replication release. The differentially private replication release file would be made available in the data set and end users would be able to download it, while the original sensitive data set would be protected and not accessible by end users except through the existing processes as above.

3. Enable statistical analysis of sensitive data sets accessible through the repository

For additional flexibility, the data depositor of a sensitive data set could allow for any researcher (end user) to be able to run any statistic available through the OpenDP interface. In this case, the data depositor would configure the allocation of privacy-loss budgets through the OpenDP interface before releasing the data set. Once the data set is published, an end user would be able to click "explore" for the sensitive data file, and the OpenDP statistical query interface would open. The user would not have access to the original sensitive data file but would be able to run the statistics of their choice—up to the point that the established privacy-loss budget allows.

Referring to some of the other design choices discussed in Appendix A, the vision outlined above fits into the curator model of differential privacy, as researchers depositing data in the repository have typically already been trusted to collect the sensitive data. It is part of a tiered access model meant to augment rather than replace the existing methods of accessing restricted data. Use Cases 1 and 2 involve noninteractive releases, whereas Use Case 3 allows for interactive queries. Many of the other key choices associated with implementing differential privacy are left to the data depositor, who cannot be expected to have expertise in differential privacy. Thus, the software tools must provide a clear user interface to guide the depositor in their decisions. There should be a tutorial on the concepts of privacy loss, privacy–accuracy trade-offs, and budgeting, including recommended choices of privacy-loss parameter ε according to different categories of data and sensitivity. The depositor should also be guided in defining the granularity of privacy appropriate for their data and the trade-offs between offering per-analyst budgets for interactive queries versus a global budget for all queries. Domain knowledge will be required of the depositor (and the analyst in Use Case 3) in deciding which statistics to release and which ones to prioritize for accuracy. For the research use cases described above, it will be important that the differentially private analyses offered provide uncertainty estimates whenever possible.

About the Authors

Micah Altman is a social and information scientist at MIT's Center for Research in Equitable and Open Scholarship. Dr. Altman conducts research in social science, information science and research methods – focusing on the intersections of information, technology, privacy, and politics; and on the dissemination, preservation, reliability, and governance of scientific knowledge. Dr. Altman has authored over 100 scholarly works. This work has been recognized with the Pizzigati Prize from the Tides Foundation, the Brown Democracy Award, awards from professional organizations, citations by the U.S. Supreme Court, and coverage by numerous local and national media organizations.

Kobbi Nissim is McDevitt Chair in the department of Computer Science, Georgetown University and affiliated with Georgetown Law. Nissim's work is focused on the mathematical formulation and understanding of privacy. His work from 2003 and 2004 with Dinur and Dwork initiated rigorous foundational research of privacy and in 2006 he introduced differential privacy with Dwork, McSherry and Smith. Nissim was awarded the Caspar Bowden Award for Outstanding Research in Privacy Enhancing Technologies in 2019, the Gödel Prize In 2017, the IACR TCC Test of Time Award in 2016 and in 2018, and the ACM PODS Alberto O. Mendelzon Test-of-Time Award in 2013.

Salil Vadhan is the Vicky Joseph Professor of Computer Science and Applied Mathematics at the Harvard John A. Paulson School of Engineering & Applied Sciences. He is Lead PI on the Harvard Privacy Tools Project and Co-director of the OpenDP software project. Vadhan's research in theoretical computer science spans computational complexity, cryptography, and data privacy. His honors include a Harvard College Professorship, a Simons Investigator Award, a Guggenheim Fellowship, and a Gödel Prize.

Alexandra Wood is a fellow at the Berkman Klein Center for Internet & Society at Harvard University and a senior researcher contributing to the Harvard Privacy Tools Project. Her research explores new and existing regulatory frameworks for data privacy and their relationship to approaches to privacy emerging from other fields. She also contributes to the development of new legal instruments, analytical frameworks, and policy recommendations to better support the sharing and use of research data while preserving privacy, utility, transparency, and accountability. She currently serves as an advisory board member for the Privacy Engineering Section of the International Association of Privacy Professionals and in 2019 she received the Caspar Bowden PET Award for Outstanding Research in Privacy Enhancing Technologies.

Disclaimer

Any opinions, findings, and conclusions or recommendations expressed in this material are those of the authors and do not necessarily reflect the views of their funders.

Acknowledgements

Work of Kobbi Nissim, Salil Vadhan, and Alexandra Wood was partially supported by the US Census Bureau under cooperative agreement No. CB16ADR0160001. Salil Vadhan was also partially supported by a Simons Investigator Award. The authors thank their coauthors on those papers, as well as Jean-François Couchot and Jean-Marc Gervais for their inquiries that led us to uncover a mistake in the calculation of Table 6.1; Mercè Crosas, Raj Chetty, and John Friedman for their comments on the case studies; Marco Gaboardi and Michael Hay for help with software tools; and Simson Garfinkel, Steven Glazerman, Michel José Reymond, Jayshree Sarathy, Anja Sautmann, Lars Vilhuber, and the members of the Bridging Privacy Definitions Working Group for their review comments on earlier drafts.

References in Chapter 6

Abadi, Martín, Andy Chu, Ian J. Goodfellow, H. Brendan McMahan, Ilya Mironov, Kunal Talwar, and Li Zhang. 2016. "Deep learning with differential privacy." 308–318. ACM. https://doi.org/10.1145/2976749.2978318.

Abowd, John. 2019. "Stepping-up: The Census Bureau Tries to Be a Good Data Steward in the 21st Century, presentation at the simons institute for the theory of computing." https://simons.berkeley.edu/talks/tba-30.

Abowd, John M., and Ian M. Schmutte. 2019. "An Economic Analysis of Privacy Protection and Statistical Accuracy as Social Choices." *American Economic Review*, 109(1): 171–202. https://doi.org/10.1257/aer.20170627.

Abowd, John, Robert Ashmead, Simson Garfinkel, Dan Kifer, Philip LeClerc, Ashwin Machanavajjhala, Brett Moran, William Sexton, and Pavel Zhuravlev. 2019. "Census TopDown algorithm: Differentially private data, incremental schemas, and consistency with public knowledge." https://github.com/uscensusbureau/census2020-das-2010ddp/blob/master/doc/20191020_1843_Consistency_for_Large_Scale_Differentially_Private_Histograms.pdf.

Aktay, Ahmet, Shailesh Bavadekar, Gwen Cossoul, John Davis, Damien Desfontaines, Alex Fabrikant, Evgeniy Gabrilovich, Krishna Gadepalli, Bryant Gipson, Miguel Guevara, Chaitanya Kamath, Mansi Kansal, Ali Lange, Chinmoy Mandayam, Andrew Oplinger, Christopher Pluntke, Thomas Roessler, Arran Schlosberg, Tomer Shekel, Swapnil Vispute, Mia Vu, Gregory Wellenius, Brian Williams, and Royce J Wilson. 2020. "Google COVID-19 community mobility reports: Anonymization process description (version 1.0)." https://arxiv.org/abs/2004.04145v1.

Alabi, Daniel, Audra McMillan, Jayshree Sarathy, Adam Smith, and Salil Vadhan. 2020. "Differentially private simple linear regression." https://arxiv.org/abs/2007.05157.

Altman, Micah, Alexandra Wood, David O'Brien, Salil Vadhan, and Urs Gasser. 2015. "Towards a Modern Approach to Privacy-Aware Government Data Releases." *Berkeley Technology and Law Journal*, 1967. https://doi.org/10.2139/ssrn.2779266.

Altman, Micah, Alexandra Wood, David R O'Brien, and Urs Gasser. 2018. "Practical approaches to big data privacy over time." *International Data Privacy Law*, 8(1): 29–51. https://doi.org/10.1093/idpl/ipx027.

Blum, Avrim, Cynthia Dwork, Frank McSherry, and Kobbi Nissim. 2005. "Practical privacy: the SuLQ framework." 128–138. ACM. https://doi.org/10.1145/1065167.1065184.

Blum, Avrim, Katrina Ligett, and Aaron Roth. 2013. "A learning theory approach to noninteractive database privacy." *Journal of the ACM*, 60(2): 12:1–12:25. https://doi.org/10.1145/2450142.2450148.

boyd, danah. 2020. "Balancing data utility and confidentiality in the 2020 US Census." Data & Society. https://datasociety.net/library/balancing-data-utility-and-confidentiality-in-the-2020-us-census/ (accessed 2020-12-15).

Bun, Mark, Kobbi Nissim, Uri Stemmer, and Salil Vadhan. 2015. "Differentially Private Release and Learning of Threshold Functions." *IEEE Computer Society*. https://doi.org/10.1109/FOCS.2015.45.

Bureau of the Census, Department of Commerce. 2018. "Soliciting feedback from users on 2020 census data products." *Federal Register*, 83(139). https://www.federalregister.gov/documents/2018/07/19/2018-15458/soliciting-feedback-from-users-on-2020-census-data-products.

Calandrino, Joseph A., Ann Kilzer, Arvind Narayanan, Edward W. Felten, and Vitaly Shmatikov. 2011. ""You Might Also Like:" privacy risks of collaborative filtering." 231–246. IEEE Computer Society. https://doi.org/10.1109/SP.2011.40.

Chen, Bee-Chung, Daniel Kifer, Kristen LeFevre, and Ashwin Machanavajjhala. 2009. "Privacy-preserving data publishing." *Foundations and Trends® in Databases*, 2(1–2): 1–167. https://doi.org/10.1561/1900000008.

Chetty, Raj, and John N. Friedman. 2019. "A Practical Method to Reduce Privacy Loss When Disclosing Statistics Based on Small Samples." *Journal of Privacy and Confidentiality*, 9(2). https://doi.org/10.29012/jpc.716.

Chetty, Raj, John N. Friedman, Nathaniel Hendren, Maggie R. Jones, and Sonya R. Porter. 2018. "The Opportunity Atlas: Mapping the Childhood Roots of Social Mobility." National Bureau of Economic Research Working Paper 25147, https://doi.org/10.3386/w25147.

Crosas, Mercè. 2011. "The Dataverse Network®: An Open-Source Application for Sharing, Discovering and Preserving Data." *D-lib Magazine*, 17(1): 2. https://doi.org/10.1045/january2011-crosas.

Crosas, Mercè. 2013. "A Data Sharing Story." *Journal of eScience Librarianship*, 1(3): 7. https://doi.org/10.7191/jeslib.2012.1020.

Crosas, Mercè. 2019. "Dataverse, DataTags, and a decade building a widely-used data repository platform." https://securelysharingdata.com/whitepapers.html (accessed 2020-12-15).

de Montjoye, Yves-Alexandre, César A. Hidalgo, Michel Verleysen, and Vincent D. Blondel. 2013. "Unique in the Crowd: The privacy bounds of human mobility." *Scientific Reports*, 3(1): 1376. https://doi.org/10.1038/srep01376.

Desai, Tanvi, Felix Ritchie, and Richard Welpton. 2016. "Five Safes: Designing data access for research." https://uwe-repository.worktribe.com/output/914745 (accessed 2020-01-30).

Dinur, Irit, and Kobbi Nissim. 2003. "Revealing information while preserving privacy." 202–210. ACM. https://doi.org/10.1145/773153.773173.

Dwork, Cynthia, Adam Smith, Thomas Steinke, and Jonathan Ullman. 2017. "Exposed! A survey of attacks on private data." *Annual Review of Statistics and Its Application*, 4(1): 61–84. https://doi.org/10.1146/annurev-statistics-060116-054123.

Dwork, Cynthia, and Aaron Roth. 2014. "The algorithmic foundations of differential privacy." *Foundations and Trends® in Theoretical Computer Science*, 9(3-4): 211–407. https://doi.org/10.1561/0400000042.

Dwork, Cynthia, Frank McSherry, Kobbi Nissim, and Adam D. Smith. 2016. "Calibrating noise to sensitivity in private data analysis." *Journal of Privacy and Confiden-*

tiality, 7(3): 17–51. https://doi.org/10.29012/jpc.v7i3.405.

Dwork, Cynthia, Nitin Kohli, and Deirdre Mulligan. 2019. "Differential privacy in practice: Expose your epsilons!" *Journal of Privacy and Confidentiality*, 9(2). https://doi.org/10.29012/jpc.689.

Fluitt, Aaron, Aloni Cohen, Micah Altman, Kobbi Nissim, Salome Viljoen, and Alexandra Wood. 2019. "Data protection's composition problem." *European Data Protection Law Review*, 5(3). https://doi.org/10.21552/edpl/2019/3/4.

Foote, Andrew David, Ashwin Machanavajjhala, and Kevin McKinney. 2019. "Releasing earnings distributions using differential privacy: Disclosure avoidance system for post-secondary employment outcomes (PSEO)." *Journal of Privacy and Confidentiality*, 9(2). https://doi.org/10.29012/jpc.722.

Gaboardi, Marco, James Honaker, Gary King, Kobbi Nissim, Jonathan Ullman, and Salil P. Vadhan. 2016. "PSI (ψ): a private data sharing interface." *CoRR*, abs/1609.04340. http://arxiv.org/abs/1609.04340.

Ganta, Srivatsava Ranjit, Shiva Prasad Kasiviswanathan, and Adam D. Smith. 2008. "Composition attacks and auxiliary information in data privacy." 265–273. ACM. https://doi.org/10.1145/1401890.1401926.

Garfinkel, Simson. 2016. "De-Identifying Government Datasets (2nd Draft)." National Institute of Standards and Technology NIST Special Publication (SP) 800-188 (Draft). https://csrc.nist.gov/publications/detail/sp/800-188/draft (accessed 2021-02-01).

Garfinkel, Simson L. 2017. "Modernizing disclosure avoidance: Report on the 2020 disclosure avoidance subsystem as implemented for the 2018 end-to-end test (continued)." https://www2.census.gov/cac/sac/meetings/2017-09/garfinkel-modernizing-disclosure-avoidance.pdf (accessed 2020-12-15).

Garfinkel, Simson L., John M. Abowd, and Christian Martindale. 2019. "Understanding database reconstruction attacks on public data." *Communications of the ACM*, 62(3): 46–53. https://doi.org/10.1145/3287287.

Garfinkel, Simson L., John M. Abowd, and Sarah Powazek. 2018. "Issues encountered deploying differential privacy." *WPES'18*, 133–137. New York, NY, USA:Association for Computing Machinery. https://doi.org/10.1145/3267323.3268949.

Harris-Kojetin, Brian A., Wendy L. Alvey, Lynda Carlson, Steven B. Cohen, Steve H. Cohen, Lawrence H. Cox, Robert E. Fay, Ronald Fecso, Dennis Fixler, Gerald Gates, Barry Graubard, William Iwig, Arthur Kennickell, Nancy J. Kirkendall, Susan Schechter, Rolf R. Schmitt, Marilyn Seastrom, Monroe G. Sirken, Nancy L. Spruill, Clyde Tucker, Alan R. Tupek, G. David Williamson, and Robert Groves. 2005. "Statistical Policy Working Paper 22: Report on Statistical Disclosure Limitation Methodology." U.S. Federal Committee on Statistical Methodology Research Report. https://nces.ed.gov/FCSM/pdf/spwp22.pdf (accessed 2020-12-15).

Hawes, Michael B. 2020. "Implementing differential privacy: Seven lessons from the 2020 United States Census." *Harvard Data Science Review*, 2(2). https://doi.org/10.1162/99608f92.353c6f99.

Kasiviswanathan, Shiva Prasad, Homin K. Lee, Kobbi Nissim, Sofya Raskhodnikova, and Adam D. Smith. 2011. "What can we learn privately?" *SIAM Journal on Computing*, 40(3): 793–826. https://doi.org/10.1137/090756090.

Kenthapadi, Krishnaram, Nina Mishra, and Kobbi Nissim. 2013. "Denials leak information: Simulatable auditing." *Journal of Computer and System Sciences*, 79(8): 1322–1340. https://doi.org/10.1016/j.jcss.2013.06.004.

King, Gary. 2007. "An introduction to the dataverse network as an infrastructure for data sharing." *Sociological Methods & Research*, 36(2): 173–199. https://doi.org/10.1177/0049124107306660.

King, Gary. 2014. "Restructuring the Social Sciences: Reflections from Harvard's Institute for Quantitative Social Science." *PS: Political Science & Politics*, 47(1): 165–172. https://doi.org/10.1017/S1049096513001534.

Machanavajjhala, Ashwin, and Daniel Kifer. 2015. "Designing statistical privacy for your data." *Communications of the ACM*, 58(3): 58–67. https://doi.org/10.1145/2660766.

Muise, Daniel, and Kobbi Nissim. 2016. "Differential Privacy in CDFs." Harvard University Presentation. https://privacytools.seas.harvard.edu/files/dpcdf_user_manual_aug_2016.pdf (accessed 2020-12-15).

Narayanan, Arvind, and Vitaly Shmatikov. 2008. "Robust de-anonymization of large sparse datasets." 111–125. IEEE Computer Society. https://doi.org/10.1109/SP.2008.33.

Narayanan, Arvind, Joanna Huey, and Edward W. Felten. 2016. "A Precautionary Approach to Big Data Privacy." In *Data Protection on the Move*. Vol. 24, , ed. Serge Gutwirth, Ronald Leenes and Paul De Hert, 357–385. Dordrecht:Springer Netherlands. https://doi.org/10.1007/978-94-017-7376-8_13.

Nissim, Kobbi, Aaron Bembenek, Alexandra Wood, Mark Bun, Marco Gaboardi, Urs Gasser, David R O'Brien, Thomas Steinke, and Salil Vadhan. 2018. "Bridging the gap between computer science and legal approaches to privacy." *Harvard Journal of Law & Technology*, 31(2): 687–780. https://privacytools.seas.harvard.edu/publications/bridging-gap-between-computer-science-and-legal-approaches-privacy.

Ramachandran, Aditi, Lisa Singh, Edward Porter, and Frank Nagle. 2012. "Exploring re-identification risks in public domains." 35–42. https://doi.org/10.1109/PST.2012.6297917.

Stemmer, Uri, and Haim Kaplan. 2018. "Differentially private k-Means with constant multiplicative error." 5436–5446. http://papers.nips.cc/paper/7788-differentially-private-k-means-with-constant-multiplicative-error.

Sweeney, Latanya. 1997. "Weaving technology and policy together to maintain confidentiality." *The Journal of Law, Medicine & Ethics*, 25(2-3): 98–110. https://doi.org/10.1111/j.1748-720X.1997.tb01885.x.

Sweeney, Latanya, Mercè Crosas, and Michael Bar-Sinai. 2015. "Sharing Sensitive Data with Confidence: The Datatags System." *Journal of Technology Science*. https://techscience.org/a/2015101601/ (accessed 2020-12-15).

The OpenDP Team. 2020. "The OpenDP white paper." https://projects.iq.harvard.edu/files/opendp/files/opendp_white_paper_11may2020.pdf (accessed 2020-12-15).

The Statutes at Large of the United States of America. 1909. "An Act To provide for the Thirteenth and subsequent decennial censuses." Public Law 61-2. https://www.loc.gov/law/help/statutes-at-large/61st-congress/c61.pdf.

US Census Bureau Center for Economic Studies. n.d.. "US Census Bureau Center for Economic Studies Publications and Reports Page." https://lehd.ces.census.gov/data/pseo_experimental.html (accessed 2020-12-16).

US Social Security Administration. 2011. "Actuarial Life Table: Period Life Table." http://www.ssa.gov/oact/STATS/table4c6.html (accessed 2020-12-15).

Wang, Yu-Xiang. 2018. "Revisiting differentially private linear regression: optimal and adaptive prediction & estimation in unbounded domain." 93–103. AUAI Press. http://auai.org/uai2018/proceedings/papers/40.pdf (accessed 2020-12-15).

Willenborg, Leon, and Ton De Waal. 1996. *Statistical disclosure control in practice.* Vol. 111, Springer Science & Business Media.

Wood, Alexandra, Micah Altman, Aaron Bembenek, Mark Bun, Marco Gaboardi, James Honaker, Kobbi Nissim, David R. O'Brien, Thomas Steinke, and Salil Vadhan. 2018. "Differential Privacy: A Primer for a Non-Technical Audience." *Vanderbilt Journal of Entertainment and Technology Law*, 21(1). http://www.jetlaw.org/journal-archives/volume-21/volume-21-issue-1/differential-privacy-a-primer-for-a-non-technical-audience/ (accessed 2019-04-23).

Appendix

A discussion of different technical approaches to disseminating data with differential privacy and key design choices, the implications of differential privacy for data collection, use, and dissemination, and a list of selected tools and resources for implementing differential privacy protections can be found in the Online Appendix at admindatahandbook.mit.edu/book/v1.0/diffpriv.html#diffpriv-appendix

Case Studies

CHAPTER 7

Institute for Employment Research, Germany: International Access to Labor Market Data

Dana Müller (Institute for Employment Research)
Philipp vom Berge (Institute for Employment Research)

7.1 Summary

This chapter describes the Research-Data-Center in Research-Data-Center (RDC-in-RDC) approach, which is a project that implemented decentralized data access to confidential German labor market data provided by the Research Data Center at the Institute for Employment Research (RDC-IAB)[1] in Nuremberg, Germany via data access points at collaborating research data centers (RDC), research institutes, and universities. RDC-in-RDC improves data access for researchers who want to work with confidential data but are unable to come to

---

Copyright © Dana Müller and Philipp vom Berge.
Cite as: Müller, Dana, and Philipp vom Berge. "Institute for Employment Research, Germany: International Access to Labor Market Data." In: Cole, Shawn, Iqbal Dhaliwal, Anja Sautmann, and Lars Vilhuber (eds.), *Handbook on Using Administrative Data for Research and Evidence-based Policy*. Cambridge, MA: Abdul Latif Jameel Poverty Action Lab. 2020.
[1] https://fdz.iab.de (accessed 2020-06-15).

CHAPTER 7

Nuremberg to work with the data on-site. The project started in 2010 and was funded by the German Federal Ministry of Education and Research (BMBF). The chapter covers the challenges involved in developing standardized procedures in an international context in order to ensure user-friendly and sustainable data access in compliance with legal requirements.

The RDC-IAB, founded in 2004, is a research department of the Institute for Employment Research (IAB), which belongs to the Federal Employment Agency (BA) of Germany. The RDC-IAB has three core functions: creating standardized research data for the scientific community, providing access to these data, and conducting research with and about IAB data. Various kinds of standardized labor market data are provided by the RDC-IAB. Administrative research data are based on the notification procedure of the German Social Security System and process-generated data are based on the BA. Additionally, surveys conducted by the IAB or partner institutes become part of the data portfolio. Furthermore, linked data between surveys and administrative data are produced. All data products are specifically created for the purpose of allowing external researchers access to the data. Different data access modalities with varying degrees of data anonymization balance analytical flexibility on the one hand with access restrictions on the other. The data provided by the RDC-IAB are used both for labor market research in general as well as for the evaluation of specific labor market policies. The main services of the RDC-IAB are funded by the staff budget of the BA and provided free of charge to the research community. However, the RDC-IAB raises third-party funds to generate new innovative data products, infrastructure projects, and research projects. Currently, nearly half of the 26 employees working at the RDC-IAB are financed by third-party funded projects.

Improving access to data for the research community is a joint task. On the national level, the RDC-IAB is in regular exchange with other RDCs through the national network organized by the German Data Forum (RatSWD). On the international level, cooperation takes place within the framework of the International Data Access Network (IDAN).

The authors of this chapter were not directly involved in the initiation of the RDC-in-RDC project and its early implementation. However, they were responsible for its further expansion and sustainability since 2016. With this case study, the authors encourage institutions with confidential administrative data to find similar ways to broaden access for the international research community.

7.2 Introduction

7.2.1 Motivation and Background

RDC-IAB is the RDC of the IAB in Nuremberg, Germany. One of its core functions is the provision of access to various surveys and administrative data products for external researchers who want to conduct labor market research. Improving data access through the RDC-IAB for external researchers (i.e., not employed by the IAB) provides benefits beyond those to the scientific community. A larger, more vibrant research community increases the amount of scientific output, improves the understanding of labor markets, and therefore ultimately benefits the BA and other policymakers.

This section will outline the RDC-IAB project RDC-in-RDC approach. The project goal was to improve data access for the domestic and international scientific community. Additionally, because Germany was lagging behind other countries such as Denmark and Finland in remote access due to national data protection legislation, this approach also helped to close some of the gap to countries with existing remote access systems (Bender and Heining, 2011; Wirth et al., 2019). The project started in October 2010 and was funded by the BMBF with the aim to implement decentralized, on-site data access within RDCs. The budget was €1 million over three years with an interim evaluation. The project was realized as a part of a continuous effort to expand and improve the services already provided by RDC-IAB. Later sections in this chapter discuss more of the institutional and legal background of the operation of RDC-IAB as well as provide an overview of the various data products and data access modalities. These sections aim to put the scope, challenges, and achievements of the project into perspective.

While establishing the RDC-IAB in 2004 significantly improved data access possibilities for the research community, there were still major obstacles. Access to restricted micro data via on-site use was only possible in Nuremberg at the RDC-IAB itself, which led to high opportunity costs for researchers living far away. For international researchers, the language barrier, contractual hurdles, and the long distances were often prohibitive. Since scientific discourse, however, thrives the most when the community is large, the RDC-IAB tried to overcome these obstacles.

The basic idea for the RDC-in-RDC approach is that researchers get data access that is similar to the on-site use at the RDC-IAB in Nuremberg but at a different data access point located in a guest RDC. This approach requires a clear delineation of tasks and responsibilities between the RDC-IAB and the guest RDC. The guest RDC must fulfill the same security criteria as the RDC-IAB, which means a safe room with restricted entry and regular monitoring. Furthermore, the workspace must be protected and other users must not easily be able to observe the screen of the access device. The guest RDC only needs to provide a network point for internet connection. All other access responsibilities reside with the RDC-IAB. With the internet connection, a secure, remote, desktop connection between a thin-client computer (which is optimized for server-based computing) in the safe room and the server at the RDC-IAB in Nuremberg is established. Staff members at the guest RDC do not have data access. They are responsible for ensuring data confidentiality using organizational and technical measures, which are regulated in a contractual agreement between the RDC-IAB and the guest RDC.

The thin-clients used for data access are initially provided by the RDC-IAB and are configured before they are sent to the guest RDC. The thin-client is the user interface utilized to establish an encrypted connection to the server at the RDC-IAB using the Access Gateway software by Citrix. Therefore, it is equipped with a limited amount of hardware and software. The thin-client solution ensures that data are neither stored nor processed at the guest RDC and makes it impossible for data users to remove data or output files at any time. All tasks regarding requests for data access, data use agreements (DUAs), administration of users, administration of the RDC-IAB server, and disclosure control is undertaken by the RDC-IAB. Since 2018, guest RDCs can also use their own hardware instead of a thin-client as long as certain client specifications are met.

The RDC-in-RDC project required coordination of different departments of the BA and IAB as well as different departments of the guest RDCs. First, the technical solution was conceptualized with the colleagues of different IT departments at the BA and the Data and IT Management department of the IAB. It was necessary to include a third-party company to conduct hardware checks and shipping of the thin-clients. Including a third-party company required a tender to be executed by the purchasing department of the BA. The IT departments implemented the final technical concept. Second, administrative matters were discussed with support of the legal advisory departments of the IAB and the guest RDCs before the collaboration contracts between the RDC-IAB and guest RDCs were established. In addition, the standardized DUA had to be expanded to allow data access within secure rooms of other collaborating RDCs. A data sharing arrangement with the guest RDCs was not necessary since the research data do not get transferred.

Five data access points were established in Germany at several guest RDCs of the Statistical Offices of the Federal States (Berlin, Bremen, Düsseldorf, Dresden) and at the University of Applied Labour Studies of the BA in Mannheim in 2011 and 2012. The goal was to achieve a good spatial coverage in Germany and to reduce travel times for external researchers. The first data access point abroad was established at the Institute for Social Research (ISR) of the University of Michigan in Ann Arbor, Michigan, US in 2011. This guest RDC was selected both because of the importance of ISR for social science research in the US and good relationships with the ISR faculty.

The implementation of the data access point at ISR was more difficult in comparison to the German data access points. First, a collaboration contract in English with specifications regarding the German and US legal system required an intensive exchange between the legal departments and the RDC-IAB contact person. Second, because of the legal framework, only de-facto anonymized data are accessible from the United States.[2] An RDC-IAB staff member, who was funded by the project, generated individual de-facto anonymized data sets for each approved project. ISR provided support for this staff member to work on-site at ISR enabling quick progress of the project and on-site resolutions of all IT and legal matters. It was therefore possible to inform students, PhD students, and interested researchers about the possibility of using German labor market data quickly and extensively. Furthermore, this personal contact made it easier to communicate with other interested universities such as Cornell University, Princeton University and the University of California, Berkeley, who later obtained their own RDC-in-RDC on-site locations.

After the termination of the original RDC-in-RDC project, follow-up funding was raised from the National Science Foundation (US) under program SES-1326365 and as part of the project Data without Boundaries within the Seventh Framework Programme of the European Union (Heining and Bender, 2012). Based on the funding, it was possible to keep one staff member of the RDC-IAB on-site at ISR to assist researchers accessing the RDC-IAB data there. The on-site staff member was employed at both IAB and ISR. The second funding source enabled the RDC-IAB to be part of the initiative to improve data access within Europe.

When the follow-up projects ended, the operation of the successful data access points was transferred to the regular work routines of the RDC-IAB. Without funding, it was necessary to find solutions to conserve personnel resources, especially since the RDC-IAB established further data access points in Canada, Europe, and the United States. Thus, standardization procedures concerning collaboration contracts, DUA, and anonymization rules were implemented.[3] Although these standardizations helped streamline the process to add new data ac-

---

[2]See section 7.5.4 for more information.

[3]The standardizations for data use agreements and anonymization rules are discussed in more detail in section 7.5. The standardized contract for guest RDCs can be provided to institutions also interested in establishing similar decentralized data access infrastructure upon request.

cess points at guest RDCs, negotiations and administrative processes at each institution still take time. New collaborations, therefore, take up to a year to be established.

While it was possible to fund several data access points during the funding period of the RDC-in-RDC project, this was no longer possible when the project ended. Therefore, all guest RDCs now must be willing to maintain data access points without financial support by the RDC-IAB. After the project ended, a few access points were initially provided with additional funds to compensate for high user demand and the RDC-IAB intermittently asked guest RDCs for a small amount of compensation for the initial implementation of data access points. These interim solutions are no longer in place.

The RDC-IAB is very grateful for all the volunteer support of the participating institutions and guest RDCs helping to improve data access to German labor market data for the scientific community. We make efforts to minimize expenses on-site. A webpage only accessible to guest RDC staff provides information about users, user guidelines, and organizational matters. Furthermore, an on-site calendar to facilitate the registration process has been implemented. The RDC-in-RDC approach is very successful. There are now sixteen data access points in various guest RDCs in Canada, France, Germany, the United Kingdom, and the United States, and more will follow.

7.2.2 Data Use Examples

The data provided by the RDC-IAB are used both for labor market research in general as well as for the evaluation of labor market policies to scientifically monitor and review the implementation of labor market reforms. The government's interest in evidence-based policy advice is demonstrated by the fact that the results are acknowledged in the reports of the respective ministries. Researchers have used the RDC-IAB data to examine the effects of the minimum wage introduced in 2015, for instance. The Minimum Wage Commission used these finding for their regular reporting and their decision to adapt the minimum wage (Mindestlohnkommission, 2016b,a). In addition, the results on the risks of various atypical occupations for career development and income based on RDC-IAB data were used in *The German Federal Government's 5th Report on Poverty and Wealth* (Bundesministerium für Arbeit und Soziales, 2017; Rheinisch-Westfälisches Institut für Wirtschaftsforschung, 2016). Furthermore, the *Second Gender Equality Report* of the German Government included research findings on gender wage gaps based on the RDC-IAB data (Bundesministerium für Familie, Senioren, Frauen und Jugend, 2017; Boll, 2015).

Due to the comprehensive coverage of individuals and establishments,[4] the RDC-IAB data offer great potential for various research questions, which is reflected in the use of the data in many scientific publications. In particular, the ability to take both the employee and employer perspective into account simultaneously has sparked interest from international researchers. The following paragraphs present a selection of recent studies from external researchers who used the RDC-IAB data to exemplify the breadth of topics covered. More details about the data products used in these studies are listed in Table 7.1. Overall, this selection illustrates how a facilitation of data access can spur scientific output.

Bradley and Kügler (2019) published the article "Labor market reforms: an evaluation of the Hartz policies in Germany" in the *European Economic Review*. They examine the response of workers and establishments to the German Hartz reforms using the Sample of Integrated Labour Market Biographies (SIAB). The Hartz reforms were introduced gradually starting in 2003 with the aim to reform public employment services and make labor market policy in Germany more efficient. The authors used a structural model with a sample of 430,000 workers in 340,000 establishments. According to their results, the reforms shortened unemployment durations without decreasing unemployment as a whole. In addition, the reforms led to wage losses. Low-skilled workers were particularly affected.

---

[4]The term establishment (*Betrieb*) is rather peculiar and needs some explanation. It is defined as a regionally and economically delimited unit in which employees work. An establishment may consist of one or more branch offices and several establishments may belong to one company. The authors decided against using *firm*, *company*, or *enterprise* as a translation as these terms usually mean something different.

Riphahn and Schrader (2019) used the SIAB for their article "Institutional reforms of 2006 and the dramatic rise in old-age employment in Germany" that was published in *ILR Review*. The authors examine the effect of a cut in unemployment benefit payout periods on labor market transitions of older workers. They compare a younger reference group of 40- to 44-year-olds with stable payout durations to an older treatment group with reduced benefit payout durations during 2004 and 2007 by using a difference-in-difference approach. Their results show for the treatment group with reduced payout durations a lower job exit rate and higher rates of finding a new job in comparison to the reference group with stable payout durations. The authors conclude from their findings that the reform is a possible explanation for the recent increase in old-age employment in Germany.

Schumann (2017) used the Establishment History Panel (BHP) for his article on "The effects of minimum wages on firm-financed apprenticeship training" published in *Labour Economics*. He examined the short-term effects of the minimum wage on apprenticeship training for the construction sector because apprentices were exempted from the minimum wage regulation. The author assumes that the minimum wage may have incentives for firms to cut their costs on apprenticeship training expenditures. By using a difference-in-difference approach and synthetic controls, the author's results show that the minimum wage reduces the probability that firms will train new apprentices when labor turnover is high.

Based on a reform in 2004, which exempted small firms from dismissal protection, Lücke (2018) examines the risk of leaving an establishment if there is no protection against dismissal. Her results have been published in *Labour* with the title "When protection puts you in jeopardy—How removing small-business clauses affects employment duration." Based on linked employer-employee data (LIAB, longitudinal model) the author compared employment durations of workers with and without dismissal protection by using survival analysis techniques. Her results indicate that dismissal protection leads to a higher risk of cessation in the first six months and a lower risk afterwards.

Table 7.1 provides a selective overview of research data available at

RDC-IAB by focusing on the data products used in the examples above. It summarizes the data source and sample population, outlines the available time period, and links to the full data documentation. A more detailed discussion of the available data products can be found in Müller and Möller (2019) and Müller and Wolter (2020). A complete list is available on the IAB website.[5]

7.3 Making Data Usable for Research

Administrative research data offered by RDC-IAB are based on two main sources. One source is the notification procedure of the German social security system. Every employer has to submit information about employees so that all social insurance agencies are able to fulfill their legal duties, such as calculating claims from contribution payments or official statistics. The second source is individual information on the unemployed, job seekers, and participants in labor market programs collected by all German employment agencies and job centers.

Before being customized by the RDC-IAB, these source data already undergo extensive preparation by the BA and the IAB. The statistics department of the BA prepares the raw administrative data for statistical purposes and then submits the data to the IAB's department of Data and IT Management. Separate histories for the various groups (e.g., employed, unemployed) are prepared and then combined into one comprehensive SQL database called the Integrated Employment Biographies (IEB). The IEB is the universe of all employees covered by social security and all registered unemployed, job seekers, and participants in labor market programs. At the time of writing this Handbook chapter, it covers the period between 1975 and 2018.

These prior data processing steps imply that RDC-IAB staff can rely on intermediate data sources that already ran through several quality and plausibility checks and are consistently formatted and internally documented. This makes the preparation of final research data products much easier and frees up resources for other downstream tasks. The

---

[5]https://fdz.iab.de/en/FDZ_Overview_of_Data.aspx (accessed 2020-06-15).

Table 7.1: Selected RDC-IAB Data

Sample of Integrated Labour Market Biographies (SIAB)	
Population / Sample Size	2 percent random sample (more than 1.8 million individuals) of the Integrated Employment Biographies, a database which includes records from: - 1975 onwards: employment subject, receipt of benefits in accordance with Social Code Act III - 1999 onwards: Marginal part-time employment - 2000 onwards: participation in an employment or training measure - 2007 onwards: Registered jobseeker
Time Period covered and frequency	1975 until 2017 for West Germany, 1992 until 2017 for East Germany, updated every 2nd year by RDC-IAB
Additional information	DOI: 10.5164/IAB.SIAB7517.de.en.v1
Establishment History Panel (BHP)	
Population / Sample Size	Repeated cross-sectional dataset (640,000-1.5 million establishments) on June 30, on all establishments with at least one employee liable to social security (until 1988) and/or at least one marginal worker (since 1999), and thereof a 50 percent random sample
Time Period covered and frequency	1975 until 2018 for West Germany, 1992 until 2018 for East Germany, annual updated by RDC-IAB
Additional information	DOI: 10.5164/IAB.BHP7518.de.en.v1
Linked Employer-Employee Data (LIAB)	
Population / Sample Size	Worker information from administrative data are linked to the IAB-Establishment Panel, an annual representative survey since 1993 in West Germany and 1996 in East Germany including approx. 16,000 establishments per year. Stratified sample of all establishments with at least one employee liable to social security on June 30 of the year before by establishment size, industry, and federal state. There are two versions of LIAB: - LIAB cross-sectional model: all establishment surveys combined with administrative worker data as of June 30 (establishment: 67,407 in total; individuals approx. 12.5 million in total) - LIAB longitudinal model: selection of repeatedly interviewed establishments (2009-2016) combined with longitudinal worker biographies (establishment: 41,777 in total; individuals approx. 1.7 million in total)
Time Period covered and frequency	LIAB Cross-sectional model: 1993-2017 LIAB longitudinal model: 1975-2017
Additional information	DOI: 10.5164/IAB.LIABQM29317.de.en.v1 DOI: 10.5164/IAB.LIABLM7517.de.en.v1

Notes: The time period covered by each data set represents the status as of 02 June 2020. For a complete list of all data products see the RDC website.

same is true for surveys conducted by the IAB (or partner institutions) that become part of the RDC-IAB data portfolio. An internal guideline specifies the division of responsibilities between the RDC-IAB and the research department conducting the survey, making sure that data quality checks are already performed and documentation (including questionnaires, codebooks, and summary statistics) is complete before the data are submitted. Note that institutions that want to build an RDC that also performs initial data preparation and documentation will need additional staffing resources.

The RDC-IAB provides a variety of standardized data sets for labor market research based on these source data. Additionally, RDC-IAB offers access to various linked data products. These are data where survey and administrative information are linked via a unique identifier or record linkage techniques for consenting respondents. Record linkage is performed by the German Record Linkage Center (GRLC) within RDC-IAB. For more details on the preparation of standardized research data products, see section 7.5.4.

The RDC-IAB provides detailed metadata for all data products in both German and English. These metadata are based on the available internal data documentation and are tailored to fit the final data product. One important aim is to harmonize variable names and values across all administrative data products. There is a designated data steward for each data product and at least one additional staff member for assistance and double-checking. All data documentation are published as a standardized data report in a report series called *FDZ-Datenreport*.[6] A data report includes an introduction and outline, a description of all administrative data sources, a description of data preparation and sampling procedure, information on data quality and problems, a description of all variables, references, and if necessary, an appendix. Frequency tables, codebooks, and test data are provided in separate files online. These separate files are generated in a standardized way from the final data product using Stata scripts. This way, their preparation can be used as part of the quality control process.

---

[6]https://fdz.iab.de/en/FDZ_Publications/FDZ_Publication_Series/FDZ-Datenreporte.aspx (accessed 2020-06-15).

Currently, researchers must search for relevant metadata in different PDF-documents. In 2012, the RDC-IAB established a new system to collect all metadata in one single metadata base. It includes an online information system with a search engine for all data products. The underlying data base relies on SQL with a web application that allows entering the metadata easily. The documentation standard is called Data Documentation Initiative (Vardigan, Heus and Thomas, 2008).[7] Although DDI was only a standard for survey data at the beginning of the project, it was adopted for documentation of administrative data with the assistance of DDI experts. It is now possible to import XML-files containing variable names and codebooks that were generated in the data production process. Thus, the metadata base covers all relevant information on the data life cycle, including internal information. The online information system can also be used to create custom data reports including only the information that is relevant for a specific research project. Currently, the data products are gradually being added to the metadata base and the online information system is being tested.

7.4 Legal and Institutional Framework

7.4.1 Institutional Setup

The IAB is the research department of the BA. It has a statutory mandate to conduct scientific labor market and occupational research and advises the BA and various ministries on issues regarding labor market policy.[8] The IAB is also legally required to provide confidential labor market data to the research community. This requirement is broadly outlined in the German Social Code (*Sozialgesetzbuch*, SGB), but the details of a researcher-friendly implementation have been developed by the BA and the IAB over time. This includes the founding of the RDC-IAB and the improvement of access for domestic and international researchers through the RDC-in-RDC approach.

---

[7]See https://ddialliance.org/ for more details (accessed 2020-06-15).

[8]The institute is scientifically independent. Freedom of research and publication is guaranteed. More information can be found on the Institute's website: https://www.iab.de/en/iab-aktuell.aspx (accessed 2020-06-15).

In 2000, the government-appointed "Commission on Improving the Information Infrastructure between Science and Statistics" recommended implementing a RDC at each public data producer of microdata (Kommission zur Verbesserung der informationellen Infrastruktur zwischen Wissenschaft und Statistik, 2001). The BA adopted this recommendation and set up an RDC at the IAB in 2004 with financial support from the BMBF provided over three years. Since the successful evaluation of the RDC in 2006 by the RatSWD, the RDC-IAB has been financed from the staff budget of the BA. Today, the RDC-IAB is one of 38 such RDCs in Germany (German Data Forum, n.d.).

The RDC-IAB is a research division with three core functions, namely data production, data access services, and research. First, data production includes the generation of various standardized administrative data products, which are updated regularly. Furthermore, RDC-IAB links survey data with administrative data if respondents or establishments give their linkage consent. Second, numerous services are offered. They include the provision of survey data from different IAB research departments; detailed online documentation for each data set in German and English; additional materials to help researchers working with these data; different access modes in compliance with the German and the European General Data Protection Regulations (GDPR); advice on data selection, application, and analysis; and disclosure control of outputs. Third, the RDC-IAB carries out its own research to improve data quality and to develop new data sets. Research projects also serve to deepen the expert knowledge on research data provided by the RDC-IAB in order to improve the advice given to users. Data access for researchers is free of charge. As long as the BA finances the personal and technical capacity of the RDC-IAB, the RDC-IAB has the duty to find solutions to improve data access under the given circumstances.

The RDC-IAB also helps the BA and other stakeholders by facilitating access to the research carried out using IAB data. For example, all ongoing user projects are listed on the RDC-IAB webpage. Submitted and published papers using IAB data are available in a literature database, which is also available online. Furthermore, the RDC-IAB generates statistics documenting data usage to inform the BA, the IAB, the RatSWD, and the data users.

7.4.2 Legal Context for Data Use

Research data provided by the RDC-IAB are based on social data and therefore subject to special data privacy protection. Detailed regulations on the collection and processing of social data are provided by German law.[9] Article 282, SGB, Book III is especially relevant for the use of research data (Sozialgesetzbuch Drittes Buch III, 1997). It permits the IAB to use administrative data available at the BA for research purposes and to conduct surveys (subparagraph 5). It also allows and regulates the long-term storage of research data (subparagraph 6). Finally, it states that anonymized research data can be made available to scientific institutions if required for the purpose of labor market and occupational research (subparagraph 7).[10] This effectively restricts access to the scientific community within certain research areas without specifying the occupational background of the data user. Data access for commercial entities is strongly restricted and limited to special cases in which the requesting entity can prove a significant background in scientific research and shows clear intention to publish research results in a way that makes it accessible for the scientific community. Data access for freelance researchers is not possible.

Data use is also embedded in the broader regulatory context of the Federal Data Protection Act (*Bundesdatenschutzgesetz*, BDSG) and the GDPR of the EU. Pseudonymization is defined (Article 5, paragraph 5, GDPR) and the requirements for anonymous data are outlined (recital 26, GDPR).[11] Anonymity depends on the means reasonably likely to be used for re-identification, so the RDC-IAB takes the context of data access into account while preparing its research data. For example, weakly anonymized data products include more sensitive information,

---

[9]These are the SGB books II, III, and IV as well as the German Data and Transmission Act (*Datenerfassungs- und -übermittlungsverordnung - DEÜV*). The authors are not aware of a complete official translation of all relevant sections.

[10]Access to non-anonymized data is regulated by article 75 SGB Book X.

[11]Available at https://gdpr-info.eu/ (accessed 2020-06-15).

because they are provided in a computing environment where the technical infrastructure restricts the use of additional information. De-facto anonymized data, however, reduce the amount of information more strongly, as data users are only bound by contractual obligations (further details in section 7.5).

RDC-IAB does not have its own legal experts to ensure compliance with these regulations but is advised by the legal departments and data protection officers of both IAB and BA. All RDC-IAB personnel are employees of a federal agency and are therefore formally committed to their responsibility to protect social data. A violation of these responsibilities can be fined or lead to imprisonment.

The RDC-IAB must carefully balance two constitutional principles when preparing and granting access to research data: academic freedom and the right to informational self-determination. This is especially relevant since the social data at the core of the RDC-IAB data products are not collected from subjects voluntarily but on a mandatory basis.[12] In practice, this leads to a conflict of objectives because the goals of maximum analytical potential and maximum data protection have to be weighed against each other. The RDC-IAB solves this conflict (and addresses additional goals such as simplicity of data use, comprehensibility, reproducibility, and a streamlined data access management system) by offering standardized data products and three different data access modes. Those will be discussed in detail later with the outline of how RDC-IAB implements the five safes framework.

7.4.3 Legal Framework for Granting Data Access

Access to RDC-IAB data is regulated by a DUA. The RDC-IAB only enters into DUAs with scientific institutions not individuals. Individual researchers with data access are listed in the DUA and pledged to data secrecy by their employer. They also sign a statement that they were made aware of the provisions for data access through the RDC-IAB.

---

[12]This is not true of the surveys, where participation is voluntary.

DUAs are standardized to ensure equal contractual rights and obligations for all requesting institutions. In the case of a project team consisting of researchers from several institutions, separate DUAs are necessary.

Neither the RDC-IAB nor the BA assert intellectual property rights on the original data or any derivative data, and co-authorship is not required. Researchers, however, are bound by the DUA to correctly cite their source data. After statistical disclosure control (SDC), the released output is *approved output* and considered as open data. Therefore, no additional approval is needed for removal, transfer, and publishing in consistency with academic standards.

In case of a breach of the DUA, sanctions can be imposed on both users and institutions, ranging from temporarily blocking the user account to financial and reputational penalties. Fines can reach up to €60,000, and users and entire institutions can be barred from access for up to two years. Information on the breach can also be shared with other RDCs. In case of severe misconduct, additional penal consequences might follow that are not regulated by the DUA but follow from German and/or European law. However, the RDC-IAB always tries to maintain a good relationship with the data users that is grounded in the understanding that researchers have no interest to circumvent security barriers and disclose personal data willfully. Most incidents that come to the RDC-IAB's attention amount to misunderstandings and inattentions with no implications for the security and anonymity of the data. These cases can usually be handled by a brief period of restricted access and cautioning users to be more careful in the future.

The decision to expand data access facilities outside Germany led to several challenges. From a legal perspective, two main issues arose. First, making on-site access to RDC-IAB data outside of Germany involved a re-evaluation of the different pillars of the portfolio for data security and data anonymity used by the RDC-IAB when working with data products derived from social data. The adjustments necessary for data access outside Germany is discussed in section 7.5. Second, entering into DUAs with foreign institutions not only required overcoming language barriers but also reaching a shared understanding of the legal aspects involved. Legal staff at the institutions requesting data access often had questions regarding details of the contract or the German legal system and there were numerous requests to change the DUA, especially from US institutions. Since the RDC-IAB does not have the resources for a legal team that can handle individual contract negotiations, especially with a steadily increasing number of international users, it was decided to incorporate the lessons learned from the pilot phase of the project into a revised standard DUA template. The revised template is comparable for German and international institutions and available in German and English.[13] It is specifically tailored for data access through RDC-IAB and currently differs from DUAs entered into by other German RDCs. DUAs are now required on a non-negotiable basis, and adjustments to the standard template are infrequent and when they are relevant for all future requests. While this decision means that some researchers might be excluded from data access because their institutions decline signing the standard DUA, RDC-IAB's experience is that this is a very rare occurrence.

One consequence of the standardization of DUAs is that sanctions are equal for both German and non-German institutions. While this should not pose a problem for the more common sanctions like temporary blocking of data access, the enforcement of financial penalties outside German jurisdiction are a different matter. Fortunately, the RDC-IAB has not yet been confronted with a case of misconduct that would have made such a test necessary.

7.5 Protection of Sensitive and Personal Data: The Five Safes Framework

The anonymity of individuals and establishments within the RDC-IAB research data is not guaranteed by a single measure, rather, a portfolio approach is followed (Hochfellner, Müller and Schmucker, 2014). The portfolio's goal is to ensure that de-anonymization would only be

---

[13]The template can be provided to institutions interested in establishing decentralized data access upon request.

possible with a disproportionate amount of time, expense, and effort. This approach combines measures that are implemented before, during, and after data use. These measures include the examination of access requirements, regulations or technical restrictions on data access and use, pseudonymization and coarsening of research data, and the monitoring of results. The individual measures in these areas are explained in more detail below. It should be noted that anonymity is created by the interaction of all measures (i.e., they must be viewed and evaluated as a whole).

7.5.1 Safe Projects

The RDC-IAB facilitates access to research data according to the legal mandate imposed on the BA. The evaluation of applications for appropriateness is therefore regulated by the relevant provisions and includes the following aspects:

- *Research topic:* The project must address topics concerning labor market research, occupational research, and social security, as well as have a clearly defined scope.
- *Relevance:* The project must generate a benefit for the scientific understanding of labor markets.
- *Applicants:* Access can only be granted to researchers from institutions performing tasks defined as independent scientific research. Institutions must be located in a secure third country as defined in the GDPR.[14] Access is only granted to researchers who directly work with the data.
- *Suitability:* The research questions can be answered using the requested data.
- *Necessity:* The requested data are necessary to carry out the research project. In particular, there are no other data equally suited for the project.
- *Time:* Data access is limited to the time necessary to finish the project. Accordingly, the end date for the contract must be chosen in an appropriate manner.

---

[14] https://gdpr-info.eu/issues/third-countries/ (accessed 2020-06-15).

The RDC-IAB uses a formal application process to assess requests for data access. Applicants are provided with a standardized application form as well as written rules and guidelines for completion. Senior researchers of RDC-IAB are responsible for reviewing the applications. These staff members are also involved in the production of the research data and conduct their own scientific research. This ensures that the scientific merit and appropriateness of the data for the project can be assessed to the best possible extent. The legal department of the IAB is consulted in difficult cases. RDC-IAB staff also guides applicants through the revision process if the request is still incomplete or insufficient.

Currently, applications are managed using a semi-formal workflow without a specialized custom IT program. Over the last few years, however, there has been a drastic increase in projects and communication with data users. The RDC-IAB is therefore working on updating and restructuring the application process including a switch to the commercial software product Jira. Currently, the RDC-IAB receives up to 500 applications a year (excluding those that do not lead to a DUA, which are currently not recorded). A team of four senior staff members works on tasks related to project approval and contract management for DUAs. The team meets twice a week to discuss and assign new applications. While members of the contract team do not work full time on contract management, the group still rotates bimonthly so that each staff member can focus on other tasks such as updating data, SDC, project work, or research.

The approval process for users from German institutions usually takes between a few days to a month. As data are not currently collected on the elapsed time between initial contact and final approval, more detailed information is unavailable. The time until the research data can be accessed depends on the data access route (with access via transferring a Scientific Use File being somewhat quicker) but it is mostly driven by the revision of the application form. RDC-IAB staff try to answer requests concerning applications within one working week or sooner, but applications often have to be revised several times until they fulfill all requirements. The swiftness of the approval process is supported by the fact that the Federal Ministry of Labour and Social Affairs (*Bundesministerium für Arbeit und Soziales*, BMAS), as the supreme federal authority, does not request a separate institutional review board (IRB) approval for each individual project after the evaluation through RDC-IAB staff. In addition, a member of the contract team is allowed to sign DUAs as a representative of the director of the IAB.

Today, ensuring safe access for projects proposed by international users is similar to the process for German institutions. Application forms and DUAs are harmonized and available both in German and English. Some applications take longer than usual, especially when counterparty legal departments have no prior experience with the process. Apart from these first-time user disadvantages, most international users gain access to the requested data within a month. Deciding whether a requesting institution is indeed a scientific institution is usually not a problem, as the majority of requests come from researchers associated with public or private universities and research institutes with strong credentials. In these cases, the decision process on whether the institution is considered scientific is usually kept relatively informal. It is only in borderline cases that the RDC-IAB requests further proof, for example, by asking for written statutes of the institution.

7.5.2 Safe People

The RDC-IAB currently does not use a circle of trust model to establish who can access its research data. Researchers employed at scientific institutions are considered trusted by virtue of their affiliation. Exceptions are made for students who write their theses at universities. In these cases, access is granted as long as their supervisor and institution agree and sign the DUA on their behalf. No further training is necessary to access the data. Citizenship or professional restrictions do not apply, and background checks are not performed. This is true both for users from Germany and from foreign institutions. Users sign a statement that they were made aware of the provisions for data access, including

CHAPTER 7

sanctions, which becomes part of the DUA.[15]

7.5.3 Safe Settings

The RDC-IAB offers the following main data access modes to its users:

- *On-site* provides access to weakly anonymized microdata at separate workstations within the secure computing environment of the RDC-IAB in Nuremberg or from one of the guest RDCs. Weakly anonymized data are de-identified microdata. In addition to pseudonymization, other highly sensitive information is deleted or coarsened to obscure indirect identifiers. Still, the risk of indirect identification might be rather high in some cases if the data were analyzed outside the secure computing environment.
- *Remote execution* allows the submission of analysis code that runs on weakly anonymized microdata without seeing the microdata directly.
- *Scientific Use Files (SUF)* are de-facto anonymized microdata that are submitted to scientific institutions. Compared to weakly anonymized data, the amount of information is further reduced through additional coarsening or deletion to reduce the risk of indirect identification outside the secure computing environment of the RDC-IAB.

For *on-site* access, users must book a free slot in advance and clear an identity check at the respective location to ensure that they have a valid and ongoing project. The data can then be accessed in a designated room at a designated secure workstation.[16] The workstation does not provide access to the Internet or the internal network of the BA. At data access points, access is managed via a (thin) client solution using Citrix. There are certain software requirements for Windows PCs and Apple Macs with an installed HTML5 capable browser, as well as network requirements for a stable internet connection. Printers or similar devices cannot be connected to the client. Access to external websites

---
[15] See section 7.4.3.
[16] More details about the safe room are described in section 7.2.1.

is prevented. IT experts from RDC-IAB and guest RDCs carefully set up each client and monitor over time. Within the secure computing environment, the user's access rights are restricted to a personal folder containing the approved research data sets, approved statistical software (usually only Stata, sometimes also R or GNU Octave) and guidelines, data reports, and working tools. Users cannot install packages for Stata or R on their own; these are provided upon request by RDC-IAB staff. Other user provided software is not allowed. Usage of users' own laptops, phones, mass storage, and (picture) recording devices is prohibited and external communication is not possible. Users can upload external aggregated data, for example, unemployment rates, after data protection review and approval through RDC-IAB staff. Program code for data analysis (e.g., Stata do-files) and research output (in the form of Stata log-files) can be exported after SDC and approval via the Job Submission Application (JoSuA) platform. This way RDC-IAB staff has full control over every piece of data, code, or output that enter or exit the secure computing environment.

In 2015, the RDC-IAB acquired JoSuA, which was provided by the Institute of Labor Economics (IZA), to manage submissions for remote execution. This allows users to prepare program code using fake test data and then upload this code to the secure computing environment to have it run on the original research data. Test data are prepared by RDC-IAB staff for the various data products and can be downloaded from the website.[17] Users can login to JoSuA from everywhere.

The main innovation behind JoSuA is that it is no longer necessary to perform manual SDC for most output. JoSuA distinguishes between an internal use (IU) mode and a presentation/publication (PP) mode. In the IU-mode, users can upload their program code and preview their output once the program is finished. A combination of a script-based automated SDC, an IT solution that prevents downloading the results, and contractual obligations ensure that these results are only used for code development. In the PP-mode, users have to wait for RDC-IAB staff to conduct a manual SDC, which usually takes up to five working days, after which they may export their results as safe output.

---

[17]See section 7.5.4.

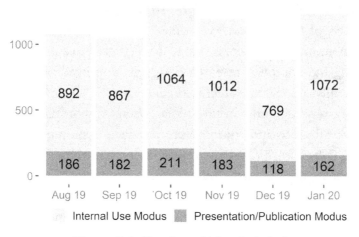

Figure 7.1: Number of jobs via JoSuA

Although influenced by expansion of data access points, the decision to switch from a model where every job submission was manually reviewed to the JoSuA model was made separately. The steadily increasing number of projects meant that more time had to be spent on SDC, and much of the workload fell on preliminary output that was not yet meant for publication. The IU-mode of JoSuA allows for more flexibility and increased speed in project development for users while freeing up resources and maintaining full control over the inputs and exported outputs. Today, about 80 to 90 percent of submissions for remote execution are in IU-mode (Figure 7.1).

Some of the data products offered by the RDC-IAB can also be downloaded as SUF and used within the premises of the requesting institution. Anonymization for these data must be stronger than in the weakly anonymous versions. The research data are stored in the Stata file format and can be downloaded from a secure download platform after signing the DUA. Details about storage and data use are specified in a data security concept that becomes part of the DUA. In this concept, the requesting institution declares that it will ensure suitable technical and organizational measures when dealing with de-facto anonymized data in compliance with data protection legislation. These measures include not sharing the data, restricting access to authorized personnel, ensuring sufficient security, using secure servers, and protecting hard drives against theft using modern encryption standards and deleting data securely at the end of the project period. Demand for SUF has been decreasing relative to weakly anonymized data products in recent years, partly driven by the improvements in access to both on-site and remote executio. Downloading and storing SUF outside of Germany is possible as long as the other "safes" are adhered to.

7.5.4 Safe Data

The data products provided by the RDC-IAB are specifically created for the purpose of allowing external researchers access to the data. Before being customized by the RDC-IAB, these source data already undergo extensive preparation by the BA, the IAB, or the partner institutes.[18] Still additional steps have to be taken before the data products can be accessed by external researchers. The sensitivity of RDC-IAB data products depends on the chosen access mode.

For *weakly anonymous* data, the data processing steps include the following:

- Drawing samples (administrative data, not surveys)
- Pseudonymization[19]
- Coarsening of highly sensitive information (e.g., exact date of birth, residential community)
- Omission of highly sensitive information that cannot be coarsened (e.g., disability status)
- Providing higher levels of coarsening as a standard and only allowing lower levels in justified cases (e.g., 3-digit industry codes instead of 5-digit, federal state instead of district)

For *de-facto anonymous data*, additional data processing steps are as follows:

- Checking whether certain characteristics that might be used for re-identification show rare values
- Additional coarsening and/or censoring

---

[18] See section 7.3.
[19] The source data used by the RDC-IAB are already pseudonymous.

- Omission of broader categories of data (e.g., omission of detailed establishment information in individual worker data sets)

These additional steps further reduce the disclosure risk for the data product and therefore enable data access via SUF. The increased safety for the research data is traded against weaker requirements for safe settings. As a result, the research data can now be stored outside the RDC-IAB secure computing environments while the portfolio of data security measures still ensures data protection.

Creating safe data for external data users is one of the main tasks of the RDC-IAB, and it is done with the users explicitly in mind. Data products are still standardized and not produced on demand. Depending on the data product, updates are performed annually, biennially, or irregularly. In case of linked data products, the linkage is done during data generation since users are not allowed to perform further linkage at a later stage (except for the linkage of aggregate statistics). Fake test data are produced for most data products that can only be accessed on-site or via remote execution so that users can prepare and test their code efficiently (Jacobebbinghaus, Müeller and Orban, 2010). These test data, however, do not meet the standards of a high-quality synthetic data product, and they should exclusively be used for code preparation.

Data are not only sampled, prepared, anonymized, and quality checked but also labelled and documented.[20] Data reports seek a good balance between accuracy and comprehensibility. They must convey important aspects about data origin and quality without drowning researchers in too much technical detail.

Total costs for the preparation of these data products are hard to measure because of several steps performed before the data are transferred to the RDC-IAB. The final step of making the standardized data accessible, including data preparation, anonymization, documentation, and test data preparation, usually requires between fifteen and sixty fulltime-equivalent working days per data set. These numbers already take into account that some data sets build upon each other, so that

---

[20] See section 7.3.

complementary effects can be exploited. New data products, however, need more time and they are usually developed as parts of third-party funded research projects. Continuation or updates of those new data products then depends on follow-up funding or compatibility with the regular data production cycle of the RDC-IAB core staff.

Producing safe data for access outside the RDC-IAB safe room is complicated by the current legal assessment prohibiting on-site access to weakly anonymous data outside the EU, even using the technical solutions outlined above.[21] This means that a choice had to be made between keeping analytic potential as high as possible and offering equal data access from all data access points. In the end, a decision was reached that the safe data concept for data access within the EU would not be changed and that additional processing of the data would be conducted when users request access to the data from non-EU data access points. To mitigate limitations in the analytical potential for research data outside the EU, additional data processing steps are individually agreed upon together with the data users before the project starts. Since the RDC-in-RDC project showed that international users often requested similar information for their research purposes, a modularized data anonymization concept was developed for all major data products to facilitate this coordination of the final anonymization strategy. This means that the process of coordination at the beginning of the project takes more time and that research teams sometimes must make tough decisions to make their projects feasible.

Since the RDC-IAB only provides standardized data products, it cannot serve more individual project needs like special samples, additional and more detailed variables, or special linkages. While an alternative, fee-based data access mode for social data exists, this mode is not operated by the RDC-IAB and it is only available for German institutions. For international researchers, cooperation with the IAB or another German research institution might prove to be the only way to conduct such research projects.

---

[21] See sections 7.3 and 7.5.3.

7.5.5 Safe Outputs

The way safe output is ensured at the RDC-IAB depends on the data access mode for the research project. For SUF, the responsibility to ensure safe output rests entirely with the requesting institution and the data users. The institution is mandated to refrain from any action that might compromise the anonymity of the statistical information contained in the data and is required to instruct data users accordingly. Thus, no statistical output that is not sufficiently anonymized is allowed to be published. The institutions can find assistance on what is meant by secure output in BA guidelines (Statistik der Bundesagentur für Arbeit, 2018) or ask the RDC-IAB for assistance.

When data are used on-site or via remote execution, both the RDC-IAB and data users work together to ensure there is no re-identification of the data. The goal is that only completely anonymous (non-sensitive) results leave the safe computing environment. As a first step, data users are urged to keep their research output clean, clear, comprehensible, and well documented according to RDC-IAB guidelines. These guidelines describe in detail how program code has to be set up (including templates), what kind of documentation is needed, and in what file format output must be stored (usually as Stata log files and graphs but with some exceptions). Data users should also restrict their output to what is necessary and ensure that output can be exported without compromising anonymity or being rendered useless after the necessary SDC. These preparations should be made during on-site visits or in IU-mode to reduce the amount of manual SDC required by RDC-IAB staff. The rules for documentation also require that all output considered for export must be generated from a script started by a single master file in the remote execution. This procedure ensures that all output is reproducible and all steps documented.

As a second step, the RDC-IAB has developed a list of relatively simple rules that statistical output must satisfy. These rules might be overcautious in some cases but ensure that SDC can be done quickly without having to consider all eventualities. The most important pillars of these rules are as follows:

- There is no disclosure of information based on one single observational unit (e.g., individual, household, or establishment). Every result must be based on at least twenty observational units. Primary cell suppression is used in tables that do meet this criterion.
- Secondary cell suppression is used, which prevents the identification of information via subtotals and/or marginal totals. Secondary cell suppression might also be necessary in linked tables.

RDC-IAB has developed some automated cell suppression routines that automatically pre-scan all output.[22] These routines are used both for the IU-mode and the PP-mode output and reduce the amount of time needed for manual SDC considerably. These routines, however, cannot account for all eventualities found in the same output files, so the manual SDC by RDC-IAB staff is still needed before output can be released. Excessive production of output or cases where manual SDC would become too time consuming are discussed bilaterally with the data users to find solutions that are easier to review and still satisfy the needs of the data users.

As a third step, rules for safe output are incorporated into the DUA. The agreement commits data users to review their approved output to make sure inferences on single observational units are impossible. In case of any suspected violations, publication or transfer to third parties must be avoided until the case can be resolved with the assistance of the RDC-IAB and the Legal Department of the IAB. All approved results are documented and archived via the JoSuA software.

Rules for on-site data access or remote execution are equal for all on-site locations as well as users from within and outside of Germany. Therefore, rules for safe output were not changed as a result of the RDC-in-RDC project.

---

[22] The script is based on Perl and was written by a staff member. It runs independently within JoSuA.

7.6 Data Life Cycle and Replicability

7.6.1 Preservation and Reproducibility of Researcher-Accessible Files

RDC-IAB versions, curates, and archives all its data products and older data products are currently not deleted. The IAB department of Data and IT-Management curates IAB source data. Preliminary data management and sampling is done at the RDC-IAB using SAS. Most final data refinement are performed using Stata. RDC-IAB preserves all master files to enable the traceability and reproducibility of each data product.

RDC-IAB provides the latest available data version to users. Older, archived versions of data sets are only available for the purpose of replication studies, or in exceptional cases, if the request is duly substantiated. It is also possible to change to the latest updated version during an ongoing research project.

7.6.2 Preservation and Reproducibility of Researcher-Generated Files

All research results generated at the RDC-IAB, both on-site or via remote execution can by restored as long as users follow the RDC-IAB guidelines and program their code accordingly. Not following those guidelines will often lead to code termination so that users have an interest in keeping their code error-free and well-structured. Each remote execution job in JoSuA is started from a master file, which opens all underlying analysis code and sub-routines. At the end of each on-site use, researchers need to follow the same procedure in JoSuA to obtain code and results. It is not possible to get intermediate code versions or results without using JoSuA. The RDC-IAB preserves user generated code and original data for ten years. Only the original data have a persistent digital identifier. Users can also export and store their code from JoSuA after a manual check by RDC-IAB staff. RDC-IAB does not store intermediate data generated during a user project but such data should be reproducible using the preserved code. Access to user generated files or output is only possible with the permission of the original researchers and a DUA. In case of misconduct or perceived misconduct, the IAB follows its procedure for good scientific practice for data access and code.[23]

7.7 Sustainability and Continued Success

7.7.1 Outreach

The RDC-IAB uses different channels to inform interested researchers about the data products and data access possibilities. Most importantly, extensive information is available online at the RDC-IAB website.[24] Additionally, the RDC-IAB newsletter keeps data users updated on news, such as new data sets or data updates. A continuous user survey helps to identifying any problems with the flow of information to the data users and adjustments can be made to the website. RDC-IAB staff presents data and data access options at conferences, workshops, and seminars. Users, RDC-IAB staff, and IAB colleagues also present their research at national and international research conferences and publish in journals in various disciplines. These conference engagements often lead to questions or data requests from other researchers. International collaborations with high-ranking scholars boosted the interest in RDC-IAB data considerably (Card, Heining and Kline, 2015; Schmieder, von Wachter and Bender, 2016). The expansion of data access points in Germany and abroad also exemplified the importance of word of mouth advertising. Quite often, users report their experiences with RDC-IAB data to their colleagues, leading to small clusters of researchers from the same institution working with the data.

RDC-IAB is a partner in IDAN. IDAN is a collaboration between six RDCs from France, Germany, the Netherlands, and the UK with the aim to enable working remotely with data from each partner at all partnering data access points, thus facilitating access and enabling

---

[23] https://www.iab.de/en/daten/replikationen.aspx (accessed 2020-06-15).
[24] See footnote 1.

cross-country comparisons. This allows parallel (but separate) analysis for different countries. Appending data sets from different countries into a common database is legally forbidden and technically prevented. The *Centre d'accès sécurisé aux données* (CASD) in France and the RDC-IAB, for instance, have already prepared documentation to make researchers more aware of the possibilities for cross-country comparisons (Laible et al., 2020). A joint conference in 2019 promoted the exchange between researchers, data providers, and stakeholders from different ministries in both countries and demonstrated the importance of access to administrative data and surveys.[25]

7.7.2 Revenue

There are no fees for RDC-IAB data users, neither for data access nor for SDC of research results. The RDC-IAB and its services are financed by a BA budget. This follows the recommendation of the RatSWD, which is responsible for the accreditation of all German RDCs. Special mention should also be made of the free assistance provided by institutions that have a data access point to RDC-IAB data.

The RDC-IAB tries to finance projects for new data products through the acquisition of third-party funds. While third parties sometimes provided funding for generating new standardized data sets at the RDC-IAB,[26] today most funding is only available for genuine research projects and generating a new data set is a by-product of a larger research goal. Funding is sometimes available for infrastructure projects like the RDC-in-RDC approach or Data without Boundaries.[27]

Additional funding possibilities arise from linking survey data of collaborating institutions with the IABs administrative data (as long as consent to linkage was provided by the survey respondents). In 2011, the RDC-IAB established the GRLC in cooperation with the University of Duisburg-Essen to conduct research on record linkage and to provide services with record linkage applications (Antoni and Schmucker,

---

[25] For more information on IDAN, see https://idan.network/ (accessed 2020-06-15).
[26] One example is the data set "Biographical Data of Social Insurance Agencies in Germany (BASiD)" (Hochfellner, Müller and Wurdack, 2012).
[27] See section 7.2.1.

2019). The implementation of the GRLC was funded by the German Research Foundation (DFG) for three years. Today, the RDC-IAB receives financial support from the collaborating institutes to perform the linkage, prepare and document the final linked data sets, and advise data users. One example of this kind of collaboration is the linked National Educational Panel Study (NEPS) created with the Leibniz Institute for Educational Trajectories (LIfBi).

7.7.3 Metrics of Success

The RDC-IAB generates statistics to inform the IAB, the BA, the RatSWD, and researchers about data use at the RDC-IAB. These statistics reflect both the success of the data and the effort involved. The RDC-IAB provides statistics on active user projects, number of remote execution jobs, and on-site uses each month/year online. A literature database informs about papers based on RDC-IAB data.[28] Not all data users, however, submit their papers to the RDC-IAB after the project ends, and data sets are not always cited correctly. Therefore, the actual number of papers using RDC-IAB data is underestimated in this database. As a result, RDC-IAB measures its success by looking at the number of users and user projects rather than number of papers or citations.

As shown in Figure 7.2(a), the numbers of users and user projects at the RDC-IAB continues to increase every year. In 2019, around 1,500 users worked in more than 700 projects.[29] The average duration of a research project is around three years. Bachelor theses or master theses usually do not take longer than six months.

Since the implementation of the additional data access points, the proportion of international users is constantly growing. Figure 7.2(b) shows the percentage share of contractual partners from Germany, the US, and other countries. While in 2012, less than 30 percent of all user

---

[28]https://fdz.iab.de/en/FDZ_Publications/FDZ_Literature_Database.aspx (accessed 2020-06-15).
[29]In Figure 7.2(a), researchers who work in different projects are counted more than once.

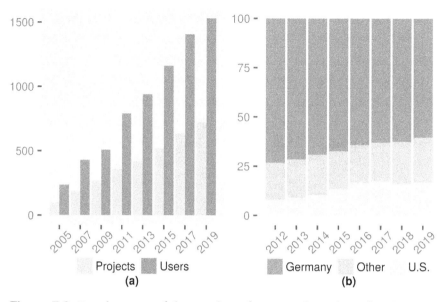

Figure 7.2: Development of the number of users and number of projects at the RDC-IAB, 2005–2019 (left) and contractual partners of the RDC-IAB by country, 2012–2019 (right)

projects were from a non-German facility, seven years later the value increased to 40 percent.

Additional statistics are also submitted to the annual activity report for all RDCs in Germany published by the RatSWD (German Data Forum, 2019). Table 7.2 shows all publications with RDC-IAB data in 2018, including publications from IAB staff. There were 60 published papers in scientific journals in 2018, 45 of these in peer-reviewed journals. Additionally, 44 papers were published as working papers or reports and RDC-IAB data were used and cited in 41 books. As mentioned above, these numbers underestimate the true number of relevant publications in 2018.

Apart from these general statistics, RDC-IAB also gathers user feedback to learn what the users think about service quality, data documentation, data access modes, and additional user needs. At first, this was done using irregular user surveys (Wolter and vom Berge, 2018), but currently two regular online user surveys are conducted. One survey focuses on service quality during the application phase. This survey is

Table 7.2: Number of publications in 2018, including all publications with RDC-IAB data (excluding Bachelor and Master theses)

Publications	Numbers
Papers	60
Peer-reviewed papers	45
Books	41
Papers in anthologies	8
Grey literature (e.g., working papers, technical reports)	14

conducted shortly after the signing of the DUA by the requesting institution. It is addressed to the researchers using the data, since they are usually more deeply involved in the application process than the representative providing the signature. The second survey covers user experiences after completed projects.

In general, user ratings are very good. For example, Figure 7.3 shows the ratings of data documentation and personal data advice. More than 90 percent of the survey respondent are satisfied (very good and good) with the data documentation. While 40 percent of all participants did not use personal data advice, nearly all others are satisfied. User suggestions, ideas, and critiques are essential to improve data access further to the extent possible given available resources.

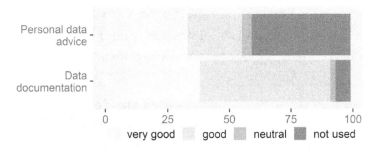

Figure 7.3: User satisfaction with RDC-IAB services, by percentage (options bad and very bad have not been chosen by respondents)

About the Authors

Dana Müller is the Head of the Research Data Center (RDC-IAB) of the Federal Employment Agency (BA) at the Institute for Employment Research (IAB) in Nuremberg, Germany. Previously, she was a researcher at the IAB and the Chemnitz University of Technology. In these positions, Dana Müller has worked with survey data, administrative data, and big-data; she has developed a deep knowledge and extensive experience in linkages of social security records, administrative information, and survey data. She has led many initiatives, including the project "Quality of work and economic success" and "Biographical data of selected social insurance in Germany." Both projects were linking different administrative and survey data to advance social science research.

Dana has published several articles in leading social science journals and books. Her main research interests include sociology of the family and gender inequalities on the labor market, as well as linkage and confidentiality of administrative data. Her research on family and gender inequalities addresses repercussions of motherhood on labor market participation and discrimination as well as the influence of family-friendly arrangements in establishments on labor market behavior of mothers and fathers. Her work on research ethics addresses data confidentiality and methods of protecting privacy in the presence of an increasing demand of data in social sciences. She is IAB's representative at the *Statistik Netzwerk Bayern* and elected member of the executive board of the DDI Alliance.

Philipp vom Berge is the Deputy Head of the Research Data Center (RDC-IAB) of the Federal Employment Agency (BA) at the Institute for Employment Research (IAB) in Nuremberg, Germany. He studied economics at the University of Regensburg, where he received his doctorate in 2013. Philipp has contributed to numerous IAB projects on data quality and data refinement. In recent years, his work on innovative research data focused on improving administrative labor market data and linked survey data to enhance their usability for minimum wage research.

Philipp's main research interest lies at the intersection of labor and regional economics. He has contributed to the emerging scientific literature on minimum wages in Germany and led several policy evaluation projects funded by the German government to accompany the introduction of the national statutory minimum wage. He has also worked on local spillovers, segregation, and policy evaluation using geocoded administrative research data.

References in Chapter 7

Antoni, Manfred, and Alexandra Schmucker. 2019. "The Research Data Centre of the German Federal Employment Agency at the Institute for Employment Research (RDC-IAB) - Linked Microdata for Labour Market Research." *International Journal of Population Data Science*, 4(2). https://doi.org/10.23889/ijpds.v4i2.1141.

Bender, Stefan, and Jörg Heining. 2011. "The Research-Data-Centre in Research-Data-Centre approach: a first step towards decentralised international data sharing." FDZ Methodenreport 07/2011 (en). http://doku.iab.de/fdz/reporte/2011/MR_07-11_EN.pdf (accessed 2020-10-05).

Boll, Christina. 2015. "Entstehung des Gender Pay Gap im Lebensverlauf." *Neue Zeitschrift für Familienrecht*, 23: 1089–1093. https://www.iab.de/de/informationsservice/informationssysteme/infoplattform/infoplattform-publikationsdetails.aspx/Publikation/k151214321 (accessed 2020-12-07).

Bradley, Jake, and Alice Kügler. 2019. "Labor Market Reforms: an Evaluation of the Hartz Policies in Germany." *European Economic Review*, 113: 108–135. https://doi.org/10.1016/j.euroecorev.2018.12.008.

Bundesministerium für Arbeit und Soziales. 2017. "Lebenslagen in Deutschland. Der Fünfte Armuts- und Reichtumsbericht der Bundesregierung." Bundesministerium für Arbeit und Soziales. https://www.armuts-und-reichtumsbericht.de/SharedDocs/Downloads/Berichte/5-arb-langfassung.pdf?__blob=publicationFile&v=6 (accessed 2020-12-07).

Bundesministerium für Familie, Senioren, Frauen und Jugend. 2017. "Zweiter Gleichstellungsbericht der Bundesregierung." Bundesministerium für Familie, Senioren, Frauen und Jugend. https://www.bmfsfj.de/bmfsfj/service/publikationen/zweiter-gleichstellungsbericht-der-bundesregierung/119796 (accessed 2020-10-05).

Card, David, Jörg Heining, and Patrick Kline. 2015. "CHK effects." FDZ Methodenreport 06/2015 (en). http://doku.iab.de/fdz/reporte/2015/MR_06-15_EN.pdf (accessed 2020-10-05).

German Data Forum. 2019. "Activities Report 2018 of the Research Data Centres (RDCs) accredited by the German Data Forum (RatSWD)." German Data Forum. https://doi.org/10.17620/02671.44.

German Data Forum. n.d.. "Research Data Centers: Data Access for Science and Research – the "Research Data Centre" success story." https://www.ratswd.de/en/data-infrastructure/rdc (accessed 2020-06-15).

Heining, Jörg, and Stefan Bender. 2012. "Technical and organisational measures for remote access to the micro data of the Research Data Centre of the Federal Employment Agency." FDZ Methodenreport 08/2012 (en). http://doku.iab.de/fdz/reporte/2012/MR_08-12_EN.pdf (accessed 2020-10-05).

Hochfellner, Daniela, Dana Müller, and Alexandra Schmucker. 2014. "Privacy in Confidential Administrative Micro Data: Implementing Statistical Disclosure Control in a Secure Computing Environment." *Journal of Empirical Research on Human Research Ethics*, 9(5): 8–15. https://doi.org/10.1177/1556264614552799.

Hochfellner, Daniela, Dana Müller, and Anja Wurdack. 2012. "Biographical data of social insurance agencies in Germany - improving the content of administrative data." *Schmollers Jahrbuch*, 132(3): 443–451. https://doi.org/10.3790/schm.132.3.443.

Jacobebbinghaus, Peter, Dana Müeller, and Agnes Orban. 2010. "How to use data swapping to create useful dummy data for panel datasets." FDZ Methodenreport 03/2010 (en). http://doku.iab.de/fdz/reporte/2010/MR_03-10-EN.pdf (accessed 2020-10-05).

Kommission zur Verbesserung der informationellen Infrastruktur zwischen Wissenschaft und Statistik. 2001. "Towards an Improved Statistical Infrastructure: Summary Report of the Commission set up by the Federal Ministry of Education and Research (Germany) to Improve the Statistical Infrastructure in Cooperation the Scientific Community and Official Statistics." *Schmollers Jahrbuch*, 121(3): 443–468. https://www.ratswd.de/dl/downloads/kvi_e_0.pdf.

Laible, Marie-Christine, Marine Seilles, Maria Alkhoury, and Raphaëlle Fleureux. 2020. "New opportunities for comparative cross-country research in France and Germany." FDZ Datenreport 03/2020. https://doi.org/10.5164/IAB.FDZD.2003.en.v1.

Lücke, Christine. 2018. "When protection puts you in jeopardy. How removing small-business clauses affects employment duration." *Labour*, 32(4): 213–236. https://doi.org/10.1111/labr.12124.

Mindestlohnkommission. 2016a. "Erster Bericht zu den Auswirkungen des Gesetzlichen Mindestlohns. Bericht der Mindestlohnkommission an die Bundesregierung nach § 9 Abs. 4 Mindestlohngesetz." Mindestlohnkommission. https://www.mindestlohn-kommission.de/DE/Bericht/pdf/Bericht2016.pdf?__blob=publicationFile&v=4 (accessed 2020-10-05).

Mindestlohnkommission. 2016b. "Zweiter Bericht zu den Auswirkungen des Gesetzlichen Mindestlohns. Bericht der Mindestlohnkommission an die Bundesregierung nach \S 9 Abs. 4 Mindestlohngesetz." Mindestlohnkommission. https://www.mindestlohn-kommission.de/DE/Bericht/pdf/Bericht2018.pdf?__blob=publicationFile&v=6 (accessed 2020-10-05).

Müller, Dana, and Joachim Möller. 2019. "Giving the International Scientific Community Access to German Labor Market Data: A Success Story." In *Data-Driven Policy Impact Evaluation: How Access to Microdata is Transforming Policy Design.*, ed. Nuno Crato and Paolo Paruolo, 101–117. Cham:Springer International Publishing. https://doi.org/10.1007/978-3-319-78461-8_7.

Müller, Dana, and Stefanie Wolter. 2020. "German labour market data - Data provision and access for the international scientific community." *German Economic Review*. http://doi.org/10.1515/ger-2019-0127.

Rheinisch-Westfälisches Institut für Wirtschaftsforschung. 2016. *Risiken atypischer Beschäftigungsformen für die berufliche Entwicklung und Erwerbseinkommen im Lebensverlauf.* Berlin:Bundesministerium für Arbeit und Soziales (BMAS). https://www.armuts-und-reichtumsbericht.de/SharedDocs/Downloads/Service/Studien/endbericht-risiken-atypischer-beschaeftigung-2015.pdf?__blob=publicationFile&v=4.

Riphahn, Regina T., and Rebecca Schrader. 2019. "Institutional reforms of 2006 and the dramatic rise in old-age employment in Germany." *Industrial & Labor Relations Review*, 73(5). https://doi.org/10.1177/0019793919863378.

Schmieder, Johannes, TIll von Wachter, and Stefan Bender. 2016. "The Effect of Unemployment Benefits and Nonemployment Durations on Wages." *American Economic Review*, 106(3): 739–777. https://doi.org/10.1257/aer.20141566.

Schumann, Mathias. 2017. "The Effects of Minimum Wages on Firm-financed Apprenticeship Training." *Labour Economics*, 47: 163–181. https://doi.org/10.1016/j.labeco.2017.05.002.

Sozialgesetzbuch Drittes Buch III. 1997. "§ 282 SGB 3 Arbeitsmarkt- und Berufsforschung." http://www.gesetze-im-internet.de/sgb_3/__282.html (accessed 2020-12-15).

Statistik der Bundesagentur für Arbeit. 2018. "Grundlagen: Definitionen - Statistische Geheimhaltung: Rechtliche Grundlagen und fachliche Regelungen der Statistik der Bundesagentur für Arbeit." https://statistik.arbeitsagentur.de/Statischer-Content/Grundlagen/Rechtsgrundlagen/Statistische-Geheimhaltung/Generische-Publikationen/Statistische-Geheimhaltung.pdf (accessed 2020-10-05).

Vardigan, Mary, Pascal Heus, and Wendy Thomas. 2008. "Data Documentation Initiative: Toward a Standard for the Social Sciences." *International Journal of Digital Curation*, 3(1): 107–113. https://doi.org/10.2218/ijdc.v3i1.45.

Wirth, Heike, Ulrike Rockmann, Dana Müller, Jan Goebel, and Tatjana Mika. 2019. "Remote Access zu Daten der amtlichen Statistik und der Sozialversicherungsträger." Rat für Sozial- und Wirtschaftsdaten (RatSWD) RatSWD Output 5 (6). https://doi.org/10.17620/02671.42.

Wolter, Stefanie, and Philipp vom Berge. 2018. "Die FDZ-Nutzerbefragung 2017 - Ergebnisse und Herausforderungen." FDZ Methodenreport 05/2018. https://doi.org/10.5164/IAB.FDZM.1805.de.v1.

CHAPTER 8

Ohio and the Longitudinal Data Archive: Mutually Beneficial Partnerships Between State Government and Researchers

Joshua D. Hawley (Ohio State University)

8.1 Summary

The Ohio Longitudinal Data Archive (OLDA) is a collaborative arrangement between the State of Ohio and the Ohio State University (OSU). Operated jointly by the John Glenn College of Public Affairs and the Center for Human Resource Research (CHRR), the OLDA stores data from five agencies (Education, Higher Education, Housing, Job and Family Services, and Opportunities for Ohioans with Disabilities) in Ohio. These data are available to government agencies as well as to external researchers. *By providing access to both networks, Ohio creates a community focused on generating evidence-based research that is used by government for both research and public policy.*

Copyright © Joshua D. Hawley.
Cite as: Hawley, Joshua D. "Ohio and the Longitudinal Data Archive: Mutually Beneficial Partnerships Between State Government and Researchers." In: Cole, Shawn, Iqbal Dhaliwal, Anja Sautmann, and Lars Vilhuber (eds.), *Handbook on Using Administrative Data for Research and Evidence-based Policy*. Cambridge, MA: Abdul Latif Jameel Poverty Action Lab. 2020.

The OLDA is an example of long-term partnerships between state government and research communities. The data system has increased its holdings to include longitudinal microdata from education, labor, housing, and disability services. Data are made available through a secure platform. The entire system is governed by a memorandum of understanding that is renegotiated every two years.

The initial idea for the data system emerged in 2007 out of a partnership between faculty at the university, which resulted in an MOU giving OSU access to state data.[1] The OLDA is a linked to a college research center, the Ohio Education Research Center[2] (OERC). The OERC is a policy research and evaluation unit at the Glenn College and conducts contract research with state and local government. The OLDA and OERC are actively used at Ohio State University in teaching education policy, data sciences, and simulation and modeling.[3]

The OLDA is broadly used to conduct research into outcomes of education and training, with additional foci on human services, housing, and health care as need arises. The core data holdings from the wage records and all public education and higher education providers enable researchers to answer critical questions such as (1) what are the employment outcomes of higher education, (2) what kinds of industries are growing or shrinking, and (3) how does employment depend on major or credential?

The data are available to outside researchers within Ohio and other states. Existing research agreements cover everything from infant mortality to the impact of lead exposure on education to extended unemployment on labor market success.

---

[1]The original research team that wrote the concept paper to the State of Ohio included Randall Olsen (Professor Emeritus of Economics, OSU) and Kathryn Sullivan (Former Director, Battelle Center for Mathematics and Science Education Policy, John Glenn College of Public Affairs, OSU). Sullivan subsequently went on to lead the National Oceanic and Atmospheric Administration (NOAA) under President Obama, and Olsen ran the National Longitudinal Surveys for the Department of Labor (DOL) for over 25 years. At the State of Ohio, the original partnership included the Ohio Departments of Education, Higher Education, and Job and Family Services.

[2]http://www.oerc.osu.edu/ (accessed 2020-12-10).

[3]For an example of simulation work using Ohio data, see our project on infant mortality (Hosseinichimeh et al., 2017).

The OLDA was started with federal grants from the US Departments of Labor and Education to the State of Ohio and Ohio State University. Between 2009 and 2013, the Ohio State University supported state development of the OLDA with Race to the Top and Workforce Data Quality Initiative (WDQI) funds. These funds enabled the state of Ohio and the university to build a strong working relationship around data. During these years program implementors developed a governance system that allows external and internal research teams to propose innovative research work.

After the core federal funding ended, the OLDA has persisted through a combination of funding from state agencies, federal research contracts, and private foundation grants. The operating budget on an annual basis is between US$1.5 to 2 million. We have approximately twelve full-time employees currently, including three research scientists, database administrators, and policy or evaluation staff.

8.2 Introduction

8.2.1 Motivation and Background

Historical Background on Use of Administrative Data in Ohio

State agencies revised the administrative code to develop longitudinal data systems over time. As education organizations (e.g., schools or colleges) in the 1990s moved to using databases to manage regular business—such as registration, course enrollment, or testing—state agencies supervising these schools developed the data systems to help schools and universities carry out the day-to-day work. During these years, the key data systems for education, including the Education Management Information System, the Adult Workforce Education Data System, the Adult Basic Education Data System, and the Higher Education Information System were formally developed to capture data submitted by individual education organizations. These data systems were developed by agencies and often under contract with an external consulting firm. The legal basis for these data systems came from Ohio Revised Code.[4]

The unemployment insurance wage record system controlled by the Ohio Department of Job and Family Services pre-dated the OLDA and reflects earlier federal efforts. The legal foundation of the current wage record system is based in the Federal Unemployment Tax Act of 1937, which set up a federal tax to cover unemployed workers. As part of the tax, states were asked to build (over time) a way of reporting earnings on a quarterly basis. Statute at the federal level currently establishes the framework for employers to report wage records as part of the administration of Unemployment Insurance (Workforce Information Council, 2014).

The motivation for building newer research databases in each of these government agencies varies. In the 1990s, government experienced an expansion of technology. IT systems were being used more broadly as states, such as Florida, built database systems to manage key administrative data (e.g., education data). Many states also created data systems that required local schools or universities to submit administrative data using a planning schedule, thereby building the local capacity for data systems. A second major reason for expanding data systems was an increasing demand from researchers for unit record data. As awareness of administrative data became more widespread in the 1980s and 1990s, faculty and professional researchers increasingly requested confidential microdata from states (Borus, 1982; Pfeiffer, 1998; Stevens, 1989, 2012).

University Role in Building the Data System

OSU worked with the Department of Job and Family Services on a periodic basis between 1995 and 2010 to conduct studies using wage records in combination with a wide range of other data files, including those from Aid for Families with Dependent Children and Workforce Investment Act programs (Center for Human Resource Research, 2001).

---

[4]The Ohio Revised Code section on the Education Management Information System describes the system and its legal basis (ORC, Chapter 3301-14).

The increase in data use for research purposes was directly related to federal policy changes. For example, the US Department of Labor established the Administrative Data Research and Evaluation Project (ADARE) for states to collaborate on research and evaluation projects. The ADARE states, including Ohio, worked together to improve access to labor, training, and education data among the research community (Stevens, 2012).

The research team worked on a series of projects linking wage and education records that laid the basis for longer-term commitment between state agencies and the research community. The group included a former state director of Labor Market Information, the current (now retired) Labor Market Information director, a deputy chancellor (and former state finance director) and several professors, including the director of the Center for Human Resource Research. There was even a former astronaut involved in the project work in the early phases!

Both of these activities, legal and technical, help to sharpen one's understanding of the political nature of data-based decision-making in modern government (Stone, 2012). Governors, the legislature, technical staff in the executive branch, and the additional stakeholders—including academic communities—work within a common political environment. Staff circulate among government offices bringing ideas and advancing priorities. This circulation of staff has proved particularly important in economic and workforce development policy where progress requires extensive collaboration among business and the public sector. For example, individual staff will work for a chamber of commerce, subsequently move to a higher education institution, and might move to an executive role in state government. These moves ensure that the system can learn and improve.

The legislative process, including the biennial operating and capital budgets in Ohio, creates regular demand for research using state data. In addition to regular demand for data on the employment outcomes of education, the legislature and executive branch frequently demand specific reports on a wide range of topics that are mandated by law. There are exceptions, but the majority of the time, research projects are requested and delivered in one- or two-year cycles. This time limited nature means that the work that state agencies request from Ohio universities tend to be short-term and related to constantly changing state policy priorities. For example, the state will often request a report on short-term employment outcomes because it can show results before the next budget is written as opposed to initiating a long-term study.

Role of Targeted Federal Funding in Supporting Use of Administrative Data

OSU worked with the state to build the OLDA to help increase access to administrative data for research purposes. The university conducted research on an ad hoc basis between 1995 and 2010. Several of these projects relied on data from across institutions as well as different state agencies. For example, in 2002 to 2003, the state commissioned a study of the outcomes of adult workforce education (Hawley and Sommers, 2003; Hawley, Sommers and Meléndez, 2003, 2005). In 2007, the state also asked for a study of developmental education (Hawley and Chiang, 2013, 2017). In both cases the university received data on an ad hoc basis, straining both the technical systems to ensure security for private student records and the legal frameworks in Ohio. OSU's legal staff worked directly with the Ohio Attorney General's Office.

The ad hoc projects built some confidence among the researchers at the university and the state levels. OSU received the extracted data from the agency data systems from two separate longitudinal data systems independently. Subsequently, the agencies provided these data extracts to the research team. At Ohio State, the team created the technical approach to merging state data, doing probabilistic matching, and standardizing data reporting rules. Researchers at other ADARE institutions, including the Upjohn Institute and the University of Missouri, were very important resources for each other (Stevens, 2012).

The Workforce Data Quality Initiative provided funding for the establishment of the OLDA longitudinal data system in Ohio. Ohio's application for first round of the Workforce Data Quality Initiative was submitted in August 2010, leading to six years of direct funding from the USDOL for Ohio to build a state longitudinal data system. That original proposal was a collaborative effort between the Ohio Department of Job and Family Services, the Ohio Board of Regents, and OSU. The proposal declared that the team would "... aid the State of Ohio to incorporate workforce information into longitudinal data systems, to help follow individuals through school, into and through their work life."[5]

This federal funding was dramatically expanded after the State of Ohio hired OSU to build the Ohio Education Research Center as a deliverable for the Race to the Top Project in 2012. The Race to the Top proposal was delivered in January 2012 and included a deliverable to expand the OLDA to include K12 education data. There were several features of this proposal that dramatically increased research use of the administrative data in Ohio. First, almost all doctoral granting institutions in the State of Ohio were collaborators in the original proposal.[6] Second, Race to the Top required a prodigious number of independent research and evaluation studies that made use of administrative data between 2012 and 2017. The Ohio Education Research Center website maintains an archive of research studies conducted under the Race to the Top project.

Lessons From the Establishment of the OLDA

There are some lessons from this story that are relevant to other states attempting to build integrated data systems. Federal money can be transformative, because it provides scarce resources in moments where radical technical and administrative change is scary. It is natural to think federal financial support is mostly used to pay staff and buy technology. However, the funding can also help convince skeptical senior staff in state government. This research has found, at critical junctures in making arguments to link confidential microdata, that states will of-

---

[5] Ohio Department of Job and Family Services (2010). Ohio Workforce Data Quality Initiative Proposal (pp. 1)

[6] Ohio State University, Ohio University, University of Cincinnati, Wright State University, and Case Western Reserve University were all partners in the Race to the Top Proposal, as well as a number of nonprofit organizations.

ten follow the lead of federal agencies. One example of this is states such as Ohio explicitly changed state law to enable them to receive funding under Race to the Top. This policy action at the state level was necessary to ensure that school funding was provided under the American Recovery and Reinvestment Act ARRA mechanism.

Because of the budget process in individual states, state government has specific reasons why they support use of administrative data. State and local government offices are often asked to participate in long-term research in collaboration with the federal government. For example, in 2011 the data at the OLDA was used to support a collective evaluation of the Registered Apprenticeship program in multiple states. Another example concerns longitudinal analysis of employment for welfare to work that the Center for Human Resource Research provided in the mid- to late-1990s. (Center for Human Resource Research, 2001; Reed et al., 2012). In both cases, the primary motivation for the analysis of state administrative data was an external demand from the federal government. Federal requirements for evaluations, particularly in the Department of Labor, are important reference points for legal and program officers in state agencies, as the federal laws allow for use of data to evaluate a public program (Code of Federal Regulations, 2006).

8.2.2 Data Use Examples

The OLDA is composed of microdata from a core group of State of Ohio agencies, as well as project-specific data from federal and local government, and occasionally, the private sector. Therefore, a description of the data holdings will shift over time as the memorandum of understanding that govern data exchange are altered to meet the policy priorities of government and the needs of specific researchers.

In 2019, the data holdings came from the following state agencies:

1. Ohio Department of Job and Family Services;
2. Ohio Department of Higher Education;
3. Ohio Department of Education;
4. Ohio Housing Finance Agency; and
5. Opportunities for Ohioans with Disabilities.

Table 8.1: Specific files maintained at the Ohio State University

Agency	Datasets	Years Available	Records
Ohio Department of Job and Family Services	Unemployment Insurance Wage Data, Quarterly Census on Wages and Employment, Job Seeker Information, Workforce Investment Act Standardized Record Data, Unemployment Insurance Claimant Data	From 1995 to present (varies based on files)	130 million wage records
Ohio Department of Higher Education	Higher Education Information (Student, Course, and Faculty), Ohio Technical Centers, Adult Basic and Literacy Education	From 1999 to present (varies based on files)	2 million unique students in higher education
Ohio Department of Education	Education Management Information System	From 2001 to present (varies based on table)	1.8 million unique students in K12 education
Ohio Housing Finance Agency	Ohio Housing Tenant Files	From 2014 to present	200,000 unique individuals
Opportunities for Ohioans with Disabilities	Vocational Rehabilitation	From 2011 to present	100,000 unique individuals

Notes: The full list of data files is maintained on the Ohio Longitudinal Data Archive website and changes over time. This is a selected list of core data holdings.

Within each agency, the data resources include the core agency-specific files for federal and state administered programs, such as the Workforce Innovation and Opportunity Act (WIOA). The specific files maintained at the Ohio State University are detailed in Table 8.1.

The uses of the data resources can be separated into three distinct areas: research use, government use, and training use. Initially, there are some similarities across the data uses. These three data users all make use of the OLDA for both analytical and evaluative reasons. For example, researchers most often wish to make use of the data for explicit analysis of the outcomes of Ohio programs, such as the impact of higher education on employment.

Research Use

The research uses of the OLDA depend on the programs that contribute microdata. These data allow researchers to analyze the impacts of state or federal policies on economic or educational outcomes. The specific data a researcher acquires and then uses depends on the analysis and the questions proposed.

The following topics are representative studies.

Education data

- Student dropout from high school
- Progression of STEM students through high school

Workforce data

- Impact of long-term unemployment on workforce participation
- Workforce outcomes of higher education programs

Table 8.2 provides example titles from approved research projects. Researchers obtain the Ohio data by completing a standardized set of documents and obtaining Institutional Review Board (IRB) approval. The paperwork for the researchers requires an outline of the methodological approach and a formal description of the data sets and variables, in addition to a formal IRB review.

Case Study: Registered Apprenticeships

The following case study provides an example of research use under the OLDA. One of the data resources the OLDA maintains is the Registered Apprenticeship Partners Information Data System (RAPIDS) file. This file contains data on all individuals from Ohio who enrolled in registered apprenticeship as covered by the US Department of Labor (DOL). Research teams at OSU have received approval from the State of Ohio to employ RAPIDS data to examine the employment outcomes of apprenticeships. In 2012, the Ohio State University used this data as part of a ten-state study of apprenticeships coordinated by Mathematica (Reed et al., 2012). During this project, a doctoral student

Table 8.2: Examples of approved studies using the Ohio longitudinal data

Type of Study	Example Project Title
Program evaluations	Wage Pathway Evaluation Study (Hawley et al., 2019)
	Ohio TechNet TAACCC Grant Evaluation (New Growth Group & The Ohio Education Research Center, 2018)
	GEAR UP Evaluation[1]
Descriptive and multivariate studies	College Credit Plus (Harlow, 2018)
	Academic Momentum and Undergraduate Student Attrition (Kondratjeva, Gorbunova and Hawley, 2017)

[1] This project is in progress and described at https://www.ohiohighered.org/gearup (accessed 2020-12-10).

also extended this work with the RAPIDS data in Ohio (Hsu, 2013). In 2018, a postdoctoral researcher at the Ohio State University received funding from the DOL to conduct work on the employment outcomes of the registered apprenticeship program.

The registered apprenticeship work conducted in collaboration with the State of Ohio and the DOL required detailed microdata from RAPIDS as well as the Unemployment Insurance Wage Records and the Quarterly Census on Wages and Employment. Additional work included matching educational outcomes from the Higher Education Information System to the RAPIDS files to see which apprentices got degrees or credentials and then linking to the WIOA file to examine which apprenticeships received job training. This project exemplifies the ways that a data system can be the foundation for a consistent research project that can assist state and federal government. On the basis of this work, the State of Ohio has begun to examine how apprenticeships can be expanded to improve economic outcomes for workers without college degrees.[7]

---

[7] The author discusses this topic in an op-ed for the Fordham Foundation (Hawley,

Government Use

The OLDA makes no distinction between research and government use of data from a data access perspective. Researchers based in government apply to use data through the same procedures as researchers in universities. While there are no formal differences in application, there are some dissimilarities in terms of the kinds of data that government requests and the projects they propose. Government officials tend to propose projects that are strongly related to public policies in state or local government. For example, researchers from Ohio Housing Finance Agency (OHFA) are currently collaborating with researchers at the Ohio State University on an experimental analysis of housing supports on employment. A second example focuses on the workforce data tools dashboard. In collaboration with the Ohio Department of Job and Family Services, researchers have built a dashboard to compare supply and demand on workers in the state.

Case Study: Workforce Success Measures (See Appendix for Example)

Initially completed in 2013, the Workforce Success Measures (WSM) is a dashboard and provides an example of how government uses this data. The Center for Human Resource Research team built the dashboard and maintains it. The tool is available on an OSU website.[8] Under the terms of the Workforce Development Strategic Plan that the state provided for the Governor's Office of Workforce Transformation, Ohio is required to provide annual comparative and standardized outcomes for participants in training and education programs funded through a range of federal workforce efforts. The WSM includes information on all of the programs included under the federal Workforce Innovation and Opportunity Act.

The purpose of the WSM is to give administrators the ability to monitor program performance on key metrics and compare program performance across type of program and geography. The measures used include the number of individuals completing the program, the number

---

2017).

[8]https://workforcesuccess.chrr.ohio-state.edu/home (accessed 2020-12-10).

of these individuals subsequently employed in Ohio, the median earnings of these individuals, employment stability, college enrollment, and education and training credentials earned. The dashboard is populated with data that is currently reported in administrative records (i.e., existing records collected in the course of routine operations) provided by the Ohio Department of Job and Family Services, the Ohio Department of Higher Education, and Opportunities for Ohioans with Disabilities.

8.3 Making Data Usable for Research

The OLDA data are available through a purpose-built and proprietary software system that is maintained by the Center for Human Resource Research at the Ohio State University. This system is called the investigator and provides a standardized process for researchers to examine the metadata. Individuals begin to analyze data by selecting a data source (e.g., higher education) and subsequently limiting the number of variables and time periods.

The investigator is a resource for experienced researchers. With this system researchers get access to a range of information on the relevant data. For example, each file is documented in a standardized manner in the investigator so that individual researchers can compare the kinds of variables they will receive. There is also a search function for variable names and pre-coded topics.

Data are also made useable because the research team provides guided support for applicants. When an individual proposes a research project or has trouble with data use, individual researchers can contact the staff for support.

The metadata are published in an open application on the center website. Access is through a guest account or a designated user account.[9] The metadata include all files that have been ingested and documented, up to and including wage record files, K12 education data, and higher education enrollments. Technically, the metadata

---

[9]https://www.chrr.ohio-state.edu/investigator/pages/login (accessed 2020-12-10).

include all variable names, values, and counts or other summary statistics for variables. It is possible to learn, for example, what is the cohort size of each group of high school graduates over time in Ohio. The metadata also include a sophisticated search feature, allowing identification of variables and types of data, including created variables.

8.4 Legal and Institutional Framework

8.4.1 Institutional Setup

The OLDA is a collaborative project between the State of Ohio and the Ohio State University that is categorized as a funded research project at the university; as such, it operates within a university institution. The OLDA project must comply with the typical rules for academic research projects. For example, all projects using the OLDA must include an IRB to comply with this institutional framework. Secondly, all staff directly working on the OLDA are OSU employees and must adhere to policies, including data security training.

The institutional setup for the OLDA is advantageous for several reasons. First, working within a university setting is somewhat insulated from the day-to-day politics, compared to being embedded in a state agency. Second, staffing is easier in the university environment—as hiring happens through students, recent graduates, and research scientist roles—as opposed to limiting recruitment to state government human resource systems. Finally, there is an openness to university life that enables more innovation with data science. Students and faculty bring a fresh perspective to using data to improve government that supplements what state and local government agencies can implement.

8.4.2 Legal Context for Data Use

There are several federal legal frameworks that govern data access, the Family Educational Rights and Privacy Act (FERPA) and the Code of Federal Regulations 20 (Section 603). These two overarching legal documents govern the rules for both government and external researchers. FERPA prohibits the release of individual student data, barring certain exceptions. Explicit consent must be in place for students before any data are released. FERPA includes an audit and evaluation exception that allows for state or local education authorities to cooperate with an integrated data system (IDS) to access student records to ensure that evaluations of government programs receive the linked data needed (Privacy Technical Assistance Center, 2017).

The Code of Federal Regulations includes Section 603, which governs the use of wage records or unemployment insurance data. Section 603 limits the use of wage record data outside of the Unemployment Insurance Program, but the federal Workforce Innovation and Opportunity Act (WIOA) rules explicitly encourage the use of the wage record data to the extent that is practical. The WIOA rules are focused on increasing the use of wage record data to study specific programs (e.g., Vocational Rehabilitation or Title I).

As states built the technical systems to document state data, the federal government worked to establish a legal framework for accessing administrative records to conduct research. Federal rules such as FERPA (enacted in 1974) were amended over time to allow greater research access. The amendments in 1994 allowed the federal and state government to allow access to student data under some conditions. Later revisions of FERPA allowed use of student records in integrated data systems when specific exceptions are met in use of the data for audit and evaluation and the data system is providing a service or function to school districts. Both the Code of Federal Regulations 20 (Section 603) and the final regulations of the WIOA (Final Rule) are necessary in legal agreements when wage records and job training data are to be used. WIOA makes it clear that states are required to participate in evaluations to the extent possible. (Office of the Federal Register, 2016).

Through a study of the employment outcomes of individuals enrolled in welfare, researchers have also learned (in recent years) that state rules vary in how they interpret data access to the Supplemental Nu-

Table 8.3: Important legal documents to review for the research community

Law or Administrative Regulation	Document
Family Educational Rights and Privacy Act (FERPA)	Audit and Evaluation Rules, Privacy Technical Assistance Center (2017)
Workforce Innovation and Opportunity Act (Final rule)	https://www.doleta.gov/wioa/about/final-rules/ (accessed 2020-12-10)
Joint Guidance on Data Matching to Facilitate WIOA Performance Reporting and Evaluation	https://www2.ed.gov/policy/gen/guid/fpco/pdf/final-ferpa-tegl-report.pdf (accessed 2020-12-10)
Unemployment Insurance and the Workforce Innovation and Opportunity Act of 2014	https://wdr.doleta.gov/directives/attach/UIPL/UIPL_20-15.pdf (accessed 2020-12-10)

trition Assistance Program (SNAP) and the Temporary Assistance for Needy Families (TANF). In some states, such as Illinois or Texas, these data are shared with researchers, while in Ohio both federal programs' data are largely off-limits to the research community.

Formal Governance Process

The OLDA is governed by a formal memorandum of understanding (MOU) and a data sharing agreement that is completed on an annual or biannual basis. This MOU is initiated by one of the member agencies (Ohio Department of Job and Family Services), signed by all the remaining agencies (Education, Higher Education, Housing Finance, and Opportunities for Ohioans with Disabilities), and thereafter by the Ohio State University. The overarching legal agreement establishes three governance committees that oversee the rules of the MOU. The Policy Council governs larger questions about how the data system can be used and includes representatives from the senior management of all of the executive agencies as well as the governor's office. The Data Stewards govern specific data systems included in the OLDA and serves as a technical resource for the analysts proposing and completing projects. The Governing Committee is a single point of contact between the center director and the lead agency (ODJFS).

Governance has evolved over time. At the outset there were frequent meetings between policy level staff, particularly during times of transition in the governor's office. In recent years, the Policy Committee meets at least once a quarter and the Data Stewards meet monthly. The kinds of decisions these committees can make vary, but the Policy Committee is responsible for big questions, such as what data files should be included in the archive. The Data Stewards are concerned with detailed questions, such as how should significant changes in the definitions of variables be handled.

All projects must be approved by each of the agencies which own data that is requested. A parallel approval process is in place for review of findings. All authors must submit studies to the research team for disclosure review by the agencies that own the data. It is worth noting that there is a thirty-day review period in the governance rules, but agencies often deal with the review more quickly.

8.4.3 Legal Framework for Granting Data Access

Technically, data are available in a de-identified format by secure transfer to approved researchers. Standard rules have been developed both to govern the transmission of data as well as to ensure that individual identification cannot occur. Individual researchers must limit use to approved computers and computing environments. Changes in personnel, such as the addition of a research assistant, must be negotiated ahead of time. Access is also limited to specific data elements and research questions. Individual researchers must declare the focus of the study, determine which variables they require to answer the question, and limit publications to these elements.

Access is also time limited. All researchers sign legal assurances that they will delete the data provided after a certain period of time. They affirm that researcher staff will only retain outputs for support of research publications. Researchers must ensure that the university research system they use for the data analysis must support encryption and be audited on a periodic basis.

There are five forms that the individual researcher must file to apply for access: (1) a data use procedures and checklist, (2) a confidentiality form, (3) a data use agreement, (4) the Collaborative Institutional Training Initiative (CITI) responsible research use certification document, and (5) an institutional review board (IRB) approval letter.

8.5 Protection of Sensitive and Personal Data: The Five Safes Framework

8.5.1 Safe Projects

The research supports safe projects by overseeing the application process. Individual researchers apply and declare the research questions. Projects must be related to either policy or research priorities of state and local government. The specific language is to "provide public benefits." The governing policy council values research that can help understand the impact of priority state policies, such as eliminating social promotion in third grade or reducing infant mortality. A safe project is one that addresses a policy priority that the state is also invested in understanding

Determining which projects are appropriate is complex and changes over time. In the early stages of the OLDA, individual access was limited to studies that were explicitly encouraged under the Race to the Top or Workforce Data Quality Initiative applications. In other words, because the topics and data required were described in overarching federal agreements, these subjects were supported. In later years, the research team broadened the application to topics that could be user identified (projects the State of Ohio had not yet conceived). As the team gained experience, there was a shift from more directed calls for research in specific areas to research on topics that addressed priorities that came directly from researchers without any guidance.

Currently, there is a multi-stage review mechanism in place that screens safe and unsafe projects. Individuals complete a one-page project description to ensure that a project is acceptable without requiring technical details on variables. Projects can be rejected at this point, a stage akin to a "desk reject" from a journal. A second stage of review for safety is conducted with a more formal application, which allows the research team to make the case to state agencies as to why the project is appropriate. At this stage, a safe project is one that has a topic of interest to one or more state agencies by virtue of advancing knowledge of a specific state policy as well as one that is possible to carry out with the data maintained under the OLDA.

8.5.2 Safe People

Safety in terms of personnel is ensured in a number of specific ways. Safe users are described as qualified, trustworthy individuals. Qualification is determined in part by role, where faculty and professional researchers are preferred over students. Student data access is only allowed under the supervision of a faculty member because data access often takes a year or more. The adopted safe person rule has a requirement if a student applies: it is only under the supervision of a researcher and that they understand the extensive time it might require to wait for data access.

Safe people are primarily determined by completion of an Institutional Review Board application and forwarding these approval letters as part of the application. There is no option to submit an application for data without this letter being available ahead of time, unlike with National Science Foundation (NSF) or National Institute of Health (NIH) proposals. Researchers might receive an exemption from the IRB but must still provide this information as part of the application.

There is also an obligation that researchers complete several OSU research review forms, even if they have completed these at another institution. For example, under the terms of the research they must complete OSU's CITI training for human subjects as well as the security policy and confidentiality agreement that is held by the Center. These affirmations are necessary to ensure that researchers are in compliance and aware of explicit security rules.

8.5.3 Safe Settings

Data access is allowed on the work computer that individuals declare in the application process. The office location of the computer at the place of work is collected and it is required that it is a desktop, not a laptop computer. Individuals are forbidden from using USB or flash drives with this data and receive data only through a secure file transfer protocol (SFTP) directly to the computer they declare in the application. Some users may access the data on computers at the center directly, if the file sizes present a problem for their personal computers or if the agencies require access to certain data items be limited to OLDA offices. There is no option for remote access or virtual access to items that are limited by physical location.

8.5.4 Safe Data

Data in the OLDA are de-identified by staff and at all times when used by researchers. The process of de-identification removes clear personally identifiable information (PII), such as full date of birth, social security number, or name. Depending on the data file, staff make some changes to ensure that the data do not identify high-earners or people enrolled in very small enrollment programs. Because PII is also created by combining data files, recombining data generated from the OLDA with data that comes from other sources is prohibited. This is necessary to state because supplementing the data with additional survey or administrative files might make it possible to identify people.

8.5.5 Safe Outputs

Disclosure review is required for all analyses or reports. Researchers submit all files to the OLDA at Ohio State, which coordinates approval with the data owners in state agencies. In these cases, OLDA requires thirty days for review. In addition to outputs, the research team reviews the actual written reports or publications. This is necessary to ensure that any findings or results from the study are communicated to the data owners prior to being published or presented to other groups.

Traditionally the researchers pay attention to cell size and geographic level of disaggregation.

Safe data also require that researchers maintain cell counts of a certain number (for example, ten or less for data from the Unemployment Wage Records). Furthermore, safe data mask the employer or industry at a specific level and limit the geographic level of analysis. For example, it is not allowed to reveal a cell of employment for a specific industry where there are three or fewer establishments in a geographic area or employment in a firm makes up 80 percent or more employment in a geographic region.

8.6 Data Life Cycle and Reproducibility

All data that are part of the OLDA are preserved within the existing data agreements. Technically, these files are not replaced over time; additional years or quarters of data are added to the existing file structure. It is possible that the data will be deleted (subject to the legal agreement from the agency). OLDA has had occasions where the data for specific projects must be deleted but not the underlying microdata. However, if an agency requires deletion of the data, OLDA's legal MOU requires compliance.

Researcher extracts are maintained permanently on OLDA systems. This is easy to accomplish as the files are simply combinations of existing microdata. Moreover, even without the extracts OLDA staff can easily reconstruct data files from the metadata system. Individuals submit these queries for data extracts, and these data dictionaries are maintained in individual user accounts as well as by the research team.

OLDA does not keep researcher generated files except for those submitted to the disclosure review process. Individual files that generate statistical results for publications are maintained by approved researchers. In fact, these must be deleted at the end of the approved period of time. If a researcher has a year to use the data, they must delete the files at the end of that year. Individuals complete and notarize a data destruction certificate that must be forwarded to the research team.

8.7 Sustainability and Continued Success

8.7.1 Outreach

At the creation of the formal data center, OLDA staff conducted a range of outreach activities to socialize educational administrators in Ohio and external researchers. Between 2008 and 2015, we conducted presentations on the data system for many different local groups, including associations of deans from different disciplines and Ohio specific research associations, such as the Ohio Association of Career and Technical Education and the Job and Family Services Director's Association. These meetings included a range of published materials, videos, and dedicated websites for researchers.

Outreach in these early years was quite formal. There was a research advisory committee that included tenured faculty from almost all schools in Ohio. The committee developed materials, solicited applications, and served as cheerleaders for data use at their individual campuses. Since the end of the Race to the Top and Workforce Data Quality Initiative, OLDA has worked on outreach with established research teams as well as responding to individuals directed to our team by agencies. Some of the Ohio agencies actually direct researchers to OLDA systems.

Outreach was also supported by presentations at national meetings, such as the National Center for Education Statistics (NCES) STATS-DC Data Summit and Workforce Data Quality Initiative convening in Washington, DC. OLDA presented for approximately six years at these meetings to states, serving to get the word out about state level use of research data to improve programs. Additionally, OLDA teams made presentations for the US Department of Labor, the Data Quality Campaign, and the National Skills Coalition.

8.7.2 Metrics of Success

Overall Qualitative Outcomes

There are a relatively small number of research centers with state administrative data in the United States. There are two models of administrative data centers, States such as Kentucky maintain an administrative data center inside state government. In contrast, centers such as the Indiana Business Research Center and OLDA are maintained within colleges or universities. Therefore, grading the progress made is difficult.

While metrics (addressed below) are important, overall developing the capacity to work with state government as a partner is the primary outcome. Metrics that measure the organizational capacity of the research center are much more difficult to quantify. For example, Kentucky has a superior legal situation because the state laws formally designate a state office (Kentucky Statistics) as the data system. Ohio's program is entirely governed by MOUs. However, being imbedded in state government also potentially limits research use of data, making the data system tied to state policy priorities in direct ways and preventing the open use of data by academics and policy researchers. There are trade-offs to having a data system within government.

A second measure of organizational capacity might be staffing or longevity. In Ohio, researchers have been lucky to have an operation that goes back in one form or another to 2000 and even further back for some research projects. In the case of Florida, Illinois, Maryland, Texas, and a handful of other states, the data systems have existed for at least as long as Ohio's in some form or fashion. Staff continuity is critical to longevity.

Organizational success also requires consistent political support. Ohio has had over ten years of consistent political leadership on data and workforce developing, leading to strong foundations for research work in collaboration with state and local government. What seems important is that government must see data as a resource to improve outcomes as opposed to something to limit access to.

Metrics

OLDA researchers monitor a number of metrics (somewhat informally), including (1) the number of data sets provided, (2) the number of projects completed, and (3) the number of websites and dashboards. The following are examples of recent accounting on these metrics.

Data sets. The OLDA maintains data from five different state agencies. The newest one was added in 2017 and the oldest one prior to 1999. Within each agency the number of data sets expands each year as the agencies increase holdings. For example, the Ohio education data began in 2001 and now includes data through 2019. It is updated annually. The LMI workforce data are added every quarter and started in 1995 with the unemployment wage record data. The volume of the data sets is significant, more so because some of the files have over 100,000 variables rather than because of the volume of storage OLDA maintains.

Projects completed. Research output includes 28 published studies in the last five years. These include academic articles, working papers, and presentations submitted to the research center. The list is maintained in a bibliography[10] and is not inclusive of in-progress work or work that has been submitted to the center but not yet reviewed or finalized.

Dashboards. The OLDA team works extensively on supporting state and local government in Ohio with dashboards and scorecards. The team has built several that are maintained every year for over five years and some that are more recent. OLDA keeps website hit traffic for these dashboards to examine the location and overall use of the dashboards in the state.

---

[10]https://www.chrr.ohio-state.edu/content/olda_bib/olda_bib.html (accessed 2020-12-10).

About the Author

Joshua D. Hawley is a professor in the John Glenn College of Public Affairs at the Ohio State University (OSU). He also serves in leadership roles at two research centers of OSU: director of the Ohio Education Research Center at the Glenn College and Associate Director for the Center for Human Resource Research (CHRR). The focus of both centers is state level administrative data. Since approximately 2009 the centers have partnered with the State of Ohio to store Ohio administrative records. The primary project for the Ohio Analytics Partnership is the Ohio Longitudinal Data Archive. Professor Hawley currently serves as the lead faculty for this effort. In addition, he teaches classes in Education and Workforce Development policy and Data Sciences.

References in Chapter 8

Borus, Michael E. 1982. "An inventory of longitudinal data sets of interest to economists." *Review of Public Data Use*, 10(1-2): 113–126.

Center for Human Resource Research. 2001. "Report on the Ohio closed cases study." The Ohio State University Report. http://chrr.ohio-state.edu/content/surveys/closed_cases/reportpart1.pdf (accessed 2020-12-07).

Code of Federal Regulations. 2006. "20 CFR Part 603 - Federal-State Unemployment Compensation (UC) Program; Confidentiality and Disclosure of State UC Information." https://www.ecfr.gov/cgi-bin/text-idx?SID=2856c3aa5841ccc6a84addf28920d3ad&mc=true&node=pt20.3.603&rgn=div5 (accessed 2020-12-10).

Harlow, Kristin. 2018. "Evaluation of College Credit Plus: Dual Enrollment in Ohio." PhD diss. The Ohio State University. https://etd.ohiolink.edu/!etd.send_file?accession=osu1543312670683351&disposition=inline (accessed 2020-10-05).

Hawley, J. D. 2017. "Making good on the apprenticeship promise will require major investments in states." *Ohio Gadfly Daily*. https://fordhaminstitute.org/ohio/commentary/making-good-apprenticeship-promise-will-require-major-investment-states (accessed 2020-10-05).

Hawley, J. D., and Shu-Chen Chiang. 2013. "Developmental Education for Adults and Academic Achievement." In *International Guide to Student Achievement*. , ed. John Hattie and M. Anderman, Eric, 19–23. Florence, KY:Taylor and Francis. https://visible-learning.org/2013/02/international-guide-to-student-achievement/ (accessed 2020-12-07).

Hawley, Joshua D., and Dixie Sommers. 2003. "Ohio's adult workforce education system: an initial investigation using administrative data." Center on Education and Training for Employment, The Ohio State University Report.

Hawley, Joshua D., and Shu-Chen Chiang. 2017. "Does developmental education help? The academic performance of adult undergraduate students in community colleges." *Community College Journal of Research and Practice*, 41(7): 387–404. https://doi.org/10.1080/10668926.2016.1194237.

Hawley, Joshua D., Dixie Sommers, and Edwin Meléndez. 2003. "The Earnings Impact of Adult Workforce Education in Ohio." Community Development Research Center.

Hawley, Joshua D., Dixie Sommers, and Edwin Meléndez. 2005. "The Impact of Institutional Collaborations on the Earnings of Adult Workforce Education Completers." *Adult Education Quarterly*, 56(1): 21–38. https://doi.org/10.1177/0741713605280140.

Hawley, Joshua D., Tian Lou, Randall J. Olsen, and Christopher Spence. 2019. "Report on the Evaluation of Ohio's Wage Pathways Program." The Ohio State University Report. https://chrr.osu.edu/projects/wage-pathways (accessed 2020-10-05).

Hosseinichimeh, Niyousha, Rod MacDonald, Ayaz Hyder, Alireza Ebrahimvandi, Lauren Porter, Rebecca Reno, Julie Maurer, Deborah Lines Andersen, George Richardson, Joshua Hawley, and David F. Andersen. 2017. "Group model building techniques for rapid elicitation of parameter values, effect sizes, and data sources." *System Dynamics Review*, 33(1): 71–84. https://doi.org/10.1002/sdr.1575.

Hsu, Yun-Hsiang. 2013. "Training Externalities and Institutional Determinants: Assessing Rentention in Ohio Apprenticeship Programs." PhD diss. The Ohio State University. https://etd.ohiolink.edu/!etd.send_file?accession=osu1366224121&disposition=inline (accessed 2020-10-05).

Kondratjeva, Olga, Elena Gorbunova, and Joshua D. Hawley. 2017. "Academic Momentum and Undergraduate Student Attrition in US and Russian Universities." *Comparative Education Review*, 61(3): 607–633. https://doi.org/10.1086/692608.

New Growth Group & The Ohio Education Research Center. 2018. "The Ohio Technical Skills Innovation Network (Ohio TechNet)." New Growth Group Report. https://ohiotechnet.org/wp-content/uploads/2018/10/Ohio-TechNet-Evaluation-Final-Report.pdf (accessed 2020-10-05).

Office of the Federal Register. 2016. "Federal Register." 81(161). https://www.govinfo.gov/app/details/FR-2016-08-19.

Pfeiffer, Jay. 1998. "From Performance Reporting to Performance-Based Funding: Florida's Experiences in Workforce Development Performance." *New Directions for Community Colleges*, 1998(104): 17–28. https://doi.org/10.1002/cc.10402.

Privacy Technical Assistance Center. 2017. "Integrated Data Systems and Student Privacy." https://studentprivacy.ed.gov/resources/integrated-data-systems-and-student-privacy (accessed 2020-10-05).

Reed, Debbie, Albert Yung-Hsu Liu, Rebecca Kleinman, Annalisa Mastri, Davin Reed, Samina Sattar, and Jessica Ziegler. 2012. "An Effectiveness Assessment and Cost-Benefit Analysis of Registered Apprenticeship in 10 States." Mathematica Policy Research Report. https://www.mathematica.org/our-publications-and-findings/publications/an-effectiveness-assessment-and-costbenefit-analysis-of-registered-apprenticeship-in-10-states (accessed 2020-10-05).

Stevens, David W. 1989. "Using State Unemployment Insurance Wage-Records to Trace the Subsequent Labor Market Experiences of Vocational Education Program Leavers." Human Resource Data Systems, Inc. Report.

Stevens, David W. 2012. "Documents and Presentations Enabled by or Related to the Administrative Data Research and Evaluation (ADARE) Project 1998-2012." Jacob France Institute, University of Baltimore Report. http://www.jacob-france-institute.org/wp-content/uploads/ADARE-publications-presentations-compendium-11-8-12.pdf (accessed 2020-10-05).

Stone, Deborah. 2012. *Policy Paradox: The Art of Political Decision Making.* . 3rd ed., New York:WW Norton.

Workforce Information Council. 2014. "Enhancing Unemployment Insurance Wage Records: Potential Benefits, Barriers, and Opportunities - A Summary of First Year Study Activities and Finding." Workforce Information Council, U.S. Department of Labor Report. https://www.bls.gov/advisory/bloc/enhancing-unemployment-insurance-wage-records_fy.pdf (accessed 2020-10-05).

CHAPTER 8

Appendix

Appendix A: Resources and Dashboards

Appendix A can be found in the Online Appendix at admind atahandbook.mit.edu/book/v1.0/olda.html#olda-appendix.

Appendix B: Case Study (Workforce Success Measures)

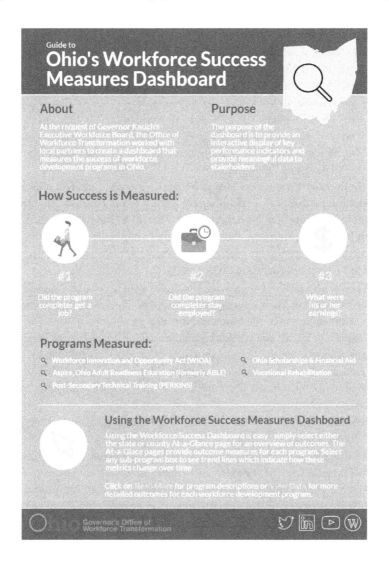

CHAPTER 9

New Brunswick Institute for Research, Data and Training: A Ten-Year Partnership Between Government and Academia

Donna Curtis Maillet (University of New Brunswick)
James Ted McDonald (University of New Brunswick)

9.1 Summary

This case study describes the establishment and development of the New Brunswick Institute for Research, Data and Training (NB-IRDT) in Fredericton, NB, Canada. NB-IRDT is a provincial research data center and data custodian as defined in NB legislation and is the product of an extensive and ongoing collaboration between the Government of New Brunswick (GNB) and academic members of the University of New Brunswick (UNB) among others. Launched in 2015 with the delivery of the first data set, NB-IRDT now holds and provides research access to more than 45 linkable person-level data sets from across the

---

Copyright © Donna Curtis Maillet and James Ted McDonald.
Cite as: Curtis Maillet, Donna, and James Ted McDonald. "New Brunswick Institute for Research, Data and Training: A Ten-Year Partnership Between Government and Academia." In: Cole, Shawn, Iqbal Dhaliwal, Anja Sautmann, and Lars Vilhuber (eds.), *Handbook on Using Administrative Data for Research and Evidence-based Policy*. Cambridge, MA: Abdul Latif Jameel Poverty Action Lab. 2020.

spectrum of service provision in NB. This includes access to data on health, social assistance, education and training, aged care, and workers compensation. Data sets are provided from government agencies and other public bodies as well as non-profit organizations. The case study highlights notable or unique aspects of NB-IRDT and describes the context of how those aspects came to be part of NB-IRDT policy. Aspects of particular note are (1) the legal authority NB-IRDT has to receive, hold, and provide access to personal level linkable data from across NB public bodies, (2) data access that is not restricted to academic users but also users from government, the non-profit sector, and the private sector without a required affiliation to UNB, and (3) active engagement with senior government decision-makers in collaborative research programs focused on government priority areas.

9.2 Introduction

9.2.1 Motivation and Background

The impetus for the collaboration that would lead to the establishment of NB-IRDT was a recognition by certain key senior provincial civil servants following the financial crisis of 2007 to 2008 that evidence to support much government expenditure to deliver healthcare, education and training, and social programs[1] was lacking. Although large amounts of data were being collected by government agencies, institutional barriers such as separate IT systems, and legal barriers such as restrictions on inter-institutional data sharing, meant that personal data could not easily be shared between those agencies. At the same time, successive years of civil service cutbacks had markedly reduced government's capacity to undertake research and program evaluation itself. In the words of one deputy minister, "we have spent CA$2 billion over the last ten years on programs and still have no idea what

---
[1]In Canada, provincial governments have responsibility for providing services in these three key areas and as a result, spending on health, education, and income support consumes much of a province's budget. For 2019, two-thirds of the NB budget was forecast to be spent in these areas.

has worked."[2] Compounding the need for action were mounting fiscal and demographic pressures on the provincial budget: NB is small (population in 2019 was less than 750,000), is almost 50 percent rural, has one of the most rapidly aging population profiles in Canada, and has relatively high rates of obesity and chronic disease such as diabetes and chronic obstructive pulmonary disease (Statistics Canada, 2020). At the same time, researchers seeking to undertake work using provincial administrative data were required to follow a time-consuming and opaque process that put significant resource demands both on the applicant and on the department from which data were sought. Opportunities to access linked data from multiple departments and public bodies were negligible. Similarly, internal government staff faced similar difficulties with gaining access to data from multiple agencies, meaning that most of the research that did occur was siloed within particular agencies.

Although it would be five years between initial conception of the idea for NB-IRDT and receipt of the first administrative data set in 2015, certain core principles guided development. The first of these was that any research undertaken should be credible, independent, transparent, and rigorous. This would lead to more informed decision-making where the public and other stakeholders would have confidence that sound and unbiased research had been provided to those decision-makers. The institute would thus be situated in a university where the institute leadership answered to the vice president (research) and not government. It would also be empowered to act as data custodian and have the right to grant and control access to administrative data for legitimate research purposes. Furthermore, while government would have an active role in the setting of research priorities and in the review of particular proposals, it would not have veto power, nor could it veto the dissemination of research results. Instead, a rigorous approval process was jointly developed that respected privacy, ensured only legitimate research (where research is broadly defined) was conducted, and that academic freedom was enshrined. As NB-IRDT developed,

---

[2]Personal correspondence between Ted McDonald and Jean-Marc Dupuis, March 2018.

CHAPTER 9

these policies continued to evolve to reflect the five safes framework to be discussed in more detail below.

The second principle was that NB-IRDT would be a resource for the Province of NB and would not be only a UNB facility. With four major universities, two medical schools, and two regional health authorities all research active in the health domain, this data resource would need to be available to all. Although it would be established within UNB, right of access to data for research was not restricted to UNB researchers nor even academic researchers. As long as the proposed research had legitimate research inquiry goals, there were no restrictions on who could request access to the data: individuals from academic, public, private, and non-profit sectors from NB and elsewhere could all do so as long as they followed the prescribed data access protocol. At the same time, NB-IRDT was left to develop its own fee structure to support the longer-term sustainability of the Institute.

The third principle was that for government to reap the full benefits of providing data to support policymaking, data needed to be linkable at the individual level and span the range of government service provision. Thus, the Province of NB undertook to support data transfer to NB-IRDT where the onus would be on individual agencies to demonstrate why particular data elements would not be transferred rather than on NB-IRDT to justify why they should. In other words, the government committed to the eventual transfer of all research-relevant data, and this was extended to include all public bodies in NB. NB-IRDT would in turn assume the responsibility of ensuring minimum required data disclosure to researchers for approved projects. Parallel to this, although NB lacked a universal personal identifying number for all government services, there was agreement that the provincial health insurance (Medicare) number would provide the index backbone to allow all data to be made linkable at the individual level. The Department of Health undertook to provide this corporate function for NB-IRDT and public bodies seeking to disclose data so that although researchers could access linked data files, neither NB-IRDT nor researchers accessing data through it would see Medicare numbers.

A fourth principle was that no government department or public body would be compelled to enter into data sharing agreements with NB-IRDT, though if they did it was understood that they would transfer close to complete data sets to the NB-IRDT platform. In every case, the decision to transfer data to NB-IRDT would remain the decision of the agency's senior decision-maker (deputy ministers in the case of GNB departments). It would fall to NB-IRDT, its Government champions, and the wider research community to make the case that doing so would be in the interest of the disclosing entity.

9.2.2 Data Use Examples

NB-IRDT represents a transformation in health and social science research infrastructure in NB and as of June 2020 holds more than forty administrative data sets spanning hospitalizations, immigrant arrivals, cancer screening, post-secondary training, long term care facilities, K–12 school report cards, and many other topics. In addition, more than fifty research projects have been initiated, are in progress, or have been completed since 2015, involving academic, clinical health, government, and private sector researchers.[3] Much of the research in the health domain has been undertaken under the auspices of a research collaboration with the Department of Health through the Canadian Institutes of Health Research (CIHR)[4] Strategy for Patient-Oriented Research (SPOR).[5] The SPOR Support Unit program, of which the Maritime SPOR SUPPORT Unit (MSSU) is a key element, involves equal contributions of federal and provincial funding and is described in detail elsewhere. Projects underway or completed include examinations of the impact of surgical experience on patient outcomes, the effects on health service use of rural hospital closure, and a series of projects on the effects of air quality, living in proximity to green space and blue space, and industrial emissions on different dimensions of health and mortality. Another project underway in 2020 undertakes program evaluation of support services and medical treatment to individuals with

---

[3]See the NB-IRDT website for more details: https://www.unb.ca/nbirdt/ (accessed 2020-12-10).
[4]https://cihr-irsc.gc.ca/e/45859.html (accessed 2020-12-10).
[5]http://www.spor-maritime-srap.ca/ (accessed 2020-12-10).

Hepatitis C who engage in high-risk behavior. The project will consider cost savings not just in terms of healthcare but also reliance on social assistance and other social programming and interactions with the court and corrections systems.

While the social value of this research and data access is significant, it does not in and of itself justify the provincial government's significant investment of time, money, and resources in an environment of fiscal restraint and government cutbacks to services. To ensure that work directly relevant to government's policy priority areas would be undertaken, two core departments entered into multi-year research agreements with NB-IRDT, in addition to the collaboration with the Department of Health through MSSU . These agreements specified funding for research and the structure of a governance model that would identify and monitor projects of direct relevance to those departments. It is noteworthy that through partnership with NB-IRDT, particular agencies could gain access to linked data collected by other agencies for research and program evaluation that would not otherwise be accessible. An additional benefit of the research agreements was that internal government resources were mobilized to support on data preparation and transfer, and data so transferred would also be available to the broader research community.

The first research agreement signed was with the New Brunswick Department of Post-Secondary Education, Training and Labour (PETL) and runs from 2018 to 2022 inclusive. Research questions identified by the governance board as being of highest policy relevance included determinants of immigrant attraction and retention (in particular those coming to NB as provincial nominees), retention and labor market outcomes of individuals participating in government-funded training and skills development programs, and topics around labor market demand and supply for employers, entrepreneurs, and recent graduates. Related work underway in 2020 involves linking K–12 school data with post-secondary education data and Medicare registration data to assess factors affecting the transition of NB school children into higher education and subsequent retention of those highly trained graduates in NB. Projects have used a range of quantitative and qualitative research methods as determined by the research team and dictated by the nature of the question and the data available but usually involve analysis of secondary data.

The second research agreement signed was with the New Brunswick Department of Education and Early Childhood Development (EECD) and involved two large scale program evaluations of two key EECD policy initiatives. The first involved evaluation across a range of outcomes of the introduction of a longer school day for younger children (K–2 inclusive), while the second involved evaluation of a subsidy for lower income families with children in regulated early learning centers. In each case, it was the department that introduced the particular program and NB-IRDT conducted the program evaluation using routinely collected data. Both short- and long-term impacts were of interest and both research programs involve linked longitudinal data from a number of public bodies. Such evaluation of these initiatives would not have been possible prior to the creation of NB-IRDT.

It is instructive to highlight one dimension of these research collaborations that was particularly important to government; namely, an analysis of immigrant retention. Although responsible for immigrant attraction and retention, PETL has no internal means to observe how many immigrants actually settled in NB and how many remained after a given period of time, even though immigration remains a cornerstone of the province's economic development plan. This is primarily because PETL did not have access to data on other service use that would indicate continued presence in NB nor the means to link the data even if they did so. However, by linking records on the granting of permanent residency through the provincial nominee program to immigrants to their Medicare registration data, researchers at NB-IRDT have been able to identify and report on key retention measures.[6] These include when or whether those granted permanent residency (in particular those nominated through the provincial nominee program) actually settled in NB, how long they remained in NB, and what fac-

---

[6]NB-IRDT signed a data sharing agreement with the Federal Government's Immigration, Refugees and Citizenship Canada agency (IRCC) who have provided landing records on all permanent residents to Canada not just provincial nominees.

tors (visa category, country of origin, age, family connections, prior education) influence those outcomes. The timeliness of the Medicare registration data has meant that retention outcomes can be observed without the substantial delays that accompany seeking access to other data sets such as tax filer data. Results from NB-IRDT reporting have helped PETL target more precisely where their international recruitment efforts should be aimed.

In recognition of the increasing depth of the collaboration between NB-IRDT and GNB, the parties entered into a memorandum of understanding in 2018 that committed both parties to achieving the long-term sustainability of NB-IRDT, to the transfer of all research-relevant data that GNB collected to NB-IRDT, and to recognizing NB-IRDT as a researcher of choice for GNB.

9.3 Making Data Usable for Research

As is often the case with administrative data, the development of curated, documented databases ready for use by researchers is a resource intensive process. Information systems of most provincial data custodians in NB are designed around funding for services, and extraction of data for purposes other than regular reporting and monitoring is rarely straightforward. Even when the transfer of a data set to NB-IRDT is a high priority for the disclosing agency and when all regulatory and legal questions about transfer of the data have been resolved, the agency may lack the human resources to dedicate to data preparation. And while much work on data documentation, cleaning, and validation can be conducted by dedicated personnel at NB-IRDT once files are received, significant work must still be undertaken at the disclosing agency. Furthermore, it may be that only the largest agencies have the necessary data and programming expertise to undertake this work in-house. Thus, in most cases without externally funded resources the pace of data transfer would be extremely slow. There have been a few notable exceptions, the most notable being the Discharge Abstract Database (DAD) of in-patient hospital stays. The DAD was an exception because hospital inpatient systems report systematically to the Department of Health in a standard form for subsequent disclosure to the Canadian Institute for Health Information (CIHI). CIHI then returns a curated data set back to the disclosing province.

As the success of these research programs would be contingent on timely data access, data transfers to NB-IRDT were made much more efficient with the signing of various master data sharing agreements (MDSA) and the standardization of data transfer and access templates. NB-IRDT entered into an MDSA with the Department of Health in 2014, with both of NB's regional health authorities in 2017, with the Department of Post-Secondary Education, Training and Labour (PETL) in 2018, with the Department of Education and Early Childhood Development (EECD) also in 2018, and with the Department of Social Development (SD) in 2019. Paralleling those agreements was the development and approval of a standard mechanism for departments and other public bodies to share identifying information with the Department of Health for data matching purposes.[7]

One successful approach taken by NB-IRDT is the secondment of NB-IRDT data specialists—analysts with expertise in administrative data—to particular agencies where the specialists are able to access the system data as if they were agency employees. While embedded, the specialists work closely with agency subject matter experts and IT specialists to understand the data systems and compile the data. Upon developing this case study, NB-IRDT personnel are embedded in PETL, SD, and both regional health authorities. The arrangements typically involve 50 percent of the analysts' time spent with the government partner and the other 50 percent at NB-IRDT. Terms are for one year and renewed as required. The host departments do not pay for this work directly as salaries are covered by MSSU or other funding sources as appropriate. Once transferred to NB-IRDT, data sets are checked for errors and completeness and then data codebooks (i.e., dictionaries) are completed according to a standard template.

Since NB-IRDT does not receive Medicare numbers and so is unable to do its own data linkage, the Institute has adopted, in partnership

---

[7]The role of undertaking all data matching taken by the Department of Health will be discussed in more detail later in the chapter.

with the New Brunswick Department of Health (DH), the creation of a crosswalk file process by DH. To create this crosswalk file, data custodians are required to assign an interim record ID to all records identified for transfer. Prior to transfer, the data set is divided into two parts, a *program* that contains only variables of research interest to be sent to NB-IRDT and a source ID file containing only the unique identifiers to be sent to DH. It is at the Department of Health that a unique Institute ID is attached to every interim ID, creating a crosswalk file that when transferred to NB-IRDT replaces the interim id in the program file. Using the Institute ID, a specific project data folder may then be created for an approved project by matching the Institute IDs across data sets. The Institute ID is universal, though on its own does not convey any identifiable information nor can it be reverse engineered to determine an underlying Medicare number. However, since the Institute ID is what makes data sets linkable, specific safeguards applied to this process include non-disclosure by DH of how Institute IDs are assigned, the complete deletion of all crosswalk files by DH thirty days after transfer to NB-IRDT, limited staff and access permission for creation of project folders, and the replacement of the Institute ID with an arbitrary number prior to access by researchers.

With the NB-IRDT data platform established and the ongoing addition of data sets, resources are now being dedicated to the development of metadata best practices. Six initiatives have been implemented. First, an experienced data analyst has been assigned the role of data manager to ensure the integration of metadata conventions and standards. Second, data documenting the transfer, receipt, and addition of all data sets to the NB-IRDT platform are systematically recorded, which facilitates necessary processes for the curation, updating, retention, and auditing of data sets. Third, all data sets transferred to the NB-IRDT are assigned a point person from the data team. It is their responsibility to develop a data set codebook for publication on the Institute public website.[8] Functioning as data dictionaries, codebooks describe the general content of the data set and date ranges. They also list

---

[8] See NB-IRDT website Data Holdings at https://www.nbirdt.ca/holdings for examples of available codebooks (accessed 2020-12-10).

the data variables available including definitions and format information. They do not, however, contain frequencies. Whenever possible codebooks are developed in partnership with original data set business owners, although existing documentation from the business owner is often quite limited or nonexistent. To assist in this development, original data owners must provide the name and contact information of a data steward for consultation on the specific data set. Codebooks include a description of the data set, a complete listing of variables, and their descriptors and related codes. A fourth initiative is the development of data set concept dictionaries. Currently only available to staff and to approved users in consultation, these tools guide researchers in the selection of the appropriate data sets and variables when seeking to derive a particular variable. For example, these tools outline and explain retention (whether citizen retention, university retention, etc.), the appropriate data sets, variables, and suggested algorithms for derivation. In the near future, concept dictionaries will be made publicly available through the NB-IRDT website. Code banks are a fifth initiative under development for access and use within the secure facilities. Code banks provide a point of reference for data sets on known variable concerns, suggested algorithms, and syntax solutions. While all data staff and approved users may contribute to code banks, the NB-IRDT data manager and the senior data analyst (who serves as the database administrator) oversee the systematic development and monitoring of content. For example, they ensure solutions are made available in the various statistical programming languages supported by the platform. Finally, NB-IRDT is developing metadata best practices through both informal and formal consultation. Through networking with key staff located at other Canadian research data centers and by participating in national workshops, NB-IRDT has identified areas of metadata development requiring immediate attention and is developing a roadmap for the strategic implementation of an ongoing data management program.

9.4 Legal and Institutional Framework

9.4.1 Institutional Setup

The authority for NB-IRDT to make available de-identified personal health and personal information to researchers is provided for in the New Brunswick Personal Health Information Privacy and Access Act (PHIPAA). By entering into both originating and operating agreements with the provincial government as prescribed in PHIPAA, NB-IRDT became a research data center. A research data center is defined in legislation as "a public body that compiles and links personal information or personal health information for the purposes of research, analysis or evidence-based decision-making." (Government of New Brunswick, 2020). In addition, as a research data center, NB-IRDT may serve as a data custodian, agent, and/or information manager. All three of these roles provide for the collection, maintenance, use, retention, or provision of information management services with respect to personal health information.

As a custodian, a research data center has the authority to access personal health information for the purpose of assisting with health care provision, treatment, planning, management, or delivery of health care programs by way of research or program evaluation. Serving as an agent, as defined in PHIPAA, NB-IRDT may also work on behalf of a custodian of personal health information and offer information manager services such as processing, storing, and archiving personal health information or providing information technology services.

It is through written agreements signed between the University of New Brunswick, NB-IRDT's host public body, and the original custodian that NB-IRDT may receive data sets. These data sharing agreements speak to the terms and conditions of the secure retention of data including whether it will be available on the data platform and so available to data access applications from other users. Agreements also address the provision of the opportunity for data business owners, as the original custodians, to remain informed of any request for access and use of their data. All data business owners are invited to send a representative to all data access application review meetings evaluating requested access to their data.[9] In addition, NB-IRDT has adopted a mandatory thirty day embargo period prior to the release of any research products (e.g., manuscripts, presentations, reports) intended for dissemination, which provides data business owners the opportunity to review work prior to dissemination. While this opportunity does not allow for a veto of any research work, it does extend to the data business owner the opportunity to address any potential concerns they may have with data usage and results interpretation. Upon developing this case study, there have been no instances where major concerns have been raised about the public release of such information.

Central to its authority to hold personal and personal health information, NB-IRDT may not receive or add to its data platform any personally identifiable data such as names, addresses, social insurance numbers, or Medicare health insurance numbers. The original data custodian must remove all unique identifiers prior to data transfer to NB-IRDT. It is notable that the data sharing between departments is limited only to identifying information necessary for data matching and no program data can be transferred to DH. See Figure 9.1 *Data transfer to NB-IRDT* for a diagram of the steps required for data transfer. The practice of data matching and data linking of personal and personal health information is addressed differently across Canadian jurisdictions. Most commonly these practices are strictly prohibited as a privacy protection measure to reduce risk of identification or re-identification of individuals. Modifications to PHIPAA introduced in the establishment of NB-IRDT, however, specifically provide for the disclosure of personal health information to the minister of the Department of Health for the express purpose of performing data matching for approved research projects. This permission allows for the creation of the essential crosswalk file. The personal health information permitted for this purpose is an individual's Medicare number. The Medicare number, a product of the provincially administered health care plan enacted in 1971, not only facilitates access to health care services for most NB residents, but also serves as a unique identifier for each resi-

---

[9]See section 9.6.1 for detailed description of this committee.

CHAPTER 9

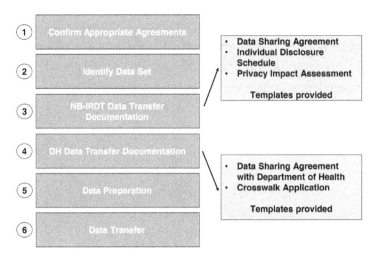

Figure 9.1: Data transfer to NB-IRDT

dent within the province.[10] Prior to the necessary legislative changes supported by key senior government decision-makers, use of the Medicare number for this purpose was expressly prohibited. This use, however, provides the key to protecting individual privacy while enabling linkage between data sets at the individual level not only within departments but across departments and public bodies.

These principles were made operational through several legal agreements and legislative changes. First, changes were made in 2012 to the PHIPAA (Government of New Brunswick, 2020), NB's provincial legislation covering appropriate use of an individual's personal health information, which allowed for the creation of a provincial research data center and defined such an entity as a data custodian. Foundational legal agreements between UNB and the Department of Health (acting as a signatory on behalf of the province) established NB-IRDT as a research data center and defined rights, responsibilities, and reporting requirements, including an originating agreement and an operational agreement both signed in 2013 (the text of which are confidential). The concept of a provincial research data center did not previously ex-

---

[10]All Canadian citizens and permanent residents of Canada moving to NB are eligible for NB health insurance after a three-month waiting period. Certain classes of temporary residents are also eligible, including international students and those temporary residents with a work permit issued after completing NB higher education.

ist and so was defined through this legislation as a facility that could provide secure data access to third parties for research purposes. Following that there were other changes to PHIPAA and to the Medical Services Payment Act, commonly known as the Medicare Act (Government of New Brunswick, 2017b), to allow the Medicare number to be used for data matching purposes in 2015. The next major legislative change was entitled An Act Respecting Research (Government of New Brunswick, 2017a). that was proclaimed into law in May 2017. The act defined a clear legal authority for prepared personal information to be transferred to NB-IRDT from many provincial government departments and public bodies by simultaneously modifying numerous other pieces of legislation. Just as importantly, the act also defined the authority for the Department of Health to receive identifying personal information from other agencies but only for the purpose of data matching for disclosure to a research data center.[11] Where the Medicare number was not available in the disclosed data, the Department of Health would use probabilistic matching methods. This was followed by a second Act Respecting Research that was proclaimed in June 2019 and addressed some legislative gaps in the first act.[12] It is worth noting that this pathway to current practice was not predetermined but rather evolved incrementally as successive obstacles and problems arose and were resolved. Similarly, at the time that the concept of a research data center was defined, there was no template for what would be required to establish and operate one and this, too, evolved over time. What was consistent throughout the time period was a commitment to achieving the vision of a research data center as a facility to make available for research linkable data from multiple government departments and public bodies.

9.4.2 Legal Context for Data Use

Disclosure of de-identified personal and personal health information for research purposes is authorized in the NB Right to Information and Protection of Privacy Act (RTIPPA) and PHIPAA, respectively. Access

---

[11] See section 9.3 for a detailed description of a crosswalk file development.

[12] See section 9.4.1 for the legislative authority for NB-IRDT to operate.

for research purposes is subject to a set of specific yet customizable security safeguards including administrative, physical, and technical practices and procedures.[13] These safeguards seek to ensure the confidentiality, security, accuracy, and integrity of all data held in custody. In order to comply with these legislative requirements, NB-IRDT has adopted a set of eleven data privacy and security policies to embed privacy best practices through all data access, use, disclosure, and retention processes.[14] These best practices are drawn from the Canadian Standards Association's ten privacy principles (Government of Canada, 2000; Office of the Privacy Commissioner of Canada, 2019), which mirror the Organization for Economic Co-operation and Development (OECD) guidelines. This embedding of legislation and privacy principles into all data policy and procedures is in itself in keeping with the international best practice of Privacy by Design, the incorporating of data protection into all processes, services, and levels of an organization, institution, or service provider (Hertzman, Meagher and McGrail, 2012). By adopting and following these policies, NB-IRDT is able to implement a set of criteria to be met for researchers to become approved users prior to accessing the data. Criteria include legislated safeguard requirements such as criminal record checks, signing of confidentiality agreements, and ongoing participation in privacy training. See Figure 9.2 *NB-IRDT approved user criteria* for an outline of requirements.

Data access for research purposes does not only require scrutiny over potential users but over the potential research and the actual data requested for access. A particular strength of PHIPAA is its Section 43, which speaks to the disclosure of data for research purposes. Similarly, data access by NB-IRDT staff for data curation purposes is also guided by legislation that defines the purposes for which access is granted.

In recognition of significant contributions that can be derived from research outcomes enabled by research access to administrative data sets, NB legislation includes a consent waiver clause. Custodians may

---
[13]See section 9.6 for detailed description of safeguards.
[14]See NB-IRDT website Data Privacy and Security at https://www.nbirdt.ca/data-privacy-and-security for the complete set of policies (accessed 2020-12-10).

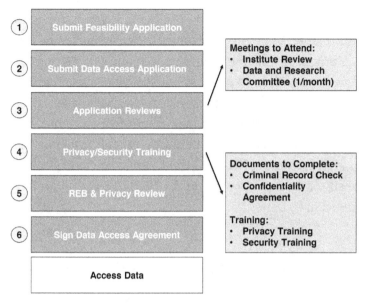

Figure 9.2: NB-IRDT approved user criteria

grant access to personal information for research purposes without an individual's consent when it would be unreasonable or impractical for researchers to obtain such consent. While this permission applies to the accessing of de-identified personal information, the impracticality of seeking consent must be justified within the compulsory review process and cannot simply be a matter of inconvenience.

9.5 Legal Framework for Granting Data Access

While data sets transferred to NB-IRDT remain under the authority of the disclosing body, the research products that arise from data access are typically the intellectual property of the principal investigator for the project unless otherwise noted in a research contract or agreement. Intellectual property rules must also conform to UNB policy, the basis of which is that research activity undertaken by a faculty member is the property of the faculty member, since NB-IRDT is part of UNB. A standard acknowledgement phrase that must be included in all disseminated research products is required by NB-IRDT. There is no requirement for co-authorship on any research using administrative data on the NB-IRDT platform. In certain circumstances for some data sets provided by a data user (such as data collected by a physician in private practice), the data owner may require co-authorship should another researcher seek to use that user-provided data, but no data received from public bodies carries any such requirement. Furthermore, while most research products remain the intellectual property of the project's principal investigator, there is a general principle that all research undertaken using NB-IRDT data should be made public. Reports undertaken for GNB are posted on the NB-IRDT website following the required embargo period.[15]

9.6 Protection of Sensitive and Personal Data: The Five Safes Framework

9.6.1 Safe Projects

All requests to access administrative data sets held on the NB-IRDT platform begin with submission of a feasibility application. This is an initial review identifying the appropriateness of the requested data sets for the proposed work and the resource requirements to undertake that work. If deemed feasible (sometimes after modification), applicants are invited to submit a complete data access application package to the NB-IRDT project coordinator. Applications are verified for completeness, and NB-IRDT staff are alerted to the pending project.

Following the initial processing, the application undergoes a number of sequential reviews. First, an Institute review is undertaken. This review covers basic privacy compliance, peer to peer review of general methodology with respect to data requirements, appropriateness of data set requests, and confirmation of necessary funding and re-

---

[15]Unless specifically undertaken through a contract, reports for government remain the intellectual property of the researcher. NB-IRDT strongly encourages publication of all research reports but the ultimate decision resides with the author(s). Publication of work undertaken in fulfillment of a contract will depend on the terms of the contract.

source needs.[16] Editing of the application is normally required as a result of this meeting and recommendations are provided in writing to applicants. After concerns and comments are addressed, a meeting of the NB-IRDT Data and Research Committee (DRC) is scheduled. In attendance at the DRC meeting are committee core members, representatives of the original data business owner of requested data sets (optional), the data access applicant, and representative Institute staff. During this meeting original data business owners are given the opportunity to inquire about the appropriateness of requested data access, data usage, and to discuss the proposed project in detail. These are productive discussions often resulting in important modifications to the applications. Applicants receive a written summary of the meeting's outcomes and recommendations. Once necessary edits have been made, the applicant is then invited to apply to the University of New Brunswick Research Ethics Board (UNB REB) for research project approval. The condition of approval by a research review body is just one among many safeguards required for legislative compliance.[17]

The REB reviews data access applications for their compliance to six requirements laid out in Article 5.5 of the Policy for secondary use of identifiable information without consent of the original contributors. In addition, the REB also seeks compliance with the UNB University Policy on Research Involving Humans (UPRIH) (Office of Research Services, University of New Brunswick, 2011). Evidence of mitigation to resolve any concerns or risks identified by any previous REB reviews in relation to the proposed project must be submitted with the REB application.

REB requirements include ensuring the following conditions are to be

---

[16] In the interests of expediency, the project application process typically begins prior to a contract or MOU being signed, although data analysis does require such an agreement to be in place.

[17] The UNB REB, defined by the Tri-Council, carries out the role of the research review board. The Tri-Council is composed of Canada's three federal research agencies: the CIHR, the Natural Sciences and Engineering Research Council of Canada (NSERC), and the Social Sciences and Humanities Research Council (SSHRC). The Tri-Council authors the *Tri-Council Policy Statement: Ethical Conduct for Research Involving Humans (TCPS or the Policy)* (Government of Canada, Interagency Advisory Panel on Research Ethics, 2020) governing all research involving human subjects inclusive of secondary use of administrative data.

met: do the risks of data access outweigh any potential intrusion of privacy; has it been determined that the research cannot be accomplished without the access; will the data be provided in its most de-identified form; are the appropriate safeguards to protect privacy of individuals and security of the data in place; and will access and dissemination of research results be consistent with the purposes for which the access was granted. See Figure 9.3 *NB-IRDT data access for researchers* for an outline of the process at NB-IRDT.

While in general, projects submitted to UNB REB require at least one research team member to be affiliated with UNB, this is not required for projects submitted to NB-IRDT where only secondary data access is being requested. Following the REB review, the application is then systematically reviewed against legislation for privacy compliance by the NB-IRDT privacy officer. Finally, a letter of support is prepared from the institute director and the application and supporting documentation are submitted to the University Office of Research Services where it is given approval by the vice president (research).

Following data access approval, principal investigators (PIs) are required to enter into a data access agreement with the University of New Brunswick. This agreement reiterates the appropriate safeguards to be followed, establishes the accountability of the PI for the research team, and confirms commitment that the use and disclosure will be consistent with approved access.

For data sets already at NB-IRDT, the typical processing time from receipt of the feasibility request to signing the data sharing agreement is about three months. Actual processing times can be significantly longer when they involve the incorporation of new data sets from the researcher or a public body. As the volume of applications continues to increase, NB-IRDT is adapting its application process to meet the demand. For example, in February 2020 an expedited review process was introduced by the Data and Research Committee (DRC) to review applications likely to be straightforward. In this process, applications are sent for review to a subset of the DRC and review results communicated to the researcher by e-mail. Currently, NB-IRDT staff are undertaking a broader process improvement evaluation to consider all

Using Administrative Data for Research and Evidence-Based Policy

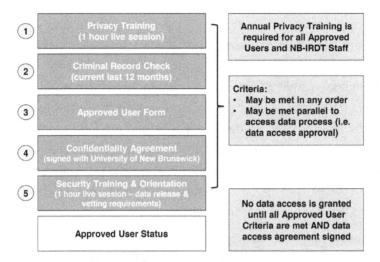

Figure 9.3: NB-IRDT data access for researchers

stages of the application process, to identify potential bottlenecks, and to determine how to address these potential delays.

9.6.2 Safe People

All potential users of the NB-IRDT and staff members regardless of their roles (e.g., managers, support staff, data analyst, etc.) are required to follow a set of administrative safeguards in keeping with legislative requirements. These include evidence of a criminal record check completed within twelve months of the data access application and a signed confidentiality agreement indicating their commitment to adhere to NB-IRDT policies, privacy principles, and best practices.[18] Individual users and staff must also participate in a one-hour administrative data privacy training session and an additional data security and results vetting request session to remind users of their obligations. Training sessions are offered twice monthly through an online platform and content is revised in keeping with legislation and privacy best practices. The principal investigator for each project is also required to provide a current curriculum vitae and sign a data access agreement with the University. This agreement attests to their responsibility for their

---

[18] See section 9.4.2 for legal and policy details.

actions and those of their research team members in relation to data access and use while in an open project relationship with NB-IRDT.[19] Penalties for violating NB-IRDT policies will vary depending on the nature and frequency of the action but can include warnings and temporary or permanent suspension of data access. More severe violations would be the purview of the University of New Brunswick Office of Research Services.[20] Additionally, all staff and approved users must attend annual privacy training sessions to review the material covered, as part of the project approval process, as a mitigating measure against potential privacy breach or incidents.

A unique strength of the New Brunswick legislation is its lack of requirement for data access applicants to hold an academic affiliation. In lieu, it is the role of the review processes to determine whether access adheres to permitted research purposes. The lack of a specific academic affiliation requirement applied in tandem with the obligatory safeguards embedded in the NB-IRDT data access application process means that opportunities for research work extend beyond traditional academic boarders. This permits access to users from government, non-profits, and private sectors.

9.6.3 Safe Settings

Currently, users must access their project files on site in one of three secure facilities (a central and two satellite sites) in NB and access is gained through the assignment of both a dedicated entry card and unique PIN. Inside the secure facility, several additional physical and technical safeguards are in place. Approved users and staff may only access data sets within specific project folders. Each user has their own unique username and password, and a separate log-in and password is required for each project such that a user cannot access two project

---

[19]Though not codified, sufficient criteria may include one or more of the following: successfully completing projects using administrative data, securing competitive research funding, or using administrative data for program evaluation or research as part of regular employment.

[20]It is notable that NB has no statistics act that may prescribe criminal sanctions for data breach such as fines or imprisonment. An example of such an act in Canada is the Canadian Statistics Act of 1985 (Government of Canada, 1985)

data sets at the same time. All workstation ports are disabled except for USB ports for a mouse and keyboard that can only accept these devices. Within the central location, workstations operate on a closed network and there is no connection to external networks (i.e., there is no internet or wireless capabilities). Project work or data cannot be saved to the local workstations and can only be saved to the local server. Security software runs in the evening and every weekend to ensure no data or files are saved to local hard drives or desktops. Users in the satellite sites use thin clients and at no time are users working on local workstations. All sites are alarmed and locked with deadbolts after working hours. Project data set access at the two satellite sites is through a zero-client model by which the satellite locations are connected to the central server by dedicated secure fiber-optic cable. Thus, the network is air gapped with respect to the wider internet. The zero-client framework for the satellites was implemented mainly for confidentiality reasons so that NB-IRDT data files remain on the secure servers in Fredericton. Zero-client analysis can also offer significant computational advantages and NB-IRDT is in the process of planning for eventual migration of the Fredericton workstations to the same zero-client environment. Approved users may access the facility during regular business hours of 9:00 a.m. to 5:00 p.m. while staff are permitted limited after-hours access based on job requirement.

Mobile devices are not permitted inside the secure facilities and approved users and staff are asked to take phones calls and similar outside of the facilities. Two exceptions are permitted: emergency IT work conducted by the NB-IRDT systems administrator and immediate assistance to approved users provided by data analysts. These exceptions are monitored by staff surveillance and incidents are reported to the NB-IRDT privacy officer for mitigation.

As a final physical safeguard, all textbooks and related print material deemed necessary for project work within the lab as well as physical notes must be vetted through the NB-IRDT senior data analyst. Approved users and staff must send such documentation to the senior data analyst electronically for vetting and addition to appropriate project folders. Written notes made while in the lab are taken on designated blue paper, may not be removed from the secure facilities, and are securely shredded when no longer needed.

Physical access within the secure facility is governed by staff roles and responsibilities. Approved users are permitted to work using one of the eleven workstations in the main lab of the secure facility. Limited access to a lockable, inner staff-office is available to the NB-IRDT data manager, systems administrator, and as needed the data analysts. The NB-IRDT senior data analyst is stationed in an adjacent, inner office where the server and media safe are housed. Only the senior data analyst and systems administrators have keys to this room. The server is held in a locked cage and both the server and the safe are bolted to the floor. The safe requires two individuals to be present for opening: one person with a key and one with a passcode.

In the NB-IRDT data lab, researchers have routine access to Stata, R, SAS, ArcGIS, and SPSS and may request other commercial software packages to be installed. Data access fees are based on a standard fee schedule that specifies rates per project and per hour of work, so total project fees vary depending on the scope of work.

9.6.4 Safe Data

All personal information and personal health information, regardless of format (identifiable or de-identified, i.e., pseudonymous) or stage of the data life cycle, is treated and given an equal level of protection. There are no distinctions or classes of data in the legislation for data that are considered personal information or personal health information. This lack of distinction, with the exception of truly anonymous data (i.e., no possibility of re-identification) that is not covered under the legislation, ensures consistent safeguards are followed and reduces the potential risks of identification, re-identification, inappropriate use, access, or disclosure.[21]

---

[21] A curious feature of privacy legislation in NB, which may result in some confusion, is that in the English version of the legislation the term used is 'de-identified' but in the French version the term used is 'anonymous'. Since NB is an officially bilingual province, all legislation must be in both French and English.

Project data sets are prepared files that include only those data elements required to undertake the project and those approved for release to the researcher. The Institute ID[22] is replaced by a study number; these numbers are specific to projects so they cannot be used to link multiple data sets. Since the project data set is a single data set that comprises approved data elements from one or more NB-IRDT data set(s) assembled by the senior data analyst working as the database administrator, the researcher is not required to do any data linkage or merging. In the review stage, the researcher was required to provide a rationale for why each data element would be required for the project. The prepared file will contain only those variables approved for access or derivations from underlying variables whose release would be considered especially sensitive. For example, a full postal code (often sufficient to identify an individual street in urban areas) is rarely required by researchers for their project work. Instead, the prepared data set may have only the first three digits of the postal code but also include derived measures of travel distances. Similarly, derived variables may include duration of stay in hospital but only the month and year of admission to hospital are included.

9.6.5 Safe Outputs

Once project work is complete, a researcher must add a vetting request file to their project folder for review by the NB-IRDT senior data analyst. Output requested for vetting and release may include regression results, cross-tabular results, graphs, and related output. Person-level data cannot be released for any reason. The senior data analyst applies both a basic set of vetting rules (i.e., no release of cell counts less than five) as well as a more exhaustive set of vetting practices and considerations to avoid residual disclosure of identifiable information if other output has been released previously. Vetting rules are based on those used in the Statistics Canada research data centers though the rules are adapted for NB administrative data.[23] Although multiple disclosure

---

[22] See section 9.3 for more details

[23] Vetting rules are not published but are discussed with the research team at project launch as part of the mandatory information sessions for researchers with newly ap-

requests are permissible for a particular project, researchers are discouraged from doing so because of resource implications and the fact that earlier releases may restrict what can subsequently be released. For output that does not meet requirements for disclosure, the senior data analyst will typically consult with the research team to discuss options such as reformatting tables, aggregating categories, or the use of random rounding. Only the NB-IRDT has the capacity to download and release project results to the principal investigator. Questions and challenges to the vetting procedure or results approved for release can be raised with the NB-IRDT Vetting Committee whose membership includes the NB-IRDT director, privacy officer, a research associate, and at least two data analysts. Decisions are recorded for transparency and future reference. The NB-IRDT *Dissemination of Research Findings Policy* requires all research projects to build in a thirty-day embargo period prior to the release of any first-release research results. During this time, Institute staff and the DRC members who approved the data access application are able to review the material or publication for appropriate data use, access and as well as privacy compliance.

9.7 Data Life Cycle and Replicability

9.7.1 Preservation and Reproducibility of Researcher-Accessible Files

The data life cycle of all platform and project data sets files must comply with both legislative requirements for data access for research purposes and the standards set by privacy principles. To ensure compliance, NB-IRDT follows a set policy on data retention, destruction, and restoration. NB-IRDT administers two data life cycles.

First, the data life cycle of all data sets transferred to NB-IRDT are retained and made accessible within the terms and conditions prescribed in their related written agreements. The conditions speak to the limiting of access for research purposes and the requirement for a stated

---

proved projects.

rationale for data access as well as to the terms of ongoing retention for the lifetime of the Institute. The agreements also refer to potential retraction or partial retraction. Terms of retraction are generally in relation to a data business owner's data quality concerns or noncompliance on the institute's part. In good faith and in recognition of the researcher process, however, clauses permitting project data set access until project closure have been secured in most agreements.

The life cycle of project data sets are administered following set parameters. Project data sets for approved research projects are created once all criteria for approved users' access have been met and the principal investigator signs a data access agreement with the university. The start date of the project aligns with the approval date from the REB. Generally, research ethics approval is for three to five years with annual progress reports submitted to the REB.

Access to dedicated project folders is for the life of the project or until the end of the project's research ethics approval, whichever comes first. Project extensions are permitted through renewal of REB approval. Access to projects data sets is withheld until REB confirmation is received.

While the REB process governs project data access, complete project data sets as well as vetted results are stored on the NB-IRDT secure server for a period of three years immediately following the project end date. The three-year timeline is considered sufficient for researchers to make revisions to academic papers or other reports for dissemination as required as part of a peer review process for publication.

Physical receipts are issued to data business owners for all data sets transferred to the secure custody of NB-IRDT. In addition, any necessary returns to business owners (e.g., corrupted files on delivery) are also given a return receipt. Should a data business owner or custodian request disposition of a data set from the NB-IRDT servers (e.g., at the close of an information manager agreement) a certificate of secure destruction is provided. A bonded third-party shredding service who has been vetted for standard compliance completes destruction of physical media. A certificate of secure destruction is provided.

9.7.2 Preservation and Reproducibility of Researcher-Generated Files

In addition to the retention of the complete data set and results, project specific syntax, coding, and related information are retained for an additional seven years. Secure disposition of this file takes place following the seven years.

New Brunswick legislation does not permit access to personal information or personal health information for any longer than is needed to complete the purpose for which permission to access was granted. As a result, project data sets cannot be retained for an unlimited time nor can they be reused for purposes other than originally permitted. This does not preclude, however, the retention of syntax that does not include variables or results information. Approved users seeking to reuse such information may request its release through the secure vetting request process. They may also choose to add such information to the shared code banks accessible to all approved users for particular data sets.

9.8 Sustainability and Continued Success

9.8.1 Outreach

Outreach is vital to the continued operation of NB-IRDT in at least four ways. First, NB-IRDT has regular reporting requirements to original data business owners, custodians, and funders around data access, finances, and related operational issues. Second, NB-IRDT engages with other prospective data custodians (for example, other government agencies) about the benefits of sharing data with NB-IRDT and how the Institute can support them in that process. Third, NB-IRDT engages with prospective research partners across the spectrum including academics, clinicians, trainees/students, and members of both non-profit and private sectors who may be interested in accessing linkable administrative data to support their work. Fourth, NB-IRDT engages in extensive knowledge translation and dissemination activities in order to demonstrate the impact that work undertaken by NB-IRDT's own research staff—academic publications and presentations, reports for government, graduate student theses, and contracted research—is having in supporting evidence-informed policy and practice.[24]

Outreach activity takes many forms. Disseminating research outcomes to funders uses both formal and informal channels. Formal channels include annual reports, annual research days specifically for particular departments and public bodies, and an annual open house conducted collaboratively with GNB's Executive Council Office. The most recent open house was attended by close to 100 GNB employees. The PETL research day, for example, includes research presentations on those projects indicated to be of most interest to PETL's senior management team and is attended by the deputy, assistant deputy ministers, program directors, and departmental research staff. Informal channels include the production research bulletin reports that are posted on the NB-IRDT website and academic and public presentations.

Research impact is communicated to the public through public showcases and events, through the production of press releases, and through social media, with research results presented in a readily understandable form for the intended audience.

Outreach to prospective partners and users also employs both formal and informal methods. Tailored information sessions have been given to almost every GNB Department, usually at the invitation of the Deputy Minister. Similar sessions have been given to other public bodies, non-profit organizations, and private sector and trade groups provincially, nationally, and internationally. For example, NB-IRDT is a central component of NB's engagement with pharmaceutical companies interested in investing and researching in NB at the annual Biotechnology Innovation Organization (BIO) international trade convention. At the other end of the spectrum, NB-IRDT has conducted several facilitated sessions with non-profit groups and charities on NB-IRDT's capacity to support needs assessments and program impact

---

[24]See NB-IRDT website "Research, Publications" at https://www.nbirdt.ca/publications and "News, Events" at https://www.nbirdt.ca/nbirdt-events for links to previous public events (accessed 2020-12-10).

evaluations. One ongoing collaboration is with Living SJ, a nonprofit organization that supports charities in Saint John, NB. This collaboration, funded by GNB, will see NB-IRDT supporting data collection, transfer, and program analysis for up to twelve SJ-based charities.

For academic users, including students and trainees, information on what is available and how to get access is communicated through on-line resources and in-person information sessions conducted across the province. Venues include health, social science, and statistics departments of NB's universities, both NB medical schools (for clinicians and medical students), and research groups' centers in the regional health authorities.

9.8.2 Revenue

The funding model for NB-IRDT's operations has been evolving since its launch in 2015. Initial infrastructure funding came from a Canada Foundation for Innovation (CFI) grant but funding to establish NB-IRDT as an institute came through the MSSU research agreement jointly funded by CIHR and the Department of Health. CFI funding covered renovations to build a secure lab at UNB, hardware and software purchase, installation, and configuration; MSSU funding covered salaries for the first personnel hired to develop the range of policies and procedures that needed to be in place before a research data center could operate. MSSU funding also covered associated expenses including external threat and risk assessments and privacy impact assessments. These direct costs to establish NB-IRDT do not include the significant value of in-kind work provided by a host of GNB personnel to establish NB-IRDT as a data custodian. This work took the form of drafting legislation, co-designing legal agreements, extensively contributing to and reviewing policies and procedures, and establishing (in law and in practice) the process by which the Department of Health would take on the function of data matching for all data destined for transfer to NB-IRDT. This was a major undertaking given the expectation that NB-IRDT would eventually host all research-relevant data on NB residents.

As of 2020, NB-IRDT has revenue from grants, contracts, and fee-for-service work of approximately CA$2.5 million, which reflects increasingly diversified funding sources. While UNB provides in-kind support for the physical operation of the facility (space, utilities) and for financial, human resources, and legal services, all other operating costs must be met from external sources. An increasingly important source of operating costs is data development. The extraction, curation, and transfer of data from government departments and public bodies is often resource intensive, and those agencies rarely have personnel to devote to the work of data preparation for NB-IRDT. To address this NB-IRDT has seconded data specialists into various agencies to undertake the bulk of this data preparation work.

MSSU funding is still a significant proportion of revenue, but it is supplemented with a number of other revenue lines. These include contributions to operating and research costs from other line departments at GNB, funding from other research grants and contracts awarded to the NB-IRDT director, researchers and affiliated scientists, and fee-for-service. Prospective users are informed of the requirement for cost recovery upon making contact with NB-IRDT. The fee schedule is an internal document and is not publicly available. Fees for each project are computed based on estimated hours of work plus a facility access fee. Researchers undertaking their own data analysis would pay only for data preparation and project and data access fees. Fee levels reflect the cost per hour of the research services requested including administrative support. Applicable fees may be lower than published levels in certain circumstances at the discretion of the director if the research collaboration offers additional benefits to NB-IRDT (for example, through the addition of new data sets to the NB-IRDT platform or by establishing a new partnership with a public body). It should be noted that work undertaken through MSSU as a provincial priority project or as part of an established funding agreement with a government partner does not typically involve additional fees. All academic and public sector users face the same fee schedule regardless of academic affiliation, although there is a higher fee schedule for users from the private sector to compensate for the use of publicly funded infrastructure.

9.8.3 Metrics of Success

Since its originating date, the NB-IRDT has been collecting metrics in two main categories: the development of the Institute's data assets and its capacity to support research. While some of the metrics captured are required under the terms and conditions of agreements, others have been invaluable performance indicators identifying service gaps and growth opportunities for NB-IRDT to become a sustainable research data center.

Without administrative data sets secured from government departments, public bodies, and other key data business owners, NB-IRDT would not be able to fulfill its mandate. The Institute's capacity to grow its data platform and make those data available for research and program evaluation requires ongoing attention. Numerous hours and events have been spent networking and fostering relationships with potential partners. These efforts are indicated in the number of data sets received as well as in their depth of coverage and diversity. Both the number of partnerships and data sharing agreements are recorded in addition to the actual number of data sets made available on the platform for data access application. As of early 2020, excluding data sets held under information manager agreements, there are approximately forty data sets currently available for data access application with an additional forty at various stages of transfer and receipt. In addition, several of these are coming from first-time partnerships under master data sharing agreements indicating partner intent to share additional data sets.

A second key area of measurement for NB-IRDT examines its ability to support research. Statistics are captured along the entire data access application process, to inform key stakeholders of capacity and for internal performance measures and process improvement. Measuring starts with the number of feasibility applications submitted followed by the full data access applications that are submitted. In turn, the number of applications actually pursued to full project status is also recorded. By way of example, in 2019, sixteen feasibility requests were reviewed resulting in twelve data access applications leading to six approved data access projects as of the end of the year. Most of the feasibility requests will eventually become approved applications although delays may arise for various reasons. As of June 2020, ten projects are also currently in the beginning of the data access application process. By default, the number of full applications submitted also reflect the number of institute and privacy reviews conducted and the number of Data and Research Committee meetings held. They do not reflect the number of major amendments to projects, which are triggered by changes to the approved data access. These amendments can range from changes in research team membership (which requires REB approval) to changes in project scope or the addition of data sets held by partners not previously consulted; thus, additional REB approval DRC meetings are needed. There were twelve such amendments in 2019, however, the overall need continues to decrease as researchers become more familiar with administrative data research work and the support documentation for data sets strengthens.

Additionally, the length of time between process stages is measured. This measure serves as both an indicator to prospective researchers as well as a performance measure for project coordination and management. Application processing time from start to finish, often the first question asked by potential researchers, has proved to be the most challenging of measurements. Though internal processes are examined and modified for efficiency, the barrier is controlling for external factors. External factors include unforeseen delays in data sets transfer triggered by specific project needs, incompletion of safeguard measures by potential researchers, scheduling of review meetings with numerous partners at the table, researchers' completion of necessary edits or updates following reviews and application resubmission, delays in REB submissions, and working around funding requirements and deadlines. As internal processes continue to improve, ongoing communication and education about these processes to researchers, as well as addressing their responsibility to fulfill application requirements, is key decreasing overall application time.

Audits of data sets accessed and data project activity are a requirement of data sharing with NB-IRDT as well as a legislated safeguard. Reporting at this level allows not only for the monitoring of appropriate data access but also provides partners with an indicator of the usage of their data. A final metric for NB-IRDT is the number of disseminated research results or outputs from data access. Not only are the requests for first-time disclosure captured but also efforts are made to identify subsequent publications or sharing of results in additional formats beyond the relationship with NB-IRDT.

About the Authors

Donna Curtis Maillet has been the Privacy Officer for the NB Institute for Research, Data and Training since it originated in 2015. In addition to a background in library and information sciences, she holds an interdisciplinary PhD and has research work experience in science and technology studies and legal pluralism. Dr. Curtis Maillet has been a part-time lecturer in sociology and public policy at St Thomas University since 2014.

James Ted McDonald is a professor of economics at the University of New Brunswick in Fredericton. He holds a PhD in economics from the University of Melbourne, Australia. He is the founding director of the NB Institute for Research, Data and Training, New Brunswick's only provincial administrative data center. He is the chair of the Canadian Research Data Centre Network Academic Council, he is a member of the CRDCN Board, and he is the academic director of the NB Statistics Canada Research Data Centre. Dr. McDonald is also on the executive committee of Health Data Research Network Canada and is the New Brunswick lead of the Maritime SPOR SUPPORT Unit (MSSU). Dr. McDonald is a UNB research scholar for 2020 to 22 and previously held that title in 2012 to 14. In 2019 he was co-winner of the Mike McCracken award for Economics Statistics, awarded by the Canadian Economics Association.

Curtis Maillet and McDonald each contributed equally to all sections of this case study.

References in Chapter 9

Government of Canada. 1985. "Statistics Act, RSC 1985, c S-19." http://canlii.ca/t/532pk (accessed 2020-06-13).

Government of Canada. 2000. "Principles Set Out in the National Standard of Canada Entitled Model Code for the Protection of Personal Information, CAN/CSA-Q830-96." Personal Information Protection and Electronic Documents Act S.C. 2000 c 5. https://laws-lois.justice.gc.ca/eng/acts/p-8.6/page-11.html (accessed 2020-10-05).

Government of Canada, Interagency Advisory Panel on Research Ethics. 2020. "Tri-Council Policy Statement: Ethical Conduct for Research Involving Humans – TCPS 2 (2018)." https://ethics.gc.ca/eng/policy-politique_tcps2-eptc2_2018.html (accessed 2020-10-05).

Government of New Brunswick. 2017a. "An Act Respecting Research, SNB 2017, c 29." http://canlii.ca/t/53944 (accessed 2020-06-13).

Government of New Brunswick. 2017b. "Medical Services Payment Act, RSNB 1973, c M-7." http://canlii.ca/t/53p70 (accessed 2020-06-13).

Government of New Brunswick. 2020. "Personal Health Information Privacy and Access Act, SNB 2009, c P-7.05." http://canlii.ca/t/54c8h (accessed 2020-06-13).

Hertzman, Caitlin Pencarrick, Nancy Meagher, and Kimberlyn M McGrail. 2012. "Privacy by Design at Population Data BC: a case study describing the technical, administrative, and physical controls for privacy-sensitive secondary use of personal information for research in the public interest." *Journal of the American Medical Informatics Association*, 20(1): 25–28. https://doi.org/10.1136/amiajnl-2012-001011.

Office of Research Services, University of New Brunswick. 2011. "University Policy on Research Involving Humans Policy." https://es.unb.ca/apps/policy-repository/_resources/php/download-policy.php?id=YZqi (accessed 2020-10-05).

Office of the Privacy Commissioner of Canada. 2019. "PIPEDA Fair Information Principles." https://www.priv.gc.ca/en/privacy-topics/privacy-laws-in-canada/the-personal-information-protection-and-electronic-documents-act-pipeda/p_principle/ (accessed 2020-10-05).

Statistics Canada. 2020. "Health characteristics, annual estimates." Table 13-10-0096-01. https://doi.org/10.25318/1310009601-eng (accessed 2020-08-28).

CHAPTER 10

The Private Capital Research Institute: Making Private Data Accessible in an Opaque Industry

Josh Lerner (Harvard Business School)
Leslie Jeng (Private Capital Research Institute)
Therese Juneau (Private Capital Research Institute)

10.1 Summary

Look up!

The Private Capital Research Institute (PCRI) is a non-profit corporation that seeks to understand the fundamental economics of private capital.[1] A wide variety of forms of private capital are examined, including angel investors, venture capital and private equity organizations, and public providers of private capital (e.g., sovereign wealth funds).

Copyright © Josh Lerner, Leslie Jeng, and Therese Juneau.
Cite as: Lerner, Josh, Leslie Jeng, and Therese Juneau. "The Private Capital Research Institute: Making Private Data Accessible in an Opaque Industry." In: Cole, Shawn, Iqbal Dhaliwal, Anja Sautmann, and Lars Vilhuber (eds.), *Handbook on Using Administrative Data for Research and Evidence-based Policy*. Cambridge, MA: Abdul Latif Jameel Poverty Action Lab. 2020.

[1] The PCRI is a non-profit corporation devoted exclusively for charitable purposes within the meaning of Section 501 (c)(3) of the Internal Revenue Code of 1986 as amended.

CHAPTER 10

The PCRI grew out of a multi-year research initiative sponsored by the World Economic Forum that studied the economic impact of private equity.[2] The PCRI received initial support from the Ewing Marion Kauffman Foundation and continues to be funded through grants and strategic relationships.

The principal activities of the PCRI are (a) build data sets related to private capital that can be made available to researchers for analysis,[3] (b) build up a community of scholars and sponsor independent academic research on the nature and effects of private capital, and (c) disseminate the findings of this research to policymakers and the public at large to foster deeper understanding of the role that private capital plays in the economy and society.

The PCRI collects data from commercial data vendors as well as the private equity firms themselves. In addition, the PCRI collects data from primary sources, such as publicly available filings. One of the more recent projects is the gathering of public filings called Certificates of Incorporation (CoIs) from states of incorporation.

The PCRI databases are available to all academic researchers with a credible research agenda. Additionally, safeguarding PCRI's independence from outside influence is critically important. Thus, the PCRI only accepts funding from entities or individuals who recognize that the value of the PCRI's research and analysis depends on an analytically rigorous and unbiased process.

10.2 Introduction

10.2.1 Motivation and Background

The level of interest in alternative investments, and private capital in particular (which encompasses both venture capital (VC) and private equity), has been intense over the past decade. This interest has

---
[2]This work was collected in Anuradha Gurung and Josh Lerner, editors (2008).
[3]See Appendix A for summary information on the PCRI database.

stemmed from both investors' desires for attractive returns and the policy questions around this rapidly growing asset class.

Returns from the United States publicly traded equities, the mainstays of investment portfolios for individuals and institutions, are projected by many analysts to be substantially weaker going forward, while exceedingly low interest rates suggest limited future returns for bonds (Perianan, 2020). Many other classes of alternative investments, such as hedge funds and real estate, have struggled in recent years to match market benchmarks. Concurrently, many public pension funds are facing severe shortfalls, and other institutional investors—from university endowments to sovereign wealth funds—are seeking additional funds to fulfill ambitious agendas. As a result, institutions are increasingly looking to private capital investments such as venture capital, buyout, and growth funds. The global private capital pool reached US$714 billion in 2018, up from US$324 billion a decade ago (Bain & Company, 2019).

This growth has, in turn, raised questions about the consequences of these investments for companies, workers, and the economy more generally (Private Capital Research Institute, 2017). In particular, policymakers have enacted and proposed several initiatives in the past decade to address the perceived harms of private equity. For example, the European Union implemented an Alternative Investment Fund Managers Directive to prevent asset stripping from private firms after acquisition by private equity or other financial sponsors (see Chapters IV and V, especially Chapter V, Section 2, Articles 26–30).[4] As another example, the European Central Bank (ECB) guidance on leveraged transactions[5] requires stringent internal review of "all types of loan or credit exposures where the borrower is owned by one or more financial sponsors."[6] Additionally, in 2019 United States Senator Eliz-

---

[4]See the directive: https://eur-lex.europa.eu/legal-content/EN/TXT/PDF/?uri=CELEX:32011L0061&from=EN (accessed 2020-12-11).

[5]See the guidance: https://www.bankingsupervision.europa.eu/ecb/pub/pdf/ssm.leveraged_transactions_guidance_201705.en.pdf (accessed 2020-12-11).

[6]See Section 3 of the ECB Guidance, which states that "Syndicating transactions presenting high levels of leverage ... should remain exceptional ... and form part of the credit delegation and risk management escalation framework of the credit institution."

abeth Warren introduced the Stop Wall Street Looting Act (see Section 3(13) of the Act) to broadly regulate private equity in the United States.[7] Fears about the high indebtedness of buyouts and their potential risk to the stability of the financial system animated United States regulatory guidance of leveraged lending to facilitate buyouts and post-buyout activities of target firms.

Although the global economy and individual investors are increasingly dependent on private capital, much remains poorly understood about these investments. A salient aspect of private capital is that it is indeed private. Traditionally, the general partners (GPs) who manage these funds have not disclosed much information to the United States Securities and Exchange Commission, other regulators, or even to their own investors (limited partners, or LPs). A shortage of reliable industry data leads to an unappealing setting where industry advocates make sweeping claims about the benefits and critics make broad charges on very shaky empirical foundations (Kaplan and Lerner, 2017).

This lack of transparency has led to two important barriers to private capital research. First, there have been barriers to entry: it has been difficult for academic researchers, graduate students and junior faculty, to get access to these records. Second, much of the research has been undertaken using commercial databases (most notably, Thomson Reuters, which has a licensing program, and Burgiss, which has made its data available to the Private Equity Research Consortium[8]) based at the University of North Carolina at Chapel Hill or else using data provided to researchers directly by limited and general partners on a one-off basis (e.g., Gompers and Lerner, 1997).

It is typically difficult to compare any but the basic facts about the various commercial databases, as these databases draw from different sources, some of which may be proprietary.[9] As a result, there are contradictory findings on a number of important topics, such as the

---

[7]See the act: https://www.warren.senate.gov/imo/media/doc/2019.7.17%20Stop%20Wall%20Street%20Looting%20Act%20Text.pdf (accessed 2020-12-11).

[8]http://uncipc.org/index.php/initiativecat/private-equity/ (accessed 2020-12-11).

[9]For recent efforts along these lines, see Brown et al. (2015), Maats et al. (2011), and Kaplan and Lerner (2017).

risk-adjusted performance of private equity and the extent of persistence of performance of funds: the differences in results appear to be at least in part a function of the differences between databases. On the former topic, see Korteweg (2019); on the latter, see Braun, Jenkinson and Stoff (2017), Harris et al. (2014), and Korteweg and Sorensen (2015). These issues are akin to the more general issues of access to private data raised by the American Economic Association's Committee on Economic Statistics.[10]

The Private Capital Research Institute (PCRI) was initially founded to address these data issues and to provide a greater fact-based understanding of private capital's global impact. Thus, the PCRI's goal is to create a standardized database on the private capital industry. Since 2010, an important part of the PCRI effort has been the building of a series of comprehensive private capital databases to serve as the foundation for independent analysis of the economic impact of private capital and the performance of funds and individual transactions.

The PCRI uses two strategies to gather data. One approach is to collect data directly from primary and secondary sources: the private capital firms themselves and commercial data vendors, respectively. Thus, a large part of this process has been formulating licensing agreements with the two types of data providers. An alternative strategy to further address these data issues is to gather data on private firms from public filings.

An example of this second strategy is a recent initiative of the PCRI: the creation of a library of CoIs and related documents to allow more researchers to explore the important topics in this area. A few academic papers have utilized the information found in CoIs to explore questions around capital structure and contractual terms of private capital investments and corporate governance issues. These studies, however, have used extremely limited proprietary data sets, making it difficult to replicate or refute the studies.

---

[10]The American Economic Association's Committee on Economic Statistics issued a report in March 2020 illustrating some of these points (AEA Committee on Economic Statistics, 2020).

For example, one of the pioneering academic papers to explore topics in this area is Kaplan and Stromberg (2003), which examines 213 venture capital investments in 119 portfolio companies by fourteen VC firms and provides an empirical analysis of the contracts used. To obtain the data for this study, the researchers created a proprietary data set by asking fourteen VC firms to provide detailed information on their portfolio companies, which included financing terms, the firms' equity ownership, and contingencies to future financing. Two concerns—acknowledged by the authors—were that the firms that were willing to share their data were not necessarily representative of the universe of venture firms and that these firms may select non-representative transactions to share. A similar critique can be offered of Lerner and Schoar (2005), which employed a very related methodology.

Furthermore, an alternative approach has been to use a selected sample of CoIs for firms collected by VC Experts, a commercial data vendor that collects data on a contractual basis. For instance, Bengtsson (2011) studies the restrictive covenants in 182 venture capital contracts. Chernenko, Lerner and Zeng (2019) study the implications of mutual funds making private investments in firms, an activity that has historically been done by venture capital firms. Again, they use VC Experts data, focusing on approximate unicorn (or near-unicorn) firms (privately held companies with valuations greater than US$1 billion) While these authors have been able to negotiate for access from VC Experts, the process was protracted, expensive, and highly limited in scope. Other academics have attempted to get access to these data and been unable to obtain it. Moreover, the representativeness of the sample of CoIs collected by VC Experts seems unclear. Given the substantial access problems associated with this data source, the PCRI believes there is a huge opportunity to create a resource that is a broadly available resource to academics.

The PCRI's CoIs collection process mitigates these concerns. First, the PCRI does not rely on proprietary data from specific VC firms who are willing to share their data. Instead, the PCRI creates a random sample of venture-backed portfolio companies and manually collects the CoI documents from the states in which the firms were originally incorporated. However, as a result, researchers only interested in studying a specific set of companies would unlikely find the companies' documents available in the PCRI CoI library. Second, the PCRI makes its CoI database available without charge to all academic researchers with a credible research agenda.

It is virtually impossible to pinpoint the exact size of the private equity industry or to verify the completeness of any data set. However, the PCRI universe is one of the most comprehensive and complete databases on private capital funds and transactions.[11] The unique feature of the PCRI database is that it draws from multiple data sources, including the private capital firms themselves, several commercial data vendors, private capital associations, limited partners, and the PCRI's own research.

10.2.2 Data Use Examples

The PCRI databases are available for use by academic researchers for academic research purposes only. As of May 2020, over 25 academic researchers were using PCRI databases.

As mentioned, one of the primary objectives of the PCRI is to promote a better understanding of the private capital industry. The PCRI hopes to encourage research in this area through access to its databases. Highlighted below are research projects that have been submitted for publication or are near completion:

- Researchers Steven J. Davis (University of Chicago), John Haltiwanger (University of Maryland), Kyle Handley (University of

---

[11]The Private Equity Growth Capital Council (2013) reported that 2,800 private equity firms were headquartered in the US investing in buyout, growth equity, infrastructure, and energy funds. Over the same time period, the PCRI database has recorded 1,600 US private capital firms that solely invest in buyouts. In addition, the National Venture Capital Association reported 874 US venture capital firms were in existence in 2013 with 1,331 VC funds and US$192.9 billion under management. By comparison, for 2013, the PCRI database has 2,082 US venture capital firms seeking investments. Some of the differences between the PCRI database and the reports can be explained by different firm-type classifications (for example, it is challenging to distinguish growth equity firms, which are often classified as venture capital), as well as the fact that the PCRI is missing firm type for about 30 percent of the data (Jeng and Lerner, 2015).

Michigan), Josh Lerner (Harvard Business School), Ben Lipsius (University of Michigan), and Javier Miranda (United States Census Bureau) completed a major project titled "The Social Impact of Private Equity Over the Economic Cycle" (Davis et al., 2019). They explored the broader economic effects of private equity buyouts over business cycles, a topic in which there has been very little investigation but is critical to understand for the regulation of private equity buyouts as well as leveraged bank lending. Using the PCRI's private equity buyout transaction data matched to Census Bureau microdata, their research answers some important questions about how private equity buyouts affect employment growth and the pace of job reallocation and wages.

- Professor Andrea Rossi at the University of Arizona's Eller College of Management submitted for publication his paper titled "Decreasing Returns or Reversion to the Mean? The Case of Private Equity Fund Growth" (2019). In April 2019, Rossi presented this paper at the European Investment Forum held at the University of Cambridge and sponsored by FTSE Russell and was awarded a runner-up award (best five papers, technically). This paper explores the phenomenon that when a private equity firm raises a larger fund, performance tends to decline relative to the previous funds it managed. Rossi uses the PCRI's data on portfolio investments to study the relationship between the amount of investments a fund makes and the fund's size.

- Jun Chen from California Institute of Technology completed his study on the scale, scope, and dynamics of non-VC early-stage financing markets. In particular, the paper "What role does angel finance play in the early-stage capital market" (2017) used PCRI data to examine the interaction between the ways in which angel investors complement and substitute for venture capital financing and the broader economic implications on how to promote economic growth and entrepreneurship. In this paper, Chen assembles the first comprehensive data set on angel financing and characterizes its size, scope, and role in the early-stage capital market.

- PCRI data was used in 2017 in the latest research on Smart Societies and the accompanying *Harvard Business Review* article of the Digital Planet initiative at the Fletcher School at Tufts University (Chakrovorti and Chaturvedi, 2017).[12] PCRI data helped form part of a benchmark that would assist policymakers to better identify their country's investment environment. The PCRI data are combined with several measures to provide a more complete view of what is actually happening in terms of investments, especially investments in technology.

10.3 Making Data Useable for Research

10.3.1 Collecting Data on the Private Capital Industry

The PCRI collects information on private capital firms, funds, portfolio companies, transaction data, and investment exits. In particular, the Institute focuses on buyouts, growth equity, and venture capital investing. One of the main strengths of the data collection strategy is that it relies on gathering data from multiple sources to mitigate sample selection biases. In the future, the PCRI would like to include more information on angel investments and sovereign wealth funds.

PCRI's first goal is to gather data directly from the private capital firms. In the outreach to these firms, the Institute has relied primarily on the relationships of its team members with the individual private capital firms. Thus, the PCRI has had to approach each private capital firm one at a time—a time-consuming endeavor. To date, the Institute has approximately fifty groups that have provided data or are in the process of contracting to do so. It might be questioned why private equity firms would be willing to share data with the PCRI when the commercial databases have often struggled to get data from these institutions. There are several answers:

- There are constraints that the PCRI places on the use of the data. In particular, the PCRI is designed to be a project run by academics

---

[12]For research reports, see https://sites.tufts.edu/digitalplanet/ (accessed 2020-06-21).

and for academics. The information is used exclusively for academic research rather than for any commercial purpose.
- The research protocol simultaneously allows academics to undertake high-quality research while protecting the confidentiality of the data provided by the private equity firms. The PCRI follows the model employed by the Census Bureau for making information available: academics can undertake detailed cross-tabulated analyses but not download or view individual data entries. Essentially the academics are able to upload queries and download results without "touching" the individual data entries.
- The private equity industry has been under much scrutiny. In particular, in the aftermath of the financial crisis there has been much greater attention to institutions such as hedge funds and private capital groups that traditionally were exempt from most regulatory oversight in the United States and Europe. As a result of these pressures, industry leaders have increasingly appreciated the need for high-quality independent research.

Gathering information directly from private capital firms has its own limitations. Even if every active group chose to participate, there would still be some groups that have gone out of business and no longer keep their records or would be difficult to contact. In addition, as the PCRI began collecting data from individual private capital firms, one of the major concerns raised was that it would take too long for the PCRI to get a database large enough to disguise the data to preserve anonymity. The PCRI thus realized the importance of quickly building a large foundation for the database. As a result, the Institute is complementing the data that is gathered from the private capital firms with data from commercial sources, even if it is not always of the same quality as that provided directly by the general partners.

The commercial sources include the Emerging Markets Private Equity Association (EMPEA), Alternatives Data Cell ("Alternatives"), Refinitiv (formerly Thomson Reuters Financial & Risk), Unquote (a UK-based data collection company acquired by Mergermarket), Start-Up Nation Central (a company that focuses on collecting data on Israeli private equity transactions and funds), and Venture Intelligence (a leading

Table 10.1: Number of distinct private capital firms provided by source of information

Vendor	Distinct Private Capital Firms
EMPEA	2,964
NYPPEX	6,100
Thomson Reuters	11,491
Unquote	5,291
PCRI Unique	**17,633**

Note: As of 2015. Source: Jeng and Lerner (2015).

source of information on private company financials, private capital transactions, and their valuations in India). Table 10.1 provides the coverage of information for the PCRI's original top four sources.[13] Refinitiv has the largest coverage of private capital firms with 11,491 firms. By combining the sources and eliminating duplicates, the PCRI finds that the overlap of private capital firms in the databases is roughly 32 percent.[14] After eliminating duplicates, the PCRI combined data set contains 17,633 *unique* private capital firms. Figure 10.1 shows a diagram of the overlap between the sources. The key features of the PCRI database are summarized in Jeng and Lerner (2015).

10.3.2 Processing of Data Received From Data Vendors or Primary Sources (LPs or GPs)

The process of combining and cleaning the various data sources is an arduous task. At the PCRI, the research staff consists of one full-time director of research, two full-time research associates, and approximately six part-time undergraduate research assistants. Research

---

[13] PCRI focuses on the four original sources: EMPEA, Alternatives, Refinitiv, and Unquote. Start-up Nation Central and Venture Intelligence were added later and represent a small fraction of the total database.

[14] As of 2015. The majority of the overlap in the data is between the Alternatives and the Refinitiv data sets. By not including the Alternatives database in this analysis, the number of unique private capital firms is 16,190 (Jeng and Lerner, 2015).

CHAPTER 10

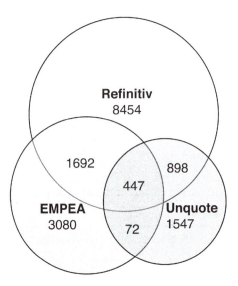

Figure 10.1: Overlap of private capital firms in PCRI database by source of information

associates work to understand, clean, and research the various data sources as well as to make those sources consistent and to develop a file-matching protocol. Part-time undergraduate research assistants help with name matching, researching missing data items, and manually collecting data.

The PCRI databases include data for over 17,000 private capital firms, 33,000 private capital funds, and 110,000 portfolio companies covering a time span from the early 1970s to 2018. The portfolio companies are geographically diverse with over 50 percent outside the United States, including 32 percent in Europe and 10 percent in Asia (Jeng and Lerner, 2015). The PCRI database contains eight different data tables: company, deal, exit, fund, fund performance, fund quarterly cash flow, general partner (GP), and investment. See Appendix A for more information on the database. Figure 10.2 provides details on the tables, including the variables in each data table and the relationship between the tables. For more information on the PCRI databases, please see the data user manual available on the PCRI website.

The PCRI has developed an internal data processing system that is used as a training guide for new research associates. The PCRI database

Figure 10.2: Table relationship diagram of PCRI database

is a relational database. When new data are received from either a commercial vendor or a private capital firm, the new data are separated into variables and put in a consistent format to be read in by Stata. Various rudimentary tables are created that correspond to tables in the PCRI database (e.g., investment, exit, GP, fund). For each data item in a table, the PCRI then identifies a key that is a unique identifier specific to a data provider. This key is then mapped to a unique identifier for each unique observation within that table (the source ID). This process, whereby the key of the data provider is mapped to a source ID, is referred to as local aliasing. These newly created source IDs are then mapped to a unique identifier within the larger PCRI database (the ID). This process is called global aliasing. The global aliasing file contains the unique identifier-name-source link.

Once this step is complete, all variables are processed in Stata to match existing codes in the PCRI database. For instance, country names are standardized to match the PCRI standard names in the supplemental tables (e.g., *Fr* would be converted to "France").

The resulting tables are stored as Stata data files in a file location specific to that data provider. Next, in the append file, all the data files are aggregated into a set of long tables containing data collected from all data providers and independently researched information. The append file saves these files to the pre-stacked file location as .csv files. This is where the PCRI eliminates formatting inconsistencies (e.g., date formatting). Once these operations have been completed, the files are saved to a file location called Stacked within each data vendor's directory, once again in .csv format.

The final consolidation stage is handled using a Python MySQL script. Wherever there are multiple sources for a variable, the PCRI creates a ranking system to determine the information to keep. An internal pecking order determines this ranking: PCRI internal research data ranks the highest, then GP-provided data, and finally commercial vendor data. The Python program also keeps track of discrepancies between data providers that meet certain thresholds (e.g., if a dollar amount invested differs by more than 10 percent, this data item is flagged). Discrepancies are added to a file for further research.

The Python script then runs a SQL query that builds the Merged Files. The data are anonymized (i.e., names and other identifiers are removed). Lastly, these .csv files are converted to Stata data files in the CSV to DTA do-file and saved to the Uploaded Files folder where they are accessible to researchers.

10.3.3 Collaboration for Certificate of Incorporation Data Acquisition

In October 2018, we signed a memorandum of understanding with the Stanford Graduate School of Business (GSB) to collaborate with GSB Professor Ilya Strebulaev. The memorandum supports the development of a library of venture capital–backed firms' CoIs and related documents and a database of the information contained within these documents. Additionally, the memorandum encourages the diffusion of the library and database to academic researchers.

Using an agreed-upon methodology, the PCRI and Stanford GSB created an initial random sample of 622 venture-backed companies. In the summer of 2019, the PCRI completed collecting CoIs for this random sample and has made these documents available to researchers through an electronic library hosted on a new platform at the Harvard Business School (HBS) called SmartRoom. At the same time, Professor Strebulaev and his team are completing the coding of the documents for this random sample. This data set will also be made available for approved researchers via the National Opinion Research Center (NORC) at the University of Chicago. The NORC houses all of the PCRI databases behind a secure firewall.

The PCRI is currently working with the GSB to collect and code CoIs for a second random sample of 250 venture-backed companies. The Institute has created the list of companies for this sample and has received and processed half of the CoIs. In addition to these two random samples created in collaboration with the GSB, the PCRI independently has collected CoIs for another 750 companies, including many unicorns. The final sample will contain almost 2,500 companies.

10.3.4 Certificate of Incorporation Document Acquisition Process

This section provides the details on the creation of the PCRI CoIs library. A CoI is a public legal document filed with the state in which the company is incorporated. It is essentially a license issued by a state government for a company to form a corporation. In addition, whenever a corporation receives private capital funding, an amended CoI is filed with the state in which it is registered. The availability of CoIs varies by state. Some states make this document available online. Other states require a written request and payment of a fee to obtain a copy (Masters, n.d.).

Based on consultation with academics interested in CoIs and colleagues at the GSB, the PCRI has opted to get a complete set of CoIs for each funding date/portfolio company pair because it gives a comprehensive overview of the firms' financing histories. To begin the process of obtaining CoIs, a PCRI research associate prepares a list of corporation names, addresses, and investment dates in an Excel spreadsheet. A research associate then determines where each corporation is incorporated/registered by going to the state website for any state in which a corporation maintains a business location. Once it is determined in which state a corporation is registered, a research assistant orders the appropriate documents from that state's website for business incorporations.

As seen in Table 10.2 below, the vast majority (82 percent) of companies in the database are registered in Delaware, which has been the focus of most of our efforts. To obtain documents for corporations registered in Delaware, order forms must be filled out and submitted online. Delaware charges US$10 for the first page of a document and US$2 for each additional page. On average, one document costs around US$30 dollars, but sometimes a single document could cost up to hundreds of dollars. On average, the total cost to obtain all the documents for one company is approximately US$125. In the case of Delaware, a hard copy of a CoIs arrives within several weeks of submitting a request.

Other states, such as New York, accept orders by mail. In the case

Table 10.2: Breakdown of state of incorporation of the 622 venture-backed portfolio companies

State	Percentage
Delaware	82.0%
California	10.0%
Georgia	1.0%
Washington	1.0%
Texas	0.7%
Colorado	0.7%
Other States	4.6%

of New York, a form must be filled out for each request. The cost is US$5 for each plain copy of a document. Processing takes ten to twelve business days, not including shipping, and the copies are sent thereafter. For an unusually large order, arrangements can be made in advance, but the work is still performed on a first-come, first-serve basis. For other states, the CoIs are usually available online for no cost. Thus, the PCRI can access the business entity database for those states (e.g., California and Massachusetts) and download copies of the documents.

In most states, the Corporations Division of the Secretary of State's office handles business incorporations and related filings. In a handful of states, business registrations are handled by a different state agency. The United States Small Business Administration maintains a list of state business registrars to help find the appropriate state agency. When the PCRI receives a hard copy of a CoIs, the file is scanned and loaded to be stored electronically. At this time, Delaware and some other states only provide hard copies of documents, making the CoI acquisition process more laborious.

10.3.5 Metadata

Information about metadata is available in a PDF version of the PCRI Data User Manual on its website for use by academic researchers.[15] The PCRI has a staff dedicated to maintaining the PCRI databases. The Institute revises the databases annually to account for data updates from the data provider and then places updated researcher-accessible files in a designated folder for users to access. The PCRI data are stored as Stata data files. The manual provides a detailed description of the eight different data tables, specifically company, exit, fund, fund performance, fund quarterly cash flow, GP, investment, and deal tables. This reference also cites the location of the files and the size of each file (i.e., number of rows). Additionally, the manual catalogs the names of the different variables and the definitions contained within each table. Furthermore, the manual indicates whether a data item is a Primary Key or Foreign Key. This distinction provides the link between two tables, facilitating the merging of different data tables. Primary Keys are unique within a table, whereas Foreign Keys are not unique but link to another table. Since the PCRI does not permit users to look at the data, the Institute provides a small, artificial sample of each data table in the manual.

10.4 Legal and Institutional Framework

10.4.1 Institutional Setup

The PCRI is an independent non-profit organization, which seeks to provide a greater fact-based understanding of private capital's global impact. The PCRI is governed by a Practitioner Advisory Committee, which is comprised of experts in the private capital industry, and an Academic Advisory Committee, consisting of leading researchers in the field. Representing diverse affiliations, these two committees provide guidance on the data collection process and periodically review

---

[15]http://privatecapitalresearchinstitute.org/images/news/pcri_manual_2_4.pdf (accessed 2020-12-11).

and provide advice on the administration, finances, and research program of the PCRI. A subcommittee of the Academic Advisory Committee meets to approve research proposals requesting access to the PCRI databases. Projects are approved as long as they have a credible research agenda, are not for commercial purposes, and do not jeopardize the security of the data. The Practitioner Advisory Committee is not able to veto approved projects. A list of members of the Practitioner Advisory Committee[16] and Academic Advisory Committee[17] is available on the PCRI website.

10.4.2 Legal Context for Data Use

One of the biggest challenges faced in the data collection effort was creating a standardized licensing agreement for all data sources, in particular for the private capital firms. By working closely with the PCRI's lawyers at Debevoise & Plimpton and a few prominent private capital firms, a standardized licensing agreement was developed. The agreement not only allowed the PCRI to obtain, use, and administer highly confidential data but also alleviated the major concerns (i.e., confidentiality and data security) of the private capital firms. The authors highlight some of the chief features of the Private Equity Sponsor Data Agreement.[18]

First, the data licensing agreement grants the PCRI a royalty-free, non-transferable license. Second, the PCRI is permitted to receive, store, reproduce, and combine the data. Third, since the PCRI is a project run by academics and for academics, the PCRI database is to be used exclusively for academic research rather than for any commercial purpose. In accordance with the licensing agreement, the PCRI carefully reviews research proposals and monitors output files to ensure that data are being used appropriately. Additionally, as a primary objective of the PCRI is to promote unbiased, academic research, the licensing agreement

---

[16] List available at http://privatecapitalresearchinstitute.org/advisory-committee.php (accessed 2020-12-11).

[17] List available at http://www.privatecapitalresearchinstitute.org/academic-advisory-board.php (accessed 2020-12-11).

[18] A sample agreement can be found in the Online Appendix.

mandates that the data sponsors would not be able to limit the areas of academic research. However, under the licensing agreement, data sponsors can obtain a preview of working papers and are also given the option to be acknowledged for their contribution to the PCRI research effort. Lastly, the licensing agreement allows either party to terminate the agreement.

In cases where data disclosure harms data sponsors, liability issues were a major source of discussion in the creation of this licensing agreement. Given the limited resources of the PCRI, the licensing agreement puts a cap on PCRI's liability at US$1,000, which only applies in cases not resulting from gross negligence, strict liability, fraud, misconduct, or misrepresentation on the part of PCRI. In such cases, there would be no liability cap. Also, the PCRI agrees not to bring any claims against any of the data sponsors.

While the PCRI has been successful with private equity groups, venture capital organizations have been much more resistant to sharing information. Thus, with a grant from the Alfred P. Sloan Foundation, the PCRI is taking an alternative approach to obtain information for researchers to understand venture capital activity. As mentioned previously, the Institute has been developing a compilation (and an associated taxonomy) of CoIs over the past two years. Extremely detailed information on venture capital transactions is available in CoIs, which are typically compiled by regulators in the state of the firms' incorporation. These corporate filings include important details on deal structure (i.e., the capital structure and key terms) as well as important valuation information. While this information is publicly available, the costs to obtain these documents are prohibitively expensive. For example, in some locations, a request for these documents must be made in person, and US$1.00 to US$2.00 is charged per page. As a parallel process, the PCRI is working to create a data set containing the twenty to thirty most critical variables contained in these documents.

10.4.3 Collaboration with the Census Bureau

Over the past several years, the PCRI has been working with the Census Bureau team regarding ways in which the PCRI data could be integrated with the Longitudinal Business Database (LBD). In the spring of 2016, the PCRI signed a confidentiality agreement that allowed it to tie certain portfolio-company level data to the LBD in a way that would respect the various confidentiality restrictions on the government and PCRI data but greatly increase the usefulness to researchers. The agreement established between the Census Buerau and the PCRI allows for the sharing of specific PCRI data items, which include portfolio company name, location information, and a PCRI source code (PCRI Data). The purpose was to link the data to the Census Bureau Business Register. As of May 2020, one academic is using the Census-PCRI linked data to explore the effect of acquisitions of startups on their newly acquired employees.

10.4.4 Legal Framework for Granting Data Access

Approved data users interested in using either PCRI data or the coded CoIs data are required to sign a data use agreement (DUA) between both the PCRI and its data host, the NORC. The contract is standard and has been vetted by a few users, but there is some flexibility for negotiation. If changes are made, they are reviewed extensively by the NORC legal staff and the PCRI. However, very few users have requested any changes. Data users are granted access for a term of one year; at the end of the term they are able to request an extension. Access to the data can be revoked if the NORC deems that any aspect of the DUA is violated. The NORC and PCRI reserve the right to ensure that the PCRI data are used in compliance with the agreement. The output is reviewed to ensure that it preserves the anonymity of the individual observations and that the analyses match the original intent of the research proposal. Additionally, according to the DUA, both the user and the NORC have the right to terminate the DUA without cause at any time. Currently, there is no cost to accessing the PCRI databases, as the fixed fee paid by the PCRI to the NORC accommodates a generous number of users.

The PCRI maintains the intellectual property (IP) rights on the architecture, computing systems, and computing environment of the data enclave, including the data set and all other data, information, documents, programs, trade secrets, and confidential information. However, the PCRI does not assert IP rights on products created by the data user, such as research papers and independent data analyses.

10.5 Protection of Sensitive and Personal Data: The Five Safes Framework

10.5.1 Safe Projects

Before obtaining access to the data, interested academic researchers are required to submit a two-to-three-page written research proposal. This proposal must clearly state the objective of the project, the PCRI data that would be used in the study, and the research methodology. A subcommittee of the PCRI Academic Advisory Committee evaluates research proposals submitted to the PCRI. The subcommittee safeguards the data by ensuring that the proposals use the data for only academic research purposes. Users may not use the PCRI databases for commercial purposes. The review process typically takes less than a week and is free of charge. The PCRI is not required by the DUA to obtain consent from the data providers before approval of a research project.

For researchers interested in gaining access to linked Census-PCRI data, the same protocol is used—researchers are required to submit a research proposal for approval by a subcommittee of the PCRI Research Advisory Committee. Again, the subcommittee reviews projects to ensure the safety of the data and that the data use is for only academic research purposes. For the combined data stored at the Census Bureau, approved researchers also need to follow the access protocol at the Census Bureau.

10.5.2 Safe People

Only approved users are granted access to the PCRI databases. The PCRI primarily accepts research proposals from academic researchers from accredited universities, not-for-profit research organizations, and research groups of government organizations. Academic researchers applying for access do not need to obtain special training to use the data. Additionally, to protect the confidentiality of the data, approved academic researchers must sign a DUA with the PCRI and the NORC. Currently, the PCRI does not place a limit on the number of users that it is able to host.

10.5.3 Safe Settings

The security of the PCRI data is paramount. The Institute's ability to obtain data from the various data vendors and private equity firms rests primarily on the ability to maintain the security and confidentiality of their data. The PCRI has designed a protocol that simultaneously allows academics to undertake high-quality research while protecting the confidentiality of the data provided by the data sponsors. To this end, PCRI's first step was to host the PCRI databases at the NORC, which has experience hosting highly sensitive federal (e.g., Medicare) and private sector data (e.g., hedge fund data used by federal investigators as part of the Financial Crisis Inquiry Commission). The PCRI initially explored creating its own platform on its own servers, but it was too costly to construct and maintain. As mentioned in section 10.4.4, the PCRI and NORC reserve the right to ensure that the PCRI data are used in compliance with the DUA agreement. Thus, privileges to access the data may be revoked if the NORC deems that any aspect of the DUA is violated.

The data are accessed using a secure remote access protocol. Users login through the NORC portal, which requires a two-factor authentication: a password and a security token password. The PCRI provides Stata software to the researcher to access the data files. To ensure safety, the PCRI employs a methodology whereby academics can undertake detailed cross-tabulated and regression analyses but not download or view individual data entries. Also, for added security, the Institute disables certain features of Stata (e.g., outsheet, list, and browse commands) that could allow the user to identify companies in the database. The cost of hosting the data at the NORC is around US$40,000 per year.

The Census data typically can only be accessed at Federal Statistical Research Data Centers (FSRDCs). Researchers require approval from both the PCRI and the Census Bureau.

For the CoIs library, the PCRI has created a searchable database using SmartRoom, a content management platform, for researchers to view, but not download, the documents. The Institute does not charge for the use of this CoIs library or the ultimate coded database that the Stanford GSB is creating. The cost to use the SmartRoom is about US$10,000 per annum and varies depending on the number of users. The Institute choses to use this platform not only because of its security features but also its user-friendly interface.

10.5.4 Safe Data

To make the data safe, the PCRI databases are anonymized (i.e., data are de-identified), and only PCRI research staff have access to identified data. Furthermore, researchers cannot see the data as they are unable to print, browse, or outsheet the data. Researchers are only able to run queries and view the results of analyses.

External data sets can be linked to the PCRI databases. Data sets can be uploaded to the NORC platform, requiring a PCRI staffer to do the matching. Only in exceptional circumstances can data be downloaded from the servers and matched to an external database. For instance, in collaboration with the Census Bureau, certain PCRI variables were linked to Census data and then stored with the Census Bureau. The Census Bureau assumes an obligation to use the PCRI data for only statistical purposes and requires maintaining data confidentiality.

10.5.5 Safe Outputs

The PCRI-NORC DUA outlines how the PCRI data can be used. Essentially, the researchers can upload queries without "touching" the individual data entries. Even though the data are anonymized, the PCRI further protects the data by prohibiting the viewing of individual observations. The NORC helped us limit STATA so that only summarized outputs can be viewed provided there are at least 100 observations used in each analysis. Outputs can be downloaded off the NORC platform but must first be approved by a PCRI staff member. Furthermore, software program log files provide a paper trail of activity, which is monitored periodically by NORC staff and PCRI to ensure that the data are being used for research purposes.

10.6 Data Life Cycle and Replicability

10.6.1 Preservation and Reproducibility of Researcher-Accessible Files

The PCRI periodically releases new versions of the databases. As of May 2020, the database is on Version 2.5. The versioning is based on content and, if necessary, structure updates. Each version is preserved and archived and can be made available upon request for replication purposes. When a new version is released, it is copied and uploaded to a separate folder for sharing on the NORC data platform.

Researcher-accessible files can be regenerated. The data are processed using a series of Python and Stata scripts to unpack raw data files from the various sources and to put them in a useable format. The PCRI receives new data feeds periodically and thus regenerates the data files annually.

10.6.2 Preservation and Reproducibility of Researcher-Generated Files

Researcher-generated files are preserved within each researcher's directory/folder and are backed-up regularly. Files are not shared amongst the researchers unless a researcher gives permission subject to PCRI approval.

10.6.3 Disposal of Data

The PCRI is not required to delete data from data providers. Upon termination of any agreements, the PCRI would be required to purge the sponsor's data from future versions of the databases within a reasonable time frame. However, any previously approved researcher would continue to have access to the previously consolidated databases. Also, the data sponsor agreements could be reassigned to another non-profit such as another academic institution, provided the PCRI gives the data sponsors prior written notice.

10.7 Sustainability and Continued Success

10.7.1 Outreach

As mentioned in section 10.3.1, outreach to private equity sponsors is a slow process because each potential data provider is contacted individually. Moreover, these private equity firms are very wary of sharing data and need to have their legal departments review the data provider agreement, necessitating frequent communication between the parties. One benefit of participation that is highlighted to the data sponsors is that they would be able to obtain a preview of working papers and would be invited to attend PCRI conferences featuring the Institute's research.

Going forward, PCRI hopes to make this process more efficient by working with some organizations that are already actively collecting information from general partners. Such organizations include a large custodian bank with whom the PCRI has signed a data sharing agreement and national venture capital associations.

To create more awareness of the PCRI databases and to get more researchers using the databases, a call for research proposals has been posted on the SSRN (Social Science Research Network). In addition, the PCRI has participated in numerous conferences (American Economic Association, the American Library Association, and the National Association for Business Economics) to present the PCRI's mission and talk more about the PCRI databases. Lastly, the PCRI hosts conferences twice a year to bring together industry leaders, academics, and policymakers to discuss relevant topics in the private capital industry. For outreach purposes, summaries of the conferences are released on the PCRI's website.[19]

A recap of some of the more recent dissemination activities is highlighted here:

- On October 11, 2019, the PCRI, along with the Private Capital Project at Harvard Business School, sponsored a small workshop entitled "The Rise of the Asset Owner-Investor in Private Markets" on the HBS campus. The past decade has seen an extraordinary surge of interest on the part of asset owners in direct investing in private markets. Not only are these institutions investing in traditional funds, but they are eager to build up their own capabilities to invest. The motivations for these initiatives include a desire to avoid the fees charged by traditional partnerships, the belief that their long-run time horizons will facilitate the identification of attractive investment opportunities, and the quest to better manage the assets in their portfolios.
- On June 21, 2019, the PCRI partnered with the PBC School of Finance, Tsinghua University to bring together a group of industry thought leaders in Beijing to share perspectives on the changing landscape of private capital in China. Over the past three decades, the private capital industry in China has grown and evolved: it is now a US$1.6 trillion industry with over US$94 billion in private equity investment value last year alone. The maturing of the industry has challenged both Chinese GPs and LPs to rethink their value creation strategies and their relationships with each other.
- On September 11, 2018, the PCRI partnered with the Private Capital Project and the Impact CoLaboratory (Impact CoLab), both at

---

[19] http://www.privatecapitalresearchinstitute.org/ (accessed 2020-12-11).

the Harvard Business School, to bring together a group of industry thought leaders—comprised of prominent limited partners, general partners, and academics—to discuss the rise of impact investing. While some investors understand the basic concept of impact investing, there is still widespread confusion about the practice, its various approaches, and the difference it can make.
- On June 15, 2018, the PCRI and the Institute for Business Innovation (of the Haas School of Business at the University of California, Berkeley) co-sponsored a roundtable discussion on "New Models of Entrepreneurial Finance." Industry leaders (GPs and LPs) and academics were brought together to discuss new developments in early-stage (e.g., syndicated angel investments) and later-stage (e.g., direct investments by sovereign funds) financing, how venture groups are responding to increased competition, and what the implications are for entrepreneurs and society more generally.

10.7.2 Revenue

The PCRI is a non-profit that relies entirely on grants and strategic partnerships to fund its endeavor. It currently receives funds from the Alfred P. Sloan Foundation and the HBS Private Capital Project.

The PCRI does not charge a fee for the use of its databases as the fixed fee agreement with the NORC allows for a certain number of users. If the maximum number of users is exceeded, there would be a charge to cover additional costs.

10.7.3 Metrics of Success

The PCRI gauges success on three fronts: (1) building a comprehensive database of private capital information; (2) sponsoring independent academic research on questions of relevant policy interest; and (3) arranging thought leadership forums that bring together academics, policymakers, regulators, investors, and industry practitioners to examine private capital's role in the economy.

To date, the PCRI database contains global information on approximately 23,000 general partners, 44,000 funds, 141,000 portfolio companies, 432,000 investments, 229,500 private capital deals, and 36,000 private equity exits that are tied to deals. Given the strategy of combining data from multiple sources, this is one of the most comprehensive private capital databases currently available. As of May 2020, the PCRI has more than 25 active academic researchers utilizing the PCRI databases, resulting in several successful research papers submitted to academic journals.

10.7.4 Concluding Remarks

An increasing share of economic activity today is taking place in settings that elude traditional federal data collection mechanisms or fail to capture the richest of the activity at work. Against this backdrop, economists are increasingly turning to private data. This chapter underscores the experience of the PCRI, specifically the process of creating a database to facilitate access to private equity information for academics to address the myriad major concerns regarding private data. While this effort is certainly a work in progress, hopefully the experience can guide researchers who want to address similar issues in other fields.

CHAPTER 10

About the Authors

Josh Lerner is the PCRI Director and the Head of the Entrepreneurial Management Unit and the Jacob H. Schiff Professor of Investment Banking at Harvard Business School. He graduated from Yale College with a special divisional major that combined physics with the history of technology. He worked for several years on issues concerning technological innovation and public policy in various settings, including the Brookings Institution, a public-private task force in Chicago, and Capitol Hill. He then earned a PhD from Harvard's Economics Department. Much of his research focuses on venture capital and private equity organizations. (This research is collected in three books: *The Venture Capital Cycle*, *The Money of Invention*, and *Boulevard of Broken Dreams*.) He also examines policies on innovation and how they impact firm strategies. (That research is discussed in the books *Innovation and Its Discontents*, *The Comingled Code*, and *The Architecture of Innovation*.) He co-directs the National Bureau of Economic Research's Productivity, Innovation, and Entrepreneurship Program and serves as co-editor of their publication *Innovation Policy and the Economy*.

Leslie Jeng is the PCRI Director of Research and has been with the PCRI since its inception. She graduated from the University of Pennsylvania with degrees in finance and mathematics and has a PhD in Business Economics from Harvard University. In addition, she has work experience in academia as well as the private sector in investment banking and quantitative investment research. Her areas of interest are corporate finance, financial institutions and regulation, and public policy. Her publications include "The Determinants of Venture Capital Funding: Evidence Across Countries," *The Journal of Corporate Finance*, 2000 and "Estimating the Returns to Insider Trading: A Performance-Evaluation Perspective," *The Review of Economics and Statistics*, 2003.

Therese Juneau is a Research Assistant at the PCRI. She graduated from the University of Texas at Austin in 2019 with a bachelor of science and arts degree in mathematics.

Acknowledgements

We would like to thank the Kauffman, Sloan, and Smith-Richardson Foundations, as well as numerous data sources, for their support of PCRI.

References in Chapter 10

AEA Committee on Economic Statistics. 2020. "Successful Private Firm-Academic Researcher Arrangements for Access to and Replicable Use of Private Data." American Economic Association report. https://www.aeaweb.org/content/file?id=11794.

Bain & Company. 2019. "2019 Global Private Equity Report." https://www.bain.com/contentassets/875a49e26e9c4775942ec5b86084df0a/bain_report_private_equity_report_2019.pdf (accessed 2020-10-05).

Bengtsson, Ola. 2011. "Covenants in Venture Capital Contracts." *Management Science*, 57: 1926–1943. https://doi.org/10.1287/mnsc.1110.1409.

Braun, Reiner, Tim Jenkinson, and Ingo Stoff. 2017. "How persistent is private equity performance? Evidence from deal-level data." *Journal of Financial Economics*, 123: 273–291. https://doi.org/10.1016/j.jfineco.2016.01.033.

Brown, Gregory W., Robert S. Harris, Tim Jenkinson, Steven N. Kaplan, and David Robinson. 2015. "What do different commercial data sets tell us about private equity performance?" SSRN 2701317. https://ssrn.com/abstract=2701317 (accessed 2020-10-05).

Chakrovorti, Bhaskar, and Ravi Shankar Chaturvedi. 2017. "The "Smart society" of the future doesn't look like science fiction." *Harvard Business Review*. https://hbr.org/2017/10/the-smart-society-of-the-future-doesnt-look-like-science-fiction (accessed 2020-10-05).

Chen, Jun. 2017. "What role does angel finance play in the early-stage capital market?" California Institute of Technology Ph.D. thesis Chapter 1. https://doi.org/10.7907/3mg0-2622.

Chernenko, Sergey, Josh Lerner, and Yao Zeng. 2019. "Mutual funds as venture capitalists? Evidence from unicorns?" European Corporate Governance Institute Finance Working Paper 675/2020. http://doi.org/10.2139/ssrn.2897254.

Davis, Steven J., John Haltiwanger, Kyle Handley, Ben Lipsius, Josh Lerner, and Javier Miranda. 2019. "The social impact of private equity by buyout type and stage of the economic cycle." https://www.aeaweb.org/conference/2019/preliminary/paper/5nsZRYTz#:~:text=Abstract%3A%20We%20study%20the%20impact,per%20worker%2C%20and%20labor%20productivity.&text=Slower%20GDP%20growth%20after%20the,a%20widening%20of%20credit%20spreads.

Gompers, Paul, and Josh Lerner. 1997. "Risk and reward in private equity investments: The challenge of performance assessment." *The Journal of Private Equity*, 1(2): 5–12. https://www.jstor.org/stable/43503183.

Gurung, Anuradha, and Josh Lerner. 2008. "Globalization of alternative investments." World Economic Forum Working papers.

Harris, Robert S., Tim Jenkinson, Steven N. Kaplan, and Ruediger Stucke. 2014. "Has persistence persisted in private equity: Evidence from buyout and venture capital funds." Darden Business School Working Paper. https://ssrn.com/abstract=2304808.

Jeng, Leslie, and Josh Lerner. 2015. "Insights into the private capital industry using the private capital research institute database. Part 1: Data sources and overview of private capital firms, funds, and portfolio companies." http://www.privatecapitalresearchinstitute.org/images/news/data_description%20article%201.pdf (accessed 2020-10-05).

Kaplan, Steven N., and Josh Lerner. 2017. "Venture capital data: Opportunities and challenges," chapter in measuring entrepreneurial businesses: Current knowledge and challenges." National Bureau of Economic Research Working Paper w22500. https://www.nber.org/papers/W22500.

Kaplan, Steven N., and Per Stromberg. 2003. "Financial contracting theory meets the real world: An empirical analysis of venture capital contract." *The Review of Economic Studies*, 70(2): 281–315. https://doi.org/10.1111/1467-937X.00245.

Korteweg, Arthur. 2019. "Risk Adjustment in Private Equity Returns." *Annual Review of Financial Economics*, 11(1): 131–152,. https://doi.org/10.1146/annurev-financial-110118-123057.

Korteweg, Arthur, and Morten Sorensen. 2015. "Skill and luck in private equity performance." *Journal of Financial Economics*, 124(3): 535–562. https://doi.org/10.1016/j.jfineco.2017.03.006.

Lerner, Josh, and Antoinette Schoar. 2005. "Does legal enforcement affect financial transactions? The contractual channel in private equity." *Quarterly Journal of Economics*, 120(1): 223–246. https://doi.org/10.1162/0033553053327443.

Maats, Frederike H.E., Andrew Metrick, Ayako Yasuda, Brian Hinkes, and Sofia Vershovski. 2011. "On the Consistency and Reliability of Venture Capital Databases."

Masters, Terry. n.d.. "How to obtain a copy of a certificate of incorporation." https://legalbeagle.com/12717162-how-to-obtain-a-copy-of-a-certificate-of-incorporation.html (accessed 2020-10-05).

Perianan, Veerapan. 2020. "Why market returns may be lower and global diversification more important in the future." https://www.schwab.com/resource-center/insights/content/why-market-returns-may-be-lower-in-the-future#:~:text=The%20main%20factors%20behind%20the,investing%20in%20a%20diversified%20portfolio. (accessed 2020-10-05).

Private Capital Research Institute. 2017. "The consequences of private equity on employment and management." https://www.hbs.edu/private-capital/Documents/ILPA-PCRI-Roundtable-2017.pdf (accessed 2020-10-05).

Private Equity Growth Capital Council. 2013. "2013 Annual Report." https://www.slideshare.net/pegccouncil/pegcc-annual-report825x825012314a2 (accessed 2020-10-05).

Rossi, Andrea. 2019. "Decreasing returns or reversion to the mean? The case of private equity fund growth." SSRN. https://ssrn.com/abstract=3511348 (accessed 2020-10-05).

Appendix

Appendix A

Summary Information of the PCRI Private Capital Database

The following tables and figures, from Jeng and Lerner (2015), provide a summary overview of the data collected on private capital firms, funds, and portfolio companies. In particular, the PCRI focuses on buyouts, growth equity, and venture capital investing.

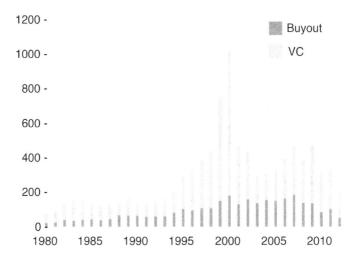

Figure 10.3: Number of private capital firms by year founded

Table 10.3: Private capital firms by location of company headquarters and year founded

Regions	1980-1989	1990-1999	2000-2009	2010-2015	Total
Africa	0.3%	1.3%	1.7%	1.0%	1.3%
Asia	9.0%	10.4%	18.2%	27.6%	15.3%
Eurasia	0.0%	0.6%	1.0%	2.3%	0.9%
Europe	22.0%	24.5%	27.1%	22.0%	25.2%
Middle East	1.0%	2.4%	2.7%	1.9%	2.3%
Multi Geography	0.1%	0.0%	0.2%	0.2%	0.1%
North America	4.1%	5.6%	5.5%	4.6%	5.2%
Oceania	1.2%	2.2%	1.9%	0.9%	1.8%
South America	0.5%	1.1%	1.7%	1.7%	1.4%
United States	62.9%	51.8%	40.1%	37.9%	46.5%

Notes: As of 2015. Source: Jeng and Lerner (2015).

Table 10.4: Private capital firms by location of company headquarters split by year founded

Fund Type	1980-1989	1990-1999	2000-2009	2010-2015	Total
Buyout	19.0%	26.0%	27.3%	26.4%	26.1%
Growth Equity	0.9%	0.7%	1.9%	8.5%	2.3%
Other	21.5%	9.4%	14.2%	11.9%	13.4%
Second	0.1%	0.4%	0.3%	0.2%	0.3%
VC	58.6%	63.6%	56.3%	53.0%	57.9%

CHAPTER 10

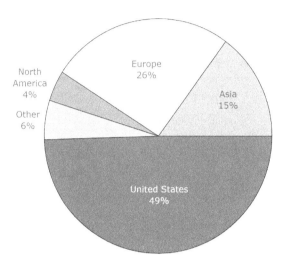

Figure 10.4: Funds by region (N = 25,238)

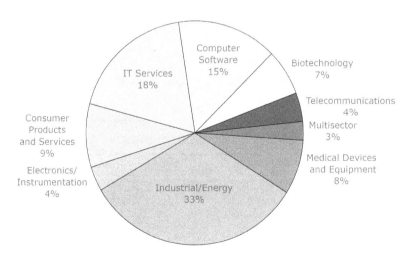

Figure 10.5: Funds by industry (N = 12,333)

Table 10.5: Portfolio companies by region and year founded

Regions	1980-1989	1990-1999	2000-2009	2010-2015
Africa	0.6%	0.6%	0.5%	0.1%
Asia	11.5%	13.5%	14.9%	10.3%
Eurasia	0.1%	0.5%	0.5%	2.2%
Europe	31.2%	25.8%	30.3%	32.5%
Middle East	0.9%	1.4%	1.8%	1.9%
Multi Geography	0.0%	0.0%	0.0%	0.0%
North America	7.3%	4.9%	3.7%	2.8%
Oceania	2.5%	1.5%	1.2%	0.6%
South America	0.7%	0.8%	0.7%	0.6%
United States	45.2%	51.1%	46.4%	49.0%

Notes: As of 2015. Source: Jeng and Lerner (2015).

Appendix B and Appendix C

A sample data sponsor agreement and sample list of certificate of incorporation variables can be found in the Online Appendix at admindatahandbook.mit.edu/book/v1.0/pcri.html#pcri-appendix

CHAPTER 11

Aurora Health Care: Using Electronic Medical Records for a Randomized Evaluation of Clinical Decision Support

Laura Feeney (J-PAL North America, Massachusetts Institute of Technology)

Amy Finkelstein (Massachusetts Institute of Technology)

11.1 Summary

This chapter is a case study that describes the process for sharing and using individual-level data from electronic medical records (EMR) for a randomized evaluation with Aurora Health Care. Aurora is a large, private, not-for-profit, integrated health care provider in Wisconsin and Illinois, comprising fifteen hospitals and more than 150 clinics in thirty communities.

Researchers from the Massachusetts Institute of Technology (MIT) and the Abdul Latif Jameel Poverty Action Lab's (J-PAL) North America of-

Copyright © Laura Feeney and Amy Finkelstein.
Cite as: Feeney, Laura, and Amy Finkelstein. "Aurora Health Care: Using Electronic Medical Records for a Randomized Evaluation of Clinical Decision Support." In: Cole, Shawn, Iqbal Dhaliwal, Anja Sautmann, and Lars Vilhuber (eds.), *Handbook on Using Administrative Data for Research and Evidence-based Policy*. Cambridge, MA: Abdul Latif Jameel Poverty Action Lab. 2020.

fice partnered with Aurora Health Care to conduct a randomized evaluation of clinical decision support software on the ordering of high-cost imaging (e.g., MRI or CT scans) by health care practitioners (Doyle et al., 2019).

Having worked to establish data sharing agreements and worked with data from a variety of other health care partners, the authors believe this case study is representative of the process and some of the challenges of data sharing and data use in similar contexts. Since completing this research study, one of the co-authors, as well as other researchers associated with J-PAL, continue to work closely with Aurora-based researchers to develop and identify opportunities for research collaboration.

In this case, the delivery of the intervention and the measurement of outcomes were conducted through the EMR system, making access to administrative data a critical feature of the research project. The data used for this research included characteristics of patients and health care providers, an indication for the patient's health problem (e.g., headache), scan orders (e.g., x-ray, CT scan, MRI), and a score indicating the relative appropriateness of the scan order. The data set included this information as related to scans ordered between November 1, 2015 and December 15, 2017 and covers the study population of 3,511 Aurora providers.

Aurora shared in the motivation to conduct research and may have benefited operationally from the insights gained throughout the process of obtaining approval to share data and preparing data for transmission. Nonetheless, the research team had to overcome concerns over protecting patient and provider confidentiality and the cost of providing data access to researchers. The research team addressed these challenges by providing funding for data extraction and by agreeing to take possession of only de-identified data.

The case describes the process by which the research team sought approval to conduct the study and access data, worked to understand data not originally designed for research, and addressed the challenges of working with de-identified data.

Approval to conduct the research and share data took several months to obtain. The data necessary for this research was complex and drawn from multiple tables and systems not designed for research. Gaining access and then making the data usable for research in de-identifiable form required a significant amount of work from analysts at both Aurora and MIT and required strong communication and trust between teams.

11.2 Introduction

11.2.1 Motivation and Background

This case study describes the process for sharing and using individual-level data from EMRs for a randomized evaluation of the effect of clinical decision support software on the ordering of high-cost imaging. The evaluation was conducted at Aurora Health Care—a large, private, not-for-profit, integrated health care provider in Wisconsin and Illinois—by researchers affiliated with the MIT, J-PAL North America, and Aurora.

Research was the motivation for making data available in this case study. In 2014, the US Centers for Medicare & Medicaid Services (CMS) announced an impending mandate that in order to be reimbursed for high-cost scans for a Medicare beneficiary, such scans must be ordered using an approved clinical decision support (CDS) system. CDS is software that consults clinical guidelines to deliver assessments of procedure appropriateness to providers at the time of order entry. CDS generates appropriateness scores for scan orders and other practices, such as prescribing medication, given clinical indications and patient demographics. If a scan order meets a set of criteria, CDS generates a best practice alert (BPA) that is shown to the provider. While several observational studies have been conducted to assess the impact of CDS on provider behavior, there had been no large-scale randomized evaluations.

The impending mandate from CMS to use a decision support mechanism for imaging orders generated the motivation to engage in this particular research project.[1] Researchers affiliated with MIT and J-PAL North America—Sarah Abraham, Joseph Doyle, Laura Feeney, and Amy Finkelstein—as well as a radiologist at Aurora—Dr. Sarah Reimer—conducted a randomized evaluation of CDS on scan ordering at Aurora Health Care. Aurora is the largest health care system in Wisconsin, comprising fifteen hospitals and more than 150 clinics in thirty communities. In December 2016, the research team enrolled 3,511 Aurora health care providers in the study and randomly assigned half of them to receive CDS (treatment group) and half to order as usual (control group). For the evaluation, CDS software was configured to trigger a best practice alert (BPA) when a scan order met a set of criteria and was ordered by a provider assigned to the treatment group.

Aurora Health Care was planning to implement a CDS system in order to prepare for the CMS mandate; participating in the study enabled the institution to gain practical knowledge for internal decision-making and planning. The timing of the study allowed the research team to provide information and evidence relevant to the upcoming policy change.

Aurora was an active collaborator on this study. The research team included a co-investigator from Aurora, and Aurora Health Care houses the Aurora Research Institute (ARI), which is committed to supporting research that leads to new and improved ways to care for people and manage community health. The result was that this relationship was a mutually beneficial research partnership, not simply a data exchange between a provider and a research team.

Nonetheless, leadership at Aurora had significant concerns about making data available to external parties. The costs of creating and maintaining health care data for administrative purposes (i.e., even before preparing such data for use by external researchers) are significant. These costs are driven by factors such as time spent by clinicians entering data, time spent by IT administrators supporting the system,

---

[1] At the time of the study's design, the mandate was to be implemented in January 2018. Implementation was later delayed until January 2020 with penalties for noncompliance to be implemented in January 2021 (Hentel et al., 2019; Centers for Medicare & Medicaid Services, 2018).

infrastructure costs of computing, and time spent by analytics teams extracting and interpreting data. Although the data exist as a natural byproduct of health care administration, some raised concerns about giving away data without compensation given the value of the data to researchers or other external parties.

The team addressed leadership concerns in two ways:

First, the research team made the case that sharing data with the external research team would enable rigorous research that would itself be valuable to Aurora Health Care. Aurora would learn about the effects of CDS in advance of the mandate. Moreover, because the team partnered with a researcher from ARI, Aurora benefited from the research generation process in terms of producing publications and publicity.

Second, the research funding from Arnold Ventures (then known as the Laura and John Arnold Foundation) included funds for a sub-award to Aurora to support the randomized evaluation of the CDS system. Part of this award compensated Aurora's business intelligence and data analytics teams for their time spent extracting, transforming, and preparing the data for this project and working with the research team to ensure a full understanding of the data. The award also provided funding for server space needed to store the snapshots and extracts of the data created for this project. Although it did not compensate the costs of the initial creation and maintenance of the data, external funding with an allowance for overhead helped to alleviate leadership concerns and secure buy-in for the project.

11.2.2 Data Use Examples

The research team analyzed scan order outcomes across the treatment and control groups to determine the impacts of CDS on the ordering behavior of providers. Aurora's administrative data, which are primarily housed within its EMR and linked by design, provided information on scan orders and completions, patient encounters and patient demographics, provider employment and demographics, and health care encounters when the BPA was shown. The team also received data on appropriateness scores, alternative scans, and the version of the ruleset used within Aurora's instance of the CDS.

The outcome measures are based on scan-request level data that contain the indication and imaging order requested as well as the score and set of alternative scans available (for each scan request ordered by one of the study's providers). These data allow researchers to identify the appropriateness of the order as well as whether the BPA would be shown if the provider were in the treatment group. A data set of ordered imaging scans allowed the team to link each request for a scan to the provider associated with the order. Researchers received an alert-level data set that allowed the team to observe which orders showed a BPA and to confirm that a BPA was shown only when the order was entered by a treatment provider and according to the criteria set for displaying the BPA.

More details on this study can be found in Doyle et al. (2019) and are summarized in a J-PAL Evaluation Summary.[2]

11.3 Legal and Institutional Framework

11.3.1 Institutional Setup

The parties to the data access mechanism in this case study are Aurora Health Care (the data provider and custodian) and MIT (the research team's academic institution). These institutions executed the legal agreement necessary to gain access to the data and approved the underlying research activities. Some of the data needed for the study was collected by a third party, the National Decision Support Company (NDSC), which built the clinical decision support software that integrates with Aurora's Epic EMR. This data, which did not contain direct personal identifiers, was sent to Aurora, linked to the Aurora data by Aurora analysts, and then transferred to the research team. Existing

---

[2]https://www.povertyactionlab.org/evaluation/clinical-decision-support-radiology-imaging-united-states (accessed 2020-12-11).

business and data sharing agreements between NDSC and Aurora covered this arrangement; no additional agreements or amendments were needed for this evaluation.

11.3.2 Legal Context for Data Use

In the United States, the Privacy Rule of the Health Insurance Portability and Accountability Act (HIPAA)[3] regulates the sharing of health-related data generated by health care entities such as Aurora Health Care. It allows, but does not require, sharing data for research. Implications of the HIPAA Privacy Rule for research, as well as a list of guides maintained by the US Department of Health and Human Services, are discussed in Using Administrative Data for Randomized Evaluations (Feeney et al., 2015).

The Privacy Rule is complex, with different requirements and obligations depending on the purpose of a data sharing arrangement. Even experienced legal professionals have difficulty interpreting its requirements with respect to research. In this environment, and with strict penalties and liability for non-compliance, many entities subject to HIPAA (referred to as covered entities) are very cautious about how and with whom they share data. Entities not already subject to HIPAA may hesitate to obligate themselves to comply with the Privacy Rule's stringent requirements.

The Privacy Rule defines three levels of data: research identifiable data, limited data sets, and de-identified data. Identifiable data may only be

---

[3]The HIPAA Privacy Rule (45 CFR Part 160 and Subparts A and E of Part 164) provides regulation for the use, storage, and sharing of medical records and other protected health information (Code of Federal Regulations, 2000c,b). It holds health care providers, health insurance providers, researchers, and others accountable for safeguarding certain types of health information in the United States. Compliance requirements differ based on the party, such as individuals, researchers, or health care providers or insurers; the purpose of the data usage; and on stipulations or structure of data use agreements. The US Department of Health & Human Services provides a detailed guide at https://www.hhs.gov/hipaa/for-professionals/special-topics/research/index.html (accessed 2020-06-23) to the requirements associated with research and identifiable health data, how the HIPAA Privacy Rule applies to research, and a guide at https://www.hhs.gov/hipaa/index.html (accessed 2020-06-23) to understanding HIPAA for all types of users (U.S. Department of Health & Human Services, n.d., 2018).

shared for research purposes with individual authorization from each patient involved or a waiver of such authorization approved by an institutional review board (IRB) or privacy board (a process similar to informed consent or waivers of consent as required by the Common Rule).[4] Limited data sets may be shared either with individual authorization or with a waiver of authorization from a privacy board or IRB and with a data use agreement (DUA) outlining the purpose of the data share, the conditions under which data will be stored, and other stipulations. HIPAA permits health care providers to share de-identified data for research purposes without further obligations (U.S. Department of Health & Human Services, 2018).

Neither limited data sets nor de-identified data sets may contain direct identifiers such as name, medical record number, or other account numbers. For research purposes, one of the most consequential differences between these data types is the treatment of dates. In a limited data set many elements of dates are allowed. In a de-identified data set all of the following must be excluded: all elements of dates (except year) for dates directly related to an individual, including date of birth, admission date, discharge date, and date of death; and all ages over 89 and all elements of dates (including year) indicative of such age, except that such ages and elements may be aggregated into a single category of age 90 or older.

11.3.3 Legal Framework for Granting Data Access

To accommodate the preferences of both Aurora's and MIT's legal teams, the research team did not attempt to access identifiable data for health care providers or patients. While the team initially pursued access to a limited data set, which would have allowed the inclusion of dates of health care encounters and scan orders, to accommodate the preferences of Aurora's legal team researchers used a data set

---
[4]The US Federal Policy for the Protection of Human Subjects or the "Common Rule", located in 45 CFR Part 46 https://www.hhs.gov/ohrp/regulations-and-policy/regulations/45-cfr-46/index.html (accessed 2020-06-23), provides regulatory guidance for research involving human subjects and governs institutional review boards (IRBs), which approve research (Office for Human Research Protections, 2018).

that was de-identified. This enabled the use of a relatively simple non-disclosure agreement (NDA), rather than the more stringent data use agreement requirements associated with limited or identified data sets. This was also important for gaining the agreement of several satellite sites of Aurora, which were wary about sharing data for this study. Their agreement was crucial, as their data was thoroughly integrated with the rest of the system and could not feasibly be excluded from the study.

The NDA was supplemented by a sub-award contract between MIT and Aurora that included additional provisions typically found in a data use agreement. For example, the sub-award contained a provision pertaining to intellectual property derived from confidential information, obligations for return of information upon request, survival of obligations of confidentiality, and provisions pertaining to the publication of a public data set and the scholarly work to be produced using the data.

The research team satisfied the HIPAA definition of de-identified data using the Safe Harbor method (Code of Federal Regulations, 2000a). Under this method, 18 identifiers of the individual, or of relatives, employers, or household members of the individual, are removed from the data set, and the data provider must "not have actual knowledge that the information could be used alone or in combination with other information to identify an individual who is a subject of the information."

Because the study involved data from an intervention with living individuals, Aurora required review of the intervention and the data sharing agreement by their IRB. The Aurora IRB required the removal of minors from the data set and requested that the team use their best effort to exclude the data from prisoners and pregnant women from the data sent outside of Aurora, but recognized that imprisonment and pregnancy are variable statuses that cannot always be readily discerned.

Through the sub-award agreement, Aurora retained intellectual property rights to their confidential information but permitted the publication of a public data set (see Doyle et al., 2018). The prime award between the Laura and John Arnold Foundation (now Arnold Ventures) and MIT required that the research team publish the data set and code needed to replicate the analysis in a repository to the "maximum extent" allowed by privacy laws, IRBs, and applicable binding agreements. During negotiation of the sub-award to Aurora, the MIT and Aurora teams negotiated acceptable terms to meet this requirement. Those terms, which outlined the level of aggregation and anticipated variables to be included in the data set, are copied in the appendix to this chapter.

Both the NDA and the sub-award recognized that the purpose of the agreement and data sharing was to generate an academic research paper, and both required the provision of a thirty-day period for Aurora to review outputs before publication. Aurora's review was limited to ensuring that confidential information was not disclosed; this satisfied MIT's legal team and the research team's desire to maintain academic freedom to publish without any perception of the possibility of censorship.[5] Clearly specifying the intended purpose of the research and the intended output of an academic paper (rather than, for example, a patent, process, or product) may have expedited agreement to terms involving intellectual property and publication.

11.4 Making Data Usable for Research

Making the data usable for research required overcoming several hurdles and a significant amount of time from both Aurora- and MIT-based data analysts. First, the team worked to identify relevant data sets, tables, and variables for the study; to extract data from these tables; and to understand how to create a linked panel data set. Second, researchers had to interrogate the data generation process in order to understand each variable beyond existing documentation. Third, the team created a process to link individual-level data from multiple sources and generate indicators for relative dates in order to create a panel data set that would comply with HIPAA's de-identification standards.

---

[5] See the text of these clauses in the Appendix.

11.4.1 Identifying Relevant Data

Aurora uses the Epic EMR system,[6] the most common in the US, which includes an industry standard radiology information and order entry system. ACR Select, which is a third-party software designed by NDSC, integrates with Epic to generate best practice alerts, using a ruleset developed by the American College of Radiology (ACR).

A massive amount of data are stored and/or generated by Epic and integrated services such as ACR Select. These data include patient and provider characteristics, information entered during health care visits (termed in Epic as "encounters"), medications prescribed, images ordered, and many other topics. Much of the data from the EMR is created automatically through user interactions and is used for operational purposes. For example, data produced when a health care provider orders a radiology image is used to generate a best practice alert if orders meet certain criteria, to send information to the radiology department about the order, to generate information for billing purposes, and to tie the scan order to the correct patient information. These data are not typically used after these automated processes occur. Data are stored in a relational database structure (SQL in the Aurora instance) with a primary key (a field that uniquely identifies each entry) and foreign keys (a column or group of columns that provides a link between data in two tables).

In this structure, linking between tables is straightforward, but identifying the correct table(s) of interest can be a challenge. Depending on the use case for the data, data may be stored or accessed in a production database, a reporting database, or an interactive records viewer. The data frames are updated with different frequencies, and some historical data may only be accessed through the data warehouse. Access to these systems is distributed across multiple teams within Aurora and within the software companies.

Data for this project came from the Epic reporting database, Clarity. Given the wide number of use cases for the data, the breadth of patient and health information stored, and the history of provider ac-

---

[6]https://www.epic.com/ (accessed 2020-12-11).

tions recorded within the database, Clarity contains an overwhelming number of tables.[7] Many of these had not been explored previously by Aurora analysts. For example, the research team wanted to confirm through data whether a BPA had been displayed in order to confirm that random assignment had been implemented properly. Because there had never been a business use for this data set, analysts at Aurora did not know whether these data would exist. Confirming the existence of these data and the name of the table was a team effort between MIT, Aurora, and NDSC.

11.4.2 Understanding Beyond Documentation

The research team gained a deeper understanding of the data through observing and speaking with providers about their interactions with the EMR and through detailed discussions with the data analytics team at Aurora. During several visits to Aurora, the research team directly observed various health care providers interacting with the EMR and spoke with them about how they interact with the system and interpret the data entry fields. Researchers learned, for example, that there are several points at which providers are asked to enter a health indication (e.g., headache, broken bone). These include a visit diagnosis used for insurance billing, a separate indication to attach to a radiology scan order, and an optional field for additional instructions to a radiologist. Speaking with health care providers helped researchers to understand which of these indications was least likely to be impacted by an intervention, and which of these indications they spent relatively more time reviewing to ensure precision and accuracy. Observing and discussing the order in which providers entered data and moved through screens and pop-ups also enabled the team to better interpret patterns in the data, such as how a cancelled or revised scan order may appear in the database.

While some documentation of variable definitions exists, this documentation is targeted to users with the original data use-case (i.e.,

---

[7]Penn Medicine, for example, reports that their instance of Clarity has over 18,000 tables (Penn Medicine Information Systems Data Analytics Center, n.d.).

health care operations and delivery), not to researchers. In addition, the research team found that definitions and terminology may vary based on context and familiarity with data. For example, scans receive an appropriateness score ranging from one to nine. The underlying data set records a numerical value outside of that range under certain circumstances. The MIT team initially referred to those scores with the numerical value, while analysts familiar with the CDS system would refer to them as "unscored." Similarly, within a health care setting, a health care "encounter" can describe any interaction between a provider and patient, regardless of clinical setting. However, on an initial reading of data documentation by someone without a clinical background, an "encounter" may connote an in-person interaction between provider and patient. Through frequent communication with Aurora's data and clinical experts, the MIT team was able to develop a much deeper understanding of the data and definitions than relying solely on written documentation.

Both processes of locating and interpreting data required substantial input from analysts and providers at Aurora as well as strong communication between multiple teams with varying perspectives and backgrounds in research and data analysis. In-person site visits were key to developing strong, trusting work relationships that enabled the team to make the data usable for this research. Making in-person connections and explaining the scope of the project with the Aurora teams enabled them to engage deeply and think critically about how to prepare the data for research and to make suggestions that may not have occurred to the MIT-based team. Without these connections, data tasks may have been assigned without context, precluding the ability to make adjustments to improve the quality or relevance of the task. These relationships enabled open dialog for discussing data questions. In-person meetings fostered trust and a shared vision, affirming the dedication of all teams to the project success. In this commitment, the Aurora team was readily available to approach even the most difficult data questions and actively participate on weekly project calls.

By combining MIT's insight on the planned analysis with the clinical and systems expertise brought by Aurora, the team could determine whether additional information or data checks were necessary, ensuring that the results from potential analyses were fully justified by the underlying data and their accurate representation of clinical practices. If additional data were necessary to improve the quality of analyses, Aurora was willing to check IRB compliance and quickly send the new data to the MIT team.

11.4.3 Linking De-Identified Data

Under the data sharing agreement, researchers were not able to receive patient, provider, or encounter IDs. In order to support a stable identifier for these entities (to allow for a replicable process as well as the appendage of additional data) a surrogate mapping process was created and verified by data analysts at Aurora. The mapping process populated a two-column table for each entity: the first column represents the source system identifier, and the second column represents the surrogate mapping ID produced by a random number generating procedure within SAS. Every ID that is extracted from the source data is merged into the mapping table for its respective entity. If an ID does not match an existing entry in the table, the ID is inserted, and a new unique surrogate mapping ID is produced for the source ID. The MIT research team wrote pseudo code and template SAS code for the Aurora team to use to verify that the de-identification and linking processes produced consistent results and accurate linkages. For example, pseudo code and documentation described a process to run the same merge twice and assert that the resulting data sets are identical. Other parts of the code print the number of unique records in each data set to be merged, the number of records from each data set that were successfully linked, and the number of unique IDs at each stage. This process was followed on-demand at regular intervals throughout the study period.

Aurora maintained this crosswalk and confirmed the stability of IDs within data pulls by running and re-running the code and ensuring identical outputs. Data from Aurora were sent in cumulative batches; batch two would be a superset of batch one and new data since the creation of batch one. By comparing these cumulative data sets, researchers confirmed the process was stable across data pulls.

No action was taken to remove or de-duplicate records in this case, as a small number of duplicates was unlikely to cause issues given the provider-level analysis planned. Ensuring each patient is uniquely identified by a single Aurora internal ID is as much a priority for health care administration as it is for research. As an additional validation exercise, however, the Aurora data team created an algorithm to identify potential duplicates. First, a set of criteria was defined for assessing potential duplicates: same first and last name; same medical record number (MRN); same social security number (SSN); same Medicare number; same Medicaid number; same date of birth or four-decimal address geocode plus first and last initials. All potential duplicate matches were evaluated in terms of their similarity on previously standardized identifiers. Where possible, edit distance scores were calculated to capture the number of changes that would have to be made to a comparison identifier to turn it into the target (e.g., the last names Smith and Smyth have an edit distance of 1, reflecting that one letter would have to be changed to turn each into the other). Records with sufficient difference in identifiers were ruled out as potential duplicates. From the remainder of records, researchers estimated that a maximum of 0.998 percent of records could be duplicates, with the actual proportion likely to be between 0.376 percent and 0.607 percent. Given the type of analysis planned, these ranges did not cause concern.

11.4.4 Working with Relative Dates

Under HIPAA, de-identified data may not contain exact dates. However, for the planned analysis, researchers needed at least some information on the relative sequence and time period of scan orders. For example, the team needed to identify scan orders from the pre-intervention period and for three-month periods within the year-long intervention period. Aurora developed a patient-specific reference date, converted each date variable into the number of days from that reference date, and sent only the relative days from that date to the

MIT research team. The patient-specific reference date was necessary, as normalizing all dates to the same intercept would reveal more individual-level information and add specificity that would increase the risk of potential re-identification. Aurora maintained a crosswalk of patients' IDs and reference dates throughout the study to ensure consistency and replicability within the study period. Finally, Aurora created a series of binary variables to indicate the timeframe of an encounter or scan from the beginning of the intervention (binned in 2-month periods).

Though the MIT research team provided draft code, the process for making the data usable for research without identifiers or dates required significant processing of the study data by Aurora staff. Aurora's analysts created queries to extract data, merge data across tables, exclude data from certain patient groups as required by the IRB (further description in the Legal Framework for Granting Access section), and de-identify the data. This required a substantial time investment by the Aurora analyst team, which was enabled, in part, by adequately budgeting for and reimbursing the time spent by these analysts in the research sub-award. Further, from the MIT research team's perspective, this amount of preprocessing without the ability to directly review the queries and data transformations required strong communication and trust between the two teams.

Two primary teams at Aurora had access to data and skills to process data. One team's primary mission was business intelligence: mainly safeguarding data and developing routine reports on demand. Another was housed within the Aurora Research Institute with a broader research mission. Identifying analysts who thought about data like researchers and who found personal or professional interest in learning new research or analytic techniques helped to facilitate the data preparation and research process.

11.5 Protection of Sensitive and Personal Data: The Five Safes Framework

In this case study, the research team describes the sharing of data for a single research project, rather than the development of an overarching framework for providing secure access to data. Aurora had an established process for some steps; others were developed to meet the specific needs of the clinical decision support evaluation. Overall, assessments and approvals for the project as a whole took several months, during which researchers were cautious about devoting additional resources to a project that might not be approved. As such, the time for assessments and approvals pushed back the timeline for the research study. This timing is consistent with experience from other efforts to access administrative data and is typically reflective of long pauses or delays in response in between rounds of iteration or document review. Converting data from a raw, identified form into a linked, de-identified, and usable form ready to share with the MIT-based team may have taken a greater number of person-hours than working through the approvals process. However, this process of preparing data for transfer and use did not have a significant impact on the timeline of the study, since the team was able to simultaneously make progress on other aspects of the research.

11.5.1 Safe Projects

The application and review process for the research and data sharing involved several formal steps established by Aurora. A research coordinator and team of regulatory support staff supported coordination between the Aurora principal investigator (PI) and various teams and review systems at Aurora. Informally, gaining support and generating enthusiasm among leaders at Aurora helped to facilitate the process and maintain the momentum needed to work through concerns. Much of the credit for the approval of the study is attributed to having the support of key leaders within Aurora and the ability of the research team to anticipate and address the unarticulated concerns and motivations of Aurora reviewers.

Initially, the academic research team connected with Dr. Sarah Reimer (the Aurora PI) through a memo describing the proposed research design. The Aurora Research Institute requires any potential research projects to receive Research Administrative Preauthorization (RAP) before proceeding to IRB review; Dr. Reimer, in collaboration with the MIT investigators, prepared and submitted an application for review. Limited information about this process is available on Aurora's public website (Aurora Health Care, n.d.); additional information is available to potential Aurora investigators via e-mail or contact with Aurora's compliance and regulatory staff. Proposed research should be clinically and scientifically significant, be feasible to execute, and have sufficient resources available. Proposals are reviewed by the service line director under which the project falls; proposals are assessed to ensure they are of the highest quality and align with Aurora's philosophies and values. This proposal was reviewed by the director of Investigator-Initiated Research.

Once the RAP is approved, projects that are determined to involve human subjects must be reviewed by Aurora's IRB.[8] For this research study, the IRB requested that the team submit two separate protocols: one for a retrospective review of historical data and another for the intervention and prospective data. The review board required additional documentation of the scientific justification for the research design as well as a detailed description of data security experience and plans.

The research (including the use of data and the steps involved in implementing the randomized evaluation of the Clinical Decision Support (CDS) system) had to be approved by the entire medical group, the primary care council, three informatics committees, the executive committee of a subset of Aurora hospitals, the finance group, the chief medical officer, the chief transformation officer, chief compliance officer, the chief information officer, the research legal team, the data security team, and the IRB. This process took several months, multiple iterations, and justification at each stage.

---

[8]MIT's IRB ceded review to Aurora.

The RAP application was submitted, and it received approval in December 2015; IRB applications were submitted in January 2016; conditional IRB approvals were received in February and March 2016, which enabled the research team to proceed with project planning and to begin negotiating a data use agreement. The full approval process required iteration between IRB and data sharing review committees (a requirement for full approval by the IRB was a finalized data use agreement, and a requirement for approval of a data use agreement was approval by an IRB). The team executed an agreement to receive a limited amount of data in the fall of 2015; they finalized an agreement to share more detailed data necessary for the full research study in September 2016 with additional variables added through a modification in January 2017.

11.5.2 Safe People

Aurora does not have a routine process for assessing researchers that is publicly available. As a part of the request for data and IRB approval, a memo was sent to Aurora describing the previous experience of the MIT team's two lead investigators—Amy Finkelstein and Joseph Doyle—with using confidential data and protected health information for research while maintaining high levels of security; this was accompanied by their CVs to demonstrate significant and relevant research experience. All investigators and research assistants completed CITI[9] or NIH[10] training in human subjects research, which are commonly used in the United States to certify that researchers understand the rules and procedures governing ethics and safety when conducting human subjects research.

Only de-identified data were shared with non-Aurora researchers, resulting in a straightforward data handling procedure without further inspection or oversight from Aurora.

---

[9]https://about.citiprogram.org (accessed 2020-12-11).
[10]https://nexus.od.nih.gov/all/2018/09/07/protecting-human-research-particip ants-phrp-online-tutorial-no-longer-available-as-of-september-26-2018/ (accessed 2020-12-11).

11.5.3 Safe Settings

The data sharing agreement allowed the MIT team to access only data sets that were de-identified per the HIPAA Safe Harbor method. These data were shared via Secure File Transfer Protocol (SFTP) and stored on a secure, encrypted server maintained by IT professionals at the MIT Department of Economics. Researchers accessed this server using an encrypted Secure Shell (SSH) protocol after connecting to the MIT VPN, which utilizes an independent authentication system.

The MIT investigators and data analysts made several visits to Aurora to meet with the data teams but were not permitted to directly interact with or view the raw data. Access to raw, identified data may have expedited the process of linking data sets and ensuring a replicable and consistent de-identification process. However, this level of access likely would not have reduced the time spent by either team in understanding and interpreting the data.

11.5.4 Safe Data

As described in section 11.3.2, most of the data generated by a health care provider is protected by the HIPAA Privacy Rule. Pricing and billing data, even when completely de-identified, are considered sensitive, as they could be used by competing health care systems or by insurance companies during pricing negotiations. The specifications of the data that would be released outside of Aurora, and that which could be released in a public use file, were negotiated specifically for this project. The specifications are included in the Appendix.

In this case, it was possible to conduct the analysis on data that were de-identified at the patient and provider level per the HIPAA Safe Harbor method. This process was conducted by analysts at Aurora. As discussed in section11.4, a process was defined and followed specifically for this research study, and the MIT-based team consulted with the Aurora analysts to ensure record linkages would be replicable and stable throughout the research process.

11.5.5 Safe Outputs

The agreements between Aurora and MIT explicitly acknowledged and permitted the publication of scholarly work that would include analytic results based on the confidential information (i.e., the de-identified data shared by Aurora).[11] The sub-award agreement also permitted the creation of a public data set that would be able to replicate the published results.

To mitigate against disclosure risk, the public data set was aggregated to the provider rather than scan-order level.

The data sharing agreement between Aurora and MIT gave Aurora a thirty-day period to review any scholarly work for disclosure of confidential information. This review period was used to review both the written manuscript and the public data set. The manuscript was reviewed by Dr. Sarah Reimer, the Aurora-based investigator. The data set was reviewed by Dr. Reimer as well as by the manager of Research Analytics who oversaw data preparation throughout the study. The manager reviewed each measure in the data set to ensure patient and provider privacy and requested approval from the vice president of Research Development & Business Services and the president of the Aurora Research Institute. Per the data sharing and sub-award agreements, this assessment was limited to reviewing for disclosure of confidential information. This limitation is often required by academic institutions such as MIT to mitigate against the risk of suppressing results or otherwise interfering with or casting doubts upon academic freedom and integrity.

Any future outputs from the shared data would need to undergo the same review process initiated by the research team; one example is described below.

---

[11] For example, the NDA included a clause that read, "Aurora acknowledges that MIT is receiving Confidential Information in anticipation of its faculty preparing written scholarly work." Although all data shared were de-identified, all agreements reference the data as confidential information.

11.6 Data Life Cycle and Replicability

11.6.1 Preservation and Reproducibility of Researcher-Accessible Files

Aurora Health Care does not actively maintain the researcher-accessible de-identified files made available for this research study. The files sent to MIT were snapshots of a data warehouse, which is periodically updated, with the potential for certain values to be over-written; for example, the status of a scan order will change as the scan is performed, changed, or canceled. The MIT team did not receive the code used by Aurora to extract data nor did the team request that this code be maintained in perpetuity.

Within the study period, the MIT team received data in regular updates, typically every two to four weeks. These data were created when an analyst at Aurora manually initiated a query to extract data. Each data extract built cumulatively on the last, enabling researchers to quantify the extent of any changes. For each data extract, the team documented the date it was received, the description of the files and variables received, and the e-mail communications related to this extract.

11.6.2 Preservation of Researcher-Generated Files

Research-generated data files and code are preserved on MIT's secure servers. Researchers do not have permission to share the raw de-identified data nor the intermediate or final disaggregated data sets. The data use agreements require that MIT return or destroy confidential data upon request by Aurora; however, to date no such request has been made.

The public data set, described in section 11.5.5, contain data aggregated at the provider level—including the number of high-cost scan orders, treatment assignment, provider type and characteristics, and aggregate patient and financial information—along with documentation and replication code. These were published on J-PAL's Dataverse, which is part of the Harvard Dataverse repository (Doyle et al., 2018).

As the team worked on data extraction, cleaning, and analysis, they generated their own documentation of the data and the indicators or derived variables they created. This culminated in a step-by-step guide on how to run the data pipeline from processing raw data to producing analysis tables. However, without a clear use case for this level of internal documentation (particularly given the complexity of the process and underlying data, that the data are not public, and the uniqueness of the purpose for which the data were prepared), researchers did not prepare this full level of documentation for publication or for use by the general public.

The Public Use Files are sufficient to replicate all published results. However, due to the aggregation and limited fields of the data set, the possibilities for further analysis may be limited. For example, the team received a request to report on the impact of CDS on musculoskeletal scans by another research team conducting a meta-analysis. Because this could not be produced from the public data set, the MIT team sought and received approval from Aurora to publish the new results from analysis conducted on the nonpublic data. The MIT research team is willing to field requests for additional analysis and seek approval from Aurora to share data if the request has merit and relates to the original purpose of the research collaboration. However, these extra steps are limitations of the arrangement stemming from the agreement to only publish aggregated data.

11.7 Sustainability and Continued Success

11.7.1 Revenue

The research on clinical decision support received funding from the Laura and John Arnold Foundation (now Arnold Ventures). Through a sub-award from MIT to Aurora Health Care, the research team provided funding on a cost-reimbursable basis for data extraction and preparation as well as support for interpreting the data. While this award seemed to garner goodwill for the project, the sub-award would have accounted for an extremely small fraction of Aurora's annual operating budget.[12]

11.7.2 Metrics of Success

The research team attributes much of the success of this data sharing and research collaboration to clear communication, strong relationships, and patience. As the team negotiated data use agreements and IRB review, they relied on their prior work with hospitals and health records as well as a familiarity with the HIPAA Privacy Rule and IRB review process; this allowed the researchers to anticipate and thoroughly respond to concerns of the Aurora review committees and to identify data sharing procedures that met the needs of both safety and research. After receiving approval for the study, frequent in-person meetings fostered trust and a shared vision and affirmed the commitment of all teams to the project success. By investing in the relationship, researchers were able to communicate about the data openly and clearly in order to develop a strong understanding at all stages of the pipeline. Recognizing that Aurora's analyst teams likely had competing priorities and limited time, the MIT team was as directly helpful as possible by generating code, pseudo code, or step-by-step instructions. Throughout the study, the MIT team had touchpoints with leadership at the Aurora Research Institute who were enthusiastic about the research partnership and helped to facilitate approvals within Aurora.

The research team and the ARI executives hoped that this research and data sharing collaboration would pave the way for future collaborations with external researchers through clarifying processes, setting precedents, and demonstrating the value of sharing data. From conversations after completion of the CDS intervention, the experience on this project contributed to an interest in further collaboration on research and in bringing deeper research expertise on staff at Aurora.

---

[12]For example, Aurora's operating income was $339.1 million in 2017 (see Aurora Health Care, Inc. and Affiliates, 2018).

As an example demonstrating this interest, Aurora's Vice President of Research Development and Business Services, Kurt Waldhuetter, visited the MIT team at J-PAL North America to discuss how to do more collaborative research work as well as to discuss a planned center on outcomes research.

After the clinical decision support project, two of the key executives at ARI left the institute, and Aurora underwent a merger with Advocate Health Care. These changes—and the resulting shift in focus at Aurora—makes it hard to determine the ultimate impact of this project on future data sharing opportunities or research.

Beyond process, the Aurora analysts who worked on data extraction gained insight into the data and techniques for processing data that have improved their efficiency. For example, the best practice alert data used for this project is not commonly analyzed by the health care system; however, the analysts stated that understanding these data has helped them respond to internal requests from the pharmacy information systems group on how to analyze their alert data. As another example, many internal reporting and assessment projects at Aurora require matching data across data systems, and the need for, and complexity of, linking data has increased as the teams must now integrate data from the Advocate systems. The Aurora analyst team has applied their knowledge gained on the CDS project of how to match patient names or other records in a string format to these internal projects.[13]

---

[13]For example, the Aurora team gained a strong understanding of how to use the concept of edit distance (a way of quantifying how dissimilar two strings are to one another by counting the minimum number of operations required to transform one string into the other) to match such records.

CHAPTER 11

About the Authors

Laura Feeney is the Associate Director of Research and Training at J-PAL North America. She provides strategic direction to the research and training team in efforts to support researchers and improve the quality and efficiency of randomized evaluations. She works with researchers, partners, and staff to develop and promote best practices in research, build the capacity of policymakers and research staff, and encourage the use of administrative data for research.

Laura has managed evaluations of health services and policies both internationally and domestically. Prior to her work at J-PAL North America, Laura worked with Innovations for Poverty Action (IPA), Shoulder to Shoulder (a network of health clinics based in rural Honduras), and the US Bureau of Labor Statistics. Laura holds an MA in economics from the University of British Columbia and a BA in economics from the University of Florida.

Amy Finkelstein is the John & Jennie S. MacDonald Professor of Economics at the Massachusetts Institute of Technology. She is the co-founder and co-scientific director of J-PAL North America. She is also the co-director of the Health Care Program at the National Bureau of Economic Research and the founding editor of *American Economic Review: Insights*. Amy has led a number of randomized evaluations of health care policies, including the Oregon Health Insurance Experiment and a study of healthcare "hotspotting." She holds a PhD in economics from MIT, an MPhil in economics from Oxford, and an AB in government from Harvard.

Acknowledgements

We are grateful to a research grant from the Laura and John Arnold Foundation for the original research underlying this case study. We received feedback from many of the original data analysts, research assistants, and study co-authors, including Andrew Marek, Noah Pearce, and Sarah Reimer from Aurora, and Sarah Abraham, Joseph Doyle, Jesse Gubb, Andelyn Russell, and Sam Wang from the J-PAL and MIT research teams. We acknowledge and thank them for their time, input, and perspective. The interpretations expressed are solely those of the authors and do not represent the views of our funder nor Aurora Health Care.

References in Chapter 11

Aurora Health Care. n.d.. "Research Administrative Preauthorization (RAP)." https://www.aurorahealthcare.org/aurora-research-institute/researcher-resources/research-administrative-preauthorization (accessed 2020-06-23).

Aurora Health Care, Inc. and Affiliates. 2018. "Unaudited Consolidated Financial Statements and Other Information For the Year Ended December 31, 2017." Aurora Health Care. https://www.aurorahealthcare.org/-/media/aurorahealthcareorg/documents/annual-report/2017-annual-financial-information-and-operating-data.pdf (accessed 2020-06-23).

Centers for Medicare & Medicaid Services. 2018. "Medicare Program; Revisions to Payment Policies Under the Physician Fee Schedule and Other Revisions to Part B for CY 2019." *83 Fed. Reg. 59452*, (Nov. 23, 2018). https://www.federalregister.gov/documents/2018/11/23/2018-24170/medicare-program-revisions-to-payment-policies-under-the-physician-fee-schedule-and-other-revisions (accessed 2020-01-30).

Code of Federal Regulations. 2000*a*. "45 CFR Part 160 - General Administrative Requirements." https://www.ecfr.gov/cgi-bin/text-idx?tpl=/ecfrbrowse/Title45/45cfr160_main_02.tpl (accessed 2020-12-11).

Code of Federal Regulations. 2000*b*. "45 CFR Part 164 - Security and Privacy." https://www.ecfr.gov/cgi-bin/text-idx?tpl=/ecfrbrowse/Title45/45cfr164_main_02.tpl (accessed 2020-12-11).

Code of Federal Regulations. 2000*c*. "45 CFR § 164.514 - Other requirements relating to uses and disclosures of protected health information." https://www.ecfr.gov/cgi-bin/text-idx?node=se45.1.164_1514&rgn=div8 (accessed 2020-12-11).

Doyle, Joseph, Sarah Abraham, Laura Feeney, Sarah Reimer, and Amy Finkelstein. 2018. "Clinical decision support for high-cost imaging: a randomized clinical trial [Data set]." *Harvard Dataverse*. https://doi.org/10.7910/DVN/BRKDVQ.

Doyle, Joseph, Sarah Abraham, Laura Feeney, Sarah Reimer, and Amy Finkelstein. 2019. "Clinical decision support for high-cost imaging: A randomized clinical trial." *PLOS ONE*, 14(3): e0213373. https://doi.org/10.1371/journal.pone.0213373.

Feeney, Laura, Jason Bauman, Julia Chabrier, Geeti Mehra, and Michelle Woodford. 2015. "Administrative Data for Randomized Evaluations." J-PAL North America. https://www.povertyactionlab.org/resource/using-administrative-data-randomized-evaluations (accessed 2020-01-30).

Hentel, Keith D., Andrew Menard, John Mongan, Jeremy C. Durack, Pamela T. Johnson, Ali S. Raja, and Ramin Khorasani. 2019. "What Physicians and Health Organizations Should Know About Mandated Imaging Appropriate Use Criteria." *Annals of Internal Medicine*, 170(12): 880–885. https://doi.org/10.7326/M19-0287.

Office for Human Research Protections. 2018. "Revised Common Rule Regulatory Text." https://www.hhs.gov/ohrp/regulations-and-policy/regulations/revised-common-rule-regulatory-text/index.html (accessed 2020-10-05).

Penn Medicine Information Systems Data Analytics Center. n.d.. "Epic Clarity." Data Analytics Center, Perelman School of Medicine at the University of Pennsylvania website. https://www.med.upenn.edu/dac/epic-clarity-data-warehousing.html (accessed 2020-01-30).

U.S. Department of Health & Human Services. 2018. "Health Information Privacy: Research." https://www.hhs.gov/hipaa/for-professionals/special-topics/research/index.html (accessed 2020-01-28).

U.S. Department of Health & Human Services. n.d.. "Health Information Privacy." https://www.hhs.gov/hipaa/index.html (accessed 2020-06-23).

CHAPTER 11

Appendix

The following are excerpts from Sub-Award or Non-Disclosure Agreements

Public Use Data Set

The following clause was included in the sub-award agreement between Aurora Health Care (the Sub-awardee) and MIT permitting the publication of a data set upon completion of the study

> "Notwithstanding the foregoing, a subset of the Subawardee Confidential Information will be made public according to the terms set forth in this section ("Public Data Set") and will not be treated as Subawardee Confidential Information once made public. The Public Data Set will not include patient, encounter, and financial level data elements. It will only include provider level data elements and may include aggregate patient and financial information. The exact nature of the Public Data Set will be determined at the end of the Research as it may depend on the findings. The Public Data Set is anticipated to be a provider-level data set with physician characteristics including provider type (MD, DO, NP, PA), specialty, age bins and average patient characteristics, along with outcomes including the number of scans that would trigger the best practice alert (BPA) being evaluated in this Research, the number of high cost scan orders, the number of scan orders with a score of 1-3, the number of scans with a score of 4-6 and the number of low cost scans. The outcomes will be measured over various timeframes such as 0-1 month, 0-3 months, 0-6 months, 0-9 months, and 0-12 months. The Public Data Set may be made available on the OSF and DataVerse websites and may be available to the public indefinitely. The exact list of data elements and aggregate

data to be made public will be agreed upon by both Parties in year 3 of the Research and prior to the Public Data Set being made public."

Publishing

The following is from the sub-award agreement:

"If and to the extent that each Party has contributed to the results of the Research, the two Parties may work together in good faith to publish the results jointly, as appropriate. The foregoing notwithstanding, both MIT and Subawardee shall have the right to publish the results of the Research arising from such portion of the Research performed solely by such Party, along with any background information about the Research that is necessary to be included in any publication of results or necessary for other scholars to verify such results. Prior to publication of Research performed solely by one Party, the publishing Party must provide the other Party with at least thirty (30) calendar days advance notice for the non-publishing Party to review the manuscript in order to identify patentable subject matter or the inadvertent disclosure of Subawardee Confidential Information."

The following is from the NDA:

"Aurora acknowledges that MIT is receiving Confidential Information in anticipation of its faculty preparing written scholarly work ("Scholarly Work"). In the event MIT personnel seek to publish a Scholarly Work, Aurora will have a thirty (30) day period to review the Scholarly Work for any disclosure of Confidential Information. Aurora shall, within the thirty (30) day period, give MIT notice identifying specifically any Confidential Information it believes would be disclosed in the Scholarly Work. If Aurora does not provide timely notice, it will be deemed to have waived any objection to disclosure of Confidential Information."

CHAPTER 12

The Stanford-SFUSD Partnership: Development of Data-Sharing Structures and Processes

Moonhawk Kim (University of California, Berkeley)

Jim Shen (J-PAL, Massachusetts Institute of Technology)

Laura Wentworth (California Education Partners)

Norma Ming (San Francisco Unified School District)

Michelle Reininger (University of Colorado at Boulder)

Eric Bettinger (Stanford University)

12.1 Summary

Research-practice partnerships (RPPs) have a growing reputation for making important connections between the worlds of research and

---

Copyright © Moonhawk Kim, Jim Shen, Laura Wentworth, Norma Ming, Michelle Reininger, and Eric Bettinger.

Cite as: Kim, Moonhawk, Jim Shen, Laura Wentworth, Norma Ming, Michelle Reininger, and Eric Bettinger. "The Stanford-SFUSD Partnership: Development of Data-Sharing Structures and Processes." In: Cole, Shawn, Iqbal Dhaliwal, Anja Sautmann, and Lars Vilhuber (eds.), *Handbook on Using Administrative Data for Research and Evidence-based Policy*. Cambridge, MA: Abdul Latif Jameel Poverty Action Lab. 2020.

practice in education (Farley-Ripple et al., 2018; Farrell, Coburn and Chong, 2019). These partnerships are long-term, mutualistic, and strategic relationships between researchers and practitioners in education: the product is research that is both related to practical challenges and generalizable to the broader field (Coburn, Penuel and Geil, 2013; Coburn and Penuel, 2016). An essential component of some of these partnerships is the data management and data sharing needed for operationalizing research, yet there is little documentation for how to develop and maintain the data infrastructure to support these partnerships.

To improve the field's understanding of the data infrastructure needed for RPPs, this chapter describes the data infrastructure within the partnership between Stanford University Graduate School of Education (Stanford GSE) and San Francisco Unified School District (SFUSD). The partnership was started in 2009 with SFUSD administrative data being shared on a project-by-project basis.[1] In 2010, given the number of requests for administrative data by Stanford faculty and researchers to be used in research studies with SFUSD, the Stanford-SFUSD Partnership developed an approach to warehousing regular extracts of SFUSD administrative data within a data warehouse at Stanford University. SFUSD administrative data housed at Stanford University captures data on over 55,000 students, over 3,500 PreK–12 teachers, and a total of almost 10,000 staff from the academic year 2000/2001 to the present. Since 2011, when the data warehouse was started, the number of Stanford research projects with SFUSD requesting data from the CEPA Data Manager has tripled from three projects to nine projects in 2018.

The chapter describes the development of the data infrastructure to meet that demand within the Stanford-SFUSD Partnership from its infancy in 2009 to its present state in 2020. The chapter starts by giving the motivation and background as well as cases of data use in research. Then the authors describe SFUSD leaders' ways of conceptualizing the different uses of data as well as capacities and personnel to prepare

---

[1]See Wentworth, Carranza and Stipek (2016) for a description of the Partnership's origins.

and supply these data to the Stanford-SFUSD Partnership and other researchers in general. The chapter addresses the legal frameworks guiding the decisions related to the design of infrastructure and agreements, and it explores the case of the Stanford-SFUSD Partnership data infrastructure through the lens of the five safes framework. Finally, the authors summarize some lessons learned that are mentioned throughout the chapter, which could be helpful for the field more broadly and especially for research-practice partnerships that analyze administrative data.

The authors represent current and former members of the Partnership who worked to launch, maintain, or revise the necessary structures and agreements to support the data preparation and exchange. They include Michelle Reininger, the former Executive Director of the Stanford Center for Education Policy Analysis (CEPA) and research faculty at Stanford GSE, who is now at the University of Colorado; Laura Wentworth, the Director of Research Practice Partnerships at California Education Partners, who continues to direct the Stanford-SFUSD Partnership; current and former administrators in SFUSD who helped improve the agreements and district-side data infrastructure within SFUSD, including Norma Ming, SFUSD's Supervisor of Research and Evaluation in SFUSD's Research, Planning, and Assessment (RPA) division, and Moonhawk Kim, formerly the Supervisor of Analytics in SFUSD's RPA division and now at UC Berkeley; as well as other current and former members at Stanford who helped operationalize the data infrastructure, including Jim Shen, who formerly managed the CEPA data warehouse and is now at J-PAL, and Eric Bettinger, one of the faculty whose research team has accessed and used the data from the warehouse and who is now the faculty director of CEPA where the data are housed at Stanford.

CHAPTER 12

12.2 Introduction

12.2.1 Motivation and Background

This chapter describes the development, design, and use of the data infrastructure for the Stanford-SFUSD Partnership. While both institutions have worked with multiple other partners, this chapter focuses specifically on the partnership between Stanford and SFUSD. Established in 2009, the Stanford-SFUSD Partnership supports an average of 25 to 30 active projects at any given time, many of which require administrative data as part of the research. The Partnership maintains a data warehouse at Stanford University that includes data from the academic year 2000/2001—ten years prior to the start of the arrangement—to the present on information related to SFUSD's over 55,000 students across 133 schools and nearly 10,000 staff. The CEPA data warehouse includes information about SFUSD student demographics, school attendance, special programs (e.g., English learner services, Special Education, or after-school programming), academic outcomes (e.g., grades, standardized test scores), behavioral outcomes and interventions (e.g., attendance, office referral), and key milestones (e.g., graduations). These data have been used in projects examining a range of topics such as ethnic studies courses (Dee and Penner, 2017), human capital (Dizon-Ross et al., 2019), and large-scale school reforms (Sun, Penner and Loeb, 2017). The partnership started when a number of Stanford GSE faculty were working on projects with SFUSD, and a local funder supporting these research projects asked the SFUSD and Stanford leaders whether they found their work together useful enough to create a more formal partnership that could provide coordination of the different relationships. The funder offered to hire a Partnership director to work with Stanford faculty and SFUSD administrators to support the two organizations when working on research together in hopes of producing mutually beneficial outcomes: generalizable research.

From the outset, the partnership was designed to encourage two institutions—Stanford University GSE and SFUSD—to work together differently, thereby changing some of the status quo practices within each institution and in their collaborations. These included establishing some new processes and agreements for governing the data infrastructure. This started with creating a data warehousing agreement and data use agreement (DUA) template and evolved to include an annual meeting where SFUSD and Stanford leaders convene to discuss data use and research with the goal of calibrating and aligning their efforts.

The processes for governing the data infrastructure evolved over time in response to needs. In the beginning of the partnership, Stanford researchers and the SFUSD research department administrators felt challenged by the volume of data exchanges and the time and resources needed to prepare those data extracts. Also, it took time to develop the DUAs for each project, which had to be reviewed individually by the Stanford and SFUSD legal departments. While SFUSD worked with many researchers, the Stanford-based research projects constituted a significant share of all requests for administrative data from SFUSD. This high volume of requests for administrative data led to an agreement to warehouse SFUSD administrative data at Stanford.

In 2011, the Partnership director worked with the SFUSD research department, Stanford GSE Dean's office, and the leadership of CEPA to streamline the agreements needed for data use and access to address the challenges with data exchange. To do this the two institutions' legal departments created a standardized DUA template, which Stanford researchers could easily fill out when submitting data requests to SFUSD. With such a template, the Stanford and SFUSD legal teams would not need to review every project's DUA. An even larger commitment to this partnership came when both SFUSD and Stanford established an umbrella warehousing agreement between Stanford University GSE, CEPA, and SFUSD to house SFUSD data and distribute the necessary data for their research projects to all Stanford researchers with an approved DUA. The warehouse would require personnel and management beyond hiring a Partnership director. This undertaking was key in moving the Stanford-SFUSD Partnership from a federation of projects to an actual partnership.

12.2.2 Data Use Examples

Here three cases of research supported through the Stanford-SFUSD Partnership's data infrastructure are described.[2] This infrastructure has enabled descriptive as well as quasi-experimental and experimental research. While the Stanford-SFUSD partnership has not used its data infrastructure to conduct randomized control trials (RCTs), the school district has occasionally, although rarely, partnered with other research organizations to conduct RCTs. For SFUSD, the operating constraint on whether it conducts experiments is not the technical aspects of the data sharing infrastructure, but rather the ethical and pragmatic considerations for implementing the proposed experiment.

Two of the three cases analyze only secondary administrative data collected by SFUSD: the first used descriptive statistics and regression modeling and the second used the method of implementing a quasi-experimental design. The third case collected primary survey data in combination with analyzing secondary administrative data. These cases were selected for a number of reasons. First, these cases represent Stanford researchers and SFUSD leaders who have been working together on lines of inquiry for a substantial amount of time. Second, the research has been influential in SFUSD leaders' decision-making as well as at the state and national levels. Third, these cases showcase some of the statistical methods that the authors thought would be of interest to the audience for this Handbook.

Study of English Learner Programs

This first case describes an example of research using descriptive statistics and regression modeling using de-identified administrative data. To better serve English learners, SFUSD leaders had adopted four different types of language programs, which provide English language development as well as instruction in another target language. Yet SFUSD leaders lacked reliable local evidence comparing the effectiveness of their bilingual and English-only language programs for English

---

[2]Please note that not all of the journal articles are cited from this research to maintain anonymity of the school district in some specific studies.

learners. To address this, SFUSD Special Assistant to the Superintendent Christina Wong and Chief of Research, Planning, and Assessment Ritu Khanna partnered with Stanford GSE Professor Sean F. Reardon, a sociologist, to examine the impact of SFUSD's programs on English learners' education outcomes. Reardon and his team worked with SFUSD research department staff to validate and organize the variables in the data across SFUSD's language pathways. With the help of the Strategic Education Research Partnership and the Stanford-SFUSD Partnership director, Khanna, Reardon, Wong, and their teams met about every other month to examine descriptive data reports and preliminary results, to address questions by the researchers, and explore interpretations of the data by the district leaders. The research suggested that over time, English learner students in dual-language programs using both English and their native language developed English and academic skills faster than those immersed in English-only instruction. In addition to producing eight articles published in peer-reviewed academic journals and other types of policy and practice publications, the research helped SFUSD leaders to evaluate and ultimately justify continued implementation and support for their bilingual programs. These findings have been presented at the state level in California and at U.S. conferences, helping to change California's policies in support of bilingual education.

Evaluating the Impact of a Course in Ethnic Studies

This second case describes an example of research applying a quasi-experimental design to analyze administrative data from the data warehouse. The SFUSD school board adopted a policy to support an ethnic studies course in their high schools in hopes that the course would help reduce absenteeism and narrow opportunity gaps, in addition to influencing other outcomes like high school dropout rates, truancy, and graduation. A set of SFUSD high schools was selected to pilot the course, and Assistant Superintendent of High Schools Bill Sanderson was in charge of overseeing the pilot and reporting back to the school board on the outcomes. Through the Stanford-SFUSD Partnership, Bill Sanderson collaborated with Stanford GSE Professor

Thomas Dee, an economist, to evaluate the ethnic studies course pilot using SFUSD administrative data from the CEPA data warehouse. Applying a regression discontinuity design, Professor Dee's research suggested that the ethnic studies courses in SFUSD's pilot program improved students' GPA and attendance significantly compared to similar students not enrolled in the course (Dee and Penner, 2017). Along with other information presented to the school board, this research helped motivate the board to pass resolution 1410-28A4, "Institutionalizing Ethnic Studies into the San Francisco Unified School District" (San Francisco Unified School District, 2014) to offer an ethnic studies course at all SFUSD high schools. This research has been cited by other school districts (Cuevas, 2019) and states (Ragland, 2017) to justify policies that support ethnic studies courses, including California policymakers as they consider requiring ethnic studies courses across all California high schools.

Evaluating Changes to Human Capital Policies

This third case describes an example of research combining primary survey data about teachers' perspectives on conditions influencing turnover and retention with secondary SFUSD administrative data from the warehouse. In 2009, San Francisco voters passed the Quality Teacher and Education Act (QTEA), which supported a parcel tax providing additional funding for teacher salaries in SFUSD among other things (Hough, 2009). Since that time, SFUSD's Human Resources department has been tasked with implementing the teacher salary increases and teacher bonuses meant to support teachers working in hard-to-staff positions and schools. SFUSD Chief of Human Resources, Daniel Menezes, has partnered with Professor Susanna Loeb to undertake research to inform this work. Loeb and her research team launched an evaluation of the effects of the increases in SFUSD teacher salaries in 2009, finding some positive influences on teacher recruitment, but less impact on teacher retention (Hough and Loeb, 2013). In partnership with SFUSD, Loeb started surveying all SFUSD teachers, principals, and assistant principals in 2009, and even with her transition to Brown University in 2017, has continued the partnership. Since then, Loeb and her colleagues have conducted multiple studies using the teacher and administrator survey data and SFUSD administrative data on students and teachers (Dizon-Ross et al., 2019). Loeb and her colleagues used quasi-experimental designs to evaluate the effects of the QTEA and other pertinent human capital policies in SFUSD (Sun, Penner and Loeb, 2017). Chief Menezes and many other leaders have referenced Loeb's research when justifying key human capital decisions. For example, in 2019, San Francisco Mayor London Breed wanted to put city funding towards a research-backed practice, and cited Loeb's research as a rationale for providing increased stipends to teachers working in hard-to-staff schools in San Francisco (Waxmann, 2019). What has been particularly valuable about this arrangement is having an external research team analyze the teacher survey data in conjunction with other teacher characteristics and outcomes in the administrative data, thus preserving the confidentiality of individual teachers' survey responses.

12.3 Making Data Usable for Research

A robust data infrastructure must be established for research-practice partnerships to reliably produce studies such as those discussed above. Prior to sharing data for research, both SFUSD and Stanford needed to prepare and process the data. This section describes frameworks to guide data management, SFUSD's and Stanford's approaches for processing the administrative data and building a data infrastructure, and finally, the processes for exchanging the data.

→ use this as a preface for CDM

12.3.1 Framework for Converting Operational Data to Analytical Data for Research

In school districts, as in other large organizations, data serve multiple purposes. While Solberg et al. (1997) distinguish between using data for accountability, improvement, and research, the authors of this chapter add service provision and evaluation as two additional purposes (San Francisco Unified School District, 2019). Whereas *research* is expected to be generalizable, *evaluation* may sometimes be narrowly focused on a local initiative. *Improvement* may draw from both research and evaluation, but it prioritizes informing the local implementers rather than external audiences. *Service provision* is inherently local, using data for such activities as enrolling students, determining program eligibility, or adapting staff caseloads. *Accountability* provides reports to the public, funders, or others in the broader community, summarizing such data as the numbers of students served per school, or staff with different credentials. These purposes may be mapped on to the distinction between enumerative studies, which describe the current state, and analytical studies, which draw inferences to apply to a future state (Deming, 1953; Provost, 2011). Accountability and service provision rely on enumerative studies about the past or present state. Some research and evaluation studies may likewise provide enumerative snapshots, such as by tabulating students experiencing homelessness, characterizing teacher diversity, or describing the participants in a given program. Research and evaluation also often constitute analytical studies intended to generalize more broadly, as when developing early warning indicators or evaluating the impact of a pilot program. Improvement may qualify under either category depending on the distance of transfer.

These distinctions are important because the types of activities require different data and their interpretations of data are varied (illustrated in Figure 12.1). Operational data describe the current state and undergo continuous updating to accurately reflect changing conditions, while analytical data capture consistent and comparable snapshots of the operational data according to a set of predetermined parameters. Staff rely on operational data in real time to provide services. For example, students may switch into and out of an ethnic studies course, shift from one section to another, or even change schools while maintaining enrollment in ethnic studies. Operational data need to reflect these changes in real time for schools and teachers to accurately maintain records of students' course-taking and provide services. By contrast, analytical data need to freeze the operational data to ensure consistent

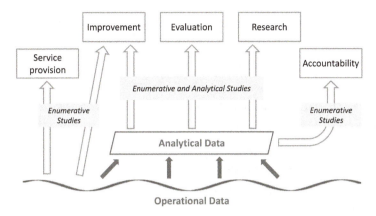

Figure 12.1: Relationships between purposes of data use, study types, and the data systems that support them.

accountability reporting, and to facilitate reproducible and replicable research and evaluation studies. Evaluating the impact of ethnic studies requires specifying the sample of students who took the course as defined by some criteria, such as enrollment by a specific date and for a minimum percentage of the school year.

Ultimately, the differentiation between operational data and analytical data is important for the usability of data, not only in terms of researchers accessing data but also regarding whether the data can be used to generate reliable and meaningful evidence for district decision-making.[3] Thus, any data-sharing arrangement must closely manage the process of generating analytical data from operational data to ensure high-quality data throughout.

12.3.2 Processes for Compiling Operational Data and Converting to Analytical Data

Although SFUSD has been working toward streamlining the data systems and workflows in the district, it does not yet have a tightly integrated and coordinated system for collecting and housing analytical data. In recent years, the district has been consolidating various

---

[3]Accountability and improvement work have largely been implemented internally within the district.

disparate systems and standardizing practices surrounding data. In addition to technical changes in the software, these efforts have also included refining the social infrastructure, such as establishing clear data governance and crafting shared definitions and approaches for data analysis. Given the diversity of the data systems, the data transfer arrangement from the district to the university has consisted of two tracks: one highly systematized track from the main student information system (SIS) and a second, less regularized track for various data beyond those stored in the SIS, which necessitated the establishment of new routines.

The standard track has a well-established workflow for extracting from the operational data and generating analytical data files. Every fall, an analyst at SFUSD's research office pulls and processes a set of data from a Microsoft SQL database server, which contains tables extracted from the district's SIS for the previous school year. These are internally referred to as the RPA tables, named after the district's research office. The data capture snapshots from the end of each school year. For example, the data for the 2018–2019 school year would be prepared in fall 2019. The elements include various student-level data, such as their enrollment, courses, grades, and assessment results. These data elements are documented in internal codebooks, which list the variables included in each data file, the description of the field, and their possible values. The district shares this codebook with the CEPA Data Manager and Stanford researchers. Similarly, the employee information system (EIS) database has its own set of documentation that comes from the Human Resources division.

The second track, for data outside the primary and established mode of transfers described above, has become more refined in recent years. Nevertheless, the workflows for generating analytical data for these are still less institutionalized than the main track. The current routines require the Supervisor of Analytics at SFUSD's research office, who manages the district's data sharing processes, to work with data owners around the district to obtain, process, and transfer the data. Data owners would (1) use the applicable aspects of the SIS, thereby making their data accessible to the research department, or (2) periodically transfer data to the research department. The Supervisor of Analytics documents the definition, the population, and the value descriptors in collaboration with the data owners and shares the documentation with the university.

This second track of compiling and processing data became necessary over time due to the proliferation of data systems and underutilization of SIS functionalities. This led to numerous data elements contained in the umbrella DUA being located with specific departments and staff that oversaw, inputted, or generated the data. Thus, the first step toward making data usable was to track down and obtain data elements from the appropriate owners. In 2017, when the Supervisor of Analytics took on the role of coordinating data exchanges on the district side, the investigation took a significant amount of time and effort. Examples of these investigations included compiling data from the Early Education Department (EED) (serving children ages 3 months through 5 years), which uses a different SIS due to distinct reporting and management needs, and the homelessness data, which involve multiple definitions of homelessness and service providers.

The operational data collected in these manners require various processing to be converted to analytical data. Three generic types of processing are necessary for the data gathered from the district's departments: restructuring data extracted from different systems to make them congruous with the main data; compiling, comparing, and contrasting different methods and data tracking the same phenomenon; and eliminating data errors. We discuss an example for each of these here. First, EED's SIS has its own particular schema for organizing student data. In that system, the data are structured differently, with column headers and value descriptors that are distinct from the district's main SIS. For example, the sets of values capturing students' race/ethnicity differ between the systems. Second, data about homelessness demonstrate another type of gap between school operations and education research. The district maintains two sets of data for students' housing statuses. One is based on students' participation in the housing program administered by the city and the county. The other, following the state's accountability reporting requirements, is based on students' housing arrangement at home. However, research based on a student-year unit of observation requires an indicator of students' annual status, and neither data set comprehensively captures students' challenges; both can vary within a school year, and the two track different aspects of students' experiences. The district does not choose which series to use. Instead, it makes all the various metrics available to the CEPA data warehouse. Lastly, even the official state assessment results files—such as those for the English Language Proficiency Assessments for California (ELPAC, formerly known as the California English Language Development Test)—might contain multiple records for some students that must be systematically unduplicated.

Analytical data generated through this second track are not documented in the main internal codebook associated with the RPA tables. The district owners of each set of data provide the Supervisor of Analytics with the necessary information, who then passes it along to Stanford. Data that originate from external sources, such as the state or third-party testing services, have their own documentation prepared by the respective source. Infrequently, metadata about some variables are not yet fully documented by the time researchers request them for a project. In such cases, the project stands by while the Supervisor of Analytics works with the appropriate data owner in the district to obtain the information.

All the data throughout the district that have been obtained and processed into analytical data files through these two tracks are then transferred to the Stanford data warehouse. Operational data used in the generation of the analytical data are not transferred to the warehouse. At the warehouse, the data undergo further structuring as described below. While the analytical data are archived at the district's research department, no process presently exists at the district to rigorously structure the archived data into a database system. This is a significant gap that should be resolved, as doing so would facilitate research and evaluation by district staff as well as other research partners beyond Stanford.

One key lesson learned comes from the variation in the Partnership's management of these processes over time. These sometimes followed a predictable schedule for data extractions and sometimes permitted ad hoc extractions for individual projects or newly-integrated data sources. These exceptions have led to complications when reconciling discrepancies in external research and internal accountability reports with partial overlap in their data source, date, or definition. The Partnership strives for greater consistency in routines for conducting, documenting, and compiling extractions from operational data to analytical data and encourage other agencies and partnerships to invest much more heavily in this area. This would ensure accuracy in the findings and promote confidence in the interpretations for action.

12.3.3 Processes for Organizing and Storing Analytical Data

After the operational data have been converted to analytical data, they need to be organized and stored in an accessible manner. The Stanford-SFUSD partnership established a data warehouse at CEPA to serve this function, although the warehouse could have been set up elsewhere. The warehouse encrypts and stores the data on servers under the direct control of the Data Manager, reducing the likelihood that unauthorized users can gain electronic access to the data. While no security arrangement is foolproof, taking steps to safeguard the data is important not only because of the organization's contractual obligation to do so, but also as part of its ethical responsibility to the students and staff of SFUSD as well as to ensure that Stanford is a trustworthy research partner.

Upon being notified by SFUSD that a data transfer has taken place, the CEPA data manager downloads and removes the data from the Google Suite for Education's shared drive. One of the key tasks for the Data Manager is to organize the analytical data to allow for rapid responses to researcher data requests. As of mid-2019, the warehouse uses a self-documenting folder naming system that tracks the year and month of receiving the data files and the type of data received. For example, staff data files received in April 2018 would be placed in a folder named "201804_Staff." This system is self-documenting by making it apparent which folder contains what set of raw analytical data and when the data were received. This file naming system was chosen because of the timing and frequency of the data transfers. The warehouse does not receive data sufficiently frequently where tracking the data at more than a monthly interval is necessary. The warehouse also places documentation files that accompany the raw data into the folder.

To make use of the analytical data files, the data warehouse processes the data into master data sets as an intermediate step before providing the data to research teams. The Data Manager imports the data to Stata for cleaning and processing, with the code for the data cleaning process saved as Stata do-files (also known as syntax files). The master data files are cleaned versions of the annual analytical data that are organized into longitudinal data files and serve as the source of the data provided to researchers. This is done for the data files most commonly used by the research teams at Stanford, such as the annual student data extracts and the biannual staff data extracts. By pre-processing the analytical data from the district into the master data files, the warehouse is generally able to significantly reduce the turnaround time between receiving a data request from a research team and providing a research team with the data that they have requested. The only instance in which this does not hold true is if a research project requests data that the warehouse does not already hold and requires SFUSD to transfer the files to the warehouse specifically for that research project.

12.4 Legal and Institutional Framework

As alluded to above, making the school district's administrative data usable for research involves staff members in various roles, social and technical structures for collaboration, and legal arrangements to comply with systems protecting student privacy. This section first describes the current institutional set-up and some lessons emerging from its evolution, before proceeding to discuss the legal contexts and structures for sharing and using data.

12.4.1 Institutional Setup

The Stanford-SFUSD Partnership's infrastructure for sharing data involves the two partnering organizations—the school district and the university—and a facilitating third-party, non-profit organization, California Education Partners ("Ed Partners"). This section begins by describing the agency data infrastructure where the data originate; followed by the data warehouse where the data are stored; and finally, the staffing to support both infrastructures.

Agency Data Infrastructure

As described above, converting operational data into research-ready analytical data requires processing by the agency that produced the data. This motivates the need for a robust data infrastructure within the agency for organizing and maintaining the authoritative versions of the analytical data. Strengthening the upstream processes of data governance and data management within the agency would accrue benefits for all subsequent analyses, regardless of who conducts those analyses. Focusing investments downstream, in the processes of transferring data to the research partner and any corresponding cleanup of the data, would lead to other consequences. Such efforts may overlook and thus inherit the challenges that result from inconsistencies in the agency's data infrastructure. This section discusses some key issues for strengthening the upstream portion of data systems within the agency.

The first issue to consider is how much and in what way the agency might centralize the internal data systems. In school districts, including SFUSD, data systems likely proliferate and diversify over time as different departments procure tools to best meet their needs. Such proliferation poses a challenge when operational data from various sources need to be compiled and transformed into analytical data. One approach to minimizing this challenge is to consolidate and reduce the number of distinct systems. Other advantages of this may be in making the data more available for on-demand analysis and better aligned with other data systems. While this approach would be the most sustainable, it may require some investments of time and money to establish, and it may not be suitable if a select few platforms for collecting and managing data cannot meet the diverse needs of the agency. Thus, an alternate approach might be to centrally coordinate the efforts of data teams dispersed throughout the agency. This is the approach SFUSD took with some limited success. The Supervisor of Analytics collaborated with other data leaders throughout the district to develop a common culture and practices for working with data. The shared language and relationships among analysts facilitated conversations when compiling the decentralized data.

The second and related issue is to invest in data governance and data quality management within the agency. Establishing sound data governance takes time, because it requires identifying appropriate staff to own, steward, and manage the data, as well as devising processes for gathering, inputting, processing, and analyzing data. While implementing and improving data governance may be a resource-intensive investment, it ultimately offers greater flexibility and sustainability over time, as robust processes and documentation for managing data quality can help mitigate challenges arising from multiple and new data systems, as well as staff turnover.

Lastly, there are smaller investments that the agency partner can consider making beyond these two larger investments. One is to systematically create snapshots of operational data at fixed time points throughout the year. In the school context, the two main time points are the census day (the state-mandated day on which the count of students enrolled at each school site is taken) and the last day of the school year. These snapshots should be created from as many data systems as possible throughout the agency, so if a research question requiring some variables arises in the future, necessary analytical data files can be generated. The other strategy is to systematically record and document all notes about data. Such records would entail notes not only about the source, date, and definition of measures, but also any errors discovered and how they are addressed, changes in the definition or methodology, and how these impact downstream data analysis.

While these are simpler strategies that invest in the agency partner's internal data capacity rather than streamlining decentralization and improving data governance, they still require substantial investment into the hardware and software for archiving data and require appropriate staffing. A staff person would need to (1) collaborate with appropriate departments and teams to coordinate the periodic archiving of snapshot data, (2) compile and organize data on a durable server using software that can accommodate different types of data, and (3) document issues and fixes as well as the typical codebook information. In this respect, agency staffing is a critical investment for prospective partnerships to consider.

Data Warehouse

The initial choices that the Partnership made focused on addressing the demands for data from the district. Rather than investing in the upstream (the district's data infrastructure) the Partnership started by establishing a warehouse of SFUSD data which Stanford faculty could more easily access. The decision to host the warehouse at Stanford rather than at SFUSD was due to a number of factors including active faculty research projects, pre-existing infrastructure at Stanford, and an institutional commitment to creating and sustaining a long-term data warehouse within CEPA. A number of faculty already were doing work with SFUSD and had access to large portions of the SFUSD administrative data sets. Second, CEPA had a number of data managers and analysts on staff who were previously familiar with the SFUSD data. Finally, faculty within CEPA work with several research partners and were committed to building a warehouse that would support research with multiple school districts; they were happy to include the data infrastructure for the Stanford-SFUSD Partnership as well.

While the Partnership's focus on refining the data-sharing infrastructure has contributed to its continued productivity, developing these infrastructures has been a double-edged sword. A positive aspect is that a process is now well established for researchers and practitioners to create projects collaboratively so that a list of appropriate data elements can be identified and arranged. A less favorable development has been how the initial choice about the infrastructure constrained potential choices about it down the road. Whereas the infrastructure was developed as part of Stanford's interests in conducting research at SFUSD and other agencies, SFUSD's needs for data sharing with other institutions have likewise grown. One specific challenge emerged in the context of anonymizing student identities. From the onset, the last part of data processing and algorithmic replacement of the student ID numbers took place at the CEPA data warehouse. Over time, this has complicated data-sharing agreements, as some of Stanford's researchers have relocated to other institutions while continuing their projects with SFUSD data and SFUSD's partnerships with researchers at other institutions have expanded. New and young partnerships should consider how the research and partnership needs of the agencies may evolve in the future when building their data infrastructures, as initial investments will limit future choices.

For a district with partnerships across multiple institutions, hosting the data warehouse at the district would bring additional benefits to data quality and management. One reason is that it would ensure maintaining all the master research data files at the district without subsequent processing occurring elsewhere. In such an arrangement, the district—the data-producing agency—would continue to own the authoritative analytical data files, managing any necessary corrections as well as any procedures for converting operational data into analytical data. Increasing the efficiency of data management can then improve data accuracy by removing the need to review and update multiple versions of the same data (i.e., at the district and then at the warehouse). Maintaining a single analytical data base for all external research and evaluation would improve consistency across multiple partners whose analyses may draw upon overlapping sets of data. It could also streamline communication upon creating standard metadata documentation that could be easily shared across multiple partners. In addition, having such research-ready data housed internally would facilitate more rapid internal analysis by district staff in conjunction with the analysis done by external researchers. With improved consistency of data between research and accountability reporting, this increases transparency and trust of the research. Such internal analyses could further strengthen district leaders' and practitioners' understanding of the data, as well as the district's ability to use the resulting research.

One new challenge that would emerge from hosting the research data files at the data-owning agency would be how to manage the workload of data requests and transfers. When the volume of requests from a research institution becomes sufficiently high, it may become worthwhile to mirror the entirety of data files at the requesting institution, and dedicate a data manager at that institution to fulfill data requests originating from there. While the infrastructure for exchanging data would look very much like the existing arrangement between SFUSD and Stanford, the final data processing would be completed at the district, so that the district owns the official data and the external warehouse would only serve as a mirror.

More generally, new and prospective partnerships should consider the following questions when deciding how to establish their data infrastructures:

- What is the expected longevity of the partnership?
- How likely are the researchers at the research organization to move to different institutions?
- What is the agency's anticipated number of other external research partners?
- What are the costs of establishing and maintaining multiple warehouses or mirror sites?
- What might be the time costs of managing multiple, disparate procedures for de-identifying/scrambling data?
- How might the agency's needs for research change over time to include greater diversity in methodological and content expertise, potentially at different institutions?
- What might be the necessary investment in building agency capacity for maintaining data infrastructure and managing data transfers?

The factors that the editors of this volume identify in the introductory chapter are important to consider. An agency that plans to have the bulk of its analysis conducted by a single external partner may find it more efficient to invest in the downstream processes of data cleanup and transfer. A similar calculation would apply if a research entity partners with multiple agencies. In contrast, an agency that anticipates developing long-term partnerships with researchers across multiple entities or that conducts its own analyses in-house may reap greater benefits from investing in upstream data management and governance within the agency.

Staffing

Staffing the data-sharing infrastructure appropriately is critical to the fluid functioning of the arrangement, along with having clear processes and workflows. At SFUSD, the supervisor of research and evaluation in RPA manages the overarching process of co-designing, vetting, and approving research projects as well as guiding researchers and practitioners to interpret and act on the findings. Since 2017, the supervisor of analytics in RPA has been the point person for managing and housing SFUSD data for research, devoting about 20 percent of the role's time to data management, including supplying data to Stanford and other research institutions. For Stanford, the data manager at CEPA is the point person for managing and housing SFUSD data within the university, with about 50 percent of their allocated time focused on maintaining the data infrastructure for the Stanford-SFUSD Partnership. For Ed Partners, the Partnership director of the Stanford-SFUSD Partnership manages day-to-day activities, ensures the agreements and operations are properly functioning to support the data exchange, and supports the Supervisor of Analytics and the Data Manager in the data compilation and exchange. The Partnership director devotes about 10 to 20 percent of the role to supporting data infrastructure.

Having a single dedicated data contact person at the district has been helpful for facilitating data exchanges. Previously, the supervisor of research and evaluation and the Partnership director managed DUAs and investigated data issues without having in-depth knowledge about effective data management practices or the district's data systems and issues. Under the new infrastructure, the supervisor of analytics at

SFUSD and the data manager at Stanford communicate routinely and manage inquiries at their respective institutions.

The Stanford-SFUSD Partnership experience, however, raises a potential question for the sustainability of the staffing infrastructure. In August of 2019, both the supervisor of analytics and the data manager left their respective positions and institutions. Filling the vacant positions subsequently required approximately two months at SFUSD and one month at Stanford. While this turnover has provided an opportunity for the Partnership to review and improve the robustness of its data management processes, it does pose a strain on both institutional partners and on research projects. In addition, because of the gaps in continuity, such churn also requires training new staff to learn highly contextualized knowledge at their respective institutions.

This raises three important questions for prospective partnerships to consider for staffing the data exchange work stream. First, how many staff members will be involved and with which institution will they be affiliated? The Partnership has designated staff members at both institutions to support the data transfer, each responsible for communicating with stakeholders at their respective institutions. For partnerships with multiple data managers, how might the roles and responsibilities be distributed efficiently across institutions? Similarly, for government agencies and research organizations with multiple partners, how might they allocate staff and responsibilities across their multiple partnerships? What are the implications of these circumstances for the number of data managers hired, and whether they reside at the agency or the research organization? How much data sharing would have to happen to justify the cost of hiring a data manager at each institution? The considerations behind the choice of the location of staff would echo those about the location of the CEPA data warehouse (discussed in section 12.4.1).

Second, how might the staff members obtain the knowledge and skills necessary to facilitate smooth data sharing? These responsibilities demand a blend of technical skills, interpersonal skills, and contextual knowledge—a combination which requires considerable training and experience. The relevant technical expertise includes not just skills with data management, but also understanding of social science research methods. Interpersonal skills encompass the ability to communicate clearly and efficiently with practitioners and researchers about issues related to how the data were collected and how they will be used for the research. Moreover, data managers benefit from being deeply embedded in their respective contexts to be acculturated and understand the structures and norms guiding how their organizations function.

Third, how should partnerships recruit, train, and retain staff members with the necessary background to minimize turnover and repeated training? How should they manage through staff transitions? What alternate arrangements might they consider for distributing responsibilities across roles to maximize the value from these specialized skill sets and interests? These are critical considerations for partnerships, both because personnel constitute significant ongoing costs and because they influence the social infrastructure and relational dynamics.

12.4.2 Legal Context for Data Use

In addition to the umbrella warehousing agreement between Stanford University GSE, CEPA, and SFUSD, the partners also created a project-level DUA template, which Stanford researchers could easily fill out when submitting data requests to SFUSD. With this DUA template, the Stanford and SFUSD legal teams would not need to review every project DUA, as the template maintained consistent legal language agreed upon by both Stanford and SFUSD legal counsel. Both the umbrella agreement and DUA template are reviewed and edited every three years.

The elements included in the original umbrella agreement, which warehoused the SFUSD data at Stanford, were compiled according to the data needed for existing research projects between Stanford researchers and SFUSD administrators. Based on the original negotiated projects, these data included student and staff identifiers that are anonymized and scrambled for each project, K–12 student data, early education data, staff data (teachers and principals), and other types of student and school level data allowable by the Family Educational Rights and Privacy Act (FERPA). Currently, the umbrella agreement does not include survey data, which are instead maintained by researchers for their individual projects. One variable that is commonly included in other districts' DUAs for research, but which SFUSD does not share with any researchers, is the indicator of whether a student is eligible to participate in the free and reduced-price meal program. SFUSD does not share these data for research since California state regulations limit the use of these data solely to administer the program.

To keep the umbrella agreement updated, the Stanford research department, the Partnership director, the SFUSD supervisor of analytics, and the Stanford and SFUSD legal departments needed to amend the agreement when Stanford research projects required additional elements.[4] From 2011 to 2014, the umbrella agreement was amended three times; from 2014 to 2017, it was amended once.[5] Similarly, project DUAs often needed to be amended to add new data elements or to extend the time frame of the research. Sometimes researchers forgot to request a variable of interest, while other times projects expanded in scope and required additional data elements not previously requested or not previously collected by the district. Therefore, SFUSD's research department and both institutions' legal teams developed an amendment template that project leaders could fill out and sign.

The benefits of the CEPA data warehouse and streamlining of agreement formation and access are threefold. First, it simplifies and standardizes research support operations for SFUSD, as they can supply data to their Stanford research partners a handful of times a year, rather than providing data for one project at a time. Second, for Stanford, this reduces the amount of time Stanford researchers wait for data extracts and provides a data manager on campus whom researchers can ask questions to help clarify their understanding of the data. Third, for SFUSD as well as the broader public and research

---

[4] See Online Appendix A for an example of the language in the Stanford-SFUSD Partnership's most recent agreements between Stanford and SFUSD.

[5] See Online Appendix B for an example of one of the amendment templates.

community, increasing the efficiency of conducting this research allows more time to focus on strengthening the quality and usefulness of the research produced, to better improve district decision-making, and inform the field of education.

12.4.3 Legal Framework for Granting Data Access

To access this data infrastructure as a researcher operationalizing a project (like the ones described above), there is a set of agreements related to the data access, exchange, and use for the Stanford-SFUSD Partnership. Guiding the overall governance of the Stanford-SFUSD Partnership is what is called a handshake agreement, or a non-binding written document, which outlines the goals, activities, and commitment of resources by all the key leaders guiding the partnership: the SFUSD superintendent; SFUSD deputy superintendent; the SFUSD chief of Research, Planning, and Assessment; the Stanford GSE dean; and the leaders at California Education Partners. While this is not a legal document, it guides the governance, structures, and resources committed to the Partnership.

The three legal agreements used to guide the partnership are a data warehousing agreement between SFUSD and Stanford, referred to as the umbrella agreement above; research approval processes conducted by Stanford University's Institutional Review Board (IRB) and SFUSD's research department; and a project-level DUA. First, the leaders at Stanford GSE (in this case the dean), at Stanford CEPA, and at SFUSD's research department negotiate the data warehousing umbrella agreement as described above.

Second, Stanford and SFUSD both have their own review processes for research involving human subjects (see sections 12.5.1 and 12.5.2 for more detail). Stanford researchers must fill out extensive paperwork to file for IRB with Stanford; in addition, SFUSD requires all researchers to submit a separate application for district review. Over time, SFUSD has streamlined their research application and developed a more consistent review process.

Third, there is a project-based DUA template with fixed legal language, which is reviewed and approved by the Stanford and SFUSD legal counsel. This template is used to develop project-level agreements for Stanford faculty to access SFUSD data through the CEPA data warehouse. For approved projects that will use administrative data, researchers must also complete a DUA specifying the data elements and years of data they will be permitted to access. The duration of these DUAs varies by project, and researchers can amend or renew those DUAs as needed through another template with pre-approved legal language. There are strict provisions for Stanford to abide by, including SFUSD asking Stanford to destroy the data at the end of a study.

Barriers and Challenges Encountered

While the procedures discussed thus far generally work well, one continued challenge involves deviations from the standard process. At times, projects have bypassed or sought to bypass the official data transfer procedures. Various Stanford researchers communicate directly with SFUSD departments to address questions about the data. Prior to establishing the DUAs and strict procedures for data exchange, some departments sent data directly to the researchers at Stanford, not realizing the need to go through the district's research office and the CEPA data warehouse. When this happened, the data were frequently transferred through unsecured means, such as district staff e-mailing unencrypted/unscrambled data spreadsheets to researchers.

While this was easy and efficient for the individual departments and researchers, it sidestepped the data safeguards built into the RPP and the CEPA data warehouse workflow. As noted, data were not properly encrypted or transferred in a manner to properly protect the personal information of the people represented in the data. Further, such transfers also made it difficult for the CEPA data warehouse to support the researchers in the future if and when they approached the warehouse for (1) subsequent longitudinal data to join to their original data or (2) any issues about the data quality or definitions. This also complicated efforts to maintain consistent analytical data, as extractions occurred at irregular points in time and were not documented routinely.

Although such deviations have been rare, the demand for them typically has arisen out of two sources: urgency or lack of awareness on the part of practitioners or researchers. The most prevalent has been lack of awareness of the standards for data exchange among individual departments and researchers. For instance, researchers and district staff may not understand that all projects need centralized approval not only from Stanford's Research Compliance Office IRB but also from SFUSD. In other cases, SFUSD staff or Stanford researchers may seek to expedite the data transfer for reasons such as the district wanting results for time-sensitive policy decisions or Stanford researchers needing to make deadlines for publications or conference submissions. Such urgency has sometimes resulted in the data owners/researchers bypassing the established process. For either of these scenarios, the Partnership has endeavored both to halt the irregular transfers and to strengthen the knowledge and understanding among staff and researchers.

Another challenge to the established and evolving data-sharing arrangement has emerged from the success of its long-term functioning. Over time, Stanford researchers (both faculty members and graduate students) have moved to other institutions but sought to continue their research using SFUSD data. Because the data-sharing infrastructure is designed only to serve researchers working within the Stanford-SFUSD Partnership, maintaining an appropriate arrangement has been a challenge. The two stopgap remedies that the Partnership has implemented thus far are to (1) create a multi-party data-sharing agreement between SFUSD, Stanford, and the third-party academic institution or (2) require the researchers at a new institution to be sponsored by or to formally collaborate with a current Stanford faculty member. Both approaches are inelegant solutions to the need for efficient and effective data sharing. This issue is revisited/readdressed at the end of the chapter.

During the earlier years of the Partnership, each DUA was drafted, negotiated, and executed anew, as noted above. SFUSD's Legal Department then had to approve each DUA, which impeded the efficiency of the data exchange process. Eventually, the Partnership invested time into creating a DUA template with standardized language approved by the legal teams on both sides. Now, the template provides common and consistent provisions for data sharing, and the researchers need only fill in their project details and requested data elements. Furthermore, the agreements can be approved without requiring any attorneys' signatures, significantly speeding up the administrative process. Any research partnership that will work on multiple projects over time should invest in creating such a DUA template in the preliminary stages.

12.5 Protection of Sensitive and Personal Data: The Five Safes Framework

12.5.1 Safe Projects

In addition to requiring documentation of university IRB approval prior to reviewing any research projects conducted in the district, SFUSD's research department also engages additional scrutiny to ensure safe projects. As mandated by FERPA, SFUSD's research department requires all research requests using administrative data to establish a formal legal agreement specifying the parameters of the data sharing. These parameters are the purpose, scope, and duration of the study; the data elements needed; and the research organization that will receive and secure the data. SFUSD applies these expectations to all research studies, even when administrative data are de-identified; this is due to the potential for individual student-level data to become identifiable upon combining different student and school characteristics and due to the desire to closely monitor external data-sharing given the risks posed with sharing data.

While the function of requiring documentation of external IRB exemption or approval is to ensure adherence to ethical standards for all research, whether federally funded or not, the purpose of SFUSD's internal review before approving research applications is to evaluate the compatibility with district priorities. Projects must demonstrate their benefit to the district and justify their need for district administrative data. The expectations SFUSD applies are summarized as the alignment, benefits, and costs (ABCs) of the proposed research. First, the research must be closely aligned with the district's strategic plan and learning agenda. Second, the project must be likely to yield benefits to policy or practice, meaning that key district decision-makers must be prepared to use the research results to yield a positive impact on relevant stakeholders with the benefits being sustainable. Third, conducting the research must incur minimal costs, in terms of time, resources, and burden to people. Costs may include the efforts needed to obtain informed consent prior to collecting primary data or releasing personally identifiable secondary data, the time required to collect and process the data, or ethical considerations regarding who bears the burden as the subject of the research.

SFUSD evaluates these dimensions by surveying the relevant district leaders most closely connected to the topic of the study who would sponsor the research, along with having its research department staff review the proposal to determine whether the design is likely to provide valid and useful findings on a timeline that can help inform the desired practical decisions. This internal review also includes a close inspection of the data elements requested in order to confirm their availability and their necessity to answer the research questions of interest. Thus, SFUSD maintains a higher bar for research approval than required by federal code.

Prior to submitting applications, researchers are instructed to consult the district website for information on its long-term vision and current strategic plan. In some cases, researchers may have the opportunity to engage directly with district staff during the development of a potential research project, whether initiated by the district in seeking research on a particular question or initiated by a researcher pitching a specific idea. Thanks to additional funding for the research-practice partnership, Stanford researchers have greater access to such guidance through the Partnership director as well as an annual grant mechanism to incentivize Stanford-SFUSD research. One challenge is that this creates inequities between research organizations. SFUSD's research department is working to correct this through stronger institution-wide messaging both within and beyond the district about research interests and opportunities, circulating requests for proposals, formalizing more of its relationships with other partners, and establishing standard processes to use across partnerships for developing research ideas.

SFUSD's research department is also continuing to strengthen its practice of assessing the cost-benefit tradeoffs of research projects. While many projects can be executed with minimal efforts using the existing archive of administrative data, other projects accrue significant costs in primary data collection, linking primary data with secondary administrative data, or processing and manipulation of administrative data. In such cases, the potential benefit of the research may be offset by the costliness involved in obtaining or providing the data. SFUSD's research department has been exploring methods for quantifying these costs more systematically, as well as guiding district sponsors to consider the opportunity costs of engaging in research projects prior to committing their support. As described further under section 12.7.3, the Partnership is simultaneously seeking to improve the measurement of benefits. With the field of scientific research developing better metrics of success for research impact and RPP effectiveness, the Partnership anticipates piloting and adopting some of these measures, along with other methods for assessing the use of research evidence. Within SFUSD, the Partnership is working to capture more consistent documentation of how research and data are used to inform practice in order to motivate greater selectivity and efficiency in efforts, including opportunities to better support the progress of active projects. The Partnership hopes to further systematize the analysis of such costs and benefits during the project development phase.

12.5.2 Safe People

Stanford University researchers who wish to utilize SFUSD administrative data for their prospective projects must fulfill several requirements prior to obtaining approval from SFUSD and receiving their data. The first requirement for researchers is to complete Stanford's human subjects training. In the event non-Stanford researchers are included on a project, they can complete their own institution's human subjects training, contingent upon the approval of the Stanford IRB. Stanford participates in the Collaborative Institutional Training Initiative (CITI) Program, which offers a certification course in human subjects research to familiarize all non-medical principal investigators and research staff about the Common Rule and IRB requirements. Researchers must complete the course prior to being added to an IRB protocol at Stanford, which SFUSD requires for approving a project proposal and DUA. All members of a project must be listed in the IRB protocol.

Separate from the general Stanford IRB requirement, Stanford researchers who receive data from the data warehouse must sign an internal access agreement that outlines their responsibilities and acknowledges that they may be held personally liable for any financial costs incurred due to a data breach for which they are responsible. The Data Manager tracks these internal access agreements and ensures that each member of the research team has completed their access agreement before transferring the data to the researchers. Once the data have been transferred to the researchers, it is the responsibility of the principal investigator to maintain data security and safety and ensure that their research staff are in compliance with the conditions set in the access agreement. As these conditions also reflect requirements set forward by Stanford University's IT security requirements, compliance tracking is left to Stanford GSE's IT staff as part of their routine auditing. To increase the transparency of all who might access and work with the shared data, starting in late 2019, the principal investigators are required to list the names of all staff anticipated to work with the data in appendices to the project-level research application and DUA.

In 2019, with an increasing number of alumni students and faculty with ongoing research projects utilizing SFUSD data, Stanford GSE and SFUSD leaders initiated a refinement of the process to more closely monitor non-Stanford researchers continuing their projects. Stanford and SFUSD developed a third-party agreement that alumni and Stanford collaborators could sign if they continued to work on projects with SFUSD. These alumni and collaborators would still need to maintain a

Stanford sponsor and Stanford IRB to access the data for their projects. The template for these third-party agreements is included in Online Appendix A.

12.5.3 Safe Settings

The Partnership has three separate settings to consider for security: data at rest, data in use, and data in transit. The storage of the data at the CEPA data warehouse and the storage of the researcher-accessible data pertain to data at rest and data in use. The mechanism for transferring data between SFUSD, the CEPA data warehouse, and the researcher pertains to data in transit.

The warehouse stores the data received from SFUSD on an encrypted desktop computer with two hard drives configured in a mirrored array, to limit the possibility of data loss in the event of a hard drive failure. An additional backup of the data is kept on an encrypted external storage drive that is kept in a locked cabinet; the backup is scheduled for each time the warehouse receives data from the district. Keeping the data files off of servers that are outside the direct control of the Data Manager reduces the likelihood that unauthorized users can gain electronic access to the data. Encrypting all of the computers and drives where the data are stored reduces the possibility that an adversary can access the data even if they gain direct physical access to the computer. Both the original analytical data and the prepared master data are stored locally on the encrypted warehouse computer and backup drive. However, the syntax files used to prepare the master data are backed up onto Stanford servers, as the syntax files themselves do not contain any sensitive information.

On the researcher side, the standard DUA template used by each research project specifies the appropriate storage mechanisms for handling the data. Separately from the DUA requirements, Stanford IT also maintains a data risk-classification system[6] for all data stored on university systems with corresponding access and storage requirements for each type of data. SFUSD data are classified as high-risk data

---

[6]https://uit.stanford.edu/guide/riskclassifications (accessed 2020-12-11).

due to the legal requirements for protecting the data and the requirement to report any breaches to SFUSD, which is a government actor. In practice, the dual requirements from the DUA and Stanford risk-classification means that researchers must store the data on Stanford servers or specific cloud services approved by Stanford University IT. Access to the storage location is provisioned by the Stanford GSE IT department via Stanford single-sign-on user accounts. Stanford-based researchers have accounts as a matter of course, while guest accounts can be provided in the event that non-Stanford-based researchers are collaborating on a Stanford-based project. The data should only be accessed from computers that utilize Stanford BigFix (a centralized operating system patch management service) and whole-disk encryption. Neither Stanford nor SFUSD place any restrictions on the location from where researchers can access the data, the software researchers use, or analysis methods.

Transferring data from SFUSD to the CEPA data warehouse and from the CEPA data warehouse to researchers utilizes the same service. The CEPA data warehouse maintains Stanford-provisioned Google shared drives, which are made available by an institutional contract between Google and Stanford University and approved by Stanford University's IT department for handling high-risk data; access is granted to the appropriate directories for SFUSD staff and Stanford researchers. One shared drive is used to transfer the complete analytical data from SFUSD to the CEPA data warehouse and to transfer researcher-generated files back to SFUSD as requested. Only SFUSD staff (including the Supervisor of Analytics, and any additional staff as requested by SFUSD) and the Data Manager have access to this shared drive. Each research project has its own separate shared drive for data transfers to and from the CEPA data warehouse; access is provisioned to research staff included on the project DUA.

Between 2014 and 2019, the CEPA data warehouse used a secure file transfer protocol (SFTP) server to handle data transfers. The switch to Google shared drive was prompted by a Stanford GSE IT department security analysis of its existing infrastructure alongside the planned shutdown of the SFTP server. The server was maintained by Stanford

GSE IT staff, while the Data Manager had administrative privileges to manage user access. The organization of the server was identical to the current arrangement. Prior to 2014, data files were transferred physically from San Francisco to Stanford on CD-ROMs. Taking advantage of existing and well-established technologies has helped make data sharing in the Partnership much more efficient and secure than before.

One future goal of the SFUSD-Stanford partnership may be to decentralize the fulfillment of data requests such that researchers can generate custom datafiles on demand through an automatic interface. Such web applications already exist for national education data systems, such as the National Center for Education Statistics (NCES). The challenge would be in implementing a similar system for data at smaller scales, such as at the level of school districts. Coordinating on a standardized data schema—such as the Ed-Fi standard in education, which provides rules for how data in education are to be formatted and exchanged between data systems—may provide the foundation for a scalable self-service data request solution in the future.

12.5.4 Safe Data

The primary concern over sensitivity of student data is embodied in FERPA. The law places the authority to grant third parties access to students' educational records and data to students' guardians, which constrains the district's ability to share student-level data to highly circumscribed and exceptional scenarios. In each stage of sharing the data, from SFUSD to the CEPA data warehouse and from the CEPA data warehouse to the researcher, the data are restricted according to the relevant DUA.

The data transferred from the district to the CEPA data warehouse includes the full set of data that may be required for SFUSD-approved research projects as defined in the CEPA data warehouse umbrella DUA. The data transferred to the CEPA data warehouse includes student names, district ID numbers, and other identifying information to facilitate the matching of data between different data sources and on

CHAPTER 12

behalf of research projects that collect primary data (e.g., survey responses). To enable its role as a data access provider on behalf of the district, the CEPA data warehouse DUA includes a provision that allows it to store data not explicitly listed in its own DUA if SFUSD has approved a research project to receive those data.

After SFUSD approves a research team's DUA, the data manager provides the appropriate sample of data as outlined in the DUA. The research team's DUA restricts the number of years of data and variables out of each data file that they are allowed to receive for each project. For data that exist in the master data files, this is as simple as extracting the appropriate subset of data as defined in the DUA. For data that are not already in the master data or not held at the CEPA data warehouse, which are typically data rarely used by researchers, the Data Manager additionally cleans the data before initiating transfer, ensuring that only the approved subset is provided to the research team. While Stanford researchers can renew and extend their DUA if the project needs to continue past its initial agreement, they must destroy the data upon final expiration of the DUA.

Data files provided to researchers utilize district-defined student identification numbers scrambled using an algorithm developed at Stanford. Such a scheme for maintaining a consistent unique identifier for students is critical for researchers to join data from multiple sources and to carry out longitudinal studies in which cohorts of students are analyzed over time. Sometimes, for research findings to guide instruction or operations, calculated measures or analyzed results at the student level must be returned to the district. In such cases, researchers provide the data manager a data file with scrambled IDs. The Data Manager *unscrambles* the identifiers to restore district ID numbers before transferring the file to the district.

To comply with the law and to protect student privacy, students' and parents'/guardians' names are generally not provided to researchers. For linking data to external data, SFUSD and the CEPA data warehouse can perform linking services on behalf of researchers. This is typically done by having the researcher provide the CEPA data warehouse with the identifying information on individuals in the data to be linked and having the data manager or the supervisor of analytics perform the linkage. In rare cases, with explicit approval in the DUA, research teams may receive data such as names or official ID numbers that would enable researchers to individually identify students. Such exceptions are made only for the purposes of linking primary data to administrative data and only when all other strategies for linking the data anonymously have been exhausted. Moreover, the district requires that researchers delete the primary keys once the data files are joined.

12.5.5 Safe Outputs

District practice is to review all research products prior to submission for public dissemination. Before publishing study designs, data, or findings in open research registries, researchers must submit any data, source code, or manuscripts for SFUSD to review to verify that they have fully anonymized SFUSD data. Although analytic results are typically aggregated and reported at a level higher than individual students, these must still be reviewed to preserve anonymity. In some cases, interactions between these dimensions may yield small cell sizes or additional information is presented in the report that risks indirectly identifying individuals. Given that FERPA's standards for "personally identifiable information" are based on whether "a reasonable person in the school community" could identify the student, having district staff review the manuscript can offer this perspective to safeguard the privacy of individuals involved in the research. If projects need to provide student-level results and calculations to improve instruction or intervention, such results are shared only with district staff through the secure transfer channels rather than being publicly released.

Beyond protecting privacy, a second reason for this review is to ensure accurate accounting of the district context and practices that may be relevant in explaining the results, similar to member-checking in qualitative research. This reflects the Partnership's emphasis on the value of co-production at multiple stages throughout the research process, including presentations and publications. The Partnership's experience is that asking the administrators and practitioners most familiar with the project to review the manuscript elicits additional information that may only have been incompletely captured previously. While this is an informal expectation rather than a legal requirement, the district makes this request of its research partners as a good-faith commitment to mutual respect and partnership. It has also been found that this supports greater dissemination and use of the research, as district leaders develop a deeper understanding and appreciation of the research through increased communication about it.

A third reason for this review is to determine whether it is appropriate to identify the district in the publication. This step is important for the district to manage consistency of messaging across its many initiatives and interests, which may be competing for attention, so that communication is aligned with strategic priorities. The DUA template includes this language: "Research Organization agrees that SFUSD shall not be named or otherwise identified in the study, unless written permission to do so is granted by SFUSD for a specific project only."

A fourth reason for review is to check for consistency between the research results and analyses conducted either internally for evaluation or accountability or by other research teams. While the Partnership does not yet have a formal process for verifying the validity of the analyses in all research products, some ad hoc review mechanisms have emerged. However, not all publication submissions always undergo this review, possibly due to the tight timelines for submission or lack of awareness. The Partnership is working toward increasing awareness of this expectation for review prior to publication, which can strengthen not just the validity and privacy protections for the reports, but also the timeliness and breadth of awareness of the research findings. More recently, the Partnership has also begun encouraging research teams to more systematically share findings with other university colleagues and research groups as a form of informal review of the analyses. While some researchers already have internal peer review processes in their own labs and centers, this has varied across projects. Engaging all projects in such a review process is especially important for results that do not undergo publication and therefore academic peer review, as the district values the reassurance of rigor in any findings that it may use to inform decision-making.

For all of these reasons, as well as to promote greater use of the research, the Partnership encourages, but does not require, co-authorship with the district sponsors most involved in the research. The Partnership would like to improve the consistency and robustness of the processes for ensuring not just safe outputs, but useful outputs that are carefully vetted and well understood by both the research team and the practitioner partners. For the sake of validity and value, the first audience for all research products should be the members of the partnership most invested in the work with the external audience being secondary. Ideally, feedback from the peer review process should then inform subsequent conversations with the practitioner partners, so that they have the opportunity to learn from relevant interests and concerns expressed by others in the field about the research and its implications.

12.6 Data Life Cycle and Replicability

12.6.1 Preservation and Reproducibility of Researcher-Accessible Files

The data generation and cleaning process produces a set of master data sets that are cleaned versions of the yearly raw analytical data organized into longitudinal data files. The warehouse maintains all of the analytical data received from SFUSD indefinitely with the only exception being specific data files that the district requests to be deleted after transfer to researchers. The CEPA data warehouse also maintains all of the scripts used to generate any researcher-accessible files and the version of the files last transferred to the researchers. This allows for rapid updates of the files as well as reproducing the latest version of the files transferred to the researchers on demand. In practice, this is of negligible concern regarding the master data since updates to those files are usually for additions to the longitudinal data rather than for corrections to historical data. Researchers are responsible for maintaining the data files that they receive.

12.6.2 Preservation and Reproducibility of Researcher-Generated Files

The CEPA data warehouse itself is not responsible for maintaining researcher-generated files, as the warehouse does not have routine access to those data. Researchers are not allowed to share these data with outsiders without the permission of SFUSD. Research team agreements require that they delete their data at the termination of a research project. Historically, enforcement tends to fall on routine audits of user accounts by IT staff, although the Partnership is establishing more regular processes for following up with researchers after projects are completed to request documentation of data destruction.

12.7 Sustainability and Continued Success

The social and technical infrastructure for sharing data within the Stanford-SFUSD Partnership is an important piece facilitating the RPP. However, that infrastructure is embedded in a broader context that contributes to the sustainability and the continued success of the Partnership. Through outreach, researchers at Stanford and practitioners at SFUSD regularly interact with one another, strengthening relationships for collaboration. The steady funding of the key staff positions by Stanford GSE has also helped to maintain continuity. Lastly, the Partnership has continuously monitored the progress of research production and use, which is the ultimate goal of the data sharing arrangement between the institutions. These three elements are discussed in turn.

12.7.1 Outreach

Stanford GSE faculty and researchers learn about the Stanford-SFUSD Partnership's research priorities and SFUSD data available for that research through a number of channels. First and foremost, they learn from the Partnership director who on-boards new faculty and hosts the Stanford-SFUSD Partnership Annual Meeting, which all faculty are invited to attend, where research produced by the Partnership is showcased. At this meeting, both the Stanford GSE dean and the SFUSD superintendent speak about how the Partnership supports their vision for their respective institutions. The Partnership director also presents information about the research conducted in the Partnership to Stanford GSE students on an annual basis. Faculty and students also can meet with the Partnership director to discuss the data in the CEPA data warehouse, as the Partnership director has an office at Stanford GSE and is on campus one to two days a week. Second, Stanford faculty and researchers learn about SFUSD data through the CEPA data manager. SFUSD leaders and the Partnership director often send faculty and researchers to talk to the CEPA Data Manager if they have questions about the SFUSD data that are warehoused at CEPA. Third, Stanford GSE faculty and researchers also hear about the data from their peers in presentations about the SFUSD research at an on-campus annual meeting showcasing the Partnership projects. Finally, in some cases, Stanford GSE faculty and researchers communicate directly with SFUSD leaders or analysts to discuss questions about the data, such as the nuances of how the data were collected or what specific values mean, particularly when the data are owned by other departments beyond RPA.

To date the Partnership has not publicized the types of data available from the district for several reasons. Of paramount importance is promoting theory-driven research rather than studies that merely mine data for correlations. Another reason is to encourage direct communication between researchers and district leaders about the research questions and the relevant data. However, the district is now revisiting this decision in the interest of standardizing documentation and streamlining communication about the data. Continuing to maintain strict review processes can help ensure that all projects are aligned with district priorities rather than simply being an impersonal transaction of data for analysis with limited connection to practical realities or benefits.

12.7.2 Revenue

As mentioned above, the arrangement for data-sharing between SFUSD and Stanford University is part of a broader research-practice partnership between the district and the university. The Partnership is funded by Stanford University Graduate School of Education through private donations, and Stanford researchers are not charged a fee for their data requests. The district has occasionally charged fees for data requests for those coming from outside the Stanford-SFUSD Partnership, depending on scope and complexity. SFUSD is now implementing a more systematic and permanent fee structure for data requests from researchers outside of established partnerships with the district.

On the university side, the Stanford GSE funds roughly half of the CEPA Data Manager position as well as the hardware infrastructure necessary for the data management. On the district side, Stanford GSE funds a significant portion (about 70 percent) of the Supervisor of Analytics position. In 2018, some of the residual funds at the district were used to make significant upgrades to the hardware infrastructure at the research office for storing and archiving data.

Since 2014, Stanford GSE has made a long-term commitment to funding the Partnership through its development efforts and commits at minimum US$500,000 a year to the Partnership for research and data infrastructure. Faculty also pursue research grants to fund research with the Partnership from private foundations and public grants offered through the US Department of Education, which also provides steady, although variable, funding for partnership research.

12.7.3 Metrics for Measuring Success

Together the SFUSD research department and Partnership director monitor progress and measure success in several ways. Beyond counting access to data, the SFUSD research department and the Partnership director are most interested in the quality and impact of the research, particularly on SFUSD policy and practice. The SFUSD research department and Partnership director monitor access to ensure that the research projects are mutually beneficial to both the faculty and the district leaders involved and that the research meets a certain level of quality; the research has the potential to produce generalizable research that influences the field of education as well as producing research that informs decisions by SFUSD district leaders. While the Partnership has not yet adopted a formal measurement model, the approach is compatible and overlaps with SAGE Publication's (2019) models of research impact and Henrick et al.'s (2017) framework for assessing RPP effectiveness. In particular, the Partnership attends to academic and practical outcomes and shifts in understanding of research.

First, Partnership outputs are measured by examining each project's research products. External products may include peer-reviewed publications, policy briefs, conference presentations, and other reports, while internal products may include informal presentations and write-ups.

Second, the impact of the research is measured not just on the field but more immediately within SFUSD. As noted previously, the Partnership measures broader research impact by considering the type of publication as well as its audience. For impact within SFUSD, which is what the Partnership values most highly, they look for evidence of instrumental use of research through changes in policy and changes in practice (preferably at more than one school or classroom); they then note whether these led to changes in student outcomes. Following Weiss and Bucuvalas (1980), the Partnership also considers conceptual use of the research by district leaders, recognizing its importance in influencing leaders' thinking as they plan future policy and practice. The SFUSD research department sends short survey questions to school and district leaders working with researchers on the projects, both when research findings are presented and when projects conclude, to assess what leaders learned and applied from the research. The survey includes questions about the anticipated sustainability and scale of the changes to begin to assess longer-term impact. Survey questions record audience attendance at research presentations and gauge knowledge of the research project, enriching measurement of the scope of research impact. The Partnership also administers its own survey to both researchers and practitioners.[7] Notes from these discussions also inform the assessment of how district leaders and researchers are thinking about the use of the research.

Third, the capacity to engage in partnership is tracked by monitoring the number of Stanford faculty or graduate students with completed or active projects, as well as the number of SFUSD departments and leaders engaged in the Partnership. Since 2011, the quantity of research projects that access data from the warehouse at Stanford has tripled from three projects in 2011 to nine projects in 2018. Another measure of the scope of data access is the number of SFUSD departments and the number of data elements included in the umbrella DUA, which have grown over the years as research interests and projects have increased. As another process measure, SFUSD has also recently begun gathering data on time spent on extracting data and communicating about data with researchers in the interest of optimizing research impact and efficiency.

12.8 Concluding Remarks

Looking across the findings of this case study of the Stanford-SFUSD Partnership data infrastructure, there is a set of implications for the field and for the Partnership's future work. For emerging and developing partnerships interested in establishing a data infrastructure to support their work, institutional leaders should consider their short-term and long-term answers to several guiding questions:

1. Why: What purpose will the data partnership serve? What kinds of questions will the data be used to answer?
2. What: Which data are needed to answer those questions? How are they organized? What is the quality of those data? What processing is needed to organize and ensure the quality of the data?
3. Who: Who needs to be involved in discussing the data, across all stages of data gathering and use? Who will be analyzing the data?

---

[7] See Wentworth, Mazzeo and Connolly (2017) for a description of the Partnership's survey development.

At which institutions, how many, and where (both internal and external, with respect to each institution)? Who will be transferring the data?
4. When: How frequently, and at what time points, will the data need to be refreshed in order to support analyses?
5. Where: Where will the data reside?

The answers to the first four questions shape the answer to the critical last question about where to locate the data infrastructure. This echoes the framework presented in the introduction to this volume (see section 1.3.3), which contrasts one-to-one, one-to-many, many-to-one, and many-to-many arrangements between data-producing agencies and data-analyzing research institutions. Locating the data infrastructure at the institution with many partners, whether at an agency with multiple research partners or at a research organization with multiple agency partners, will facilitate taking advantage of the benefits of specialization and economies of scale. Partnerships where both institutions have multiple other partners will want to consider how to resolve these tensions prior to anticipated future growth.

Once established, any partnership using shared data will need to *continually improve the ways in which data are collected and archived*. For example, in SFUSD, although spreadsheet files gathered from various departments are systematically archived on an internal server, they are not processed to create robust databases. One critical step toward pursuing this improvement is to maintain a clearer separation between operational and analytical data systems. Along with better integration of the operational data systems that sit across distinct databases in the school district departments, the Partnership would also establish firmer timelines for finalizing the extracts of analytical data from these systems. Maintaining authoritative analytical data files for research at SFUSD would also significantly improve data quality, consistency in analyses, and efficiency in data management across the multiple analysts and researchers who use those data. On the Stanford side, the data manager could implement an intermediate step of data organization and storage between the raw data receipts from the district and the master data files that are used to provide data to research teams.

CHAPTER 12

About the Authors

Eric Bettinger is a Professor at Stanford University Graduate School of Education, a senior fellow at the Stanford Institute for Economic Policy Research (SIEPR), and the Faculty Director of CEPA.

Moonhawk Kim is the Director of Research-Practice Partnerships and Community Engagement at the Graduate School of Education, University of California Berkeley. He worked in the RPA division at SFUSD from May 2016 to August 2019. From September 2017 to August 2019, he was the Supervisor of Analytics at RPA and served as the school district's point of contact for data exchanges for the Stanford-SFUSD Partnership.

Norma Ming has worked as Supervisor of Research in SFUSD's RPA division since September 2014; she manages the district's research portfolio and oversees internal evaluation projects. This includes reviewing and supporting all external research partnerships and projects from initial development to incorporation into decision-making to ensure alignment with district priorities.

Michelle Reininger is the Director of Research Partnerships and Data Initiatives at the Crown Institute at the University of Colorado at Boulder. Michelle was the Executive Director of CEPA from 2010 to 2019; she worked with the Stanford legal team on the MOUs and DUAs for the partnership and managed the creation and day-to-day operations of the CEPA data warehouse for the Stanford-SFUSD Partnership.

Jim Shen is the Senior Manager for the Innovations in Data and Experiments for Action Initiative (IDEA) at the Abdul Latif Jameel Poverty Action Lab based at MIT. He was the Data Manager for the Center for Education Policy Analysis (CEPA) from January 2015 to August 2019 where he managed the CEPA data warehouse. He was responsible for the day-to-day operations of the CEPA data warehouse, serving as the point of contact for Stanford researchers utilizing San Francisco Unified School District (SFUSD) data and SFUSD staff for data exchanges. Jim holds a BA in history and international relations and an MA in political science from the University of California, San Diego.

Laura Wentworth is the Director of Research Practice Partnerships at California Education Partners. The RPP program at Ed Partners supports three partnerships with Stanford University and SFUSD, Stanford University and nine school districts neighboring the campus, and UC Berkeley and Oakland Unified School District. Since 2009, Laura has managed the day-to-day operations and relationships of the Stanford-SFUSD Partnership.

References in Chapter 12

Coburn, Cynthia E., and William R. Penuel. 2016. "Research–Practice Partnerships in Education: Outcomes, Dynamics, and Open Questions." *Educational Researcher*, 45(1): 48–54. https://doi.org/10.3102/0013189X16631750.

Coburn, Cynthia E., William R. Penuel, and Kimberly E. Geil. 2013. "Research-Practice Partnerships: A Strategy for Leveraging Research for Educational Improvement in School Districts." William T. Grant Foundation. https://wtgrantfoundation.org/library/uploads/2015/10/Research-Practice-Partnerships-at-the-District-Level.pdf (accessed 2020-10-05).

Cuevas, Eduardo. 2019. "'A sense of identity': Salinas high schools to require ethnic studies in fall 2020." *The Californian*. https://www.thecalifornian.com/story/news/education/2019/04/05/salinas-high-requirements-ethnic-studies-class/3365548002/ (accessed 2020-10-05).

Dee, Thomas S., and Emily K. Penner. 2017. "The Causal Effects of Cultural Relevance: Evidence From an Ethnic Studies Curriculum." *American Educational Research Journal*, 54(1): 127–166. https://doi.org/10.3102/0002831216677002.

Deming, W. Edwards. 1953. "On the Distinction between Enumerative and Analytic Surveys." *Journal of the American Statistical Association*, 48(262): 244–255. https://doi.org/10.1080/01621459.1953.10483470.

Dizon-Ross, Elise, Susanna Loeb, Emily Penner, and Jane Rochmes. 2019. "Stress in Boom Times: Understanding Teachers' Economic Anxiety in a High-Cost Urban District." *AERA Open*, 5(4). https://doi.org/10.1177/2332858419879439.

Farley-Ripple, Elizabeth, Henry May, Allison Karpyn, Katherine Tilley, and Kalyn McDonough. 2018. "Contents Full Article Content List Abstract Background Applications of the Framework Implications Notes References Figures & Tables Article Metrics Related Articles Cite Share Request Permissions Explore More Download PDF Rethinking Connections Between Research and Practice in Education: A Conceptual Framework." *Educational Researcher*, 47(4): 235–245. https://doi.org/10.3102/0013189X18761042.

Farrell, Caitlin C., Cynthia E. Coburn, and Seenae Chong. 2019. "Under What Conditions Do School Districts Learn From External Partners? The Role of Absorptive Capacity." *American Educational Research Journal*, 56(3): 955–994. https://doi.org/10.3102/0002831218808219.

Henrick, Erin C., Paul Cobb, William R. Penuel, Kara Jackson, and Tiffany Clark. 2017. "Assessing Research-Practice Partnerships: Five Dimensions of Effectiveness." William T. Grant Foundation. https://wtgrantfoundation.org/library/uploads/2017/10/Assessing-Research-Practice-Partnerships.pdf (accessed 2020-10-05).

Hough, Heather J. 2009. "The Quality Teacher and Education Act in San Franscisco: Lessons Learned." Policy Analysis for California Education Policy Brief 09-2. https://edpolicyinca.org/sites/default/files/PB.09-2.pdf (accessed 2020-10-05).

Hough, Heather J., and Susanna Loeb. 2013. "Can a District-Level Teacher Salary Incentive Policy Improve Teacher Recruitment and Retention?" Policy Analysis for

California Education Policy Brief 13-4. https://edpolicyinca.org/sites/default/files/PACE%20Policy%20Brief%2013-4_LowRes.pdf (accessed 2020-10-05).

Provost, Lloyd P. 2011. "Analytical Studies: A Framework for Quality Improvement Design and Analysis." *BMJ Quality and Safety*, 20(Supplement 1): i92–i96. https://doi.org/10.1136/bmjqs.2011.051557.

Ragland, James. 2017. "Students might get a kick out of a proposed new ethnic studies course for Texas schools." *The Dallas Morning News*. https://www.dallasnews.com/opinion/commentary/2017/02/11/students-might-get-a-kick-out-of-a-proposed-new-ethnic-studies-course-for-texas-schools/ (accessed 2020-10-05).

SAGE Publishing. 2019. "The Latest Thinking About Metrics for Research Impact in the Social Sciences." SAGE Publishing White Paper. https://doi.org/10.4135/wp190522.

San Francisco Unified School District. 2014. "Agenda: Regular Meeting of the Board of Education." https://archive.sfusd.edu/en/assets/sfusd-staff/about-SFUSD/files/board-agendas/Agenda1292014.pdf.

San Francisco Unified School District. 2019. "Guidelines for Conducting Research in SFUSD."

Solberg, Leif I., and Gordon Mosser. 1997. "The three faces of performance measurement: Improvement, accountability, and research." *The Joint Commission Journal on Quality Improvement*, 23(3): 135–147. https://doi.org/10.1016/S1070-3241(16)30305-4.

Sun, Min, Emily K. Penner, and Susanna Loeb. 2017. "Resource- and Approach-Driven Multidimensional Change: Three-Year Effects of School Improvement Grants." *American Educational Research Journal*, 54(4): 607–643. https://doi.org/10.3102/0002831217695790.

Waxmann, Laura. 2019. "Teacher stipends could attract new talent to underserved schools." *San Francisco Examiner*. https://www.sfexaminer.com/home/teacher-stipends-could-attract-new-talent-to-underserved-schools/ (accessed 2020-10-05).

Weiss, Carol H., and Michael J. Bucuvalas. 1980. "Truth tests and utility tests: Decision-makers' frames of reference for social science research." *American Sociological Review*, 45(2): 302–313. https://doi.org/10.2307/2095127.

Wentworth, Laura, Christopher Mazzeo, and Faith Connolly. 2017. "Research practice partnerships: a strategy for promoting evidence-based decision-making in education." *Educational Research*, 59(2): 241–255. https://doi.org/10.1080/07391102.2017.1314108.

Wentworth, Laura, Richard Carranza, and Deborah Stipek. 2016. "A university and district partnership closes the research-to-classroom gap." *Phi Delta Kappan*, 97(8): 66–69. https://doi.org/10.1177/0031721716647024.

CHAPTER 12

Appendix

Links to the "Agreement for Confidential Data Exchange Between San Francisco Unified School District and Stanford University" and the "Data Use Agreement Between San Francisco Unified School District and Stanford Research Organization" can be found in the Online Appendix at admindatahandbook.mit.edu/book/v1.0/sfusd.html#sfusd-appendix.

CHAPTER 13

City of Cape Town, South Africa: Aligning Internal Data Capabilities with External Research Partnerships

Hugh Cole (City of Cape Town)

Kelsey Jack (University of California, Santa Barbara)

Derek Strong (University of Southern California)

Brendan Maughan-Brown (University of Cape Town)

13.1 Summary

The day-to-day administration of policies and programs in the City of Cape Town (CCT), South Africa generates a large amount of data. In recent years, decision-makers in CCT have begun to think strategically about how to leverage these data resources to tackle multiple and interrelated municipal policy challenges, including the sustainability of utility services (e.g., energy and water); rapid urban transformation;

Copyright © Hugh Cole, Kelsey Jack, Derek Strong, and Brendan Maughan-Brown.
Cite as: Cole, Hugh, Kelsey Jack, Derek Strong, and Brendan Maughan-Brown. "City of Cape Town, South Africa: Aligning Internal Data Capabilities with External Research Partnerships." In: Cole, Shawn, Iqbal Dhaliwal, Anja Sautmann, and Lars Vilhuber (eds.), *Handbook on Using Administrative Data for Research and Evidence-based Policy*. Cambridge, MA: Abdul Latif Jameel Poverty Action Lab. 2020.

investments in transportation, housing, and infrastructure; the informal economy; and public safety. Specifically, CCT has made initial investments in enhancing data capabilities by adopting and implementing a data strategy and establishing a Data Science unit to facilitate greater data sharing (including through data engineering), enhanced tools for analysis (including open-source tools and data science environments), and advanced analytics. This builds on many years of investment in research, data, statistical analysis, and corporate (as opposed to fragmented) GIS capability. It also builds on the development of sophisticated policy and strategy capacity and a single policy development process for the whole organization. These steps have laid the groundwork for a broad-based effort to adopt evidence-based policymaking for greater impact and more cost-effective solutions.

Evidence-based policymaking is built on research informed by policy-relevant data sets. Practically, this requires making data available to researchers both within the municipal government and outside of it, primarily but not exclusively in academia. Data access presents numerous new challenges associated with the scale and scope of administrative data and the human resource and technological capabilities to use and share data. Specific concerns, common to many administrative contexts but particularly challenging at the municipal level, include (i) the security challenges of data sharing, (ii) the legal risks associated with greater data access, and (iii) the time and resource investment required to maintain the data architecture and governance systems that enable the sharing and use of data by various actors.

CCT maintains active research collaborations with numerous partners, which have helped to identify policy and program strengths and areas for improvement. This chapter emerges out of such a collaboration, between CCT and researchers at the Abdul Latif Jameel Poverty Action Lab (J-PAL) and University of California, Santa Barbara (UCSB), and reflects contributions from both sides of the research-policy interface. The authors describe ongoing efforts to develop a more streamlined system for cataloging, accessing, and sharing administrative data with external researchers and with analysts and decision-makers within CCT. The partnership has worked together over the past two years to advance CCT's vision for streamlined data sharing. Bringing researchers into the planning and implementation process helps to ensure that data sharing solutions work for both policy and research. The end goal is a single, cloud-based, data sharing platform for both public-use and restricted-use data sets, documented in a browsable catalog with standardized metadata. The single platform would be used by researchers both inside and outside of the city government. A streamlined process for research permission and data access would increase researcher accountability, including the reciprocal sharing of research output, analysis code, and cleaned and new data sets. The work is still in progress and the descriptions in this chapter reflect the evolving situation.

13.2 Introduction

13.2.1 Motivation and Background

Municipalities in South Africa play numerous roles: first, providing democratic and accountable government for local communities; second, ensuring service provision to communities in a sustainable manner; third, promoting social and economic development; fourth, encouraging the involvement of communities and community organizations in the matters of local government. The City of Cape Town is no exception. It serves a population of over 4 million people and provides a mix of basic services (electricity, water, sanitation, and refuse removal) and supporting services (transport, housing, safety, emergency services, primary healthcare, environmental health, community development, environmental services, and digital infrastructure) with a 2020 operating budget of around US$3 billion (City of Cape Town, 2020). Relative to many municipalities around the world, CCT's data systems are well organized and well maintained. For example, all formal commercial and residential properties are registered on cadastral maps and assigned a unique parcel number to which other municipal records, including property taxes, water, electricity and refuse billing, and other services are linked. This has facilitated administrative innovations, such as *consolidated billing*: many businesses and residents receive a single bill for their municipal account, which streamlines the process of collections and accounting. However, these data remain under-utilized for purposes other than administration and operations. Specifically, while capacity for data analytics and research within CCT continues to grow, even internal staff struggle to identify, obtain, and process the necessary data.

Recent crises, including the 2017–18 water crisis ("Day Zero") and the 2020 COVID-19 pandemic, highlight the importance of internal data sharing and analytics. They also revealed challenges. For example, staff in one department may be unaware of the data collected by another department, unsure of how to link data sets across departments, and unfamiliar with the staff members who manage the other data. Parallel challenges arise around research partnerships with external actors whose specific and often one-off data requests impose a time burden on CCT staff; these actors often lack engagement both in developing research questions and sharing results. Historically, the data sharing process for external parties has proceeded on a case-by-case basis. This ad hoc approach is costly for both data providers and researchers, and it often depends on personal relationships. These relationships may unravel if CCT staff change jobs and result in opportunistic collaborations that may miss some of the most high-value opportunities. Additionally, the actual transfer of data is not always secure (e.g., sometimes involving unencrypted flash drives). In spite of these challenges, CCT has engaged in successful research collaborations with external partners on topics including water conservation, municipal tariffs, electricity metering, youth employment, and more.

The situation has started to change. In 2016, Cape Town's municipal government underwent a restructuring process. As part of that process, CCT leaders looked to other cities around the world to collect innovative ideas for how to better run a fast-growing urban hub in a middle-income country. A theme emerged: leveraging the data created as part of regular administration and operation had the potential to uncover opportunities and efficiencies, leading to more effective governance and policymaking. The restructuring created two new units that are central to the activities described in this chapter: (1) a Policy and Strategy Department and (2) a Data Science unit. Craig Kesson, now executive director of Corporate Services at CCT, was a champion and architect of steps to strengthen evidence-led decision-making and data capabilities. Hugh Cole (one of the authors on this chapter) was recruited from the International Growth Centre (IGC) at the London School of Economics to lead the Policy and Strategy Department. While at the IGC, Hugh saw first-hand the potential for evidence to inform and improve policy and the crucial role that administrative data play in opening up collaborations between policymakers and researchers. Within the CCT, he began to advance an agenda for streamlining research collaborations, building internal research capacity, and making data more accessible to researchers both inside and outside of the CCT government.

In parallel, Kelsey Jack (another author on this chapter) had developed a series of collaborative research activities with CCT and researchers at the University of Cape Town where J-PAL's Africa regional office is based. As described in greater detail in the Data Use Examples, these collaborations revealed both the strengths of CCT's administrative data and areas for improvement. Kelsey and Hugh were in regular contact about the challenges of identifying, accessing, and working with CCT data sets. In 2018, Kelsey hired Derek Strong (a third author on this chapter) to work with both the Policy and Strategy and Data Science units within CCT to identify and advance solutions to these challenges. Importantly, the barriers faced by external researchers, both internationally and in Cape Town, were paralleled by researchers and data analysts within the municipal government. Thus, any progress toward data organization and access would be of immediate value to both internal and external actors.

While efforts to streamline data access in CCT are ongoing, including the expansion of remote access to data, substantial time and resources have already been invested under the CCT, J-PAL, and UCSB collaboration. From the researchers' perspective, the motivation appears clear: access to high-quality administrative data from a globally important city presents exciting opportunities. Furthermore, remote access to data also enables more convenient, international collaborations and even removes the need for a physical presence in Cape Town.

CCT's motivation to devote time and resources to such an endeavor stems both from a desire to uncover creative solutions to combat persistent, urban challenges and to establish terms for research partnerships that are more collaborative, building internal capacity and filling data gaps. As an example of the former, the investment of time and expertise by external researchers can uncover new policy insights that go beyond the scope of internal data analytics. Similarly, more accessible and user-friendly data resources lower the cost of incorporating data and evidence into the internal decision-making process. As an example of the latter, high levels of informality in the housing, transport, and economic sectors lead to persistent gaps in administrative records. Research collaborations involving primary data collection and analysis relevant to the informal sector complement administrative data and help inform a more relevant and responsive regulatory and service delivery environment for the most vulnerable residents. However, streamlined data sharing and reciprocal agreements are needed to achieve this collaborative vision.

The desire to fully capture the value of data and to streamline data sharing led CCT to adopt and implement a *Data Strategy* in June 2018.[1] This strategy recognizes administrative data as a "collection of public assets that should be managed in a way to maximize public benefit and organizational growth." It describes how CCT intends to transform its data for greater utilization and the management and processes surrounding CCT data to support meaningful strategic and operational decision-making. As part of the Data Strategy, CCT is currently developing more streamlined data management processes along with tools to lower the cost of sharing and coordinating across data sets both internally and externally. The Data Strategy resulted in the creation of the new role of chief data officer, which is a role fulfilled by Craig Kesson (in addition to his executive director functions).

A *Research Framework* adopted in 2019, also clarifies procedures for

---

[1] A summary of implementation activities associated with the Data Strategy is provided at Strong (2020b).

sharing data with external partners by integrating data access into broader research management practices to ensure reciprocal exchange of value and the translation of knowledge into policy.[2] As described in the Research Framework, research needs are evaluated in the development or revision of all CCT policies, strategies, and bylaws. The identified research needs are then incorporated into CCT's *Research Agenda* to inform what research CCT procures or pursues in the form of partnerships.

By aligning internal data capabilities with external research partnerships, the Data Strategy and Research Framework facilitate collaborative research. Primary issues raised in these documents include data accessibility (lack of documentation and mechanisms to identify and obtain data), data quality (multiple versions of related transactions), data custodianship (uncertain or ambiguous accountability), data security (lack of consistent guidelines and practices), and data analytics (lack of capabilities).

13.2.2 Data Use Examples

This section discusses three data use examples that have been catalytic for the collaboration underpinning this chapter and occurred prior to the streamlining efforts described, then introduces a third case that highlights ongoing challenges. The first data use example describes in detail the challenges and opportunities around making data available to external research partners. The other two exemplify the importance of data for internal analytics and decision-making and raise many of the same lessons described under the external data use example. These examples are intended to provide grounding for the challenges and potential solutions discussed in the rest of the chapter.

---

[2]The City's Research Framework outlines a collection of systematic approaches to help the effective and efficient production, flow, and use of information and knowledge in the organization. The framework comprises a research vision, research value chain, and enablers (research principles, objectives, and activities), and includes a high-level CCT Research Agenda that outlines the City's priority research themes. As of the time of publication, the document is not yet publicly available.

CHAPTER 13

Case 1: Impacts of Pre-Paid Electricity Metering

Like many research partnerships, this first example arose out of an existing research relationship. As part of his master's thesis at the University of Cape Town (UCT), Grant Smith had collaborated with Professor Martine Visser on a project involving water billing data (Smith and Visser, 2014) and expanded his research to include analysis of both water and electricity data as part of his PhD dissertation. To facilitate this work, Grant Smith (through UCT) established a data use agreement (DUA) with the water and electricity departments of CCT that allowed for broad access to utilities data. Kelsey Jack was added to this existing DUA through an addendum process once she and Grant began collaborating. The research project arose out of an initial interest in understanding how prepayment for electricity affected residential customers. Prepaid metering of electricity is common across Africa but little research had been done to understand how it impacts customers or electric utilities. A series of meetings between the researchers and staff in CCT's electricity department revealed an opportunity for a randomized controlled trial to measure the impacts of prepaid electricity metering relative to monthly billing. The experiment utilized an existing program, which replaced several postpaid or conventional meters with prepaid meters, by randomizing the order of meter replacement. The origin story of this case highlights the role of personal relationships and familiarity with available data, along with the value of genuine collaboration to identify questions and opportunities for research partnerships.

The project required data provisions by three distinct parties. First, billing data were accessed through the Systems Applications and Products in Data Processing (SAP) server (used to manage household bills) under the Enterprise Resource Planning department. Second, prepaid electricity data were accessed from the server used to administer the point of sale vending system under the Electricity department. Finally, GIS data necessary to support the spatial randomization design were accessed through the GIS team in the Electricity department. In parallel, researchers worked closely with operational staff unfamiliar with the details of data management, access, and processing. Researchers therefore iterated between data extraction requests (typically done in-person with the relevant data manager and involving file downloads on to CDs or flash drives) data cleaning, and design decisions. This process highlighted the value of centralized data inventories and a streamlined process for data sharing to lessen the time burden on both sides.

Once data were obtained from CCT, the process of integrating the data with the logistics of a field experiment was extremely time consuming. The RCT involved around 4,000 customers, but the data sets covered all residential electricity customers in CCT. These were used as inputs to the randomization to ensure balance on observable characteristics such as electricity use and property values. In addition, researchers worked with the operational staff to ensure adherence to the randomization and to match implementation details with the administrative outcome data on the back end. In practice, this involved daily visits to the office of the contractor hired to implement the meter replacements to reconcile their records with those of the research team.

Administrative records were used not just as an input to the randomization but also as the primary source of outcome data. This required numerous steps to ready the data for analysis. First, the most complete format for accessing billing records involves text files associated with printing a household's bill. Bill formats change periodically, and bills can be printed in three different languages. Extracting the relevant information from these files required extensive processing. Second, once households were switched from electricity billing to prepaid metering, the system used to track their electricity use changed from the SAP-based billing records to the prepaid point-of-sale vending records. Linking these two systems relied on property identifiers. Third, in lieu of shareable metadata to explain the data sets, the principal investigators (PIs) and research assistants relied on extensive direct communication with data managers, including in-person meetings, e-mails, and telephone calls. In many cases, these conversations were prompted when efforts to clean or organize data hit roadblocks. As a result, the cleaning process was less efficient and the communication less streamlined than if more complete metadata had been available at the start. Similar requests are likely fielded from other researchers working on the same or related data, forcing CCT staff to repeat information.

Given the nature of the study design, data could not be completely de-identified. In particular, it was necessary to retain both meter numbers (for prepaid and postpaid data sets) and property identifiers, which were used to match across data sets and implement the spatial randomization. However, all other identifiers (names, addresses, etc.) were removed in an initial step of cleaning done at UCT on a secure server. In some cases, requests were made at the time of data extraction to only share the necessary identifiers. However, it was often easier for the CCT data manager to impose minimal filters on the data at the time of extraction rather than customizing the fields for each request, and it was left to the UCT-based research team to complete the de-identification process prior to cleaning and analysis. As a result, the information loaded onto flash drives and CDs often contained detailed information, including names and addresses.

Upon completion of the project, the PIs solicited feedback from CCT on the research findings through (1) a presentation to the Electricity department, (2) a presentation to the head of the utilities division, and (3) sharing the draft manuscript with a request for comments. The DUA required CCT be given thirty days to review the manuscript for disclosure of confidential information. No specific comments were directed toward confidentiality or disclosure control. Efforts on the part of the researchers to solicit feedback above and beyond the required confidentiality review were voluntary and organized by the researchers.

The paper was published in a journal that requires non-confidential data be published alongside the manuscript (Jack and Smith, 2020). The PIs provided code, detailed metadata, and instructions for how to request the data for replication directly from CCT. However, providing instructions with sufficient detail for actual replication was near-impossible. Standardized data sets shared through a streamlined data sharing platform would facilitate replication: code could be published along with instructions referencing specific data sets and variables.

Case 2: Data Use for Planning and Policy During Cape Town's Drought

The recent drought in Cape Town (2015–18) required CCT to engage with both external researchers and with its own data in new ways to support decision-making in a time of crisis. In this case, a crucial step involved sharing and visualizing data on water supply and consumption to keep Cape Town's population informed and spur collective action to conserve water. Specifically, CCT made use of data visualization to keep citizens informed by developing a Water Dashboard[3] that reflected dam storage percentages, weekly dam level changes, and average daily production. Additionally, a city water map known as the Green Dot map depicted household water consumption levels across specified bands of kiloliter usage.[4] This provided a neighborhood lens on water usage and allowed for targeted communication and peer influencing to motivate behavior change (reducing household water consumption).

Furthermore, by harnessing and monitoring detailed, high-frequency data, the City was able to increase the efficiency of existing water infrastructure. For example, pressure reducing valves (PRVs) were used to provide data on pressure and flow in order to inform and optimize the operation of the water infrastructure. Through the use of PRVs, demand and leakage within a distribution system was managed more efficiently by reducing pressure in a discrete zone. The installation of PRVs provided valuable data that helped to improve reliability of service delivery, decrease infrastructure damage and water losses, and forecast and budget for repairs. Subsequent advanced analytics using PRV data were, however, limited by the data provisions in the PRV supplier contracts; CCT will seek to avoid this in future contracts.

The drought highlighted the complexity and importance of spatially explicit, real-time data access, the value of visualization, and the issues

---

[3] https://coct.co/water-dashboard (accessed 2020-12-11).
[4] Though the map has been removed from CCT's website, information on the map is available at http://www.capetown.gov.za/Family%20and%20home/Residential-utility-services/Residential-water-and-sanitation-services/cape-town-water-map (accessed 2020-12-11).

with combining different data sources. Data sharing was crucial to CCT's success in reducing water consumption to a level that allowed CCT to make it through the drought. The drought also illuminated data challenges, such as data sharing between departments, data ownership (some key data sets were owned by contractors), and the translation of technical data nuances for public communications.

Case 3: Responding to and Recovering From the COVID-19 Pandemic

Many of these same challenges (and some new ones) are emerging in the CCT response to the COVID-19 pandemic. The Social Vulnerability Index (SVI) developed for the Water Disaster Plan has been repurposed to inform planning for quarantine and isolation sites across Cape Town as well as for guiding the humanitarian response. Economic impact modelling is being used to understand the impact on the Cape Town economy and to generate financial scenarios for the City. The City has worked closely with the Western Cape Government Department of Health to secure quality, granular, spatialized Covid-19 case data to inform the response. Epidemiological modelling has been used to inform planning, including logistics modelling for health and fatalities responses. Data sharing across spheres of government and between city departments has been a challenge but one made much easier by investments made in recent years in data capability and systems. The data challenge of the pandemic response is compounded by the deterioration of data quality, requiring the City to access and understand new data sets as the crisis unfolds. For example, in the early stages of the epidemic in Cape Town, the response was guided by COVID-19 case data (positive tests), but as community transmission was established and testing demand exceeded capacity (requiring a focus on testing in-hospital patients and healthcare workers), the focus shifted to using death data to track the pandemic. As systems for managing fatalities came under pressure, data quality and speed degraded. This required CCT staff to understand data systems they had not worked with before and to build data collection systems not reliant on slow or poor-quality official data from other parts of government.

Improved data systems will lower the costs (and increase speed) of leveraging data resources to manage crises in the future. Recognizing this, enhancing knowledge management and data use is one of the goals of the CCT Resilience Strategy (City of Cape Town, 2019b).

These data use examples highlight challenges and potential associated with the historical reality of data use and research in CCT. Throughout the remainder of this chapter the authors contrast historical experiences and practices with the on-going aspirations and initiatives toward a streamlined data sharing process.

13.3 Making Data Usable for Research

As discussed earlier in this chapter, a collaboration was developed between CCT and researchers at J-PAL and UCSB to help CCT identify, develop, and implement sustainable solutions for streamlining the sharing process both internally and with external researchers. Figure 13.1 depicts the high-level data sharing process that CCT is working toward.[5]

The process of identifying potential technical solutions for data streamlining has followed best practices by (1) perceiving and identifying various barriers to data access and use (Connelly et al., 2016; Goerge, 2018; Lane and Shipp, 2008; Petrila, 2018; Abraham, 2019), (2) assessing new tools and approaches for secure and remote access to data (Lane and Shipp, 2008; Culhane et al., 2018; Foster, 2018), and (3) understanding diverse user needs (Lane, 2018; Abraham, 2019).

Other important considerations and activities have revolved around the following areas listed in Table 13.1. In all of these tasks and in implementation, investments in human capital with respect to data skills of CCT staff as well as network-building internally and externally are perceived as crucial to success.

---

[5]Current research request guidelines and a web form can be found at http://www.capetown.gov.za/City-Connect/Access-information/Submit-a-research-request (accessed 2020-12-11).

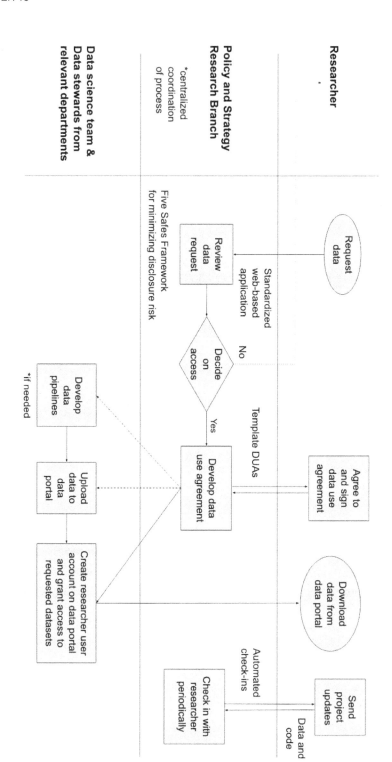

Figure 13.1: Data sharing process

Table 13.1: Areas of consideration and associated activities

Technical solutions	- Finding a data sharing platform with sufficient metadata and access control capabilities to support researcher-specific use restrictions
	- Integrating said platform with CCT data systems
Data infrastructure	- Development of metadata standards
	- Assessment of self-hosting options versus cloud computing with the appropriate attention given to security concerns.
IT architecture	- Addressing tensions between existing and newer approaches and technology stacks
	- Ensuring that legacy systems do not create barriers to effective data sharing
Governance	- Process improvement evaluations
	- Processes for integrating data use agreements with the data sharing platform
Data privacy	The evolution of CCT's understanding and application of applicable data laws and data ethics considerations must keep pace with CCT's increasingly open data environment

13.3.1 Metadata

A major initiative to facilitate data use is the development and implementation of structured metadata standards to be applied to all CCT data. CCT's Data Science team together with the Information and Knowledge Management department have developed standards comprising a minimal required set of metadata elements along with additional, recommended elements (Strong, 2020a). The minimal set of elements is similar to the Dublin Core but with unique considerations for administrative data. The intent of the required minimal set is to minimize the burden on data stewards and to maintain quality metadata. Core fields include a summary of the data set, update frequency, data access rights, reasons for restriction, data format, spatial coverage, temporal coverage, and information about the source and stewardship of the data set.

CCT is investigating the process for making a publicly available catalog of all available CCT data that also contains basic metadata. This catalog could include both public-use and restricted-use data sets with the former providing direct access links and the latter providing information on how to request access to the data. An initial internal data inventory has been created, cataloging over 1,000 distinct data resources. Over 500 unique data resources come out of the SAP system used for revenue management and other administrative purposes. The GIS data system (run on ESRI software) is the second biggest source with nearly 500 unique data resources. Metadata creation and further classification are needed before it can be made public. Once completed, this data catalog will make it easier for researchers both inside and outside of CCT to identify specific data of interest and to include them in research requests: this will reduce the burden on CCT staff when processing requests. Additionally, the tacit knowledge gained by researchers through the experience of working with a particular data set can be codified by contributing back metadata and longer-form documentation. In particular, researchers' assessment of the quality and usability of the data is especially important (Connelly et al., 2016).

13.3.2 Data Processing

CCT data are generated, in most cases, in the course of administering day-to-day municipal functions. Data typically need to be transformed to be useful for researchers. Historically, as described in the first data use example, raw data were extracted from various source systems and shared with researchers who then invested in cleaning and organizing the data for their research purposes. For example, residential billing data come from the files used to print household bills. These are text files with variables stored in strings and multiple languages (Afrikaans, English, and Xhosa). A large amount of code is needed to convert these files into formats appropriate for analysis. Researchers face a trade-off between cleaning all the available data, which would allow for future analyses, and only developing the specific data set they need for their immediate research goals.

Going forward, CCT's intent is to develop data pipelines that transform raw data into more readily usable forms. The process involves collaboration between CCT's Data Science unit and the specific CCT departments where data originates. Where relevant, it will also involve researchers who have invested previously in processing specific data sets. CCT is actively promoting the potential multi-use of data in the design of major data gathering efforts undertaken by the municipality. For example, the municipal building and land use application system is currently being reviewed and restructured to accommodate data access and analysis by multiple CCT departments as well as external research partners. For many of CCT's large data sets, however, significant data engineering work is needed, and it is often difficult to establish consistent identifiers across data sources depending on the relevant unit of observation. Challenges also arise in communication across software platforms, such as the SAP billing platform, the ESRI spatial data platform, and the point-of-sale prepaid electricity vending server. Transitioning more of CCT's administrative systems toward open-source software would help address some of these issues, but long relationships with proprietary platforms such as SAP and ESRI make that difficult. Discussions surrounding the feasibility of these transitions are underway.

CCT strives for a balance between maintaining good data practices throughout the organization through the establishment of standards and rules as well as ensuring that there is not an unsustainable burden falling on those tasked with data generation and maintenance. The greater the number of actors anticipated to use the data, the more effort is required to collect, structure, and maintain the data. Relying on office and field staff to generate and prepare data to a specific standard while maintaining the status quo with their current job assignments may easily overburden them: in turn this could jeopardize overall data quality and create resistance to increased data sharing. Current plans anticipate investing in data processing in response to data use requests, but in a manner that anticipates multiple uses of the data; once data are extracted and processed, the same steps do not need to be repeated for future requests. Minimal processing to preserve flexibility across future users involves transforming data into tabular formats with standardized variable names as well as other modifications like storing dates and times in ISO 8601 format.

The primary barriers to developing data pipelines include (i) lack of access internally within CCT, (ii) lack of basic data documentation and (iii) time constraints of staff with the necessary skills. The goal is to expand the use of APIs (Application Programming Interface) within CCT to address (i) and increased metadata creation to address (ii). Both should help address (iii).

13.4 Legal and Institutional Framework

13.4.1 Institutional Setup

CCT is both the custodian and provider of administrative data. External researchers submit requests for data that also outline their research aims, and the Research Branch within the Policy and Strategy Department reviews the application. The Research Branch filters requests based on their research priorities and other criteria established in the Research Framework and liaises with relevant departments within the City to assess the availability of data and appropriateness of the request. The volume of requests is considerable: in FY20, CCT received 136 research applications.

CCT has established an inter-departmental Data Coordinating Committee (DCC) led by the chief data officer. Each department has a representative on the DCC, nominated by the executive director. The rest of the committee is composed of workstream leads, key directors/managers who are responsible for resources key to the strategy, and technical specialists. This committee provides governance, structure, and oversight of CCT's data, specifically with regards to the following three areas:

- Improved governance—to facilitate the development of a CCT data strategy and the establishment of clear accountability, roles, and responsibilities for the management of information
- Technology—to ensure the development of Information Technology platforms and tools to support and enable the management

and integration of CCT data and information (also addressing issues of usability)
- Content—to set in place policies, guidelines, and standard operating procedures (SOPs) for the management of CCT data and information content (City of Cape Town, 2018)

The mandate of the DCC includes the following:

- Identifying data gaps and priorities
- Working toward one source of custodianship of data
- Managing the potential duplication of data and reporting
- Ensuring the availability of data

The Data Strategy sets forth many desired outcomes including (i) data sets available in a usable format; (ii) an IT architecture that accommodates diverse data types (volume, variety, velocity); (iii) SOPs for good data practices; (iv) skilled personnel able to adapt to changing data and software environments; and (v) a widespread recognition of the value of data throughout CCT.

To achieve these outcomes five key, interlinked workstreams were established: data culture, data capabilities, data collaboration and partnerships, data architecture, and data governance (City of Cape Town, 2018). A workstream on economic analysis was added in 2019 to reflect the emphasis in the data strategy of improving the use of a wider range of economic analysis tools in CCT decision making. The Data Science unit focuses primarily on the technical and architectural components of the Data Strategy.

13.4.2 Legal Context for Data Use

The primary data privacy law in South Africa is the Protection of Personal Information Act (POPI) of 2013 (Republic of South Africa, 2013). Though the law is technically in effect, it has yet to be implemented and enforced: this has introduced uncertainty around how to comply with the law. It is expected to be implemented sometime in 2020 and includes a one-year grace period such that strict enforcement would begin in 2021 (Giles, 2020). Because there is no precedent, there is little guidance on what practical measures to take in order to comply, though the law is similar to the European Union's General Data Protection Regulation (GDPR).

POPI has two primary clauses that affect the use of data containing personally identifiable information by researchers. First, it states that sufficiently de-identified data leads to compliance with the law. This is also often required by university human subjects research review boards in situations where consent is difficult to obtain, such as with administrative records. The law is somewhat ambiguous as to what sufficiently de-identified data means as well as with the point at which de-identification must occur. Second, POPI states that legitimate research use of personally identifiable data is exempt from the law.[6] The precise interpretation of the limitations imposed by POPI for research purposes is still under discussion by lawyers in Cape Town and elsewhere. In practice, CCT intends to de-identify all shared data unless access to personal identifiers is essential to the proposed research and is governed by a data use agreement that ensures confidentiality and restricts further dissemination.

To comply with POPI, CCT currently uses a combination of de-identification techniques and a disclosure control framework that filters and prioritizes legitimate research requests (described in section 13.4.3). Looking ahead, CCT data custodians will flag data sets with personally identifiable information through a tag in the metadata, applied to either the entire data set or specific variables within it. Additionally, data custodians may also categorize the sensitivity of the data set based on criteria still under development. This metadata will provide a streamlined and systematic approach to managing confidentiality concerns and POPI compliance.

While standards for managing most administrative records are still evolving, standards around spatial data are more entrenched. The

---

[6]For example, Condition 4, section 15 (3) on the further processing of personal information states: "The further processing of personal information is not incompatible with the purpose of collection if— ... *(e)* the information is used for historical, statistical or research purposes and the responsible party ensures that the further processing is carried out solely for such purposes and will not be published in an identifiable form."

Spatial Data Infrastructure Act of 2003 delineates the ways that spatial data and metadata are collected, maintained, and published by public bodies in South Africa, primarily to ease integration of various data sources and to minimize costs (Republic of South Africa, 2003). CCT complies with these standards and regulations when sharing spatial data of any kind. Given that property identifiers are often used for linking across different administrative data sets, spatial data linked to these identifiers are particularly sensitive in the case of CCT.

13.4.3 Legal Framework for Granting Data Access

At the time of writing, CCT employs DUAs to stipulate what data sets can be accessed by external users and how the data can be used, as well as to convey related management issues including non-disclosure. Typically, the DUAs are developed with input from CCT's Research Branch and Legal Services Department, as well as the specific operational departments that generate the data. The focus of the DUAs is ensuring data confidentiality. In the absence of legal repercussions for violation of the agreement, their efficacy depends on trust between the parties, as well as reputational considerations and a desire for future collaboration (Sexton et al., 2017).

The negotiation and establishment of bespoke legal agreements to underpin data and research partnerships was found to be a considerable disincentive for CCT and its partners to collaborate, and uneven and inconsistent terms created risks to both parties. CCT's legal department has prioritized the development of a series of template collaboration agreements to be available to all departments as an *off-the-shelf* governance tool to use in establishing data and research partnerships. Data sharing can work in both directions: in most cases, CCT provides the partner with access to administrative data and the partner shares output and analytical code or improved data sets at the end of the project. In some cases, however, CCT explicitly looks to partnerships to fill data gaps. The following types of research and data partners are accommodated within this series of template agreements.

- *Research partners* include academic institutions or individuals seek-

ing to conduct research utilizing administrative data. Template agreements will cover both embedded research or active collaborations and more hands-off data access for desk-based analysis.
- *Knowledge partners* are organizations (private or public) who have data expertise and want to partner with CCT on specific projects.
- *Data partners* include government departments, businesses, and organizations who have data that the CCT requires to gain the insights necessary for better decision making. These agreements involve data sharing in the opposite direction (CCT is the recipient).
- *Donors* are funders who wish to support initiatives around data access.
- *Public sector partners* are public entities who can offer CCT technical support in implementing the City's Data Strategy, such as the National Treasury's CCT Support Programme and the UK Foreign Office-funded Future Cities Programme.
- *Contracted service providers* are contractors involved in implementing policies, programs, and day-to-day operations. Data sharing goes in both directions with contractors accessing CCT records and sharing data sets resulting from their activities back with CCT.

CCT's Intellectual Property Policy provides guidance on Intellectual Property (IP) from publicly funded research and development, which is subject to case-by-case review (City of Cape Town, 2019*a*). For non-commercial research output, CCT does not typically exert any IP ownership. IP of the original and derived data (not including statistical outputs) is retained by CCT, and acknowledgement of data sources is required in any resulting publications or public materials.

13.5 Protection of Sensitive and Personal Data: The Five Safes Framework

CCT balances the need to extract value from data with the need to protect the privacy and interests of residents, as well as the security of CCT's physical assets. New approaches in data sharing must be accompanied by stringent security measures and robust data governance for the municipality to fulfil its responsibility to respect and protect its residents.

As part of the Data Strategy, CCT is pursuing a secure distribution model for sharing data, primarily as downloads via a secure, access controlled, cloud-based data sharing platform, which allows more flexibility than a data enclave model but carries a greater disclosure risk. While CCT has had existing disclosure control practices, they have not been motivated by an explicit framework or conceptual model. Currently, CCT is re-evaluating its practices as guided by the Five Safes framework (Desai, Ritchie and Welpton, 2016). In contrast to a data enclave model, secure distribution arguably relies more heavily on project selection and data use agreements to minimize disclosure risk, relative to technical means that place strong limits on where data can be stored and analyzed. The choice of secure distribution results from concerns over the costs of implementing a data enclave model, and restrictions on access if implemented as a physical enclave. In addition, risks are mitigated by the relatively low assessed risk of most CCT data that is shared for research purposes.

A data sharing platform—defined here as a centralized, cloud-based location for securely cataloging, describing, uploading, controlling access to, and downloading data sets—facilitates numerous aspects of the proposed streamlining. In order to achieve a streamlined process, the platform should integrate both the technical aspects of securely storing and distributing data with the governance aspects of controlling access to data. Additionally, as a data catalog at the core, the platform should serve as a data discovery tool based on the available metadata for both internal and external research purposes. Currently, CCT is working toward adopting a modified version of CKAN, which is a popular open-source data sharing platform. CKAN is primarily designed and used for sharing open data sets, so modifications are needed to extend its access control and security capabilities.

The authors assess each of the Five Safes in light of CCT's reworking of the data sharing framework (1 = least important, 5 = most important).

13.5.1 Safe Projects

Importance = 5; Cost = 5

In the future, project selection will be based on a formal application that specifies research questions and required data, though historically this has not always occurred. The Research Branch reviews the applications for appropriateness and alignment with the Research Framework and research priorities (Strong, 2020c).[7] Currently, the review workflow has associated SOPs, though areas of improvement have been identified, especially with respect to integration with the entire data sharing process. For example, the application process could trigger determination of security levels (linked to tags in the metadata) and eventual access restrictions. The application form is being redesigned as a web-based form to make it more accessible to external researchers and to help reduce processing time. Domain experts, analysts, and lawyers may all review applications, and applications are reviewed in the order that they are received. Where necessary, the research application triggers the development of a DUA, as described in section 13.4.3. In the future, a rule may be added that institutional review board (IRB) approval is needed before access is formally granted to academic researchers: a requirement that benefits from publicly accessible metadata.

13.5.2 Safe People

Importance = 5; Cost = 3

CCT accepts applications from what it views as trusted researchers with institutional affiliations. Many of the filters applied to identify trusted researchers are anticipated by the template agreements described in section 13.4.3. Under current practices, the specific cost of verifying trusted researchers is lower than the overall assessment of a proposed project. Because CCT will use a secure distribution model, it places additional importance on selecting safe people. However, there are no specific requirements or training needed apart from having a relevant

---

[7] See section 13.4.1.

qualification, demonstrable research experience, and an institutional affiliation: all of which signal a basic competency in data management and analysis. Drawbacks of this approach include (a) that some early career or less well-established researchers may be overlooked and (b) guidelines for implementation remain subjective.

13.5.3 Safe Settings

Importance = 4; Cost = 3

If a research application is accepted, a DUA is then developed. The primary purpose of this agreement is to ensure the nondisclosure of confidential information by describing the specific data that can be used and how it can be stored and analyzed. It is intended that data will be distributed primarily through secure downloads, but other means like encrypted flash drives may also be used in certain cases. This improves flexibility in the location of the actual research. The agreements make it clear, however, that the responsibility for properly and securely managing data falls on the researcher who is liable for any breaches or disclosures. The selection of trusted researchers helps minimize the risk in this area, though additional requirements such as (third-party) training in safely accessing and storing confidential data would further reduce risks.

13.5.4 Safe Data

Importance = 4; Cost = 2

Safe data is ensured by initially assessing the risk of requested data for individual data sets and their combination. Additionally, data containing personally identifiable information are de-identified when possible, and aggregated data may also be made available instead (when appropriate to the research design). The data use agreement also stipulates that the data must be used exclusively for research purposes and may not be used for economic or other advantage or distributed to others. Once again, the selection of trusted researchers helps minimize the risk in this area.

Making data safe is less costly than the existing procedure of extracting and processing data for each individual request, which often involves repeating extractions that other researchers have requested in the past. To populate the secure data platform following an approved research request, raw or minimally processed data will be extracted, organized, and shared on the platform with complete metadata to ensure users are familiar with the data generating process and interpretation of the data content. CCT is currently working to develop data pipelines that will help reduce the internal burden of processing and de-identifying data and not require re-extractions of the same data. The sensitivity of a data set will be ranked and tagged in metadata to enable quicker risk assessments, and less sensitive versions of data sets may be generated by, for example, aggregating or averaging across observations. However, currently there are no plans to use additional methods such as sampling or adding noise to the data. Beyond these steps, the burden of transforming data into a research-ready format falls on the researcher, and it is intended to require researchers to share code and processed data through the data platform for use by CCT.

13.5.5 Safe Outputs

Importance = 2; Cost = 1

Safe outputs are ensured by a review of papers and other research outputs by CCT staff, though the onus primarily falls on the researcher. DUAs typically state that the researcher should provide a manuscript to CCT prior to publication and CCT then has 30 days to review and respond with respect to disclosure issues. Researchers do not always comply because research relationships are often one-off, deadlines are not clearly defined, and CCT is left to chase after researchers who fail to supply a manuscript. Specific deadlines could be added via the researcher's login to the data sharing platform, and access could be limited if research output is not shared on time. Going forward, CCT intends to catalog all research that is produced from CCT data. The data sharing platform can be leveraged to streamline this process.

13.6 Data Life Cycle and Reproducibility

13.6.1 Preservation and Reproducibility of Researcher-Accessible Files

As mentioned previously, the data sharing process will eventually be embedded in broader research management practices by CCT. To some extent, such as with the metadata standards, data, and code curation practices are also under development. Because of the costs in terms of personnel time and resources, these practices are currently limited. The proposed data sharing platform will maintain access to data indefinitely, but more thought needs to be given to long-term preservation in terms of storage, persistent identifiers, version control, and access permissions. This is an area where partnership with research organizations could be fruitful.

13.6.2 Preservation and Reproducibility of Researcher-Generated Files

The reciprocal sharing of researcher-generated files back to CCT is desired and intended to be explicitly embedded in DUAs, but it remains to be seen how to share materials effectively. CCT places greater emphasis on code sharing because code documents the analysis workflow and derived data files can always be re-generated, though this depends on how robustly CCT preserves source data sets. In addition, code typically does not need to be access controlled and could be publicly shared, ideally via Git repositories. By detailing the workflow, this would increase research transparency, reproducibility, and productivity (Playford et al., 2016). Integrating exchange of code via the data sharing platform is also under consideration.

CHAPTER 13

13.7 Sustainability and Continued Success

13.7.1 Outreach

The Policy and Strategy Department, especially its Research Branch, implements the research management functions for CCT for both internal and external activities. These functions include reviewing data requests and project proposals and developing data use agreements.

In addition, the data platform being developed provides an access point to CCT's data both in terms of metadata as well as secure downloads. A web-based data request form is also in development.

Apart from managerial functions, the Policy and Strategy department and its Research Branch also facilitate and coordinate institutional research partnerships and knowledge networks. These networks include a diverse set of researchers and organizations covering multiple disciplines, geographies, levels of experience, and research interests. CCT collaborates with the Cape Higher Education Consortium[8] and has other long-standing research partnerships (e.g., with Mistra Urban Futures[9] and the African Centre for Cities[10]). CCT is building on this foundation by actively seeking new research partnerships locally and internationally; the City is seeking to establish formal collaborations with universities where there is already evidence of research partnering with multiple researchers at an institution.

13.7.2 Revenue

CCT chooses not to charge access fees to researchers, primarily because doing so would only serve to restrict access. Though CCT incurs costs to share data with researchers, it expects value returned in the form of useful knowledge and related products, such as cleaned data sets and analysis code. Supporting research (and students) is also treated as

---

[8] http://www.chec.ac.za (accessed 2020-12-11).
[9] https://www.mistraurbanfutures.org (accessed 2020-12-11).
[10] https://www.africancentreforcities.net (accessed 2020-12-11).

creating a public good. Charging fees would likely disadvantage many researchers in South Africa and other developing countries.

CCT's rationale for investing in a more streamlined process for data sharing and collaboration is premised on cost-saving rather than revenue generation. A lack of internal capacity for data science, statistics, and economic analysis means that CCT needs to harness partnerships with external researchers to realize the value of its data. One of the five pillars of the Data Strategy is the fostering of research partnerships to mitigate the risk of overburdening CCT staff or overutilizing expensive consultant time. Additionally, CCT recognizes that it can never recruit and retain all the knowledge and specialized skills it needs to understand and respond to complex urban challenges. Where incentives can align, research partnerships give access to this expertise and insight.

13.7.3 Metrics of Success

CCT's Research Framework outlines monitoring and evaluation indicators for both internal and external research projects, although operationalizing the indicators is a work in progress. Metrics include the number of research analyses that directly inform CCT strategy, policy and by-law processes and operations, the number of CCT programs influenced by research analyses, and the number of CCT-supported research engagements. In addition, metrics will cover the number of specialist research studies initiated by CCT staff (experimental, modelling, evaluation, feasibility, longitudinal, predictive) and the number of CCT research platforms and tools accessed, among others.

In lieu of revenue generated by selling data, CCT intends to track the monetary value of research funding raised through its partnerships (even if the funds stay with the researchers) and the estimated value of the services provided by researchers. These values will be calculated by pricing the estimated hours of external researcher time according to the standard consultancy rate for the level of skills and tasks completed. In addition, CCT will estimate the monetary value of external expertise gained in the form of time and tools, techniques, models, and systems developed. These metrics will be useful in building the business case for investment in external partnerships by CCT.

More directly related to data sharing between CCT and researchers, metrics will track the number of data sets made available to strategic partners (with necessary agreements in place) and the time required for external partners to gain access to CCT data; where possible, metrics will be tracked according to sensitivity rankings (open, sensitive, confidential).

13.8 Concluding Remarks

This case study provides a snapshot—taken in the midst of a dramatic transformation in Cape Town—where the municipality is purposefully implementing a Data Strategy and Research Framework and creating a unique and secure data sharing platform. Importantly, this platform will meet the needs of internal users, lowering the cost of in-house data discovery and exchange. At the same time, these internal efforts are being leveraged to streamline data sharing with external researchers whose research proposals have been vetted by CCT staff. Using the platform, researchers will be able to search for available data, securely download data to which they have been granted access, and contribute metadata, analysis code, and other files.

The benefits of streamlining the data sharing process include an increased volume of research on policy relevant questions, greater accountability of researchers to report findings and share cleaned data or new data sets with CCT, and a more secure and standardized approach to transferring data to researchers. These benefits come at a cost, which is largely front-loaded and associated with establishing the data sharing platform, as well as centralizing and standardizing the diverse set of administrative data sets used by CCT. This stage is still ongoing, and the interim picture provided here is rapidly changing. Lessons will continue to be learned and unresolved issues solved. CCT will carefully balance data privacy concerns with the need to generate bodies of evidence that inform municipal policies and support enhanced service delivery and improved outcomes for residents of Cape Town.

CHAPTER 13

About the Authors

Hugh Cole has been director of Policy and Strategy at the City of Cape Town since 2017. The Policy and Strategy Department contains four branches: Strategic Policy, Strategic Planning, Research, and Economic Analysis. He reports to the executive director of Corporate Services (also the Chief Data Officer). Prior to joining CCT, Hugh was the Director responsible for Country Programmes at the International Growth Centre (IGC) based at the London School of Economics (LSE). Hugh is a graduate of the University of Cape Town and the LSE where he is Visiting Fellow of the School of Public Policy.

Kelsey Jack is an Associate Professor of Environmental and Development Economics at the University of California Santa Barbara's Bren School of Environmental Science and Management. She has conducted research, including RCTs and observational studies, in collaboration with CCT since 2013. She co-chairs J-PAL's Environment, Energy, and Climate Change sector and is on the advisory board for J-PAL Africa's IDEA Lab. She is also lead academic for IGC Zambia and a Faculty Director of UCSB's Environmental Market Solutions Lab (emLab).

Derek Strong is currently a Research Computing Associate with the Center for Advanced Research Computing at the University of Southern California. Prior to this, he worked with Kelsey Jack at UC Santa Barbara and with the City of Cape Town to identify and implement solutions for streamlining municipal data sharing with researchers. His interests include research computing, open science, and meta-research.

Brendan Maughan-Brown is an interdisciplinary social scientist with expertise on: the uptake of HIV-prevention and treatment services; behavioral economics; and the social and behavioral determinants of HIV risk. He is a Chief Research Officer at the Southern Africa Labour and Development Research Unit, University of Cape Town.

Acknowledgements

The authors thank Gordon Inggs, Yogini Jivanji, Craig Kesson, Kayleen Simpson, Carol Wright, Joshua D. Hawley, and the IDEA team at J-PAL for support of the collaboration and for constructive comments on the draft.

References in Chapter 13

Abraham, Katharine G. 2019. "Reconciling Data Access and Privacy: Building a Sustainable Model for the Future." *AEA Papers and Proceedings*, 109: 409–413. https://doi.org/10.1257/pandp.20191108.

City of Cape Town. 2018. "Data Strategy." City of Cape Town.

City of Cape Town. 2019*a*. "Intellectual Property Policy (Policy Number 45412)." https://resource.capetown.gov.za/documentcentre/Documents/Bylaws%20and%20policies/Intellectual_Property_Policy.pdf (accessed 2020-12-14).

City of Cape Town. 2019*b*. "Resilience Strategy." https://resource.capetown.gov.za/documentcentre/Documents/City%20strategies%2C%20plans%20and%20frameworks/Resilience_Strategy.pdf (accessed 2020-12-23).

City of Cape Town. 2020. "2019/20 Adjustments Budget." http://resource.capetown.gov.za/documentcentre/Documents/Financial%20documents/1920AdjBudget_Ann1_1_OpexAdjSummary_May2020.pdf (accessed 2020-12-23).

Connelly, Roxanne, Christopher J Playford, Vernon Gayle, and Chris Dibben. 2016. "The role of administrative data in the big data revolution in social science research." *Social Science Research*, 59: 1–12. https://doi.org/10.1016/j.ssresearch.2016.04.015.

Culhane, Dennis, John Fantuzzo, Matthew Hill, and T C Burnett. 2018. "Maximizing the Use of Integrated Data Systems: Understanding the Challenges and Advancing Solutions." *The ANNALS of the American Academy of Political and Social Science*, 675(1): 221–239. https://doi.org/10.1177/0002716217743441.

Desai, Tanvi, Felix Ritchie, and Richard Welpton. 2016. "Five Safes: Designing data access for research." https://uwe-repository.worktribe.com/output/914745 (accessed 2020-01-30).

Foster, Ian. 2018. "Research Infrastructure for the Safe Analysis of Sensitive Data." *The ANNALS of the American Academy of Political and Social Science*, 675(1): 102–120. https://doi.org/10.1177/0002716217742610.

Giles, John. 2020. "When is the POPIA deadline in South Africa?" https://www.michalsons.com/blog/when-is-the-popia-deadline-in-south-africa/39672 (accessed 2020-12-11).

Goerge, Robert M. 2018. "Barriers to Accessing State Data and Approaches to Addressing Them." *The ANNALS of the American Academy of Political and Social Science*, 675(1): 122–137. https://doi.org/10.1177/0002716217741257.

Jack, Kelsey, and Grant Smith. 2020. "Charging Ahead: Prepaid Metering, Electricity Use, and Utility Revenue." *American Economic Journal: Applied Economics*, 12(2): 134–168. https://doi.org/10.1257/app.20180155.

Lane, Julia. 2018. "Building an Infrastructure to Support the Use of Government Administrative Data for Program Performance and Social Science Research." *The ANNALS of the American Academy of Political and Social Science*, 675(1): 240–252. https://doi.org/10.1177/0002716217746652.

Lane, Julia, and Stephanie Shipp. 2008. "Using a Remote Access Data Enclave for

Data Dissemination." *International Journal of Digital Curation*, 2(1): 128–134. https://doi.org/10.2218/ijdc.v2i1.20.

Petrila, John. 2018. "Turning the Law into a Tool Rather than a Barrier to the Use of Administrative Data for Evidence-Based Policy." *The ANNALS of the American Academy of Political and Social Science*, 675(1): 67–82. https://doi.org/10.1177/0002716217741088.

Playford, Christopher J, Vernon Gayle, Roxanne Connelly, and Alasdair J G Gray. 2016. "Administrative social science data: The challenge of reproducible research." *Big Data & Society*, 3(2): 1–13. https://doi.org/10.1177/2053951716684143.

Republic of South Africa. 2003. "Spatial Data Infrastructure Act of 2003." https://www.gov.za/documents/spatial-data-infrastructure-act (accessed 2020-12-11).

Republic of South Africa. 2013. "Protection of Personal Information Act 4 of 2013." https://www.gov.za/documents/protection-personal-information-act (accessed 2020-12-11).

Sexton, Anna, Elizabeth Shepherd, Oliver Duke-Williams, and Alexandra Eveleigh. 2017. "A balance of trust in the use of government administrative data." *Archival Science*, 17: 305–330. https://doi.org/10.1007/s10502-017-9281-4.

Smith, Grant, and Martine Visser. 2014. "Behavioural Nudges as a Water Savings Strategy: Report to the Water Research Commission." Water Research Commission 2091/1/13. http://www.wrc.org.za/wp-content/uploads/mdocs/2091-1-13.pdf.

Strong, Derek. 2020*a*. "Core metadata elements for municipal datasets – June 2020." https://osf.io/2a7ev/ (accessed 2020-12-14).

Strong, Derek. 2020*b*. "Research Branch project review criteria, based on Research Framework prioritization - June 2020." https://osf.io/2a7ev/ (accessed 2020-12-14).

Strong, Derek. 2020*c*. "Summary of Data Strategy Implementation - June 2020." https://osf.io/2a7ev/ (accessed 2020-12-14).

CHAPTER 14

Administrative Data in Research at the World Bank: The Case of Development Impact Evaluation (DIME)

Arianna Legovini (World Bank)
Maria Ruth Jones (World Bank)

14.1 Summary

DIME evaluates impact. Evaluating impact is a good organizing principle for constituting high-quality data sets. It helps researchers structure the content and characteristics of data sets to enable policy analysis. This is not the case for administrative data, which are designed to monitor processes. The vector of variables and the selection of observations into administrative data can restrict its use for analysis. Low research capacity in government agencies further limits the use of administrative data even for its intended purpose. This chapter describes how the Development Impact Evaluation (DIME) department of the World

---

Copyright © Arianna Legovini and Maria Ruth Jones.
Cite as: Legovini, Arianna, and Maria Ruth Jones. "Administrative Data in Research at the World Bank: The Case of Development Impact Evaluation (DIME)." In: Cole, Shawn, Iqbal Dhaliwal, Anja Sautmann, and Lars Vilhuber (eds.), *Handbook on Using Administrative Data for Research and Evidence-based Policy*. Cambridge, MA: Abdul Latif Jameel Poverty Action Lab. 2020.

Bank[1] combines an evaluative and capacity-building approach to secure access to existing administrative data, then fuses it and integrates it with other existing or newly collected data, to make administrative data analysis-ready and provide added value to country clients.

As a global research program, DIME provides tailored impact evaluation services to governments. Each set of services support governments in conceptualizing policies and programs, developing data plans, conducting field experiments to guide mid-course corrections, and evaluating the impact of policy interventions in the medium to longer term. With about 200 long-term collaborations with government agencies across sixty countries, DIME works with governments to develop the data infrastructure and know-how to improve the evidence-base for public policy over time. In partnership with about thirty multilateral and bilateral organizations, DIME also invests in transforming the way development finance is used.

DIME uses administrative data across its thematic programs: economic transformation, public sector governance, infrastructure and climate change, fragility and conflict, and gender. Among these, administrative data features most prominently in public sector governance programs. This is because the recent investments countries have made in their e-government systems are generating a massive amount of transaction-level data. DIME's multi-country justice program, Data and Evidence for Justice Reform (DE JURE) (World Bank Group, 2020a), leverages investments in smart courts and associated data systems to increase the economies of scale of knowledge generation on the quality and efficiency of judicial proceedings. Similarly, ieProcure accesses data from e-procurement systems to study the economics of public procurement and ways to improve the quality-to-cost ratio of procured goods and services. These programs develop analytical tools that can be adapted to different country contexts with the aim to support a tailored experimental research agenda in each context.

In country programs, DIME's use of administrative data leverages economies of scope and partnerships across agencies in different

---

[1] https://www.worldbank.org/en/research/dime (accessed 2020-12-14).

sectors. The researchers develop spatially integrated, cross-sector data infrastructure and research to help optimize government economic policy, planning, and evaluation functions. The administrative data included in these data sets can include data from land registries, road networks, infrastructure investments, tax, energy billing, or social transfers. Administrative data are complemented with an array of other data sources—survey, census, remote sensing, and crowdsourcing—to create multi-sector, georeferenced data sets, maps, and dashboards that are tailored to each specific country context and policy interest. These data sets can be augmented over time to respond to new and evolving economic analysis needs. The Rwanda case is described below (World Bank Group, 2020c).

When an administrative data system does not exist or is not yet in digital format, DIME invests in piloting digital systems that can later be scaled up by government. The first experience working with the justice sector, for example, was in the context of the Dakar courts in Senegal where the research team digitized massive quantities of paper records to identify bottlenecks in the legal chain and measure the impacts of a legal reform on procedural efficiency. The patient safety and road safety impact evaluations in Kenya provide examples of digital pilots.

This chapter will describe how DIME generates demand from government agencies and supplies them with research services that augment their data, program management, and policy functions. It presents examples from the DIME portfolio that demonstrate a spectrum of administrative data usage. It ranges from developing a pilot administrative data system, to digitizing paper-based administrative data, to leveraging existing cross-sector administrative data to develop a country data set, and to developing sector-specific data sets across multiple countries. In all cases, the aim is to establish capabilities for impact evaluation analysis and investing in data as a public good to enable greater speed and frequency of policy experimentation and knowledge generation. These capabilities include long-term client relationships and local capacities that put knowledge into action.

14.2 Introduction

14.2.1 Motivation and Background

The experience in DIME shows that the issue of *access* to administrative data is not easily decoupled from the larger objective of creating capabilities for administrative data generation and use. The examples in this chapter demonstrate the role that research can play in developing better data systems—systems that are designed to support research on important policy questions—thus increasing their value for policymaking. The role of research in shaping data, or the fact that data are both research outputs and inputs, is not always well understood.

Most efforts to collect data are driven by statistical agencies, not by research institutions, and statistics-driven data are on average a suboptimal input into research. To optimize data sets as an input into research, the data output itself should be research driven. When planning to evaluate the impact of a policy intervention, DIME researchers develop data sets based on a specified measurement framework. The data sets include the vector of variables and variable characteristics that are aligned to the theory of change of the policy intervention and that have the sample size, power, representativeness, and coverage required to conduct the analysis.

[margin note: Selection of Variables]
[margin note: → need to include in report]

The source for each variable might vary. Sometimes more than one source is viable. When more than one source can be used for the same variable, comparisons can inform the understanding of data quality and the tradeoff between costs and quality. The resulting data set might fuse administrative data with survey, census, remote sensing, or crowdsourced data. This output is then an input to data analysis and research products. The novel data sets are analyzed to understand the economic problem the research team is trying to solve, develop testable hypotheses, and test them by implementing field experiments designed to narrow down the causal pathways of programs and policies.

In no small part, DIME engagements seek to build administrative data systems that create research-quality data. Data integration increases

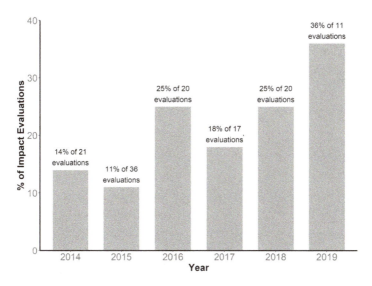

Figure 14.1: Percent of DIME impact evaluations using administrative data, out of all impact evaluations that started in a given year

value for research and policymaking and helps sustain longer-term efforts for data generation. While in the past, impact evaluations relied heavily on baseline and follow-up surveys, today's data sets include spatially integrated data at various frequencies that are increasingly tailored to support a process of adaptive research and policymaking. As a result, the use of administrative data has increased in recent years, as shown in Figure 14.1, from about 15 percent of impact evaluations to more than 35 percent. And whereas administrative data in the past could be used mainly for A/B testing, integrated data sets can be used to assess biases in coverage and to evaluate policy impact.

DIME secures access to administrative data and resources to collect supplementary data by generating demand for impact evaluations from government agencies. Developing joint research agendas with government counterparts motivates government provision of administrative data. Adding value to governments in the form of data trainings, analytics, and tools secures continued access to the data and establishes open channels for policy discussions. Sharing analytical outputs early and often with the data provider is a critical step to sustainable data access. The administrative data analytics are often useful for increas-

Figure 14.2: The DIME model for the adoption of data- and evidence-informed policy

ing efficiency in government functions, and they help generate testable hypotheses (highlighted in the case of road safety in Nairobi below).

The impact evaluations follow a co-production model in which the research team and the government counterparts work closely together on a shared agenda. The DIME model seeks to address constraints to data- and evidence-informed policymaking through multiple channels (illustrated in Figure 14.2). This includes building skills to create informed consumers, using group dynamics to create cross-country communities of practice, subsidizing research services while counting on governments to finance data to address the public and private good elements of research, and addressing reputational and aspirational considerations by documenting successes and helping countries improve their abilities to save and improve lives.

14.2.2 Data Use Examples

DIME's data sets and tools are tailored to the needs and requirements of evaluating the impact of a specific set of policy interventions. The data sets can be loosely categorized as project, spatial (country or city), or sector data, recognizing that each investment in data starts small and grows over time, sometimes cutting across these categories. For example, household survey data collected in Afghanistan for the impact evaluation of the Targeting the Ultra-Poor (project) is now being used to ground truth algorithms that use telecom-provider data to identify the ultra-poor in Afghanistan (spatial) and develop data tools that can potentially be applied by social protection agencies in different countries to administer their social protection programs (sector) (Aiken et al., 2020).

The administrative data component of these data sets come from government systems. In reality, only some of these systems are digital: some are paper-based and others simply do not exist. DIME's work adapts to these conditions by either using existing data, digitizing paper-based reports, or developing data system pilots. In the justice example, DIME leverages investments in e-courts that were financed by World Bank projects. Where these investments have not been made, as in the case of patient safety in Kenya, a patient safety e-checklist and facility monitoring system were developed from the ground up. The chapter presents these and some other examples to highlight where DIME (1) developed a pilot administrative data system where none existed; (2) digitized paper-based administrative data to fill data gaps; (3) leveraged existing administrative data to develop a spatially integrated country data set; and (4) used recent investments in e-government to develop unique sector-specific data sets.

Piloting New Administrative Data Systems and the Case of Patient Safety in Kenya

With no systematic data available on compliance with patient safety standards in Kenyan health facilities, lack of clear rules of the game, and inadequate monitoring or enforcement of regulation, the DIME research team worked on developing an understanding of patient safety and experimentally tested a new inspection regime. In a partnership with the Kenyan Ministry of Health, the Kenya Patient Safety Impact Evaluation (KePSIE) piloted a high-stakes health inspection system for private and public facilities (Bedoya, Das and Dolinger, n.d.). It consisted of a new regulatory framework with clear rules of the game, a scoring system, and enforcement of warnings and sanctions where facilities were provided time to improve or face the risk of closure.

To test such an intervention, an associated electronic inspection and monitoring system was created. To give some context, systems to report and diagnose constraints to patient safety are underdeveloped, even in high-income countries (Wachter, 2010; Longo et al., 2006), and of 45 countries in the Africa region with legislated quality inspection, only five actually implement any type of inspections, and those are mostly for private health facilities (International Finance Corporation, 2011).

The KePSIE's system was piloted and evaluated in three counties of Kenya representing 7 million health visits per year and a population of 4.5 million people. The 273 health markets, covering all facilities, were randomly assigned to one of three groups: (1) high-stakes inspections; (2) high-stakes inspections plus scorecards disclosing the score of the facility; and (3) control. The trial demonstrated that a new inspections regime that includes clear rules, monitoring, and enforcement is effective at improving patient safety in both public and private facilities (15 percent higher patient safety scores in treated relative to control facilities). The government is scaling up the inspection system at the national level with the support of a new World Bank Group (WBG) health operation.

This case is a proof of concept of the value of supporting governments in developing data systems to evaluate sector-wide improvements in accountability and governance, especially when guided by researchers who invest in understanding issues such as, in this case, the role of national policies on safe healthcare practices and how data systems can support corresponding monitoring and enforcement systems (World

Health Organization Regional Office for Africa, 2014).

This work produced more than twenty operational outputs, three published papers, two forthcoming reports, five briefs and blogs, and ten dissemination events. The operational outputs include technical support to develop the new regulations, operational guidelines, trainings of health inspectors, training materials and manuals, and detailed inspection protocols. This example demonstrates the value that a research team can bring to the development of a monitoring system that is well integrated with effective regulation and a system of warnings and sanctions.

Digitizing Administrative Data to Fill Data Gaps and the Case of Road Safety in Kenya

Many countries face insurmountable barriers to prioritizing their investments to reach their Sustainable Development Goals (SDG). This is even more difficult in areas with severe data limitations, such as the SDG target on halving mortality on the roads. The WHO estimates that only around 22 percent of road accident fatalities are captured in official records. To learn how to close this data gap, DIME invested in piloting high-frequency data systems for cities as part of its thirty country ieConnect for Impact program in transport. Generating data on crash locations and characteristics can help cities prioritize investments to reduce car crashes, road injuries, and deaths.

Kenya ranks among the countries with the highest road traffic deaths per capita in the world. Working in Nairobi, DIME undertook a massive effort to collate multiple different data sources to tackle this challenge. The researchers obtained administrative data through a data sharing agreement with the National Police Service (NPS). The NPS provided access to paper records stored in police stations across the city. A total of 12,546 crash records were manually digitized from a nine-year period across the city of Nairobi. The reports include crash details, location, and severity; these were then mapped to show crash hot spots.

A preliminary finding showed that 98 percent of these reports included injuries or deaths, indicating that crashes without injuries or deaths had not been reported or stored. To supplement these records, the team then used crowdsourced crash data processed through machine learning algorithms to identify and geolocate crashes reported by an established platform on Twitter feeds (Milusheva et al., 2020). To ground truth the crashes reported on Twitter, an app-based delivery firm was contracted to dispatch motorcycle drivers to the crash location within minutes after the crash was reported.

The researchers also integrated private sector data on speed, road events, weather conditions, and land use from AccuWeather, Google Maps, Uber, and Waze. Data from Uber and Waze were accessed through a combination of publicly available data and specific partnerships leveraging the World Bank Development Data Partnership (DDP) initiative. The administrative data was combined with primary survey data collected at 200 hot spots to ascertain infrastructure conditions and video analytics were used to ascertain road user behavior, which generated in excess of 100 new variables on high-risk locations.

Integrating all these sources into one data set provides unique insights into the contributing factors leading to a high concentration of crashes in specific locations. The analysis helped turn a seemingly intractable problem into something more manageable. For instance, it is now clear that 200 of the 1,400 crash sites across the city account for over half of road traffic deaths. This represents 150 kilometers of the 6,200-kilometer road network that can now be targeted for road safety interventions.

The data creates an opportunity to design a randomized control trial to demonstrate how to prioritize scarce infrastructure and enforcement resources for high-risk locations and times to achieve the SDG on road safety, and is informing the road safety component of a large development project in Kenya. DIME is exploring applications of the lessons from this project in Liberia, Mozambique, and Sierra Leone.

Leveraging Country Investments in Administrative Data Systems and the Case of Spatially Integrated Country Data Systems in Rwanda

Governments often lack the capacity to extract relevant sectoral information from their administrative data or to integrate data across sectors to conduct economic analysis. Country programs, a recent innovation for DIME that is currently being piloted in various countries, build deep country-level data ecosystems. These leverage a combination of administrative data and primary data collection to support a government strategy across one or multiple sectors of the economy. The more advanced case is that of Rwanda where DIME has worked for the last eight years. What started as a research collaboration with the Ministry of Agriculture and Animal Resources (MINAGRI) exploring multiple constraints to the adoption of production technologies in agriculture (Jones and Kondylis, 2018; Jones et al., 2019) grew across multiple government agencies, including the Ministry of Infrastructure and the Rwanda Revenue Authority.

The Rwandan Feeder Roads Impact Evaluation is a canonical example of how survey and administrative sources of data can be brought together in a country program to answer questions beyond the scope of traditional impact evaluations. This impact evaluation began as a partnership with the government to evaluate the impact of the national feeder road rehabilitation program across multiple donor investments and involved significant effort by the research and operational teams to coordinate across projects. In this spirit, a similar collaboration was launched with the government to harmonize the market price survey data. Data collected in rural markets in the catchment of targeted feeder roads were combined with the administrative e-Soko price data, collected at major markets nationally. The market locations are integrated into a geographical information system including maps of the road network and village boundaries. This enables the evaluation of the impacts of feeder road rehabilitation, and of national road construction more broadly, with all data sources in a harmonized platform.

A key component of country programs is leveraging this assembled data infrastructure to both increase client capacity for analytics and impact evaluation and to inform policy decisions in real time. To these ends, the team developed open-source dashboards to facilitate access to the data and support data analytics. The team also trained government officials in the development and use of these dashboards in a continuing effort to strengthen their monitoring and evaluation function. In addition, the country-level data system informs policymakers on the impacts of policies at-scale and helps operational partners coordinate evidence-based policy actions. In a recent example, the data ecosystem has informed MINAGRI on the impacts of the COVID-19 pandemic on food prices, which is guiding the optimal targeting of social protection response to the crisis.

Leveraging Investments in Government Systems and the Case of Data and Evidence for Justice Reform (DE JURE)

Governments that have invested resources in e-government, sometimes with World Bank support, are now demanding the analytics and research services that help them reap benefits from their investments. DIME works with procurement agencies and judiciaries, for example, to analyze e-procurement and e-justice data to improve the functional quality and efficiency; research is used in combination with tax data and firm surveys to understand important economic questions such as the demand effect of public procurement on firm growth or the effect of judicial efficiency on firm valuation. Investments in e-government have transformed the opportunities for analysis of the functioning of government. DIME is working with public administrations from low- to higher-income countries to analyze transaction level data on procurement, civil service, tax, customs, and courts proceedings to inform reforms aimed at increasing efficiency and quality of services.

One example is DIME's DE JURE program. DE JURE aims to develop a global data infrastructure for the justice sector, expand artificial intelligence (AI) tools to produce interpretable data from unstructured text, and produce experimental evidence to inform justice reforms (Ash et al., 2018). Large-scale data sets of all court proceedings and machine learning tools are being used to address whether judicial rulings betray systematic biases, arbitrariness, or inefficiencies in the administration of justice. Working in a diverse group of countries including Bangladesh, Brazil, Chile, Croatia, Estonia, India, Kenya, Pakistan, Peru, and Senegal, the program aims at increasing the amount and depth of the empirical research in justice, which has historically been limited by the lack of administrative data systems and tools to analyze massive amounts of transcripts (Kondylis and Stein, 2019).

The value of justice sector administrative data is expanded when it is merged with other sources: human resources data to obtain the characteristics of court administrators; surveys of court administrators and users, run by the judiciary annually, to record perceptions and satisfaction; and firm-level data linked to the court data through firm's tax identifiers. In Africa and Latin America, DIME is collaborating with two judiciaries on three RCTs that leverage existing technological platforms to improve judicial performance and reduce court congestion. The first two evaluate what kinds of low-cost, actionable information reduce judicial delays. These RCTs test mechanisms for a better way to onboard AI (Babic et al., 2020). The third evaluates whether a telework program with congestion pricing using non-financial incentives might reduce court backlog.

The team is also working on a project that evaluates how justice impacts economic outcomes. Leveraging the random assignment of cases to tribunals, the research team is evaluating the impact of differences in judicial speed on the outcomes of firms and their employees in two countries in Latin America and Eastern Europe. This builds off a machine learning methodology for causal inference developed in the judicial context (Babic et al., 2020). In Latin America, the current focus is an RCT of training judges amid a pedagogical transition from theory to case-based teaching (possibly based on the history of their past decisions) and includes self-reflection exercises (which embeds social-emotional learning interventions). Prior analysis of economics training of US judges found the training shifted the direction of legal precedent by 10 percent (Galletta, Ash and Chen, 2019). The team is also launching RCTs of legal analytics for firms, addressing questions such as whether information that facilitates investment decisions lead to legal innovation (Chen, 2015).

In South Asia, DIME measures textual slant in the manner in how judges from different castes describe litigants from the same or another caste (Ash et al., 2019). The team also uses gender-based violence prevention reported through mobile applications to assess missing cases. In Eastern Europe, the team studies when judicial decisions can be successfully automated. The DE JURE initiative is exploring how, collectively, these insights can spur e-justice solutions.

14.3 Making Data Usable for Research

There are many challenges to making administrative data usable, and these challenges are similar across many different contexts in which DIME works. Often administrative data are available in hard copy only; data sets are not interoperable due to inconsistent or omitted numeric identifiers; data generation is decentralized and there is no aggregation at the national level; and administrative data coverage is limited or biased. As a result, integrating data requires multiple trips to field offices, coding and digitization, painstaking efforts to merge on available variables, and careful validation with other data sources. Cases from DIME's portfolio illustrate some of these problems:

The data are available in hard copy only. In Senegal and Kenya, the court records were originally in paper version only, and the DIME research team invested more than one year in coding and digitizing several years-worth of case records. Initially, it was difficult to estimate the time required to digitize the data, which injected some uncertainty in the impact evaluation process. Also, this work required a substantial amount of resources, including involvement of DIME researchers and consultants and the judiciaries' central and local staff. In practice, this type of task falls on the research team. It was not before analytical results were shared that the value of using this type of data was appreciated.

There are data sets that are not interoperable. In Chile and Croatia, access to the data was substantially easier as both countries' judiciaries have an advanced case management system, which generates vast amounts of granular data about each aspect of every case. As such, administrative data were shared with a smooth and fast process and only required standard data cleaning to make data usable for research. However, significant challenges arose when merging the court level data with firms' data and tax records. The administrative data systems at different institutions were not interoperable and merging the different types of data took significant time and effort. In DIME's experience, the interaction between research and governments can demonstrate the utility of a common and consistent system of record identification and can spur governments to improve systems.

There is decentralized data generation. In Rwanda, as in most contexts, each line ministry generates their own administrative data with little knowledge of, or interaction with, data from other ministries. There is no centralized repository, so even learning what data sets are available requires a significant investment of time. Making the individual data sets useful for research required linking across ministries and incorporating detailed data from local government that are never centralized. Getting all different agencies to agree to share data requires building relationships with each agency and customizing outputs to meet the expectations of each one.

There are data sets that are limited or biased in coverage. In the case of Nairobi road traffic crashes, the comparison between administrative and crowdsourced data demonstrates that data from a specific source, whether administrative or crowdsourced, cannot be assumed to be representative of the underlying population. The police data was found to be limited to a specific subsample of the population (crashes with injuries or deaths) while crowdsourced data was found to be unequally distributed across time and location.

There is a lack of administrative data systems. Perhaps the most extreme challenge is a case where there is no system to record administrative data. In Kenya, the process for health inspectors checking compliance with patient safety lacked clear rules, and as there were no full-time inspectors, it only covered a small portion of the facilities each year. The DIME data pilot made it possible, to have a wide-reaching and comprehensive system that achieves the following: record detailed information of more than 300 items for all facilities in a standardized manner; generate scores and classify facilities by the end of the inspections to let the facilities know their performance; and provide facilities with warnings, sanctions, and next steps. This facilitated the government's capacity to monitor and enforce safety standards by improving inspection regulation, monitoring standards, and enforcement in the pilot regions. The policy insights generated from the work convinced the government of the utility of scaling up the inspection system nationally (financed by a World Bank project).

Even when pilots are demonstrated to be effective, the institutionalization of new data systems by government might fail due to either resource constraints or the lack of capacity for successful operation. In these cases, the gains from using data effectively are short-lived. As opposed to health in Kenya, the courts in Senegal did not continue digitizing records or transition to electronic case management. As a result, data-driven management of the court was imperiled. As the Kenya example shows, development finance must supplement the work of DIME to build and scale up systems. While researchers can make explicit the value of data and data systems, the effort required for fully adopting effective data systems in government are beyond the scope of limited research funding and capacities. It thus falls on governments to use their own resources or demand support from development institutions to build these systems.

14.4 Legal and Institutional Framework

14.4.1 Institutional Setup

DIME has a global portfolio of 123 active impact evaluations. The portfolio is supported by a team of twenty research economists, twenty other permanent staff, and co-authors from academic institutions. The portfolio generates correspondingly large amounts of data with more than 300 surveys completed over the past six years and many projects relying on high-frequency data, satellite data, and administrative data.

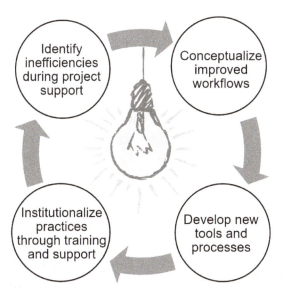

Figure 14.3: DIME Analytics uses an iterative process to expand technical capacity throughout the research cycle.

Standardizing and enforcing protocols for high-quality research across such a large portfolio and team is challenging. DIME chose to address this by investing in DIME Analytics as an institutional, portfolio-wide solution. DIME Analytics is a centralized unit responsible for developing and ensuring adoption of best practices in data collection and analysis across DIME's portfolio. In DIME's experience, centralizing resources and reducing the private costs of adopting reproducible research practices is key to ensuring high-quality, reproducible research. DIME Analytics identifies inefficiencies and practices that compromise research quality, develops improved workflows, creates and tests tools needed for their adoption, and then provides the training and technical support necessary to sustain adoption (illustrated in Figure 14.3).

DIME Analytics ensures the credibility of DIME research by developing best practices, providing implementation tools and workflows, and monitoring compliance across all research teams. Research assistants (RAs) follow a formal annual training program designed to teach recent graduates the skills they need for a future in research. The program includes ten full-day courses, twelve seminar-style continuing education courses, and customized academic development through office hours. The training program covers standard data structures, safe and reproducible data practices, data collection and cleaning workflows, and the tools created by DIME Analytics to implement these standardized practices.

Institutionalizing RA recruitment and training means that researchers spend less time onboarding staff and that technical skills are standardized across the portfolio, so research assistants can more easily be assigned to different tasks across an impact evaluation portfolio without significant retraining. The approach facilitates portfolio-level improvements to reproducible research. For example, when RAs follow consistent coding conventions, reviewing code is more efficient. The training program provides a mechanism to address problems and inefficiencies identified by DIME Analytics and to disseminate newly developed tools and workflows. In 2019 alone, DIME Analytics offered 28 reproducible research trainings.

In addition to the standardized training program, DIME Analytics offers regular *bootcamps* to achieve real-time technology adoption. These hands-on sessions directly transition projects to improved workflows. A recent bootcamp focused on safe handling of confidential data for all active projects. Participating project teams implemented updated data security protocols to achieve full adoption across the DIME portfolio by the end of the bootcamp session. An earlier bootcamp transitioned all research teams to reproducible workflows, such as using git/GitHub to manage and version-control all analytical code for DIME projects.

By investing in DIME Analytics, DIME aims to improve both its own portfolio and the quality of development research more broadly. All the resources developed by DIME Analytics are shared publicly through the DIME Wiki,[2] Development Research in Practice: The DIME Analytics Data Handbook (World Bank Group, 2020b), and the annual Manage Successful Impact Evaluations course.[3] There are few other development research institutions that develop and publicly share research protocols and trainings. DIME adheres to this unusual standard of

---

[2]https://dimewiki.worldbank.org/ (accessed 2020-12-14).
[3]https://www.worldbank.org/en/events/2019/06/10/manage-successful-impact-evaluations (accessed 2020-12-14).

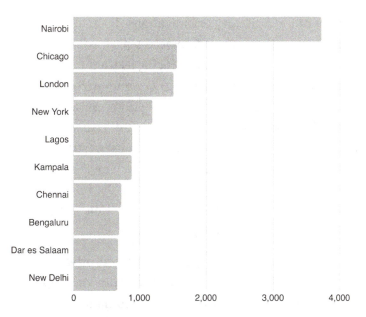

Figure 14.4: Global DIME Wiki usership: most active cities (outside the Washington D.C. area)

transparency so that the practices are continuously improved through public scrutiny and feedback and so that high-quality research tools and practices are globally available and accessible. There is significant demand for such public goods: Figure 14.4 shows the global reach of the DIME Wiki, which has attracted more than 128,000 global users since it was established in 2018.

14.4.2 Legal Context for Data Use

DIME has historically relied on informal data sharing agreements based on relationships with government counterparts and clearly established, shared objectives. However, the process is becoming more formalized. In 2018, the World Bank issued a procedure for Development Data set Acquisition, Archiving and Dissemination which provides staff with specific guidance and a template data license agreement (World Bank Group, n.d.c). The template data license agreement specifies the specific objectives of the data sharing and whether the data can be used only for the established purpose or for other objectives consistent with the mandates of the signatory organizations. It establishes the terms of the agreement and the type of data access protocols. Protocol options include open data, licensed use, official use only (access limited to World Bank staff), access restricted to pre-authorized WB staff, access restricted to pre-authorized WB staff working on a specified project or a specified output, or access restricted to a specific business unit or individuals. The data provider may impose restrictions to sharing derivative works and any or all of the metadata. The agreement also specifies the required citation for the data. As this template is pre-approved by the World Bank's legal team, and thus fast-tracks the data sharing process, most partners agree to use it.

DIME researchers also often negotiate with the private sector for access to proprietary data, typically with a letter of support from the government. The World Bank has negotiated data license agreements with global companies with data of broad interest for development research, through the Development Data Partnership (DDP).[4] Current partners include Digital Globe, the European Space Agency, Facebook, Google, LinkedIn, Uber, and Waze. Under the terms of the standard DDP license agreement, data sets are provided for the World Bank's use for any objective consistent with the World Bank's mandate.

World Bank governance does not compromise DIME independence in its research. Impact evaluation reports are reviewed through a World Bank process, but research papers do not require World Bank or governments' clearance. They are published with authors' disclaimers and are not considered official documents of the World Bank.

14.4.3 Legal Framework for Granting Data Access

As per the World Bank Procedure on Development Data Acquisition, all development data sets acquired by the World Bank are to be deposited in the internal Development Data Hub and classified as either public or restricted access. Deposit is to be made no later than six months after the data are acquired with the provision to later deposit any revisions

---

[4]https://datapartnership.org/ (accessed 2020-12-14).

or updates. Once deposited, staff may choose to embargo dissemination pending the publication or release of any derivative work(s). Staff are encouraged to provide data in an open format and public license to facilitate re-use.

Data archival is a requirement for funding under the Impact Evaluation to Development Impact (i2i) Trust Fund.[5] To qualify for i2i funding, data must be cataloged in the year in which it was collected. Typically, that data are embargoed (i.e., cataloged but not released) until publication of the research results. In some cases, teams release data prior to publication but embargo the variables identifying the random assignment or non-experimental design. These embargoes apply both internally and externally. The expectations around the timeline for data publication were established with low-frequency survey data; there are not yet clear policies in place governing the publication of high-frequency data.

DIME publishes all data that can be made publicly available, as per the terms of the agreement with the data provider, to the World Bank's Microdata Catalog.[6] On the Microdata Catalog, staff choose the terms of use (World Bank Group, n.d.*b*). Options include open access; direct access (data are freely available under basic conditions); public access (data are available to registered users who consent to respect a list of core conditions); or licensed files (users request data access for a specific purpose directly from the data owner). DIME data sets are typically catalogued as licensed files. To access licensed files, interested individuals must disclose the intended use of the data and a list of expected outputs, and no other uses are permitted without prior written consent from the World Bank.

Much of the administrative data used by DIME are classified as restricted access, as per the terms of the license agreements, and cannot be made publicly accessible. Restricted access data are classified into three tiers of internal access: data classified as *strictly confidential* are accessible only to specific individuals; data classified as *confidential* are

---

[5]https://www.worldbank.org/en/research/dime/brief/i2i-fund (accessed 2020-12-14).

[6]https://microdata.worldbank.org/index.php/home (accessed 2020-12-14).

accessible on a need-to-know basis; data classified as *official use only* are accessible to all staff in the institution. DIME often shares (de-identified) data on a need-to-know basis with operational colleagues, such as questions around placement or targeting of new World Bank operations. As there is no publication incentive in this case, issues of intellectual property are less salient. In cases where the data cannot be published publicly, publishing the research is a way to demonstrate to researchers that the data exist (and the types of linkages are possible). DIME also aims to incentivize policymakers to increase their use of that data and their willingness to collaborate with other research teams.

14.5 Protection of Sensitive and Personal Data: The Five Safes Framework

14.5.1 Safe Projects

Creating a safe project involves a collaboratively developed research agenda that serves each entity involved in the project and a shared understanding of how data will be used. This is core to DIME's co-production model. The researchers, government, and any implementing partners start from a problem in which they are all invested and work together toward a solution, rather than pursuing a research question pre-determined by the researchers.

To evaluate the appropriateness of potential projects, DIME considers three factors:

1. Does the research collaboration contribute to the public good, and is it policy-relevant?
2. Is the approach technically valid?
3. Is the proposed approach transparent and ethically sound?

DIME projects are governed by the i2i trust fund. Proposed projects are evaluated through an external double-blind review process at both the *expression of interest* and the full *concept note* stage. The review assesses the policy contribution and the technical merits and flags potential ethical issues.

To assess policy relevance, proposed i2i projects are scored by World Bank operational departments at both the *expression of interest* and the *concept note* stage. They evaluate proposed projects on their potential to contribute to evidence gaps, potential to influence the design and/or scale-up, and potential to influence prioritization of current and future development interventions. Impact evaluation *concept notes* go through a formal World Bank approval process, which concludes with a review chaired by either the country manager or the practice manager and two external reviewers (usually a subject-matter expert and an operations expert). This ensures ongoing relevance of DIME's work to World Bank and country policy priorities.

To evaluate technical merit, all proposed i2i projects go through a double-blind review by external academics. Final decisions are made by a technical committee comprised of experienced research economists from the World Bank. The review process is a meaningful mechanism for selecting appropriate projects and cuts off a substantial portion of the distribution. This is demonstrated in Figure 14.5 (technical ratings are given on a scale of 0 to 3 with 3 being highest quality). From the first seven open calls, just over 50 percent of proposals were accepted as i2i projects.

To evaluate ethical soundness, the technical review flags projects with potential ethical issues; these projects must go through Institutional Review Board (IRB) approval and any issues must be addressed by the researchers before funding is released. i2i promotes registration of all impact evaluation studies. Currently, 42 percent of DIME studies are registered, which is a figure that is increasing over time. Additionally, the *concept note* template requires detailed explanation of data acquisition strategies and data quality controls. Once projects are underway, research teams must submit annual updates to MyIE, DIME's internal monitoring system. This is a unique mechanism to validate compliance with DIME protocols, as research teams are required to document study registration, updates to research design, data sources and use, and policy influence.

CHAPTER 14

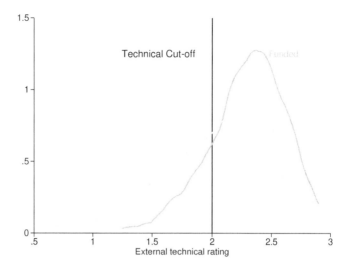

Figure 14.5: The distribution of technical ratings of funded vs. unfunded impact evaluation proposals. Technical ratings are assigned during double-blind proposal review.

14.5.2 Safe People

The World Bank has well-established relationships with its member states and a reputation for high-quality analytical work. DIME researchers work on public good research, which fosters mutual trust and accountability to clients. Much data sharing occurs initially under the auspices of the larger relationship with the World Bank and is sustained through the ongoing collaboration.

At DIME, researchers have a special ethical responsibility: to generate scientifically valid and credible research that is actionable. Upholding high research standards is secured through competitive selection of research economists on the academic market and high standards of competitive hiring for all other staff involved in the production of impact evaluation products. For example, in DIME's most recent recruitment for research assistants and field coordinators, the rigorous evaluation process (including objective evaluation of software skills) resulted in less than 5 percent of applicants being offered a position.

To maintain high ethical standards, in addition to the IRB process, all researchers working on i2i-funded projects are required to submit documentation of successful completion of ethics training on conducting human subjects research from recognized providers such as CITI[7] or PHRP.[8] Human subjects research certification is also required for any team member who is expected to work with personally identifiable data.

World Bank employment contracts govern intellectual property rights and specify that any works produced, or materials acquired, during the course of the appointment belong to the World Bank. As research assistants and field coordinators typically work with confidential data, DIME requires the signature of non-disclosure agreements (NDA)[9] at the start of their tenure. The NDA has specific provisions for maintaining full confidentiality and safeguarding private information. As a condition of employment, personnel commit to keeping all research information confidential, to blind any identifying information, to handle all data securely, to use secure technologies for encryption-at-rest and encryption-in-transfer, and to destroy all local copies of data and research outputs at the end of the contract unless given written authorization by the research staff. New hires are also required to review DIME's Data Security Standards and pass an assessment on the content (World Bank Group, n.d.*a*).

14.5.3 Safe Settings

DIME has recently formalized its Data Security Standards, which apply to all confidential data. Confidential data include all data that are categorized as restricted access, due to terms of license agreements or inclusion of personally identifying information. The Data Security Standards are intended to ensure that confidential data are accessible to only the specific research team members listed on the Institutional Review Board approval.

---

[7]https://about.citiprogram.org (accessed 2020-12-14).
[8]https://phrptraining.com/ (accessed 2020-12-14).
[9]https://github.com/worldbank/dime-standards/blob/master/dime-research-standards/pillar-4-data-security/data-security-resources/dime-data-nda.md (accesssed 2020-12-14).

World Bank computers are encrypted, and the enterprise version of OneDrive encrypts all data on the fly; however, since DIME works extensively with external partners, additional protocols have been self-imposed. These protocols include encryption-in-transit required for any data transferred over the Internet, encryption-at-rest required for data stored on any server (from data collection servers to longer-term storage options), and encryption-at-rest required for local folders used to store confidential data (whether shared or not).

Larger data sets are stored in secure servers in the World Bank's cloud environment, with access limited to specified World Bank staff and consultants using World Bank–controlled credentials through a single sign-on process. The strong encryption protocols are necessary given frequent domestic and international travel by research team members, which necessitates the use of laptops and prevents a physical infrastructure solution.

Research assistants and field coordinators are trained in DIME Data Security Standards, and they in turn work closely with government counterparts and implementing partners to make sure that the standards are applied. Field coordinators play a particularly important role in identifying data security challenges and helping to implement secure protocols, as the field coordinators are physically present with partners. DIME Analytics offers customized support to DIME project teams for setting up secure data infrastructure and provides advising on safe handling, transfer, and storage of confidential data.

In terms of safe data acquisition from external providers, data are typically uploaded from a provider to a WB OneDrive (enterprise) folder. Two-factor authentication with an on-demand, single-use code is sent by e-mail. The encryptions-in-transit protocol is HTTPS and data are encrypted-at-rest immediately on the WB-controlled OneDrive (enterprise) server. Larger data sets sent directly to a cloud environment are typically pulled into those environments using an SFTP protocol.

When digitizing administrative data, case-by-case protocols are developed to ensure data security. In the example of the Nairobi road safety evaluation, the team set the following protocols: paper records were scanned at the police department headquarters, so physical copies never left the premises; the records were scanned by a DIME field coordinator, who was subject by contract to standard provisions of data confidentiality and ownership; the field coordinator physically transferred the scans to the firm hired to digitize them; the contract for the firm included standard provisions requiring that the firm or any of its employees cannot use or disclose the information being digitized; and personally identifying variables were not digitized.

14.5.4 Safe Data

The key to ensuring safe data is respecting privacy rights. In many cases, DIME accesses data that is confidential and therefore requires secure sharing protocols. Protocols for data security are detailed in the chapter on Data Acquisition in Development Research in Practice: The DIME Analytics Data Handbook (World Bank Group, 2020b). DIME encourages research teams to de-identify confidential data as early as possible in the process to reduce access restrictions. This simplifies workflows (i.e., avoids frequently handling encryption keys to access data) and limits risk of possible access breaches. This typically involves stripping identifiers not directly used in the analysis and keeping only encoded versions of constructed indicators. All variables tagged as potential identifiers are removed from data before publication, although this creates a trade-off in terms of data usability. Discussions are ongoing with the World Bank Data Group on possibly implementing more sophisticated disclosure protocols, such as differential privacy. Stripping spatial information, while important for maintaining privacy, decreases the value of the data, as it limits integration with other data sources.

The digitization of administrative data is done using vetted software platforms that offer secure encryption. Digitization is typically done by a consultant or firm that is contracted by the World Bank; contracts include clear stipulations of intellectual property and data ownership. When digitized, the data are submitted directly to servers hosted by the World Bank, rather than a third-party. DIME typically uses SurveyCTO for manual data digitization, because of the tools for safe data (e.g. tools to encrypt data, publish subsets of data, and limit access to sensitive data based on user profiles).

14.5.5 Safe Outputs

The primary mechanism for ensuring safe outputs at DIME is rigorous protocols for assessing disclosure risk in analysis data sets. When outputs are generated from data sets that are rigorously de-identified, disclosure risks for outputs are minimized. In cases where analysis relies on identifying variables, more care is needed to mitigate disclosure risk. As a safeguard, one of the checks in DIME's pre-publication code review process is to check all outputs and tabulations for disclosure risk, particularly outputs concerning subsamples.

14.6 Data Life Cycle and Replicability

14.6.1 Preservation and Reproducibility of Researcher-Accessible Files

Version control and transparent workflows are critical to ensuring reproducibility. As discussed in section 14.4.1, DIME has instituted clear workflows to transparently document all modifications to data after initial receipt. DIME has recently established new reproducibility standards and implemented those through a hands-on *reproducibility bootcamp*. These standards include keeping all projects on GitHub or (version control more generally); establishing protocols for project documentation, data storage, and identifiable information management; and establishing protocols for the extent that sensitive data can be shared for replication and reanalysis. While most of these elements are common across types of data, secure storage solutions and access protocols for identifiable data are of greater concern with administrative data because of the size of the data and number of subjects.

Accessibility to a second user and long-term data engagements are potential benefits of administrative data. Documentation is critical to allow for continued usage; tracing and recording the process of gaining data access, developing data sets, and preparing data for research, and recording the relationship histories and the people involved in the project. Since relationships with data providers and individual researchers are often the point of first access, preservation of research projects involves knowing the story behind the data access. At this point, there is not a technical solution to facilitate this documentation, but the hope is to advance on this when infrastructure allows.

14.6.2 Preservation and Reproducibility of Researcher-Generated Files

Prior to publication, all DIME research papers undergo a computational reproducibility check completed by DIME Analytics. This verifies that using the same materials and procedures provided, a third-party can exactly reproduce the tables and figures in the paper. DIME Analytics has developed a detailed checklist for this purpose, which is completed by the research team at submission, verified during the reproducibility check, and returned to the team for inclusion in an online appendix. The completed checklist clearly indicates the reproducible research standards with which the project complies. Adopting reproducible workflows from early in project implementation simplifies the final reproducibility check. DIME recently scaled up this service to be available to all World Bank staff.

Once reproducibility is verified, DIME Analytics supports the project team in publishing the code and data for the project. All data that can be made public (per the terms of the data license agreement) are published to the World Bank Microdata Catalog. Code is typically published to the World Bank's GitHub site.

Data that are *official use only*, or more restricted access, are archived on the internal data hub, which provides information on metadata and is accessible to World Bank staff. For the Microdata Catalog, documentation and cataloging are done in accordance with the Data Documentation Initiative (DDI) metadata standard—an international, XML-based standard for microdata documentation—and based on

CHAPTER 14

the guidelines for data archival described in the Quick Reference Guide for Data Archivists (Dupriez, Castro and Welch, 2019). It also complies with the XML Dublin Core Metadata Initiative (DCMI) Specifications for documenting external resources (questionnaires, reports, programs, etc.).

Preservation also requires effective management of storage media. Stata is used as a standard internal format, and a policy on managing migration to later versions is under development by the Microdata Catalog team. The Microdata Catalog does not require a disposal protocol. Obsolescence of media is not thought to be a concern. DIME has no active disposal protocols at this time.

14.7 Sustainability and Continued Success

14.7.1 Outreach

A shared research agenda and continuous engagement over the lifetime of an impact evaluation are key to DIME's outreach strategy to its clients. Generating timely descriptive outputs and creating accessible data interfaces builds trust and interest. This facilitates government counterparts' access to their own data and increases the relevance of partnerships with DIME to their day-to-day work. DIME does extensive capacity building activities, such as hands-on trainings in data management and descriptive analysis, to increase counterparts' direct engagement with the data. Training is a means to sustainably maintain engagement with the research question by building practical staff knowledge of the researcher-generated data outputs.

A typical DIME outreach strategy is as follows. First, the research team agrees on the research agenda with the client and maps the existing data landscape (as discussed above). Second, the research team integrates various data sources to create the data sets, which will ultimately be used to generate original research outputs. Third, where useful, DIME creates accessible, open-source interfaces for government counterparts to interact with administrative data sources, such as Shiny[10] dashboards. Fourth, the research team engages with the data provider to generate new insights and ways for the data provider to understand how they can improve the use of their data and to build capacity for internal data-driven operational evaluations and program evaluation. The end goal is to demonstrate the utility of the data sets and to catalyze investments in institutionalized data systems with formal access protocols and well-developed data security infrastructure.

The data use examples illustrate DIME's outreach strategy:

In the *Rwanda* case, the feeder road evaluation is part of the research team's broader collaboration on impact evaluations with the Government of Rwanda, which has been ongoing since 2012. Team members travel to Rwanda quarterly and regularly engage in high-level policy discussions. Results are presented to the minister as they become available. This ensures that research impact resonates at the highest level of government. DIME has invested in significant capacity building with counterparts at the Rwanda Transport Development Agency and the Ministry of Agriculture and Animal Resources by providing hands-on trainings on data management and analysis and providing frequent descriptive analytical outputs to help improve data collection systems and answer policy questions. The research team worked with the government to develop an open-source Shiny dashboard as an accessible way for government officials to engage with data. Dashboards are more of a data interaction than a data extraction, but they can preserve engagement with data and facilitate use of data for policy decisions that go beyond the original research agenda.

The *KePSIE* experience illustrates that the DIME co-production model with national counterparts can be sustained over a six-year period, overcome many delays and much turnover of key stakeholders and still secure substantial success. DIME strengthened the Ministry of Health's data systems by developing an electronic checklist to collect inspection records and by creating a pilot web-based monitoring and planning system that aggregates inspections results and allows for real-time access to patient safety monitoring and inspections implementation. The

---

[10]https://shiny.rstudio.com/ (accessed 2020-12-14).

checklist and score system that DIME helped develop for the evaluation became the national regulatory health facility inspection system for both private and public facilities.

In the *Nairobi road safety* case, the DIME team established a broad collaboration with members of the Kenya Working Group on Transport that includes Kenyan ministries, departments, and agencies in the transport sector, as well as interested development partners and the National Police Service. Team members engaged in high-level policy discussions with this multi-stakeholder group and engaged in operational discussions with specific members to develop collaborations and pilot ideas such as an electronic-crash record system with the police.

The work with the *justice sector in Kenya* has included a collaboration with the highest levels of the judiciary to develop score cards, analyze data, and introduce reforms. After the digitization of court records was completed, the Judiciary of Kenya has started to use the judge-level data as part of their performance management process and to keep judges and other key court staff updated on key indicators, such as case backlog. Finally, insights from the data are informing the design of reform and testing of pilot interventions.

14.7.2 Revenue

DIME impact evaluations are financed through grants, including the i2i Trust Fund. Primary data collection is typically financed by World Bank operations. Data acquisition from government counterparts is typically shared on a no-fee basis through a data license agreement. Private sector data are either provided pro bono, in exchange for research services, or procured through research grants. Data made available through the Development Data Partnership incurs no usage fees for World Bank staff. For example, in the Nairobi road safety project, Uber and Waze data were made available at no cost through the DDP. Data that are financed through lending operations, such as the e-government interventions, are made available for the research team at no additional cost. For example, the DE JURE projects make use of the large amounts of data generated by e-government investments in partnership with the World Bank operational teams.

14.7.3 Metrics of Success

A successful DIME impact evaluation is one that improves counterpart data systems, influences policy decisions, and is fully reproducible.

What Clients Say About DIME

To objectively measure success, DIME conducted a carefully designed survey for 44 engagements in 22 countries (106 respondents) (Legovini et al., n.d.). Analysis of the survey responses—from 33 implementing agencies as well as World Bank project managers, known as Task Team Leaders—suggests that the technical support provided throughout the design and implementation processes has had positive effects on data systems (e.g., monitoring and evaluation capacity) and policy design.

With regards to data systems the surveys showed positive feedback:

- 100 percent of respondents from implementing agencies and 93 percent of World Bank TTLs documented instances where DIME contributed to monitoring and evaluation capacity.
- 82 percent of respondents from implementing agencies and 94 percent of World Bank TTLs documented how the baseline analysis contributed to policy design.

In terms of policy influence the surveys showed the following results:

- 68 percent of respondents from implementing agencies and 79 percent of World Bank TTLs reported that a proven treatment intervention was adopted by the government.
- 62 percent of the respondents from implementing agencies and 13 percent of the World Bank TTLs reported the engagement motivated scale-up and/or scale-down of the government intervention.

CHAPTER 14

- 71 percent of respondents from implementing agencies and 52 percent of World Bank TTLs reported that the engagement had a positive spillover effect on other projects as well.
- More broadly, 89 percent of respondents from implementing agencies and 85 percent of World Bank TTLs thought the engagement helped rationalize the design process of the relevant policy, and 94 percent of all respondents thought the engagement with DIME added value to their units.

Reproducible Data Projects

Since 2018, DIME has required that all working papers pass a computational reproducibility check before they are published; DIME Analytics has to be able to reproduce the exact results from the paper using the data and code provided.

Reproducibility Skels

Institutionalizing this requirement has led to big gains. In 2018, only 17 percent of working papers met the computational reproducibility standard, and half of the papers required significant revisions to achieve it. In contrast, by 2019, nearly two-thirds of DIME working papers met the reproducibility standard and less than ten percent required significant revisions. This increase reflects both significant efforts by DIME Analytics to identify reproducibility challenges and offer targeted trainings and tools as well as a significant mindset shift for research teams.

Currently, DIME is well above the norm in the field. An analysis of 203 economics papers published in top journals in 2016 showed that less than one in seven provided all data and code needed to assess computational reproducibility (Galiani, Gertler and Romero, 2017). More recently, at the American Economic Review, only two out of five accepted papers passed the computational reproducibility check on first pass (Vilhuber, 2019).

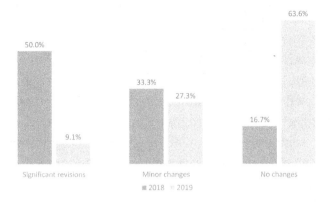

Figure 14.6: DIME computational reproducibility check results

14.8 Concluding Remarks

DIME has worked with client countries for the past fifteen years to strengthen their capacity for evidence-informed policy decisions. The DIME model is to support governments throughout policy design and implementation processes and invest heavily in the production of research-led data sets that can be applied to understanding the economic problems governments are trying to address. By striking a delicate balance between generating high-quality evidence and remaining responsive to policy processes on the ground, DIME has been able to build trust relationships with government clients. By helping governments build capacity for data and evidence-intensive policymaking, DIME secured broad access to administrative data and the opportunity to improve its quality.

CHAPTER 14

About the Authors

Arianna Legovini heads the Development Impact Evaluation (DIME) Department of the World Bank. She established this group in 2009 based on a model of collaboration between research and operations to optimize project design, secure higher returns to development investments, and empower governments to generate contextually relevant evidence to guide their policymaking process. She successfully aligned US$200 million in donor and government client financing to support a systematic approach to data analytics and causal evidence across a large program of World Bank and other development banks operations. She now presides over a team of 186 people conducting research in sixty countries across all sectors, working with 200 agencies, and shaping US$20 billion in development finance. She started similar groups with the Inter-American Development Bank and the Africa region of the World Bank. She provides advisory services to the thirty largest multilateral and bilateral development agencies in the world.

Maria Ruth Jones is a Survey Specialist in DIME. Maria co-founded and now leads DIME Analytics, which is an initiative to support transparent, high-quality, and reproducible research at DIME. She also works on impact evaluations in agriculture and transport; current research projects focus on the impacts of large-scale, rural infrastructure projects in Rwanda. Maria joined the World Bank in 2009. Previous roles at DIME include coordination of the Global Agriculture and Food Security Program impact evaluation portfolio (2012–16) and a program of impact evaluations with the government of Malawi (2009–11). Maria has an MA in international relations / development economics from the Johns Hopkins School of Advanced International Studies, and a BA in economics and Spanish from Amherst College.

References in Chapter 14

Aiken, Emily, Guadalupe Bedoya, Aidan Coville, and Joshua Blumenstock. 2020. "Targeting development aid with machine learning and mobile phone data." Unpublished manuscript. http://jblumenstock.com/files/papers/jblumenstock_ultra-poor.pdf (accessed 2020-10-05).

Ash, Elliott, Daniel Chen, Raul Delgado, Eduardo Fierro, and Shasha Lin. 2018. "Learning policy levers: Toward automated policy analysis using judicial corpora." Unpublished manuscript. https://users.nber.org/~dlchen/papers/Learning_Policy_Levers.pdf (accessed 2020-10-05).

Ash, Elliott, Sam Asher, Sandip Bhupaitiraju, Daniel L Chen, Paul Novosad, Arianna Ornaghi, and Bilal Siddiqi. 2019. "Algorithmic justice for development: Using machine learning to identify and mitigate bias in Indian courts." https://users.nber.org/~dlchen/papers/Implicit_Bias_in_the_Indian_Judiciary_slides.pdf (accessed 2020-12-07).

Babic, Boris, Daniel L Chen, Theodoros Evgeniou, and Anne-Laure Fayard. 2020. "A better way to onboard AI." *Harvard Business Review*, July-August. https://hbr.org/2020/07/a-better-way-to-onboard-ai.

Bedoya, Guadalupe, Jishnu Das, and Amy Dolinger. n.d.. "Randomized Regulation: The impact of minimum quality standards on health markets." https://www.aeaweb.org/conference/2020/preliminary/1846 (accessed 2020-12-07).

Chen, Daniel L. 2015. "Can markets stimulate rights? On the alienability of legal claims." *The RAND Journal of Economics*, 46(1): 23–65. https://doi.org/10.1111/1756-2171.12076.

Dupriez, Olivier, Diana Marcela Sanchez Castro, and Matthew Welch. 2019. "Quick Reference Guide for Data Archivists — Guide for Data Archivists documentation." https://guide-for-data-archivists.readthedocs.io/ (accessed 2020-12-15).

Galiani, Sebastian, Paul Gertler, and Mauricio Romero. 2017. "Incentives for replication in economics." National Bureau of Economic Research, Inc. Working paper 23576. https://doi.org/10.3386/w23576.

Galletta, Sergio, Elliot Ash, and Daniel L Chen. 2019. "Causal effects of judicial sentiment: Methods and application to U.S. circuit courts." *SSRN*. https://dx.doi.org/10.2139/ssrn.3415393.

International Finance Corporation. 2011. "Healthy partnerships: how governments can engage the private sector to improve health in Africa." World Bank. https://hdl.handle.net/10986/2304.

Jones, Maria, and Florence Kondylis. 2018. "Does feedback matter? Evidence from agricultural services." *Journal of Development Economics*, 131(C): 28–41. https://doi.org/10.1016/j.jdeveco.2017.10.

Jones, Maria, Florence Kondylis, John Loeser, and Jeremy Magruder. 2019. "Factor market failures and the adoption of irrigation in Rwanda." World Bank Policy Research Working Paper WPS9092. http://documents.worldbank.org/curated/en/496531576687282363/Factor-Market-Failures-and-the-Adoption-of-Irrigation-in-R wanda.

Kondylis, Florence, and Mattea Stein. 2019. "The speed of justice." World Bank Policy Research Working Paper WPS8372. http://documents.worldbank.org/curated/en/455021521720861143/The-speed-of-justice (accessed 2020-10-05).

Legovini, Arianna, Guadalupe Bedoya, Özsel Beleli, and Chloë Fernandez. n.d.. "DIME model for informing policy decisions: Portfolio results and case studies." Manuscriptavailableonrequest.

Longo, Daniel R, John E Hewett, Bin Ge, and Shari Schubert. 2006. "The long road to patient safety. A status report on patient safety systems." *Missouri Medicine*, 103(5): 545–552. https://doi.org/PMID:17133761.

Milusheva, Sveta, Robert Marty, Guadalupe Bedoya, Elizabeth Resor, Sarah Williams, and Arianna Legovini. 2020. "Can crowdsourcing create the missing crash data?" 305–306. ACM. https://doi.org/10.1145/3378393.3402264.

Vilhuber, Lars. 2019. "Panel 3: Practical steps to credibility and transparency in research: who should do what?" https://www.worldbank.org/en/events/2019/09/10/transparency-reproducibility-credibility.

Wachter, Robert M. 2010. "Patient safety at ten: Unmistakable progress, troubling gaps." *Health Affairs*, , (29): 165–73. https://doi.org/10.1377/hlthaff.2009.0785.

World Bank Group. 2020*a*. "Data and Evidence for Justice Reform (DE JURE)." http://pubdocs.worldbank.org/en/923891592406548876/DE-JURE-Brief.pdf (accessed 2020-12-15).

World Bank Group. 2020*b*. "Development Research in Practice: The DIME Analytics Data Handbook." https://worldbank.github.io/dime-data-handbook/ (accessed 2020-12-15).

World Bank Group. 2020*c*. "Rwanda: Program Brief." http://pubdocs.worldbank.org/en/703511592406882534/Rwanda-Program-Brief.pdf (accessed 2020-12-15).

World Bank Group. n.d.*a*. "DIME Standards, Pillar 4." https://github.com/worldbank/dime-standards (accessed 2020-12-15).

World Bank Group. n.d.*b*. "Microdata Library Terms of Use." https://microdata.worldbank.org/index.php/terms-of-use (accessed 2020-12-15).

World Bank Group. n.d.*c*. "Policy & Procedure Framework." https://policies.worldbank.org/en/policies/all/ppfdetail (accessed 2020-12-15).

World Health Organization Regional Office for Africa. 2014. "Guide for developing national patient safety policy and strategic plan." World Health Organization Technical documents 9789290232070. https://hdl.handle.net/10665/148352.

CHAPTER 15

The Use of Administrative Data at the International Monetary Fund

Era Dabla-Norris (International Monetary Fund)

Federico J. Díez (International Monetary Fund)

Romain Duval (International Monetary Fund)

15.1 Summary

This chapter describes the use of administrative data at the International Monetary Fund (IMF, the Fund) in the context of its three main operations: macroeconomic surveillance and research, lending to member countries, and technical assistance to build capacity in policymaking in member countries. The chapter notes how the Fund has a long-standing tradition of using administrative data in some activities, but the systematic use for monitoring economic developments in member countries and research is still in its infancy. This is partly because the use of administrative data for macroeconomic analysis remains relatively recent, is resource-intensive, and often comes with

Copyright © International Monetary Fund.
Cite as: Dabla-Norris, Era, Federico J. Díez, and Romain Duval. "The Use of Administrative Data at the International Monetary Fund." In: Cole, Shawn, Iqbal Dhaliwal, Anja Sautmann, and Lars Vilhuber (eds.), *Handbook on Using Administrative Data for Research and Evidence-based Policy*. Cambridge, MA: Abdul Latif Jameel Poverty Action Lab. 2020.

strings attached. Several examples of interactions with government authorities (the ultimate providers of administrative data) in the context of specific projects are provided; these show wide variation in the degree of collaboration with national authorities, as well as in the procedures and (legal and technical) constraints in accessing and using the data. These country examples also highlight the challenges and opportunities, some of them unique to the institution, for IMF staff to obtain and work with such data. On the legal front, for example, while traditional judicial enforcement mechanisms for data use agreements are not applicable, since the IMF as an international organization is immune from the judicial process, potential partners that provide administrative data are comforted by other features of the IMF's immunities that provide strong protections to confidential information—and staff can and do negotiate one-off data access agreements with national authorities. The IMF's specificities also show in how it can ensure safe projects, people, settings, data, and outputs. For example, staff can leverage the institution's strong credibility, infrastructure, and procedures along these safe dimensions, but there is still wide variation in practices depending on individual member countries' requirements, and overall success in accessing and using administrative data is easier to achieve in a technical assistance context where demand for IMF analysis and research originates from the source country itself. In the future, through its bilateral engagement with its 189 member countries, participation in international data initiatives, and partnerships with universities and research networks, the IMF has the potential to gradually enhance the comparability, access, and use of (selected) administrative data produced by national authorities.

15.2 Introduction

15.2.1 Motivation and Background

The IMF, as an international organization, works closely with the country authorities of its membership. These include tax administrations, central banks, and financial supervisory authorities that generate administrative data of immense value. As such, the Fund has potential access to a wealth of administrative data through its engagement with 189 member countries.[1] However, overcoming the financial, institutional, and technical hurdles to access administrative data remains a key challenge to unlocking the potential for research purposes. Building capacity to utilize administrative data at the IMF and within member countries would enable the IMF to better answer a series of long-standing research questions in macroeconomic, financial, and structural arenas.

The IMF's interactions with members involve three main activities. First, the IMF conducts macroeconomic surveillance, which entails monitoring of economic and financial developments in each member country and the provision of policy advice. Second, the IMF provides financing to members with balance of payments problems. Finally, the IMF provides technical assistance and capacity development programs in its areas of expertise.[2] In addition, the Fund's work in economic research and statistics supports all three of these activities. Each of these operations can potentially lead to IMF staff accessing and working with administrative data owned by a national government. As such, the Fund has a long-standing tradition in the use of administrative data that is tightly linked to its core functions. However, the intensity with which this kind of data are used varies significantly across different lines of Fund operations.

The use of administrative data is most common in the case of technical assistance requested by agencies or instrumentalities within member countries. For example, when analyzing the impact of tax reforms or weaknesses in existing tax systems, social programs, or banking sector reforms, Fund staff are likely to have access to confidential administra-

---

[1] The Fund has several frameworks in place regarding data. Under Article VIII, Section 5 of its articles of agreement, certain data must be provided to the Fund. Under the Data Standards Initiatives, members voluntarily subscribe to certain standards for data publication. This chapter refers solely to data that are voluntarily provided to the Fund and that fall outside of these other frameworks.

[2] While the surveillance and policy recommendations are normally conducted annually and for every member country, IMF financing and technical assistance are demand-driven and can only be initiated at the request of country authorities.

tive data (e.g., tax records for specific taxes, government spending programs, or credit registry and bank loan-level data) to assess the impact of the policies being evaluated. Technical assistance missions on statistics often work with authorities to develop the use of granular administrative data alongside or in place of survey data (e.g., the use of tax data to estimate GDP by production as described in Rivas and Crowley, 2018); these data can then be used by IMF staff for policy evaluation. Similarly, in the context of provision of IMF financing, country authorities often make confidential administrative data available to Fund staff to better assess program performance and compliance with conditionality linked to IMF financing or to assess and evaluate the impact of policies that are intended to affect certain groups or activities.

There is growing recognition within the IMF that the systematic use of administrative data could also be beneficial for macroeconomic surveillance and research, a key pillar of its activities. This could allow for quicker and better-targeted policy responses to changes in business conditions and more granular assessment of member country policies. For example, using administrative data would enable IMF staff to better assess the implications for consumption and income distribution of alternative tax policy recommendations in a country.

The systematic use of administrative data, however, is less common in the context of IMF surveillance and research than for the Fund's two other main activities. One reason is that the use of micro-administrative data for macroeconomic analysis (and surveillance) has only become a routinely used tool within the last ten years, even in academia. Another reason is that utilizing administrative data is resource-intensive both in terms of the direct financial costs involved and staff time required to access and process the data. Further, even with interest from the Fund, national authorities can be unwilling to share the data for surveillance and research purposes, as the benefits to them are not always clear-cut. In these instances, and lacking any systematic institutional protocols, obtaining data rests on personal efforts by IMF staff to approach and potentially partner with national authorities.[3] Finally, in many instances, legal constraints and

---

[3]Moreover, it can be particularly challenging to develop and maintain longer-term

confidentiality concerns pose challenges to accessibility. For example, countries often require that IMF staff be physically present to access the data or grant access indirectly through collaboration with a local staffer.

15.2.2 Data Use Examples

This section provides concrete examples where Fund staff has used administrative data for policy and surveillance work that have broader relevance for the research community, highlighting the procedures followed for securing data access from authorities, the challenges faced by staff, and the outputs from the projects.

Marrying Research and Technical Assistance: the Case of Peru

Peru's electronic invoicing (e-invoicing) tax reform study offers an interesting example of how policy questions raised in the context of IMF's technical assistance activities, and relationships built with country authorities in the process, were leveraged to develop research projects using administrative data. The Peruvian government faced challenges with value-added tax (VAT) compliance as identified by the IMF's Revenue Administration's Gap Analysis Program (RA-GAP) Assessment.[4]

The 2015 RA-GAP analysis for Peru had highlighted weaknesses in VAT collections and pointed to the recent introduction of electronic invoicing (e-invoicing) as a potential tool for increasing revenue collections. The VAT is particularly susceptible to compliance risks arising from

---

personal relationships with national authorities since IMF staff tend to rotate jobs within the Fund.

[4]The RA-GAP assessment provides a systematic evaluation of the revenue administration's operations for the VAT, assessing which group of taxpayers are contributing to tax gaps—the difference between potential and actual revenue collections—and identifies potential causes and sectoral gaps (Hutton, 2017). The assessment itself requires detailed tax return records, tax payment and refund records, and customs data. This information is combined with tax registration information and detailed National Accounts data and input-output or source-use tables. The tax authority or the ministry of finance in the country shares the confidential administrative data with an IMF team electronically during a field visit, but in an anonymized manner.

overclaiming of input tax credits by submission of false or altered invoices. By digitalizing transaction data, the presumption was that e-invoicing should allow for greater oversight and review of tax refund applications by the firm and its suppliers, increasing the probability of evasion detection and thereby encouraging greater voluntary compliance. A key question of interest to the Peruvian tax authority (SUNAT) was whether the e-invoicing reform had achieved its intended objectives and for which types of firms compliance had improved the most. From the IMF's perspective, this question was of broader relevance as a number of emerging market and developing economies have introduced e-invoicing in recent years, but there were few studies assessing its efficacy.

The electronic transmission of invoice information in Peru required a substantial overhaul of tax administration and taxpayer IT capabilities. Until 2014, the SUNAT promoted voluntary use of e-invoices, relying primarily on paper invoices. From 2015 onwards, a schedule for the mandatory incorporation of firms into the e-invoicing system was introduced: the first reform waves focused on larger firms and priority industries, while smaller firms were given more time to comply. This sequential introduction of the reform provided a useful empirical identification strategy. Moreover, assignment of firms to each group was based on a revenue threshold and other firm characteristics, which could allow for assessing the heterogenous reform effects. However, the reform evaluation itself fell outside the purview of the IMF's standard technical assistance activities and required additional funding.

Around this time, the Bill & Melinda Gates Foundation had entered into a partnership with the IMF's Fiscal Affairs Department to advance research and practice on using digital advances to improve public finance in emerging market and developing economies. Financial support was provided by the foundation to advance this agenda within the Fund and showcase this more broadly to the Fund's membership. The IMF research team outlined a proposal to use these funds to evaluate the impact of e-invoicing reform in Peru, exploiting the quasi-experimental variation in the reform rollout. The reform design allowed a precise comparison of firms that were already required to digitalize against similar ones that had yet to do so. In addition to specific findings for Peru, the project aimed to shed light on the implementation of digital technologies for tax administrations in emerging market and developing economies more broadly. The team's proposal identified how the study could provide insights for IMF technical assistance on the efficacy of e-invoicing mechanisms and their interaction with other tax compliance tools, which could feed into the design of e-invoicing rollouts by other countries. The project was approved by an internal IMF committee and funding was provided for travel by the research team to organize joint workshops and conferences with the tax authority.

To evaluate the reform, the IMF team needed to draw from the comprehensive data set of all firms' monthly tax reports in Peru. Due to the sensitive nature of taxpayer data, it was clear at the outset that the team would not have direct access to the data, and the project itself would require buy-in from SUNAT. The IMF's strong relationship with SUNAT, thanks to ongoing provision of technical assistance, led not only to the endorsement of the study by the tax authority but also a commitment by SUNAT on a close collaboration to advance the empirical analysis.

The IMF team agreed with SUNAT to design the analysis and work remotely. The size and confidential nature of the data called for an innovative collaboration: the IMF put together a team of experts in different fields and from the Inter-American Development Bank (IDB) and different departments within the IDB who had used similar data to discuss the broader policy questions and work strategy. The database remained on servers in Peru while the work was conducted across countries via remote communication. The IMF team relied on remote processing and sent scripts to a staff member designated by SUNAT as the *point-person* within the tax authority. This point-person had some in-house skills to run the scripts, but this was complemented by a concerted effort from the IMF research team to provide coaching and guidance on econometric packages. To facilitate the process, the IMF team constructed mock databases to test and troubleshoot the scripts.

It was also clear from the outset that exclusively remote working would not suffice to advance the project. Inevitably, the project would require on-site work to refine the analysis and resolve potential hurdles encountered. As a result, the funding request has explicitly budgeted several short visits to Peru for fieldwork and discussions with counterparts in the tax authority. The engagement with SUNAT was further strengthened through workshops and joint seminars to discuss initial findings, share know-how on working with administrative data, and solicit inputs from various stakeholders, which culminated in a co-authored IMF working paper with the authorities (Bellon et al., 2019). The understanding with SUNAT was that the paper would be subsequently revised by the IMF team for journal publication (as of this writing, the *Journal of Public Economics* requested the IMF to revise and resubmit the paper).

SUNAT found the interaction to be useful for presenting findings to ministerial level decision-makers as well as highlighting the value of the research conducted by the tax administration. Given the success of the first-round engagement, SUNAT was eager to further exploit the value of administrative data for research. The initial capacity building investment by IMF has led to repeated engagements and to the Peruvian tax administration to be more open to outside researchers also utilizing the tax administration's data, using similar data sharing and use protocols as for the IMF team. An ongoing follow-up project uses transaction-level data to examine and quantify spillovers in technology adoption by different types of firms (Holtsmark and Misch, 2020).

Enhancing Surveillance: The Case of Vietnam

Ongoing projects with the General Statistics Office (GSO) of Vietnam are examples of using administrative data to inform policy in the context of IMF's surveillance activities and fostering buy-in from the data provider for continued engagement. Census data and other labor and household surveys are confidential in Vietnam and not easily made accessible to researchers or even IMF staff. The IMF country team on Vietnam wanted to examine corporate vulnerabilities arising from the COVID-19 pandemic, but obtaining access to the firm census data was not straightforward.

As a first step, the contours of the project were explicitly outlined in a letter to the highest level of the GSO, and assurances provided that data would only be used for their intended purpose. It was understood that the Washington D.C.-based IMF team would not have direct access to the census data and would need to work remotely with a designated point-person in the GSO. One challenge was that the GSO office hosting the census data was not well-versed in different statistical packages, particularly Stata. The IMF team would have to hire someone locally to provide on-site training on Stata before the work could begin, but funding for this type of research activity is not readily available in the IMF. After much internal deliberation, a small pot of discretionary funds was found. This was used by the IMF team to hire a Vietnamese university professor known to GSO staff. The professor provided on-site training and served as facilitator between the two teams, helping with the running of scripts prepared by the IMF team.

The GSO team initially shared a 10 percent anonymized sample from the firm census that served as the basis for developing the scripts and agreed to share detailed summary statistics and moments of the data requested by the IMF. The IMF team worked closely with the GSO, sharing scripts, receiving summary tables and statistics, and exchanging views on the results.[5] This initial engagement culminated in a policy note that was jointly co-authored with staff from the GSO and widely shared within the Vietnamese government, including at the ministerial level. The publicity garnered by the project and the close working relationship fostered trust and resulted in buy-in from the GSO on continued future engagement.[6] The IMF team and the GSO are in the pro-

---

[5] In other cases, access to the administrative data occurred without IMF staff working along with authorities on a joint project. For instance, Fund researchers have utilized both the confidential social security and economic census data from Mexico. For the economic census data, IMF researchers had access to the underlying confidential survey data, but this required travel to Mexico to access the data. Brazil, Canada, Colombia, Denmark, France, Luxembourg, Slovakia, and South Africa are examples of other countries where the IMF has had access to administrative data for research purposes.

[6] An ongoing project with the Norwegian authorities is another example of using administrative data for joint research to inform policy in the context of IMF's surveillance activities. Using novel administrative data covering the universe of registered electric cars combined with detailed information of the owners, the project with the

cess of organizing seminars to more widely disseminate the results of their joint work in Vietnam and have outlined a series of future projects that will shed light on policy questions of relevance to the Vietnamese government.

15.3 Legal Framework

Some of the main challenges to accessing administrative data include understanding the legal frameworks regarding the usage (and potentially transfer) of the data and overcoming any associated confidentiality issues. IMF staff face most of the constraints that other users of administrative data must overcome, as well as several issues unique to the IMF.

As mentioned above, IMF staff working on technical assistance projects and IMF-supported programs in member countries often require administrative data to perform the necessary analyses. In these instances, the country usually has a straightforward process for making the data available to the IMF. Often, the IMF's existing confidentiality framework—grounded in the articles of agreement by which all members agree to abide—is sufficient to address any domestic legal requirements on sharing information. However, as in the case of engagement with the statistical authority in Vietnam, the Fund may also agree that the data will be used only for stated purposes and not for any other research activities.

In some cases, however, the IMF may also wish to perform follow-up research utilizing the data that are outside of the scope of the original activities, for instance, to generalize lessons learned in one country across other countries. These projects require reaching additional agreements with the country authorities. The terms and sophistication of these agreements, as well as the authorities' willingness for further engagement, vary significantly across contexts.

A legal issue unique to the IMF and other similar organizations (such as the World Bank) is its status as an international organization with

Norwegian authorities analyzes the environmental effects, economic costs, and distributional consequences of electric cars (Holtsmark and Misch, 2020).

immunity from judicial process. All members of the IMF have committed to granting this immunity by signing the IMF's articles of agreement and enacting domestic laws that give effect to the privileges and immunities set forth in the IMF's articles of agreement.[7] In practice, because the IMF's immunities, traditional judicial enforcement mechanisms are not applicable for data use agreements with the IMF. Fund staff do not have the authority to waive the IMF's immunities in any agreement with a member or domestic agency to use its administrative data. While this unique characteristic may initially lead to reluctance on the part of potential partners to provide data to the IMF for research purposes, countries are usually comforted by the IMF's other immunities that provide strong protections to confidential information. For example, pursuant to the immunities of the Fund under Article IX of the Fund's articles of agreement, information and documents provided by members (or any other party) to the Fund form part of the Fund's archives, which are inviolable. "Inviolability" has been applied to mean that all non-public information or documents generated within or received by the Fund from members or other parties are protected by the Fund's immunities and would only be disclosed (including in response to a subpoena) with the approval of that member or other party and in accordance with the Fund's policies.

In addition to the data accessed through circumstances unique to the IMF, such as technical assistance programs, the IMF also accesses administrative data for research purposes through existing mechanisms of data access or one-off agreements between the IMF and individual countries. In the Peru and Vietnam cases described above in section 15.2.2, data access rested on one-off agreements that were subsequently extended to cover multiple projects. With the Mexican statistical agency (INEGI), IMF researchers can use existing access mechanisms that INEGI has established for academic and non-academic institutions to work with data on-site. In the framework of this agreement, researchers can establish individual bilateral arrangements with INEGI

---

[7] In the United States, Section 11 of the Bretton Woods Agreements Act (public Law 171-79th Congress, 59 Statutes at Large, page 512 et seq., approved July 3, 1945, 22 U.S.C. Section 286h), gives full force and effect to the privileges and immunities of the IMF set out in its articles of agreement.

by completing a form listing the project details and the supervisor who has approved the project.

15.4 Making Data Usable

While most countries generate increasingly rich administrative data, making them readily available is challenging for various reasons. Since administrative data already exist and are usually collected on a regular or pre-set frequency, government agencies do not incur additional costs for data collection. However, country authorities may not have the proficiency and data management expertise to clean, anonymize, and organize the data into the format required for analysis. Often the issue stems from a lack of financial resources to build the technical capacity as seen in the Vietnam case. There is also the concern that confidential data could be de-anonymized and released into the public domain. Secondary disclosure (identification via deduction, particularly in concentrated markets) is also a concerning issue.

In some instances, the process of making data accessible is made easier by providing technical assistance on how to extract and prepare the data as in the case for the VAT revenue gap assessment. This revenue gap assessment itself is conducted by experts from the IMF and other international institutions working closely with a local team familiar with tax administration operations, tax design and policy, and statistical data. The first step in the technical assistance program is to identify available data and assess the quality, including by ensuring that data are accurately classified.[8] The simple task of reviewing the quality and scope of available tax record data can help tax administrations make the data more usable for their own analysis and in some instances, make data more research usable. As a second step, more harmonized tools and templates are used to extract the information required to conduct the tax gap analysis.

---

[8]There is a key initial and ongoing role here for national statistical agency staff familiar with industry/product coding to ensure that data are accurately classified and routinely reviewed to avoid mismatches and double counting.

In some cases where data are made accessible, the IMF provides technical assistance and training on data cleaning, for example, by employing an in-house developed algorithm. In other cases, IMF staff can spend considerable time cleaning and processing the data, particularly in instances where there is a lack of documentation, or the data already had been prepared for other purposes. This can be challenging given the relatively short time horizons for many IMF projects, which results in IMF staff often not having time to invest in data sets requiring significant cleaning and manipulation before becoming operative.

The IMF is usually interested in conducting cross-country analysis in order to have broad-based evidence on which to base the recommendations provided to its members. However, using administrative data on a cross-country basis is extremely challenging, since countries collect data in different formats and with different measures of outcomes, resulting in the IMF not using administrative data for these purposes. These issues transcend any individual country's data collection methods and can only be (fully) addressed through international standards for data classification and comparability. One possible long-term path to addressing this issue would be to follow the approach the IMF has taken with its balance of payments manual that provides guidance on how to compile balance of payments and related data. A similar approach toward how countries collect, document, and disseminate administrative data would be a potential path forward in improving the use of administrative data.

The IMF together with the Financial Stability Board (FSB) in collaboration with the Inter-Agency Group on Economic and Financial Statistics (IAG) have been leading the work on the G20 Data Gaps Initiative (DGI) since 2009. A second phase of the DGI (DGI-2), which started in 2015, sets more specific objectives for G20 economies to compile and disseminate minimum common data sets. While assisting countries in implementing DGI-2 recommendations, the IMF has been underscoring the importance of administrative data.

In recent years, the IMF has been entering into partnerships with universities and research networks to expand the availability of cross-country, comparable data— which can be used for policy-relevant analysis—for countries in specific regions. For instance, firm-level data for countries in Asia are not readily available for researchers and policymakers. This has resulted in a partnership with the Productivity Research Network (PRN) at the National University of Singapore. Through this collaboration PRN will allow IMF staff to access the PRN's firm-level data set, based on country-level industrial censuses, for all available countries, and to access the underlying scripts. In exchange, the IMF will support the expansion of country coverage by reaching out to relevant country authorities and statistical agencies, encouraging them under their privacy policy to work with PRN in the data collection exercise. The PRN will be allowed to mention the IMF as a partner along with other international financial institutions involved in the project, and the IMF will be at liberty to publish analytical pieces based on data compiled by PRN, along with the adequate attribution and referencing of data sources, without prior consent. Making use of such collaborations to access harmonized administrative data (and not just survey-based data) will be the next frontier.

15.5 Protection of Sensitive and Personal Data: The Five Safes Framework

15.5.1 Safe Projects

As noted in section 15.3, one of the common ways that the IMF gets access to administrative data is through providing technical assistance. As these activities are undertaken at the request of agencies or instrumentalities within member countries, they are by definition considered safe projects by the member country.

Performing program evaluations can be more challenging. Projects that can highlight potential issues and weaknesses with member countries are often sensitive, requiring buy-in from bureaucratic and political leadership in member countries. Given the ad hoc nature of proposing these research programs, each member country has different circumstances and criteria for evaluating research proposals. The IMF is generally most successful when proposing research projects on issues that the member nation wants to address. In the Peru example, the tax administration was interested in evaluating the effectiveness of their revenue mobilization program. When the IMF proposed a research project that addressed the specific question, it was easy for IMF staff to find buy-in at the tax administration for the project. In the Vietnam experience, the research project was undertaken in collaboration with the country authorities in the context of the IMF surveillance activities. It was considered *safe* as the project was part of IMF country engagement.

Given the prerequisites of having member nations sign-on to research projects and the lack of a systematic mechanism for having them evaluate prospective projects, it is incumbent on the IMF staff to take the first step on conveying the merits of projects to countries. The reliance on interpersonal relations and existing engagements with government officials to initiate projects also means that getting the projects off the ground rests on personal initiative. The difficulty in identifying partners and securing buy-in can also limit the topics and types of projects that IMF researchers attempt to pursue. In an effort to address these issues, there have been attempts at cataloging the institutional history with different partners to identify those that are willing to share data for research purposes.

15.5.2 Safe People

From the perspective of member countries, international organizations such as the IMF are perceived as *safe*, although the determination of what type of staff should be given access to confidential data and for what purposes is heavily dependent on the specific member country. While IMF staff are always subject to general IMF policies on the protection of confidential information, when working on data through technical assistance programs or research projects, IMF researchers may agree to additional confidentiality. In some instances, tax authorities might agree to provide detailed records, including data at the enterprise level, only to designated IMF staff and their managers.

Internally, the IMF maintains confidentiality requirements upon its staff to ensure that it maintains its reputation as a trusted advisor. Disciplinary measures that apply in case of breaches of security are clarified in internal protocols. Significant efforts are made to educate IMF staff around issues of data confidentiality, including IMF staff receiving training in information security and ethics as part of their general employee training. Related to this, the IMF also maintains an intranet for researchers that outlines data sets that are accessible to internal researchers and the requirements for access to each data set.

The IMF occasionally brings in outside researchers for projects on a contractual basis. When outside researchers are contracting with the IMF, they are covered under the same confidentiality understandings, rules, and procedures that IMF staff operate.

15.5.3 Safe Settings

Depending on each individual member country and specific project, requirements for accessing and storing data can vary. The access mechanisms span a range of options from traveling to a secure facility in the member country to being allowed to download the data via a secure connection to IMF servers. In the case of some technical assistance missions, access to the data can be restricted to those given explicit authorization by the data authorities. The data can also be encrypted in such a way that even the IT personnel who service the server cannot see the data on it.

In the instances where the IMF is authorized to store the data, the data are placed on a secure server with access-controlled folders. IMF IT staff place access controls on the server to restrict data access to staff with proper approval. The IMF maintains this infrastructure for many of its technical assistance missions, which require that relevant staff and researchers have ongoing regular access to data from the member country. Staff and researchers have access to a wide range of IT resources and statistical software (SAS, Stata, Python, and R, among others) to choose from for their analysis. Data providers are consulted on the software available to share common platforms for the analysis.

15.5.4 Safe Data

As with the other aspects of the five safes framework, the determination of what constitutes safe data is up to the member country for each project in which the IMF is involved. In some cases, the data can be highly sensitive. This is particularly the case for individual tax records, data on recipients of specific government spending programs, or bank loans to individual firms and households. More generally, any data on individual reporting units or specific transactions/instruments, which in most cases allow the identification of individual entities, are therefore considered confidential. In these cases, governments themselves often make modifications to the raw data before sharing with the IMF, with links that could be used to identify individuals or other entities typically stripped for security reasons.

To encourage the sharing of sensitive information and documents, IMF staff share the institution's data protocols that describe procedures aimed at preventing unauthorized access to, and disclosure of, sensitive information and documents obtained through the country engagement.

In some instances, the same data provider will have different access requirements based on different types of data. For example, in Brazil and Mexico, accessing firm-level data requires that researchers travel to a data center, while more aggregated data can be downloaded instead. Usually, staff directly involved in a given project will have access to the same data, but access to these data will be restricted to them and their managers. In contrast, other Fund staff would only see aggregated data.

15.5.5 Safe Outputs

The decision on what outputs are acceptable is mostly at the discretion of the member country. While the existence of most technical assistance missions is public information, whether a country makes its diagnostic public is at its own discretion, even if it does not involve the use of administrative data. Under IMF policy (International Monetary

Fund, 2013), the recipient of technical assistance makes the decision of whether they would like to make the final advice public. Government agencies and instrumentalities are typically reluctant to make public the state of their government finances, banking system, or health public information. At the same time, the IMF encourages the wider dissemination and publication of technical assistance information.

In many cases, countries require that IMF researchers follow standard statistical disclosure precautions such as mandating a minimum number of observations when countries allow results to be published. Agencies in different countries also have varying levels of familiarity with research and publications, which can require that IMF staff spend additional effort in detailing the different instances of the publication process and preparing the output for their approval. In agencies where the supervisors and data analysts are also familiar with academic research, this process tends to be easier.

15.6 Sustainability and Continued Success

Any Fund project involving the use of administrative data is assessed in terms of its costs and its performance. In regard to the former, much of the cost involved in generating and sharing (or eventually transferring) administrative data to the IMF is borne by the member country. In low- and middle-income countries, it is often the case that the agencies that might provide data suffer from a lack of financial resources to hire sufficient data staff. From the IMF's standpoint, the main costs usually are in terms of staff's time and traveling costs, whenever data access requires physical presence in the country. The direct financial costs for accessing administrative data, such as fees, are relatively minor, especially compared to those incurred by the IMF to purchase large firm-level data sets.

Regarding performance, the metrics used vary significantly with the nature of the project as each of the IMF's core activities (macroeconomic surveillance and research, lending, and technical assistance) entail different objectives. That said, the ultimate goal is to provide valuable (and in some cases, actionable) information to senior IMF and national authorities to help them develop appropriate policy recommendations and actions, respectively—advice that would not be as detailed if access to administrative data was lacking. Another metric of success is the instance of a given project leading to follow-up projects (as in the example of Peru and Vietnam). This indicates a confirmation by the authorities of the *modus operandi*: continued engagement speaks to success in creating deeper linkages with the data providers. Successful engagement in some countries could also be shown as an example that encourages other data providers to offer access to their data.

15.7 Concluding Remarks

The intensity and frequency with which administrative data are used at the IMF depends on whether these are used for technical assistance, lending-related purposes, or for macroeconomic surveillance and research. While the use of administrative data usage is common in the first two areas it is much less so in the latter. In the absence of institutional protocols and incentives, the use of such data for research purposes depends on staff initiative in approaching national authorities/data providers. There is an increasing recognition, however, of the benefits of using these kinds of data for Fund's surveillance and research leading to several successful engagements such as the ones described in this chapter. At the same time, the Fund's unique status as an international organization creates opportunities. In particular, in the future, through its bilateral engagement with its 189 member countries, participation in international data initiatives and partnerships with universities and research networks, the IMF has the potential to gradually enhance cross-country comparability, access, and use for (at least some) administrative data produced by national authorities for research purposes.

About the Authors

Era Dabla-Norris is the mission chief for Vietnam and division chief at the IMF's Asia-Pacific Department. Previously, she was a division chief at the IMF's Fiscal Affairs Department.

Federico J. Díez is an economist at the Structural Reforms Unit of the IMF's Research Department. Previously he was an economist at the Research Department of Federal Reserve Bank of Boston.

Romain Duval is the Head of the Structural Reforms Unit and an Advisor to the Chief Economist in the IMF Research Department. Previously he was the Division Chief for Regional Studies of the IMF Asia-Pacific Department and, prior to joining the Fund, the Division Chief for Structural Surveillance at the OECD Economics Department.

Disclaimer

The views expressed in this paper are those of the author(s) and do not necessarily represent the views of the IMF, its Executive Board, or IMF management.

References in Chapter 15

Bellon, M., J. Chang, E. Dabla-Norris, S. Khalid, F. Lima, E. Rojas, and P. Villena. 2019. "Digitalization to Improve Tax Compliance: Evidence from VAT e-Invoicing in Peru." International Monetary Fund Working Paper 19/231. https://www.imf.org/en/Publications/WP/Issues/2019/11/01/Digitalization-to-Improve-Tax-Compliance-Evidence-from-VAT-e-Invoicing-in-Peru-48672 (accessed 2020-10-05).

Holtsmark, B., and F. Misch. 2020. "Learning from the Global Leader: An Analysis of Electric Car Subsidies in Norway."

Hutton, Eric. 2017. "The Revenue Administration—Gap Analysis Program: Model and Methodology for Value-Added Tax Gap Estimation." International Monetary Fund Technical Notes and Manuals 17/04. https://www.imf.org/en/Publications/TNM/Issues/2017/04/07/The-Revenue-AdministrationGap-Analysis-Program-Model-and-Methodology-for-Value-Added-Tax-Gap-44715 (accessed 2020-10-05).

International Monetary Fund. 2013. "Staff Operational Guidelines on Dissemination of Technical Assistance Information." https://www.imf.org/external/np/pp/eng/2013/061013.pdf (accessed 2020-12-23).

Rivas, Lisbeth, and Joe Crowley. 2018. "Using Administrative Data to Enhance Policymaking in Developing Countries: Tax Data and the National Accounts." International Monetary Fund Working Paper 18/175. https://www.imf.org/en/Publications/WP/Issues/2018/08/02/Using-Administrative-Data-to-Enhance-Policymaking-in-Developing-Countries-Tax-Data-and-the-46054 (accessed 2020-10-05).

CHAPTER 16

Using Administrative Data to Improve Social Protection in Indonesia

Vivi Alatas (Asa Kreativita)

Farah Amalia (J-PAL Southeast Asia, University of Indonesia)

Abhijit Banerjee (Massachusetts Institute of Technology)

Benjamin A. Olken (Massachusetts Institute of Technology)

Rema Hanna (Harvard Kennedy School)

Sudarno Sumarto (SMERU Research Institute and National Team for the Acceleration of Poverty Reduction)

Putu Poppy Widyasari (J-PAL Southeast Asia, University of Indonesia)

16.1 Summary

This chapter describes a long-run engagement, conducted over more than a decade, between researchers and the Government of Indone-

Copyright © Vivi Alatas, Farah Amalia, Abhijit Banerjee, Benjamin A. Olken, Rema Hanna, Sudarno Sumarto, and Putu Poppy Widyasari.
Cite as: Alatas, Vivi, Farah Amalia, Abhijit Banerjee, Benjamin A. Olken, Rema Hanna, Sudarno Sumarto, and Putu Poppy Widyasari. "Using Administrative Data to Improve Social Protection in Indonesia." In: Cole, Shawn, Iqbal Dhaliwal, Anja Sautmann, and Lars Vilhuber (eds.), *Handbook on Using Administrative Data for Research and Evidence-based Policy*. Cambridge, MA: Abdul Latif Jameel Poverty Action Lab. 2020.

sia to use randomized evaluations combined with administrative data to understand and improve the delivery of social protection programs. Like many countries worldwide, Indonesia provides citizens with social protection programs to help combat extreme poverty and reduce inequality. These types of programs take many forms: from social safety net programs that provide cash or in-kind goods to poor households, to subsidized and/or contributory health and unemployment insurance programs, to active labor market programs providing wage subsidies or public employment placement services.

Social protection programs are rapidly being expanded throughout many low- and middle-income countries. In just the past decade, the number of low- and middle-income countries running conditional cash transfer programs, which condition benefits on households making human capital investments in their children, has more than doubled, with more than sixty low- and middle-income countries currently administering programs of this type (World Bank, 2018). There is reason to believe that programs will be expanded even further as countries continue to grow: for example, as countries become wealthier, a greater share of GDP usually goes to social transfer and insurance programs (Chetty and Looney, 2006).

Given the scope and importance of such government programs in the lives of citizens, it is imperative to understand how to ensure that these programs deliver on their intended goals. As Hanna and Karlan (2017) lay out, the details of social protection program design matter considerably in terms of the cost-effectiveness, scope, and reach of these programs and policies. For example, suppose a government aims to provide cash transfers to the poor. This sounds simple enough, but there are many questions and policy decisions that the government needs to take into account: How do we define who is poor? Once we have defined that criteria, how do we identify people and determine whether they match our criteria and are hence eligible? Then what is the best way to let people know that they are indeed eligible? How much money should we provide, and should we provide different amounts of money to different people? What should be the frequency and mechanism of the transfer? Should the transfer be conditioned on certain positive behaviors (e.g., vaccinating children, school attendance), and if so, what should these conditions be? How do we ensure that transfers are not lost to various forms of leakage? Getting the answers right is crucial—optimal targeting alone, for example, could improve the welfare gains of citizens from social assistance programs by as much as 57 percent (Alatas et al., 2019).

Well-designed randomized experiments can help provide governments with the answers to these questions and more to help them design programs that meet citizen needs.[1] There is, however, a key challenge: many studies use household survey data to measure outcomes. Household surveys have many advantages—they allow the researcher to ask questions on any topic of interest and to target a particular population. But they are by no means perfect. In-person household surveys are costly, particularly in middle- and higher-income countries and in remote locations. In remote areas, the cost of surveying can be upwards of US$70 per household, and costs are often even higher in high-income countries. While survey and evaluation costs are still a very small fraction compared to the level of funding and benefits that are distributed in social protection programs (and small relative to the potential losses from running programs ineffectively or incurring leakages), these costs can lead to small sample sizes and be a real deterrent to evaluating some programs.[2] Beyond cost, household surveys can be

---

[1] Some of the first social science experiments of social protection programs occurred in the US, such as the Negative Income Tax Experiments carried out in the late 1960s and early 1970s and the RAND health insurance experiment (Newhouse, 1993). Then, in 1997, a randomized experiment began to test the impact of Mexico's conditional cash transfer program, PROGRESA, providing a model for incorporating experimentation into government programs in low- and middle-income countries (for example, see Behrman and Todd, 1999; Gertler, 2004), which has subsequently been replicated in many countries around the world.

[2] For example, Banerjee et al. (2018) evaluated a new pilot program in conjunction with the Indonesian government designed to improve transparency in its social protection programs by mailing households a social protection card. The costs of multiple rounds of surveying to understand whether the pilot program had impacts and to test which variant would have the largest impacts was approximately US$750,000. The pilot showed that the program could increase the subsidy received by low-income households by 26 percent. As the program was subsequently scaled up and 14.38 million households received the program, this implied about a US$110 million increase in effective subsidy *per year*. In short, the evaluation costs were small relative to scope of the program and potential societal gains.

plagued by recall bias, measurement error, and Hawthorne effects.

This chapter details a long-standing collaboration between the Government of Indonesia and a team of researchers based both in Indonesia and abroad, which include the chapter's authors. The research team includes researchers from the Abdul Latif Jameel Poverty Action Lab (J-PAL) and its Jakarta-based regional office, J-PAL Southeast Asia (J-PAL SEA), as well as the National Team for the Acceleration of Poverty Reduction (TNP2K) and the World Bank. J-PAL is a global research center based at the Massachusetts Institute of Technology (MIT) that aims to reduce poverty by providing scientific evidence for policymaking and conducts randomized impact evaluations around the world. Rema Hanna and Benjamin Olken are the scientific directors of J-PAL SEA and Abhijit Banerjee and Benjamin Olken are both directors of J-PAL. Putu Poppy Widyasari is a research manager at J-PAL SEA, and Farah Amalia is a senior training associate at J-PAL SEA. TNP2K is an Indonesian government-affiliated think tank, under the vice president's office, whose mandate is to assist with the implementation, evaluation, and development of anti-poverty programs in Indonesia. Sudarno Sumarto is senior research fellow at the SMERU Research Institute and a policy adviser at TNP2K. Vivi Alatas was lead economist at the World Bank during the work discussed here. The research team worked with an array of government partners, including Bappenas (the National Development Planning Agency), Statistics Indonesia (BPS, the government statistics bureau), the Ministry of Social Affairs, and the Social Security Agency (BPJS Kesehatan).

The collaborative engagement between the researchers and the Government of Indonesia is quite unique in its extensive use of **administrative data to experimentally evaluate social protection programs**. In the process of administering these programs, governments generate considerable amounts of data just about the functioning of the programs—from who receives the program, to what they experienced, to actual outcomes. As the digitization of government data is on the rise, these new big administrative data sets can be utilized instead of household surveys, even in low- and middle-income country environments. Leveraging administrative data can improve data collection in several ways: (1) cheaply increasing effective sample sizes to ensure sufficient statistical power to measure policy-relevant changes in outcomes, (2) allowing for national samples that improve external validity, and (3) providing real outcomes rather than self-reported data. As the chapter will show, administrative data can be useful in other ways as well.

Indonesia has been a leader in experimentally evaluating social protection programs and, in particular, using administrative data to design more expansive and creative experiments to deepen the understanding of the mechanisms through which these programs function and can hence be improved. Importantly, working together, the researchers and the government have designed innovative experiments that use administrative data in three distinct ways, each of which will be discussed here.

First, **administrative data have been used to implement and monitor treatments that were part of the research.** For example, this includes using program eligibility lists to determine the sample for an experiment or to check whether treatment assignments were implemented in practice through actual policy changes.

Second, **administrative data have been used as a substitute for survey data in measuring program outcomes.** For example, in experimentally evaluating variants in the promotion and pricing of Indonesia's national health insurance program, the researchers ascertained the impacts of different treatment conditions on health outcomes using insurance claims data rather than a long endline survey.

Third, researchers have **studied the process of collecting administrative data.** Studies have focused on how best to determine who should be eligible for anti-poverty programs and, in running programs, how the design of administrative data collection tools could affect subsequent behavior. For example, a classic question in economics is whether the targeting of programs based on socio-economic data collection to determine household eligibility provides disincentives to work or causes other distortions in behavior. Thus, building experiments into these data collection mechanisms can help economic researchers understand whether the data collection itself distorts behavior and impacts program outcomes.

The remainder of this chapter will focus on Indonesia's experiences in using administrative data in large-scale policy experiments along these three key dimensions. While this is an example of how these methods were used to evaluate social protection programs, the lessons learned can be relevant to the administration of government programs as well. The chapter will describe how administrative data have increased what can be learned from experimentation to feed into the policy decision-making process. Moreover, the authors will discuss the processes of accessing and using the data (e.g., how to ensure stakeholder buy-in for data use and how to preserve anonymity) to help provide a guide to researchers and policy practitioners who would like to follow Indonesia's lead and incorporate administrative data into their experimental policy designs.

16.2 The Use of Administrative Data to Implement and Monitor Experimental Treatments

Administrative data can be used to implement the treatment arms in a social experiment, as well as to monitor whether the experimental treatments were implemented properly.

16.2.1 Using Administrative Data to Implement an Experimental Treatment

An important policy question is how to ensure that beneficiaries actually get their intended program subsidy. There may be many reasons beneficiaries do not—ranging from a lack of information on their own eligibility or what benefits they are eligible for, to outright theft of program funds, or clientelism in public service delivery.

Indonesia launched a national rice subsidy program in 1998, which eventually came to be known as the *Raskin* (Rice for the Poor) program. Until recently, it was Indonesia's largest social assistance program. Raskin was designed to deliver fifteen kilograms of rice per month at a subsidized price to 17.5 million households, which is about 30 percent of the country. In reality, beneficiaries received far less than they were actually entitled to. According to the research team's survey estimates, beneficiaries received only 32 percent of the intended subsidy and paid 42 percent more than the official copay, or subsidized price (Banerjee et al., 2018).

In 2014, the government of Indonesia planned to cut fuel subsidies and increase the scope of social protection to help alleviate the shocks this could cause. They wanted to both improve the efficiency of current social protection programs and create a temporary cash transfer program to mitigate any price shocks for the poor. TNP2K proposed a new nation-wide intervention dubbed "Social Protection Cards." Cards would be directly mailed to beneficiaries to give them information about their eligibility and hence improve transparency across the programs. However, there was substantial risk inherent in this idea: it would not work if the eligibility information did not reach participants or if lack of information was not the key constraint preventing beneficiaries from receiving their subsidies—the cards could have been a waste of funds, squandering money that could be better spent in other ways to improve the programs.

In assessing the proposed cards program, the vice president of Indonesia requested that concrete evidence be generated—and provided to him within six months—on whether this would work before it was expanded nationally. The J-PAL-affiliated research team, including this chapter's authors, worked with TNP2K to design an experimental pilot with the Raskin program to test the impact of the card on Raskin receipt, as well as different variants to understand the best way to implement it (e.g., what should be written on the card, should it include coupons, how much additional advertising is required, etc.). The experimental design and experimental findings are detailed in Banerjee et al. (2018).

In order to run the experiment, the researchers used individual administrative data on eligibility from Indonesia's Unified Database (UDB), which was housed at TNP2K. The UDB is a census that the government periodically conducts to capture socio-economic data from households.

These data are then fed into a formula to calculate predicted consumption levels for each household through a proxy-means test that determines eligibility for social protection programs based on ownership of a variety of common household assets (see Alatas et al. (2012) for more details on the proxy-means test). The database thus includes names, addresses, asset information, proxy-means scores, and eligibility statuses.

The administrative data was first used to implement the experiment: the beneficiary listing identified the eligible households to whom to mail Raskin cards in treatment villages (see Figure 16.1). Second, the administrative data allowed the researchers to identify eligible and ineligible households in the survey conducted at the end of the experiment to learn how the treatments differentially affected both types of households.

Obtaining the beneficiary list data from the Unified Database (UDB) was key to implementing the experiment. The main goal was to test whether program delivery was hindered because people did not know their official eligibility status, and there was no way to identify the officially eligible population without access to the underlying administrative data.

Importantly, this is very sensitive data, as it includes the names and addresses of individuals, along with their income and assets. Therefore, both the government and the researchers instituted strong data sharing and storage protocols to ensure that the information was protected. First, the research team obtained institutional review board (IRB) approvals on processes to use, store, and handle data. Second, only two local staff members from the research team accessed and handled the identified beneficiary data, and both were required to sign non-disclosure agreements with the government. Third, all data with personally identified information were stored in encrypted folders, and personal identifiers were removed from the data as soon as possible. After the UDB data were merged to the endline survey data, all personal identifiers were stripped from the files by select team members, and only de-identified data were shared with the rest of team for analysis.

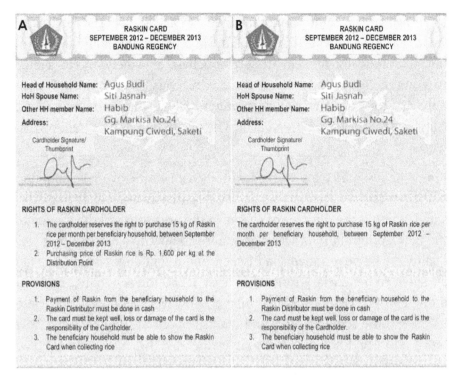

Figure 16.1: Sample Raskin cards. The names and addresses in these sample cards are fictitious and for demonstration purposes only.

16.2.2 Using Administrative Data to Monitor an Experimental Treatment

The government of Indonesia (GoI) aims to convert its five principal social protection programs, known as *Bantuan Sosial*, to electronic voucher distribution by 2022. Collectively, these programs reach over 15 million of Indonesia's poorest households. According to a Presidential Decree issued in June 2016, the Raskin rice program was slated first to make the transition.

Beginning this process, the government of Indonesia transitioned Raskin from an in-kind transfer to e-vouchers. Under the new system, called BPNT (*Bantuan Pangan Non-Tunai*/Non-Cash Food Assistance), beneficiary households are transferred electronic vouchers directly to an account in their name that they can access using a debit card, smart card, or mobile money platform. Recipient households can then theoretically redeem these e-vouchers at a network of agents (registered shops or vendors) for rice or eggs. These include both public-sector agents as well as private retailers who are recruited and equipped to accept BPNT e-vouchers by one of Indonesia's state-owned banks.

While the research team worked with the GoI on the overall evaluation of the reform (see section 16.3.2), the researchers also aimed to understand whether the number of agents in the area affected the quality of the BPNT program (i.e., whether a more competitive market improves quality). The government had issued initial guidelines specifying (1) an agent to beneficiary ratio of at least 1:250 in each village and (2) a minimum of two agents per village. However, very few areas were meeting these requirements, and it was important to understand how much effort and how many resources the government should exert to increase compliance.

In 2016, working with the GoI, the research team identified 216 districts where the BPNT reform had already happened or was in progress. The team then randomized the districts into two experimental groups. In one group, the districts are asked to exert extra effort to try to meet the agent coverage requirements. In the second group, districts were told that one of the two coverage guidelines was no longer required. The banks tasked with recruiting private BPNT agents and district officials learned of each district's treatment status through the normal processes for sharing programs and policies with stakeholders: letters from the government, a series of explanatory meetings, and phone calls to reinforce the treatment.

As part of the design, the researchers had to monitor the experiment and understand whether the number of BPNT agents actually changed as a result of treatment activities (e.g., letters, meetings), and whether villages met the GoI-issued requirements.

Given the spread of the districts across the nation, surveying villages across the 216 districts (and visiting each one multiple times to capture

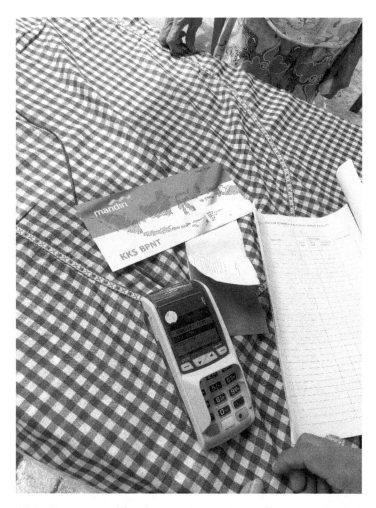

Figure 16.2: State-owned banks recruit private retailers to serve as BPNT agents and outfit them with equipment to process BPNT e-voucher transactions and sometimes to provide other basic banking services. These recruited agents then appear in bank administrative data.

changes over time) would have been prohibitively expensive. Instead, the research team used administrative data to monitor the experiment.

The researchers obtained detailed administrative data from the banks tasked with the recruitment of BPNT agents, collected by Bank Indonesia (Indonesia's Central Bank) to learn how many agents existed within each village, with snapshots twice a year starting March 2018. This

CHAPTER 16

data on bank agents is provided by each of the government banks participating in the program as part of regular administrative data reporting on their agent recruitment activities.

In an example of the kind of troubleshooting often required when working with administrative data, once the research team ascertained that the data are available and could be used to monitor the intervention—and, more generally, the reform—the team discovered that the form and codes of cataloguing villages and districts were not consistent across banks, nor consistent with the government's official codes. This made it difficult to match data both across different data sets and across time. The research team provided support to the government and the banks to clean the data and work with the institutions to draft guidelines to make the data consistent across various data sets going forward. In this case, collaboration between the research team and the government resulted in improvements to the data collection process, facilitating further research and program implementation.

16.3 Using Administrative Data to Measure Outcomes

In most experimental program evaluation designs, one measures the *actual outcomes* of both the control and treatment groups by conducting an endline survey. This can be costly. For example, a basic, two-hour endline survey across households for the Raskin card example costs about US$60–$70 per household surveyed, not including additional independent survey monitoring costs. The expense of these surveys can add up quickly when surveying a large sample or measuring program impact at various points in time (e.g., short-run versus long-run outcomes). The following two sections describe how two different forms of administrative data (program use data and national sample surveys) were used to measure program outcomes.

16.3.1 Utilizing Program Use Data to Measure Outcomes

In January 2014 the GoI introduced a national health insurance scheme, Jaminan Kesehatan Nasional (JKN), with the objective of achieving universal insurance coverage by 2019. JKN is a contributory system run by the Social Security Agency (BPJS Kesehatan). Non-poor informal workers are mandated to individually register for JKN and make monthly payments, but the mandate is hard to enforce. Unsurprisingly, BPJS Kesehatan has faced low take-up among this group. Those who do enroll tend to be those who have high levels of claims, so the revenues generated by premium payments do not cover the high cost.

A discussion began among researchers, TNP2K, BPJS Kesehatan, and Bappenas in 2014 to understand how to address this take-up issue. An experiment was designed to test whether temporary price subsidies could boost enrollment among healthier individuals, driving down the government's cost per individual enrolled.[3]

The experiment and data collection process in the two sample cities (Medan and Bandung) ran roughly as follows. Since there was no list of non-poor, informal workers who were not enrolled in JKN, researchers first went door-to-door to find individuals. Through this method, the research team identified about 6,600 target households for the sample. The researchers then conducted a short baseline survey that included the NIK (national ID number) of each household member, so that the sample could be matched to the BPJS administrative data. After the survey, households were individually randomized into different arms of the experiment through the survey app, and the survey enumerator administered the corresponding subsidy treatment (if any).

To understand the effect of the treatments on take-up, enrollment (i.e., selection), and ultimately the per person cost of insurance to the government, the researchers matched the NIK numbers of sample respon-

---

[3]Additional treatments were also designed to understand how both non-monetary sign-up costs and informational barriers affected take-up (see Banerjee et al. (2019) for more details on the experimental treatments and results).

dents to the BPJS administrative data on enrollments, monthly premium payments, and claims over the subsequent 32 months to answer three questions (for both the treatment and control groups):

1. Did the household enroll?
2. Did the household stay enrolled (i.e., did they continue to make their monthly premium payments)?
3. Did the household utilize the insurance? More specifically, did they visit a health care provider? What was the visit for? How much did the government need to reimburse the provider (i.e., the value of the health claim)?

The administrative data had several advantages over conducting a conventional household survey. First, it was much cheaper, since the data used were collected as part of the program administration, instead of just for the experiment. Second, recall bias was not a concern with the administrative data. Imagine the researchers had run an endline survey two and a half years after the treatment instead of using the administrative data. People could have easily forgotten the exact month when they visited the doctor and for what reason. To mitigate recall bias in a survey context, one would conduct frequent endline surveys to capture timely data, but this strategy can easily double or triple survey costs. Instead, with the administrative data, the research team had dated information for the 32-month follow-up period that was not subject to recall bias. Third, an endline survey may have been subject to differential response bias: households who received the treatment might feel indebted or grateful to the researchers and thus more inclined to respond positively to questions about the insurance. The administrative data obviated this concern, as it recorded actual, observed insurance outcomes for everyone.

Appendix A describes the close collaboration between the research team and the GoI that ultimately ensured the safe use of Indonesia's national health insurance data in this research project. In the end, the systems put in place to facilitate data use paid off in terms of policy impact. The research collaboration provided key insights to the Indonesian government on their insurance pricing systems—Bappenas credited the collaborative study on the national health insurance system when determining insurance premium pricing in 2016.

16.3.2 Building Questions into the National Sample Survey to Measure Outcomes

As discussed in section 16.2.2, the government of Indonesia has transitioned Raskin from an in-kind transfer of rice to e-vouchers redeemable for rice or eggs. This system was introduced in 44 of the largest cities in 2017 as a pilot, with a larger rollout in 54 cities and selected districts in 2018, and a national rollout in 2019.

The GoI asked for assistance to assess the impact of the reform on the quality of services that beneficiaries receive, which was to be studied around the 2018 phase-in of the reform. Given the budget allocation for 2018 to serve about 8.3 million beneficiaries with BPNT, the government needed to choose about 40–45 districts from 105 districts that were ready to receive the program during the 2018 roll-out, with the remaining districts to be treated under the budget allocations for 2019. Thus, the researchers randomized 42 districts to receive BPNT in 2018, with the rest treated in mid-2019.

A key question was how to survey citizens to evaluate the reform. The experiment spanned 105 districts across the country, making conventional household survey methods infeasible as discussed in section 16.2.2. With the GoI, the research team identified an alternative. Since 1963–64, the Statistics Bureau of the Government of Indonesia (BPS) has conducted a biennial national sample survey called the National Socioeconomic Survey (SUSENAS). It is administered to over 250,000 households and collects data on health, education, fertility, consumption and expenditures, and housing, among others. SUSENAS data are used for various purposes including planning, monitoring, and evaluating government programs. The researchers thus developed an idea to add questions to the SUSENAS to evaluate the BPNT reform. The SUSENAS is particularly well-suited for this use, as it covers all districts and is representative at the district level (the researchers' unit of randomization).

Appendix B describes the process of adding questions to the national sample survey through careful collaboration with many stakeholders. A challenge was ensuring that the timelines matched between the program implementation and the survey. The national sample survey has a set schedule determined by BPS, while the schedule for the transition of districts to BPNT (the treatment in this experiment) was decided by other ministries. Coordination was necessary to ensure that the treatment groups were transitioned to BPNT sufficiently before the surveys were fielded and that the control groups were treated afterwards.

The national sample survey represents a hybrid between administrative data and experiment-specific survey data. The survey is in the form of a conventional household survey but is administered by the government in order to inform its policies, regardless of the specific research projects described here. More generally, note that using national sample survey data of this sort has benefits and limitations. Benefits include large geographic scope and representative samples. The survey constitutes a panel of districts, and so control variables at the district level from previous years can be included in regression models to gain additional statistical power. In terms of limitations, as one can imagine from the process above, adding questions to a national survey may not provide all the variables that would be desired in a two-hour, evaluation-specific endline survey. In fact, the new Block XVI on Social Protection was only one page long, so questions needed to be designed very carefully.

16.4 Studying the Collection of Administrative Data Itself

As described in section 16.2.1, a number of programs in Indonesia use the UDB—a unified database of the households that are eligible for government programs. A series of studies conducted by members of this research team explored a variety of ways how to do this best (in particular Alatas et al., 2012, 2016).

16.4.1 Administrative Data Collection for Program Targeting

Governments are often worried about whether social assistance reaches the poorest households. In 2005, the government of Indonesia announced cuts to fuel subsidies, which were to be offset by increased transfers to the poor and near-poor. Program targeting emerged as an important policy priority, as the government sought to ensure that these transfers reached their intended recipients. In 2011, to further improve the targeting of social protection programs, Indonesia set out to establish a national targeting system.[4] This national targeting system, the Unified Data Base (UDB), is essentially a unified registry of actual and potential beneficiaries, which aims to provide high-quality data for all programs to access, facilitate complementarities between programs, reduce costs by avoiding duplicated targeting efforts across programs, and mitigate fraud, corruption, and the unintended duplication of benefits. While the potential advantages of such a system are large, switching targeting methods introduces the risk that some households could be systematically excluded from social assistance. The technical and administrative challenges of such a multi-program effort are extensive, and the risk of information manipulation may increase with the scale of the effort.

To mitigate these risks, careful decisions on data collection and selection were needed, and a number of options for collecting this administrative data were considered. In particular, there was debate as to whether to conduct a survey sweep with hard data collection enabling the use of a proxy-means test (see sections 16.2.1 and 16.4.2),

---

[4]Indonesia has historically used a blend of methods. For example, BLT, a cash transfer program launched in 2005, relied mostly on community assessment, self-assessment. and pre-existing lists to collect data and has relied mostly on PMT (proxy-means test) scores and community input to select beneficiaries from the resulting pool. The village head nominated poor individuals, and theoretically, this nomination data was combined with pre-existing lists of family planning data. However, in practice, frequently only the village head nominations were used. In 2008, data collection methods for the cash transfer program were supposedly modified to use consultative community meetings to update lists, identifying households that had moved, died, or were no longer poor. However, in practice, these meetings were generally restricted to village officials, rather than the broader community, and households were only removed for death or relocation, not for no longer being poor.

community-based targeting, or some combination of both. In collaboration with the government, researchers from J-PAL and the World Bank conducted a randomized control trial to test these targeting methods against each other (Alatas et al., 2012).

The results of the experiment informed the creation of the Data Collection for Social Protection Programs (PPLS11) registry, which was finalized in December 2011, covering the 25 million poor and vulnerable households constituting Indonesia's bottom 40 percent. It was subsequently endorsed by a cabinet-level committee, which instructed all central agencies to use it as the basis of their beneficiary lists. The registry has since been used for the national health fee waiver program (Jamkesmas) that aims to cover the poorest 76 million individuals and a conditional cash transfer program that now covers 10 million households, as well as for targeting unconditional cash transfers to qualifying households during further fuel subsidy reductions (see section 16.2.1). The establishment and widespread use of this registry significantly reduced the exclusion of poor households from government assistance, marking a critical milestone in Indonesia's development of an integrated social safety net. Furthermore, since the adoption of PPLS11, Indonesia has continued to improve its administrative data systems, and thus the social protections that rely on those systems, through empirical research that relies on both experimental and administrative data. One follow-up study focused on the potential of using self-selection to help determine inclusion in the proxy-means test screening process (Alatas et al., 2016).

16.4.2 Using Administrative Data as a Research Treatment to Improve Data Collection

In 2014, the government of Indonesia set about updating the UDB, which forms the basis of eligibility of social protection programs. The UDB contains data from a semi-census where Census Bureau enumerators collect information from households on socioeconomic characteristics and assets. These data are then fed into the proxy-means test formula used to identify poor households and target them for social programs.

One important question in both the economics literature and policy space is whether these data collection processes used in program targeting have distortionary effects. In high-income countries, where means testing is done based on employment and income status, the question often revolves around whether targeting leads to individuals working less for fear of becoming disqualified from benefits programs. Since targeting is based on assets in low-income countries (as income and employment are hard to verify), the question becomes whether households would choose not to invest in assets (or hide assets) for similar reasons. This could have real implications on household well-being, for example, if the asset is a better water source that can affect health or a productive asset (like a cow) that can affect household consumption.

Working in partnership with the government of Indonesia, the researchers built a randomized controlled trial directly into the 2015 UDB data collection—which collected data on 25 million households, generating data on 92 million individuals nationally—to ascertain whether adding additional asset questions to the UDB data collection would incentivize households to reduce asset acquisition.

Specifically, the researchers randomized questions about two additional assets onto the UDB questionnaire. The randomization was done at the province-level, since that is the level at which the surveys are printed and the enumerators are trained. To ensure that everyone received the same number of survey questions, each province was randomized into one of two options: in half the provinces, households received (1) either a question on flat-screen television ownership or a question on the number of rooms in their house and (2) either a question on how many active cell-phone SIM card numbers the household had or whether they had a modern toilet installed. Importantly, TVs and cell phones can be hidden from enumerators far more easily than rooms and toilets. Thus, the researchers could test whether being exposed to a particular question affected citizens reported and actual asset ownership.

Inserting different variables for randomization required the approval from the BPS deputy in charge of social statistics. For the data collection, BPS had to train approximately 100,000 enumerators, which spanned central, provincial, and district level trainings. Having different versions of the questionnaire within the same data collection was a new exercise for BPS and so was the idea of randomization. Despite the challenges that the new data collection posed, the researchers were able to convince the BPS deputy to implement the randomization because of a long history of engagement and collaboration between BPS and TNP2K, along with a presentation to BPS leaders on the rationale and future benefits of the study. Additionally, the BPS deputy also benefited from the opportunity to check the quality of SUSENAS data. In order to understand the treatment impacts on actual cell phone ownership, the researchers obtained administrative data on yearly SIM card subscribers from all major Indonesian telecommunications companies through the Ministry of Communications and Informatics (KeMenKomInfo). Following formal written requests from TNP2K and presentations regarding the study's objective to KeMenKomInfo officials, they finally agreed to release the data strictly for the purpose of the study. The study found that households randomized to receive the TV question were less likely to report TV ownership, but actual TV sales were unaffected, suggesting that households may have responded by hiding the asset, not changing their consumption.

16.5 Concluding Remarks

The experiences discussed here suggest that administrative data has a number of roles to play in conducting research on social protection policies. The projects described use administrative data as an outcome variable, allowing the scalable use of high-quality data. Even beyond that, the researchers used administrative data to implement treatments and in addition studied how to improve administrative data collection itself.

Several key lessons emerge. Given that governments own most administrative data sets, it is important to determine research questions and priorities together with the government so that the study is policy relevant. It is imperative to keep in mind that there are often multiple stakeholders; researchers must make sure that everyone understands the study goals, the exact data that are needed, the manner data will be used, and the responsibilities on both sides. Given the sensitivity of some data, having strong data storage protocols that meet IRB standards is important.

It is of course worth noting that administrative data-based experiments do not work in all cases and have some costs. For example, in some instances, an intervention would need to be designed, randomized, and implemented at a much larger scale (e.g., district level rather than village level) in order to match the available data. In other cases, the types of questions needed may not be available in existing data sets (for example, self-reported health status is not available in health insurance claim data). Notwithstanding, the projects and resulting policy actions described here would not have been feasible without leveraging administrative data through collaborations with many stakeholders—a crucial resource for researchers and policymakers seeking to generate and use experimental evidence for social good.

CHAPTER 16

About the Authors

Rema Hanna and Benjamin Olken are the scientific director of J-PAL SEA, and Abhijit Banerjee and Benjamin Olken are both directors of J-PAL. Putu Poppy Widyasari is a research manager at J-PAL SEA, and Farah Amalia is a senior training associate at J-PAL SEA. Sudarno Sumarto is senior research fellow at the SMERU Research Institute and a policy adviser at TNP2K. Vivi Alatas was lead economist at the World Bank during the work discussed here.

Acknowledgements

We thank the many J-PAL SEA staff members who contributed to the projects discussed here, in particular Lina Marliani for many years of outstanding leadership of J-PAL Southeast Asia and Alexa Weiss and Jenna Juwono for comments and input on the draft. We thank our many partners in the Government of Indonesia, in particular Bambang Widianto, Suahasil Nazara, Pungky Sumadi, Vivi Yulaswati, Andi ZA Dulung, Tubagus A Choesni, Fachmi Idris, Mundiharno, Tono Rustiano, Wynandin Imawan, Rahmi Artati, Maliki, Elan Satriawan, Gantjang Amanullah, M.O Royani, Nurul Farijati, Herbin, Dwi Martiningsih, Andi Afdal, Citra Jaya, Thoman Pardosi, Sri Kusumastuti Rahayu, and Fiona Howell for outstanding cooperation. Funding for the research described here came from the Australian Government Department of Foreign Affairs and Trade, the World Bank–Royal Netherland Embassy Trust Fund, 3ie, KOICA, and the Harvard Ash Center, along with in-kind support from the Government of Indonesia. We thank Survey Meter and Mitra Samya for outstanding data collection, project implementation, and fieldwork. Alatas was a Senior Economist at the World Bank during the work discussed here, and Sumarto works as a Policy Advisor to the Indonesian Government through TNP2K. The views expressed here are those of the authors alone and do not necessarily represent any of the institutions or individuals acknowledged here.

References in Chapter 16

Alatas, Vivi, Abhijit V. Banerjee, Rema Hanna, Benjamin A. Olken, and Julia Tobias. 2012. "Targeting the Poor: Evidence from a Field Experiment in Indonesia." *American Economic Review*, 102(4): 1206–1240. https://doi.org/10.1257/aer.102.4.1206.

Alatas, Vivi, Abhijit V. Banerjee, Rema Hanna, Benjamin A. Olken, Ririn Purnamasari, and Matthew Wai-Poi. 2019. "Does Elite Capture Matter? Local Elites and Targeted Welfare Programs in Indonesia." *AEA Papers and Proceedings*, 109: 334–339. https://doi.org/10.1257/pandp.20191047.

Alatas, Vivi, Abhijit V. Banerjee, Rema Hanna, Benjamin A. Olken, Ririn Purnamasari, and Matt Wai-Poi. 2016. "Self-Targeting: Evidence from a Field Experiment in Indonesia." *Journal of Political Economy*, 124(2): 371–427. https://doi.org/10.1086/685299.

Banerjee, Abhijit, Amy Finkelstein, Rema Hanna, Benjamin A. Olken, Arianna Ornaghi, and Sudarno Sumarto. 2019. "The Challenges of Universal Health Insurance in Developing Countries: Evidence from a Large-Scale Randomized Experiment in Indonesia." Working Paper 26204. https://doi.org/10.3386/w26204.

Banerjee, Abhijit, Rema Hanna, Jordan Kyle, Benjamin A. Olken, and Sudarno Sumarto. 2018. "Tangible Information and Citizen Empowerment: Identification Cards and Food Subsidy Programs in Indonesia." *Journal of Political Economy*, 126(2): 451–491. https://doi.org/10.1086/696226.

Behrman, Jere R, and Petra E. Todd. 1999. "Randomness in the Experimental Samples of PROGRESA (Education, Health, And Nutrition Program)." International Food Policy Research Institute Discussion Paper 125777. https://www.ifpri.org/publication/randomness-experimental-samples-progresa-education-health-and-nutrition-program (accessed 2020-10-05).

Chetty, Raj, and Adam Looney. 2006. "Consumption Smoothing and the Welfare Consequences of Social Insurance in Developing Economies." *Journal of Public Economics*, 90(12): 2351–2356. https://doi.org/10.1016/j.jpubeco.2006.07.002.

Gertler, Paul. 2004. "Do Conditional Cash Transfers Improve Child Health? Evidence from PROGRESA's Control Randomized Experiment." *American Economic Review*, 94(2): 336–341. https://doi.org/10.1257/0002828041302109.

Hanna, Rema, and Dean Karlan. 2017. "Designing Social Protection Programs: Using Theory and Experimentation to Understand How to Help Combat Poverty." In *Handbook of Field Experiments*. Vol. 2, 515–553. https://doi.org/10.1016/bs.hefe.2016.07.002.

Newhouse, J. P. 1993. *Free for all? Lessons from the Rand Health Insurance Experiment*. Cambridge, Mass:Harvard University Press. https://doi.org/10.7249/CB199.

World Bank. 2018. "The State of Social Safety Nets 2018." The World Bank. http://hdl.handle.net/10986/29115.

CHAPTER 16

Appendix

Appendix A

Collaborating to work with Indonesia's health insurance records

First, researchers and government partners discussed the research questions, study priorities, and treatments. This ensured that the study questions were useful for policy. This is an important first step for any evaluation collaboration to be successful, regardless of whether administrative data are used.

Second, the relationship was formalized through two agreements that clearly outlined the research design and plan, the data that would be shared with the researchers, and the responsibilities of each actor. The initial agreement was a memorandum of agreement between BPJS Kesehatan (who owned the data), Bappenas (who was facilitating the research from the policy side), and J-PAL SEA (who represented the researchers). This agreement included the study design, broad data to be shared, and the study protocols. The other agreement was a separate cooperation agreement between BPJS Kesehatan and J-PAL SEA that spelt out each entity's roles and responsibilities in detail. Both agreements required a series of official meetings that occurred over the course of six months.

Next, the official data request was submitted to BPJS Kesehatan. This included the exact variables to be shared, the frequency of data sharing, the de-identification process, and the data security protocols in place. The administrative data from the national insurance program are sensitive. They contain not only insurance status but also health records. Therefore, it was very important that both the government and researchers followed these data protection principles: (1) to ensure that the data were used for the stated purposes only, (2) that all parties were in agreement on those purposes, and (3) that strict data security protocols were followed. At this point, the research team was working closely with BPJS Kesehatan to understand the structure of the data, how it could be extracted, which departments within BPJS were responsible for the different component data sets, and so forth.

After an official letter was issued to grant data access, the research team maintained a close relationship with the BPJS team to continue to discuss the data use and ask questions about the data sets themselves. In addition, periodic updates on the results were presented to the BPJS team so that they could learn from the experiment as it was happening.

Appendix B

Collaborating to embed questions in Indonesia's official national sample survey

Adding questions to a national sample survey seemed like a straightforward idea, especially since the survey was being conducted anyway and the evaluation itself was commissioned by the government. But as with most things in life, things are never so simple.

It is important to keep in mind that the government comprises many different actors and each has a stake in the data, as they have their own policy information needs. Thus, the first challenge was to identify the stakeholders in this data set and generate buy-in. One clear stakeholder is BPS (the census bureau), who is in charge of conducting the sample survey and ultimately decides what to include.

However, many different ministries use the SUSENAS data, submit their own sets of questions to BPS, and have input and feedback on the overall survey. Moreover, given that BPS has a fixed budget to field the survey, there are constraints on the survey length. If questions are added, it likely means that others are removed. Therefore, the research team had to ensure buy-in from other ministries that would be interested in the BPNT reform to increase the probability that the submitted questions were included.

Therefore, in addition to numerous meetings and discussions with BPS to explain the importance of adding the questions and maintaining them over several rounds, the research team also conducted a series of meetings with other stakeholders, including Bappenas, TNP2K, the Ministry of Social Affairs (MoSA), and the Coordinating Ministry for Human Development and Cultural Affairs (PMK).

CHAPTER 16

A second challenge was to follow the right timeline for stakeholder engagement and attend the right meetings where decisions were made. For example, the research team found that in order to include new questions in the regular SUSENAS data collection in March, discussions with related ministries and institutions need to start at the latest in July or August of the previous year, before survey preparation begins in September. Inter-ministerial coordination usually occurs in October when the ministries propose their own questions for SUSENAS. This coordination workshop is crucial, since this is where the decisions to keep or drop questions are made. The research team therefore obtained permission to attend the workshop.

The first draft of the questionnaire from the inter-ministerial meeting is then workshopped internally by BPS and circulated with several representatives from each relevant institution in early November. During this process, modifications are still highly possible. Since the activity is usually not public (i.e., only between BPS and each ministry or institution separately), regular follow-up with BPS is necessary to understand the current stage of the process. By following up with government partners, such as TNP2K and Bappenas, the research team was able to access several drafts of the questionnaires and provide inputs as necessary. Ultimately, the additional questions proposed by the research team were approved by BPS and included in the socioeconomic survey, specifically in Block XVI on Social Protection, a new section in the SUSENAS used to track the reform.

Index

45 CFR 46, 117, 129
  45 CFR 46 Part A (Common Rule), 115, 392, 448
  45 CFR 46.111, 121–125

accountability, 425, 426
Act Respecting Research, 325
adversarial actor, 40
aliasing, global, 360
aliasing, local, 360
analytical data, 426–434, 436, 443, 449, 450, 455, 461
analytical studies, 426
anonymization, 150
anonymous data, 257
attribute disclosure, 148
Aurora Health Care, 18, 28, 385–416

Bantuan Pangan Non-Tunai, 571–573, 577, 578, 587
Belmont Report, 115, 117, 119, 123
biometric authentication, 51
Bundesdatenschutzgesetz, 257
Bundesministerium für Arbeit und Soziales, 263

California Consumer Privacy Act, 150
Canada Foundation for Innovation, 340
Canadian Institute for Health Information, 319, 329

capacity building, 532, 533, 537, 541, 543, 548
categories of IRB review
  exempt research, 131, 133–135, 138, 139, 301, 445
  non-exempt research, 117, 121, 129–131, 134, 135, 138
categorization of data access mechanisms, 57–78
cell suppression, 154
Center for Education Policy Analysis, 421, 435
Centre d'accès sécurisé aux données, 166, 274
certificates of incorporation, 348, 351, 352, 361–363, 366, 367, 370
City of Cape Town, 5, 23, 27, 467–501
cloud storage, 42, 450, 469, 489, 528
coarsening, 155
code bank, 321, 338
Code of Federal Regulations, 115, 297, 391, 392
codebook, 89, 151, 254, 255, 319–321, 428, 430, 435
complementary suppressions, 154
computational reproducibility, 531, 536, 537
concept dictionary, 321
confidentiality, 148
covered entity, 391

criteria for IRB review, 121

data access control, 46–47
data access point, 243, 246–249, 264, 266, 269, 273–275
data analyst, 176, 320, 331, 333, 334, 336, 394, 398, 404, 411, 471, 558
data at rest, 449
Data Coordinating Committee, 484
data custodian, 86, 146, 147, 160, 164, 311, 313, 318, 320, 322–324, 338, 340, 486
data dictionary, 89
data documentation, 22, 252, 268, 270, 274, 277, 318, 321, 333, 343, 394, 396, 397, 407, 428–430, 432, 434, 436, 473, 482, 484, 531, 553
Data Documentation Initiative, 255, 531
data enclave, 368, 489
data in transit, 449
data in use, 449
data intermediary, 86
data management plan, 120, 132, 210
data manager, 320, 334, 431, 435, 437–441, 452, 453, 457, 461, 475, 476
data protection plan, 132
data provider, 85, 88, 95, 145, 147, 153–155, 163, 191, 203, 221, 274, 351–372, 390, 393, 470, 507, 522, 523, 531, 533, 548, 557, 559
data requestor, 86
data sharing agreement, 120, 139
data sharing platform, 469, 476, 489, 492, 493, 496

data sharing process, 428, 470, 479, 490, 493, 496, 522
data sponsor, 366, 369, 372, 383
data use agreement, 14, 56, 80, 85–112, 120, 121, 174, 176, 210, 218, 247, 248, 258–260, 262–264, 271, 273, 277, 300, 367–369, 371, 391–393, 403, 406, 408, 421, 429, 438, 440–445, 448–454, 460, 474, 476, 486, 487, 489–494, 542, 551
 data access agreement, 330, 331, 337, 542
 data license agreement, 521, 522, 531, 534
 data sharing agreement, 315, 319, 322, 342, 386, 391, 521
 data transfer agreement, 120
 licensing agreement, 365, 366
data warehouse, 395, 406, 418–420, 423, 430–433, 435, 436, 439, 441, 443, 448–452, 455–457
Data without Boundaries, 248, 274
database administrator, 285, 321, 335
de-facto anonymized, 248, 258, 264, 266, 267
de-identification, 8, 18, 19, 132, 150, 152, 176, 177, 203, 206, 219, 228, 302, 394, 398, 404, 476, 486, 586
de-identified data, 133, 177, 189, 211, 226, 264, 299, 302, 322, 325, 327, 330, 334, 370, 386, 391–393, 399, 401, 403–406, 422, 445, 476, 486, 491, 524, 530, 570
Development Data Partnership,

512, 522, 534
Development Impact Evaluation, 24, 503–540
  Data and Evidence for Justice Reform, 504, 514, 516, 534
  DIME Analytics, 519, 520, 528, 529, 531, 536
  i2i, 523–526, 534
  ieProcure, 504
differential privacy, 14, 146, 150, 158, 173–239, 529
direct identifiers, 152
Discharge Abstract Database, 318
disclosure, 148
  disclosure risk, 160
  inferential disclosure, 149
Dublin Core, 481, 532

e-government, 504, 509, 514, 534
Ed-Fi, 451
electronic medical record, 385, 387, 389, 390, 395, 396
employee information system, 428
encryption, 13, 43–46, 57, 79, 181, 217, 267, 299, 449, 450, 527–530
engagement, 91, 95
English learner, 422
enumerative studies, 426
equivalent protections, 119
Establishment History Panel, 251
ethnic studies, 420, 423, 426, 427
evaluation, 425

Family Educational Rights and Privacy Act, 119, 121, 181, 221, 296, 297, 441, 445, 451, 453
Federal Employment Agency, 244–275
Federal Statistical Research Data Center, 74–75, 370

field experiment, 153, 504, 506
Five Safes Framework, 260–271, 300–303, 328–336, 368–371, 401–405, 445–455, 488–492, 524–530, 554–558
  Safe Data, 267–269, 302, 334–335, 370, 404, 451–453, 491–492, 529–530, 557
  Safe Outputs, 270–271, 302–303, 335–336, 371, 405, 453–455, 492, 530, 557–558
  Safe People, 263–264, 301, 331–332, 369, 403, 447–449, 490–491, 526–527, 555–556
  Safe Projects, 261–263, 300–301, 328–331, 368, 401–403, 445–447, 490, 524–525, 554–555
  Safe Settings, 37–84, 264–267, 302, 332–334, 369–370, 404, 449–451, 491, 527–529, 556

General Data Protection Regulation, 92, 118, 133, 150, 216, 256, 257, 261, 486
generalizing, 155
German Data Forum, 244, 256, 257, 274–276
German Federal Ministry of Education and Research, 244, 245, 256
German Record Linkage Center, 254, 274
German Research Foundation, 275
Government of Indonesia, 5, 28, 563–588
  national sample survey, 574, 577, 578, 587
  Unified Database, 569, 570, 578–581
guest RDC, 246–249, 264, 265

health insurance, 314, 323, 324, 391, 575, 576, 583, 586
Health Insurance Portability and Accountability Act, 121, 150, 153, 391–394, 399, 404, 408
 individual authorization, 392
 Privacy Rule, 391, 404, 408
 protected health information, 391, 403
 Safe Harbor, 393, 404
homelessness data, 429
human research, 113–115, 118, 127, 129, 135, 283, 307
 not human research, 127, 129
human subjects, 301, 329, 392, 402, 403, 442, 486, 527

identity disclosure, 148
impact evaluation, 340, 504–535, 566
improvement, 425
Indonesia Census Bureau, 580
informed consent, 123, 124, 126, 130, 135, 392, 446
Institute for Social Research, 247, 248
institutional review board, 15, 94, 95, 113–144, 150, 210, 218, 263, 292, 296, 300, 301, 392–403, 408, 442–449, 490, 525–527, 570, 583
 central IRB, 117
 commercial IRB, 117
 ethics board, 95
 independent IRB, 117
Integrated Employment Biographies, 252
intellectual property, 368, 488, 524, 527, 529
internal data processing system, 358

International Data Access Network, 244, 273, 274
International Monetary Fund, 24, 26, 541–561
 articles of agreement, 543, 550, 551
 RA-GAP, 545
 revenue gap, 552
 surveillance, 541, 543–545, 548, 549, 555, 558, 559
 technical assistance, 541, 543, 545–547, 550–559
international research, 114
IP address restriction, 48, 302

Job Submission Application, 265, 266, 271, 272

k-anonymity, 155
Kenya Patient Safety Impact Evaluation, 510, 533
Kullback-Leibler divergence, 163

Lei Geral de Proteção de Dados, 150
Leibniz Institute for Educational Trajectories, 275
licensing agreement, 351, 365
limited data set, 391, 392
linked employer-employee data, 251

Maritime SPORT Support Unit, 315, 316, 319, 340, 341
masking, 155
measurement framework, 506
Medical Services Payment Act, 325
Medicare Act, 325
memoranda of understanding, 86
metadata standards, 481, 493
minimal risk, 116, 131, 135

multiple imputation, 159
Nairobi road safety study, 528, 534
National Center for Education Statistics Restricted-Use Data License, 77
National Educational Panel Study, 275
National Opinion Research Center, 361, 367, 369–371, 374
Natural Sciences and Engineering Research Council of Canada, 329
New Brunswick Institute for Research, Data and Training, 27, 70–71, 311–346
noise infusion, 158
  input noise infusion, 158
  output noise infusion, 158
non-disclosure agreements, 120, 393, 394, 405, 415, 527, 570
non-statistical disclosure limitation, 151

Office for Human Research Protections, 115, 127, 128
Office of Sponsored Research, 94
Ohio Longitudinal Data Archive, 18, 20, 23, 26, 27, 73, 283–310
on-site access, 244–246, 248, 249, 259, 264–265, 268–272, 275, 548, 549, 551
operational data, 426–431, 433, 434, 436, 461

partnership director, 420, 421, 423, 438, 441, 446, 456–459
Personal Health Information Privacy and Access Act, 322–325
personally identifiable information, 7, 18, 25, 27, 133, 178, 181, 219, 220, 302, 453, 486, 491
physical access card, 51–52, 332
physical data enclave, 54–55, 264–265, 332–334, 370
pq percent rule, 154
privacy board, 120, 392
Privacy by Design, 326
privacy officer, 330, 333, 336
Private Capital Research Institute, 24, 25, 73–74, 347–383
program targeting, 579
project coordinator, 328
project data set, 333, 335–337
propensity score, 163
Protection of Personal Information Act, 485
proxy-means test, 570, 579, 580
pseudonymization, 257, 261, 264, 267
python, 59, 164, 360, 361, 371, 556

Quality Teacher and Education Act, 424
quasi-identifiers, 150, 155, 162

R, 147, 164, 265, 556
Race to the Top, 285, 289, 290, 300, 304
randomized evaluation, 2, 385–387, 389, 402, 410, 564–566, 572
Raskin, 568–571, 574, 577
re-identification, 87, 93, 122, 132, 139, 150, 151, 155, 158, 160, 162, 176–179, 203, 257, 267, 270, 323, 334, 400
record linking, 153
regression discontinuity, 152
regression models, 152

remote desktop, 48–49
remote execution, 53–54, 264–266, 268, 270–272, 275
research associate, 336, 357, 358, 362
research data center, 243–245, 247, 254, 256, 259, 260, 273, 274, 276, 311, 321, 322, 324, 335, 340, 342
Research Data Center at the Institute for Employment Research, 18, 22, 23, 27, 71–72, 147, 243–282
  Research-Data-Center in Research-Data-Center, 243
research proposal, 365, 367–369, 372, 496, 554
Research, Planning and Assessment tables, 428, 430
research-practice partnerships, 417–419, 425, 443, 447, 456, 459
researcher-provided infrastructure, 56–57, 264, 266–267, 302, 404, 449–451, 491
Right to Information and Protection of Privacy Act, 325

SafePod Network, 76
Sample of Integrated Labour Market Biographies, 250, 251
sampling, 157
SAS, 75, 272, 334, 398
Scientific Use Files, 264, 266–268, 270
secure file transfer protocol, 46, 48, 302, 450
secure room, 52, 264, 332
security threat, 38–41
  adversarial actor, 39
  internal threat, 40

unintentional breach, 40
senior data analyst, 321, 333–335
service provision, 425, 426
social protection program, 509, 564–571, 579, 580
Social Sciences and Humanities Research Council, 329
Sozialgesetzbuch, 255, 257
Stanford-SFUSD Partnership, 22, 23, 26, 417–466
Stata, 147, 164, 254, 265, 266, 270, 272, 334, 360, 361, 364, 369–371, 432, 532, 549, 556
statistical disclosure limitation, 13, 145–172, 176, 177, 179, 182, 186, 218, 227, 259, 262, 265, 266, 270, 271, 274
Statistics Act, 332
Statistics Canada Real Time Remote Access, 75
Strategy for Patient-Oriented Research, 315, 346
student information system, 428
supervisor of analytics, 438, 439, 441, 453
supervisor of research and evaluation, 438
suppression, 153
survey data, 159, 255, 256, 274, 422, 424, 425, 441, 505, 509, 512–515, 518, 523, 544, 549, 565, 567, 570, 578
swapping, 156
synthetic data, 159, 186, 268
systems administrator, 333, 334

thin client, 49–50, 264, 333
threat models, 160
Tri-Council, 329

Unemployment Insurance Wage

Records, 286, 293
United States Census Bureau, 158, 159, 177, 178, 222, 224–227, 233, 354, 356, 367, 368, 370
University of New Brunswick University Policy on Research Involving Humans, 329

verification servers, 163

virtual data enclave, 55–56, 369–370
virtual private network, 47, 404

weakly anonymous, 257, 264, 266, 267, 269
Workforce Data Quality Initiative, 285, 288, 300, 304

CPSIA information can be obtained
at www.ICGtesting.com
Printed in the USA
BVHW040313120521
607043BV00001B/6